The Syriac Version of the Old Testament
An Introduction

While the Syriac version of the Old Testament, known as the Peshitta, was translated from a Hebrew text, it was preserved by the eastern churches alone. In his book, M. P. Weitzman argues that the translation was put together in around 200 CE by a small Jewish community estranged from the Rabbinic majority. This community eventually embraced Christianity and brought the Peshitta with them. This remarkable theory is the prelude to a comprehensive analysis of the Peshitta itself, which covers all the books of the Bible, surveys the existing scholarship and explores the relationship between the translation and the original Hebrew text. Apart from the philological detail, the book also examines the translations' historical links with Judaism and early Christianity. As a wide-ranging introduction to the subject, the book will appeal to biblical scholars and religious studies students as well as to philologists and historical linguists.

M. P. WEITZMAN was Reader in Hebrew and Jewish Studies at University College London.

UNIVERSITY OF CAMBRIDGE ORIENTAL PUBLICATIONS 56

A series list is shown at the back of the book

The Syriac Version
of the Old Testament

An Introduction

M. P. WEITZMAN

CAMBRIDGE
UNIVERSITY PRESS

PUBLISHED BY THE PRESS SYNDICATE OF THE UNIVERSITY OF CAMBRIDGE
The Pitt Building, Trumpington Street, Cambridge CB2 1RP, United Kingdom

CAMBRIDGE UNIVERSITY PRESS
The Edinburgh Building, Cambridge CB2 2RU, UK   http://www.cup.cam.ac.uk
40 West 20th Street, New York, NY 10011-4211, USA   http://www.cup.org
10 Stamford Road, Oakleigh, Melbourne 3166, Australia

First published 1999

Printed in the United Kingdom at the University Press, Cambridge

Typeset in 10/13pt Times NR [SE]

A catalogue record for this book is available from the British Library

ISBN 0 521 63288 9 hardback

CONTENTS

FIGURES

FOREWORD

Robert P. Gordon

Michael Perry Weitzman

It has been some consolation to the family and the colleagues of Michael Weitzman that this, the first of his projected two volumes on the Syriac Version of the Old Testament (otherwise known as the Peshitta), was already at proof stage at the time of his lamented death, at the age of fifty-one, on 21 March 1998. A number of ground-breaking essays on the subject had already given promise of what we now have in our possession – a landmark study of the Peshitta version of the Old Testament.

Michael Weitzman came up to Cambridge in 1963 to read Hebrew and Aramaic for the Oriental Studies Tripos. In the entrance scholarship examination at St John's College he was awarded an Open Scholarship in Hebrew, Greek and Latin. This was just the beginning of a brilliant undergraduate career in which he achieved first class honours in both parts of the Tripos (1965 and 1967), while simultaneously studying for an external degree in mathematics from London University, where he obtained a first class in 1968. During his time in Cambridge he won several college and university prizes, crowning these successes in 1971 when he returned to sit the examination for the rarely awarded Tyrwhitt's Hebrew Scholarship and Mason Prize for Biblical Hebrew.

In his undergraduate days Michael happily indulged his fascination with Hebrew and the Semitic languages generally, and was soon developing a complementary inter-est in the ancient versions of the Hebrew Bible. His work on his Hebrew set texts filled a succession of little notebooks with comments on philology and the renderings of the major ancient versions. These, with characteristic generosity, were afterwards passed on to contemporaries who might have a use for them in succeeding years. If a modern language became desirable for study purposes a sufficient familiarity with it would soon be acquired. And yet, alongside the gifted intellect and the erudition there was a gentleness of attitude toward other people and their limitations, and a sense of humour that delighted in finding simple things amusing, while it could just as easily erupt in a trilingual pun.

Michael's linguistic and mathematical interests combined in the doctoral disserta-tion that he wrote at University College, London, and for which he was awarded his Ph.D. in 1974. It was entitled *A Statistical Approach to Textual Criticism, with Special Reference to the Peshitta Version of the Old Testament*, ran to two volumes, and required the appointment of both a statistician and a Semitist as examiners. Here he applied himself to the study of text-critical methodology, and in particular to the analysis of manuscript relationships, developing statistical models and applying distributional criteria to the mapping of manuscripts whose genealogical relationships are no longer recoverable. The dissertation itself was never published, but some idea of its focus and method can be gleaned from several published articles, including one which takes as its starting-point the complex manuscript situation affecting Cyprian's *De Unitate*. Later work on the Peshitta Psalter also had its genesis at the dissertation stage.

This interest in the Peshitta version extended, however, to all its principal aspects. Since he believed the Peshitta to be a more cohesive translation than was apparent from previous studies of individual books, Michael set out to produce a comprehensive account of the version. Prominent among his publications over a twenty-year period were a number that addressed fundamental Peshitta questions such as the version's community background and date of origin, literary style, relation with the Hebrew textual tradition and the other ancient versions, and the characteristics of its manuscript groupings. In this regard, special mention may be made of the essay entitled, 'The Interpretative Character of the Syriac Old Testament', contributed to volume 1 of *Hebrew Bible/Old Testament: The History of Its Interpretation*, edited by M. Saebø (Göttingen, 1996, pp. 587–611).

These studies, whether published in journals or as chapters in edited volumes, were invariably substantial and significant. In them he argued for the originality of readings in the ninth-century Or Ms 58 of the Biblioteca Medicea Laurenziana, Florence (Leiden siglum 9a1), found evidence of two translation hands in the Peshitta of Samuel (a refinement more characteristic of the more advanced type of research associated with the Septuagint, the Peshitta's elder sibling), and propounded the theory that it was the poor state of the Hebrew *Vorlage* of the Syriac books of Chronicles that was responsible for the waywardness of a translation whose peculiarities have sometimes seen it classed as some kind of Syriac Targum. In one of his last studies, which has now appeared posthumously in *Targum Studies* II (ed. P. V. M. Flesher, 1998, pp. 159–93) – a volume is dedicated to his memory – this question of the status of Peshitta Chronicles is addressed and the conclusion reached that only if the term 'Targum' is seriously redefined could it embrace Peshitta Chronicles. The influence of Jewish liturgy and rabbinical thought on the Peshitta, and notably of the Qaddish prayer within the Peshitta of Chronicles, became a subject of special interest in recent years.

By a happy coincidence Michael was engaging in his research at the same time as the volumes of the Leiden Peshitta Edition were being published. He did not join the Leiden team as a collaborator but was regularly in correspondence with the editors, visited the Peshitta Institute from time to time, and had access to all draft materials held there. The present volume was written in association with the Peshitta Institute and the Leiden Institute for the Study of Religions, and in particular their 'The Hebrew Bible and Its Ancient Versions' programme. In addition, Michael was an official collaborator on the Concordance to the Old Testament in Syriac project, was one of the editors working on the new Annotated English Translation of the Peshitta, and had accepted an invitation to be an external supervisor of a Peshitta Institute/Free University of Amsterdam project dealing with the computer-assisted linguistic analysis of the Peshitta.

While his own major Peshitta enterprise was developing, Michael was publishing in other, strictly unrelated, areas, applying his statistical and linguistic skills to such matters as verb frequency and source criticism in the Hebrew Bible, statistical patterns in Hebrew and Arabic roots, the distribution and pronunciation of Hebrew root consonants, Hebrew lexicography, and the retroversion of the Greek minor versions from the Syro-Hexaplar. With the late Chaim Bermant he co-authored *Ebla: An Archaeological Enigma* (London and New York, 1979), a work of *haute vulgarisation* – he enjoyed the term! – which offered to a wider public some insight into the significance of this ancient city and its archive at a quite early stage in Ebla studies. The book was translated into five other languages between 1979 and 1986. While all this researching and publishing was going on, he was carrying a full teaching load at University College, London, where he was appointed a Lecturer in 1972 and a Reader in 1997. A good number of other institutions and examining boards, operating at both the secondary and tertiary level, benefited from his selfless interest in the promotion of Hebrew and related studies.

Hebrew and Aramaic Studies at Cambridge has produced a number of Semitists who have distinguished themselves in academic and public life during the twentieth century. None was more brilliant or more truly a scholar than Michael Weitzman, and we can but congratulate ourselves on our good fortune in having this volume by which to remember him, even if it also reminds us that we have been denied so much by his passing.

PREFACE

The Syriac version investigated here has been known, at least since the ninth century, as the Peshitta. It is not the only translation of the Old Testament into Syriac, but the others – which are in part revisions of it and in part daughter-versions made from the Greek Bible – cannot challenge the status of the Peshitta as *the* Syriac version.

The new edition of the text, under the general editorship of the Peshitta Institute in Leiden, has finally set research into the Peshitta on a sound textual basis, and has already inspired a number of important studies of individual biblical books. At the same time, however, it is important to keep sight of the impressive degree of cohesion between the different books in this biblical version. Hence the present study, which – at least in principle – is concerned with the biblical books as a whole.

The use in the book title of the Christian term 'Old Testament' for the Hebrew scriptures calls for some explanation. Whether the translators were Jewish or Christian is a matter for debate, and indeed one of the principal issues in this book. What is undeniable, however, is that the Syriac version of these biblical books has been handed down exclusively by the eastern churches, which view them as the Old Testament. I have preferred to start out from this fact, and in this concur with the Leiden editors.

The word 'introduction' also deserves remark. Elsewhere, it suggests an elementary treatment confined to areas of consensus; but in biblical studies it is traditional for an 'introduction' to enter into detail and also to expound the author's own views, whether widely accepted or not. It is in that sense that the present work aims to serve as an introduction.

Perhaps more than any other student of the Peshitta, I am indebted to each and every member of the international team of scholars whose contributions – in particular the painstaking collations – make up the new edition. I am especially grateful to Dr Piet Dirksen, Dr Konrad Jenner, former and current heads of the Peshitta Institute, who have answered my many queries and made me very welcome. In Leiden I have been much stimulated by discussions with three generations of scholars, who also include Dr Marinus Koster, Professor Arie van der Kooij and Professor Luc van Rompay, and Dr Bas ter Haar Romeny. As for Professor P. A. H. de Boer and Professor Martin Mulder, it is only to their memory that I can pay tribute.

I have also greatly benefited from discussions and correspondence with other colleagues, notably Dr Sebastian Brock, Dr Anthony Gelston, Professor Jan Joosten, Professor Robert Gordon, the Reverend David Lane and Professor J. B. Segal. Their comments on draft chapters have been especially valuable. From my students I have learnt at least as much, especially from Matthew Morgenstern and from Dr Gillian Greenberg, who has generously read through the whole text. I am grateful to them all.

To enable me to complete this work, Professor John Klier arranged for me to be relieved of undergraduate teaching duties during the academic year 1995–6. As departmental head he has been unprecedentedly supportive, and deserves my heartfelt thanks.

Constant use has been made of Dr Williams's Library, the libraries of the University of London and its schools, and the holdings of the Peshitta Institute in Leiden. The help that I have received is gratefully acknowledged.

This book is dedicated to my children Gail and Alexander, who have had to compete with the Peshitta for my attention for as long they can remember. I can only hope to have struck the right balance.

ABBREVIATIONS

AJSL	American Journal of Semitic Languages and Literature
BO	Bibliotheca Orientalis
BZAW	Beihefte, Zeitschrift für die alttestamentliche Wissenschaft
CSCO	Corpus Scriptorum Christianorum Orientalium
DJD	Discoveries in the Judaean Desert
JBL	Journal of Biblical Literature
JJS	Journal of Jewish Studies
JSS	Journal of Semitic Studies
JTS	Journal of Theological Studies
MGWJ	Monatsschrift für Geschichte und Wissenschaft des Judentums
MPI	Monographs of the Peshitta Institute, Leiden
OCA	Orientalia Christiana Analecta
OCP	Orientalia Christiana Periodica
OrChr	Oriens Christianus
OTS	Oudtestamentische Studien
PG	Patrologia Graeca
PIC	Peshitta Institute Communications
PL	Patrologia Latina
PO	Patrologia Orientalis
REJ	Revue de études juives
RSO	Rivista degli Studi Orientali
SBL	Society for Biblical Literature
SJOT	Scandinavian Journal of the Old Testament
SVT	Supplements to Vetus Testamentum
TB	Talmud Bavli
VT	Vetus Testamentum
ZAW	Zeitschrift für die alttestamentliche Wissenschaft
ZDMG	Zeitschrift der deutschen morgenländischen Gesellschaft

1
Introduction

The eastern churches have preserved a translation of the Hebrew Bible into Syriac. The Syriac language was the Aramaic dialect of Edessa (today's Urfa, in south-east Turkey) and of its province Osrhoene; and it was the medium by which Christianity spread from Edessa over Mesopotamia and the Iranian plateau. Yet internal evidence leaves no doubt that the translation was made from a Hebrew text, rather than from the Greek Bible, which had official status in the early church.[1] The translation thus has links both with early eastern Christianity and with Judaism, and the nature of those links is a question central to the origin of the version. In discussing it, we shall have to take care not to treat 'Judaism' and 'Christianity' as two simple homogeneous entities, given the variety which the archaeological discoveries of this century have revealed in either religion.

The Syriac version is not, of course, the only known case of a translation made from a Hebrew original but preserved by the church. An earlier instance was the Old Greek version, commonly called the Septuagint (or LXX). In the case of LXX, however, the general religious context is clear. First, the version is simply too early to be Christian. Moreover, a Jewish origin, at least for the version of the Torah, is acknowledged in such Jewish sources as the letter of Aristeas and the Talmud.[2] The reason for its abandonment by the Jews is also evident, namely its adoption by the church. For the Syriac version, by contrast, the evidence of date would admit Christian as well as Jewish origin. Furthermore, there is no reference to this version in Jewish sources, or rather not until the Middle Ages.[3] Its religious context is thus obscure, and in particular the silence of the Jewish sources, given that the translation was made from the Hebrew, demands explanation.

The place of origin is identified by many as Edessa, where the Syriac dialect is already attested at the turn of the era. Also popular, however, is the theory that the version originated further east, in Adiabene, whose king Izates converted to Judaism during Claudius' reign (41–54 CE). This theory, and the general question of the location of the Syriac version, are further discussed in later chapters.

---

[1] The theory that the Syriac version goes back to the Hebrew not directly but through a Jewish Aramaic translation is examined – and rejected – in chapter 3 below.

[2] See TB Meg. 9a and parallels (which shares the story of 72 translators placed by "Ptolemy" in separate cells), and Soferim 1:7 (which instead mentions just five translators, whose version of the Torah was as disastrous as the Golden Calf). On these rabbinic traditions, see most recently G. Veltri, *Eine Torah für den König Talmai*, Tübingen 1994.

[3] On the Jewish references to P from the Middle Ages, and allegedly earlier, see pp. 160–2 below.

The theory that the translation was made by or for the converts in Adiabene would imply a date in the first century CE. Even aside from that theory, the translation must pre-date the fourth-century Syriac fathers Aphrahat and Ephrem, who cite it extensively. It can in fact hardly be later than about 200 CE, since it uses a particle that Ephrem no longer understood.[4] Around the end of the fourth century, we are told that nothing was remembered of the translators' identity or circumstances,[5] and this fact likewise suggests a date hardly if at all later than 200 CE.

That the whole translation is of a single date should not be taken for granted, since differences in translation technique emerge between the different books. Native tradition too speaks of a number of different translators (though not necessarily in different eras). Thus the unity of the translation, as well as its date, place and religious background, all merit discussion.

Quite apart from its own interest, the translation has an important bearing on both earlier and later writings. In relation to the Hebrew text of the Bible, this is the earliest translation of the whole canon into another Semitic language. It is thus potentially an important witness to the biblical text, and at the very least shows how the Hebrew text was understood at a particular (if as yet unidentified) time and place. In subsequent centuries also, the translation assumes new importance as the basis of the rich literature of Syriac-speaking Christianity, while the history of its text reflects the history of the constituent churches.[6]

The name of the translation

The translation has long been known by the name Peshitta (Syriac: ܦܫܝܛܬܐ). Here the abbreviation P will be used to indicate the translation, or sometimes the translator.

The name Peshitta is first found in two works by Moses bar Kepa (c. 813–903): his Hexaemeron[7] and his introduction to the Psalms.[8] The form is a passive participle from the root ܦܫܛ, whose primary meaning is "stretch out". The gender is feminine, to agree with the noun ܡܦܩܬܐ "version" understood. The etymological sequence of different dentals /ṭt/ in the name is not tolerated in pronunciation, which would be either Pshita or Pshitta in the east and Pshito in the west.[9]

In Syriac, as in Jewish Aramaic, the meaning of the participle ܦܫܝܛ sometimes developed from "stretched out" to "straight, straightforward, simple, obvious". Its

---

[4] This is the particle ܕܝܢ in Gen. 1:1. See p. 253 below, as well as G. Goldenberg, "Bible Translations and Syriac Idiom" in MPI 8, pp. 25–39, especially pp. 28–9.

[5] See the references cited on p. 146 in the commentary on the Twelve Prophets by Theodore of Mopsuestia (c. 350–428).

[6] See the chapter entitled "Text and Context" in D.J. Lane, *The Peshiṭta of Leviticus* [=MPI 6], Leiden 1994, pp. 157–72.

[7] Syriac text with French translation cited in J.P.P. Martin, *Introduction à la Critique Textuelle du Nouveau Testament: Partie Théorique*, Paris [1883], p. 100. German translation in L. Schlimme, *Der Hexaemeronkommentar des Moses bar Kepha*, Wiesbaden 1977, vol. 1, p. 172.

[8] G. Diettrich, *Eine jakobitische Einleitung in den Psalter* (=BZAW 5), Giessen 1901, p. 115. Moses bar Kepha's authorship was demonstrated by J.-M. Vosté, "L'introduction de Mose bar Kepha aux Psaumes de David", *Revue Biblique* 38 (1929), pp. 214–28.

[9] E. Nestle, "Zum Namen der syrischen Bibelübersetzung Peschittâ" in *ZDMG* 47 (1893), pp. 157–9 argued for simple /t/; the spelling in the title was etymological only. E. König argued for a doubled /t/, in "Zum Namen der syrischen Bibelübersetzung Peschittâ" *ZDMG* 47 (1893), pp. 316–19. In the west, consonants are no longer doubled.

counterpart פָּשׁוּט in Mishnaic Hebrew likewise came to mean "straightforward". The related Hebrew noun פְּשָׁט is used from the eleventh century onward of biblical inter-pretation, and denotes the "simple" meaning, as opposed to homiletics read into the text. The name Peshitta may likewise mean "the simple (version)".[10]

An alternative explanation for the name Peshitta is that the participle instead devel-oped from 'stretched out' to mean 'widespread'. On that view, the name Peshitta would be analogous to *Vulgata* "common text".[11] No analogy, however, can be found for such usage in Syriac, and so the meaning 'simple' may be preferred.

The simplicity, according to Barhebraeus, lies in P's "rejection of ornate language" (ترك البلاغة).[12] Moses bar Kepa contrasts the Peshitta with the Syrohexapla version (based on LXX) produced in 615–17 CE; by comparison, P is indeed simple. It is unlikely, however, that the name is actually a translation of Greek ἁπλᾶ, to contrast with ἑξαπλᾶ.[13] First, only in Greek would this contrast be recognised; moreover, the term Peshitta is also used for the standard text of the New Testament, where no Hexapla existed, and the contrast is rather with the more literal Harklean version, like-wise produced in the seventh century.[14]

The framework of Peshitta research

The extant texts of P are separated from the other extant forms of the Hebrew Bible by many removes. When we study the relationship of P to these other textual witnesses, all the different stages have to be taken into account. The more we attribute to one such stage, the less can be attributed to the others: for example, in relation to the discrepan-cies between P and MT, the more are ascribed to translation technique, the fewer can be ascribed to a difference in the Hebrew *Vorlage*.

The various stages that must be considered are summarised in fig. 1. Here, some of the vertical lines represent descent by copying, while others represent mental processes, as indicated in the figure. Genealogies of this sort in studies of the biblical text are inevitably over-simplified and therefore unfashionable. In this case, for example, no account is taken of variations within MT, nor of possible variations in the genealogy between one book and another. Moreover, it sometimes happened that a scribe copying one manuscript also consulted a second manuscript from a different family, and so blurred together different lines of descent. Even so, it is important to have the basic underlying relations clearly in mind. To deny the legitimacy of any such scheme out-right is in effect to affirm that readings circulated at random, which would misrepresent matters far more seriously.

In any biblical book, the Hebrew texts that now survive and the Hebrew source (tech-nically termed the *Vorlage*) used by the translator of P are of common origin. This is

---

[10] The verb פשט and the noun פשוט are already applied in the Talmud to biblical exegesis, but there seem primarily to denote interpretation recognised as obviously authoritative rather than simple interpretation *per se*. See R. Loewe, "The 'Plain' Meaning of Scripture in Early Jewish Exegesis", *Papers of the Institute of Jewish Studies London*, ed. J.G. Weiss, Jerusalem 1964, pp. 140–85, especially p. 181.

[11] So e.g. R. Payne Smith, *Thesaurus Syriacus*, Oxford 1897–1901, col. 3319 ('versio vulgata, communis, popularis').   [12] Arabic text cited in N. Wiseman, *Horae Syriacae*, Rome 1828, p. 92.

[13] F. Field, *Origenis Hexaplorum Quae Supersunt . . . Fragmenta*, Oxford 1875, vol. 1, p. ix, n.1.

[14] Nestle, "Zum Namen", p. 159.

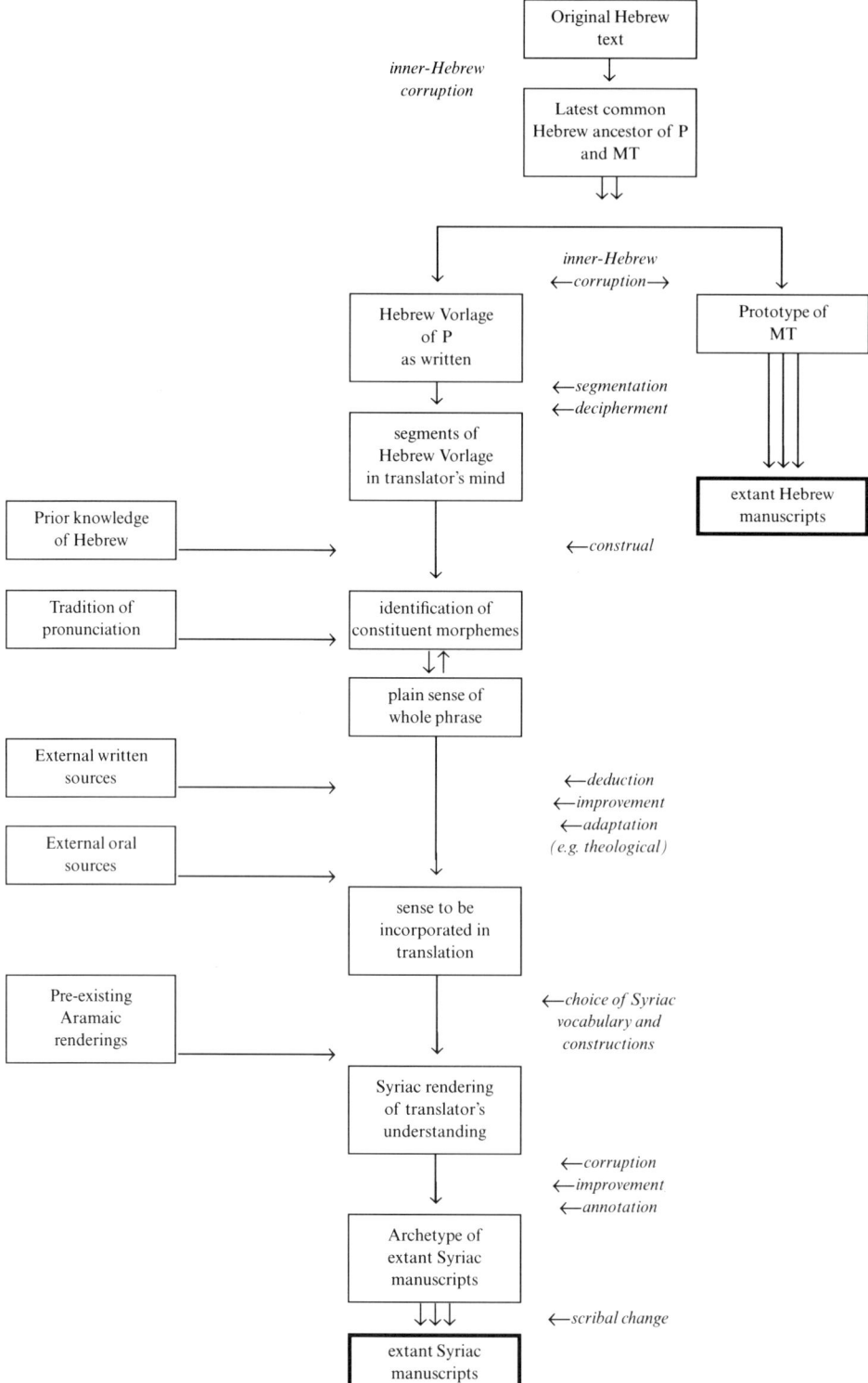

Fig.1. The relationship between the extant Hebrew and Syriac texts

not merely because both go back ultimately to the lost original text of the Bible. The lines of transmission leading down to MT on the one hand, and to the *Vorlage* of P on the other, had much in common, since MT and P share various inferior readings of which some other extant forms of the text – such as 4QSam[a] and LXX in Samuel – are free. In these cases, where an erroneous reading stands in MT and P but not in all witnesses, it is a fair conclusion that that inferior reading already stood in the latest common ancestor of both MT and the *Vorlage* of P. How many generations of copies lay between that latest common ancestor and the original Hebrew text, we cannot tell.

Further errors may have arisen in the transmission of the Hebrew between that latest common ancestor and MT. In principle, these should not be present in the alternative line of transmission leading to the *Vorlage* of P, nor in more distantly related authorities such as LXX. Conversely, errors may have arisen in the transmission of the Hebrew between the latest common ancestor and the *Vorlage* of P. We may expect these to have given rise to errors confined to P and absent both from MT and from LXX (and other more distantly related witnesses). It may prove difficult, however, to distinguish such errors in P's Hebrew *Vorlage* from errors made in the translation process itself.

Between the written Hebrew text which lay before the translator and the Hebrew text which he attempted to put into Syriac, various stages intervene. The former text may be thought of as two-dimensional: the text as set out upon the page. The latter is instead linear: the text as divided into segments, which the translator processes one by one. These segments of the Hebrew *Vorlage*, as will be shown below, normally contained more than one word. No doubt the translator made every effort to convert the written text into a linear sequence of segments accurately, but on occasion he may have inadvertently have failed. A particular difficulty was that he constantly had to read a segment in the Hebrew *Vorlage*, write down a Syriac translation in his own book, and then to return to the next segment in the Hebrew *Vorlage*. Fatigue or carelessness could have caused him to return to the wrong point, and thus to omit a particular segment, or perhaps to render it twice.

Once the translator had begun to work on a given segment, he had to read all its letters; and here too he may have encountered difficulty. In some such passages, his decipherment of any doubtful letters may have been false. There may also have been places where he could not decipher anything at all; such passages had to be treated by the same expedients as were applied to texts that could be read but not understood, as considered in detail below.

After the segment had been delimited and its letters read, the translator next had to understand it. Here the first step was to identify what morphemes (i.e. elements of vocabulary and grammar) were present. Like any other reader of an unpointed text, the translator would examine the words in turn, picking up any "pattern clues" of morphological form within the word under scrutiny and any "syntactic clues" in neighbouring words.[15]

What other sources the translators might have had, beyond the consonantal Hebrew text, and what authority they might have attached to these, will need to be discussed. One possibility to investigate is that they had a reading tradition, which indicated the

---

[15] H. Rosén, *A Textbook of Israeli Hebrew*, Chicago 1962, p. vii.

pronunciation of the Hebrew text, at least in some passages. It is also possible that they had access to LXX or to some other written form of the Greek Bible. Yet another suggestion is that they had manuscripts of one or other of the Jewish Aramaic versions, or alternatively that they drew upon orally transmitted Aramaic renderings for particular phrases in the text. However, a consonantal Hebrew text was the translators' primary source, as will become clear below.

Upon first scanning a segment of text, the translator may have found one (or more) of the Hebrew words to be patient of more than one identification. He would then check these alternatives against the resulting overall sense implied by each for the whole phrase. He may have gone through this process of re-appraisal more than once. Thus the final understanding proceeds phrase by phrase, rather than word by word.[16]

The normal outcome was that the translator found only one set of identifications of the morphemes to be viable. These would have led to the plain sense of the whole segment, without ambiguity, at least in the translator's own mind. The translator's success here would have depended on his prior knowledge of Hebrew, and his skill in applying that knowledge to the Hebrew *Vorlage*.

Having identified the plain sense uniquely, the translator usually wished to convey it precisely; but this was not always so. On occasion, he may instead have wished to improve it either on grounds internal to the text (e.g. by resolving a logical contradiction) or on external grounds (e.g. by removing an element which had become theologically objectionable, such as a reference to God changing his purpose).

It did not always happen, however, that the translator arrived at a unique plain sense. An alternative possibility is that he hesitated between two different but viable possibilities; in that case he may have chosen just one, but with some misgivings, or he may even have preserved both alternatives in a doublet translation. At the other extreme, he may have found the Hebrew so obscure as to yield no plain sense for the whole segment at all, even though he may have identified various morphemes within it. In such cases, the translator would have had recourse to special techniques or supplementary sources, since he was still expected to produce some form of translation. As special techniques, he might stretch the sense of the morphemes identified, or tacitly emend the Hebrew text in order to obtain clear sense, or guess from the context. Supplementary sources might have been other scriptural passages, other biblical versions or exegetical traditions; the possibilities are considered in detail in chapter 2.

A distinction may be drawn at this point between construal and interpretation. The construal of a segment may be defined as the derivation of its plain sense, so far as is possible. The normal outcome, as stated above, is that the whole segment yields plain sense without ambiguity. Where, however, more than one possibility for the plain sense is found, construal is the derivation of the alternative meanings; and where no plain sense for the segment can be derived at all, construal means identifying whatever morphemes one can. Interpretation is then the gap between the results of construal and the sense which the translator actually tries to express. It need not occur at every point in the text; and where it does, it can take different forms. In cases where construal yielded a unique plain sense, interpretation may modify it, e.g. in order to remove a perceived

---

[16] J. Barr, *The Typology of Literalism*, Göttingen 1979, pp. 296–7.

logical or theological difficulty. In cases where construal yielded two or more alternative meanings, interpretation consists of choosing between these; and where construal
gave no satisfactory sense, techniques such as guesswork to which the translators
resorted constitute yet another type of interpretation.

The translators' understanding of the text, once reached, had to be conveyed
through an appropriate choice of words and constructions in Syriac. This was another
side of the translators' skill, quite apart from the understanding of the text. How far
they may have drawn here upon pre-existing renderings in Aramaic, either in written or
in fixed oral form, is a question to be discussed below.

The Syriac mss extant today are separated from the translators' original work by
some generations of copying. All canonical books survive in the seventh-century manuscript 7a1 in Milan, but for most books we already have copies from the sixth century
and for a few books from the fifth. These last include the oldest dated biblical ms in any
language.[17] There are also citations of particular passages in the fourth-century fathers
Aphrahat and Ephrem, but even these are at least a century later than the translation
itself.

Even where the extant witnesses agree, they do not necessarily preserve the text that
left the hand of the translator. A number of changes – both involuntary corruptions
and deliberate 'improvements' or annotations – entered the text so early that no extant
ms is free of them. These readings can all be termed errors, in the sense that they depart
from the original text, although some were introduced deliberately. We may suppose
that, in any given biblical book, all the extant witnesses to the Syriac text derive from a
lost ancestor which already had these errors. This latest common ancestor (technically
termed the archetype) of all the extant mss was thus itself a copy, distinct from and
perhaps some generations removed from the original translation. The only hope of
removing these changes lies in conjectural emendation.

Finally, although the extant Syriac biblical mss show an impressive degree of uniformity, they are not identical. An important part of our task, therefore, is to choose
between the rival readings where the Syriac mss disagree. This will in turn require criteria which will inform the choice, and will also carry implications for the history of the
text.

However over-simplified, the above survey suffices to highlight a major difficulty in
the study of P. Of the many stages in the history and development of the text as traced
in fig.1, we can observe only two: the extant mss of MT in Hebrew, and of P in Syriac.[18]
Hence it is not always possible to identify which of the many factors considered in fig. 1
have determined the relationship between these two forms of the text in any given
passage. For example, where the translator seems aware of the sense of a rare Hebrew
word, did he have prior linguistic knowledge or make a clever deduction from the
context? Where P agrees with another version against the plain sense of MT, should we
suppose that the two versions had a different *Vorlage* from MT, or that one version has

---

[17] This is the palimpsest 5ph1, dated to 771 of the Seleucid era, i.e. 459/60 CE. Manuscript 5b1 on the
Pentateuch is dated to 775 of that era, i.e. 463/4 CE.

[18] The authorities excluded from fig.1 may be helpful here and there, but not on a regular basis, either
because they belong to families which branched off too early (e.g. LXX and various Qumran texts) or
because they are translations from a text of the same type preserved in the original language in MT (e.g.
Aquila, the Targums).

influenced the other, or that the two translators arrived at similar results independently in the face of the same difficulties in the Hebrew text? We shall constantly be weighing the probabilities of alternative explanations, without necessarily having any certain basis for a decision.

Existing research on the Peshitta

It is not necessary to present here a summary of existing research on the Peshitta, since that task has already been discharged admirably in two book-length works: the compendium (in German) prepared by Haefeli[19] and the new survey (in Italian) by Dirksen.[20] Briefer surveys have been provided by van Puyvelde,[21] Brock,[22] de Boer,[23] Goshen-Gottstein[24] and Joosten.[25] Another important tool provided by Dirksen is his very full classified and annotated bibliography, published in 1989 and updated in 1992.[26] Altogether, therefore, it is only necessary here to trace the main contours of Peshitta research.

First in logic, though only latterly accomplished, is the collation of the manuscripts. The earliest text of the Peshitta of the Old Testament to circulate among western scholars was prepared by the Maronite scholar Gabriel Sionita for the Paris polyglot of 1645. That text was based largely on the almost contemporary Paris manuscript "Syriaques 6" (Leiden siglum: 17a5), and suffered badly from errors accumulated over the centuries. Yet it formed the main basis for subsequent editions until the turn of the twentieth century. The London polyglot of 1657 added some variant readings from two mss, which, however, were again no earlier than the seventeenth century.[27] It is true that Lee's edition of 1823, often reprinted and until recently the most accessible text, claimed to draw upon earlier manuscripts; but Lee did not specify his sources, nor how he had used them, and his text offers very few corrections to that of the polyglots.[28]

In 1869, Ceriani drew attention to the existence of far older mss of P.[29] These

---

[19] L. Haefeli, *Die Peschitta des Alten Testamentes, mit Rücksicht auf ihre textkritische Bearbeitung und ihre Herausgabe* [=Alttestamentliche Abhandlungen XI.1], Münster 1927.

[20] P.B. Dirksen, *La Peshitta dell' Antico Testamento*, tr. P.G. Borbone [=Studi Biblici 103], Brescia 1993.

[21] Cl. Van Puyvelde, "Versions Syriaques", in *Dictionnaire de la Bible*, Sup. 6, Paris 1960, cols. 834–84 (Peshitta: 835–55).

[22] S.P. Brock, "Bibelübersetzungen, I.4: Die Übersetzungen ins Syrische, 4.1.1. Peschitta", in G. Krause and G. Müller (eds.), *Theologische Realenzyklopädie*, Berlin 1977–, vol. 6 (1980), pp. 182–5.

[23] "Towards an Edition of the Syriac Version of the Old Testament", *VT* 31 (1981), pp. 346–57 [= PIC 16].

[24] M.H. Goshen-Gottstein, תרגומים סוריים, in אנציקלופדיה מקראית, edited by the Bialik Institute, vol. 8, Jerusalem 1982, cols. 847–54.

[25] J. Joosten, "La Peshitta de l'Ancien Testament dans la recherche récente", *Revue d'Histoire et de Philosophie Religieuses* 76 (1996), pp. 385–95.

[26] P.B. Dirksen, *An Annotated Bibliography of the Peshitta of the Old Testament* [=MPI 5], Leiden 1989. This was updated by Dirksen in P.B. Dirksen and A. van der Kooij (eds.), *The Peshitta as a Translation* [=MPI 8], Leiden 1995, pp. 221–36; and further updates are expected.

[27] On the history of the printed editions, see W.E. Barnes, "The Printed Editions of the Peshitta of the Old Testament", *Expository Times* 9 (1897/8), pp. 560–2. A detailed study of a particular book is provided by J.A. Emerton, "The Printed Editions of the S. of S. in the Peshitta version", *VT* 17 (1967), pp. 416–29. See further the works of Ceriani, Barnes and Emerton cited below.

[28] S. Lee (ed.), *Vetus Testamentum Syriace*, London 1823.

[29] A.M. Ceriani, *Le edizioni e i manoscritti delle versioni siriache del Vecchio Testamento*. A summary was published, under the same title, in the series *Reale Istituto Lombardo di Scienze e Lettere: Rendiconti*. Serie II, Volume II, Parte 1. Milan 1869, pp. 12–14, 267–8, 291–3.

included a ms in Milan which he inclined to date to the sixth century, and which covered nearly the whole Old Testament (now known as 7a1).[30] He also noted the fine collection of mss recently acquired by the British Museum, including a ms of the Pentateuch dated to 463/4 CE (i.e. 5b1).[31] The exploitation of these resources was begun almost immediately in studies of individual books: Chronicles,[32] Psalms[33] and Isaiah.[34] Not until 1956, however, was a project lauched to prepare a new edition on the basis of the manuscript evidence, following the meeting of the International Organisation for the Study of the Old Testament in Strasbourg. The work was entrusted to an international team and co-ordinated by the newly founded Peshitta Institute in Leiden.

The first achievement of the Peshitta Institute was a worldwide list of mss of the Peshitta Old Testament.[35] Its ultimate aim was a new edition of P, which began to appear in 1972 and is now almost complete.[36] The new edition provides full collations of all the biblical mss up to and including the twelfth century, though the earliest volumes (published before 1977) also reported the readings of mss right up to the nineteenth.

A critical edition in the strict sense aims to restore the original text, and this in principle entails three tasks: to collate all the mss, to select the best reading where these disagree, and to emend the text by conjecture where none of the extant witnesses offers a satisfactory reading. The Leiden edition was designed for the first stage only, and rightly so, given the state of knowledge and opinion when it was launched.[37] The next stage, of choosing between rival readings, presupposes agreed criteria for the choice; but these did not yet exist. This point is illustrated by the scholar who berated the Leiden editors for refraining from indicating their preferred readings and thus for "leaving half the work undone":[38] his own trenchant review of a fundamental work on the textual criticism of P[39] showed how far scholarship still remained from consensus on the criteria for assessing rival readings, even in 1980, long after full publication of the textual materials.[40] Even today the necessary consensus is only gradually emerging.

Although the Leiden edition does not in principle go beyond the collation of the mss,

---

[30] Another outstanding contribution by Ceriani to Peshitta research was the publication of a facsimile edition of this ms, in 1876–83.

[31] This ms reached the British Museum in March 1843. See W. Wright, *Catalogue of the Syriac Manuscripts in the British Museum*, London 1870–2, vol. 3, p. xiii.

[32] W.E. Barnes, *An Apparatus Criticus to Chronicles in the Peshitta Version with a Discussion of the Value of the Codex Ambrosianus*, Cambridge 1897.

[33] Id., *The Peshitta Psalter according to the West Syrian Text, Edited with an Apparatus Criticus*, Cambridge 1904.

[34] G. Diettrich, *Ein Apparatus criticus zur Pešitto zum Propheten Jesaja* [= BZAW 8], Giessen 1905.

[35] *List of Old Testament Peshitta Manuscripts (Preliminary Issue)*, edited by the Peshitta Institute, Leiden University, Leiden 1961. Updates to this list have been published in VT, as "Peshitta Institute Communications". A revised edition of the *List* is being prepared by Dr Jenner.

[36] *Vetus Testamentum Syriace*, Leiden 1972– .

[37] The reading shown in the text was not necessarily that preferred by the editors. Instead it was determined by formal rules; see pp. 288, 307–8 below.

[38] M.H. Goshen-Gottstein, "Prolegomena to a Critical Edition of the Peshitta", in C. Rabin (ed.), *Studies in the Bible* [= *Scripta Hierosolymitana* 8], Jerusalem 1961, pp. 26–67; see p. 63n.

[39] M.D. Koster, *The Peshitta of Exodus. The Development of its Text in the Course of Fifteen Centuries*, Assen/Amsterdam 1977.

[40] M.H. Goshen-Gottstein, "The Peshitta and its Manuscripts: A Review", *Bibliotheca Orientalis* 37 (1980), pp. 13–16.

the editors of two particular biblical books have provided important monographs on the historical inter-relations between the mss, and the problems of choice between rival readings.[41] Two more – Gelston and Lane – have produced valuable studies which deal more briefly with those topics and also examine the translation technique.[42]

Studies of the translation technique in fact began to appear long before the new edition was conceived. Nearly every book of the Hebrew Bible in the P version has been subjected to a detailed comparison with MT and other known textual authorities. Most of these investigations were produced around the turn of the twentieth century, often as doctoral theses. They consist largely of a verse-by-verse running commentary, with a brief summary arranged by topic; details will be found in Dirksen's bibliography. Many of the authors checked the printed editions then available against the facsimile of the Milan codex (7a1). Although the Leiden edition has since revealed many further readings of importance, major discrepancies are rare, so that these studies retain much value, especially in their detailed comments on difficult passages in P.

Gelston's work on the Twelve Prophets stands apart from these earlier studies in being securely based on full manuscript collations. Arranged by topic, it provides a penetrating analysis of the relationship which P bears to the extant forms of the Hebrew and to the other textual witnesses. More recently, studies of P in Daniel[43] and Job[44] have also appeared.

Outside the Pentateuch, the only books of the Hebrew Bible on which no running commentary exists are Judges and Jeremiah. The Pentateuch is exceptional, in that investigations have been organised by topic, rather than in commentary form. Thus Hirzel in 1825 provided an overview of the translation technique of the Peshitta Pentateuch, and also examined the evidence for its original background. Hirzel argued for a Christian context, mainly on the basis of the version's supposed negligence in ritual matters.[45] This conclusion was attacked in the seminal study by Joseph Perles, who pointed out many parallels in the Pentateuch between P and Jewish Targums or rabbinic sources, and showed that many of P's renderings there presupposed knowledge of Jewish exegesis. On a smaller scale, Perles also pointed out parallels between P and Jewish sources outside the Pentateuch. In addition, he made some perceptive suggestions on the general background of P, though constraints of space sometimes forced him to leave arguments incomplete.[46] In later study of P in the Pentateuch, attention later focused on parallels (real and alleged) with the Jewish Targums – notably Onkelos and the Palestinian Targums discovered in the Cairo Geniza.[47] More

---

[41] P.B. Dirksen, *The Transmission of the Text in the Peshiṭta Manuscripts of the Book of Judges* [=MPI 1], Leiden 1972; and Koster, op. cit.

[42] A.Gelston, *The Peshiṭta of the Twelve Prophets*, Oxford 1987. D.J. Lane, *The Peshiṭta of Leviticus* [=MPI 6], Leiden 1994.

[43] R.A. Taylor, The *Peshiṭta of Daniel* [=MPI 7], Leiden 1994. This is written primarily in commentary form, with detailed comparison of the Syriac, Hebrew and Greek forms of the text, cautiously evaluated.

[44] H.M. Szpek, *Translation Technique in the Peshiṭta to Job* [= SBL Dissertation Series 137], Atlanta 1992. On this, see *JTS* 47 (1996), pp. 584–7.

[45] L. Hirzel, *De Pentateuchi Versionis Syriacae Quam Peschito Vocant Indole Commentatio Critico-Exegetica*, Leipzig 1825.

[46] J. Perles, *Meletemata Peschitthoniana*, Breslau 1859.

[47] The course of this discussion is traced in detail by P.B. Dirksen, "The Old Testament Peshiṭta", in M.J. Mulder et al. (eds.), *Mikra: Text, Translation, Reading and Interpretation of the Hebrew Bible in Ancient Judaism and Early Christianity,* Assen/Maastricht and Philadelphia 1988, pp. 255–98. See further chapter 3 below.

recently, the parallels which P bears to rabbinic literature have been examined in detail.[48] These studies are all organised by topic. No running commentary exists at all for Leviticus, Numbers and Deuteronomy, though for Genesis and Exodus a commentary in Hebrew was provided by Heller.[49]

We come finally to the two works of synthesis, by Haefeli and Dirksen. Haefeli's book provided a compendium of research up to about 1916.[50] After a summary of the existing theories on the origin of P and of its later development, Haefeli devoted separate sections to each of the different biblical books (including the Apocrypha), where he summarised and evaluated existing research. Haefeli intended his work to serve as a preparatory study for a new edition of P, and the latter half accordingly examines the character of the biblical mss, other primary sources and printed editions, as well as the methodological problems of establishing the text.

Haefeli's ideas for a new edition were shaped by Nöldeke's observation that the text of P had suffered seriously during the earliest centuries of its existence, for which we have no ms. He suggested that the text of 7a1 should be supplemented with an apparatus to show the most important variants in both eastern and western mss, and doubted whether any further progress was feasible towards the reconstruction of the translators' original work.[51]

Dirksen's new survey of the field appeared in 1993. By that time, Haefeli's plans for collating the mss of P had been largely fulfilled and indeed surpassed – owing in no small measure to Dirksen's own efforts – in that the Leiden edition provides the text of 7a1 plus full information on variant readings. Dirksen's survey treats the different aspects of Peshitta research by topic, rather than book by book. His description and evaluation of work since Haefeli's day – notably on the relationship between P and the Targums, on the character of the different witnesses to the text of P, and on the value of P as a witness to the Hebrew text – is judicious and up to date. Altogether his work is a fine complement to Haefeli's.

An important new research tool is the concordance recently completed under Strothmann's editorship.[52] Although the concordance largely ignores the Leiden collations and instead rests on the texts of the London Polyglot and Urmi editions, it remains useful because major textual discrepancies are infrequent. The volume on Psalms gives also the Hebrew equivalents. The first volume of another concordance

---

[48] Y. Maori, *The Peshitta Version of the Pentateuch and Early Jewish Exegesis* (in Hebrew), Jerusalem 1995.

[49] Ch. Heller, *Peshitta in Hebrew Characters with Elucidatory Notes. Part I: Genesis*, Berlin 1927. *Part II: Exodus*, Berlin 1929. Heller's notes (in Hebrew) address points minor and major, selected on no obvious principle. Some of them compare P's understanding with other ancient versions and medieval Jewish commentaries. Others cite at length rabbinic interpretations with which P agrees (and supposedly followed) or disagrees (and was supposedly at pains to exclude). There are some helpful remarks on translation technique.

[50] Although the book finally appeared in 1927, Haefeli explains in the foreword that publication had been long delayed.

[51] This suggestion concludes Haefeli's monograph (pp. 115–16). According to Haefeli, further progress would depend on the discovery of more ancient material either in mss or in patristic citations.

[52] W. Strothmann, with K. Johannes and H. Zumpe, *Konkordanz zur syrischen Bibel. Der Pentateuch*, Wiesbaden 1986. *Die Propheten* (1984). *Die Mautbē* (1995). N. Sprenger, *Konkordanz zum syrischen Psalter*, Wiesbaden 1976. W. Strothmann (ed.), *Wörterverzeichnis der apokryphen-deuterokanonischen Schriften des alten Testamentes in der Peschitta*, Wiesbaden 1988. These are volumes 26, 25, 33, 10:8 and 27 respectively of the series Göttinger Orientforschungen, I. Reihe, Syriaca.

which gives the Hebrew correspondences in all books and utilises the Leiden collations has now been published by the Peshiṭta Institute, covering the Pentateuch (Leiden 1997).

The present investigation

The present study re-examines the text of P and aims to be comprehensive in two senses. First, it relates to all the different stages which separate the extant Hebrew and Syriac texts and which have been traced above. Second, the investigation is based on passages drawn from the whole Hebrew Bible. Though comprehensive in these senses, the study does not of course claim to be exhaustive.

A comprehensive study of this sort has not been attempted before. Hitherto, primary scholarship was concerned with the logically prior task of collating the mss. Moreover, the likelihood that many different translators took part encouraged the examination of separate sections rather than the whole Old Testament. Yet certain advantages are unique to the comprehensive approach.

First, as already remarked, the translators aimed primarily to convey the "plain" sense of the biblical text. This left little scope for the translators to betray much of their own views. Any single biblical book will therefore offer few direct clues to the larger historical questions surrounding the origin of P. One may hope, however, to construct a viable picture by combining clues from a number of biblical books, on the assumption that these were translated within a single community.

Second, it is only by comparing different books that one can hope to notice the systematic differences between them, as well as the links which nevertheless bind them together. This evidence sheds light on the number of different translators and the degree to which they consulted together; and this too has important implications for the origin of the version.

Third, a comprehensive study forces the investigator to compare his findings in different books. For example, if he regards P's direct source in the Pentateuch as a lost Palestinian Targum rather than a Hebrew text, he must also explain how a P version exists for books like Daniel and Ezra, where no Targum was ever made. More generally, a comprehensive study provides some check against the possibility that the differences between the results reached in different books are due to differences of perception of the same facts by different investigators.

The present study will first proceed (in chapter 2) to a general description of the translation technique, on the principle that, even though more than one translator was involved, a common approach existed to the task of translation. Here we shall break down the translation process – including the treatment of Hebrew passages which baffled the translator – into its constituent stages. We shall also consider the balance struck between fidelity to the Hebrew source and the demands of clarity, logic and religious belief. The results will help to define the conditions under which a discrepancy in sense between P and MT can be ascribed to a difference between MT and the Hebrew *Vorlage* of P.

Chapter 3 examines the relationship between P and the other versions with which it sometimes agrees, in Greek and Aramaic. It will be argued that while the translators of all biblical books in P worked primarily from a Hebrew original, many also sporadically consulted the Greek Bible in written form. The parallels with the Targums, by contrast, suggest common oral tradition or mere polygenesis, rather than literary dependence of P upon any Targum. The text of P in patristic citations will also be examined, as these are often claimed to preserve a Syriac text earlier than that of the biblical mss and closer to the Targums. Parallels with rabbinic sources, given their overlap with the Targums, will also be examined.

Chapter 4 assesses the degree of consistency in the translation of different biblical books. Conservative and modern usages can be identified in the Syriac language, modern usages being correlated with readiness to consult the Greek Bible. The different biblical books vary in their preferences, and so can be ranked along a scale between 'conservative' and 'modern'. More subtle differences can also be discerned. At the same time, there is a network of linking features which suggest that the translators of the different books constituted a single school.

Chapter 5 examines the historical context. Internal evidence implies that the translators valued prayer and faith but lacked enthusiasm for sacrifice or the other ritual demands of Judaism. In some books, they identify themselves with the Jews as a people, but in others they seem an introspective group. It is argued that they represent a non-rabbinic Jewish community, which eventually accepted Christianity. In this way they preserved their values of faith and prayer while gaining a rationale for rejecting Jewish ritual. The roots of their non-rabbinic Judaism, and the factors leading to their conversion, are also considered. As to the setting of the version, the evidence suggests that the work spanned perhaps one or two generations, towards the end of the second century CE, and that the likeliest location is Edessa.

The last chapter discusses the establishment of the text. The manuscripts and other textual witnesses are not everywhere unanimous, and at some points the original reading may have been lost. A policy for discriminating between rival readings is developed, and the implications noted for the history of the biblical text. The scope for conjectural emendation is also considered. The recovery of the original Syriac text can be approached from two directions: not only backwards through its descendants, the extant Syriac mss, but also sideways through its cousins, the extant forms of the Hebrew text. An appendix shows how the inter-relations of the manuscripts of P in two sample books of P can be investigated by statistical methods.

In strict logic, the establishment of the text should have been discussed first of all. Fortunately, however, serious instances of variation among the textual witnesses or of corruption in all of them are not so frequent as to disturb the analyis in the earlier chapters.

The study draws gratefully upon existing research, particularly the new edition of the Syriac text. It will also examine existing scholarly positions on a range of questions. As explained above, however, the task of surveying existing research in detail has already been well discharged elsewhere.

In embarking upon this study, we should be mindful of those who transmitted the version to our own age. Although the Syriac-speaking church was divided in the wake of the controversies of the fifth century, the Syriac version has to this day been transmitted by its various branches: by the Church of the East ('Nestorian') in Iraq and further east, by the Syriac Orthodox ('Jacobite') church in Turkey and Syria, and (from the seventh century) by the Maronite church in Lebanon. Until the late Middle Ages P was also the Bible of the Byzantine Syrian ('Malkite') church in Syria and Palestine, long after Arabic had begun to encroach as the sacred language of that church. Despite their divisions, these churches have transmitted the text with an impressive degree of uniformity. The comparison of this text with the texts of the Bible texts preserved by other communities, in different languages, is the task to which we must now turn.

2
The relationship between the extant Hebrew and Syriac texts

The relationship in general

For the most part, P stands close in sense to the Hebrew of MT.[1] Although we shall inevitably be paying most attention to passages where they differ, it has to be stated at the outset that close correspondence is the rule.

Undeniably, however, discrepancies appear from time to time between the sense of P and any "plain" sense which modern scholarship, for all its diversity, would attribute to MT.[2] The possible causes identified in the last chapter can in principle be grouped under three headings. First, the Hebrew *Vorlage* physically before the translator may have differed from MT. Second, the translator may have changed the sense, whether deliberately (when he "improved" it or chose to follow a different source) or inadvertently (when he misread or misunderstood the Hebrew text). Third, the text of the Syriac translation may have suffered change in transmission.

In theory, each of these could be a total explanation in itself. We could translate P back into Hebrew, and treat the result as the *Vorlage*, no matter how often it differed from MT; every discrepancy in sense would thus be ascribed to differing Hebrew texts. Or, we could assume that MT corresponds to P's *Vorlage* exactly, and the existing mss of P to the original translation; and we could assume a translation technique free enough to account for all the differences. Or, we could translate MT into Syriac, treat the result as the translator's work, and assume as much inner-Syriac change as is needed in order to reach the extant text of P.

A moment's reflection, however, shows that each of these three types of explanation has its limitations, and none can explain all the discrepancies on its own:

(a) A Hebrew text reached by retroversion must be linguistically acceptable before it can be supposed to have stood in the *Vorlage*. For example, P's statement 2 Chr. 24:16 that Jehoiada "ran many races for the Temple" is modelled on the phraseology of the Greek games rather than anything in Hebrew, and no literal retroversion can have stood in the *Vorlage*. Secondly, the Hebrew text recovered by retroversion must bear a credible relationship to MT in palaeographic terms, though we have a choice of direction: the putative Hebrew variant in the *Vorlage* may be the source of the MT reading,

---

[1] In practice, MT is almost always uniquely defined, despite some variation within the tradition; on this, see E. Tov, *Textual Criticism of the Hebrew Bible*, Minneapolis 1992, pp. 25–39.

[2] "Plain exegesis" can be defined as what "corresponds to the totality of the meaning(s) intended by the writer"; see Loewe, "The 'Plain' Meaning of Scripture", pp. 141–2.

or a development thereof, or both may be separate developments from some supposed earlier reading.[3]

(b) Translation technique is also subject to two constraints: rationality and coherence. First, any discrepancy in sense ascribed to this cause must have been reached in some logical fashion (apart from a minority due to such involuntary factors as eye-skip). Second, when all such passages are taken together, the overall impression of the translation technique in the whole translation unit[4] must show a measure of consistency. For example, in Jeremiah the Septuagint tends to be literal, so that the shorter text of the Septuagint cannot be attributed to radical translation.[5]

(c) Finally, inner-Syriac change is subject to constraints analogous to (a). First, the putative original Syriac text must bear a more direct relation to MT than does the existing Syriac text. Second, the existing text must be explicable as a scribal development of it, whether by accidental or by deliberate change.

Yet these constraints are not stringent enough to identify the correct explanation in every case of discrepancy between MT and P. We therefore have to consider what assumption to make when more than one possibility remains open. On the one hand, we could adopt a minimalist approach to translation technique. In that case, when the cause of discrepancy in sense between P and MT is in doubt, we shall invoke the first or third factors. This would mean positing a *Vorlage* that differed from MT, or emending the Syriac text. The opposite extreme is a maximalist view of translation technique. In that case, when in doubt, we shall assume that the discrepancy originated with the translator, whether consciously or not, and we shall refrain from positing different Hebrew or Syriac readings in order to attain agreement in sense. No doubt the truth lies somewhere between the extreme minimalist and maximalist positions, but it is important to know which of the two is the better starting-point.

What evidence we have supports the maximalist assumption. First, a free approach characterises other ancient translations made into Syriac, though there the source language was Greek. On the Old Syriac Gospels, for example, Burkitt observed:

Syriac is a language of very different genius to Greek, and the translator of the *Evangelion da-Mepharreshe* was far more careful to reproduce the sense of the original than to express Greek idioms in a foreign tongue. This makes his work more natural and animated, while it does not seriously interfere with its value as a critical witness in matters of importance. But in many minor points the evidence of the Syriac is really ambiguous . . . [6]

Again, the Syriac translation of Eusebius' Ecclesiastical History is characterised by McLean as follows:

Of the two qualities most desirable in a version – faithfulness and literary skill – our Syriac translator shews both in a considerable degree, but the latter more markedly than the former. His Syriac is good and idiomatic, and in many cases he has rendered freely without altering the

---

[3] These requirements are analogous to the criteria of authenticity and directionality used in discriminating between rival Syriac readings, in chapter 6 below.

[4] A translation unit is the portion of the Bible for which a single translator was responsible. As a first hypothesis, each of the 24 biblical books can be considered a separate translation unit, though we shall have reason to modify this in chapter 4 below.

[5] E. Tov, *The Text-Critical Use of the Septuagint in Biblical Research*, Jerusalem 1981, p. 52; 2nd ed. 1997, p. 19.   [6] F.C. Burkitt, *Evangelion da-Mepharreshe*, Cambridge 1904, vol. 1, p. ix.

general sense. The involved syntax and cumbrous sentences of Eusebius give place to a more perspicuous arrangement of words. On the other hand, liberties have often been taken, and misunderstandings are not uncommon, especially where unusual Greek words have to be rendered.[7]

The Old Syriac Gospels may be dated *c.* 200 CE, while the Syriac translation of the Ecclesiastical History can be no later than the early fifth century.[8] It seems perverse to argue that such translations are instead literal renderings of Greek exemplars that offered a text not known elsewhere, which particularly lent itself to translation into idiomatic Syriac.

There is a second reason for attributing the maximum to translation technique, and hence the minimum to textual change either in Hebrew or in Syriac. The transmission of the sacred text, both in Hebrew and in Syriac, was in principle intended to be faithful and mechanical. Admittedly, on the Hebrew side this is an over-simplification: as well as "model" copies, transmitted with great care, we know that in the Holy Land up to the second century CE there also circulated "vernacular" copies of the text, which were deliberately simplified and otherwise adapted for readers who spoke Hebrew.[9] Still, in general, a Hebrew variant in the *Vorlage*, or an inner-Syriac change, implies a failure somewhere in the transmission of the biblical text. By contrast, an explanation in terms of translation technique will involve the more probable eventualities of creative interpretation or of sheer misunderstanding on the part of the translator.

As noted above, there is one essential constraint to the maximalist position, namely that the overall picture of the translation technique which results must be coherent. Subject to that, the present treatment will posit the minimum of textual change, whether in Hebrew or in Syriac, and lay correspondingly greater emphasis on the various aspects of translation technique. The question will be kept under review as the data are examined, and we shall return to it on pp. 60–2. At the outset, however, we must acknowledge the inescapable uncertainty in any discussion of translation technique, in that we have no direct access either to the starting-point of the translation (i.e. the Hebrew *Vorlage*) or to its end-point (the translator's original work).

We shall now examine in detail the stages through which the translation has passed.

Perception

At any point in the text, the translator's first task was to locate in the *Vorlage* the material to be translated, before reading it. Occasionally, faulty location caused a discrepancy between the text which passed into the translator's mind and the text of the *Vorlage*. The translator was constantly switching back and forth between the *Vorlage* and the translation which he was making, and under fatigue he may on occasion have

---

[7] W. Wright and N. McLean, *The Ecclesiastical History of Eusebius in Syriac*, Cambridge 1898, p. ix.

[8] See L. van Rompay, "Some Preliminary Remarks on the Origins of Classical Syriac as a Standard Language", in G. Goldenberg and S. Raz (eds.), *Semitic and Cushitic Studies*, Wiesbaden 1994, pp. 70–89: p. 73.

[9] These include 1QIs[a], as well as some other biblical texts copied at Qumran. See E.Y. Kutscher, *The Language and Linguistic Background of the Isaiah Scroll (1QIsa)*, [= *Studies on the Texts of the Desert of Judah* VI], Leiden 1974.

picked up the *Vorlage* at the wrong point. Eye-skip through this cause between similar expressions in the Hebrew seems the cause of some of the omissions in P, e.g.

(a)   Lev. 11:40a

והאכל מנבלתה יכבס בגדיו וטמא עד הערב

The second half of this verse is identical, except that it begins והנשא את נבלתה. P has omitted the first half, apparently by accident.

(b)   Num. 13:19–20a

MT   ומה הארץ אשר הוא ישב בה הטובה הוא אם רעה
ומה הערים אשר הוא יושב בהנה הבמחנים אם במבצרים
ומה הארץ השמנה הוא אם רזה היש בה עץ אם אין

P   ܘܐܝܟ ܗܝ، ܐܪܥܐ ܕܝܬܒܝܢ ܒܗ. ܐܢ ܫܡܝܢܐ ܗܝ، ܐܘ ܐܝܬ ܒܗ ܐܝܠܢܐ ܐܘ ܠܐ

and what is the land in which they dwell: is it fertile? and are there trees in it, or not?

Here the translator's eye skipped from the first to the second occurrence of ומה הארץ. The omission of eight words at Dan. 11 – from ושב (v. 28) to ולא תהיה (v. 29) inclu- sive – which effectively reverses the sense of the remaining words of v.29, may likewise be accidental, even though the words between which eye-skip must be posited – ועשה (v.28) and תהיה (v.29) – share only the last letter.[10]

The supposed error of perception can sometimes be connected with the external layout of the text. For example, at Ps. 23:5–6 P has a curious addition:

MT   ...כוסי רויה: אך טוב וחסד ירדפוני

P   ...ܘܪܘܝܘܬܐ ܐܝܟ ܚܝܐ. ܛܝܒܘܬܟ ܘܪܚܡܝܟ ܢܪܕܦܘܢܝ

and my cup inebriates [me] *like life*. Your grace and mercy have pursued me . . .

The reference to life is explicable if we posit a *Vorlage* set out in lines of about 19 letters as follows:

...כוסי רויה אך
טוב וחסד ירדפוני כל ימי
...חיי

We may then suppose that the translator's eye skipped a line, from אך to חיי, and that these two words were rendered ܐܝܟ ܚܝܐ "like life". This would not be the only instance in Psalms where אך is identified with the similar-sounding ܐܝܟ (cf. 39:7,12 etc.). Thereafter, the translator returned to the right place at טוב, which he rendered: "Your grace . . .". He did not, however, expunge the element "life". Similarly, in Ps. 119 the omis- sion of v.91 and other dislocations may mean that the translator's eye sometimes failed to return to the right spot, within a block of eight verses all beginning in the same letter.[11]

---

[10] R.A. Taylor, *The Peshitta of Daniel* (=MPI 7), Leiden 1994, p. 278, instead inclines to view it as a "bold stroke" by the translator in the simplification of a somewhat redundant text; but such boldness would be without parallel in P-Daniel.

[11] For further detail on these and similar passages, see M.P. Weitzman, "The Peshiṭta Psalter and its Hebrew *Vorlage*", *VT* 35 (1985), pp. 341–54.

Reading

Having located the text in his *Vorlage*, the translator had to read it. This was usually straightforward, but occasionally the *Vorlage* was not fully legible, and the translator's decipherment was unsuccessful. A likely case occurs at Lam. 3:1 –

MT   אני הגבר ראה עני

P   ,אלך גלבהא שי, בזהב.

> Almighty God, look upon my enslavement!

Apparently אני was illegible, and the translator instead continued the address to God at the end of Lam. 2, drawing upon two biblical phrases from other books, at Isa. 10:21 and Gen. 29:32.[12]

Again at Job 29:18, two alternative renderings in P suggest that the translator found the *Vorlage* unclear and hesitated between two possible reconstructions:

MT   ואמר עם קני אגוע

P   והזדת לכלא הזמבא אהרא אפוזי. ואמרך הא כני ואמר.

> and I said: "I shall save a wretched people, and like a reed I shall reach an end".

Although he finally arrived at the correct reading of the last three words, the translator cannot have been at all certain, for he also contemplated the alternative restoration עם עני אושיע for the last three words, based on Ps. 18:28.

The phenomenon of difficulty in deciphering the *Vorlage* is most extensive in Chronicles, discussed in chapter 3. It is again exemplified in P in two more extensive passages in Wisdom of Solomon, viz Wis. 11:13–15b and 17:4c–16b, where semantic correspondence between the Greek original and the Syriac suddenly breaks down. It has been suggested that the original text of P in these passages was accidentally lost, and the gap filled by a reviser who knew little Greek.[13] It seems likelier, however, that these portions happened to be illegible in the Greek *Vorlage*, and that the translator himself rendered them using techniques similar to those seen in Chronicles. These passages in Wisdom are discussed in detail by the writer elsewhere.[14]

Construal

The translator's next step was to identify the lexical items and grammatical forms present in the sequence of Hebrew consonants that he had read. Here, the translator might occasionally disagree with the conventional identifications. Thus at Exod. 18:18 the verb תִּבֹּל, which most derive from root נבל 'wither', is translated by P as תחסד אנת "you will be disgraced"; the translator thus connected it rather with the noun נְבָלָה 'disgrace', rendered כאבתא at Judg. 19:23 (cf. 1 Sam. 25:25). An instance

---

[12] A. Abelesz, *Die syrische Uebersetzung der Klagelieder und ihr Verhältnis zu Targum und LXX*, Privigye 1895, pp. 36–7. On p. 33, Abelesz likewise ascribes the cryptic שמבב in P at Lam. 1:16 to misreading of a damaged Hebrew text (MT: שוממים).

[13] J. Holtzmann, *Die Peschitta zum Buche der Weisheit. Eine kritisch-exegetische Studie*, Freiburg-im-Breisgau 1903, pp. 24, 28, 97–8.

[14] "Two curious passages in the Peshitta of Wisdom", in B. Taylor (ed.), *IX Congress of the IOSCS*, Atlanta 1997, pp. 137–51.

where P agrees with LXX against the usual identification is the derivation of הסתיר, with God's face as object, from סור 'turn away'.[15]

Occasionally it is arguable that P's identification is superior to the conventional one. Thus at Num. 24:8 Heb. חציו is usually construed as "his arrows", but REB ("their backs") connects it instead with بتۯ "loins" and so agrees with P ܚܨܘܗܝ. Again, יִרְאָה at Ezek. 1:18 is rendered by P ܡܚܙܐ and so derived from ראה 'see'; and NEB likewise rendered: "the power of sight".

Sometimes these identifications contradict the vocalisation of MT, e.g.

(a)   Deut. 1:44

MT   (וַיִּרְדְּפוּ אֶתְכֶם) כַּאֲשֶׁר תַּעֲשֶׂינָה הַדְּבֹרִים

P   ܐܝܟ ܕܒܘܪܐ ܕܬܢܢܐ

"like smoked bees"

(vocalising the verb as תֶּעָשֶׁנָּה).

(b)   Judg. 20:16

The slingers of Benjamin could shoot successfully אֶל הַשַּׂעֲרָה "at a hair". However, P makes them shoot ܠܥܠܥܠܐ , finding instead the word שְׂעָרָה 'storm'. Perhaps the intended meaning was that even a storm could not disturb their aim.

(c)   1 Sam. 21:5

Here David assures Ahimelech that his young men have abstained from women (מֵאִשָּׁה). According to P, however, they had instead abstained from sacrifice (ܡܢ ܕܒܚܬܐ), the Hebrew being vocalised מֵאִשֶּׁה.

(d)   2 Sam. 23:1

MT has הֻקַם עָל "was raised above", while P renders ܕܐܩܝܡ ܢܝܪܐ "who raised the yoke", vocalising הֵקִם עֹל .

This raises the question whether the translators worked from the unpointed text alone, or whether they were aided by a tradition of pronunciation. It is true that P's understanding of the Hebrew usually agrees with that implied by the vocalisation of MT. In any given passage, however, we cannot easily decide whether he was supplied orally with that vocalisation or worked it out from his prior knowledge of Hebrew. Moreover, as just shown, there are many passages where P's construal of the consonantal Hebrew text runs wholly counter to any reading tradition; and there are a few biblical passages such as Lam. 3:1 where P seems baffled by a damaged Hebrew *Vorlage* and has no reading tradition on which to fall back. The translators cannot, therefore, have possessed a continuous reading tradition to accompany the written text.

Evidently, though, the linguistic knowledge needed in order to translate at all presupposes an education, which must have been largely oral and based on biblical texts. Hence the translators must have been exposed to a tradition of pronunciation of *parts*

---

[15] S.E. Balantine, *The Hidden God*, Oxford 1983, pp. 80–114. Gelston, *Twelve Prophets*, p. 143 provides further examples of unexpected lexical identification.

of the Bible. We may tentatively infer that any given translator had no more (and no less) than a patchy knowledge of a reading tradition, which might or might not cover parts of the book which he happened to be translating. Consequently, he found many words in the consonantal text to be of uncertain vocalisation and hence meaning.

Each lexical item identified was associated by the translator with a certain basic sense. Here we are concerned with his pre-existing knowledge of Hebrew, rather than any deductions reached in the course of the translation. That basic meaning did not necessarily agree with that upheld by modern scholarship. For example, תירוש is conventionally understood as 'wine', but P renders ܥܢܒܐ (Judg. 9:13, 2 Kgs. 18:32) or ܦܘܠܬܐ (Isa. 65:8), both meaning 'berry' or 'grape'. In this instance, P is probably right; the meaning 'grape' is supported in rabbinic sources and fits the majority of biblical occurrences better than the conventional 'wine'.[16]

More often, however, the basic meaning supposed by P is not so valuable. For example, סוללה 'siege-works' is almost everywhere understood by P to mean 'ambush' (noun ܟܡܐܢܐ or verb ܟܡܢ). Again, we find the odd rendering ܣܟܝ 'wait' for חוש, mainly in Psalms.[17] The roots עלז/עליץ are often rendered by Syr. ܥܫܢ (even in straightforward contexts like Ps. 5:12), by association with ערץ.

Of some words, the translators seemed to have had no prior knowledge, and a translation had to be reached through specific techniques developed for passages not initially understood (see pp. 36–48 below). Thus for the verb נדב (Qal and Hitpaʻel) we find guesses or deductions: ܐܬܚܫܒ 'think' (thrice in Exodus), ܐܬܟܢܫ 'gather' (1 Chr. 29:6), ܦܪܫ 'separate' (passive participle – Judg. 5:9), ܫܦܪ 'be pleasing' (2 Chr. 17:16), ܫܒܚ 'praise' (1 Chr. 29:17 and – as noun – Judg. 5:2) Even the rare renderings ܪܓ 'desire' (Ezra. 3:5, Neh. 11:12) and ܝܗܒ 'give' (1 Chr. 29:9), which come within sight of the true sense, could have been guessed from the context. Again, חליל is never recognised as a wind instrument, and is instead assigned to percussion[18] or strings,[19] though Isa. 30:29 shows the vague ܚܕܘܬܐ 'joy'.

In the case of some institutions unique to ancient Israel, the translators did not know the exact meaning and could only offer an etymology. An example is אורים ותמים, which P represents by ܢܗܝܪ ܘܓܡܝܪܐ "bright and complete" at Exod. 28:30 (and similarly at Deut. 33:8); compare ܓܡܝܪܘܬܐ "completeness" alone at 1 Sam. 14:41, where MT has תמים only. At Lev. 8:8, this etymology was interpreted as the more intelligible ܝܕܥܬܐ ܘܩܘܫܬܐ "knowledge and truth" (Lev. 8:8).[20]

Having identified each word and noted its basic sense, the translator had to consider the overall meaning of a whole phrase. This was an iterative process, since many words in the text, which was of course unvocalised, were ambiguous in themselves. The translator may thus have had to revise his initial identifications of lexical (and other) items until he obtained satisfactory sense for the phrase overall. At the end, he would hope to reach the 'plain sense' of the phrase, which he would proceed to express in Syriac. Sometimes, however, matters were not so straightforward. The translator may have

---

[16] S. Naeh and M. Weitzman, "Tirosh – Wine or Grape?", *VT* 44 (1994), pp. 115–20.
[17] Reasons for these two renderings are suggested below.   [18] ܦܠܓ – 1 Sam. 10:5.
[19] ܩܝܬܪܐ at 1 Kgs. 1:40, Isa. 5:12; ܟܢܪ at Jer. 48:36.
[20] At Num. 27:21, however, P renders the Urim by their function: ܫܐܠܬܐ 'inquiry'. Even more plainly, לאורים ולתמים at Ezra. 2:63 = Neh. 7:65 becomes "and he will ask and see".

been dissatisfied with the plain sense. Alternatively, he may not have been able to derive continuous sense at all: he might have failed to identify one of the words, or, having thought that he had identified them all, he may have been unable to form any meaning for the whole phrase. For the moment, however, let us consider how the plain sense was expressed when such difficulties did not arise.

The segmentation of the text

The two primary (and often conflicting) aims of a translation are fidelity and intelligibility. The balance struck in a given translation is often indicated by describing it as either literal or free. That distinction, however, is inadequate, as Barr has observed, since literalism has different aspects which each need separate consideration, and a translation may be 'literal' in one of these respects and 'free' in another.[21] Of these, the first is the level at which the translator segments the text. Does he translate phrase by phrase, or word by word? Of course, the translator needed to examine whole phrases in order to understand the Hebrew text at all, so that the question of segmentation applies primarily to the way that he expressed the sense in Syriac: was his aim to represent the sense of each phrase, or to provide an equivalent for each Hebrew word?

These two alternatives have sometimes been posed in relation to translations from Hebrew into Greek,[22] or from Greek into Syriac,[23] and in these cases the structural difference between the two languages allows a clear answer. The answer is less obvious, however, for a translation from Hebrew into Syriac. The general intelligibility of P suggests that the translators' first concern was to represent the overall sense of each phrase. On the other hand, the Syriac text of P usually presents a readily identifiable equivalent to each Hebrew word of MT, in more or less the same order. Did the translators proceed phrase by phrase, in which case the word-by-word correspondences are a by-product, due to the similarity of structure of the two languages? Or did they proceed primarily on a word-by-word basis, in which case the general clarity of the translation is a happy by-product of that similarity between Hebrew and Syriac?

On balance, the phrase-by-phrase approach seems likelier. First, as already noted, this is the usual approach in Syriac translations from Greek down to about the sixth century. Indeed, on the rare occasions where the Old Testament Peshitta is based on a Greek source, the translator has clearly worked with phrases rather than words. This is illustrated by various phrases from the couplets which P appended on the basis of LXX to Prov. 9:12 –

ὃς ἐρείδεται ἐπὶ ψεύδεσιν   ܐܝܟ ܕܢܣܡܟ ܥܠ ܟܕܒܘܬܐ

ὄρνεα πετόμενα   ܘܥܘܦܐ ܕܦܪܚ

or more extensively:

LXX   διαπορεύεται δὲ δι' ἀνύδρου ἐρήμου καὶ γῆν διατεταγμένην ἐν διψώδεσιν

P   ܠܓܘ ܐܪܥܐ ܨܗܝܬܐ ܕܠܝܬ ܒܗ ܡܝܐ. ܘܡܢ ܐܝܟܐ ܕܕܚܝܚܐ ܘܨܗܝܬܐ ܘܝܒܝܫܐ

---

[21] J. Barr, "The Typology of Literalism in Ancient Biblical Translations", *Mitteilungen des Septuaginta-Unternehmens* XV, Göttingen 1979, pp. 275–325.   [22] Barr, "Typology of Literalism", p. 294.
[23] S.P. Brock, "Aspects of Translation Technique in Antiquity", *Greek Roman and Byzantine Studies* 20 (1979), pp. 69–87.

That the Hebrew too was usually rendered on the level of phrases rather than words tends to be confirmed by the adjustments made for clarity's sake, and by the devices used to bring sense out of obscure Hebrew phrases, which are described below.

In general, it is only where a translator could not make sense of the Hebrew phrase as a whole that he might fall back on a word-by-word translation, as we shall see. The books where word-by-word translation is commonest are S. of S. and Qohelet, perhaps because the translators wanted it clear that they were not responsible for the eroticism of the one or the cynicism of the other.[24]

The practice of breaking a word into even smaller units is found in Aquila,[25] but is virtually alien to P, e.g.

Exod. 32:25   לשמצה; P ܐܫܡܗ ܒܝܫ, cf. T^{OF[J]N} שום ביש, analysing as שם צואה[26]

Isa. 9:1 etc.   צלמות; P ܛܠܠ ܡܘܬܐ, cf. LXX σκιὰ θανάτου

Ps. 10:10   חלכאים; P ܡܚܝܠܐ ܘܟܐܒܐ, suggesting חלי + כאבים

The first two examples seem in fact due to external influences: traditional exegesis reflected also in the Targums, and consultation of LXX, respectively. The relationship between P and these versions is examined in detail in chapter 3.

Quantitative correspondence

A second type of literalism is quantitative: its ideal is that no words are added to the text, or subtracted from it.[27] In this sense, P tends to be strictly literal, almost through-out – except in the special case of Chronicles, discussed below. Given also the close rela-tionship between Hebrew and Syriac, we usually find that each word in the Hebrew is rendered by a single word in Syriac, so that prosodic equivalence is the norm between the version and the original. Only occasionally might a single Syriac word cover two or more in Hebrew, e.g.

Lev. 11:3   ܦܣܝܩܬܐ for מעלת גרה

Job 1:22   ܨܚܐ for נתן תפלה

Ruth 1:7   ܡܬܝܒܝܢ for אשר היתה שמה.

Conversely, seldom does a single Hebrew word need two in Syriac, e.g.

Lev. 16:4   ܟܣܝ ܦܪܩܗ for יצנף

Deut. 32:24   ܢܘܢܐ ܕܡܝܐ for רשף

Exod. 8:21   ܚܠܘܛܐ ܕܟܠ ܓܢܣ "a mingling of every sort" for the plague of ערוב (but thereafter ܚܠܘܛܐ alone).

Where additions occur, P is motivated primarily by a drive to clarify the sense of the text itself, rather than to introduce extraneous matter. Sometimes the Hebrew seemed so brief or elliptic that the reader might miss the sense without guidance from the trans-lator; and P here makes insertions (italicised below), clarifying the sense on the basis of the context. Examples are Gen. 36:6 "to *the* land *of* Seir", 1 Sam. 20:12 "may the Lord God of Israel *testify*", 2 Sam. 23:11 "to *despoil* livestock", 1 Kgs. 6:6 "*and he made the*

---

[24] Alternatively, this literalism may be due to the influence of LXX, which in these books follows the style of Aquila.   [25] Barr, "Typology of Literalism", pp. 300–1.

[26] Aquila (ὄνομα ῥύπου) and Symmachus (κακωνυμίαν) analyse similarly, but an Aramaic source is likelier for P's rendering, given the number of parallels between P and the Targums in the Pentateuch.

[27] Barr, "Typology of Literalism", p. 303.

arcade", Prov. 31:1 "*who received* prophecy (MT הגשא)", Job 3:1 "the day that he was born" (MT simply יומו). A subtler device to bring out the sense was to insert enclitic particles for emphasis, e.g. at Deut. 32:27b:

MT   פן יאמרו רמה ולא י׳ פעל כל זאת

P   ܘܢܐܡܪܘܢ ܕܐܝܕܢ ܗܝ ܐܬܬܪܝܡܬ ܘܠܐ ܗܘܐ ܡܪܝܐ ܥܒܕ ܗܠܝܢ

> ... it is our hand that was raised high, and it was not the Lord who performed these things

P thus highlights the contrasting subjects, by using the enclitics ܗܝ and ܗܘܐ.[28]

The purpose of some other expansions in P is not primarily to clarify, in that there was no real danger of misunderstanding. The motive was rather stylistic: explicit and unambiguous expression was preferred in Syriac. Hence we may explain some expansions which to us might seem pedantic, e.g. 2 Sam. 23:10 "his hand cleaved to *the hilt of* the sword", 2 Kgs. 2:7 "and they both stood on *the bank of* the Jordan". The explication of pronouns, which is tantamount to addition, is often due to the same motive, e.g. Exod. 4:24 "and *Moses* was on the way", Isa. 44:9 "the craftsmen who make them" (MT has just המה).

In particular, P often marks explicitly speakers or addressees, as at Exod. 5:17, where MT has just ויאמר, while P expands: "and *Pharaoh* said *to them*". P likewise marks the onset of direct speech (e.g. 2 Sam. 18:23, Job 27:10c), where this is left in the Hebrew for the reader to infer. In these cases, the translator's basic concern may have been presentation: to leave the subject or any other part of the sentence unspecified was not acceptable Syriac style, even though an attentive reader could have worked out the sense.

There was an allied stylistic preference for regularity in wording. Thus P provides names with their standard epithets, even when these are lacking in the Hebrew, e.g. the Lord *thy God* (Deut. 6:18), Eleazar *the priest* (Josh. 24:33), Nebuchadnezzar *the king* (Dan. 1:18), Ezra *the scribe* (Ezra 7:25). Allied is the tendency to introduce standard wording from similar passages: thus at Lev. 23:26 P inserts "speak to the children of Israel" as in the other sections of that chapter.

The opposite departure from quantitative literalism is omission. As a response to a text which the translator failed to understand, this will be discussed below. Here we shall note cases where the translator consciously abbreviated a text which he had understood, though of course the separation of these two cases is somewhat subjective.

Where the Hebrew seemed so redundant that quantitative literalism would lead to unacceptable prolixity, the translators condense the text. P thus omits ויסעו (Num. 10:28), which seemed superfluous after the preceding phrase: "These are the journeys of the children of Israel . . .". P likewise at Deut. 18:1 omits כל שבט לוי, immediately after the reference to the (priests and) Levites. Job 40:12a too is omitted, following the very similar line in 11b. Parallelism caused particular problems, both because the Hebrew seemed redundant in itself and because of the lack of Syriac equivalents for the synonyms present. Sometimes the translator omitted one of the parallel words, as at Hos. 11:8 –

MT   איך אתנך כאדמה אשימך כצבאים

P   ܐܝܟ ܐܬܠܟ ܐܝܟ ܐܕܡܐ ܐܘ ܐܣܝܡܟ

---

[28] See G. Goldenberg, "Bible Translations and Syriac Idiom", MPI 8 (Leiden 1995), pp. 25–39: 31–4.

He might even omit a whole clause, as at Isa. 51:8 –

MT כי כבגד יאכלם עש וכצמר יאכלם סס

P ܡܛܠ ܕܐܝܟ ܕܠܒܘܫܐ ܘܐܝܟ ܕܠܥܡܪܐ ܢܐܟܘܠ ܐܢܘܢ ܣܣܐ

This tendency is particularly noticeable in Ezekiel, where all but four words of Ezek. 33:5 are omitted as repetition of material in the previous verse. Within the Twelve Prophets, the phenomenon is discussed by Gelston.[29]

In general, however, P is committed to quantitative literalism. That commitment is particularly evident when P is compared with the Targum(s) in poetic passages, e.g. at Judg. 5:1–

MT בפרע פרעות בישראל בהתנדב עם ברכו י׳

P ܒܦܘܪܥܢܘܬܐ ܕܐܬܦܪܥ ܐܝܣܪܝܠ ܒܬܫܒܘܚܬܐ ܕܥܡܐ ܫܒܚܘ ܠܡܪܝܐ

In the vengeance that Israel avenged, in the praise of the people, praise the Lord

Here every word in P corresponds to a word in the Hebrew, usually in a straightforward fashion (except that the sense of התנדב was guessed from the context of a song of praise). The Targum, by contrast, has expansions running to some 50 words.

Imitation of the form of the Hebrew

Yet another aspect of literalism is the extent to which the translator imitates the form of the original. Correspondence in form between the Hebrew and Syriac texts is indeed frequent, and it is not difficult to find whole phrases where every Syriac word is cognate with the corresponding Hebrew word, as at Jer. 50:6a –

MT צאן אבדות היה עמי רעיהם התעום

P ܐܝܟ ܥܢܐ ܐܒܝܕܬܐ ܗܘܬ ܥܡܝ. ܪ̈ܥܘܬܗܘܢ ܐܛܥܝܘ ܐܢܘܢ

We must ask, however, whether that correspondence was a matter of principle or a mere by-product of the similarity between the Hebrew and Syriac languages.

A brief survey – intended merely for illustration – of different areas of language shows that there was no thoroughgoing policy to reproduce the form of the Hebrew. In vocabulary, for example, the verbs הלך and שוב possess cognates in Syriac – namely ܗܠܟ (Pa‘el) and ܬܘܒ – which, however, are not commonly used. Had the translators been bent on reproducing the Hebrew form, we might have expected them to insist on these cognates. Instead, however, they normally use those verbs which most naturally express the sense in Syriac, namely ܐܙܠ and ܗܦܟ respectively. It is worth adding, though, that in the case of a few Hebrew words the translators disagreed as to whether the cognate – e.g. ܓܠܐ ‘go into exile’ for גלה – was acceptable in Syriac or not. As we shall see, their differing attitudes allow us to distinguish different hands in the composition of P.

Grammatical categories too are freely altered. Thus adjectives tend to replace abstract nouns, e.g.

Isa. 45:3 מטמני מסתרים, P ܠܣܝܡܬܐ ܟܣܝܬܐ

Verbs sometimes replace other parts of speech, e.g.

Isa. 4:5 כי על כל כבוד חפה ܡܛܠ ܕܥܠ ܐܝܩܪ ܬܛܠܠ

Amos 3:11 צר וסביב הארץ ܐܘܠܨܢܐ ܢܚܕܪܝܗ ܠܐܪܥܐ

[29] Gelston, *Twelve Prophets*, p. 133.

The Hebrew infinitive construct with prepositions is usually replaced by a conjunction and finite verb, e.g.

Gen. 2:4 בְּהִבָּרְאָם ܟܕ ܐܬܒܪܝܘ

Exod. 2:4 לָדַעַת ܘܢܕܥ

Num. 31:16 לִמְסָר מַעַל ܘܕܢܣ ܐܟܠܘ

despite a fair number of exceptions.[30] The Hebrew infinitive absolute is often ignored, as are various particles (e.g. נא גם אך). The Hophʻal conjugation in Hebrew (and biblical Aramaic) is regularly replaced by the simple stem, e.g.

Job 7:3 MT הָנְחַלְתִּי P ܝܚܬܠ

Dan. 5:13 MT הֻעַל P ܥܠ

The reason is that an Aramaic equivalent (of the type Ettaphʻal) is not found (except in certain types of weak verb) before Ephrem, in the late fourth century.[31]

In syntax too the translators often depart from the Hebrew. Explicit links between sentences are provided by the insertion of *waw*, so that in Lamentations the sobbing effect of the staccato phrases is lost.[32] Again, where Hebrew points a contrast by omitting any conjunction, P often inserts ܐܠܐ (e.g. Lev. 6:23, Num. 12:7, Deut. 1:38). P is less free in word order and so, where the Hebrew places the object before the verb, however, P moves it afterwards, e.g.

Ps. 145:19 MT רְצוֹן יְרֵאָיו יַעֲשֶׂה P, ܘܥܒܕ ܨܒܝܢܐ ܠܕܚܠܘܗܝ

In particular, interrogative sentences are often recast. The word הֲלוֹא introducing questions is often rendered by ܗܐ 'behold', or omitted, so that the question is replaced by its expected answer. Less often the rendering is ܠܐ, but presumably intended as interrogative (*nonne*).[33] Positive sentences in question form are likewise often replaced by their expected (negative) answers, e.g. at Deut. 20:19. At Exod. 32:11 Moses' question (introduced by לָמָה) likewise becomes a strong negative: "No, Lord, let not thy anger flare . . .". However, the distinction between positive and negative questions is not always clear, so that the desired and undesired fasts of Isa. 58:6 and 5 respectively are formally indistinguishable in P:

v.5: MT הֲכָזֶה יִהְיֶה צוֹם אֶבְחָרֵהוּ

v.6: MT הֲלוֹא זֶה צוֹם אֶבְחָרֵהוּ

P (both) ܗܘ ܨܘܡܐ ܕܓܒܝܬܗ

Altogether, then, imitation of the Hebrew was not in itself a policy of the translators. In conveying the plain sense, they often arrived at a Syriac text which ran close to the Hebrew, simply because of the close relationship between the languages. Seldom do they push against the limits of acceptable Syriac for the sake of preservation of the Hebrew form.

Consistency of equivalences

Yet another possible ideal of literalism is one-to-one correspondence between the vocabulary of the source text and the translation. One-to-one correspondence has two

---

[30] E.g. ܟܕܢܦܩ at Judg. 5:4, and most infinitives with *l-* in Genesis, as well as many in Samuel.

[31] C. Meehan, "Qal/Peʻal as the Passive of Hifʻil/Afʻel in Mishnaic Hebrew and Middle Aramaic", in K. Jongeling, H.L. Murre-van den Berg and L. van Rompay (eds.), *Studies in Hebrew and Aramaic Syntax Presented to Professor J. Hoftijzer on the Occasion of his Sixty-fifth Birthday*, Leiden 1991, pp. 112–31.

[32] B. Albrektson, *Studies in the Text and Theology of the Book of Lamentations*, Lund 1963, pp. 210–13.

[33] Gelston, *Twelve Prophets*, p. 137.

aspects: first, any given Hebrew word should be rendered by the same Syriac word on all occurrences, and secondly, every Syriac word should correspond to one Hebrew word only. Neither aim, however, was upheld by the translators of P.

True, there are many cases of a Hebrew word that is usually rendered by the same Syriac word, but this may simply be because the Hebrew and Syriac words have a similar range of meaning. The translators did not hesitate to depart from the regular equivalent, e.g. to enhance the clarity or attractiveness of their translation, or to resolve figurative or anthropomorphic language.

The drive for clarity

When consistent Syriac equivalents would mislead, the translators sought variety. Thus the verb זבח is normally rendered by its cognate ܕܒܚ "sacrifice"; but at Deut. 12:15, 21, which sets out to authorise slaughter other than sacrifice, P brings out the sense by instead rendering ܢܟܘܣ : "slaughter!". In Gen. 22:5, where MT uses נער both of Abraham's servants and of Isaac, P has ܥܠܝܡܐ and ܛܠܝܐ respectively; the situation in Job 1:15–19 is similar. In Josh. 2 the adjective נקי is differently rendered according as freedom from an oath is meant (ܡܚܣܝܐ – vv.17, 20) or freedom from blood guilt (ܡܚܣܝܐ ܡܢ ܚܛܝܬܐ – v.19).[34]

Even when the difference detected is one of nuance only, P may vary the rendering, as at Gen. 3:15 –

MT הוא ישופך ראש ואתה תשופנו עקב

P ܗܘ ܢܕܘܫ ܪܝܫܟ. ܘܐܢܬ ܬܡܚܝܘܗܝ، ܒܥܩܒܗ.

Thus P makes man *tread down* the serpent's head, while the serpent *smites* his foot, even though the Hebrew had used the same root for both. Further examples:

Gen. 18:12 MT ותצחק שרה בקרבה P ܘܓܚܟܬ ܣܪܐ ܒܠܒܗ̇

Gen. 21:6 MT כל השמע יצחק לי P ܟܠ ܕܫܡܥ ܢܚܕܐ ܠܝ

Thus, while the Hebrew speaks of laughter both before and after Isaac's birth, P turns the latter into rejoicing, while retaining the usual equivalent for the former.

The translators will also select a more specific word than MT – albeit on the basis of information implied by the Hebrew – if the context requires. Thus the Ashdodites at 1 Sam. 5:3 did not simply take (MT ויקחו) the fallen Dagon but restored him (ܘܐܬܩܝܡܘܗܝ،) upon his place. The threat הדמין תתעבדון (Dan. 2:5) is spelt out: "you will be cut limb from limb". The translators often replace the colourless verb היה, as at Isa. 7:24 –

MT כי שמיר ושית תהיה כל הארץ

P ܡܛܠ ܕܫܝܪܐ ܘܟܘܒܐ ܬܬܡܠܐ ܟܠܗ̇ ܐܪܥܐ

Ultimately, this selection of different equivalents for the same Hebrew word is part of the same drive for clarity already noted in connection with P's expansions.

Maintaining the reader's interest

The stylistic aim of avoiding monotony gave rise to inconsistency of rendering at Gen. 27:44–5, where Rebecca bids Jacob flee to Laban's household –

[34] Further examples are noted by P.G. Borbone, "Correspondances lexicales entre Peshiṭta et TM du Pentateuque: Les racines verbales", in MPI 8 (1995), pp. 1–23; see 9–10.

MT עד אשר תשוב חמת אחיך: עד שוב אף אחיך ממך...
P ܥܕܡܐ ܕܬܬܢܝܚ ܪܘܓܙܗ ܕܐܚܘܟ ܘܥܕܡܐ ܕܢܗܦܘܟ ܪܘܓܙܗ ܕܐܚܘܟ ܡܢܟ...
Here P renders the two occurrences of שוב differently – even though it renders חמה and אף identically. Grammatical structures may likewise be deliberately varied, as in Deut. 23:3–4:
MT גם דור עשירי (לא יבא...)
P (v.3) ܐܦܠܐ ܥܠ ܥܣܪܐ ܕܪ̈ܝܢ
P (v.4) ܐܦܠܐ ܠܕܪܐ ܥܣܝܪܝܐ[35]
To hold the reader's interest, the translators may dramatise the text, e.g.

(a) 1 Kings 3:22
MT ותדברנה לפני המלך
P ܘܢܨ̈ܝܢ ܗܘ̈ܝ ܩܕܡ ܡܠܟܐ

and they (the two harlots) were *striving* before the king

(b) Ruth 3:3
MT ושמת שמלתיך
P ܘܐܨܛܒܬܝ ܒܠܒܘ̈ܫܝܟܝ "*adorn thyself* in thy garments"
Again at Dan. 2:24 MT has כל קבל דנה "therefore", which P heightens to ܘܒܗ ܒܫܥܬܐ "at that very hour". Further examples are given on pp. 33–6 below.

The translators may also modernise the text to take account of conditions in their own day. Many names have been modernised, e.g. Qardu (Kurdistan) for Ararat, as noted below. The monetary unit שקל is occasionally modernised to ܣܠܥܐ or ܐܣܛܝܪܐ (*stater*),[36] while גרה becomes ܙܘܙܐ or ܡܥܐ. At Ezra 8:25, precious metals used as media of exchange are weighed in MT but counted (as coins) in P. Burnished or yellowed bronze is called Corinthian, the most precious bronze of the age (1 Kgs. 7:45, Ezra 8:27, 1 Chr. 29:7).[37] Nor is social change neglected. Joshua dismisses the people to their cities rather than their tents (Josh. 22:4–8).[38] The mother's precedence is replaced in P by the father's at Lev. 19:3 21:2; 'mother's son' (Deut. 13:7) likewise becomes 'father's son', as also in LXX.

Figurative and anthropomorphic language

For the most part, P retains figurative language, e.g..
Lev. 26:26 בשברי לכם מטה לחם ܘܐܬܒܪ ܚܘܛܪܐ ܕܠܚܡܟܘܢ
Here we may contrast the Targums, whose translators seem to have had little faith in their readers' ability to interpret figures aright – to the extent that they sacrifice the

[35] See further I. Avineri, "Problèmes de variation dans la traduction syriaque du Pentateuque", *Semitica* 25 (1975), pp. 105–9.
[36] The latter occurs at Exod. 21:32, 2 Sam. 24:22, 2 Kgs. 7:1, Neh. 10:32, though the vague rendering ܡܬܩܠܐ "weight" is more frequent.
[37] D.M. Jacobson and M.P. Weitzman, "What was Corinthian Bronze?", *American Journal of Archaeology* 96 (1992), pp. 237–47; idem, "Black Bronze and the Corinthian Alloy", *Classical Quarterly* 45 (1995), pp. 580–3.
[38] The same tendency is noted in LXX by J.W. Wevers, "The Interpretative Character and Significance of the Septuagint Version", in M.Sæbø (ed.), *Hebrew Bible / Old Testament: The History of Its Intepretation*, Göttingen 1996, pp. 104–5.

suspense in the parable of Isa. 5:1–7 by revealing at the outset that the disappointing vineyard is none other than Israel.

The resolution of figures is unusual. While the Hebrew of Gen. 49 calls Issachar a bony ass (v.14) and Naphtali a hind let loose (v.21), P describes them as a mighty man and a swift messenger respectively, agreeing with T^F[J]. At Gen. 44:30, קשורה בנפשו "bound up with his soul" becomes ܚܒܝܒ ܠܗ ܐܝܟ ܢܦܫܗ "beloved to him as himself" (so T^ON). At Isa. 29:22 'whiten' (of face) is replaced by 'be ashamed'; and at Ezra. 9:8 יתד is explained as 'place'.

Occasionally one metaphor is replaced by another less colourful. Thus at Isa. 66:14 the bones of the Israelites will exult rather than sprout, and at Job 40:11 wrath is poured out rather than scattered.

In the same way, bodily terms in relation to God do not in themselves trouble the translators. Thus P preserves references to God's hand and voice, although אף of God's nostril is instead taken as "anger" (Deut. 33:10, 2 Sam. 22:9, Isa. 65:5). God hears and even smells (Gen. 8:21), and men see him and the pavement beneath his feet (Exod. 24:10). Men may see God's face (Isa. 1:12, Ps. 42:3), though this expression is more often replaced (as in MT) by 'appearing before' God (e.g. Exod. 34:23, Deut. 16:16)

By contrast, terms that suggest creaturely frailty are rejected in P. Notably, references to God 'repenting' (נחם), i.e. changing his purpose, are removed. Instead, God is said to 'turn away' (Syr. ܐܗܦܟ) evil in the Twelve Prophets (Amos 7:3, Jonah 3:10,4:2, Zech. 8:14), while the translator at 2 Sam. 24:16 was equally driven to paraphrase: "and the Lord held back the angel of death who was destroying the people".[39] Divine omniscience is also affirmed: thus at Gen. 22:12 P has: "now I have made known" rather than "now I know" as in MT. Likewise at Deut. 1:33 God has no need to go before the people to spy out (MT לתור) a place for them to camp; instead he goes ܠܡܬܩܢܘ 'to establish' the place. P also insists on divine omnipotence: at Dan. 3:18 P omits והן לא, not even admitting the possibility of God failing to save. By contrast, a foreign deity is often called not a god but a thing feared (ܕܚܠܬܐ).

P also rejects figures which represent God as an inanimate object. Thus מגן 'shield' likewise becomes ܡܥܕܪܢܐ 'helper' at Gen. 15:1, Deut. 33:29, 2 Sam. 22:31, Prov. 2:7, 30:5, and regularly in Psalms. The epithets סלע and צור 'rock' become either 'helper' likewise (e.g. Ps. 19:15) or simply 'God' (Ps. 28:1 etc.), or 'trust' (Ps. 18:3), or, most commonly, 'might(y)' or 'strengthener' (Deut. 32:4, 1 Sam. 2:2, Isa. 17:10, Ps. 18:3, 62:8, etc.). At Ps. 84:12 P replaces the divine epithets שמש ומגן "sun and shield" by ܡܬܪܣܝܢܢ ܘܡܥܕܪܢܢ "our nourisher and helper".[40]

P also shows a general tendency to emphasise the gulf between God and man. The preposition ܩܕܡ is often introduced as a buffer. God is occasionally replaced by an angel (e.g. Gen. 32:31, as Targums; Ps. 8:6; 1 Chr. 14:11) or, in Chronicles, by the divine presence (ܫܟܝܢܬܐ).[41]

[39] R.J. Loewe, "Jerome's Treatment of an Anthropopathism", *VT* 2 (1952), pp. 261–72, citing Num. 23:19, Judg. 2:18, 2 Sam. 24:16, Jer. 26:3,13,19, 42:10, Ezek. 24:14, Joel 2:14, Zech. 8:14, Ps. 110:4.
[40] LXX too changes the figure, but differently: ἔλεον καὶ ἀλήθειαν ἀγαπᾷ κύριος...
[41] Gelston, *Twelve Prophets*, p. 153; N.Séd, "La Shekhinta et ses amis 'Araméens'", *Mélanges Antoine Guillaumont*, Geneva 1988, pp. 233–42.

Although many of these changes can be easily paralleled in the Targums, it is important to note that even in this area P sometimes goes its own way. Thus the expression 'walk with God' is usually changed in P to 'be pleasing (ܫܦܪ) to God', while the Targums usually write: "walk *in the fear of* God".[42] Again P softens Gen. 18:25 quite differently:

MT   חלילה לך השופט כל הארץ לא יעשה משפט

P   ܚܣ ܠܟ ܕܝܢܐ ܕܟܠܗ ܐܪܥܐ. ܠܐ ܢܬܥܒܕ ܕܝܢܐ ܗܢܐ.

> Far be it for you, judge of all the earth; let this judgment not be done.

Unlike P, T[JN] retain the question of MT: "Shall the judge of all the earth not do justice?" T[O] softens the question differently from P, by substituting a pious answer:

> . . . the judge of all the earth shall nevertheless perform justice.[43]

It has been suggested that the attitude towards anthropomorphisms varies among the biblical books, and in particular that P-Psalms exhibits "a dread of anthropomorphisms, of which the translators of the Pentateuch were free".[44] Closer inspection suggests, however, that all the translators are sensitive to the same features – notably, the comparison of God with inanimate things – and that those features happen to be especially frequent in Psalms. It is in fact in Chronicles that the translators go furthest to avoid anthropomorphisms, but in that book the translator was labouring under exceptional conditions, as discussed in chapter 4 below.

Limitations of retroversion

The other side of the consistency ideal is that every Syriac word should correspond to just one Hebrew word. This is the more important side for any attempt to reconstruct the Hebrew text behind the Syriac. However, this ideal too is not attained. Part of the reason is that the translators found Hebrew richer than Syriac in synonyms, at least in some fields. Where the Hebrew uses two words, P may be content to repeat one; P thus uses the verb ܓܥܠ for both שקץ and טמא at Lev. 11:43, or ܢܛܪ for both נטר and שמר at Jer. 3:5.[45] P likewise tends to impose some uniformity on vocabulary over extended passages: in Genesis 24, for example, ܓܠܐ (Paʿel) represents both הקרה (v.23) and הוכיח (vv.14, 44).

The relative lack of synonyms in Syriac has led to one device that works systematically against consistency of equivalence. Where two synonyms are available in Syriac, the translators may eke them out by treating one as the 'A-word' and one as the 'B-word'. If any of the Hebrew synonyms occurs alone, P tends to use the 'A-word'; if two Hebrew synonyms occur in a single verse, P tends to use the 'A-word'

---

[42] Gen. 5:22,24; 6:9,24; 17:1; 48:15; Ps. 56:14, 116:9. However, we find ܦܠܚ at Gen. 24:40, ܫܦܪ at 1 Sam. 2:30 and the literal ܗܠܟ at 1 Sam. 2:35, 2 Kgs. 20:3, Isa. 38:3.

[43] S.D. Luzzatto (אוהב גר, Vienna 1830, p. 37) defends this reading against some mss of T[O] which instead include a negative.

[44] W.E. Barnes, "On the Influence of the Septuagint on the Peshitta", *JTS* 2 (1901), pp. 186–97.

[45] For further cases in Numbers and Deuteronomy where one Syriac word covers two different Hebrew words, see P.G. Borbone, "Correspondances Lexicales", pp. 5–9.

for the first and the 'B-word' for the second. Thus the Hebrew synonyms for 'anger' (e.g. אף זעם חמה חרון עברה קצף) are covered by ܪܘܓܙܐ ('A') and ܚܡܬܐ ('B'). Similarly the various Hebrew terms for 'lion' are rendered by ܐܪܝܐ ('A') and ܓܘܪܝܐ ܕܐܪܝܐ ('B').[46]

Change in translation technique

The technique of a given translator – and in particular his balance between the demands of content and form – might evolve in the course of his task. A striking illustration can be found at the beginning of Genesis. In the opening words P renders each word of the Hebrew by a corresponding Syriac form: the first word ܒܪܫܝܬ is a transliteration, and later in v.1 the Hebrew accusative particle is rendered by the rare particle ܝܬ, which already puzzled Ephrem.[47] From the second verse onward, however, ܝܬ is dropped, never to recur in the Pentateuch, and the accusative is marked either by *l*- (as already in 1:3) or not at all.[48]

By Gen. 1:16 the translator is even ready to replace a Hebrew noun by a Syriac verb in order to avoid tautology:

1:15   יהי מארות   ܢܗܘܘ ܢܗܝܪܐ   "let there be lights"

but 1:16   והיו למארות   ܘܢܗܘܘܢ ܡܢܗܪܝܢ   "and let them be shedding light".

At other points too the translators seem to experiment with various forms of literalism, before accepting the demands of intelligibility. In Leviticus, the translator first attempts to render עולה by the cognate ܥܠܬܐ, but finally settles on ܩܪܒܐ ܥܠܬܐ, given that ܥܠܬܐ also had the undesirable alternative sense of "hillshrine". Similar hesitation in relation to the same word can be detected at the beginning of Numbers; the evidence is presented in chapter 4. Rather similarly, a translation which fully imitates the form of the Hebrew occurs at Exod. 6:10 –

MT   וידבר י׳ אל משה לאמר

P   ܘܡܠܠ ܡܪܝܐ ܥܡ ܡܘܫܐ ܠܡܐܡܪ

In later passages, however, the concluding infinitive is usually replaced by the more idiomatic ܘܐܡܪ ܠܗ (Exod. 6:29, 14:1, 25:1), and occasionally omitted altogether (e.g. Exod. 13:1, 16:11).

Similarly, Avineri identified Hebrew phrases which contain a construct, and which are rendered on their first occurrence with a Syriac construct but thereafter by an emphatic noun plus *dalath*, e.g. מעיני מים:

1 Kgs. 18:5   ܡܥܝܢܝ ܡܝܐ

2 Kgs. 3:19   ܡܥܝܢܐ ܕܡܝܐ

Apparently the translator first imitated the Hebrew form, but later preferred to follow normal Syriac idiom.[49]

---

[46] On the renderings of 'anger' and 'lion' in the Twelve Prophets, see Gelston, *Twelve Prophets*, pp. 141–2.

[47] See discussion in chapter 5, p. 253.

[48] In general, *l*- accompanies animate objects only. See Th. Nöldeke, *Compendious Syriac Grammar* (tr. J.A. Crichton), London 1904, p. 230.

[49] I. Avinery, "An Example of the Influence of Hebrew on the Peshitta Translation – The *Status Constructus*", *Textus* 9 (1981), pp. 36–8. Avinery's sole textual basis is 7a1. In some of Avinery's other examples, the mss are divided, so that it is not clear whether the variation is due to the translator or merely to copyists.

Less often, the translator moves towards literalism in the course of his task:

(a) In Josh. 2, the translator renders רדף not by its Syriac cognate (which could mean 'persecute') but by נפק בתר "go out after". From Josh. 7:5, however, the translator resigned himself to using רדף after all.

(b) At Cant. 1:13 דודי is rendered רחמ‍ but thereafter the translator settles for the neater דד despite its ambiguity.

The reason for the change in these cases was that the Syriac cognate, while less idiomatic, was the neater solution when the Hebrew word occurred repeatedly.

Sometimes we catch a translator changing his mind within a short space:

(a) In Gen. 11, בלל (of language) becomes פלג at v. 7 but בלבל at v. 9.

(b) In Gen. 13, ככר (of the Jordan valley) is rendered (דירדנ‍) אתרא in v.10 but חד in v.12. At 19:25 the rendering is different again: פחתא.

(c) Again in Gen. 13, the verb אהל becomes נטא in v.12 and אתא in v.18. Evidently the meaning was unknown, and P guessed differently on these two occasions.

(d) In Exod. 8:22 [26] one phrase is differently rendered on two occurrences:

MT   לא נכון לעשות כן כי תועבת מצרים נזבח לי' אלהינו
הן נזבח את תועבת מצרים לעיניהם ולא יסקלנו

P   It is not fitting to do thus, because from the abomination of the Egyptians (דמצריא גנsלתא) we are sacrificing to the Lord our God; and if we sacrifice the fear-objects of the Egyptians (דמצריא דחלתא) in their sight, they will stone us.

Although from an Israelite viewpoint the fear-objects of heathens are indeed abominations, the two Syriac phrases must have borne different meanings in this context, since Pharaoh – who is here addressed – would not have made that identification. Here the "abomination of the Egyptians" means most naturally the object of their contempt, unlike their fear-objects. The same term is thus given two quite different meanings within a single verse.

(e) A more complex case occurs in the description of the priestly breastplate (Heb. חשן) at Exod. 28:15–30, where the translator departs briefly from two of his usual equivalences:

(i) In earlier passages, טבעת had indicated the large rings used to hold together items of sacred furniture or even the tabernacle itself, and P had used זממתא ('large ring'). Here, however, in relation to garments, P opts for קוסקא ('small ring', also used for קרס), starting from 28:23, the first occurrence of טבעת in relation to the breastplate.

(ii) This change, not unexpected in itself, seems to have sparked off another. Up to this point the חשן itself became the bland פרסא 'outspread mantle', even as recently as v.22. In v.23, however, the translator instead rendered it: חוסיא 'atonement'. This new rendering had the advantage of similar sound, but the disadvantage of also representing כפרת, with an entirely different meaning.

By v.28, the translator has abandoned both these new usages: טבעת is again זממתא and חשן again פרסא. The rendering קוסקא for טבעת never reappears. However, חוסיא for חשן does recur – again suddenly – at Exod. 39:9–21, seven times altogether, when the breastplate is again described. Finally, the last occurrences of חשן – at Lev. 8:8 – revert to פרסא.

It has been suggested that the present text of Exod. 28:23–7 has been taken from a different source from the rest of the chapter.[50] This hypothesis, however, raises the new problems of the origin of this second source and the reason that it was preserved in just these verses. Nor does it explain the recurrence of ܚܘܣܐ – without ܩܘܣܝܐ – in Exod. 39. It seems better to assume a single translator, and to see in his alternations his struggle at rendering technical vocabulary.

Evidently, then, a translator might change his mind about the meaning of a word, particularly if it was rare. In such cases, he did not go back to change his earlier renderings, perhaps because of a scarcity of writing materials, or even of time. He instead accepted that his work could not be faultless.

For all these reasons, there is no policy in P to maintain one-to-one correspondence. Here P differs from the Syrohexapla, where this aim met with great (though not total) success.[51] If we do not appreciate this stance, we may draw precarious inferences from P's choice of words. Thus the Hebrew at Gen. 4:5 states that Cain's face fell, while P has ܐܬܟܡܪ "was darkened". P has been said here to represent Cain's face as dark and satanic;[52] but in fact 'dark' is a stock epithet for a sad face, and is likewise substituted by P at Gen. 40:6–7. A further example, at Deut. 32:10, is included in the discussion in chapter 3 of issues of method in deciding whether P has been influenced by the wording of rabbinic Midrash.

Improvement on the Hebrew text

So far we have been concerned with the manner in which the translators convey the plain sense, including even cases where that plain sense posed problems of expression (e.g. a reference to God changing his purpose). We must now consider other possibilities: either that the plain sense was not found satisfactory in itself, or that it was not clear what the plain sense might be.

In the former case, the translators may make radical changes to improve the perceived logic within the verse. At Josh. 24:19, for example, Joshua tells Israel: "you cannot serve the Lord"; P, doubting that such a categorical statement could have been intended, softens this:

ܣܒ ܠܟ ܕܠܡܐ ܠܐ ܡܫܟܚܝܢ ܐܢܬܘܢ ܠܡܦܠܚ ܠܡܪܝܐ

Take care lest you are not able to serve the Lord.

Again at Ps. 1:1, P inverts the nouns and so blesses the man who "has not walked in the *way* of the wicked nor stood in the *counsel* of sinners", to accord better with the verbs. At Isa. 44:16–17, the Hebrew states that the idolator uses half his wood for warmth, half for cooking and the rest to make an idol; P corrects the arithmetic by substituting "its coals" for the second "half".

Moreover, the translators tried to screen out problems in the Hebrew text, as in the following examples:

[50] M.D. Koster, *The Peshitta of Exodus: The Development of its Text in the Course of Fifteen Centuries*, Assen/Amsterdam 1977, p. 67.
[51] M. Weitzman, "The Reliability of Retroversions of 'The Three' from the Syro-hexapla: A Pilot Study in Hosea", in A. Salvesen (ed.), *Origen's Hexapla and Fragments*, Tübingen 1998, pp. 317–59.
[52] E. Levine, "The Syriac version of Genesis iv 1–16", *VT* 26 (1976), pp. 70–8.

(a) The words that Jacob uttered on first seeing his son's gory coat are rendered almost exactly, at Gen. 39:33 –

MT   טָרֹף טֹרַף יוֹסֵף

P   ,הֹ כֹּ סֹמֹפֹ חֹכֹנֹ אֹכֹתֹכ

    Joseph my son is surely torn

Later, when Judah explains to the vizier of Egypt (whom he does not know to be Joseph) why his father cannot live without Benjamin, the same words are used in MT of his brother's supposed death:

Gen. 44:28   אַךְ טָרֹף טֹרָף

P's translator, however, thought that this detail of the brother's supposed death would have provoked further questions from the vizier; and so here he selects general terms:

P   כֹ מֹכֹמֹ כֹ מֹכֹ לֹ

   he is surely slain

(b) At Exod. 15:17 P corrects the perfect tense reference to the Temple in Moses' day, and renders: "establish it with thy hands!".

(c) At Exod. 32:4,8 the Israelites say of the golden calf: "These are your gods". P resolves the discord of number by substituting the singular (כֹמֹ אֹלֹכֹ,).

(d) Whereas Deuteronomy speaks of priests and Levites in apposition, P distinguishes them by inserting a suitable conjunction ('and', 'or'). e.g. at Deut. 17:9, 18:1.

(f) At 1 Sam. 16:19, where Saul summons David "who is with the sheep", the translator apparently objected that Saul at that stage did not know that detail, and so he substitutes: "he is useful to me".

(g) At Job 42:11 in MT, all Job's relatives and friends came to eat with him in his house "and they grieved for him (וַיָּנֻדוּ לוֹ) and comforted him". P instead writes that they came to his house "for they had grieved for him . . ." (כֹ אֹ,זֹבֹהֹ,כֹ מֹמֹ כֹ מֹלֹכֹ,), so that Job's friends do not grieve after his restoration.

For the sake of the perceived logic the translators might even add a negative[53] or omit it.[54] Josh. 23:4 is re-cast with an added negative: "I have *not* apportioned the remaining nations, but I have apportioned those west of Jordan". This technique of converse translation has been noted in the Targums by Klein.[55]

The translators' uninhibited approach to the text is illustrated by some passages where they mistranslated a word by missing a Hebrew idiom, and sought to "improve" the text in line with this faulty understanding.

(a) At 1 Sam. 2:13 the Hebrew uses the definite article of an object not previously mentioned, where the priest's servant carried a three-pronged fork (הַמַּזְלֵג שְׁלֹשׁ הַשִּׁנַּיִם). Unfamiliar with this Hebrew usage, and, considering that the definite article required an earlier reference, P adds at the beginning of the verse: "now they [the sons of Eli] had made themselves a three-pronged fork".

---

[53] E.g. Gen. 41:54, Lev. 25:35, Deut. 29:11 33:29, Josh. 10:20, 1 Sam. 17:39, Mal. 2:16, Ps. 56:3 60:6 68:19 90:13, Job 4:16b 9:15a.

[54] Deut. 20:19, Josh. 11:13 17:17 22:20, 2 Sam. 23:5, Ps. 16:2 37:33, Job 17:4b 18:5b, Ruth 2:13, Dan. 11:18.

[55] M.L. Klein, "Converse Translation: A Targumic Technique", *Biblica* 57 (1976), pp. 515–37.

(b) At 2 Sam. 12:14 the Hebrew introduces "enemies" euphemistically:

נאץ נאצת את איבי י׳

P, however, not recognising the construction, replaced the verbs by ܪܘܪܒܬ: "you have exalted (the enemies of the Lord)".

(c) 1 Kgs. 11:18 describes Pharaoh's treatment of Solomon's foe Hadad:

ויתן לו בית ולחם אמר לו וארץ נתן לו

The translator missed the sense 'allocate' for אמר and, assuming the sense "say", supplied direct speech (ܬܒ ܠܘܬܝ). The sentence is thus understood:

and he gave him a house and bread, and said to him: *"Dwell with me!"*, and land he gave to him.

(d) Job 27:10

MT אם על שדי יתענג יקרא אלוה בכל עת

P ܐܢ ܕܝܢ ܥܠ ܚܣܝܢܐ ܢܬܬܟܠ ܘܢܩܪܐ ܠܐܠܗܐ ܒܟܠܙܒܢ ܢܥܢܝܘܗܝ، ܐܠܗܐ ܘܢܫܡܥܝܘܗܝ،

This passage concerns the wicked, and in the Hebrew both lines are questions, with אם as interrogative ("will he delight in the Almighty?..."). However, P misunderstood it as "if", and then found no apodosis, which he had to supply:

> But if he relies on the Mighty One, and calls to God at every time, *God will answer him and listen to him.*

(e) At Ruth 2:8, Boaz's words to Ruth are thus reported:

MT הלוא שמעת בתי אל תלכי ללקט בשדה אחר

P ܒܪܬܝ، ܠܐ ܫܡܝܥ ܠܟܝ ܒܡܬܠܐ ܕܒܚܩܠܐ ܕܠܐ ܕܝܠܟܝ ܠܐ ܬܠܩܛܝܢ

> My daughter, have you never heard[56] *in a proverb*: "In a field which is not yours, do not glean".

Why does P introduce a "proverb"? The Hebrew uses the perfect (שמעת) with present sense. P, however, took the perfect to refer to the past. The only way that Ruth could have heard the relevant words in the past, however, was through a proverb.

(f) Another misguided improvement, albeit not due to missing a linguistic point, occurs at 1 Sam. 23:12. Here David inquires through the ephod whether the citizens of Qeilah will deliver him up to Saul. God answers: "They will deliver up"; and David leaves the city. P, however, considered that David would not leave Qeilah without explicit instruction, and so lengthens God's reply:

ܡܫܠܡܝܢ ܠܟ. ܩܘܡ ܦܘܩ ܡܢ ܩܪܝܬܐ

They will deliver you up. Arise, go forth from the city.

Here P forgets that the ephod only provided a decision between two given alternatives, rather than a series of instructions.

In some other passages the translator made an error and proceeded to correct the text accordingly. Thus at Num. 31:28 P wrongly replaced "one in 500" (as the tribute for the Lord from the Midianite spoil) by "one in 50", by assimilation to v.30. Accordingly, he

[56] A translation of the type "has one ever . . .?" seems to suit the few instances of the verbal construction of type ܫܡܝܥ ܠܟ in P; see also Prov. 13:23, Job 38:22. For these references, I am grateful to Prof. J. Joosten, who also alerted me to the view that the construction was then entering Syriac under the influence of Persian. See E.Y. Kutscher, "Two 'Passive' Constructions in Aramaic in the Light of Persian", *Proceedings of the International Conference on Semitic Studies in Jerusalem 1965*, Jerusalem 1969, pp. 132–51:140.

had to multiply several figures in vv.37–40 by ten. At Josh. 18:21–24 the translator sub-divided in error two of the twelve city-names, and so changed the total in v.24 to four-teen. The omission of Psalm titles seems due to the same radical attitude; the titles found in the mss were added later and bear no relation to the Hebrew.[57]

In all these passages we may be confident that the translator has set out to improve on the text of his *Vorlage*; and the fact that he was capable of this has important impli-cations for any attempt to infer his Hebrew *Vorlage*, as we shall see.

There are also cases where the translator 'improves' the text in line with his theologi-cal beliefs. In view of their relevance to the origin of P, these cases are discussed in chapter 5 below. They are not so frequent as to affect significantly the description of the translation technique.

Text not believed to have been understood

In a minority of passages, the translator was unable to derive an overall plain sense at all. Nevertheless, he still had to produce a translation, and to that end allowed himself certain devices, and we must try to identify these and show their application. This, of course, is inevitably an inductive and in some measure subjective procedure.

Where a word was problematic, either in itself or in context, the translator may nevertheless use that word as his starting-point, and then make some adjustment to its usual meaning, or even to its text, in order to reach an intelligible translation. On other occasions the translation of a problematic word is instead based entirely on the context. Only occasionally does the translator abdicate his function, by reproducing the obscurity of the original or even omitting a passage.

Derivations of sense related to the Hebrew text

Where the translator knew the meaning of the words individually but made no satisfac-tory sense of them together, he might stretch the known meaning of a Hebrew word, e.g.

(a)   Gen. 4:7

MT   הלוא אם תיטיב שאת

P   ܗܐ ܐܢ ܬܫܦܪ ܡܩܒܠ ܐܢܬ

      behold, if you are fitting, I would accept (your sacrifice).

The sense 'accept' is not the obvious sense of נשא 'to bear', but is a possible interpreta-tion of it.

(b)   2 Sam. 23:7

MT   (ואיש יגע בהם) ימלא ברזל ועץ חנית

P   ܒܩܢܐ ܕܢܪܓܐ ܘܒܦܪܙܠܐ ܡܟܢܫ ܗܘ ܠܗܘܢ

      with the shaft of the axe and with iron he gathers them.

---

[57] W. Bloemendaal, *The Headings of the Psalms in the East Syrian Church*, Leiden 1960.

The rendering "gather" is just within sight of the basic meaning "fill" for Hebrew מלא.[58] The terms for the weapons are, incidentally, inverted.

Sometimes instead the sense of the Syriac equivalent is stretched beyond that area where it coincides in meaning with the Hebrew word, e.g.

(a) Judg. 5:9
MT המתנדבים בעם
P ܐܝܠܝܢ ܕܦܪܝܫܝܢ ܒܥܡܐ "the distinguished among the people".
In the Pentateuch, the noun נדבה was usually rendered ܦܘܪܫܢܐ "an offering set apart". P-Judges uses the same Syriac root, but in a wholly different sense.

(b) Jer. 20:3
MT מגור מסביב (to be Pashhur's new name)
P ܬܘܬܒܐ ܘܚܕܘܪܐ "sojourner and beggar".
Heb. סביב is often rendered by the preposition ܚܕܪ, – which, however, is here transformed to the related noun ܚܕܘܪܐ 'one who goes about', which in Syriac had developed to 'vagrant, beggar'.

Yet another way in which a translator might obtain a suitable meaning for a word, while remaining tied to its Hebrew text, was to interpret it by association with a similar word in Syriac. Examples are:

	MT	P	
Gen. 32:29	שרית	ܐܫܬܪܪܬ	you showed yourself strong[59]
Gen. 42:7	ויתנכר	ܘܐܬܢܟܠ	and he deceived
Exod. 13:4	האביב	ܗܒܒܐ	blossoms[60]
Deut. 29:20	יעשן	ܢܥܫܢ	will grow strong
1 Sam. 20:13	ייטב	ܐܛܒ	I discover
2 Kgs. 11:6	מסח	ܡܢ ܣܘܪܚܢܐ	from harm
Isa. 10:26	צור עורב	ܛܘܪ ܚܘܪܝܒ	Mount Horeb
Jer. 23:19	סערת	ܣܘܥܪܢܐ	deed[61]
Ezek. 8:12	משכיתו	ܒܛܫܐ	hidden
Mic. 2:8	וְאֶתְמוּל (עמי)	ܐܬܡܠܝ	was filled
Ps. 93:3	דכים	ܒܕܟܝܘܬܐ	in purity
Job 6:9	וידכאני	ܘܕܟܝܢܝ	and purify me

Occasionally a Hebrew word that included צ was replaced by a similar-sounding Syriac word with ܛ, apparently on the analogy of cases of true etymological correspondence between these letters. Thus התיצב is rendered ܐܬܛܝܒ 'ready oneself' at Num. 11:16 and Jer. 46:14; so also the Niph'al at Exod. 38:8. The same understanding also occurs in the Targums, though they prefer the synonym אתעתד. Likewise at Jer. 2:20 צעה is rendered ܛܥܝܐ "(you) stray".

58 The rendering ܩܝܣܐ ܕܢܘܪܐ for עץ חנית should perhaps be emended to ܩܝܣܐ ܕܢܝܙܟܐ 'shaft of the spear', as at 2 Sam. 21:19.

59 This interpretation, which takes the first consonant as Shin, differs from T[O]JGN איתרברבת, which starts out from Heb. שׂר and so takes the first consonant as Sin.

60 So also Exod. 23:15, 34:18, Deut. 16:1.

61 This passage and its duplicate at 30:23 are discussed in chapter 4.

Even in the Aramaic of Ezra, P renders **כנמא** by ܐܝܟ ܢܡܘܣܐ and **טעם** by ܛܓܡܐ or ܕܝܛܓܡܐ, from Greek (δια)τάγμα. These renderings rest on mere phonetic similarity – a sobering reflection on the degree of mutual intelligibility between Aramaic dialects.

Derivation of sense following a textual adjustment

Another device for obtaining sense in a difficult passage is tacitly to change the Hebrew text. Grammatical elements may be ignored or changed for this purpose, as illustrated below.

Gen. 20:16

Here Abimelech has told Sarah that he has given 1,000 (shekels of) silver to her (so-called) brother, and continues:

MT הנה הוא לך כסות עינים לכל אשר אתך ואת כל ונכחת

P ܘܗܐ ܐܦ ܗܘ ܝܗܝܒ ܠܟܝ ܚܠܦ ܕܟܣܝܬܝ ܥܝܢܐ ܕܟܠ ܕܥܡܝ ܘܥܠ ܟܠܡܕܡ ܐܟܣܬܝܢܝ

> and behold, it too is given to you, because you covered the eyes of all who were with me, and concerning everything[62] you reproved me.

This involves the tacit change of **אתך** to **אתי**, and of the passive **ונכחת** to an active **הֹכַחְתִּנִי**, as well as reading a past tense into **כסות עינים**.

Ps. 2:6–7

MT ואני נסכתי מלכי... אספרה אל חק

P ܐܢܐ ܐܩܝܡܬ ܡܠܟܝ...ܕܢܫܬܥܐ ܥܠ ܩܝܡܝ

> I have set up my king . . . *that he* might tell of *my* covenant.

Ps. 16:11

MT נעמות בימינך נצח

P ܘܡܢ ܒܣܝܡܘܬܐ ܕܙܟܘܬܐ ܕܝܡܝܢܟ

> and (I shall be satisfied) from the bliss of the victory of thy right hand.

Here the required sense is attained by varying the word order; note also the construal of **נצח** as "victory" rather than "eternity".

Sometimes the translator's deliberate misreading of the *Vorlage* changes a lexical rather than grammatical element, as at Ezra 4:14 –

MT מנדה בלו והלך (3 kinds of tribute)

P ܡܕܬܐ ܠܝܬ ܠܟ "There is no tribute for you."

The last two words of the text are treated as if they were **לא לך**. Likewise, at Lev. 26:16 and Deut. 28:22 **שחפת** was treated as if it were **ספחת** 'scab', and so rendered (together with the following word **קדחת**) by terms from the leprosy laws ܓܪܒܐ ܘܡܠܘܫܬܐ. Some two hundred instances of this phenomenon in the Psalter alone were collected by Vogel,[63] and a few more are mentioned in chapter 3.

[62] Or perhaps: "and in addition to all (your deception, lit. covering of eyes)".

[63] A. Vogel, "Studien zum Peshitta-Psalter Besonders im Hinblick auf sein Verhältnis zu Septuaginta", *Biblica* 32 (1951), pp. 32–56; 198–231; 336–63; 481–502: see pp. 208–13.

Such 'misreading' of the Hebrew may have been a widely acceptable exegetical device. We may compare the rabbinic Al-Tiqre which may make adjustments on the scale – though not with the frequency – observed in P, e.g.[64]

	MT	read as:	
Gen. 20:16	כסות	כהות	(TB Meg. 28a)
Deut. 32:17	שערום	שעום	(Sifre ad loc)
Ezek 16:7	בעדי עדים	בעדרי עדרים	(TB Sot. 11b)
Qoh. 8:10	קבורים	קבוצים	(TB Git. 56b)

A similar convention may have existed at Qumran, at least in passages so obscure as not to have any "plain sense". Thus at Hab. 2:4, where MT has עפלה, with which the text of 1QpHab. agrees, the commentary nevertheless explains that [the sins of the wicked] will be doubled upon them (יכפלו עליהם), as if the Hebrew had been כפלה. Again at Hab. 2:15, where MT has מעוריהם 'their nakedness', 1QpHab. instead reads מועדיהם 'their stumblings/ festivals';[65] and here again it may be that the author of the Pesher had a text no different from MT but considered it legitimate to adjust to מועדיהם to attain a desired sense.

In Job, it occasionally seems that the translator began with a Syriac equivalent of a Hebrew word and deliberately misread that, e.g. at 41:1a –

MT הן תחלתו נכזבה

P ܗܐ ܪܓܠܟ ܐܬܫܪܝܬ

> behold your foot is loosened.

Semantically, P utterly differs from MT, but the Syriac words resemble ܫܘܪܝܐ "beginning" and ܕܓܠ "deceive", which are normal renderings of the Hebrew words, if the first is vocalised תְּחִלָּתוֹ. Yet these two Syriac words, if restored, would yield poor sense, especially in context: "the beginning deceived you". The translator would hardly have presented this as his finished work. Thus the inner-Syriac change implied by the existing text seems due to the translator himself.[66] The alternative of scribal corruption cannot, however, be excluded – though that would imply, exceptionally, that the original translation was here literal to the point of obscurity.

Derivation of sense from the general context

In the cases considered above, some semantic path between the Hebrew text and its translation can be traced. There are other renderings, however, which have no basis apart from fitting the context, e.g.

---

[64] A. Rosenzweig, "Die Al-Tiqri-Deutungen", in M. Brann and I. Elbogen (eds.), *Festschrift zu Israel Lewy's siebzigstem Geburtstag*, Breslau 1911, pp. 204–53. As Rosenzweig observes, however, most Al-Tiqre readings vary vowels or vowel letters only.

[65] This was of course applied to the Wicked Priest's disruption of the sect's observance of the Day of Atonement.

[66] G. Rignell, *The Peshitta to the Book of Job Critically Investigated with Introduction, Translation, Commentary and Summary*, Stockholm: Monitor Forlaget, 1994, pp. 5, 367. (This book was posthumously edited by the author's brother, Dr K-E Rignell.) On the basis of this phenomenon, Rignell considered that the translation was executed in two stages. In the first, annotations showing the Syriac equivalents of individual Hebrew words were added to a Hebrew text between the lines or in the margin. In the second, a continuous Syriac translation was obtained from those annotations, which were sometimes misread.

Exod. 23:5
MT עזב תעזב עמו
P ܡܫܩܠ ܬܫܩܘܠ ܥܡܗ

(And when you see your enemy's donkey crouched beneath his burden, and you wish not to carry with him,) you shall indeed carry with him.

Here the usual sense of עזב 'forsake' was clearly inappropriate, but ܫܩܠ 'carry' is simply guessed from the context.

Num. 4:13
MT ודשנו את המזבח
P ܘܢܦܪܩܘܢܗ ܠܡܕܒܚܐ

and they shall dismantle the altar.

The rendering 'dismantle' well fits the context, which concerns the duties of the Kehathites when the camp moved off; but it is totally incorrect.

Guesses from the context are in fact frequent in P. The victims of the mutilations at Deut. 23:2 are (rather ironically) replaced by ܓܝܪܐ 'adulterer', because of the reference in the next verse to ממזר, which is fairly rendered ܒܪ ܓܘܪܐ "son of adultery".[67] At Isa. 9:4 סאון is guessed as ܟܠ, on the basis of the neighbouring רעש. At Amos 6:11, the obscure nouns רסיסים... בקיעים are rendered by the verbs ܘܢܙܝܥܘܗܝ ..... ܘܢܚܪܒܘܗܝ, "and will make it quake . . . and make it desolate", apparently through sheer guesswork from the general context.

On a larger scale, at Hab. 3:14, P's rendering of the problematic Hebrew words again bears no semantic relation to any of them but simply provides a suitable bridge between the preceding and succeeding phrases:

MT (נקבת במטיו ראש פרזו) יסערו להפיצני עליצתם (כמו לאכל עני במסתר)
P .... ܕܐܬܬܟܠܘ ܒܚܣܝܢܘܬܗܘܢ ....

You bored with his [own] rods the heads of his rulers, *who relied on their audacity*, that they might devour the poor in secret.

Again, a whole verse may be translated on the basis of a few words, filled out by guesswork to yield acceptable sense overall, as at Ps. 36:2 –

MT כי החליק אליו בעיניו למצא עונו לשנא
P ܡܛܠ ܕܣܢܝܐ ܗܝ ܒܥܝܢܘܗܝ ܕܢܫܒܘܩ ܚܛܗܘܗܝ ܘܢܣܢܐ ܐܢܘܢ

for it is *hateful* in his eyes that he *forsake* his sins and hate them.

Here the elements supplied by guesswork are italicised.

Sometimes the translator did not catch any definite meaning, and uses a word of vague sense, as at Hab. 1:4 –

MT כי רשע מכתיר את הצדיק
P ܡܛܠ ܕܥܘܠܐ ܕܒܪ ܒܝܫ ܒܝܫ ܠܙܕܝܩܐ

for the wicked (man) treats the righteous very badly.

[67] The rabbis defined ממזר as the offspring of a forbidden union (so e.g. Sifre ad loc.), of which adultery was the likeliest case.

Similarly, at Deut. 33:3 the difficult **אשדת** is rendered ܝܗܒ "he gave". At 1 Kgs. 1:9, **אבן הזחלת** becomes simply ܟܐܦܐ ܪܒܬܐ "great stone". Isa. 10:18 states of the invading Assyrians: **והיה כמסס נסס**, which P renders vaguely: "he shall be as if he had never been". At Prov. 7:20, the intending adulteress says that her husband will return only **ליום הכסה**; P has merely ܠܝܘܡܬܐ ܣܓܝܐܐ "after many days". Job 6:16 is again rendered vaguely:

MT   **עלימו יתעלם שלג**

P   ... ܣܓܝ ܬܠܓܐ "snow became much".

Vague guesses often involve the use of a 'drudge word'. The commonest root so used is ܚܝܠ, whose derivatives include ܚܝܠܐ 'strength' and ܚܝܠ 'strong'. Forms from this root render not only the usual words denoting strength but also many words which the translators found difficult (at least in context), such as **צל** (Num. 14:9), **תועפת** (Num. 23:22), **גור** (Deut. 32:27), **עקב** (Jer. 17:9), **חגוי** (Obad. 3), **קדימה** (Hab. 1:9), **זכר** [Hiph'il] (Ps. 20:8) and **אפיקי** (Job 40:18).

In some cases where P has a derivative of ܚܝܠ T^O has the equivalent root **תקף**, as for **דבא** (Deut. 33:25) and even the name **זוזים** (Gen. 14:5). This suggests that the use of strength terms as drudge words goes back to an older tradition on which the Targums and P both depend.[68] As Gordon has observed, such usage is already attested in the Aramaic version of Job from Qumran,[69] as at Job 30:14 –

MT   **כפרץ רהב**

11QTgJob (col. xvi 2)   **בתקף שחני**   "when my boil becomes strong (= virulent)"

Another drudge word is ܐܬܛܪܦ 'be buffeted, exhausted', representing **מזי** (Deut. 32:24) and many words in Jeremiah (**הלל** [Hitpolel], **יפח** [Hitpa'el], **ספף** and **קיה**) and in Psalms (**מוג**, **דלף** [Hitpolel], **עוף**, **עטף** [Hitpa'el], **שוח** [Hitpolel], **שפך**). In these books, ܚܝܠ and ܐܬܛܪܦ provide two basic alternative guesses for difficult words, the first being suitable when things look good for the subject and the second when they look bad.

Other drudge words are of more limited scope. The root ܫܒܚ in Psalms, because of its frequency in rendering a host of Hebrew synonyms for praise, came also to represent some words of unknown meaning, e.g.

81:8	**בסתר רעם**	ܣܬܪܐ ܕܗܠ ܕܫܒܚܟ
91:1	**בצל שדי יתלונן**	ܛܠܠܗ ܕܐܠܗܐ ܕܫܒܚ
110:3	**עמך נדבת**	ܥܡܟ ܕܫܒܚ

A drudge-word over a more limited stretch in Psalms is ܐܬܛܫܫ, serving within Ps. 35–39 for **האח** (35:25), **רפה** and **עזב** (37:8), **שכן** (37:27), **נחת** (38:3) and **בלג** (Hiph'il: 39:4). Special drudge-words appear also in sections of technical matter. Thus in the leprosy laws we find ܣܘܦܐ 'scale, scab' not only for **ספחת** 'scab' (Lev. 13:2) but also for **בהק** 'eruption' (13:39) and **שקערורת** 'hollows' (14:37). Again we are reminded of P's tendency to level the vocabulary over an extended section. Where accuracy was out of reach, this technique at least provided coherence.

In all these cases the incorrect sense makes it obvious that the translator was guessing. However, the translators' capacity for guesswork raises the suspicion that

---

[68] The nature of such common tradition is discussed in chapter 3.
[69] Compare also **בתקף** (restored) for **כארבה** at 39:20 (col. xxxiii 1). See R.P. Gordon. "The Citation of the Targums in Recent Bible Translations (RSV, JB, NEB)", *JJS* 26 (1975), pp. 50–60: 51n.

some correct renderings may likewise be guessed rather than due to pre-existing knowledge.

Derivation of sense from beyond the immediate context

In poetry, a sense might be inferred from parallelism within the verse. At Mic. 6:2, for MT איתנים, P has ܟܐܦܐ, to contrast with הרים in the parallel clause. Again, at Job 31:10 the translator missed the sexual reference in תטחן לאחר אשתי, rendering: "my wife milled for others". Hence the parallel clause ועליה יכרעון אחרין was guessed: "and she baked in another place".

Less often the translator looked to a neighbouring verse. Thus at Gen. 49:14 P renders משפתים as ܫܒܝܠܐ after ארח in v.17. At Num. 32:15 P replaces להניחו by ܠܡܛܥܝܘܬܟܘܢ "to make you wander", using the same verb as for וינעם (v.13). At Isa. 53:8, the rendering ܩܪܒܘ "they drew near" for נגע seems at least partly inspired by the translation ܩܪܒ for נגש (construed as נגש) in the previous verse. We are reminded here of the tendency noted above to impose uniform vocabulary over an extended passage, but when the sense was well understood.

The translator may look even further afield within the book. In the wise woman's plea at 2 Sam. 20:19, P did not find עיר ואם (להמית) satisfactory as it stood, and instead rendered ܡܛܠ ܘܐܡܗ, with a glance at the other wise woman of 2 Sam. 14:6.[70] At Isa. 5:17, the ruins of מחים become "rebuilt ruins" after 58:12. Again, at Nah. 1:6, MT has הצרים נתצו "the rocks were shattered" while P renders ܛܘܪܐ ܐܬܦܫܪܘ "the mountains were melted". That phrase had just occurred in P at Mic. 1:4, for ונמסו ההרים; apparently צרים recalled ܛܘܪܐ and hence the other passage.[71]

In Exodus, two words which looked similar and occurred in similar contexts (namely, of baking dough) were interpreted in the light of each other:

12:34

MT   משארתם צררת בשמלתם

P   ܠܝܫܗܘܢ ܟܕ ܨܪܝܪ ܒܡܐܢܝܗܘܢ

their uncooked dough bound up in their towels

16:23

MT   ואת כל העדף הניחו לכם למשמרת עד הבקר

P   ܘܡܕܡ ܕܝܬܝܪ ܗܘܐ ܠܟܘܢ ܛܪܘ ܠܝܫܐ ܠܨܦܪܐ

and what remains, keep for yourselves as uncooked dough till morning.

In 12:34, the mysterious משארת is preceded by a reference to dough that had not risen. In 16:23, the Israelites are authorised to cook the manna before Sabbath, but to leave the remainder as משמרת. The translator assumed that the difference

---

[70] R.P. Gordon, "The Variable Wisdom of Abel: the MT and Versions at 2 Samuel XX 18–19", *VT* 43 (1993), pp. 215–26: 222.   [71] Gelston, *Twelve Prophets*, p. 150.

between these two Hebrew forms could be ignored; compare the phenomenon of "deliberate misreading" discussed above. Hence he sought a rendering to fit both contexts equally, and produced ܩܪܝܪܐ – "uncooked (dough)", literally "cold".

On a few occasions the translator looked to a different biblical book altogether. In some such passages, it can be shown that the other biblical book is cited after the P version, and not simply from the Hebrew. These passages shed welcome light on the relationship between the different biblical books in P, and they are discussed in chapter 4.

Passages from other books may also be adduced. Thus at Job 36:20, עמים תחתם led the translator to import Isa. 43:4a: "and he will give nations for thee and peoples for thyself". At S. of S. 8:11, המון (בעל) 'multitude' in the context of a vineyard reminded the translator of Dan. 4:9, and so the phrase was rendered ܘܐܒܗ ܣܓܝ : "and its fruit was plentiful". Appeal to other biblical passages is especially common in Chronicles, where the *Vorlage* seems to have been damaged, as argued in chapter 3. The phenomenon is further discussed in chapter 4 below.

A quotation from a non-biblical source is found at the end of David's prayer at 1 Chr. 29:19 –

ܘܢܬܩܕܫ ܫܡܟ ܪܒܐ ܘܢܫܬܒܚ ܒܥܠܡܐ ܕܝ ܒܪܐ ܩܕܡ ܐܝܠܝܢ ܕܕܚܠܝܢ ܠܟ

that Thy great name be sanctified and praised in the world that Thou didst create before those that fear Thee.

This bears no resemblance to the Hebrew text, which was apparently illegible at this point. Instead, it is based primarily on the opening of the Qaddish prayer:

יתגדל ויתקדש שמיה רבא בעלמא די ברא כרעותיה

In addition, the element ܘܢܫܬܒܚ seems to reflect the third paragraph (יתברך וישתבח), while the final phrase finds a counterpart in a Hebrew re-working of the Qaddish preserved in the Jewish liturgy:[72]

כרצונו וכרצון יראיו וכרצון כל בית ישראל

(may his name be praised) in accordance with his will, and the will of those who fear him, and of all the house of Israel.

It seems that the translator knew that the illegible words concluded the prayer. He therefore cited the Qaddish, which was recited among the Jews at the conclusion of a discourse (TB Sota 49a).[73] Other extra-biblical references are doubtful; the question is discussed in chapter 5 below.

Abdication of the translator's function

In some very obscure passages the translators abdicate their function. They may translate word-for-word and so reproduce the obscurity of the original, or they may resort to omission or free composition.

---

[72] S. Baer (ed.), סדר עבודת ישראל, Rödelheim [1868], p. 224.
[73] For detailed discussion, see M.P. Weitzman, "The Qaddish Prayer and the Peshitta of Chronicles" (in Hebrew), in H. Ben-Shammai (ed.), *Hebrew and Arabic Studies in honour of Joshua Blau*, Tel-Aviv and Jerusalem 1993, pp. 261–90.

Literal obscurity is found at times in the difficult book of Job, e.g. at 11:17a –

MT   וּמִצָּהֳרַיִם יָקוּם חָלֶד

P   ܘܡܢ ܛܗܪܐ ܢܩܘܡ ܚܦܪܐ

and from noon, digging will arise.

Evidently חָלֶד was understood on the basis of חֹלֶד "mole", but readers must have been puzzled. Similarly at Jer. 6:11, while each word is rendered accurately, no satisfactory sense emerges overall:

MT...וְאֵת חֲמַת יְ מָלֵאתִי נִלְאֵיתִי הָכִיל שְׁפֹךְ עַל עוֹלָל

P   ܘܐܢܬܝ ܚܡܬܗ ܕܡܪܝܐ ܡܠܝܬܝ ܐܠܝܬܝ. ܐܫܘܕܝ ܘܟܝܠܝ ܥܠ ܝ̈ܠܘܕܐ...

and thou (f.) art filled with the wrath of the Lord, and weary. Measure and pour over children . . .[74]

The fact that the sense of P was not everywhere immediately clear has implications for Syriac lexicography. For example, it has been argued that ܬܝܒܘܬܐ, which normally means 'repentance', must also be capable of the meaning 'apostasy', since P would not otherwise make good sense in the passages where this word renders מְשׁוּבָה (Jer. 2:19, 3:2, 8:5, Hos. 14:5).[75] However, the native commentators were able to extract a meaning without being aware of any other meaning apart from 'repentance', e.g.

Jer. 2:19

MT   וּמְשֻׁבוֹתַיִךְ תּוֹכִחֻךְ

P   ܘܬܝܒܘܬܟܝ ܬܟܣܟܝ

Išo'dad[76]   ܗܘ ܗܟܝܠ ܕܬܝܒܘܬܟܝ ܬܟܣܟܝ. ܗܢܘ ܗܘ ܕܠܘ ܒܩܘܫܬܐ ܗܘܐ ܐܠܐ ܒܢܟܝܠܘܬܐ.

that is, it [your repentance] scorns and rebukes you, that it was not in truth but in dissembling.

Hos. 14:5

MT   אֶרְפָּא מְשׁוּבָתָם

P   ܐܣܐ ܬܝܒܘܬܗܘܢ

"Ephrem"   ܠܬܝ̈ܒܐ ܗ

that is, [I shall heal] those who repent.

Thus the hypothesis that P was everywhere straightforward is not a safe basis for the revision of the lexicon.

The ultimate abdication was, of course, to omit the difficult material altogether. Some elements in the text were so difficult – in themselves or in context – that the translator apparently felt that any attempt at translation would only create obscurity. Examples of difficult words or phrases which the translators were content to omit occur at Exod. 34:19 תִּזָּכָר, 1 Sam. 9:24 לֵאמֹר הָעָם קָרָאתִי, 1 Kgs. 7:28 בֵּין הַשְׁלַבִּים

---

[74] Despite unusual construal (וְאַתָּ 'and thou' against MT וְאֵת, suffixes תִי- as second person singular feminine, and הָכִיל as imperative), the translation is straightforward.

[75] Th. Sprey, "*tybwt'* – מְשׁוּבָה", *VT* 7 (1957), pp. 408–10.

[76] C. Van den Eynde (ed.), *Commentaire d' Išo'dad de Merv sur l'Ancien Testament IV. Isaïe et les Douze.* CSCO 303 (Syr 128), Louvain 1969, ad loc.

ומסגרת, Isa. 13:8 יחילון י, Ps. 51:8 בטוחות and Prov. 19:7c. In Job some particularly difficult lines or verses are likewise omitted (29:6, 30:3–4, 38:25a, 41:21a,22–24a) or compressed (39:3–4). The same phenomenon in the Twelve Prophets is noted by Gelston.[77] There are many omissions in Chronicles also, but as the passages concerned (e.g. 2 Chr. 29:10–19) are not particularly difficult, the reason here seems rather that the *Vorlage* was difficult to read, as argued in chapter 3.

Repeated avoidance of the difficulties in the Hebrew through omission (with other devices) can result in a smooth but colourless rendering of an extended passage, as in the case of Jer. 17:1–4:

1) MT   חטאת יהודה כתובה... חרושה על לוח לבם ולקרנות מזבחתיהם:

P)   ܘܚܛܝܬܐ ܕܝܗܘܕܐ... ܟܬܝܒܐ ܘܪܫܝܡܐ ܥܠ ܠܒܗܘܢ ܘܥܠ ܩܪܢܬܐ ܕܡܕܒܚܝܗܘܢ

The sin of Judah is written . . . and engraved on the tablets of their heart, and on the horns of their altars,

2) MT   כזכר בניהם מזבחתם ואשריהם על עץ רענן על גבעת הגבהות:

P   ܘܥܠ ܕܚܠܬܗܘܢ ܬܚܝܬ ܟܠ ܐܝܠܢ ܕܥܒܝܛ ܘܥܠ ܟܠ ܪܡܬܐ ܪܡܬܐ

and (on) their fear-objects, under every tree that is thick and upon every high hill,

3) MT   הררי בשדה חילך וכל אוצרתיך לבז אתן במתיך בחטאת בכל גבוליך:

P   ܘܥܠ ܛܘܪܐ ܒܚܩܠܐ. ܢܟܣܝܟ ܘܟܠܗܘܢ ܓܙܝܟ ܘܬܚܘܡܝܟ ܐܬܠ ܐܢܘܢ ܠܒܙܬܐ ܡܛܠ ܚܛܗܝܟ

and on the mountains and in the field. Your possessions and all your treasures, and your borders, I shall give for spoil because of your sins,

4) MT   ...ושמטת ובך מנחלתך אשר נתתי לך:

P   ܘܐܥܒܪܟ ܡܢ ܝܪܬܘܬܐ ܕܝܗܒܬ ܠܟ...

and I shall make you pass away from the heritage that I gave you.

Here P omits some difficult phrases (כזכר בניהם מזבחתם, במתיך, ובך), and transforms some grammatical elements, notably the word order in v.3. In this way, the impassioned phrases in the Hebrew are rolled into long and relatively dull sentences; and the result contributes little to our understanding of the original Hebrew.

A less serious abdication of the translator's role is to leave the choice open between two alternative understandings. Thus at Ruth 1:13 מכם מר (לי מאד) is first rendered "bitter concerning you" and then "more bitter than you". Such cases are common in Job; for example, Job 24:10 is rendered twice, with עמר becoming first 'bread' and then 'measure' (ܣܐܬܐ ܘܠܚܡܐ). There is also a double rendering of the second line of Job 31:35:

MT   הן תוי שדי יענני

The first rendering (brought forward to the beginning of the verse) runs:

P   ܘܬܘܝܗ, ܡܟܟܢܝ ܕܐܠܗܐ ܡܟܟܢܝ

the vexations of God humbled me.[78]

The second rendering is in the proper place:

(ܡܢ ܕܝܢ ܢܗܒ ܡܢ ܕܢܫܡܥ ܠܝ) ܐܢ ܐܝܬܘܗܝ܆ ܐܠܗܐ ܢܥܢܝܢܝ

(Who will grant one who would listen to me,) if he exists? Let God answer me.

Here the letters תוי have been mentally rearranged and so associated with Syriac ܐܝܬ. Another such case, at 1 Chr. 12:1, is discussed in chapter 3. However, the doublet at Gen. 24:21, where משתאה is rendered ܡܫܬܩܐ ܘܡܣܬܟܠܐ, is paralleled in T[N] and seems inherited from Targum tradition; see discussion in chapter 3.

Finally, unlike some other translators – notably Theodotion – P does not use transliteration to represent elements not understood. The transliteration ܬܘܗ ܘܒܘܗ at Gen. 1:2 was needed because of the lack of a Syriac term; and תבל had to be regularly transliterated as ܬܐܒܠ because ܐܪܥܐ was usually reserved for ארץ in a parallel clause. In Kings P transliterates בספר דברי הימים to indicate the title of a book: ܒܣܦܪ ܕܒܪ ܝܡܝܢ.[79]

Occasionally we find Syriac calques of Hebrew words, but these again suggest simply the lack of a native term in Syriac. Examples are ܐܪܘܢܐ for ארון, ܢܫܝܐ for גיד הנשה (Gen. 32:33), ܦܕܬܐ and even ܐܦܘܕܐ (at Hos. 3:4) for אפוד, the verb ܝܒܡ for יבם ('perform levirate marriage', at Gen. 37:8 etc.), ܥܪܘܒܐ for the plague ערוב, ܦܪܘܟܬܐ for פרכת (2 Chr. 3:14), ܨܝܨܝܬܐ for ציצת. Other apparent borrowings – e.g. ܐܡܝܢ regularly for אמן – may, however, be native Syriac words; and even the verb ܗܝܡܢ, though its form suggests borrowing from Heb. האמין, may pre-date the translation.

Combination of devices

We may now consider how these devices may be combined, in single verses and also in extended passages. Examples:

Gen. 49:22

MT בן פרת יוסף בן פרת עלי עין בנות צעדה עלי שור

P ܒܪܐ ܕܬܪܒܝܬܐ ܝܘܣܦ ܒܪܐ ܕܬܪܒܝܬܐ. ܣܩܝ ܥܝܢܐ ܒܢܝܢܐ ܣܡܝܟܐ ܕܣܠܩ ܥܠ ܫܘܪܐ.

a son of growth is Joseph, a son of growth. Go up, O well! A building supported, which goes up by a wall.

Here we find:

(a) appeal to another biblical passage, namely Num. 21:17 (MT עלי באר)

(b) tacit grammatical change, whereby בנות was taken as בנין 'building' (cf. 'wall')

(c) misreading of צעדה as סעדה, whence 'support'.

(d) otherwise close adherence to the Hebrew, despite the resulting obscurity.

2 Sam. 17:20

Here Absalom's agents are looking for Ahimaaz and Jonathan, and the texts continue:

MT ותאמר להם האשה עברו מיכל המים ויבקשו ולא מצאו...

P ...ܐܡܪܐ ܠܗܘܢ ܐܢܬܬܐ ܥܒܪܘ ܠܗܘܢ ܡܟܐ ܡܛܠ ܕܒܥܘ ܡܝܐ. ܘܠܐ ܐܫܟܚܘܢ...

The woman tells them: "They have passed on hence, because they sought water". And they did not find them . . .

[79] Contrast ܒܣܦܪ ܡ̈ܠܝ ܝܘܡܬܐ (Esther 10:2) and ܒܟܬܒܐ ܕܦܬܓ̈ܡܐ ܕܝܘ̈ܡܬܐ (Neh. 12:23).

The rare word מיכל has thus been understood through the similar-sounding but unrelated Syriac ܡܟܐ, while the verb ויבקשו has been taken as part of the direct speech. Here the result is smooth if inaccurate sense.

Isa. 66: 9
MT האני אשביר ולא אוליד יאמר י׳
P ܐܢܐ ܝܗܒܬ ܣܘܟܝܐ ܗܢܐ ܘܠܐ ܡܦܩ. ܐܢܐ ܐܡܪ ܡܪܝܐ

I have granted this expectation; and will I not bring it forth, says the Lord?

Unexpectedly, אשביר is explained through Syr. ܣܒܪܐ,[80] and the interrogative ה is ignored in this clause.
Job 40:2a:
MT הרב עם שדי יסור
P ܣܓܝܐ̈ܢ ܐܢܘܢ ܡܠ̈ܟܘܗܝ ܕܐܠܗܐ

many are the counsels of God

Here the lexical item רַב *rab* "many" rather than רִב "to quarrel" is identified, the sense of יסר is extended from "chastise" to "counsel", the preposition עם is ignored and the word order changed.
Hab.3:16b
MT אשר אנוח ליום צרה לעלות לעם יגודנו
P ܕܟܪܙ ܠܝ ܘܚܘܝܢܝ ܝܘܡܐ ܕܐܘܠܨܢܐ ܕܐܬܐ ܥܠ ܥܡܐ

for he predicts to me and has shown me the day of trouble that is coming upon the people.

This is not an accurate translation of the Hebrew, but it well continues the previous line: there the prophet is trembling, and here a reason is provided. Apparently the last word of the verse was read as יַגִּידֵנִי "he tells me". The regular Syriac equivalent of הגיד is ܚܘܝ, which, however, can also mean "show", whence: "he has shown me (the day . . .)". A phrase of similar meaning ("he predicts to me") is then supplied for Hebrew אנוח, for which no suitable sense could be found. This sense of Syr. ܟܪܙ is also found at Isa. 16:6 and Jer. 48:30 – where again, incidentally, it bears no semantic relation to any word in the Hebrew (cf. p. 193 below).

Such combinations were especially necessary when the translator was confronted by long lists of unfamiliar words. Thus Daniel 3 has repeatedly a list of seven foreign words denoting officers in the Babylonian empire. The translator uses general terms for the first three (ܫܠܝܛܐ ܪ̈ܒܝ, ܡܪ̈ܘܬܐ, ܥܠܝ̈ܠܐ); these exhausted, he transliterates the remaining four. In Isa. 3:18–23 P has to render 21 items of ladies' finery. After two vague renderings ('clothes', 'ornament'), he attempts a logical progression, from four hairstyles, through decorations of the temples and face, and a nose-ring, to four types of chain (cf. שירות earlier in the sequence) and eight types of robe, distinguished partly by colour. Here and there the influence of LXX is detectable: thus the hairstyles (for the 3rd to 6th items) recall ἐμπλόκια for the 2nd, and LXX too has some (but fewer) coloured robes.

80 Though there are a few instances of a cognate verb and noun שבר in biblical Hebrew.

Treatment of extended passages

In some difficult sections, good sense could be achieved – though not accuracy – through the expectation of logical coherence overall. At Zeph. 3:1, for example, a tacit change of grammatical elements together with an incorrect construal led to an unexpected understanding:

MT   הוי מראה ונגאלה העיר היונה

P   ܐܘܢ ܓܢܒܪܬܐ ܘܐܠܐ ܦܪܝܩܬܐ ܩܪܝܬܐ ܕܝܘܢܢ

The last two Hebrew words, each with a definite article, mean: "the oppressing city" and refer to Jerusalem. The previous chapter, however, had been concerned with Nineveh, which the translator thought was intended here too. He interprets the two difficult previous Hebrew words, accordingly, to fit Nineveh: thus ונגאלה is derived from גאל "redeem", and מראה (apparently) from ראה "see", stretched to "know", and in the passive "known, renowned". Nineveh was indeed a renowned city, which had once been delivered – from the punishment announced by Jonah. With this in mind, P ignores the definite articles in the last phrase and renders it: 'city of Jonah'. To reinforce this understanding, P links 3:1 to the preceding verse by adding ܘܢܐܡܪ:

> Everyone who passes over it will wonder, and whistle, and wave his hand, *and say:* Woe the renowned and (formerly) delivered city, the city of Jonah![81]

A still longer passage in which sense (but not accuracy) was provided through these techniques is Job 36:16–20a, discussed elsewhere.[82]

Names

The great majority of names are simply transcribed. Geographical names and adjectives, however, are sometimes modernised – or at least identified – according to traditions paralleled in the Targums, e.g. Qardu for Ararat, Matnin for Bashan, Indian for Ethiopian,[83] Arab for Ishmaelite, MPS ('Memphis') for Moph or Noph, Spain for Sepharad (Obad. 20), GBL (four times in Chronicles) for Seir. At Josh. 13:11,13, Ma'achah becomes Kuros (ܟܘܪܘܣ), while the Targum has the earlier form אפיקירוס, i.e. the Ἐπίκαιρος mentioned as one of the five cities east of the Jordan by Ptolemy V.16.9. Armenia (ܐܪܡܢܝܐ) is substituted both for מני (Jer. 51:27) and for ההרמונה (Amos 4:3). Hamath becomes Antioch at 1 Chr. 13:5, 18:9 and 2 Chr. 8:4. Apparently the translator took Hamath to symbolise the northern boundary of the promised land, as in the phrase לבא חמת (e.g. Num. 34:8), but identified that border with the Taurus Mountains (as in Gen. Apocr. 21.16).[84] These traditions are all paralleled in the corresponding Targums.

Perhaps following this last precedent, the translators claimed other places too for the vicinity of their own own neighbourhood, which, as will be argued in chapter 5, was probably Edessa. The Aramean district of Soba is thus equated with Nisibis in 1 Chr.

---

[81] Gelston, *Twelve Prophets*, p. 148.
[82] "Hebrew and Syriac Texts of the Book of Job", SVT 66(1997), pp. 381–99.
[83] This identification reappears in TB Meg. 11a, but has classical antecedents in the "Ethiopians of Asia" described by Herodotus 7.70 as straight-haired and serving with the Indians in the Persian army.
[84] N. Avigad and Y. Yadin, *A Genesis Apocryphon*, Jerusalem 1956, p. 30.

18–19.[85] Harran was substituted for Aram Ma'achah at 1 Chr. 19:6. Mabbog is specified as Pharaoh Necho's objective at 2 Kgs. 23:29 (where it is added to the text) and at 2 Chr. 35:20 (where it replaces Carchemish, in fact some 40 km to the north), in the account of Josiah's death at 2 Chr. 35:20.

At 2 Chr. 1:16, where MT has ומקוא "and from Que" (in Cilicia), P rightly detects a toponym, though the text is puzzling: ܡܢܕܐܐ ܐܠܦܐ. A similar form occurs in Tg. to Ezek. 27:6, where מאיי כתים is rendered ממדינת אפוליא.[86] The goods exported are horses in Chronicles but a "covered house for the theatre" on Tyre's ships in Ezekiel. In neither passage is Apuleia in south-east Italy particularly appropriate. At least in P-Chronicles, we could emend to Apamaea or Pamphylia, in the general region of Edessa.

The translators also introduce the great powers of their own day, without parallel in the Targums. Thus ששך at Jer. 25:26, which in fact indicates Babylon, becomes ܐܪܫܟܝܐ 'Arsaces' and at 51:41 ܐܪܫܟܝܬܐ 'the Arsacid city'. In this way the biblical antecedents of Parthia become the Babylonians rather than the benign Persians. Likewise the פרתמים 'nobles' in Esther, Daniel and Ezra become ܦܪܬܘܐ (Parthians). A reference to Rome may have been introduced through the cipher Edom at Ps. 12:9 –

MT   כרם זלות לבני אדם

P   ܐܝܟ ܙܘܐܡܐ ܕܥܠܬ ܕܒܢܝ ܐܕܘܡ

    like the vile pride of the children of Edom[87]

A noted phenomenon in P is the frequent substitution of Edom for Aram; and this too has been thought to refer to Rome. The question is discussed in an excursus at the end of this chapter.

The translators sometimes make surprising deductions about the identity of toponyms, notably:

(a) In Josh. 12–13, Geshur becomes Endor, apparently because both were mentioned as unconquered spots which lay (Josh. 17:11–12) or could have lain (Josh. 13:7, 13) in Manasseh's territory.

(b) Jaffa becomes Eilat at Josh. 19:46, and the sea of Jaffa becomes the Red Sea at 2 Chr. 2:15. The point of departure for Tarshish is named as Jaffa at Jonah 1:3 but as Etzion-Geber, close by Eilat,[88] at 2 Chr. 20:36; and the translators seem to have identified the two ports.

(c) In 2 Sam. 23, the mention of more than one "Shamma the Hararite" (vv.11,33) led the translator to distinguish them as hailing from different mountains, namely of Olives and of the King.

The translators might occasionally mistake a common noun for a name, e.g. אשדת (Deut. 3:17) as Ashdod, or מלצר as a personal name at Dan. 1:11. Conversely, sometimes the translator did not acknowledge the presence of a name, and so translated החירת (Exod. 14:2 etc.) as ܚܝܠܐ "the ditch", פתורה (Num. 22:5) as ܦܫܘܪܐ 'interpreter',

---

[85] This equation also appears in Saadiah's version of Ps. 60:2.
[86] The same name appears in some texts of Midrash to Ps. 9:7, but seems corrupt: "'The enemy are come to an end, their structures are for ever.' For example, Constantine built Constantinople, Apulus built Apulia (?), Romulus built Rome, Alexander build Alexandria, Seleucus built Seleucia. The founders have come to an end, but the cities they established endure."
[87] R. Duval, "Notes sur la Peschitto, I, Edom et Rome", *REJ* 14 (1887), pp. 49–51.
[88] Deut. 2:8, 1 Kgs. 9:26.

or מרתים (Jer. 50:21) as ܡܪܕܘܬܐ 'rebellious'. At 2 Sam. 8:18 and 20:7, P renders פלתי

...כרתי as ...ܐܪ̈ܐ ܦܠܚ̈ܐ "free men . . . workers"; apparently, פלתי was misread as part of

פלח, and a contrasting sense inferred for כרתי. The same occasionally occurs in LXX,

e.g.

Zech. 6:14

MT   לחלם ולטוביה ולידעיה ולחן בן צפניה

LXX   τοῖς ὑπομένουσιν καὶ τοῖς χρησίμοις αὐτῆς καὶ τοῖς ἐπεγνωκόσιν αὐτὴν καὶ εἰς χάριτα
       υἱοῦ Σοφονίου

When a toponym comprises or contains common nouns, P may treat the whole as a name. Thus ערבות מואב "the plains of Moab" is treated in the Pentateuch as a name: ܥܪܒܘܬ ܡܘܐܒ;[89] and for קרית יערים we similarly find the near-transliteration ܩܘܪܝܬ ܢܥܪܝܢ. On the other hand, such names are sometimes translated, e.g. מערת המכפלה as ܡܥܪܬܐ ܐܥܦܬܐ 'double cave' (Gen. 23:9 etc.), משרפות המים as ܡܝ̈ܐ ܚܡܝ̈ܡܐ 'hot waters' (Josh. 13:6), צופים (1 Sam. 1:1) as ܕܘܩ̈ܐ 'watchers'.

Intermediate between such translations of names and the usual system of transliteration is partial etymologisation. Thus ציון is rendered ܨܗܝܘܢ (cf. ܨܗܝܐ 'thirst' as from ציה 'dryness'), and רות becomes ܪܥܘܬ 'favour'.[90] The name אלקנה was rendered ܐܠܩܢܐ under the influence of ܐܩܢܐ, the term for the lattice-work in the sanctuary (1 Kgs. 7:17 etc.). Possibly the rendering ܒܘܨܪ 'defect' for בצרה, capital of Edom, is likewise intentional.

In names containing or comprising a third person singular masculine imperfect verb, the Hebrew initial *y-* is sometimes replaced by *n-* as in the Syriac conjugation, e.g. ܢܦܬܚ, ܢܓܐܠ (for יגאל), ܢܗܠܐܠ (for יהלאל). It may be that the translators adapted these names to the Syriac verb form. However, some names retain *y-* (e.g. ܝܨܚܩ); moreover, *y-* may change to *n-* in names not derived from imperfect verbs, such as ܢܕܒܐܠ (Exod. 6:22) or ܢܓܡܠ (1 Sam. 27:6 etc.). Thus it is equally possible that names based on the imperfect were left unchanged by the translators but later corrupted by copyists.

Some frequent personal names ending in *–ō* are adapted to end in *–ōn*, a far more frequent ending in Syriac; thus ܝܬܪܘܢ 'Jethro', ܦܪܥܘܢ 'Pharaoh', ܫܠܝܡܘܢ 'Solomon'. For the last, compare LXX Σαλωμων, though in P the two *ō* vowels suffered dissimilation to *ē/ō*.[91] Jonah's name is likewise extended to ܝܘܢܢ, perhaps under the influence of the accusative Ιωναν at the beginning of his book in LXX. The appending of *–n* to names is also attested elsewhere, e.g. Νωεμιν for נעמי in LXX or יודן for יהודה in Galilean Aramaic.

Divine names are usually translated. The Tetragrammaton, as well as *YH* and *'DNY*, regularly become ܡܪܝܐ (cf. LXX κύριος), in contrast with the transliterations in the Targums.[92] This shows some knowledge of a reading tradition. For the second occurrence of the Tetragrammaton at 2 Chr. 20:17, most mss have ܐܘܓܪܝ ܡܪܐ ܡܪ̈ܘܬܐ; this transliteration, however, never recurs in P, and the true reading may instead survive in ms 9a1, which has the expected brief rendering ܡܪܝܐ.[93] The combination *'DNY YHWH* usually becomes ܡܪܝܐ ܐܠܗܐ, as traditionally read, but P in Ezekiel and the Twelve Prophets instead has ܡܪܐ ܡܪ̈ܘܬܐ as written.[94]

---

[89] Contrast ܚܩܠܐ ܕܡܘܐܒ at Josh. 13:32.   [90] This may actually be the etymology of the Hebrew.
[91] However, toponyms like Jericho and Shiloh remain unchanged.
[92] Though at Exod. 15:2, YH is both transliterated and translated (ܗܘ ܡܪܝܐ).
[93] Ms 9a1 often preserves the original reading uniquely; see chapter 6 below.
[94] This serves also for *YHWH 'LHM* in Chronicles, by contrast to ܡܪܝܐ ܐܠܗܐ, which is usual elsewhere.

The name Elohim is usually rendered ܐܠܗܐ, though ܡܪܝܐ is sometimes substituted in Qohelet,[95] and the phrase בני אלהים is regularly transliterated (ܒܢܝ ܐܠܗܝܡ).[96] El too is normally translated ܐܠܗܐ but transliterated as ܐܝܠ when אלהים is also present (Gen. 46:3, Num. 16:22) but also at Isa. 10:21 14:13. El Shaddai (in Genesis and Exodus) is transliterated, but Shaddai alone usually becomes ܐܠܗܐ or ܫܕܝܐ. Both renderings can be found in Job, as Rignell noted;[97] perhaps they function as A-word and B-word respectively. In Ruth, this name is transliterated at 1:20; in the next verse 1:21, however, it is rendered ܡܢ ܕܟܠܗ ܒܐܝܕܘܗܝ (cf. LXX ἱκανός), reflecting the rabbinic etymology שֶׁדַּי.

The divine title צבאות is transliterated from 1 Sam. 1:3 (where it first occurs) to 2 Sam. 6:2, but elsewhere usually translated as ܚܝܠܬܢܐ (cf. LXX παντοκράτωρ); see pp. 00–000 below. At Exod. 3:14, אהיה אשר אהיה is transliterated in full as a divine name (cf. most witnesses to T°).

Personal names are nearly always transcribed, not translated.[98] Many, however, have suffered change. In the case of the major prophets, oral familiarity may be responsible: ܚܙܩܐܝܠ יחזקאל ܐܪܡܝܐ ירמיהו ܐܫܥܝܐ ישעיהו

More often, however, the cause is scribal error. Thus the names of three of the kingdoms in Gen. 14:1 are transliterated, but for the fourth, viz גוים, P has ܓܠܝܐ. Although a nation of Gelians is mentioned by Bar-Daisan, who places them by the Caspian Sea,[99] there was no reason for the translator to introduce them here, and the text of P is better explained as a corruption of ܓܝܝܐ, a virtual transliteration of the Hebrew (cf. the spelling גיים at Gen. 25:23, Ps. 79:10).[100]

Sometimes the corruption results from attraction to a neighbouring word. Thus the name Jael (יעל) became ܥܢܐܝܠ, since it is immediately preceded by Anat (ܥܢܬ) at Judg. 5:6. Similarly, at 2 Sam. 2:8 the name of Ish-Bosheth is partly assimilated to that of his father, in the phrase איש בשת בן שאול, and so appears as ܐܫܒܫܘܠ. Likewise, the name of Amnon (אמנון) appears in the existing text of P as ܚܡܢܘܢ, by partial assimilation to the name of his mother Ahinoam (ܐܚܝܢܘܥܡ) at 2 Sam. 4:3. Even the curious form ܪܘܒܝܠ for Reuben, from Gen. 29:32 onward, seems due to attraction to the name ܪܚܝܠ 'Rachel', mentioned in the previous verse.

What is remarkable is that the disfigured form is used – and attested by all mss of P – wherever the name occurs rather than simply in those passages where the corruption apparently originated. This implies an early revision to impose uniformity. The revisors must have worked within the closed field of P, without reference to Hebrew or even Greek sources.

Such a revision would also explain the many cases in P where a name – either personal or a toponym – differs palaeographically from MT too far to be merely corrupt,

[95] There are 16 occurrences of ܡܪܝܐ against 23 of ܐܠܗܐ, according to R.B. Salters, "The word for 'God' in the Peshiṭta of Koheleth", *VT* 21 (1971), pp. 251–4. Salters wonders whether the change aimed to identify the remote God of Qoheleth with the Lord God of Israel.

[96] The inner-Syriac variation at Gen. 6:2,4 is discussed in chapter 6 below.

[97] Rignell, *The Peshiṭta to the Book of Job,* p. 365.

[98] The form ܪܒܝ for גדלתי at 1 Chr. 25:29 is a rare exception.

[99] The text was edited with notes by F. Nau in PO I/2, pp. 490–658; see pp. 587–8.

[100] Corruption from Yodh to Lamedh occurs at Num. 13:13 (MT מיכאל, P ܡܠܟܐܝܠ); compare Codex Sinaiticus at Mark 7:26, where ܐܪܡܠܬܐ is corrupt from ܐܪܡܝܬܐ 'gentile', rendering ἑλληνίς, as noted by F.C. Burkitt, *Evangelion da-Mepharreshe*, Cambridge 1904, vol. 2, p. 282. A similar corruption from ܣܘܟܝܐ to ܣܘܟܠܐ is suggested by P. Borbone, "'Comprensione' o 'speranza'? Osea 2,17 nella Peshiṭta", *Henoch* 10 (1988), pp. 277–281.

and yet agrees with names found in P elsewhere. Thus the extant text of P shows Eliav for Lael (Num. 3:24), Sepharwaim for Aqrabim (Num. 34:4), ܐܪܡܬܐ (as at Josh. 13:37) instead of the expected ܚܡܬܐ (MT:) at Josh. 13:20, and even Ono (Syr. ܐܘܢ) for לשם (Josh. 19:47). The place names יקב זאב (Judg. 7:25) and קרקר (Judg. 8:10) have both become ܡܝܡܒ or ܡܕܒ (the mss vary), apparently through reciprocal assimilation. Personal names are merged even between the genders: so Merab is assimilated to Nadab, while the form ܝܘܟܒܪ represents Jochebed, Ichabod and David's son Jibchar (2 Sam. 5:15). A personal name is assimilated to a toponym, when Menahem is instead called ܚܣܘܡ. Apparently the revisers suspected that certain names were corrupt, and tried – albeit disastrously at times – to match them with names known elsewhere in P.

Finally, Syriac forms may be substituted for divergent Hebrew month names:

	MT	P
1 Kgs. 6:1,37	זו	ܐܝܪ
1 Kgs. 6:38	בול	ܬܫܪܝ ܐܘܝ,
Zech. 7:1 (and Neh. 1:1)	כסלו	ܟܢܘ
Esther 2:16	טבת	ܟܢܘ ܐܘܝ,
Esther 8:9	סיון	ܚܙܝܪ

Two month names for which the Syriac name is not substituted are:

Exod. 13:4 etc.	אביב	ܣܘܒܐ 'flowers' (by similarity of sound)
1 Kgs. 8:2	איתנים	ܚܠܠܬܐ 'harvests' (guessed from context)

By contrast, the expression "*n*th month" is usually rendered exactly, though at 1 Chr. 12:16(15) we find ܝܪܚ ܩܕܡܝ for בחדש הראשון.

The relationship of the *Vorlage* to the consonantal text of MT

No doubt the *Vorlage* of P sometimes differed from the consonantal text of MT. The problem is to identify those differences. We know that the translation technique was not altogether literal, and indeed we have sometimes caught the translators introducing drastic changes such as the "proverb" at Ruth 2:8. Hence, any retroversion from P into Hebrew is subject to a margin of uncertainty.

We may first consider cases where an alternative Hebrew reading other than the consonantal text of MT actually survives, whether within the massoretic tradition (notably as Qere) or in the evidence from Qumran. Here we must try to identify which (if any) of the extant Hebrew texts agreed with the *Vorlage* of P. Only then will we proceed to the retroversion of P into Hebrew in passages where MT is our only authority in Hebrew and P disagrees in sense.

Qere/Kethib

There are two types of Qere/Kethib variant.[101] In the first and less common category, the Kethib was not suitable – whether too holy or too indelicate – for reading, and a Qere which is graphically quite different is substituted. In the second category, by contrast, the

---

[101] J. Barr, "A New Look at Kethib-Qere", *OTS* 21 (Leiden 1981), pp. 19–37.

difference between the Qere and the Kethib concerns a single letter and so is graphically minimal – though the difference in sense may well be greater than in the first category.

Foremost in the first category is the Tetragrammaton, which P renders ܡܪܝܐ after the Qere. Evidently the translator was familiar with the traditional oral reading. Likewise, P in most books renders 'DNY YHWH as ܡܪܝܐ ܐܠܗܐ after Qere, though in Ezekiel and the Twelve Prophets P instead agrees with the Kethib.

However, in passages where the purpose of the Qere is instead to remove indelicacy, P tends to agree with the Kethib. Thus שיניהם at 2 Kgs. 18:27 and Isa. 36:12 is literally rendered, as against Qere מימי רגליהם. Likewise, חרייונים at 2 Kgs. 6:25 is literally rendered ܕܒܢܐ ܕܝܘܢܐ, "of dove's dung" as against Qere דביונים. Similarly the latrine of 2 Kgs. 10:27 (Kethib למחראות) is plainly translated ܒܝܬ ܚܪܝܐ, in contrast with the softer Qere למוצאות. There is just one euphemism on which P follows Qere against Kethib: where Kethib has עפלים and Qere the (less indelicate) טחרים, P follows the latter to render ܠܛܚܘܪܐ. Incidentally, the Syriac word seems to have been an anatomical rather than physiological term, to judge from the suffix ("their") at 1 Sam. 5:6 ܘܡܚܐ ܐܢܘܢ ܒܛܚܘܪܝܗܘܢ (cf. also verses 9, 12). In all these cases, P's *Vorlage* agreed with the Kethib, and the translator was not aware of any alternative reading, written or oral.

We now turn to those passages where the Qere and the Kethib differ by a single letter. In some such passages P agrees in sense with Kethib against Qere, e.g.

	Kethib	Qere	P
Jer. 6:29	מאשתם	מאש תם	ܡܢ ܐܫܬܗܘܢ
Pr. 21:29	יכין	יבין	ܡܬܒܩܐ
Job 19:29	שדין	שדון	ܕܐܝܬ ܕܝܢܐ

Here belong some cases where the difference between Kethib and Qere concerns the words לא and לו, e.g.

Exod. 21:8	אשר לא (לו Q) יעדה	ܕܠܐ ܡܫܬܒܩܐ
Isa. 63:9	בכל צרתם לא (לו Q) צר	ܒܟܠ ܐܘܠܨܢܗܘܢ ܠܐ ܐܠܨ ܐܢܘܢ
Ps. 100:3	הוא עשנו ולא (ולו Q) אנחנו	ܘܗܘ ܥܒܕܢ ܘܠܐ ܚܢܢ

In all these passages there is no reason to suppose that P knew any form of the text other than the Kethib.

On the other hand, we sometimes find P exhibiting agreement with Qere too strong to be coincidental, e.g.

	Kethib	Qere	
Gen. 30:11	בגד	בא גד	=P [ܐܬܐ ܓܕ,]
Josh. 8:16	בעיר	בעי	=P
1 Sam. 17:7	(חניתו) וחץ	ועץ	=P [ܘܩܝܣܐ]
2 Sam. 8:3	בנהר	בנהר פרת	=P
2 Kgs. 20:4	עיר	חצר	=P
Ps. 55:16	ישימות	ישי מות	=P
Job 9:30	במו שלג	במי שלג	=P

To these too we may add some cases where the difference between Kethib and Qere concerns לא and לו, e.g.

2 Kgs. 8:10   חיה תחיה (.Q לו) לא אמר הנא הנא הוא לה וכי אמר לה

Job 13:15   איחל (.Q לו) לא יקטלני הן גבר הוא מכלא הנא אסבר לה ... א

In this last passage, P agrees with Qere in a declaration of absolute faith: "Though he slay me, I hope for him alone."

How are these agreements between P and the Qere to be explained? It is unlikely that all these readings reached P through a reading tradition, for any reading tradition known to P was at best sporadic, and unlikely to have been available in all these passages. More probably, then, these Qere readings stood in P's written *Vorlage*. This is in keeping with the view that some Qere readings, despite the name, represent written variants.[102]

However, a minority of P's agreements with Qere may indeed be due to a reading tradition attached to a particular passage. Such seems the case at 1 Sam. 2:16 –

MT כי עתה תתן (.Q לא) לו ואמר   P ואמר לה לא. אלא השתא הב לה

Here P reflects both the Kethib and the Qere, suggesting that the translator had access to the written text and the reading tradition together.

It must be admitted that in most passages it cannot be determined whether P's *Vorlage* agreed with the Qere or the Kethib. In many, the variation concerns matters like Hebrew spelling or morphology too subtle to show up in translation. In some other passages the variation, though greater, is still slight enough to fall within the margin of adjustment of which the translator was capable, as at Lev. 9:22 –

MT (Qere. יָדָיו)   וישא אהרן את ידו

P   וארים אהרן אידוהי אידוהי,

Then there are cases where P agrees with the Qere which, however, can be viewed as an obvious (if occasionally misguided) correction of the Kethib, e.g.

Lev. 11:21   כרעים (.Q לו) לא אשר

Judg. 16:18   את כל לבו (.Q לי) לה הגיד כי הפעם עלו לאמר ... ותקרא

Judg. 20:13   בנימן (.Q add. בני) ולא אבו

Here too belong the cases in Gen. 24 and Deut. 22 where the Kethib has נער but the Qere has נַעֲרָה, and P understands likewise, as the context demands.

Finally, we cannot tell whether P's *Vorlage* agreed with Kethib or Qere where P is not an exact representation of either, e.g.

	Kethib	Qere	P
Zech. 14:2	ישגלנה	ישכבנה	נשתכבן
Pr. 22:20	שלשום	שלשים	הא תלת זבני

In the same way, where P agrees with a ms that differs marginally from the majority within MT, it cannot be determined whether P's *Vorlage* differed from the majority MT text or not. Such is the case at Zech. 11:13b, where a sum of thirty shekels is deposited. Most mss within MT have היוצר, but there is limited attestation of האוצר "the treasury", and P likewise has בית גזא. However, as the meaning "treasury" could readily have been inferred from the context, we cannot safely infer that P's *Vorlage* actually had האוצר rather than the majority reading of MT.

---

[102] The various opinions are discussed by E. Tov, *Textual Criticism of the Hebrew Bible*, Minneapolis/Assen-Maastricht 1992, pp. 58–63.

Hebrew texts outside the Massoretic tradition

Such is the margin of uncertainty that where a text from Qumran diverges from MT we may not be able to tell with which the *Vorlage* of P agreed. To the instances in the Twelve Prophets noted by Gelston,[103] we may add Exod. 12:39 –

MT   כִּי גֹרְשׁוּ מִמִּצְרִים

2QExod[a]5:8   כי גרשום מצרים = [104]כִּי גֵרְשׁוּם מִצְּרִים

P (7h13,12b1)   ܡܛܠ ܕܐܦܩܘܗ ܐܢܘܢ ܡܢ ܡܨܪܝܢ

P (most mss)   ܡܛܠ ܕܐܦܩܘ ܐܢܘܢ ܡܢ ܡܨܪܝܢ

The text of P – especially the majority reading – agrees closely with the Qumran fragment against MT, notably in the use of an active verb. It has been inferred that the *Vorlage* of P agreed with the Qumran fragment.[105] However, the active verb in P does not exclude a passive verb in the *Vorlage*. Active forms from the verb גרשׁ are normally rendered by the Aphel ܐܦܩ "to bring out"; but as no Ettaph'al yet existed for this verb, the translator could not have rendered גרשׁו by a Syriac passive, and was thus forced to recast the sentence in the active. Thus we could accept the majority text of P as original, and argue that P's *Vorlage* agreed with MT. The translator re-cast the verb as active, but then felt the need for a subject, as happened at Gen. 39:1 –

MT   וְיוֹסֵף הוּרַד מִצְרָיְמָה

P   ܝܘܣܦ ܕܝܢ ܐܚܬܘܗܝ, ܐܚܘܗܝ ܠܡܨܪܝܢ (cf. Gen. 37:36)[106]

Agreements between P and the biblical texts discovered at Qumran in fact raise a more fundamental problem. Most of the Qumran biblical texts appear to fall into two classes. First, there were model copies, which scribes strove to copy exactly. Beside these, however, were vernacular copies, designed to adapt the text for those who spoke Hebrew but were not expert in the biblical text. A vernacular copy thus served much the same purpose as a translation, apart from the change of language, and so exhibited much the same sorts of adjustment.[107] Thus they do not only update biblical language to a later form of Hebrew, but also replace rare or difficult terms, and generally adapt the text to improve clarity, simplicity and logical consistency. It has been estimated that 60 per cent of all the biblical texts discovered at Qumran were model texts, while 20 per cent were of the vernacular type.[108]

Are we right, then, to regard P as a rather free translation – as described in detail above – of a Hebrew text much like MT? Or is P instead a more literal translation of a vernacular copy, which already had the explanatory additions, simplifications and so on now found in P? The latter possibility seems unlikely, for a number of reasons. First, for so important an undertaking as a translation, one would expect a model rather than a vernacular text to be sought out. In his idealised account of the origin of LXX, Josephus relates that the High Priest sent to Egypt not only the seventy-two translators but also a copy of the Hebrew text, to be returned when the translation was complete.[109]

---

[103] Gelston, *Twelve Prophets*, p. 113.   [104] DJD III, p. 51.

[105] Y. Maori, "Methodological Criteria for Distinguishing between Variant *Vorlage* and Exegesis in the Peshitta Pentateuch", MPI 8 (1995), pp. 103–20: 118.

[106] On that view, 7h3 and 12b1 show an assimilation to ܡܨܪܝܢ ܡܢ earlier in the same verse.

[107] Tov, *Textual Criticism*, pp. 108–10. The term "vulgar", often used rather than "vernacular", is inappropriate for a biblical text.

[108] Tov, *Textual Criticism*, pp. 114–17 (where the remaining 20 per cent are also classified).

[109] Antiq. 12.2.6 (56).

This may preserve a memory of the use of a model text by the LXX translators. Second, the lack of any mention of vernacular copies in the Babylonian Talmud suggests that these were not known in the east; they would have served no purpose there, because scholars could understand the model copies, while the common people did not speak Hebrew.[110] Finally, as mentioned above, a rather free approach seems to have been characteristic of the oldest translations into Syriac, to judge from the other surviving examples.

The question whether the freedom evident in P originates with the translator or in his *Vorlage* is particularly acute in Isaiah, where many agreements were pointed out by Gottstein between P and the great Isaiah scroll (1QIsᵃ).[111] That scroll, as Kutscher has argued, is a vernacular copy.[112] At first sight, these agreements suggest that the Hebrew *Vorlage* of P agreed at these points with 1QIsa. against MT.[113] Instead, however, it may be that both the scribe of 1QIsa. (or one of its antecedents) and the translator of P were working from a Hebrew text close to MT, and that both independently reached the same resolution of the problems in that Hebrew text. To take two examples:

(a) 5:24

MT   ואש לוהבת וחשש להבה (ירפה), 1QIsa. ‏

P   ‏ مں ܐܠܗܒܐ ܘܢܣܒܐܬ ܐܟܠܐ (ܘܐܟܠܬ)

It looks as if P's *Vorlage* agreed with the Qumran scroll in **אש** against MT **חשש**. It is equally possible, however, that both set out from a text identical with MT. The rare word **חשש** was then guessed both by the Qumran scribe and by P to mean "fire", because of the occurrence of **אש** in the parallel line and the succeeding **להבה**.[114] The tautology created by this identification was relieved by the change of **להבה** to a kindred verb.

(b) 8:11

MT   וְיִסְּרֵנִי (מלכת בדרך העם הזה)

1QIsᵃ   יסירני ‏ "he removes me", so P ‏ ܡܥܒܪ.

P agrees with the Qumran copy, but need not have found that reading as his *Vorlage*. Both may instead start out from a text identical with MT, but reject the rare construction **יסר מן** ("chastise from") in favour of the commoner **הסיר מן**.[115]

Thus close scrutiny of the agreements in Isaiah between P and the Qumran copy against MT does not justify confidence that P's Hebrew *Vorlage* actually differed from MT.

Similar problems of deciding whether the *Vorlage* differed from MT arise when P agrees in sense with the Samaritan Pentateuch. In the well-known case of Gen. 2:2a, MT states that God completed his work on the seventh day, while P instead, together with the Samaritan Pentateuch (as well as LXX), has the sixth day. Whether the

---

[110] Kutscher, *Isaiah Scroll*, p. 86.
[111] M.H. [Goshen-]Gottstein, "Die Jesaja-Rolle im Lichte von Peschitta und Targum", *Biblica* 35 (1954), pp. 51–71.   [112] Kutscher, *Isaiah Scroll*, pp. 77–89.
[113] Such was Gottstein's general conclusion (p. 52).
[114] See the fuller discussion by Kutscher, *Isaiah Scroll*, pp. 36,221.   [115] Kutscher, *Isaiah Scroll*, p. 268.

translator found in his *Vorlage* the sixth or the seventh day cannot, however, be determined. One could claim that "sixth" is the original Hebrew reading, while "seventh" is an error peculiar to MT, which resulted from assimilation to 2b ("and he rested on the seventh day"); P was free of this error, together with the Samaritan (as well as LXX). Or, one could concede that "seventh" is the original reading, but claim that there were Hebrew texts of the vernacular type[116] which substituted "sixth" in order to resolve the obvious problem of God completing his work on the day of rest; and this easier reading "sixth" likewise stood in the *Vorlage* of P. Finally, against both the above possibilities, one could argue that the *Vorlage* of P had "seventh" as in MT, and that it was the translator who – like other translators and copyists but independently of them – made the obvious change from "seventh" to "sixth". In short, no certainty is possible.

Where the extant forms of the Hebrew text differ more markedly, however, it is often possible to determine with which P's *Vorlage* agreed. In the case of major divergence between MT and LXX, P's *Vorlage* usually resembled the former.[117] In Jeremiah, for example, P had in general the longer text rather than the shorter form reflected in some mss from Qumran (4QJer[b.d]) and in LXX.[118] In Samuel again, P's text agrees in general with MT against the text attested by 4QSam[a] and LXX.

In individual verses, by contrast, we often find agreement between LXX and P against MT. Here we have to consider whether both LXX and P reflect a Vorlage different from MT, or whether P (or at least its extant text) has been influenced by the Greek text of LXX. That question is deferred to the next chapter.

The reliability of retroversion without external support

We now consider the validity of retroverting the text of P into Hebrew when its sense differs from MT and is not supported by any other ancient witness.

In the first place, the retroversion of a Syriac reading calls for particular caution where the Syriac mss are divided and a rival Syriac reading agrees with MT. For example, according to *BHS*, P prefaces Exod. 14:15 with the words: "and Moses cried out before the Lord". However, this phrase does not appear in the oldest manuscript (5b1), which is sometimes alone in preserving the original Syriac text.[119] Apparently, the phrase was added later in Syriac tradition, in order to explain God's question: "Why do you cry to me?" Again, at Ezra 5:2 *BHS* cites P as reading "Sennacherib"; the earliest manuscripts, however, have "Esarhaddon" – albeit in the corrupt form ܣܢܚܝܪܒ – like MT.[120]

Even when the mss of P are unanimous, however, a discrepancy in sense between MT and P need not imply a different *Vorlage*, given the many ways in which the translators of P were capable of adjusting the text. The laconic notes in the apparatus of *BHS* sometimes make light of this problem. For example, Exod. 21:8 deals with a girl who is

---

[116] The Samaritan Pentateuch may be classified here; see Kutscher, *Isaiah Scroll*, p. 74.

[117] M.J. Mulder likewise concludes that "the Hebrew original of P . . . was all but identical with MT". See "The Use of the Peshitta in Textual Criticism", in N.F. Marcos (ed.), *La Septuaginta en la Investigacion Contemporanea*, Madrid 1985, pp. 37–53.

[118] See most recently P.M. Bogaert in *Revue Biblique* 101 (1994), pp. 363–406: 369–70.

[119] M.D. Koster, *The Peshitta of Exodus*, Assen 1977, p. 528.

[120] C. Moss, "The Peshitta Version of Ezra", *Muséon* 46 (1933), pp. 55–110: 104.

sold by her father as a bond-maid, but is "bad" in her husband's eyes. Here MT has
רָעָה, but P has ܣܢܝܐ 'hated'. *BHS* reports P as follows:

snj' = שְׂנוּאָה

The reason that *BHS* presents a retroversion into Hebrew may be simply that Hebrew is
the proper common denominator for reporting the text of the ancient versions.
However, if instead the reader is intended to infer that the form שְׂנואה actually stood in
the translator's *Vorlage*, then the assumption is involved that P never varied his renderings according to nuance, and so could not have rendered רעה in this context ("bad in
the eyes of . . .") by ܣܢܝܐ ("hated in the eyes of . . ."). But such an assumption is ground-
less, and in fact there can be no confidence that the *Vorlage* of P differed from MT.

It is especially important to take account of the character of the translation when
emending the Hebrew on the authority of P. In this connection it is worth considering
passages where a reading different from MT is commended in *BHS* on the authority of
P. Thus at Isa. 5:19 the objects of the prophet's condemnation are, according to MT:

האמרים ימהר יחישה מעשהו למען נראה
ותקרב ותבואה עצת קדוש ישראל ונדעה

On יחישה, *BHS* notes P's reading ܢܣܬܪܗܒ ܐܠܗܐ, and bids us to read יחיש followed by
the Tetragrammaton. The implication is that the latter was abbreviated to ה, which
came mistakenly to be combined with the previous word.

However, it is common for P to supply the subject explicitly when the Hebrew left it
implicit, so that the presence of ܐܠܗܐ in P is no guarantee that the translator found
יחיש followed by the Tetragammaton, or even יחיש ה with a space, in his *Vorlage*. In
the existing text, the insolent third person jussive and the omission of any divine name
in the first line well suit the defiance which the prophet is trying to depict. The emendation instead ensures that each verb is supplied with a subject, and may show simply that
the translator and the modern critic both had tidy minds. There is no confidence that
the recommended reading ever existed.

There are other passages where it seems likely that a retroversion of P into Hebrew
will yield the original reading and yet the likelihood remains that P's *Vorlage* agreed
with MT. Here we must remember that, even if we confine ourselves to the transmission
of a text in its original language, not every correct reading found in a ms results from
unbroken transmission direct from the original. The correct reading may instead have
been lost and then supplied by scribal conjecture; in the terminology of Kantorowicz,
not every reading which is *richtig* ('correct') is necessarily also *echt* ('authentic').[121] By
the same token, a correct reading found (in Syriac guise) in P may have been supplied
through conjecture on the part of the translator, or of the copyist of his *Vorlage* or of
one of its ancestors.

At Gen. 36:6, for example, we are told, in relation to Esau:

MT   וילך אל ארץ מפני יעקב אחיו

P   ܘܐܙܠ ܠܐܪܥܐ ܐܚܪܬܐ ܘܥܪܩ . . .

BHS would add שעיר after ארץ, on the authority of P. We know, however, that even if
P's *Vorlage* coincided with MT, the translator would have wished to specify the land,
which he could readily have identified through v.9, which states that Esau dwelt in the

---

[121] H. Kantorowicz, *Einführung in die Textkritik*, Leipzig 1921.

hill-country of Seir.[122] Even assuming that אל ארץ שעיר is the original reading, P's *Vorlage* may have agreed with MT, and the reference to Seir in P may be conjectural. Thus P's reading is probably *richtig*, but not necessarily *echt*.

Similar points arise in connection with obscure or awkward words which are found in MT and other versions but not in P, and which *BHS* bids us delete on P's authority. At 2 Kgs. 17:8, for example, the words ומלכי ישראל אשר עשו do not fit syntactically and are not found in P. A Hebrew text obtained by retroverting P may well be *richtig*; given, however, that the translators preferred to omit an awkward phrase rather than write nonsense, we can have no confidence that a text without the relevant words is *echt*. In some other cases, we cannot be confident that a text without these words is even *richtig*. At Josh. 22:14, for example, *BHS* suggests omission of the words here bracketed, on the authority of P:

ועשרה נשאים עמו נשיא אחד נשיא אחד[לבית אב] לכל מטות ישראל

ואיש ראש [בית אבותם] המה לאלפי ישראל

However, the second line does not flow well in Hebrew without the disputed words. It may instead be that the words – which relate to the בית אב – appeared P's *Vorlage* but that the translator thought it best not to trouble his readers here with that ancient institution.

Of course there may be *some* places where a reading preserved by P alone is actually *echt*, i.e. has been transmitted without change from the Hebrew original. In such cases there will be special reasons for doubting the rival possibility that the translator is responsible for the semantic divergence between MT and P. A possible example occurs at Ezra 6:3 –

MT   רומה אמין שתין פתיה אמין שתין   =LXX

P   ܘܪܘܡܗ ܐܡܝܢ ܐܫܬܝ ܘܦܬܝܗ ܐܡܝܢ ܥܣܪܝܢ

Here MT states that the ark in the Temple was 60 cubits square (the third dimension is not given), while P gives its dimensions as 60 cubits by 20 cubits. P's figures are consistent with 1 Kgs. 6:2 ($60 \times 20 \times 30$). However, if the translator had actually consulted 1 Kings, he would have been expected to include the third dimension. It is therefore arguable that he is instead following a *Vorlage* of Ezra which preserved the true dimensions, namely 60×20. In that case, the number 20 was replaced by assimilation to the preceding 60, and this error occurred independently both in MT and in LXX – which is conceivable. Here, then, is a case where there may be grounds to argue that P alone preserves the true reading.[123]

Instances of this sort, however, are rare indeed. No such cases could be identified in the recent thorough studies of P in Leviticus,[124] Judges[125] or the Twelve Prophets.[126] In Daniel, two seemingly redundant phrases in MT – אבוך מלכא at 5:11 and

---

[122] In place of אל ארץ, LXX has ἐκ γῆς Χανααν.

[123] C. Hawley, *A Critical Examination of the Peshiṭta Version of the Book of Ezra*, New York 1922, p. 15.

[124] Lane, *The Peshiṭta of Leviticus*, p. 85.

[125] The only example considered by Dirksen is at Judg. 14:18, where MT has החרסה: "(before the setting of) the sun". Here P has the puzzling ܐܬܐܠ, which seems an error for ܐܬܪܠ 'chamber', suggesting the emendation החדרה "(before he came) to the chamber". However, החרסה is likelier to be original, as it gives good dramatic sense: the Philistines produced their solution at the very end of the prescribed time. P's understanding seems rather based on deliberate misreading of the rare Hebrew form, with a glance at החדרה at Judg. 15:1.

[126] Gelston, *Twelve Prophets*, p. 128, tentatively identifies four passages where P's putative *Vorlage* was unique, but does not claim that these readings are original.

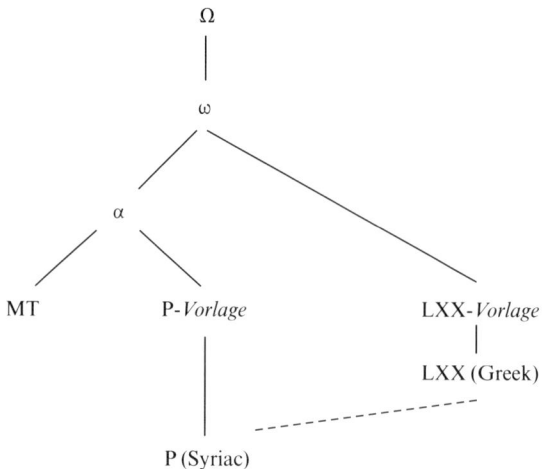

Fig. 2. Outline relationship between MT, Septuagint and Peshitta.

ואשמע את קול דבריו at 10:9 – are absent in P; but they may still have been present in P's *Vorlage*, and omitted for the sake of style.[127]

In order to understand why it is so rare for P to reflect alone the original text, we may consider the genealogical relationship between MT, P and LXX, which is basically as in fig. 2. Here ω is needed to explain the errors which are common to all three witnesses and can only be removed by conjectural emendation; and α is needed to explain those errors which are common to MT and P but of which LXX is free. The dotted line indicates the possibility of the Syriac translator being influenced by the Greek text of LXX, as considered in chapter 3.

This diagram is mainly a simplified version of fig.2 above, and does not separate out the many stages that separate P from MT. On the other hand, it is more extensive in referring also to the origins of LXX. However over-simplified, it indicates the relationship between the witnesses at most points in the text.

Just why so few correct readings survive in P alone, given the many places where the correct reading survives in MT alone or in LXX alone, can be understood through the outline genealogy below. MT is an indispensable witness, if only because there are features of the original Hebrew which even the most literal translation could not preserve, and most translators did not strive exclusively for literalism in any case. Moreover, in some books P has been influenced by LXX, as we shall see, so that errors in LXX may have infected P, in which case MT would alone (at least among these three witnesses) be correct. LXX too will preserve the true reading uniquely at times, since errors arose along the line from ω to α, and these would not normally have affected LXX. The particular value of the testimony of LXX in Samuel and Ezekiel is well known.

By contrast, in order for P to preserve the original reading against the agreement of MT and LXX, we need an exceptional combination of circumstances. Various scenarios can be imagined, but all are complex, e.g.

---

[127] *Pace* Taylor, *The Peshiṭta of Daniel*, p. 310.

(a) An error occurred somewhere along the line leading down from ω to LXX. The true text was still transmitted to α, and thence to P-*Vorlage*, and is reflected in P. However, a different error occurred independently, at that same point of the text, somewhere along the line leading down from α to MT. Thus P alone preserves the true text.

(b) The true reading survived in ω, and thence in α, and thence in P-*Vorlage* and in P. There also existed, however, a false but plausible reading. The latter was adopted somewhere along the line leading down from ω to LXX-*Vorlage*, and also by a copyist along the line leading down from α to MT. This plausible reading may have been an obvious facile correction of a difficult text, which could have occurred to more than one copyist independently; or it could have spread through the common practice whereby a scribe copying one ms would also consult another and introduce its readings.

(c) P may have had access to an additional Hebrew source, which belonged to a family now extinct which was independent of α and therefore free of ω's errors, which have been reproduced both in MT and in LXX.

Other scenarios too could be imagined. However, none of these, nor any of those just mentioned, can be expected to occur on a regular basis. In this they differ from the scenarios in which the true reading survives in MT alone or in LXX alone.

The value of P for the textual criticism of the Hebrew Bible has been variously assessed. On the one hand, Cross considers that "only rarely has the potential of the Syriac Bible as a textual tool been glimpsed".[128] On the other, Tov assigns P to the same basic category as MT, including it within the siglum м. The latter view seems closer to the mark. If anything, past use of P in the reconstruction of the Hebrew text has been excessive. The danger is that the translator has anticipated the modern critic: the very features sought by the critic in order to identify good readings may have been brought in long ago by the translator in order to foster smoothness and consistency in his version.

Thus, in the area traditionally of greatest demand, namely the provision of variant Hebrew readings, P's role is modest. For the most part, it confirms MT; less often, as we shall see, it confirms a different *Vorlage* in LXX; and seldom indeed does it preserve a Hebrew reading which cannot be derived from one or other of these. This is, in brief, because (unlike LXX) its earliest ancestry largely coincided with that of MT, and because (unlike MT) it is only a version.

The real interest of P lies elsewhere. P shows in detail how – and to what degree – the Hebrew Bible was understood in a particular community in the earliest centuries of this era. It testifies also to the beliefs of that community, whose identity remains to be discussed in chapter 5 below.

Conclusion and sequel

P can fairly be described as an idiomatic, though faithful, translation. The translators aim primarily to convey the plain sense, despite the attention given here to departures from it. However, broadly following the classical ideal, they convey not the words but the content[129]

---

[128] F.M. Cross, "Problems of Method in the Textual Criticism of the Hebrew Bible", in W.D. O'Flaherty (ed.), *The Critical Study of Sacred Texts*, Berkeley 1979, pp. 34–5.

[129] S.P. Brock, "Aspects of Translation Technique in Antiquity", *Greek Roman and Byzantine Studies* 20 (1979), pp. 69–87.

– provided that they believed that the content could be recovered. This combination of fidelity with intelligibility is the obvious ideal for the translator convinced that his readers will have no access to the Bible except through his translation.

By the seventh century, however, the literal ideal had become dominant in Syriac translation from the Bible, through the conviction that the form of the biblical original was important in its own right and needed to be conveyed no less than the content.[130] This, together with increased regard for the accuracy of LXX, led Paul of Tella in 615–17 CE to make the Syrohexapla, a literal Syriac translation of the fifth column of Origen's Hexapla. P was not displaced by this version, however, nor by the version made by Jacob of Edessa in *c.* 705 CE, which was in fact an attempt to combine the clear wording of P with the perceived accuracy of the Syrohexapla.[131] Thus P remained the principal version of the Old Testament for the Syriac-speaking church, and a mainspring of its rich and imaginative literature.

Excursus: Aram and Edom

The evidence

At least in the present form of the text of P, the name Aram and the adjective Aramean are only rarely rendered by the obvious Syriac equivalents (ܐܪܡܝܐ, ܐܪܡ). Usually, they are replaced by Edom (ܐܕܘܡ) or Edomite (ܐܕܘܡܝܐ).[132] The occurrences in the different books are as follows:

	Gen.	Num.	Deut.	Judg.	Sam.	Kgs.	Isa.	Jer.	Ezek.	Dodk.	Chr.
Aram	20	1	2	2	0	6	4	0	0	3	2
Edom	0	0	0	1	20	60	1	1	2	0	26

These figures cover the nouns (including compound names) and the gentilic adjectives together, but exclude the adverb ארמית 'in the Aramaic language', which is translated without change.

There are just four contexts where Aram is retained, but systematically so:

(a) The region east of the Euphrates which was homeland to the patriarchs and also to Balaam and to Cushan-Rish'ataim (Judg. 3:8,10). In this context the Hebrew usually has one or other of the compounds ארם נהרים or פדן ארם (or its equivalent שדה ארם at Hos. 12:13). In just two passages Aram (or its adjective) appears alone in this connection:

Num. 23:7   מן ארם ינחני בלק   ܡܢ ܐܪܡ ܕܒܪܢܝ ܒܠܩ

Deut. 26:5   ארמי אבד אבי   ܐܪܡܝܐ ܐܘܒܕ ܐܒܝ[133]

(b) The eponymous ancestor of the Aramaean people (e.g. Gen. 10:22).

(c) The early migration of the Arameans from Qir, which was to be reversed (Amos 1:5, 9:7).

---

[130] S.P. Brock, "Towards a history of Syriac translation technique", *Orientalia Christiana Analecta* 221 (1983), p. 12.

[131] M.H. [Goshen-]Gottstein, "Neue Syrohexaplafragmente", *Biblica* 37 (1956), pp. 162–83:165.

[132] The occasional change from noun to adjective is ignored for present purposes.

[133] Thus: "to Aram my father was taken". The reason that ܐܘܒܕ was chosen to render the difficult אבד may be attraction to the former passage.

(c) Narratives involving Rezin, the last king of Aram: hence the six occurrences of Aram in 2 Kgs. 15–16, and the four in Isa. 7.

Combinations of ארם with other names are not always rendered exactly. In rendering ארם דמשק, P inserts a conjunction: "Edom *and* Damascus" (2 Sam. 8:5,6; 1 Chr. 18:5). In 2 Sam. 10, MT refers to ארם בית רחוב and ארם צובה (v.6), and to ארם צובה ורחוב (v.8), as hired to fight for by the Ammonites. In P, these become Edom *son of* Rehob or Soba, sounding like personages rather than peoples.[134] Finally, the rendering "Harran" for ארם מעכה at 1 Chr. 19:6 was noted earlier.

In all cases, the biblical mss of P are unanimous as regards the choice between Aram and Edom (though they occasionally vary between noun and adjective). Aphrahat presupposes the same text, in that he denotes Ahab's opponents by Edom rather than Aram.[135] However, the commentary ascribed to Ephrem, wherever extant, has Aram like MT, or else calls the people Syrians, even though the biblical mss of P have Edom(ites).[136]

For completeness, we may note that some occurrences of Aram in MT fall within verses wholly lacking in P – in the Psalm title Ps. 60:2 (*bis*) and at 1 Chr. 2:23 7:34, 2 Chr. 28:23 – and that Aram is omitted at Isa. 7:4. At Isa. 17:3, Aram is replaced by Ephraim (ܐܦܪܝܡ), which is mentioned in the Hebrew earlier in the same verse.

Explanations

Roediger considered that P originally retained Aram, and that the change to Edom was due to copyists. He argued, firstly, that the commentary attributed to Ephrem, where it exists, always has Aram (or Syria). Secondly, the retention of Aram in a minority of passages even in the biblical mss suggests that the translation may originally have had Aram throughout. Roediger's suggested motive for the rejection of the name Aram was a shift in geographical terminology. In normal Syriac usage, the term Aram is restricted to the region (also called Assyria) east of the Euphrates. This area was, however, clearly unsuitable for most references to Aram in the Hebrew Bible, where a land bordering directly on Israel (and so located west of the Euphrates) is indicated. Copyists therefore altered the name to Edom, which was graphically similar.[137]

Against the theory of scribal change, Payne-Smith objected that, however easy the move from ܝ to ܢ, the replacement of ܐܕܘܡ by ܐܪܡ also involves the bold addition of the letter ܡ. Noting that exchange between ארם and אדם was easier in Hebrew script, he considered that the translators were themselves responsible, though he did not discuss the cause.[138]

Walker too supposed deliberate change by the translators. He suggested a political motive: to avoid friction with the Jews' pagan neighbours in the Roman province of Syria, where he assumed that the translation was made. The risk of friction arose from the fact that most biblical references to Aram occur in accounts of hostilities with

---

[134] The element 'son' was apparently justified by the one occurrence of בית.
[135] Ed. Parisot, col. 593, l.17; col. 949, l.20.
[136] See Ed. Rom. I, pp. 483–4 (ܣܘܪܝܐ), 505, 506, 531, 538, 547, 548 (all Aram or Aramaean).
[137] A. Roediger, *De Origine et Indole Arabicae Librorum V.T. Historicorum Interpretationis Libri Duo. Liber Primus, qui est De Fonte Interpretationis Librorum Iudicum . . . Arabice*, Halle 1829, pp. 22–3, esp. p. 23n.
[138] R. Payne-Smith, *Thesaurus Syriacus*, col. 35.

northern Israel. Hence the translators – whom he took to be Jews – replaced Aram by Edom, which (rather than Aram) was the traditional enemy of their forbears in the kingdom of Judah.[139]

Walker sought also to account for the distribution of passages where Aram is retained. He rightly argued that, in relation to the patriarchal homeland, the translators had no option to substitute Edom, which originated with Esau after Abraham's day. Nor could Edom be substituted for the eponymous ancestor of Aram, who likewise pre-dated Edom. As to the retention of Aram in relation to Rezin, Walker explains that Rezin is called "head of Damascus" (Isa. 7:8) and so could not be passed off as king of Edom. At Amos 1:5 likewise, according to Walker, the immediately preceding reference to Damascus was taken as a sure pointer to Aram and against Edom, and this presumably also affected 9:7.

Van der Kooij too ascribes the change to the translators, but considers that it introduced a covert reference to world politics in their own day. We know from Jewish sources and also from Aphrahat that Edom could serve as a code-name for Rome.[140] According to van der Kooij, Edom thence came to indicate the Roman province of Syria, into which biblical Aram now fell.[141] Indeed, according to Van der Kooij, the precise extent of this substitution indicates the date of the translation. The designation ܐܪܡ for the area of biblical Aram that lay beyond the Euphrates indicates, according to van der Kooij, that in the translators' day that area lay outside the Roman Empire, and hence that the translation dates from a time when Roman rule was bounded by the Euphrates. The translation must therefore be later than Trajan's eastern campaign of 117 CE, before which the Roman empire had not reached the Euphrates, but earlier than 165, when Roman rule was further extended up to the Khabur river in Mesopotamia and so came to include even the homeland of the patriarchs.[142] Van der Kooij's proposal to date the translation more precisely still, on the basis of this and other evidence, is discussed in chapter 5.

Comment

The scholars mentioned above suggest varying motives for the change from Aram to Edom, and differ also on whether the translators or later copyists were responsible. These two questions are best considered separately.

We may begin with the question of motive. Walker suggested that the change was prompted by a wish to preserve good relations between different peoples within the Roman empire. This argument loses force, however, if the translation was made (as most suppose) outside the Roman empire, whether in Edessa or further east. In any case, had the translators really wished to avoid offence to the Arameans of their own day, they would not have retained the name Aram in the passages dealing with Rezin,

---

[139] N. Walker, "The Peshiṭṭa Puzzle and its Implications", *VT* 18 (1968), pp. 268–70.

[140] Edom regularly indicates Rome in the Talmud (TB Sanh.12a, A.Z. 2b etc.). Tg. to Isa. 34:9, in a section on Edom, identifies the foe as רומי. The references in Aphrahat are discussed below.

[141] A. van der Kooij, *Die alten Textzeugen des Jesajabuches. Ein Beitrag zur Textgeschichte des Alten Testamentes*, Göttingen 1981, pp. 293–4.

[142] N.C. Debevoise, *A Political History of Parthia*, Chicago 1938, pp. 213–51. Van der Kooij does not go into the question of the passages that mention Rezin.

who launched the Syro-Ephraimitic war against Judah. Here Walker's argument that the description of Rezin as "head of Damascus" left them no choice is weakened by the fact that Edom is substituted even at 1 Kgs. 15:18 and 2 Chr. 16:2, to yield a reference to "Bar-Hadad . . . king of Edom who dwelt in Damascus".

Nor is van der Kooij's theory that Edom was intended as a code for Syria free from objection. In the first place, such a code would have created confusion with the real Edom – particularly in contexts where both Aram and Edom appear, such as 2 Sam. 8:5–14 (where David vanquishes both peoples) or 1 Kgs. 11:14–25 (where adversaries to Solomon arise from both). Secondly, although there is plentiful evidence that Edom could denote Rome itself, this is a far cry from using Edom(ite) of the land and inhabitants of Aram in biblical times, on the ground that that territory was destined later to come under Roman rule.

The evidence that Edom could have indicated the Roman province of Syria – as opposed to Rome itself – is in fact slight. The title "sons of Esau" in Aphrahat indicates not Syria but Rome (notably as the fourth beast in the vision of Daniel 2),[143] or the Romans.[144] The only evidence said to equate Edom directly with Syria is another passage of Aphrahat, which cites Isa. 11:11. That verse contains a list of places from which the Jews would be gathered back to their land, and Aphrahat quotes part of that list in a form different from that found in the biblical mss:

MT ומפתרוס ומכוש ומעילם ומשנער
P ܘܡܢ ܦܬܪܘܣ ܘܡܢ ܟܘܫ ܘܡܢ ܥܝܠܡ ܘܡܢ ܣܥܝܪ
Aphr. I 868 ܘܡܢ ܨܘܪ ܘܡܢ ܨܝܕܢ

P has Seir, which is a by-name of Edom, rather than Shin'ar as MT. It has been suggested that Seir (and hence Edom) was understood by Aphrahat to indicate Tyre and Sidon (and hence Syria).[145] However, the fact that Tyre and Sidon stand in place of no fewer than four names suggests instead that Aphrahat never attempted an exact citation of this part of the verse.[146] He may instead have been thinking of Joel 4:4–7, where Tyre and Sidon are named as centres for trading enslaved Jews; or he may have considered Tyre and Sidon more relevant than the remote locations of the original. It is worth adding that Aphrahat's Bible might not have had the reading ܣܥܝܪ at all; that reading probably arose through an inner-Syriac corruption from ܣܢܥܪ, which represents Shin'ar at Gen. 10:10 etc., and that corruption might not yet have occurred.

The treatment of the passages in Samuel and Chronicles which refer to ארם דמשק suggests that the translators did not in fact equate Edom with Syria. At 2 Sam. 8:5 = 1 Chr. 18:5, the translators insert a conjunction ("Edom *and* Damascus") which implies that Edom did not include Damascus. In the next verse, P-Samuel likewise writes that David set up overseers in Edom *and* in Damascus.[147]

Altogether, then, the most convincing motive for the removal of Aram is that

[143] Aphrahat, I, cols. 209, 220, 233, 236.
[144] ܘܡܠܟܘܬܐ ܬܘܒ ܒܡܐܬܝܬܗ ܐܫܠܡܗ ܠܝܗܘܕܝܐ ܕܐܬܦܪܩܘ ܒܢ̈ܝ ܥܣܘ (I, col. 229).
[145] Van der Kooij, *Die alten Textzeugen*, p. 294.
[146] The operative word of the citation was ܬܢܝܢܐ, earlier in the verse. The Jews would be redeemed twice, and this promise was fulfilled through their deliverances from Egypt and Babylonia; no further deliverance was ever promised.
[147] Rather differently, P-Chronicles removes any reference to Aram. He writes Damascus alone for ארם דרמשק and later in the verse replaces Aram by the Damascenes (ܕܪ̈ܡܣܘܩܝܐ).

suggested by Roediger, namely that the name had changed in scope since biblical times. It is worth adding that Edessa lay in that very region for which the designation Aram was retained. If those who made the change – whether translators or early copyists – worked in that area, they would understandably have been concerned for the correct use of the name.

Now Roediger held that the change was made by copyists, and not by the translators themselves. Hence two questions: why copyists should have rejected Aram, and why they should have chosen Edom in particular as its substitute. One possible answer is that copyists found the term Aram (in relation to all Syria) intolerably archaic; in that case, however, the obvious name to substitute would have been ܣܘܪܝܐ and not Edom, which (as argued above) never indicated Syria. Alternatively, it might be argued that the copyists viewed the form ܐܪܡ as an outright mistake – rather than an archaism – and so corrected it systematically by conformity with the graphically similar ܐܕܘܡ. It is true that some other names were corrected at least as drastically by copyists, e.g. from Menahem to Mahanaim or from Merab to Nadab. In all those cases, however, the name changed was unfamiliar to Syriac copyists, who apparently thought that it was intrinsically corrupt, or in other words that no such name existed. No Syriac copyist, however, could have thought this of the name Aram.

Thus the two questions raised by Roediger's view do not together admit satisfactory answers. Hence the replacement of Aram by Edom cannot reasonably be ascribed to copyists. The only remaining possibility is to ascribe it to the translators themselves.

Here we must recall that the letters ד and ר were not always clearly distinguished in the translator's *Vorlage*, so that there may have been real doubt as to whether Aram or Edom was intended. This ambiguity in the graphic form is borne out at 2 Chr. 20:2, where אֲרָם יָם is rendered ܝܡܐ ܣܘܡܩܐ "the Red Sea", and אֲרָם was thus mistaken for אָדֹם "red". Now where a graphic form could be read either as Aram or as Edom, the former option would be the more problematic: the translator would have either to reproduce the name as ܐܪܡ and so introduce an obsolete usage,[148] or to abandon the original form altogether by modernising to ܣܘܪܝܐ. It would be more straightforward to read the ambiguous form as Edom; and in most passages, there was no overwhelming reason against this. Even in relation to "Bar-Hadad who dwelt in Damascus", the translators could have convinced themselves that he was king of Edom rather than Aram; for the verses 1 Kgs. 11:14–25 deal at some length with the similarly named Hadad of Edom, and tell us in particular that he shared the role of adversary to Solomon with a certain Rezon who dwelt in Damascus (v.24).

Only the clearest of indications led the translators to retain Aram. These included, as Walker observed, reference to the patriarchal homeland or to the eponymous ancestor. We also need, however, to account for the retention of Aram in the two passages in Amos and also in the group of passages in Kings and Isaiah relating to Rezin, the last king of Aram. Walker's claim that Aram was retained for no reason other than the neighbouring references to Damascus is not compelling, as shown above. In the two passages from Amos, the reason for the retention of Aram seems rather that they

---

[148] Except in the minority of passages where the reference is to the eponymous ancestor or to the region east of the Euphrates.

mention Aram's early migration from Qir; this could not be made to fit Edom, which was known to have originated with Esau in Canaan. An association with Qir may also explain the group of passages associated with Rezin. In the report of Rezin's end at 2 Kgs. 16:7–9, Ahaz bribed the Assyrians to save him from the king of Aram, and they duly exiled the population of Aram to Qir, slaying Rezin. Thus Rezin is linked with the Aram which was brought up from Qir and thus distinct from Edom. This would explain why Aram is always used in relation to Rezin, while all his predecessors become kings of Edom.

It remains to explain the references to Aram or Syria in the Ephremic commentary, where the biblical mss have Edom. According to Roediger, the Ephremic commentary here preserves the original reading, while the form Edom is due to later copyists. The possibility that the Ephremic commentary alone preserves the true reading should not be dismissed out of hand. As we shall see in chapter 6, there are other instances, albeit none on so large a scale, where the true reading has survived in an Ephremic work, even in one of disputed authenticity. Yet that is not the only possible explanation. The commentaries are known today only from a *Catena Patrum*, which was compiled by Severus, a monk of Edessa, in 861 CE and which interweaves Ephrem's comments with later material.[149] It is possible that the passages which mention Aram(eans) or Syria(ns) are due to a scholar later than Ephrem. This scholar, one could suppose, based his comments on LXX – which had Syria rather than the Edom of P – and revived the ancient usage of ܐܪܡ to indicate all Syria.

All in all, it seems likeliest that the change from Aram to Edom originated with the translators. From their own viewpoint, however, there was no outright change. Rather, they found the graphic form in their *Vorlage* ambiguous, and they tended to read it as Edom rather than Aram. The reason for their aversion to Aram was that the restriction in its scope since biblical times rendered it a problematic term; and they were usually able to find some justification for the reading Edom. However, the evidence is delicately balanced; and the possibility that copyists too had a hand in the replacement of Aram by Edom cannot be excluded.

---

[149] F.C. Burkitt, *S. Ephraim's Quotations from the Gospel* [=*Texts and Studies* 7.2], Cambridge 1901, p. 87.

3
The Peshitta and other Versions

I. THE PESHITTA AND THE SEPTUAGINT

The parallels with LXX: possible explanations

Numerous parallels between P and LXX – against MT – have been observed.[1] Their incidence, however, has been found to differ strikingly from book to book. According to Haefeli's survey, LXX influence was found to be frequent in Ezekiel,[2] the Twelve Prophets,[3] Proverbs,[4] S. of S.[5] and Qohelet;[6] sporadic in Genesis,[7] Joshua,[8] Isaiah,[9] Jeremiah,[10] Psalms[11] and Esther; and insignificant or non-existent in Samuel, Kings, Job, Lamentations and Chronicles. In Daniel the parallels are rather with Theodotion, as shown by Wyngarden[12] and in greater detail by Taylor.[13] We must therefore investigate the cause of the parallels, and also explain the variation in their reported incidence between books.

In theory, there are a number of possible causes for the parallels, and the cause may have differed from passage to passage. As in the previous chapter, we may put

---

[1] For a brief but penetrating general survey, see W.E. Barnes, "On the Influence of the Septuagint on the Peshitta", *JTS* 2 (1901), pp. 186–97.

[2] C.H. Cornill, *Das Buch des Propheten Ezechiel*, Leipzig 1886, pp. 153–4.

[3] See most recently A. Gelston, *The Peshitta of the Twelve Prophets*, Oxford 1987, pp. 160–77.

[4] H. Pinkuss, "Die syrische Übersetzung der Proverbien, textkritisch und in ihrem Verhältnisse zu dem masoretischen Text, den LXX und dem Targum untersucht", *ZAW* 14 (1894), pp. 65–141, 161–222:94–109. J. Joosten, "Doublet Translations in Peshitta Proverbs", MPI 8, pp. 63–72.

[5] J.M. Salkind, *Die Peschitta zu Schir-Haschirim textkritisch und in ihrem Verhältnisse zu MT und LXX untersucht*, Leiden 1905, pp. 9–10.

[6] Janichs, *Animadversiones criticae in versionem syriacam Peschitthonianam librorum Koheleth et Ruth*, Leipzig 1869, p. 34; A.S. Kamenetzky, "Die P'šita zu Kohelet textkritisch und in ihrem Verhältnis zu dem masoretischen Text, der Septuaginta und den andern alten griechischen Versionen", *ZAW* 24 (1904), pp. 181–239:237; A. Schoors, "The Peshitta of Kohelet and its Relation to the Septuagint", in C. Laga et al. (eds.), *After Chalcedon. Studies in Theology and Church History*, Fs. A. van Roey, Louvain 1985, pp. 347–57.

[7] J. Hänel, *Die aussermasoretischen Übereinstimmungen zwischen der Septuaginta und der Peschitha in der Genesis* [=BZAW 20], Giessen 1911.

[8] H. Mager, *Die Peschittho zum Buche Josua*, Freiburg im Breisgau 1916, p. 66.

[9] See most recently A. van der Kooij, *Die alten Textzeugen des Jesajabuches. Ein Beitrag zur Textgeschichte des Alten Testamentes*, Göttingen 1981, pp. 287–8.

[10] P.F. Frankl, "Studien über die Septuaginta und Peschito zu Jeremia", *MGWJ* 21 (1872), pp. 444–56, 497–509, 545–57:547–50.

[11] A. Vogel, "Studien zum Peshitta-Psalter besonders im Hinblick auf sein Verhältnis zu Septuaginta", *Biblica* 32 (1951), pp. 32–56,198–231, 336–63, 481–502:336–63, 481–502. For a contrary view, see J. Lund, "Grecisms in the Peshitta Psalms" in MPI 8, pp. 85–102.

[12] M.J. Wyngarden, *The Syriac Version of the Book of Daniel*, Leipzig 1923, pp. 19–21.

[13] R.A. Taylor, *The Peshitta of Daniel* [=MPI 7], Leiden 1994, p. 312.

these under three main headings. First, P's Hebrew *Vorlage* may have differed from MT and agreed instead with the *Vorlage* of LXX. Second, P's agreement with LXX may have arisen in the translation process, either because the translator consulted LXX or because he came independently to the same understanding. Third, the text of P may have been altered by later copyists in conformity with the Greek text of LXX.

As before, it is safest to attribute the maximum to the translators' activity. This implies keeping to a minimum the assumption of variant readings and hence of scribal change in the copying either of the Hebrew or of the Syriac text. We shall therefore discuss the role of the translators before proceeding to consider textual explanations, whether that LXX and P shared a common *Vorlage* different from MT or that the text of P was conformed to LXX by later scribes.

If an agreement between P and LXX against the plain sense of MT is due to the translators, one possibility is that P's translator consulted LXX; but we must also consider alternative explanations. One of these is coincidence or polygenesis: a given difficulty in the biblical text may have elicited identical but independent responses from LXX and P. As the previous chapter showed, P habitually departs from literal translation of the Hebrew in certain characteristic ways, e.g. making explicit what is implicit in the Hebrew, or harmonising different passages. Where such a departure from the Hebrew brings P into agreement with LXX, polygenesis is a likely cause. Convenient collections of instances from Genesis 1–25 and Qohelet have recently been presented by Dirksen[14] and Schoors[15] respectively. Even in some striking cases of agreement, polygenesis cannot be excluded altogether, e.g.

(a)   Gen. 49:20

MT   מאשר שמנה לחמו והוא יתן מעדני מלך

LXX   . . . καὶ αὐτὸς δώσει τρυφὴν (A: τροφὴν) ἄρχουσιν

P   ܐܫܝܪ ܟܠܗ ܐܝܬܝܗ ܐܪܥܗ. ܘܗܘ ܢܬܠ ܬܘܪܣܝܐ ܠܡܠܟܐ

Asher – good is his land; and he will give nourishment to kings.

Hänel's conclusion that the word in P depends on LXX, in the corrupt form found in codex A, may well be right. Yet polygenesis cannot be ruled out, because P may instead have been guessing a meaning for the rare מעדני on the basis of לחמו "his bread" in the previous line, which he had earlier treated as a figure for "his land".

(b)   1 Sam. 17:6,45

MT   כידון

LXX   ἀσπίς

P   ܣܟܪܬܐ (v.6), ܣܟܪܐ (v.45)

Although כידון usually becomes ܢܝܙܟܐ 'spear' in P, we here find items of armour. This interpretation, according to Barnes, arose from LXX, which likewise takes כידון as a

---

[14] P.B. Dirksen, "The Peshitta and Textual Criticism of the Old Testament", *VT* 42 (1992), pp. 376–90.

[15] A. Schoors, "The Peshitta of Kohelet", pp. 347–57; see pp. 348–51.

defensive weapon in these passages alone. The possibility remains, however, that both translators reached this conclusion in v.6 independently, given that all preceding items in vv.5–6 are defensive (כובע, שריון, מצחה) and that this item was located between the shoulders. In that case, neither translator wished to introduce inconsistency by changing to an offensive weapon when the word recurred in v.45, despite the preceding context ("thou comest against me with a sword and a spear . . .").

Polygenesis cannot, however, explain the cases – exemplified below – where P and LXX agree in an interpretation for which there is little warrant in the text, or where P seems to echo the very language of LXX. Moreover, in some books the sheer number of agreements between LXX and P against MT is too high for all of them to be viewed as independent responses to a Hebrew text identical with MT.[16]

A further possible explanation of agreements between P and LXX is that both independently reflect an older exegetical tradition. This explanation well fits certain agreements attested also in other authorities, as at Num. 24:7 –

MT   יזל מים מדליו

LXX   ἐξελεύσεται ἄνθρωπος ἐκ τοῦ σπέρματος αὐτοῦ

P   ܢܦܘܩ ܓܒܪܐ ܡܢ ܒܢܘܗܝ,

T⁰   יסני מלכא דיתרבא מבנוהי (T^JFN longer but similar)

Again, at Ruth 1:21:

MT שדי, LXX ὁ ἱκανός, P ܡܢ ܕܟܠ ܡܣܬܝܟ,

LXX and P both analyse the Hebrew as "he who is sufficient" (*ša+day*), as regularly in Aquila (also ἱκανός), the Samaritan targum (ספוקה) and Saadiah (*al-kāfī*).[17]

However, not every interpretation in which P and LXX together depart from the 'plain' sense of MT can be ascribed without further ado to common tradition. One feature is necessary, and a second desirable, before common tradition can be invoked. The first is that the translation should point some lesson, or at least make good sense. The second is that the translation should find confirmation in outside sources, such as other versions or extant rabbinic or hellenistic literature. One cannot always insist on this latter condition: some traditions may crop up in LXX and P and nowhere else. However, it will be hard to believe that great numbers of traditions have been preserved by LXX and P independently, and by no other source. After all, unlike the Targums, neither LXX nor P is renowned for picking up interpretative traditions that differ from the 'plain' sense. Only a minority of passages where LXX and P agree fulfil both conditions.

Critical passages showing LXX influence upon the translators of P

There are two types of critical passage where one cannot avoid supposing that the translators themselves consulted LXX. In the first type, the only explanation of P's rendering is that LXX has been misunderstood. The translator himself must be responsible, since a reviser who set out to conform P to LXX would surely have had a better grasp of LXX. Examples:

[16] This remark applies in particular to the Twelve Prophets: see Gelston, *Twelve Prophets*, pp. 160–7.
[17] Note that P had instead transliterated ܐܠܫܕܝ in the previous verse.

(a)   Exod. 25:2

Here MT speaks of "(every man) whose heart moves him (ידבנו לבו)". P renders surprisingly: "who thinks (ܘܡܬܚܫܒ) in his heart". LXX has οἷς ἂν δόξῃ τῇ καρδίᾳ : "to those to whom it seems (good) to the heart", a fair though not literal rendering of the Hebrew. Now the Greek verb δοκέω can mean either 'seem (good)' or 'think', and P has apparently chosen the wrong sense – as if the Greek had begun in ὅς rather than οἷς. The Hebrew phrase נדיב לב is rendered by P in the same way at Exod. 35:22, and even at Exod. 35:5, where LXX does not use δοκέω.

(b)   Num. 25:3

MT   ויצמד ישראל לבעל פעור

LXX   καὶ ἐτελέσθη Ισραηλ τῷ Βεελφεγωρ

P   ܘܐܬܛܝܒ ܐܝܣܪܐܝܠ ܠܒܥܠ ܦܥܘܪ

cf. 25:5: MT הנצמדים, LXX τὸν τετελεσμένον, P ܐܝܠܝܢ ܕܐܬܛܝܒܘ

    The Syriac verb ܐܬܛܝܒ 'be completed / complete oneself' bears no relation to the Hebrew, and must be due to the Greek. However, although τελέω originally meant 'complete', it developed the sense 'consecrate, initiate', which applies in this passage: Israel was initiated into the mysterious rites of Baal Peor. P shows no awareness of this developed sense, and simply translates according to the etymology. There is no evidence that a meaning 'initiate' for ܐܬܛܝܒ ever developed in Syriac. If anything, when followed by the preposition *beth* the Syriac verb meant: 'gratify oneself with',[18] so that P here means: "and Israel gratified itself with Baal Peor".

(c)   Ruth 4:6

Here, Boaz's rival declares that he cannot perform his duty as kinsman to acquire Naomi's field and to marry Ruth. His next words to Boaz differ utterly in MT and P:

MT   גאל לך אתה את גאלתי

       perform thou my duty as kinsman.

P   ܩܢܝ ܠܟ ܐܢܬ ܡܛܠ ܚܣܝܪܘܬ ܗܝܡܢܘܬܝ, ܕܝܠܝ

       claim thou, on account of my lack of faith.

It seems that the translator was puzzled by the two forms from the Hebrew root גאל; usually this word means 'redeem', but here it bears its primary sense: 'perform a kinsman's duty'. P's translator consulted LXX, whose translation was accurate but obscure: ἀγχίστευσον σεαυτῷ τὴν ἀγχιστείαν μου. Apparently the P translator focused on the last three words, but misread ΑΓΧΙΣΤΕΙΑΝ as ΑΠΙΣΤ(Ε)ΙΑΝ 'lack of faith'. The concluding independent pronoun ܕܝܠܝ in P confirms that his source was not Hebrew but a Greek phrase ending in μου.

(d)   Ruth 4:15

Here Naomi is told that Ruth's child will sustain "thy grey hair (i.e. old age)". In P, however the child is to be a sustainer "for thy city". Apparently the P translator was

---

[18]   For this usage, compare Ephrem's comment on Gen. 4:7b, discussed on p. 289 below.

puzzled by the Hebrew (שיבתך) and consulted LXX, which had rendered literally τὴν πολιάν σου; P however misread πολιάν as πόλιν.[19]

(e) Isaiah 28:7

Here it is the text of Theodotion, rather than LXX, which the translator of P seems to have misunderstood:

MT פקו פליליה

Theod. ἠσωτεύθησαν ὑπερόγκως "they were licentious exceedingly"

P ܐܟܠܘ ܐܣܘܛܐܝܬ "they ate gluttonously"

The Hebrew complains that drunken priests and prophets "totter (in) judgment". Theodotion's adverb ὑπερόγκως probably interprets פליליה through פלא 'wonder'. His verb, however, seems a mere guess at the sense of פקו.

P's rendering here bears no relation to the Hebrew. The adverb ܐܣܘܛܐܝܬ, however, must be explained through Theodotion, especially as no derivative of ἄσωτος occurs in either version (as extant) elsewhere in Isaiah. Moreover, P's choice of verb suggests that the translator did not appreciate the full range of the Greek word: in Greek the word means "licentious" in general, but when borrowed into Syriac it acquired the specific meaning "gluttonous", perhaps because it happened to be used at Deut. 21:20 (and thence Prov. 23:20–21) to render Hebrew זולל.[20] Thus Syriac translators in other books reject ܐܣܘܛܐ as too narrow a rendering of ἄσωτος (and its derivatives). For example, at 2 Macc. 6:4 the Peshitta renders ἀσωτία by ܒܘܣ̈ܡܐ 'revelries'. The Old Syriac Gospels at Luke 15:13 render ἀσώτως (of the behaviour of the prodigal son) by ܥܡ ܙܢܝ̈ܬܐ ܦܪܝܨܐܝܬ.[21] In this difficult phrase at Isa. 28:7, however, P used the Syriac cognate, and the resulting nuance of gluttony led to the verb ܐܟܠܘ.

In the second type of critical passage, elements from both the Hebrew and LXX are welded together inextricably. One cannot posit an original text free of elements from LXX, for if the latter are removed from the existing text, the residue makes no sense. Examples:

(a) Isa. 54:15

MT הן גור יגור אפס מאותי מי גר אתך עליך יפול

P ܘܟܠ ܕܡܬܬܦܢܝܢ ܡܢ ܐܝܕܝ̈ ܢܥܠܘܢ ܠܟܝ ܘܬܗܘܝܢ ܒܝܬ ܓܘܣܐ ܠܬܘܬܒ̈ܝܟܝ

and all who convert – from my hands they will come in to you; and you will be a refuge to your sojourners

cf. LXX ἰδοὺ προσήλυτοι προσελεύσονταί σοι δι᾽ ἐμοῦ καὶ ἐπὶ σὲ καταφεύξονται

In the main, P seems based on LXX, which alone explains the elements "come in to

[19] See already A. Roediger, *De Origine et Indole Arabicae Librorum V.T. Historicorum Interpretationis Libri Duo*, Halle 1829, p. 48n; Janichs, *Koheleth et Ruth*, p. 33.

[20] At Prov. 7:11, admittedly, P describes the adulteress as ܡܪܘܕܐ ܘܐܣܘܛܐ; but this is due to the combined influence of LXX ἄσωτος and the association of the Hebrew סוררת with the epithet סורר of the rebellious – and gluttonous – son at Deut. 21:18–21.

[21] The last two words are dropped by the Peshitta in Luke, and only the Harklean is so literal as to write ܐܣܘܛܐܝܬ. This comparison was facilitated by G.A. Kiraz, *Comparative Edition of the Syriac Gospels* (4 volumes), Leiden 1996.

you" and "refuge"; yet dependence on the Hebrew at the same time is reflected in P's provision of two alternative translations of גר, each characteristic of P's translations from the Hebrew elsewhere, namely ܓܝܘܪܐ and ܪܡܘܬܐ.[22]

(b)   Jer. 4:11

MT   רוח צח שפיים במדבר

LXX   πνεῦμα πλανήσεως ἐν τῇ ἐρήμῳ

P   ܐܝܟ ܪܘܚܐ ܛܥܝܬܐ ܒܫܒܝܠܝܗ ܕܡܕܒܪܐ

    like a wandering spirit on the paths of the desert

Here the element "wandering" comes from LXX, but the next word "paths" is a frequent rendering in P of שפיים.[23] Once again, elements from the Hebrew and the Greek are intertwined.

(c)   Micah 7:3–4

MT   ויעבתוה: טובם כחדק ישר ממסוכה

LXX   καὶ ἐξελοῦμαι τὰ ἀγαθὰ αὐτῶν ὡς σὴς ἐκτρώγων

P   ܘܐܣܠܝܘ ܛܒܬܗܘܢ ܐܝܟ ܩܛܝܪܐ ܕܐܟܠܗ ܣܣܐ

    and they rejected their good, like a patch that a moth devoured

The devouring moth in P is evidently inspired by LXX. On the other hand, the verb ܐܣܠܝ 'reject' is a common equivalent of Hebrew תעב,[24] which the translator seems to have reached by misreading the first Hebrew word as ויתעבוה. Finally, 'patch' is an object supplied by P for the verb 'devoured' adopted from LXX (ἐκτρώγων).

(d)   Ps. 57:5

MT   נפשי בתוך לבאים אשכבה להטים

LXX   καὶ ἐρρύσατο τὴν ψυχήν μου ἐκ μέσου σκύμνων. ἐκοιμήθην τεταραγμένος

P   ܘܦܨܝ ܢܦܫܝ ܡܢ ܟܠܒܐ ܘܕܡܟܬ ܟܕ ܕܠܝܚ ܐܢܐ

    and he saved my soul from dogs, and I slept while troubled

Here P largely agrees with LXX, but the phrase ܡܢ ܟܠܒܐ can only have come from the Hebrew: the translator saw כלבים in בים (בתו)כלב(א), the second and third words. If a P text free from the influence of LXX once existed, and was only later revised after LXX, the reviser would not have retained the reference to dogs: contrast Syhex ܡܢ ܓܘ ܓܪܝܐ.[25]

Joosten has found such translations – which he well describes as "patchworks" from both the Hebrew and LXX –in Proverbs, e.g. at Prov. 18:8a –

---

[22] On these equivalences see further pp. 171–4 below.

[23] Again at Isa. 49:9, Jer. 3:2, 21; 7:29; 12:12; 14:6. See further A. Gelston "Some Notes on Second Isaiah", *VT* 21 (1971), pp. 517–27:519.   [24] E.g. Amos 5:10, Mic. 3:9.

[25] Other cases from Psalms where elements from the Hebrew and LXX seem to have been welded together from the first are discussed by the present writer in "The Peshitta Psalter and its Hebrew Vorlage", *VT* 35 (1985), pp. 341–54.

MT   דברי נרגן כמתלהמים

LXX   ὀκνηροὺς καταβάλλει φόβος

P   ܟܠܗܘܢ, ܘܢܚܬܘܢ ܘܢܚܝ ܠܐ ܟܒܪܐ

> The words of the slothful cast him into adversity

Although P has adopted the elements "slothful" and "cast" from LXX, the syntax differs and the element "words" evidently depends on the Hebrew.[26]

Further examples of LXX influence upon the translators

Beyond these critical passages, there are many close agreements between P and LXX in which coincidence, common tradition and a common *Vorlage* differing from MT can all be excluded, and there is no evidence that the Syriac text has been changed in transmission.[27] Such cases are most easily ascribed to LXX influence upon the translators of P, e.g.

(a)   Gen. 4:8.

Though MT states that Cain spoke to Abel, no words are quoted. Soon afterwards, however, the brothers are said to be in the field. Cain's words are given in LXX as διέλθωμεν εἰς τὸ πέδιον, and in P as ܢܪܕܐ ܠܦܩܥܬܐ "let us proceed to the plain / valley". The agreement has been ascribed to a common tradition, reflected also in the rabbinic legend preserved in Tanhuma Bereshit 9. There, Cain and Abel agreed to divide the world and parted company, but Cain then treacherously

> pursued him from mountain to valley, and from valley to mountain, until they grappled together. Abel prevailed over Cain, who fell beneath him. When Cain saw this, he began to cry: "Abel my brother! Do not harm me!"; and [Abel] had mercy and let him go; and then [Cain] stood up and killed him, as it is said: "And Cain rose up", implying that he had fallen.[28]

It is true that "valley", which is a possible meaning of P ܦܩܥܬܐ, occurs here too; but it has scant importance in the legend. Indeed alternative versions of the legend mention the mountains only. Thus in Tanhuma Mishpatim 13, the brothers agreed to allot all land to Cain and all moveables to Abel; but as Abel roamed about the world,

> Cain pursued him, saying: "Away from my portion!". [Abel] ran to the mountains, but [Cain] was after him, saying: "This is mine" – until he stood over him and killed him.

Thus the parallel in rabbinic tradition is simply too insubstantial to explain the agreement between LXX and P. Nor is a common Hebrew *Vorlage* a satisfactory explanation, since this, as Barnes observed (p. 193), would not have read "plain" but rather "field", as in the next phrase (cf. נלכה השדה in the Samaritan Pentateuch). Coincidence too is excluded: without LXX, P would not have thought of a plain,

---

[26] Joosten, "Doublet Translations in Peshitta Proverbs", MPI 8 (1995), pp. 63–72; see pp. 64–5. P's final word seems a vague guess inspired by 17:20b "he that turns his tongue will fall into adversity".

[27] The mss of P are unanimous and show no evidence of dislocation; contrast the cases of scribal change considered below.

[28] Y. Maori, *The Peshitta Version of the Pentateuch and Early Jewish Exegesis*, Jerusalem 1995, pp. 235–9.

especially as in the continuation of the verse P places the brothers in the field. We must conclude that P consulted LXX διέλθωμεν εἰς τὸ πεδίον, in which case the word ܩܥܬܐ was first intended as 'plain' – even though Ephrem, who located Paradise on a mountain (cf. Ezek 28:14), understood it as 'valley'.[29]

(b)   Num. 21:14

MT   את והב בסופה ואת הנחלים ארנון

LXX   (Πόλεμος τοῦ κυρίου) τὴν Ζωοβ ἐφλόγισεν καὶ τοὺς χειμάρρους Αρνων

        (The war of the Lord) set aflame Zoob and the torrents of Arnon

P   ܒܫܠܗܒܝܬܐ ܒܥܠܥܠܐ ܘܒܢܚܠܐ ܕܐܪܢܘܢ

        a flame in the storm and in the torrent of Arnon

The Hebrew explains P's reference to the "storm" (סופה), but not to the "flame", which seems due rather to LXX ἐφλόγισεν. Apparently the LXX translator, finding neither a subject nor a verb in the two Hebrew phrases introduced by את, detached the words "War of the Lord" from the previous verse to supply a subject. He also provided a suitable verb in place of בסופה, apparently guessed to suit the context. P was in turn puzzled by את והב; he therefore adopted LXX ἐφλόγισεν but changed it into a noun, to provide a subject.[30]

(c)   Jer. 48 [LXX 31]:34

MT   מצער עד חרנים עגלת שלשיה

P   ܡܢ ܨܥܪ ܘܥܕܡܐ ܠܚܘܪܢܝܡ ܘܥܕܡܐ ܠܩܪܝܬܐ ܕܐܠܣ ܥܓܠܬܐ ܬܠܝܬܝܬܐ

        from Zoar unto Horonaim, and unto the town of 'LS, a three-year-old heifer

P agrees with MT except in mentioning additionally a mysterious "town of 'LS". The equivalents of the last two Hebrew words in LXX vary among the mss; it seems that they were first transliterated as Αγελα Σαλασια which, though not itself attested, can be viewed as the source of the extant readings. Most mss have ἀγγελ(ε)ίαν "news" for the first word, and in most Lucianic mss the second word has become corrupted to εἰς Ελισαν. The translator found this or a similar reading in his text of LXX and took it as a city, just like the preceding Zoar and Horonaim. The same Syriac phrase also appears in the Syrohexapla.

(d)   Ezek. 21:18

MT כי בחן but LXX ὅτι δεδικαίωται, P ܡܛܠ ܕܐܬܬܪܝܨ ܗܘܐ

LXX moves from 'examine', which is the plain sense of the Hebrew, to 'find correct'. Even though this is a theoretically possible development of meaning

---

[29] Thus Ephrem writes *wa-nḥet* (and later *aḥteh*) *la-pqa'tā*; see R.-M. Tonneau (ed.), *Sancti Ephraem Syri in Genesim et in Exodum Commentarii*, Louvain 1955, p. 49 (section III.5).

[30] Conceivably LXX ἐφλόγισεν for סופה is based on Syr. ܣܦ (Aph.) "set fire", but it is unlikely that the word "flame" in P was derived independently from Syr. ܣܦ to represent סופה, since P had already rendered that word as "storm".

(compare Latin *probare*), there is no warrant in the context. P's agreement in this unexpected sense cannot be ascribed to a *Vorlage* differing from MT, nor indeed to coincidence. Nor is there any outside evidence that this understanding of בחן was traditional. The agreement between LXX and P, also found in the previous phrase:

MT יָדְ but LXX τὴν χεῖρά σου, P ܟܦܟ [=יָדֵ],

instead suggests that the translator of P was here consulting LXX.

(e)   S. of S. 4:1 and 6:7.

Here the maiden is told that her eyes are like doves –

MT   מִבַּעַד לְצַמָּתֵךְ "behind thy veil"

but LXX   ἐκτὸς τῆς σιωπήσεώς σου P ܠܒܪ ܡܢ ܫܬܩܟܝ "beyond thy silence".

LXX and P make little sense. Evidently these versions derived לְצַמָּתֵךְ not from צַמָּה 'veil', but from the verb צָמַת, which originally meant 'be silent' (so Ar. ﺻﻤﺖ).

Although in Hebrew this root is confined to the Hiph'il, which developed to 'suppress, destroy', the original meaning 'silence' was known among the ancient translators, so that at Ps. 101:8 אַצְמִית is translated by Symmachus as ἀφώνους ἐποιοῦν and by P as ܐܫܬܩ. In the passages from S. of S., however, the sense 'silence' is so unlikely that P's agreement with LXX cannot be coincidental. Nor can it be ascribed to common tradition: a traditional rendering must make sense. The likeliest explanation is that LXX decided in despair that a translation that made little sense was better than none at all. P in turn was baffled by the unusual Hebrew word and contented himself with translating LXX.

(f)   Qoh. 1:17

MT הוֹלֵלוֹת, but LXX παραβολάς, P ܡܬܠܐ

As Schoors observes, the only explanation of the agreement in the idiosyncratic understanding of הוֹלֵלוֹת as 'proverbs' is that P consulted LXX.[31]

Loanwords and calques from the Greek in P

We may here consider the significance of cases where the language of P closely echoes that of LXX. It may be that P has the same Greek word as LXX, as a loanword into Syriac; or P may have a calque which builds up through native Syriac elements a mirror of the Greek word.

Greek loanwords in P do not necessarily betoken LXX influence, since the Syriac language had absorbed a number of Greek words.[32] There are in fact many instances where P has a loanword from Greek while LXX has a quite different word, e.g.

---

[31] Schoors, "Peshitta of Kohelet", p. 354.
[32] P also exhibits a few Latin loanwords: ܛܒܠܪܐ (*tabellarius* 'courier'- 2 Sam. 15:1, Prov. 23:34 etc.), ܠܓܝܘܢ (*legio* – Num. 24:24), ܦܣܩܝܢ (*piscina* 'pond' – Neh. 3:15), ܩܪܘܟܐ (*carruca* – Exod. 14:6 etc.).

	P	**Greek source-word**	**LXX**
Gen. 42:4	ܩܘܝܪܐ	καιρός	μαλακία
Exod. 12:	ܦܪܘܣܬܐ	προστάς /παραστάς	σταθμός
Num. 18:7	ܐܣܟܝܡܐ	σχῆμα	τρόπος
Num. 35:2	ܐܓܘܪܐ	ἀγρός	τὰ προάστεια
Judg. 3:3	ܛܘܪܢܐ	τύραννος	σατραπεία
1 Kgs. 7:4	ܐܟܣܪܝ	ἐξέδρα	ἐπίθεμα
Prov. 7:10	ܐܣܟܝܡܐ	σχῆμα	εἶδος

As Perles observed, many of these Greek loanwords were also absorbed into the Jewish Aramaic dialects of the Targums and Talmuds. It is worth adding that the particles ܓܝܪ and ܕܝܢ, which usually correspond in both function and syntax with γάρ and δέ and at first sight seem loanwords, in fact show traces of quite different usage in the earliest Syriac texts (including P) and may well be Semitic in origin.[33]

It follows that even when P has the same Greek word as LXX, borrowed into Syriac, we have to consider the possibility that LXX and P reached the same sense independently, and that the Greek loanword happened to be the best vehicle to express that sense in Syriac. That explanation could sometimes be argued, e.g.

	MT	**LXX**	**P**
Gen. 3:7	חגרת	περιζώματα	ܦܪܙܘܡܐ
Judg. 3:25	המפתח	τὴν κλεῖδα	ܩܠܝܕܐ
Jer. 5:1	ברחובותיה	ἐν ταῖς πλατείαις αὐτῆς	ܒܦܠܛܘܬܗ
Ezek. 30:21	חתול	μάλαγμα 'plaster'	ܡܠܓܬܐ

There are cases, however, where the presence of the same Greek word in P as in LXX cannot be coincidental. One such case is where the Greek loanword is rare in Syriac and there is no reason to suppose its earlier naturalisation, e.g.

Amos 7:7–8

MT אנך, LXX ἀδάμας, P ܐܕܡܘܣ

This Syriac word does not recur in P and seems to have been coined to represent the text of LXX.

Ps. 18:12

MT עבי שחקים, LXX ἐν νεφέλαις ἀέρων, P ܥܢܢܐ ܕܐܐܪ

The commonest equivalent of שחק in P-Psalms is ܫܚܩ ܫܡܝܐ (36:6, 57:11, 68:35, 77:18, 89:7, 108:5),[34] though we also find ܫܚܩ alone (89:38) or ܫܡܝܐ (78:23); hence P here probably depends on LXX.

Another situation where the occurrence of the same Greek word in both LXX and P can hardly be coincidental is where P's loanword appears in LXX at a neighbouring but not identical point, as at Isa. 13:22 –

---

[33] J. Joosten, "The Use of Some Particles in the Old Testament Peshitta", *Textus* 14 (1988), pp. 175–83: see pp. 178–82.

[34] This equivalence was first coined at Deut. 33:26, in which verse the simple ܫܡܝܐ had already been used.

MT איים, P ܣܝܪ̈ܢܐ

LXX has ὀνοκένταυροι here, but the Greek source-word σειρῆνες in v.21 (for בנות יענה). LXX and P can hardly have alighted independently on the same meaning for the two different words. Rather, it seems that P, searching for an equivalent for איים, adopted the word just used by LXX for בנות יענה in the previous verse.[35]

As to calques of Greek forms, these can be recognised by being too long in relation to the Hebrew, and by corresponding quantitatively instead with the Greek, given that each element within a Greek compound word needs to be represented in Syriac. Where LXX presents a Greek word of which P shows a calque, the agreement cannot be coincidental unless the calque itself – and not just its constituent parts – can be shown to have been naturalised in Syriac. Thus LXX influence is virtually certain at Ps. 68:35 –

MT גאותו, LXX ἡ μεγαλοπρέπεια αὐτοῦ, P ܪܒܘܬ ܓܐܘܬܐ

Everywhere else, P-Psalms renders גאוה or גאות by a single word, e.g. ܒܓܐܘܬܐ (93:1). P's long and not especially precise rendering here is not explained by the Hebrew, but arises straightforwardly from the Greek.

Likewise at Ps. 53:6 –

MT חֹנָךְ, LXX ἀνθρωπαρέσκων, P ܕܐܝܠܝܢ ܕܫܦܪܝܢ ܠܒ̈ܢܝ ܐܢܫܐ.

Once again P's rendering is too long to represent the Hebrew, but perfectly fits the Greek. Direct influence by LXX has to be detected here too, simply because the wording in P could not have been inspired by any other source.[36]

In its renderings of the Hebrew adjective אכזר(י), P shows calques of two different Greek words in different biblical books. In two places, the model is ἀνίατος:[37]

Isa. 13:9	אכזרי	ἀνίατος	ܕܐܣܘ ܠܝܬ ܠܗ
Lam. 4:3	לאכזר	εἰς ἀνίατον	ܠܡܚܘܬܐ ܕܠܝܬ ܠܗ̇ ܐܣܝܘܬܐ

In three passages, however, the model is instead ἀνελεήμων:

Prov. 5:9	לאכזרי	ἀνελεήμοσιν	ܠܐܝܠܝܢ ܕܠܐ ܡܪܚܡܝܢ
Prov. 11:17	אכזרי	ἀνελεήμων	ܓܒܪܐ ܕܠܐ ܡܪܚܡ
Prov. 17:11	אכזרי	ἀνελεήμονα	ܕܪ̈ܚܡܝܢ ܠܝܬ ܠܗ

We have now surveyed cases of various sorts, where the alternative hypotheses to literary dependence of P upon LXX can be convincingly excluded. Beyond these, however, there are many more cases where literary dependence by the translators upon LXX explains the evidence as well as any other hypothesis. Here the safest explanation is that the translator was influenced by LXX. This is in keeping with the maximalist approach taken in chapter 2 to translation technique.

General arguments regarding the possibility of LXX influence

The influence of LXX, as noted above, is far from systematic. There is no difficulty, however, in supposing that P's translators made sporadic use of LXX, alongside a

[35] A similar situation occurs at Jer. 50[27]:39, where MT has ציים את איים but P ܣܝܪ̈ܢܘܣ; LXX has ἰνδάλματα ἐν ταῖς νήσοις, but later in the same verse again σειρήνων for יענה.

[36] So already Vogel, "Studien zum P-Psalter", pp. 495–6 (who is not convinced that the translator, as opposed to copyists, consulted LXX). In the opinion of Lund ("Grecisms in P-Psalms", pp. 94–102), however, these passages fall short of proving any literary dependence on LXX in the existing text of P.

[37] This Greek rendering was coined at Deut. 32:33, where it suits the context (of snake poison), though P there has the vague ܒܝܫ. See B. Albrektson, *Studies in the Text and Theology of the Book of Lamentations*, Lund 1963, pp. 176–7.

Hebrew text as their main source. Two analogies among the ancient versions for the sporadic use of a second source readily come to mind. One is furnished by the Vulgate, which, like P, agrees sporadically with LXX in most books of the Hebrew Bible. Although Jerome translated primarily from the Hebrew, he also occasionally consulted the Greek, as he tells us in his Preface to Ecclesiastes:

Sed de Hebraeo transferens, magis me Septuaginta Interpretum consuetudini coaptavi: in his dumtaxat, quae non multum ab Hebraicis discrepabant.[38]

Another translator who follows one main source but occasionally consults another is the P translator of Chronicles: for the most part, he follows the Hebrew, but he also draws upon parallel passages in earlier biblical books, apparently where he found his Hebrew text of Chronicles illegible.[39]

Given these analogies, it is wrong to argue that, because P's translator has not followed LXX consistently, he was not influenced by LXX at all. At Gen. 4:8, for example, it has been argued that, had P consulted LXX, he would not have reverted to "field" in the next phrase.[40] But this is in fact typical of the way that P's translators used LXX. They rightly worked primarily from the Hebrew, but consulted LXX at points of difficulty, promptly reverting to the Hebrew thereafter, as the above examples show.

Another general argument advanced against LXX influence upon the translators is bound up with Kahle's theory that P derives from a Palestinian Targum brought to Adiabene, and that agreements between the text of P and LXX are therefore secondary.[41] Kahle's theory of the origin of P will be considered fully in the discussion below on P's relationship with the Targums, whence Kahle drew much of his evidence. Here it need only be said that the theory is far from proven; and once we locate P closer to the west than Adiabene, there is no difficulty in supposing that the translators could have consulted the Greek Bible when they were puzzled by the Hebrew. In Edessa, in particular, Jewish grave inscriptions have been found both in Hebrew and in Greek, suggesting that the necessary expertise to translate the Hebrew Bible with aid from the Greek could be found there.[42]

The nature of LXX influence on the P translators

Even where P agrees with LXX, there are neighbouring passages where P quite differs from LXX and follows the Hebrew. The first word of P – ܒܪܫܝܬ – already testifies that P is no daughter-version of LXX, as supposed by some copyists[43] and even occasionally by modern scholars.[44] Whatever the influence of LXX, P is translated primarily from a Hebrew text.

[38] Migne, PL xxiii, coll. 1011 f.   [39] See pp. 113–20 below.
[40] S.R. Isenberg, "On the Jewish-Palestinian Origins of the Peshitta to the Pentateuch", *JBL* 90 (1971), pp. 69–81:77.   [41] P.E. Kahle, *The Cairo Geniza*, 2nd edn, Oxford 1959, p. 270.
[42] J.B. Segal, *Edessa. 'The Blessed City'*, Oxford 1970, pp. 27,42.
[43] According to a colophon in 7a1, 9a1 and other mss, the Peshitta Psalter was translated "from the language of Palestine into Hebrew, and from Hebrew into Greek, and from Greek into Syriac". Though obviously inaccurate, this statement may reflect awareness that the Peshitta Psalter rests mainly on the Hebrew but also consulted LXX.
[44] Note G.W. Anderson's passing reference to P as "a daughter-version of the Septuagint", in P.R. Ackroyd and C.F. Evans (eds.), *Cambridge History of the Bible*, vol. 1, Cambridge 1970, pp. 158–9, and other references rightly criticised by Lund, "Grecisms in P-Psalms", p. 85.

On the other hand, a rendering imported into P from LXX in a particular passage could exert influence well beyond. Thus at Gen. 45:22 the Hebrew has חֲלִפוֹת שְׂמָלוֹת, which LXX renders δισσὰς στολάς. P seems to have followed LXX here, for he renders (ܙܘܓ̈ܐ) ܙܘܓ "pair (of garments)" Now ܙܘܓ remains P's regular rendering for חֲלִפוֹת, even though the element 'twofold' never appears in LXX's renderings of חֲלִפוֹת elsewhere (even at its second occurrence in Gen. 45:22). This lack of exact correspondence between LXX and P is not surprising: P is not derived primarily from LXX, but merely utilised LXX here and there.

Occasionally, P has a double translation in order to present the sense both of the Hebrew and of the Greek, as at Ruth 1:13 –

MT   כִּי מַר לִי מְאֹד מִכֶּם

LXX   ὅτι ἐπικράνθη μοι ὑπὲρ ὑμᾶς

P   ܟܒܝܪ ܗܘܐ ܠܝ ܡܢ ܕܝܠܟܘܢ ܡܠ ܕܗܘܐ ܠܝ ܕܡܪܝܪ

Here P renders first LXX and then the Hebrew.

Such a situation has also been observed in Psalms, as at Ps. 64:8 –

MT   וַיֹּרֵם אֱלֹהִים

LXX   καὶ ὑψωθήσεται ὁ θεός [implying וְיָרֻם]

P   ܐܬܬܪܝܡ ܐܠܗܐ ܘܡܪܡ ܐܢܘܢ

According to Vogel, a doublet of this sort is more probably due to a reviser than to the translator;[45] but it is in fact quite possible that the translator, hesitating between his own understanding of the Hebrew and that of LXX, played safe by including both. It will be recalled that doublets due to such hesitancy are found even where LXX was not involved, notably in Job. Likewise in Proverbs, Joosten has called attention to double translations of certain verses (or half-verses), one based on the Hebrew, the other on the Greek.[46]

It may be added that the Greek on which P drew was not always LXX. The source is occasionally Theodotion, as already noted, while a striking parallel with Symmachus appears in Ps. 12:6 –

MT   אָשִׁית בְּיֵשַׁע יָפִיחַ לוֹ

LXX   θήσομαι ἐν σωτηρίᾳ, παρρησιάσομαι ἐν αὐτῷ

Symm   τάξω σωτήριον ἐμφανές

P   ܘܐܥܒܕ ܦܘܪܩܢܐ ܓܠܝܐܝܬ

And I shall perform salvation openly

The idea of acting openly is already present in LXX; but Symmachus and P further agree in not representing either בְּ or לְ. Apparently LXX results from a tendency, due to aural confusion between the gutterals, to take יָפִיחַ as some part of יפע (Hiph.); compare also Ps 10:5 (MT יָפִיחַ Aquila apud Syrohexapla ܢܬܚܘܐ) and Ps 27:12 (MT יָפֵחַ, Σ ἐξεφάνη). Palaeographically it seems unlikely that each of these renderings reflects a real Hebrew reading יֹפִיעַ (or the like).

As has already been observed, the influence of LXX varies from book to book, and this influence correlates with the translator's receptivity to linguistic innovation. In particular, those books which regularly have the later usage ܡܕܝܢܬܐ, rather

---

[45] Vogel, "Studien zum P-Psalter", pp. 491ff., 500.   [46] J. Joosten, "Doublet Translations", pp. 66–72.

than the older ܪܝܬܐ, to indicate 'city' – namely Ezekiel, the Twelve Prophets and the Solomonic books – owe most to LXX. Indeed, some later usages found in these books seem derived from LXX: for example, ܝܩܕܐ ܥܠܬܐ (rather than ܥܠܬܐ) for עוֹלָה is not only an innovation but an imitation of the text of LXX (ὁλοκαύτωμα).

At the other end of the spectrum stand Kings, Chronicles and Job, which preserve older lexical usages (e.g. ܚܣܕܐ 'kindness' rather than ܛܝܒܘܬܐ, or ܣܐܡܐ 'silver metal' rather than ܟܣܦܐ). The conservatism of P-Job would explain why LXX was not consulted in that difficult book,[47] though it is also possible that the translator was deterred by the many lacunae which make LXX about one-sixth shorter than MT in Job, as Origen already noted.[48] It is true that at 1 Kgs. 18:29, the extant text of P has an addition which derives from LXX:

LXX   καὶ ἐλάλησεν Ηλιου ὁ Θεσβίτης πρὸς τοὺς προφήτας τῶν προσοχθισμάτων λέγων
       Μετάστητε ἀπὸ τοῦ νῦν, καὶ ἐγὼ ποιήσω τὸ ὁλοκαύτωμά μου. καὶ μετέστησαν καὶ
       ἀπῆλθον.

P   ܐܠܝܐ ܕܝܢ ܠܒܬܐ ܢܒܝܘܗ̈ܝ ܕܣܛܪܐ ܥܡ ܘܠܗܢܐ ܡܢ ܗܝܕܐ. ܐܦ ܐܢܐ ܐܝܟ ܐܡܪܬ ܥܠܬܐ ܝܩܕܐ ܐܙܠܘ ܘܗܢ
       ܘܐܩܪܒ

The verb ܫܢܐ and the noun phrase ܝܩܕܐ ܥܠܬܐ reflect the Greek words μεθίστημι and ὁλοκαύτωμα; they do not occur elsewhere in P-Kings. They thus indicate the influence of LXX upon the existing text of P, rather than a common Hebrew *Vorlage*. Was this influence exercised on the translator or on later copyists? Walter has argued for the former;[49] but these words could in fact equally be due to a later copyist, who wished to remove the prophets of Baal before Elijah's sacrifice, and found suitable wording in LXX.

The variation between books is illustrated by P's treatment of the terms for gems in Exod. 28:17–20 and its parallel 39:10–13 on the one hand, and in Ezek. 28:13 on the other. Nine gems are common to the passages from both books. In Exodus, P's terms are Semitic in eight cases and Greek in just one. In Ezekiel, *all* the renderings are Greek loanwords (there are only eight, as one gem name is not translated). Five of these are directly borrowed (or imitated) from the Greek of LXX. The only item in P-Ezekiel which can be related to the Hebrew is ܒܗܩܐ, if this represents Heb. שֹׁהַם as in Exodus. Beyond that, P-Ezekiel shows no agreement with the renderings of the same Hebrew words in P-Exodus. The only other respect in which P-Ezekiel corresponds to the Hebrew rather than to the Greek of Ezekiel is quantitative: the list of 8 items in P stands closer to the 9 in MT than to the 14 in LXX.[50] Two items in P-Ezekiel, namely ܩܪܕܘܢܐ and ܡܙܓܬܐ, bear no obvious relation either to MT or to LXX, and may be due to guesswork. The texts may be compared as follows:

---

[47] E. Baumann, "Die Verwendbarkeit der Pešita zum Buche Ijob für die Textkritik", *ZAW* 18 (1898), pp. 305–38; 19 (1899), pp. 15–95, 288–309; 20 (1900), pp. 177–202, 264–307: see pp. 19, 27–8 of vol. 19 (1899).
[48] PG xiii 1293 f.
[49] D.M. Walter, "The Use of Sources in the Peshitta of Kings", MPI 8 (1995), pp. 187–204: 188.
[50] In Ezekiel, LXX does not correspond with MT; instead, it reproduces the list of twelve stones from LXX in Exodus, but silver and gold are inserted in the middle of the list.

MT	P-Exod.	P-Ezek.	LXX-Ezek.	Comment on P-Ezek.
אֹדֶם	ܣܡܩܬܐ	ܣܪܕܘܢ	σάρδιον	from LXX
פטדה	ܝܪܩܐ	ܛܘܦܕܝܢܐ	τοπάζιον	guessed?
יהלם	ܢܨܒܬܐ	ܐܙܡܪܓܕܐ	σμάραγδον (+ 1 stone)	from LXX
תרשיש	ܬܪܫܝܫ	-		
שהם	ܒܘܪܠܐ	ܒܘܪܠܐ	-	from Hebrew?
ישפה	ܝܫܦܗ	ܣܦܝܠܐ	σάπφειρον	from LXX
ספיר	ܣܦܝܠܐ	ܐܝܣܦܘܢ	ἴασπιν (+ silver, gold and 3 stones)	from LXX
נפך	ܟܪܟܕܢܐ	ܟܪܘܣܘܠܝܛܘܣ	χρυσόλιθον (+ 2 stones)	from LXX?[51]
ברקת	ܒܘܪܩܐ	ܡܪܓܢܝܬܐ	-	guessed?

This diversity among the P translators helps to explain the pattern of additions accepted from LXX into P. Thus the translator of Proverbs included some additional couplets found in LXX but not in MT, following 9:12; 9:18; 11:16a; 13:13; 14:22; 25:20; 27:21. The mss of P-Daniel include the LXX additions in Dan. 3, which may well have been included by the original translator. They were certainly known in Syriac early enough for Ephrem to recall how the angel – according to Dan. 3:50 (Gk.) – made the like of a "whistling dewy wind" (ὡσεὶ πνεῦμα δρόσου διασυρίζον) in the midst of the furnace:

ܐܬܪܟܢܬ ܫܒܬ ܐܪܡܢ. ܒܢܘܪܐ ܠܚܒܝܒܝܗ. ܛܪ̈ܦܝܗ ܛܥܢ ܛܠܠܐ. ܦܝܓܘܗ، ܠܐܬܘܢܐ.

(The True Bough) bent down and cast her beloved ones into the fire; her leaves bore dew; they cooled the furnace.[52]

The translator of Esther was more conservative and so excluded the additions in LXX.

As well as consulting LXX at specific points in the text, the translators of P show evidence of a more general hellenistic influence upon their language, which may have been mediated partly by LXX. Thus, even in books like Ezra, Nehemiah and Chronicles, where no textual influence from LXX has been detected, the regular translation of תורה is the Greek loanword ܢܡܘܣܐ (νόμος). The corresponding loan-word is confined in the rabbinic sources to the laws and customs of the gentiles (or Jewish law as referred to by gentiles),[53] and its usage in P for divine laws seems due to LXX. Another theological term derived from Greek is ܕܝܬܩܐ "covenant"; the usage is characteristic of LXX, rather than contemporary Greek in general, in which the meaning was instead "bequest, will" (cf. Heb. 9:16–17; so also the corresponding loanword in Jewish Aramaic). Even the fact that the divine name is translated (ܡܪܝܐ) links P with LXX, rather than with the Jewish Aramaic versions, which merely transliterate. Another such Graecism in a book betraying no direct LXX influence is P's statement (2 Chr. 24:16) that Jehoiada "ran many races" for God's temple – an idiom drawn from the Greek

51 P may have followed the sound of LXX, even though the etymology utterly differs.
52 E. Beck (ed.), *Des Heiligen Ephraem der Syrers Hymnen De Paradiso und Contra Julianum*, CSCO 174, Syr 78, Louvain 1957, p. 68.
53 E.g. Mekhilta Shir.7, Sifra Aharei 9:9, Targum on Ezek. 20:25.

games (cf. 1 Cor 9:24–27). However, the avoidance of anthropomorphisms in P-Psalms is probably not due to LXX, since this is no less a feature of P in those books in which the translators appear not to have consulted LXX at all.[54]

Agreements between LXX and P against MT: a different Hebrew *Vorlage*?

Even though the majority of the agreements between LXX and P can be ascribed to the translators' activity, some instead imply that the two versions shared a Hebrew *Vorlage* different from MT. The possibility appears stronger in those books where agreement between LXX and P is rare and there is no evidence that P consulted LXX, e.g.

	MT	LXX	P	implied Hebrew *Vorlage*
1 Sam. 28:16	עֲרָךְ	μετὰ τοῦ πλησίον σου	ܥܡ ܣܒܝܟ	עם רעך
Job 10:8	יַחַד	μετὰ ταῦτα	ܗܝܕܝܢ ܡܢ	אחר

Coincidence and common tradition cannot explain such instances, and so a common *Vorlage* may be inferred. In the same way, some of the agreements in Samuel between P and Lucian's recension of LXX – e.g. the 3,000 Philistine chariots (MT: 30,000) at 1 Sam. 13:5 and the four years' planning (MT: 40) of Absalom's rebellion at 2 Sam. 15:7 – could be taken as evidence of a local Hebrew text current in Syria – though the rival possibility that Lucian consulted P cannot be ignored.[55]

A different common *Vorlage* is particularly likely if P implies the same consonantal text as LXX but construes it differently, e.g.

	MT	LXX	P	implied Hebrew *Vorlage*
1 Sam. 20:19	תֵּרֵד	ἐπισκέψῃ	ܐܢܬ ܬܬܒܥܐ	תפקד

Here LXX apparently found in his *Vorlage* not תֵּרֵד but תפקד, which he took as Qal ("you will visit"). P likewise implies תפקד, but understood in the Niphʿal ("you will be missed"). The agreement in the implied consonantal text cannot be due to coincidence, nor – given the difference in meaning – to borrowing from the Greek text of LXX. Thus P and LXX testify independently to a different – and indeed superior – Hebrew text. In terms of fig. 2, MT in all these cases shows an error that arose along the line leading down from β to MT.

In Jeremiah, P had in general the longer text of MT rather than the shorter form attested by LXX and some Qumran copies. However, a few of the expansions that characterise MT are also lacking in P, such as

Jer. 38:28　והיה כאשר נלכדה ירושלם

Jer. 44:3　לַעֲבֹד

Here again one could well argue that P's *Vorlage* agreed with that of LXX; these particular expansions found in MT had not yet spread to the east.

At 1 Sam. 1:23, P's *Vorlage* takes an intermediate position between MT on the one hand and the text common to 4QSamᵃ and LXX on the other. Here Hannah has promised to bring her son to serve in the sanctuary all his days, and Elkanah's reply runs as follows in the different witnesses:

---

[54] *Pace* Barnes, "On the Influence", p. 197.
[55] Th. Stockmayer, "Hat Lucian zu seiner Septuagintarevision die Peschito benützt?", *ZAW* 12 (1892), pp. 218–23.

4QSam[a]   ‏[ה היוצא מפיך‎

LXX   ἀλλὰ στήσαι κύριος τὸ ἐξελθὸν ἐκ τοῦ στόματός σου

MT   ‏אך יקם י' את דברו‎

P   ܒܪܡ ܢܩܝܡ ܡܪܝܐ ܡܠܬܟ

Apparently, the text of 4QSam[a] ("what comes forth from thy mouth"), which was also in the *Vorlage* of LXX, is original: Elkanah approves the vow which "comes forth from the mouth" of his wife (cf. Num. 30:3,8), and prays that Lord should bring about its fulfilment. According to MT, by contrast, Elkanah prays for the fulfilment of the Lord's word; but this could only mean Eli's words in v.17,[56] which were in fact not so much a promise as an endorsement of Hannah's prayer for a son, and which in any case were already fulfilled by Samuel's birth. MT thus seems inferior. Now P implies a Hebrew text ‏דברך‎, thus: "However, may the Lord confirm your word." This attests an intermediate stage in the development of the text, where the technical phrase "that comes forth from the mouth" is simplified to ‏דבר‎, as in MT, but the second person suffix – and hence the general sense – is retained.[57] In terms of fig.2, the change to ‏דברך‎ had already occurred in β, whose reading P preserves, while MT ‏דברו‎ reflects a further change.

To conclude, no doubt passages exist where LXX and P shared a *Vorlage* differing from MT. Such a hypothesis, however, can only account for a fraction of the cases where LXX and P agree strikingly against the plain sense of MT. In particular, this cause would not account for the many cases where LXX and P both presuppose a consonantal *Vorlage* no different from MT and yet their common interpretation of that Hebrew text is so unexpected that two translators can hardly have reached it independently.

Influence of LXX upon copyists of P

Finally, we must consider the possibility that copyists of P were influenced by LXX. With regard to the use of the extant P text as a witness to the biblical text, it does not matter whether LXX influenced the translators themselves or later copyists; but the distinction remains important in historical terms.

Influence upon copyists rather than the translator is particularly likely if only part of P's ms tradition agrees with LXX, e.g.

Isa. 9:5

MT   ‏שר שלום‎

P   ܪܒܐ ܕܫܠܡܐ

to which mss 7a1 8a1*, as well as marginal readings in 6h5 and 9a1, add ܘܐܒܐ ܕܥܠܡܐ ܕܐܬܐ "and father of the age to come", following the widespread addition to LXX πατὴρ τοῦ μέλλοντος αἰῶνος.[58]

---

[56] "And may the God of Israel grant thy request . . ."

[57] For this analysis I am grateful to Prof. T. Fenton. For a more cautious treatment, see Tov, *Textual Criticism*, p. 176.

[58] Quoted from S.P. Brock, "Text History and Text Division in Peshiṭta Isaiah", MPI 4 (1988), pp. 49–80: 64.

Psalm 2:12

MT   נשקו בר

P   ܢܫܩܘ ܒܪܐ

but the reading ܐܘܚܢܘ ܐܘܪܚܬܐ, reflecting LXX δράξασθε παιδείας, occurs beside it in some mss, and in its stead (over an erasure) in 7a1.

Another situation where LXX influence on copyists seems likely, rather than on the translator himself, is where the mss differ in the position of the material that agrees with LXX. An example occurs at Qoh. 12:5, where for each phrase the P mss offer two renderings, which reflect both the Hebrew and LXX. However, the mss differ among themselves. The P text as found in the first hand of one early ms (8a1) may be aligned with the Hebrew and Greek texts as follows:

(a)   ܘܢܗܘܐ ܠܗ, ܫܩܝܐ   = וינאץ השקד (the first word being guessed)
(b)   ܐܪܒܐ ܩܡܨܐ   = ויסתבל החגב (the first word being guessed)
(a')   ܘܢܥܦܐ ܫܓܕܐ   = καὶ ἀνθήσῃ τὸ ἀμύγδαλον
(b')   ܘܢܣܓܐ ܩܡܨܐ   = καὶ παχυνθῇ ἡ ἀκρίς
(c')   ܘܢܬܒܕܪ ܩܦܪ   = καὶ διασκεδασθῇ ἡ κάππαρις
(c)   ܘܢܬܒܛܠ ܡܣܟܢܬܐ   = ותפר האביונה (cf. אביון 'poor')

The Syriac may be translated:

and wakefulness shall spring up over him like a locust, and the almond shall grow, and locusts will multiply, and the caper shall be scattered, and the needy woman shall be annulled

Phrases (a)(b)(c) in P seem direct attempts to translate the Hebrew, while (a')(b')(c') derive from the corresponding phrases in LXX. However, the order varies among the P mss. The oldest ms (7a1) places (a') and (c') at the end of the phrase, long after (c); and between them, rather than (b'), 7a1 has ܘܢܦܪܥ ܫܘܫܢܬܐ (w-teshwah) "and the lily shall flourish", apparently in order to replace the locust by plants, in keeping with both the preceding and succeeding lines. Two lectionary mss (9l1.3) omit (a')(b')(c') altogether. Some other mss omit (b), whose sense is largely covered by (b'). All this dislocation suggests that phrases (a')(b')(c') were added secondarily to the text, and never gained an established place.[59]

Other examples from Qohelet of LXX influence on the copyists of P are presented by Schoors (pp. 351–4). In some of Schoors's examples, it can be argued that the LXX reading with which the P mss agree is secondary within the LXX tradition and thus too late to have influenced the translator.

That LXX influence upon copyists of P was mediated by the Syrohexapla may be suspected, but not easily proved.[60] According to Koster, only a few variants in the latest mss can be safely ascribed to this cause.[61] Suspected cases in earlier mss may be otherwise explicable, as at Zech. 5:4 –

---

[59] Scribal revision after LXX – albeit with differences of detail – is likewise suggested by Kamenetzky ("Die P'šita zu Kohelet", p. 200), Schoors ("The Peshitta of Kohelet", p. 353) and by J. Göttsberger, "Koh 12,5 nach der Pešitto", *Biblische Zeitschrift* 8 (1910), pp. 7–11. For different views, see Janichs, *Animadversiones*, pp. 17–18 (LXX influence on translator) and D.J.Lane, "Lilies that fester: the Peshitta text of Qoheleth", *VT* 29 (1979), pp. 481–90.   [60] Gelston, *Twelve Prophets*, p. 101.
[61] M. Koster in *JSS* 33 (1988), p. 284.

MT   הנשבע בשמי לשקר

P (most mss)   ܘܕܝܡܐ ܒܫܡܝ ܒܕܓܠܘܬܐ

P (6h9)   ܒܫܡܠ...ܐ = Syhex.

It has been suggested that 6h9 was influenced by Syhex., and should therefore be re-dated to the seventh century. However, 6h9 may instead reflect assimilation to the similar context in Mal. 3:5, or to the third of the ten commandments (Exod. 20:7=Deut. 5:11), in all of which passages the verb ܝܡܐ appears along with ܒܕܓܠܘܬܐ in all mss.

Although LXX has exerted some influence upon copyists of P, one could not hope to explain all the parallels by that hypothesis. In particular, this would not explain the two sorts of critical passage noted above: where the Greek text was misunderstood, and where Greek and Hebrew elements are welded together inextricably.

II. THE PESHITTA AND THE EXTANT TARGUMS

The main theories

Introduction

The Targums will occupy us for longer than LXX. This does not necessarily reflect greater influence upon P, but rather greater scholarly attention to the possibility of such influence. Indeed, it is at present a common view that P is not a direct translation from a Hebrew original but based on an earlier Jewish Targum.

Many parallels exist between P and the Targums,[62] especially in the Pentateuch. To some extent, these may result from polygenesis: two translations of the same text, at about the same period, into dialects of the same language are likely often to agree. Many of the agreements, however, betoken common origin, as Perles already noted.[63]

Perles's own suggestion was that while the translators of P worked primarily from the Hebrew, they knew of Jewish traditions which were attached to isolated phrases or verses, and which also crop up in the Targums. Such a view has been re-affirmed in the recent study by Maori.[64]

Often, however, the parallels have instead been ascribed to literary dependence of P upon a Jewish Targum. On the weaker form of this hypothesis, P was still translated primarily from a Hebrew original, but the translators also consulted from time to time

---

[62] These are cited as follows:

T^O = Onkelos, in A. Sperber (ed.), *The Bible in Aramaic*, vol. I (Leiden 1959).

T^J = Pseudo-Jonathan, in D. Rieder (ed.), *Pseudo-Jonathan. Targum Jonathan ben Uziel on the Pentateuch*, Jerusalem 1974, and in E.G. Clarke (ed.), *Targum Pseudo-Jonathan of the Pentateuch: Text and Concordance*, Hoboken 1984.

T^F = Fragment Targum, in M.L. Klein (ed.), *The Fragment Targums of the Pentateuch* (2 vols) (Rome 1980).

T^P = Palestinian Targums, in M.L. Klein (ed.), *Genizah Fragments of Palestinian Targum to the Pentateuch* (2 vols), Cincinnati 1986.

T^N = Neofiti, in A. Diez Macho (ed.), *Neophyti 1: Targum Palestinense Ms de la Biblioteca Vaticana* (5 vols), Madrid 1968–78.

Tg= Targum Jonathan to the Prophets, quoted from A. Sperber (ed.), *The Bible in Aramaic*, vols II–III, Leiden 1959–62.

[63] J. Perles, *Meletemata*, 27–31.

[64] Y. Maori, *The Peshitta Version of the Pentateuch and Early Jewish Exegesis*, Jerusalem 1995, p. 298.

a written copy of a Targum. Such was the view of Silverstone[65] and of Wernberg-Møller,[66] who both identified this Targum as Onkelos (T^O). Certainly P shows more parallels with T^O than with any other extant Targum.

A stronger hypothesis of dependence upon the Targum – or at least *a* Targum – was made popular by Baumstark[67] and Kahle,[68] and by their respective pupils Peters[69] and Wohl.[70] On this view, P in the Torah is not a direct translation from the Hebrew at all. Rather, an old Jewish Targum was transposed into Syriac, and stripped of most of its exegetical additions and modifications by reference to the Hebrew. In Isaiah, Delekat likewise viewed P as a revision after MT of an older Aramaic/ Syriac version.[71] In all these books, however, the theory tells us that this revision after the Hebrew was not total. Hence parallels remain with the extant Targums, and these form part of the evidence for the theory.

In addition, evidence has been detected in further agreements which certain forms of the biblical text in Syriac *other* than the majority text of the biblical mss exhibit with one or more Targums. The relevant Syriac text forms are found in individual mss of P, and in Syriac patristic citations. Parallels between patristic citations and the Palestinian Targums have been found particularly numerous. Attention was drawn to this phenomenon by Baumstark but the data were assembled in particular detail (in the Pentateuch) by Vööbus[72] and (in Isaiah) by Running.[73] These non-standard forms of the biblical text in Syriac are said to preserve traces of the earlier Targum from which P supposedly derives.

Moreover, since Targums are often expansive, and also depart frequently from exact translation, interest has also alighted upon looser or more expansive forms of the text in Syriac, by comparison with the text familiar from the biblical mss of P. These text forms, which appear either in individual Bible mss or in patristic citations, have been claimed as traces of an early stage when – it is argued – the text of P bore a looser relationship to the Hebrew, and thus stood closer to the Targums. Such claims have been made even for biblical citations that bear no resemblance to any extant Targum, provided only that they differ from the text of the biblical manuscripts of P. Examples occur in Peters's study of the Psalms,[74] as well as the work of Vööbus and (especially) Running. On this view, P represents the end of a process of three stages: the original Targum, its transposition, and its subsequent re-working.

Kahle attached particular importance to the parallels which Syriac biblical texts (whether standard or not) exhibit with the Palestinian Targums, particularly with

---

[65] A.E. Silverstone, *Aquila and Onkelos*, Manchester 1931, p. 127.
[66] P. Wernberg-Møller, "Prolegomena to a Re-examination of the Palestinian Targum Fragments of the Book of Genesis Published by P.Kahle, and their Relationship to the Peshitta", *JSS* 7 (1962), pp. 253–66, especially p. 263.
[67] A. Baumstark, "Pešiṭta und palästinensisches Targum", *Biblische Zeitschrift* 19 (1931), pp. 257–70.
[68] P. Kahle, *Masoreten des Westens*, vol. II, Stuttgart 1930, pp. 3*–4*.
[69] C. Peters, "Peschittha und Targumim des Pentateuchs", *Muséon* 48 (1935), pp. 1–54.
[70] S. Wohl, *Das Palästinische Pentateuch-Targum: Untersuchungen zu den Geniza-Fragmenten und ihrem Verhältnis zu den übrigen Targumen und der Peschitta*, Zwickau 1935.
[71] L. Delekat, "Die Peschitta zu Jesaja zwischen Targum und Septuaginta", *Biblica* 38 (1957), pp. 185–99, 321–35:194.   [72] A. Vööbus, *Peschitta und Targumim des Pentateuchs*, Stockholm 1958.
[73] L.G. Running, "An Investigation of the Syriac Version of Isaiah", *Andrews University Seminary Studies* 3 (1965), pp. 138–57; 4 (1966), pp. 37–64, 135–48.
[74] "Pešitta-Psalter und Psalmentargum", *Muséon* 52 (1939), pp. 275–96.

the fragments of the latter which Kahle himself had discovered in the Cairo Genizah.[75] He inferred that the Targum from which P supposedly derived resembled the Palestinian Targums preserved in those fragments. To explain how this could have happened, given the eastern location of P, Kahle took up a hypothesis already suggested by Perles[76] and Marquart.[77] During the reign of Claudius (41–54 CE), the royal house of Adiabene converted to Judaism; and this provides a likely background for the origin for P, since these converts would have required a version of the Hebrew Bible in an east-Aramaic dialect. To this Kahle added a new suggestion: the converts were supplied not with a new translation from Hebrew into their own east-Aramaic dialect, but with a pre-existing translation from Palestine in western Aramaic, which they then transposed into east-Aramaic (i.e. Syriac). In this way Kahle explained the supposed affinity between P and the Palestinian Targums. This theory was further supported, according to Kahle, by supposedly west-Aramaic linguistic elements in P.

According to Kahle, T[O] was of Babylonian origin. This created a difficulty for his theory that P originated in the Palestinian Targum tradition, since P in fact shows a far closer relationship with T[O] than with any of the Palestinian Targums. This difficulty was avoided by Baumstark, who agreed with Kahle that P derived from a west-Aramaic Targum, but supposed – as subsequent scholarship has tended to agree – that T[O] too originated in the west.[78] According to Baumstark, a Palestinian Targum text brought to the east and stripped there of its exegetical additions became the common ancestor both of T[O] and of P.[79]

Finally, we have to consider the theory of Beyer, who posits before P a predominantly literal translation of the whole Hebrew Bible, made into Imperial Aramaic and begun about the fourth century BCE. This has since perished, except that the portion on Job survived at Qumran. Nevertheless, it was a common source of P and the Jewish Aramaic versions, and in particular of their shared readings. P is the result of a redaction of this Targum into literary Syriac, accompanied by revision after LXX, in the fourth century CE.[80] This is a variant of the stronger hypothesis, in that it derives P not directly from a Hebrew text but from an earlier Aramaic version, albeit one far older than that envisaged by the other theories.

Theories of literary dependence upon Targums preserved by the Jews

Let us first consider the more popular theory, namely that P derives from a lost Palestinian Targum rather than directly from a Hebrew text. An immediate challenge is that this theory fails to explain P's quantitative literalism, given that the extant

[75] Kahle, *The Cairo Geniza*, pp. 272–3. The evidence was published by Wohl, and is evaluated below.
[76] *Meletemata*, pp. 7–8.
[77] J. Marquart, *Osteuropäische und ostasiatische Streifzüge*, Leipzig 1903, p. 299.
[78] That T[O] is of Palestinian rather than Babylonian origin is now widely agreed. Particularly influential was E.Y. Kutscher, "The Language of the Genesis Apocryphon: a Preliminary Study", in C. Rabin and Y. Yadin (eds.), *Scripta Hierosolymitana 4: Aspects of the Dead Sea Scrolls*, Jerusalem 1958, pp. 1–35, esp. pp. 9–11.
[79] The (sometimes shifting) views of these scholars are traced in detail by Dirksen, *Mikra*, pp. 264–85.
[80] K. Beyer, "Der reichsaramäische Einschlag in der ältesten syrischen Literatur", *ZDMG* 116 (1966), pp. 242–54: 253.

Targums are more periphrastic and expansive, albeit in varying degrees.[81] Baumstark suggested that those who derived P from their Palestinian Targum source removed the exegetical additions from the latter by consulting the Hebrew at the same time. As Sperber retorted, however, anyone capable of that feat could more easily have translated from the Hebrew direct.[82] Aware of this objection, Vööbus suggested instead that a Palestinian Targum was first transposed into Syriac, complete with its many expansive and loose renderings, and later gradually whittled down ("*genagt und gefeilt*") by Syriac-speaking scholars, until all the exegetical additions were removed.[83] This suggestion, however, is no more convincing than Baumstark's. Syriac churchmen, cut off from the Hebrew original, would not have been able to identify which elements of the transposed Targum actually were exegetical additions. For example, what instinct guided them at Gen. 7:14 to retain the phrase "every bird of every wing" (in MT but omitted by LXX) rather than expunge it as an exegetical addition? To answer this objection, Vööbus offered a further suggestion: perhaps the process of whittling down the transposed Targum began at a time when the Syriac church was still in contact with Aramaic-speaking Jews, who were deputed to this task and could have consulted the Hebrew. However, such inter-faith collaboration seems improbable; and moreover, this hypothesis brings us back to Sperber's objection, that these Jews could more easily have provided a fresh translation directly from the Hebrew than whittle down a transposed Targum through comparison with the Hebrew. Altogether, then, the theory fails to account for the quantitative literalism that is characteristic of P.

The theory likewise fails to explain P's greater accuracy at many points, by comparison with all extant Targums, including even T⁰. Thus at Gen. 1:1, for Heb. בראשית, only P reflects the Hebrew form (as ܒܪܫܝܬ); even T⁰ is more distant (בקדמין). P again achieves a closer relation to the Hebrew in poetic passages, e.g. at Gen. 49:12 –

MT   חכלילי עינים מיין ולבן שנים מחלב

T   let his mountains be red with his vineyards; let his vats drip with wine; let his valleys be white with produce and flocks of sheep.

P   ܘܢܗܪܢ ܥܝܢܘܗܝ, ܡܢ ܚܡܪܐ. ܘܚܘܪܢ ܫܢܘܗܝ, ܡܢ ܚܠܒܐ.

his eyes glisten from wine, and his teeth are white from milk

P likewise often stands closer to the Hebrew where God has anthropomorphic epithets (see pp. 29–30 above), or where sensitive matters of doctrine arise, e.g. at Exod. 34:7 –

MT   ונקה לא ינקה פקד עון אבות על בנים ועל בני בנים

T⁰   סלח לדתביbin לאוריתיה ולדלא תיבין לא מזכי מסער חובי אבהן על בנין ועל בני בנין מרדין

he forgives *those who return to his Torah; and those who do not repent*, he does not hold innocent; he visits the sins of fathers upon *rebellious* children and children's children

P   ܘܡܚܣܐ ܠܐ ܡܚܣܐ. ܦܩܕ ܣܟܠܘܬܐ ܕܐܒܗܐ ܥܠ ܒܢܝܐ ܘܥܠ ܒܢܝ ܒܢܝܐ

---

[81] The Aramaic version of Job from Qumran shows a comparable degree of correspondence with the Hebrew, but, precisely for that reason, should not be called a Targum. Beyer's theory will be considered separately below.

[82] A. Sperber, "Peschitta und Onkelos", in S.W. Baron and A. Marx (eds.), *Jewish Studies in Memory of George A. Kohut*, 1874–1933, New York 1935, pp. 554–64: 557.

[83] Vööbus, *Peshitta und Targumim des Pentateuchs*, p. 107.

At the same time, the theory fails to explain renderings in P which differ from anything in the Targums and can only come from misunderstanding of a Hebrew text directly read, e.g.

Gen. 49:22   MT עֲלֵי עָיִן "upon a spring", P ܣܩ ܚܣܢܐ "ascend O spring"

Deut. 1:44   MT תַּעֲשֶׂינָה "(bees) do", P ܣܬܢܐ "smoked (bees)" representing תֶּעָשַׁנָּה as discussed in chapter 2.

A further argument against the theory is posed by the existence of P in Daniel and Ezra-Nehemiah. These books must have been translated without help from any Jewish Targum, for none is known ever to have existed. Evidently, then, the expertise existed to translate the other books as well directly from the Hebrew into Syriac.

Furthermore, evidence for an older expansive Syriac text, which might be compared with the Targums, has been drawn almost exclusively from patristic citations, rather than from the biblical mss of P. This would imply that those citations preserve – on a regular basis – an older text than the biblical mss. However, such a relationship is hardly credible.[84]

We now turn to the weaker form of the hypothesis, namely that the translator worked primarily from a Hebrew source but consulted a written copy of T⁰ (or some other Targum) from time to time. In that it asserts less, this hypothesis is harder to discredit; but there is no good evidence for it in the first place. Dependence on a written copy of an extant Targum would be indicated if we had passages in P which could only be explained by supposing that an Aramaic version – as opposed to the Hebrew text – had been misread or misunderstood, as was argued above in relation to LXX. However, as Rosenthal observed[85] and as further discussed below, not a single convincing example can be found.

Further evidence against all theories of literary dependence comes from those passages where P omits a difficult Hebrew phrase. Examples are frequent after the Pentateuch, and some examples were given in chapter 2 above. The translators would not have been baffled so often had they been able to consult a continuous written Targum.

Alternative explanations of the evidence adduced for literary dependence

The evidence adduced for theories of literary dependence of P upon the Targums preserved by the Jews can all be explained otherwise. Many parallels are due to polygenesis: some coincidences are inevitable when the same text, presenting the same difficulties, is translated into two dialects of the same language. Many parallels, again, can be ascribed to common dependence on a tradition of biblical scholarship in Aramaic. The only book where the parallels between P and the Targum are indeed so close and so extensive as to imply a literary relationship is Proverbs; but here it is the Targum which has drawn from P. Such borrowing from the church is not inconceivable around the tenth century CE, as we shall see.

---

[84] In the words of Goshen-Gottstein in *JSS* 6 (1961), p. 269: "we cannot take it as mere coincidence that it is in quotations that these deviating readings turn up piecemeal".

[85] F. Rosenthal, *Die aramäistische Forschung*, Leiden 1939, pp. 202–3.

Again, the looseness of biblical citations in patristic works may reflect the function of those works rather than echo a hypothetical Targum. In particular, both patristic writers and Palestinian targumists agreed in expanding the text, albeit from different motives: the former preferred not to cite proof-texts in a form so terse as to obscure their arguments, while the latter felt free to provide expansions, in the knowledge that the Hebrew original would remain available to their audience as a check. At all events, both differed from the translators of P, who felt bound by the principle of quantitative literalism to reproduce the terseness of the Hebrew.

Occasionally a single ms of P, or a patristic citation, preserves the original reading of P against the majority of witnesses. Such cases have been claimed to support theories of literary dependence of P upon an earlier Targum. In fact, however, these cases can simply be viewed as lone survivals of the original text of P, which for some reason has been lost in all other witnesses. That the original text should survive uniquely in one manuscript, or even in a citation, is an unusual event, but both phenomena are well attested for Greek and Latin textual traditions (as discussed in chapter 6 below). In none of these cases is there any reason to suppose that the original text derives from a Targum rather than directly from the Hebrew text.

We also find occasionally in patristic works a biblical citation in a form known from the Targums and differing from the text of the mss of P. In none of these cases, however, is this reading the source of the text of the biblical mss of P. Rather, it seems that a Jewish Targum rendering of some phrases or verses circulated in the Syriac-speaking church alongside P, as Brock has shown in some detail.[86]

The last two paragraphs may be thus summarised. Patristic citations sometimes preserve the original text of P – which, however, shows no sign of derivation from any Targum. Again, they sometimes preserve renderings known also in one or other of the Targums – which, however, do not represent the original text of P but rather a translation of a particular phrase that circulated alongside P. What the patristic citations do not provide is a rendering which demands recognition as the original text of P *and* stands closer than the text of the P mss to the Targums.

As to the alleged west-Aramaic origin for P, the evidence is insubstantial. The main item claimed is P's occasional use of the accusative particle *yat* – which however is also known from eastern Aramaic, and from ancient Aramaic before the split into eastern and western dialects.

Altogether, there is no reason to posit P's dependence upon any written Targum, extant or otherwise. This position must however be worked out in detail. Since scholars have been impressed by the sheer mass of material adduced for theories of literary dependence, we shall need to go through it, or at least through a representative sample. The discussion will eschew such adjectives as targumic, Targum-like, *targumhaft*, *targumartig*, and others that have been used. These terms may indicate either similarity with renderings in actual Targums, or literary dependence upon a Targum; and too often, this ambiguity has led scholars who have demonstrated the former to claim the latter.

---

[86] S.(P.) Brock, "Jewish Traditions in Syriac Sources", *JJS* 30 (1979), pp. 212–32; "A Palestinian Targum Feature in Syriac", *JJS* 46 (1995), pp. 271–82.

Parallels in the Torah attributable to polygenesis

The Targums and P translated the same text into dialects of the same language. The demands of Aramaic idiom, and the pursuit of intelligibility, will often have led them independently to the same rendering. In all the lists that follow, T[O] agrees exactly (apart from dialectal and other minor differences) with P, except where otherwise stated, and absence of reference to other Targums need not imply disagreement with P. The letter R means that P also agrees with one or more rabbinic sources; for Pentateuchal passages, references are given by Maori.[87]

Some parallels result from the demands of the Aramaic language. Thus, both P and the Targums rejected certain constructions peculiar to Hebrew. For example, both avoid the singular pronoun for a nation, preferring the plural to indicate its people (e.g. at Exod. 1:10 P=T[OJFN]) and adjusting otherwise to indicate its territory, e.g. at Num. 20:18, MT בי (לא תעבר), P=T[OJ] ܒܐܬܘܡܗ (hiat T[N]). The Hebrew usages "man and wife" for animals (Gen. 7:2), or "woman to sister" for curtains (Exod. 26:5), are likewise resolved to "male and female" and "one towards another" (P=T[OJN]).

A specifically Aramaic feature underlies the shared policy of P and the Targums in rendering לקח: *nsb* serves for taking objects and *dbr* for taking people (apart from taking a wife, in which case *nsb* is used). A similar distinction is observed in French, as in the contrasting sentences:

> j'ai *pris* un parapluie pour sortir
>
> j'ai *emmené* mon petit frère à l'école
>
> j'ai *pris* femme.

This leads P and the Targums to agree in their choice of rendering for לקח, according to the context. Thus both use *dbr* at Gen. 34:2 when Shechem takes Dinah against her will, but *nsb* at Gen. 34:4 when he asks to marry her. Both versions may even agree in adding a verb in order to conform with the demands of Aramaic, as at Gen. 43:15 –

MT	ומשנה כסף לקחו בידם ואת בנימן
T[O]	ועל חד תרין כספא נסיבו בידהון ודברו ית בנימן
P	ܠܒܢܝܡܝܢ ܘܐܡܗܘܢ ܢܣܒܘ ܟܣܦܐ ܥܦܝܦܐ ܘܚܕܐ

A more striking example at Josh. 7:24 is noted below. Such agreement does not imply, *pace* Silverstone (pp. 128–31), that P had a written copy of Onkelos before him; rather, both follow Aramaic usage.

Many Hebrew idiomatic expressions had to be modified in both Aramaic dialects, e.g.

Gen. 8:17   ושרצו, P ܘܣܓܘ, T[OJN] ויתילדון (the context is not confined to teeming creatures)

Exod. 20:7   לא תשא את שם י׳, P=T[OF] . . . ܒܡܘܡܬܐ ܐܠܗܐ ܠܐ :: T[JPN]

Exod. 32:19   תחת ההר, P=T[OJN] ܕܛܘܪܐ, ܒܫܦܘܠܘܗܝ "in the lower reaches of the mountain"

Again, in Hebrew God could be said to place (Heb. שת) a son, so explaining the name Seth; P and T[OJ], unable to reconcile this with Aramaic idiom, substitute *y(h)ab* 'gave' (Gen. 4:25; contrast T[N] שוי). This shared sensitivity to Aramaic idiom is reflected in some translations common to P and the Targums for Hebrew נפל in different contexts:

[87] Y. Maori, *The Peshitta Version of the Pentateuch and Early Jewish Exegesis*, Jerusalem 1995.

ܐܪ "(Ishmael) settled"   Gen. 25:18 (P=T^{OJFN})

ܢܙܪ "(his earlier days of Naziriteship shall) be null"   Num. 6:12 (P=T^{OJN})

ܬܬܦܠܓ "(the land which will) be allocated"   Num. 34:2 (P=T^{OJ}; ct T^N תפול).

A particular feature of the Hebrew original which both P and the Targums tend to modify is its terseness. These versions supply particles where the Hebrew constructions seemed incomplete, e.g. Exod. 19:4 ("*as* on eagles' wings" P=T^{OJFP}::T^N), Lev. 10:19 ("and *if* I ate" P=T^{OJFN}), Lev. 26:42 ("my covenant *with* Jacob" P=T^{OJF} [hiat T^N]). Again, P and the Targums agree in expanding at Deut. 8:15 –

MT   ...במדבר הגדול והנורא נחש

P   ܒܡܕܒܪܐ ܗܘ ܪܒܐ ܘܕܚܝܠܐ ܐܬܪ ܚܘܘܬܐ...

For the last two words, compare T^O אתר חיון and T^J אתר מלי חיוון; T^N too has an insertion: ארע בית חיוויין.

Both P and the Targums also added words in order to make explicit what the Hebrew left implicit and so to remove obscurity or ambiguity, e.g.

Gen. 2:24   "and *the two of them*[88] will become one flesh" (P=T^{JNG}:: T^O)

Gen. 26:18   "which *his father's servants* had dug" (P=T^J :: T^{ON})

Gen. 27:22   "and *the feel of* the hands (is of Esau)" (P=T^{JFN}:: T^O) – though different words are chosen, namely ܓܫܬܐ in P and derivatives of root מוש in the Targums.

Gen. 38:28   "*thread of* scarlet" (P=T^J :: T^{OPN})

Gen. 44:5   "this *cup*" (P=T^P :: T^{OJN}), though again the wording differs: P has ܐܣܩܦܐ and T^P כלידא

Num. 9:16   "the cloud covered it *by day*" (P=T^J, against T^{ON})

Again, both P and the Targum(s) might use a more specific expression to bring out a point implied in the Hebrew, e.g.

Gen. 29:27f   MT שבע "week (of nuptial feasting)", P ܡܫܬܘܬܐ 'feast'; T^{JFPN} add יומי משתיא :: T^O

Exod. 3:2   MT "(the bush) was not eaten", P ܠܐ ܝܩܕ 'did not burn'; so T^N לית הוא יקיד; cf. T^{FJ}, which add יקיד. However, T^O renders literally.

Deut. 17:12   MT "he will die", P=T^{OJN} ܢܬܩܛܠ "he will be put to death".

Both P and the Targums also resolve logical discrepancies in the Hebrew, e.g.

Gen. 28:9   MT "Mahalat", P "Basmat"; T^{J}R (::T^{ON}) adds הי בשמת; cf. Gen. 36:3, where the daughter of Ishmael who married Esau is called Basmat

Exod. 15:1   MT "I (shall sing)", P "we"=T^{OJFPN}, given that the Israelites sang too.

These changes too may have been made by P and the relevant Targums independently.

P and the Targums also show some agreement in style of expression:

(a) Both tend to supply elements left implicit in the Hebrew, for the sake of neat presentation, even where the meaning was never in doubt. Thus they change "row" into "first row" at Exod. 28:17, 39:10 to conform with the succeeding references to the second and later rows (P=T^{OJFN}).

(b) Both relieve monotony by introducing variation. Thus both use two adjectives (ܫܦܝܪ and ܪܓܐ) where the Hebrew repeats one (יפה), at Gen. 29:17 (P=T^{OJPN} and one manuscript of T^F), 39:6 (P=T^{OJPN}).

---

[88] As opposed to the father and mother mentioned in the previous line.

(c) Both sometimes heighten and dramatise the sense, e.g.

Lev. 24:12 MT ויניחהו "and they left him"
P ܘܚܒܫܘܗܝ "and they bound him",
so T^{O} ואסרוהי; more vaguely T^{JFN} אצנעו יתיה

Deut. 28:52 MT "until your walls fall",
P=T^{ON} ܕܢܟܒܘܫ ܫܘܪܝܟ "until he overcomes your walls" = T^{J}

Deut. 32:38 MT "let them arise", P adds tauntingly ܗܫܐ;
T^{OFPN} add כען, T^{J} adds כדון

In particular, the Hebrew verb "be" is sometimes replaced both in P and in the Targums by a more specific expression, e.g.

Gen. 13:3

MT	אשר היה שם אהלה (בתחלה)	"where his tent was (at the beginning)"
P	ܕܢܨܒ ܗܘܐ ܬܡܢ ܡܫܟܢܗ...	"where he had pitched his tent"
T^{OJN}	די פרס תמן משכניה	"where he had stretched out his tent"

Lev. 15:19
MT (שבעת ימים) תהיה (בנדתה), P ܬܬܒ, T^{J} תהי יתבא :: T^{ON}

We now come to the treatment of Hebrew expressions which posed difficulties of understanding both for P and for the Targumists. Both might have inferred the same meaning from the context, e.g.

Gen. 18:12 MT עדנה, P=T^{O} ܛܠܝܘܬܐ 'youth'; compare the references in this verse to the advanced age of Sarah and Abraham.

Exod. 1:11 MT שרי מסים, P ܫܠܝܛܢܐ ܒܝܫܐ, T^{O} שלטונין מבאישין. The taskmasters set over the Israelites are called "evil" in P and "evil-doing" in T^{O}. This agreement in a vague term could have been derived independently by either translator from the succeeding statement that the taskmasters' purpose was למען ענותו: to afflict the Israelites. The usual (though anachronistic) perceived sense 'tribute' for מס was clearly unsuitable here.

Exod. 30:32 MT מתכנתו, P=T^{OJN} ܕܡܘܬܗ, cf. following כמהו.

Num. 22:5 MT פתורה (בלעם), P ܦܬܘܪܐ, $T^{P[N]}$ פתיר חילמא; the rare toponym פתור could easily have been explained twice independently through פתר 'interpret', aptly enough for the soothsayer Balaam.

Deut. 32:27 MT לולי כעס אויב אגור פן ינכרו צרימו
P ܐܠܐ ܠܐ ܪܘܓܙܐ ܕܒܥܠܕܒܒܐ ܕܥܫܢ ܕܠܐ ܢܬܪܘܪܒܘܢ ܒܥܠܕܒܒܝܗܘܢ

were it not for the wrath of the enemy that grew strong; lest their enemies were exalted

$T^{F[N]}$ אילולי כעסא דסנאא די תקף דלא יתגברון עליהון בעלי דבביהון
The verbs in T^{O} כניש... יתרברב and T^{J} דחיל... יתרברבון agree in sense in the second line only.

Both P and the Targums might find and utilise an obvious parallel passage in the same way in order to elucidate a difficult expression, e.g.

Gen. 41:56 MT בהם אשר כל את (יוסף ויפתח)

(and Joseph opened) all that was in them

P ܐܘܨܪ̈ܐ; T[OJ]N עיבורא בהון די אוצריא
All these versions had previously used אוצרא 'store-house' in v.47, in rendering Heb. לקמצים.

Exod. 13:21 MT לנחתם "(God went before them) to lead them", P ܠܡܒܬ ܐܘܢ "to let them encamp", so T[F] משרוי בית אתר להון למתקנא (=T[OJ]). Both think of Num. 10:33, where the ark travelled before the people "to spy out a resting-place for them".

Exod. 15:16 MT קנית זו עם "the people that you created/acquired"
P and T[OFPN]: "the people that you redeemed" (ܦܪܩܬ; compare גאלת זו עם in v.13; :: T[J]).

Exod. 20:6 MT לאלפים, P=T[OJFPN] ܕܪ̈ܐ ܠܐܠܦ "to thousands of generations" (cf. Deut. 7:9).

Num. 11:4 MT והאספסף, P ܚܠܘܛܐ, T[O[N]] ועירבובין. Both versions interpret as "mixture", comparing the רב ערב of Exod. 12:38 who accompanied the Israelites.[89]

There is of course some subjectivity in attributing some of the above examples to polygenesis, rather than placing them in the next category.

Parallels in the Torah implying common origin

There are many parallels, not merely in content but in wording, too striking to be ascribed to polygenesis. As noted above, these were ascribed by Perles to common tradition.

In principle, three kinds of tradition may be distinguished. First, there are Hebrew words and particles whose proper meaning has been handed down intact from biblical times. Second, where the original meaning was forgotten (or deemed unsuitable), a meaning was deduced or invented in the post-biblical era and then handed down; this may be called an exegetical tradition. Third, where a biblical element (such as an anthropomorphism) posed problems of expression rather than understanding, a tradition may have grown up which recommended a particular choice of words in Aramaic/Syriac. Such a tradition may be termed translational. The two last terms – exegetical and translational – are based on Maori's Hebrew terminology: תרגומית מסורת פרשנית, מסורת מסורת.[90] These three types of tradition correspond to three aspects of the translator's task: to be familiar with biblical Hebrew, to apply that knowledge to the understanding of the text, and to express that understanding in Syriac. In practice, of course, these types of tradition cannot always be distinguished.

---

[89] The shared consonantal pattern ($C_1C_2C_3\,C_2C_3$) encouraged this identification.
[90] Maori, *Peshitta version of the Pentateuch*, p. 300.

Lexical traditions

Even the most elementary knowledge of biblical Hebrew had to be learnt from a teacher, and to that extent derives from tradition.[91] Thus we may speak of lexical traditions, which have carried the sense of words down from biblical times. In the case of rare words, especially for realia, these can yield striking parallels, e.g.

Gen. 30:14   MT דודאים, P=T^OJPNR ܝܒܪܘܚܐ 'mandrakes'

Gen. 30:37   MT ערמון, P=T^ONR ܕܠܘܙܐ 'plane-tree' :: T^J

Exod. 26:1 etc   MT תולעת שני, P=T^OJN ܨܘܒܥܐ ܕܙܚܘܪܝܬܐ

Exod. 30:34   MT שחלת, P= T^O ܛܦܪܐ

Lev. 3:4   MT יתרת על הכבד, P=T^OJ ܚܨܪ ܕܥܠ ܟܒܕܐ 'caul of the liver'
cf. T^N מה די ישתייר מן חצר כבדא

Lev. 11:17   MT שלך, P=T^OJNR ܫܠܘ ܢܘܢܐ 'pelican'[92] (so Deut. 14:17)

Deut. 14:5   MT אקו ודישן, P=T^OJ ܝܥܠܐ ܘܪܝܡܐ 'mountain-goat and wild ox' :: T^N

Here too belong some of the gems in Exod. 28:17–20 // 39:10–13:

MT	שהם	אחלמה	לשם	אדם
P	ܒܪܠܐ	ܥܝܢ ܥܓܠܐ	ܩܢܟܝܪܘܢ	ܤܡܩܬܐ
	=T^OJF	=T^OJ	=T^OJ	=T^OJFN

In principle, such traditions were the common property of all those who retained knowledge of the biblical text. Thus, they do not betoken P's literary dependence on any written Targum, nor indeed on any sort of post-biblical scholarship.

Traditions at least partly exegetical

Common dependence on post-biblical scholarship is, however, indicated by common renderings where the sense appears not to have been retained since biblical times but deduced through later exegesis. Most traditions of this sort relate to rare or unique expressions, where the original meaning was least likely to be transmitted.

Exegetical traditions relating to more frequent words are rare. One example relates to תחש at Exod. 25:5 and thereafter, which originally indicated a porpoise or some other animal but is rendered by P=T^OJN as ܤܣܓܘܢܐ 'many-coloured', following a tradition confirmed in the Talmud (TB Shabb. 28a) and echoed also in LXX ὑακίνθα.[93] Similarly, Heb. מורא of the terrors that accompanied the Exodus is instead rendered ܚܙܘܐ or ܚܙܘܢܐ "sight, spectacle", as if from ראה, in both P and T^OJP,[94] and similarly in LXX. The instances occur at Deut. 4:34, 26:8, 34:12; apparently the meaning "sight(s)" better fitted the preceding mention of "signs and wonders" in the first of these passages. In such cases, both the Targums and P depend on post-biblical reflection on the meaning because the original sense was lost.

---

[91] This dependence on tradition was cleverly demonstrated by Hillel to a new proselyte who asked to be taught the Written Torah but not the Oral: Hillel taught him the alphabet in correct order but at the next day's lesson reversed it, showing the teacher's oral input to be indispensable (TB Shab 31a). Whether *everything* that Hillel viewed as Oral Law is essential for an understanding of the Hebrew Bible is a separate issue.

[92] For further examples, see J.A. Emerton, "Unclean Birds and the Origin of the Peshitta", *JSS* 7 (1962), pp. 204–11.   [93] At Ezek. 16:10, however, P guesses ܡܣܢܐ 'shoes' from the context.

[94] LXX likewise has the plurals ὁράματα or θαυμάσια.

Most examples, however, are confined to single passages:

Gen. 2:8 MT מקדם, P=T^ON R ܡܢ ܩܕܝܡ "of old" following the tradition that Paradise was created before the world; cf. T^J קדם ברית עולם "before the creation of the universe".

Gen. 15:10 MT בְּתָוֶךְ, P ܒܫܘܝܐܝܬ, T^O בשוי:: T^JFN

Gen. 24:21 MT משתאה לה, P ܫܬܐ ܘܡܬܒܩܐ ܒܗ, cf. T^N שתי ומסתכל בה[95]
Both translations share a tradition to offer two alternative renderings, based on the roots שתה 'drink' and שאה 'gaze'.

Gen. 27:3 MT תליך, P= T^O ܣܝܦܟ

Gen. 30:8 MT נפתולי אלהים נפתלתי
P ܒܥܝܬ ܡܢ ܡܪܝܐ ܘܐܬܟܫܦܬ "I entreated the Lord and supplicated". T^OJPN likewise speak of prayer, connecting with Heb. התפלל 'pray', though the wording varies, e.g. T^O קביל בעותי י׳ בצלותי.

Gen. 30:28 MT נקבה, P ܦܘܪܫ T^O R :: T^JPN

Gen. 30:42 MT עטפים... קשרים, P=T^OJPN R ܠܩܝܫܝܐ... ܒܟܝܪܐ

Gen. 32:21 MT אכפרה פניו, P=T^O ܐܢܘܚ ܪܘܓܙܗ :: T^JPN

Gen. 38:14 MT בפתח עינים
P ܒܦܪܫܘܬ ܐܘܪܚܬܐ ,cf. T^J[N] בפרשת אורחין
T^O agrees partially: בפרשות עינים.

Gen. 47:21 MT לערים
P=T^ON ܡܢ ܩܪܝܐ ܠܩܪܝܐ "(Joseph moved the people) from city to city":: T^JF

Gen. 49:6 MT אל תחד כבדי, P=T^O ܠܐ ܢܚܘܬ ܡܢ ܐܝܩܪܝ, :: T^JFPN

Gen. 49:21 MT אילה שלוחה
P ܐܝܓܪܐ ܩܠܝܠܐ "(Naphtali is) a swift messenger" =T^JF R :: T^O

Exod. 1:12 MT יפרץ, P=T^OJN ܬܩܝܦܝܢ ܗܘܘ

Exod. 4:16 MT לפה, P=T^OJFN R ܡܬܪܓܡܢܐ

Exod. 21:19 MT ורפא ירפא, P=T^OJN R ܘܐܓܪ ܐܣܝܐ [ܢܬܠ]

Exod. 31:4 MT לחשב מחשבת "to invent designs"
P ܠܡܠܦܘ ܐܘܡܢܘܬܐ "to teach craft", cf. T^O[N] ...לאלפא
These renderings apparently reflect Exod. 35:34, where Bezalel has the gift להורת 'to teach'. The phrase לחשב מחשבת recurs at Exod. 35:32, where, however, P renders literally, presumably to avoid duplication with the reference two verses later to Bezalel's teaching ability.[96]

Exod. 32:25 MT לשמצה בקמיהם
P ܕܢܗܘܘܢ ܫܡܐ ܣܪܝܐ [7a1 ܒܫܪܒܬܐ] ܒܐܚܪܝܬܗܘܢ

to be a stinking name in their posterity

T^OFJN =R לדריהון, interpreting as ". . . a stinking name for those that would come after them" (cf. Deut. 29:21).

Exod. 38:8 MT צָבְאוּ, P=T^OJ ܕܐܬܝܢ ܠܡܨܠܝܘ :: T^F; cf. T^N דהוון מצליין

Lev. 5:21 MT תשומת יד, P=T^OJ ܒܫܘܬܦܘܬܐ ܕܐܝܕܐ::T^N

[95] A similar doublet occurs in T^O; see Maori, *Peshitta version of the Pentateuch*, p. 114.

[96] T^ON have 'teach' in both passages. T^J is literal at Exod. 31:4 but has לאלפא at Exod. 35:32.

Lev. 13:55 MT בקרחתו או בגבחתו
P ܒܚܕܬܘܬܗ ܐܘ ܒܒܠܝܘܬܗ

in its [the garment's] new state or worn state

Compare (albeit in reverse order) $T^{O}R$: בשחיקותיה או בחדתותיה,
T^{N} בבליותיה (בבליותיה ?) או בחדתותיה

Lev. 17:7 MT לשעירים, P ܠܫܐ̈ܕܐ, $T^{O[JN]}R$ לשידין
compare Sifra: ואין שעירים אלא שדים

Lev. 23:40 MT פרי עץ הדר, P=$T^{OJFPN}R$ add ܐܬܪ̈ܘܓܐ 'citrons', the halachic interpretation.

Num. 5:28 MT ונזרעה זרע, P ܘܬܩܒܠ ܙܪܥܐ, cf. $T^{J[N]}R$ ותתעבר בבר דכר

Num. 7:3 צב (שש עגלות), P ܟܒ̈ ܡܛܝ̈ܒܢ = $T^{J}R$[97]

Num. 19:15 MT אין צמיד פתיל עליו, P ܠܐ ܗܘܐ ܫܝܥ "was not smeared"; $T^{OFN}R$ (but not T^{J}) – though longer – have the same word.

Num. 21:18 וממדבר מתנה, P=$T^{OFJN}R$ ܘܡܢ ܡܕܒܪܐ ܐܬܝܗܒܬ ܠܗܘܢ ܒܡܬܢܐ "and from the wilderness it was given them at MTNH". The Targums agree with P, except that T^{O} lacks the last word, T^{J} has למתנה and T^{FN} have מתנה. All allude to the tradition of the well given to accompany the Israelites throughout their wanderings; cf. 1 Cor. 10:4. However, the elements מתנה, נחליאל and במות in verses 18–19, which P takes as toponyms, are interpreted in the Targums to mean that the well was a gift which accompanied them even to the valleys and mountains.[98]

Num. 21:28 MT בעלי, P=T^{OJF} ܦܠܚ̈ܝ :: T^{N} מדבחין

Num. 24:24 MT וצים מיד כתים
P ܘܠܓܝ̈ܘܢܐ ܢܦܩܘܢ ܡܢ ܐܪܥܐ ܕܟܬ̈ܝܐ
T^{FN} have the same word לגיונין, as well as אוכלוסין, and state at length that hordes will come forth from Rome, accompanied by many legions. T^{O} (סיען) and T^{J} (אוכלוסין) show general agreement.

Deut. 6:5 MT ובכל מאדך, P ܘܡܢ ܟܠܗ ܩܢܝܢܟ, cf. $T^{O[JN]}$ ובכל נכסך

Deut. 17:8 MT יפלא, P=T^{FN} (+ some editions of T^{O}) ܢܬܟܣܐ :: T^{J}

Deut. 21:4 MT (נחל) איתן, P=T^{OJN} ܒܘܪܐ 'untilled'

Deut. 21:23 MT כי קללת אלהים תלוי
P ܡܛܠ ܕܟܠ ܕܡܨܚܐ ܠܐܠܗܐ ܢܙܕܩܦ

for he that reviles God shall be hanged

$T^{O[J]}$ ארי על דחב קדם ה׳ אצטליב
P agrees with T^{O}in referring קללת to the condemned man's crime. However, P defines that crime as blasphemy, while T^{O} is utterly vague. The direct source of each was probably an exegetical tradition, reflected also in Symmachus (βλασφημίαν); Sifre *ad loc* likewise sees here a particular reference to blasphemy and paraphrases: מגדף.

[97] This results from the understanding of the root יצב as ܛܝܒ 'prepare', in both P and the Targums, as noted above.

[98] Isenberg curiously denies that the agreement could be due to shared aggadic tradition, and concludes that P is "stemmatically related" to the Palestinian Targums. See S.R. Isenberg, "On the Jewish-Palestinian Origins of the Peshitta to the Pentateuch", *JBL* 90 (1971), pp. 69–81; see p. 71.

Deut. 29:18　MT והתברך, P=T⁰ ܢܬܒܪܟ :: Tᴶᴺ

Deut. 32:11　MT אברתו, P ܘܐܝܟ ܕܓܦܘܗܝ, T⁰ᶠᴺ אברוהי תקוף (deriving the Hebrew alternatively from אביר 'strong' and אברה 'pinion'); Tᴶ also has both elements but in separate phrases.

Deut. 32:15　MT שמנת עבית כשית

P ܘܐܬܟܣܝ ܘܐܬܡܠܝ ܫܡܢ, T⁰[ᴺ] נכסין קנא תקוף אצלח

Note that T⁰ abandons the figure from the first, while P retains it for the first word.

Deut. 32:17　MT באו, P=T⁰ᴶ ܐܬܘ̈ܢ :: Tᶠᴺ

Deut. 32:36　MT ואפס עצור ועזוב, P ܘܣܠܝܩ ܘܬܪܝܨܐ ܘܪܓܡܐ, cf. Tᶠᴺ[ᴾ] דסעד וסמיך..

Common identification of place names also betokens common exegetical tradition, e.g.

Gen. 10:14　MT כפתרים, P=T⁰ᴶᶠᴺᴳR ܩܦܘܕܩܝܐ 'Cappadocians'. The link may be through the name כפתור, found in Genesis Apocryphon XXI.23 (on Gen. 14:1) to indicate Elassar in Asia Minor.[99]

Gen. 14:7　MT חצצון תמר, P=T ܥܝܢ ܓܕܝ En-Gedi. This rests on 2 Chr. 20:2 – בחצצון תמר היא עין גדי

The frequent substitution of *Matni/an* for Bashan, in both P and T⁰ (with support from other Targums), also suggests common tradition; given its distant eastern location, P is unlikely to have been independently aware of the Aramaic name for this biblical district.[100]

Occasionally these shared traditions departed from the vocalisation of MT:

Deut. 13:7　MT אשת חקך "(the wife of) your bosom", P=T⁰ ܩܝܡܟ "your covenant", as if vocalising חֻקְּךָ , to emphasise the legal rather than the physical aspect of marriage (::Tᴶᶠᴺ).

Deut. 28:54　MT again אשת חיקו; P=T⁰ render likewise (:: Tᴶᴺ); Tᶠ טליותיה avoids literal translation in a different way.

Deut. 33:2　MT וְאָתָה, P=T⁰ᴶᶠ ועמיה (vocalising Hebrew as וְאִתּֽה)

Deut. 34:7　MT לֵחֹה, P ܦܟܗ, 'his cheeks (had not shrunk)', Tᴶ=R ניבי לסתיה 'his cheek teeth (had not fallen)', both based on Heb. לְחָיִים (:: T⁰ᶠᴾᴺ)

There is no difficulty in positing traditions of understanding based on a vocalisation differing from MT, for such are also known elsewhere. An example is the understanding shared by LXX and the Jewish Passover eve liturgy (the Haggadah) of Isa. 63:8–9:

MT　　ויהי להם למושיע: בכל צרתם לו[101] צר ומלאך פניו הושיעם

> and he became for them as a saviour. In all their troubles, he was troubled, and the angel of his face saved them

LXX　　καὶ ἐγένετο αὐτοῖς εἰς σωτηρίαν ἐκ πάσης θλίψεως. οὐ πρέσβυς οὐδὲ ἄγγελος, ἀλλ᾿ αὐτὸς κύριος ἔσωσεν αὐτούς...

> and he became for them for salvation from all trouble. Neither an envoy nor an angel (*or* messenger), but the Lord himself saved them . . .

---

[99] N. Avigad and Y. Yadin (eds.), *A Genesis Apocryphon*, Jerusalem 1956, p. 34.

[100] In P, Bashan is so identified in all passages in Numbers (3x), and in most passages in Deuteronomy (15x), Joshua (13x) and Chronicles (5x). For further occurrences see Jer. 50:19 (but not 22:20) and Mic. 7:14 Nah. 1:4 (but not Zech. 11:2).　　[101] So Qere; Kethib has לא.

cf. Haggadah   And the Lord brought us out of Egypt, not through an angel, nor through a
seraph, nor through a messenger, but the Holy One, blessed be he, in his glory
and in himself . . .[102]

Unlike MT, both LXX and the Haggadah have the verse-break after צתרם; thereafter
they have לא rather than לו, vocalise צָר 'messenger' rather than צַר 'he was troubled'
(so MT), and take פניו as *ipse* (2 Sam. 17:11).[103]

Exegetical traditions emanate from scholars who sought to resolve difficulties in the
biblical text, or to read lessons into it. Their original language, at least to judge both
from rabbinic literature and the Qumran commentaries, was normally Hebrew; but
many if not most probably reached P's translators in Aramaic guise.

In theory, all these agreements between P and one or more Targums could be
ascribed to literary dependence. However, there is no need: common dependence in the
relevant passages on a tradition of biblical scholarship in Aramaic/Syriac would
suffice. This is the more economical explanation; moreover, there is no evidence – as we
shall see – of specifically literary dependence upon the written text of a continuous
Targum.

Translational traditions

We also find shared renderings in passages where the primary problem was one of
expression rather than understanding. They appear to go back to traditions that arose
specifically among translators into Aramaic/Syriac.

A subtle but striking example at Gen. 35:22 is pointed out by Maori. In the reference
to Reuben and his step-mother Bilhah, P chooses a Syriac form close to the Hebrew
וישכב, namely ܘܫܟܒ. The normal rendering in this sense P would have been ܓܢܐܥܡܗ. T[N]
comes even closer to the Hebrew, writing וישכב and so leaving the word untranslated.
Maori notes that both P and T[N] reflect the ruling for translators in Mishna Megilla
4:10, that this passage is not to be translated but only read.

Some translational traditions arose from linguistic differences between Hebrew and
Aramaic/Syriac. A neat resolution worked out by one translator might be passed on, as
at Exod. 14:25 –

וינהגהו בכבדות MT

and he (God) made them (the Egyptians) drive it (their chariotry) in heaviness

P=T[O] ܘܗܘܘ ܕܒܪܝܢ ܠܗܘܢ ܒܩܛܝܪܐ

and they were driving them (the chariots) by force

Since the causative Hebrew construction would have been cumbersome in Aramaic, a
simpler construction was produced, in which the Egyptians became the subject.[104]

Other translational traditions common to P and the Targums reflect common
concern to avoid anthropomorphisms. Hence the phraseology common both to P and

---

[102] An exposition of Exod. 12:12. This part of the Haggadah is thought to derive from Mekhilta Bo 7, which
has: "not through an angel or a messenger" but lacks the element *ipse*.
[103] P resembles MT, except in reading לא and rendering: "he did not oppress them".
[104] For a somewhat different view, see Maori, *Peshitta version of the Pentateuch*, pp. 310–11.

the Targums to distance man from God, e.g. through the addition of *qdām* when God would otherwise be the direct object, or though the statement that God "revealed himself over" those to whom, in MT, he simply appears.[105] Other examples are:

Gen. 24:40   MT התהלכתי "I walked (before God)", P=T^OJN ܦܠܚܬ "I served"

Gen. 32:31   MT "(I have seen) God", P=T^OJN ܡܠܐܟܐ "an angel" (plural in T^JN)
               Likewise at Gen. 32:29 (P=T^JPN::T^O) and 33:10 (P=T^JN::T^O), MT has '(wrestled with) God' but P renders: 'an angel' and the Targums cited (apart from T^O) have 'angels'.

Gen. 44:16   MT האלהים מצא את עון עבדיך

               God has discovered the sin of your servants

               P=T^OJP ܡܢ ܩܕܡ ܐܠܗܐ ܐܫܬܟܚ ܚܛܗܐ ܕܥܒܕܝܟ[106]

               from before God sin has been discovered unto your servants

               This rendering maintains divine omniscience; God needs no discoveries.

Num. 16:22   MT "will you be angry?", P=T^OJN ܢܗܘܐ ܪܘܓܙܐ "will there be anger?"

Deut. 1:33   MT "(of God) to spy out (a camping place for you) ", P=T^OJN ܠܡܬܩܢ "to prepare", since God needs no reconnaissance

Deut. 32:4   MT (of God) "rock", P= T^OF ܬܩܝܦܐ 'mighty'

Conversely, אלהים in relation to heathen gods is replaced by a contemptuous term, though P and the Targums differ in choice: ܕܚܠܬܐ 'objects of fear' in P but טעוותא 'errors' in T^OJ.[107] Likewise at Gen. 30:27, P imputes no success to heathen practices: Laban is made to discover God's blessing of Jacob not through divination (MT נחשתי) but by mental effort (ܒܣܘܡ = T^ONR :: T^JFP).

    A rarer shared theological motive which affected expression rather than understanding was to avoid the term 'chosen', which had encouraged sectarian division:[108]

Exod. 19:5   MT סגלה   P=T^OJFPNR ܚܒܝܒ (though T^FPN add היך סגולה)
Deut. 7:6   MT עם סגלה   P=T^OJNR ܥܡܐ ܚܒܝܒܐ (though T^N adds היך סגולה)
So also at Deut. 14:2, 26:18.

Combination of exegetical and translational traditions

In many cases – perhaps most – where P agrees in sense with one or more Targums, it also agrees in wording. No doubt the ultimate source of such agreement is an exegetical tradition, which may or may not appear in rabbinic sources. It has been argued that both P and the relevant Targum(s) draw directly and independently upon that pre-existing exegetical tradition.[109] This implies that the agreement in exact wording – as opposed to content – is coincidental. Another possibility, however, is that the exegetical tradition was followed by a translational tradition which recommended the proper Aramaic wording to express that sense; and that the latter tradition is the direct source

[105] S.P. Brock, "A Palestinian Targum Feature in Syriac", *JJS* 46 (1995), pp. 271–82.
[106] So substantially T^N also:...מן קדם י' ארעת חובתהון "from before the Lord their sin has come to light".
[107] So Exod. 12:12 22:19 23:13 etc.
[108] M.P. Weitzman, 'העם הנבחר: הופעתו והעלמותו' ("Usage and Avoidance of the Term 'Chosen People'"), *Language Studies* (Jerusalem) 4, 1990, pp. xv–xvi, 101–28.
[109] This case is argued by Maori, *Peshitta version of the Pentateuch*, pp. 298–9.

on which both P and the Targum(s) both depend. Altogether, the agreement would thus be due to a combination of two traditions: exegetical and translational. This seems better as a general explanation, since coincidence could not convincingly explain the sheer number of agreements in exact wording as well as content. Many of the cases considered above, where P and one or more Targums agree in wording as well as sense, therefore probably belong in this combined category.

The usual result was that P conveyed the sense of the exegetical tradition, through the traditional wording. One or two cases are worth noting, however, where the translator adopted the wording but probably failed to convey the underlying exegetical sense. Thus at Exod. 30:8, the time for lighting the candelabrum is specified as בין הערבים. T^O apparently took this phrase in its natural sense: "at twilight", for he writes בין שמשיא, cognate with Heb. בין השמשות.[110] Following this translational tradition, P wrote ܒܝܬ ܫܡܫܐ, though the meaning of this expression – apparently unique in Syriac – may not have been clear to P's audience.

P's rendering of Hebrew ימים in the sense 'year' seems a similar case. There was an exegetical tradition which took it to mean one year exactly to the day. Exact reckoning of time was indicated in Hebrew by מעת לעת; this often indicates an exact day, but at TB Ar. 18b it is used of exact years. The same expression ('from time to time'), rendered directly into Aramaic/Syriac, became the traditional equivalent for ימים, as at Num. 9:22 –

MT   או יֹמַיִם או חֹדֶשׁ או יָמִים

P=T^O   ܐܘ ܡܥܕܢ ܐܘ ܝܪܚܐ ܐܘ ܠܥܕܢ ܝܘܡܝܢ :: T^JN;

The same rendering appears at Gen. 24:55 (P [ms 5b1 only] = T^O:: T^JN) and similarly in P=T^OJ:: T^N at Lev. 25:29. The agreement can hardly be ascribed simply to exegetical tradition, i.e. to shared understanding of the Hebrew as an exact year; for this expression ("from time to time") is unlikely to have conveyed that specific sense – or perhaps any sense – to Syriac speakers, especially where the context gave no indication that a year rather than any other period was meant. Rather, it seems that the exegetical tradition was followed by a translational tradition, which fixed the Aramaic equivalent as "from time to time"), and was adopted by P.

The cases just considered are, however, exceptional. In most passages where the parallel between P and the Targums may reasonably be ascribed to common dependence on a combination of exegetical and translational traditions, the sense of the former as well as the wording of the latter were conveyed clearly to P's readership.

The life-setting of the traditions

Exegetical traditions may fittingly be located in the house of study, where scholars strove to understand the biblical text. By contrast, translational traditions rather suggest an origin in the synagogue, where the Hebrew lections were publicly rendered

---

[110] This is the plain sense (as Ibn Ezra carefully shows in his comment on Exod. 12:6), whereas the rabbis took the phrase to denote the period from half an hour after midday until sunset. The rabbis were concerned that this phrase at Exod. 12:6 defines the time of the Passover sacrifice, for which the period of twilight would be too brief (see Mishnah Pes. 5:1). Finding this intepretation too cumbersome to incorporate in his translation, T^O falls back on the plain sense. For a different view of T^O's procedure, see L. Ginzberg, על הלכה ואגדה: מחקר ומסה, Tel Aviv 1960, p. 102.

into Aramaic. This rendering was originally delivered *ex tempore*; thus Mishnah Meg. 4:4 required the text of the Pentateuch to be read one verse at a time, to avoid straining the translator's memory. The first stage towards fixed Aramaic versions occurred, we may surmise, when translators exchanged solutions to problematic expressions in the text and so began to build up a fund of recommended renderings of individual phrases. Thus the translational traditions, like the exegetical, were originally discrete, and did not yet form a continuous version.

We may suppose that this fund of tradition continued to circulate orally. The fact that translators were free, but not obliged, to draw upon it explains the varied allegiances – T^O now agreeing with the Palestinian Targums and now disagreeing, and P on different occasions agreeing with either, both or neither. In particular, Aramaic renderings of particular biblical phrases continued to circulate orally until well into the Middle Ages, even after continuous written Targums emerged. Such Aramaic renderings are often quoted in rabbinic literature, and cannot all have been drawn from the written Targums, if only because they sometimes differ from all such Targums.[111]

Concluding remarks

The renderings shared between P and the Targums yield clear sense. They are almost invariably consistent with the Massoretic vocalisation. Many recur in outside sources, as noted in detail above. It is for these reasons that common tradition is an acceptable explanation for these parallels, unlike most of the parallels between P and LXX.

It may of course happen that a common tradition is not transmitted with equal fidelity by P and the Targums. Thus at Num. 21:18 above, the allusion to the gift of the well is fuller in the Targums than in P. The converse occurs at Gen. 38:5. Here MT records that Judah's wife bore his third son, and adds: "and he (or it) was in Kezib (ובכזיב)", which P renders ܐܦܣܩܬ ܗܘܐ "and she ceased". P follows a tradition found also in Gen.R. 85.4 – which derives כזיב from the root כזב 'be false, cease', sometimes used of failing waters (Is 58:11, cf. Jer. 15:18), since this was the woman's last child. On this interpretation, the Hebrew literally meant "it was in cessation". Some other Jewish scholars knew the rendering *pesqat*, but erroneously combined it with the literal meaning of the Hebrew text ("and it was in Kezib"), and so concluded that Pesqat was an alternative name for Kezib. Thus T^J writes והוה בפסקת, and one Fragment-Targum manuscript (L) has similarly והוות בפסקת. It is true that other Palestinian Targum witnesses instead have a verb form. Specifically, T^N has והוה דפסקת; among manuscripts of the Fragment Targum, V agrees with T^N; and others have והוה במפסקא (ms P), and והות דפסקא (ms N). However, these verb forms seem to be *ad hoc* emendations by individual scribes who sensed a flaw in the tradition of the toponym Pesqat. Only P preserves the tradition clearly.

Finally, as will be discussed below, P shows acquaintance with some interpretations that crop up in the rabbinic sources and *not* in any known Targum. The hypothesis of literary dependence on the Targums does not explain this evidence. The alternative

---

[111] M.H. Goshen-Gottstein, *Fragments of Lost Targumim* (Hebrew with English introduction), vols. 1–2 (Ramat-Gan 1983–89).

hypothesis of common dependence on traditions attached to individual passages better accounts for these; it assumes less and yet explains more.

Alleged direct evidence for the literary dependence of P upon the Targums

The parallels between P and the extant Targums on the Torah are impressive both in quantity and in quality. However, as we saw in relation to LXX, there are only two types of case that prove literary dependence of P upon another version: first, where P misread or misunderstood the written text of that version; and second, where P inextricably combined elements from the Hebrew and from that version. Cases of the former type have been adduced as evidence of P's dependence on the Targums, but none seem convincing.

One passage that has been adduced is Exod. 8:5 –

MT	התפאר עלי (למתי אעתיר לך...)	glorify yourself over me; (when should I pray..?)
T^O	שאל לך גבורא הב לי זמן	ask for yourself a mighty act; give me a time
P	ܫܐܠ ܠܟ ܙܒܢ ܘܗܒ	ask for yourself a time
LXX	τάξαι πρός με (πότε εὔξωμαι...)	appoint for me (when I should pray . . .)

In MT, Moses addresses Pharaoh in courtly language before asking when he should pray for the plague of frogs to end. P gives straightforward sense, removing the formal introduction. T^O is longer, falling into two phrases. Silverstone claimed that P's translation could not have been derived from the Hebrew, and is "manifestly based on Onkelos" (p. 133), which P has abridged. One could equally argue, however, that P reproduces directly a traditional understanding of the text, echoed also in LXX. This tradition, we could suppose, took התפאר עלי as a mere formula, and replaced it with a substantive meaning ('ask') derived from the following interrogative: למתי. T^O then depends likewise on this exegetical tradition, but adds a phrase in order to relate this verse to the "tests" which according to Deut. 4:34 accompanied the Exodus: God was challenged to perform the mighty act (גבורא) of removing the plague at a time of Pharaoh's choosing. This exegesis is mentioned also in Rashi's comment on the latter verse:

במסות: על ידי נסיונות הודיעם גבורותיו, כגון "התפאר עלי" אם אוכל לעשות כן הרי זה נסיון.

Silverstone also considered that P misread T^O at Exod. 32:18, where Joshua hears the Israelites worshipping the golden calf:

MT (אנכי שמע) קול ענות, T^O קל דמחייכין, P ܩܠ ܕܚܛܝܬܐ 'sound of sin'

According to Silverstone (p. 136), P misread T^O מחייכין 'revellers' as מחייבין 'sinners'. Other explanations, however, are at least as likely. Perhaps the translator scanned the succeeding verses for some clue to the obscure Hebrew, and alighted on Moses' rebuke, three verses later, that Aaron had brought upon Israel great sin (P: ܚܛܝܬܐ, the same word as in v.18).[112] Again, perhaps he 'misread' ענות as עונות "iniquities", or even found this reading in his Hebrew *Vorlage*; it is firmly attested in the Samaritan tradition.[113]

---

[112] This technique of guesswork from another verse was discussed in chapter 2 above.

[113] Aram: חובין. The Samaritan reading in Greek guise is ἁμαρτιῶν; see F. Field, *Origenis Hexaplorum quae supersunt*, Oxford 1867–74, ad loc. Compare Symmachus (apud Syrohex) ܕܚܛܝܬܐ.

Again, Baumstark[114] supposed that P at Exod. 2:18 resulted from misreading of an alleged Palestinian Aramaic prototype, which agreed with Palestinian Targums extant today:

MT מהרתן בא, T^OJN^ אוחיתון למיתי "you hastened to come"

P ܐܫܩܝܬܝܢ ܒܥܓܠ "you quickly gave drink"

According to Baumstark, the copy of the Targum used by P was itself written in Estrangelo script; in the second word (ܠܡܐܬܝ), P mistook *y* (ܝ) for *sh*(ܫ), and interpreted the resulting ܠܡܫܬܝ as 'to give drink' (even though it in fact means 'to drink'; the causative requires a different root). A far easier explanation, however, is that the text of P is corrupt, for an original ܐܬܝܬܝܢ 'you have come'; an early copyist was distracted by the form ܐܫܩܝ which occurs in both the previous and the following verses (for וישק).

The Targums and non-standard Syriac texts in the Torah

In a few passages, a parallel to a rendering in one or more Targums has been detected in some 'non-standard' form of the biblical text in Syriac, i.e. a form other than the majority text of the mss of P. These Syriac renderings have been said to attest the putative Aramaic Targum from which P derives, or, as Vööbus puts it, "eine noch wesentlich targumnähere Schicht". The term 'non-standard' is here used for convenience only, without implying that the 'standard' text need be superior and without any connection with the question (discussed in chapter 6) of the emergence of a 'standard text' in the medieval history of P.

Parallels with the Targum in single manuscripts of P

Where the biblical mss of P are divided, one of the rival readings may agree with a Targum. The significance of that agreement depends on whether that reading also stands close to MT.

In cases where one of the rival readings of the P mss agrees not only with a Targum but also simultaneously with MT, it may be that that Syriac reading is the original text of P, e.g. at Deut. 32:30 –

MT איכה ירדף אחד אלף

P (9a1) ܐܝܟܢ ܪܕܦ ܗܘܐ ܚܕ ܠܐܠܦܐ

P (rell.) ܪܕܦ ܗܘܐ ܚܕ ܠܐܠܦܐ

Here, as often, the reading in 9a1 – albeit confined to a single ms – seems the original text of P. The majority text arose because of the ambiguity of the previous verse (v.29):

P ܐܠܘ ܚܟܡܘ ܘܐܣܬܟܠܘ ܒܗܕܐ ܘܐܬܒܝܢܘ ܒܚܪܬܗܘܢ

We may surmise that v.29 was intended to be self-contained: either ܐܠܘ was a conditional particle with the apodosis introduced by the conjunction *waw* ("if they were wise, they would understand . . ."),[115] or it expressed a wish ("if only they were wise and understood . . ."). The majority text, however, reflects an understanding of v.29 as one

[114] Baumstark, "Pešiṭta und palästinensisches Targum", p. 268.

[115] This common Semitic construction appears also in the Old Syriac Gospels; see F.C. Burkitt, *Evangelion da-Mepharreshe*, Cambridge 1904, vol. 2, pp. 69–74. For the uncompounded perfect in each clause, cf. P at Judg. 8:19. The resulting sense ("if they were wise, they would understand this . . .") is widely supported, e.g. by T^O^, RSV.

long protasis: "If they were wise and appreciated this and understood their end . . .". Verse 30 then had to become an apodosis, incompatible with the interrogative ܐܠܘ. That interrogative, preserved in 9a1, is a straightforward rendering of the Hebrew. There is nothing to suggest that it was instead derived from a Targum – even though an interrogative naturally appears also in the Targums, e.g. T°איכדין; it approximates to the Targums only inasmuch as these too reflect the Hebrew.[116] The category of passages where the true reading survives in a single manuscript – most often 9a1 – will be discussed in detail in chapter 6. At all events, the agreement of a variant reading with a Targum is no evidence that P is a re-worked transcription of an older Aramaic version, where that variant agrees at the same time with MT.

The case is different when the variant reading which agrees with the Targum is *not* the variant that stands closer to MT. In such cases – or at least in those cited by Vööbus – it seems that the variant which agrees with MT represents the translator's original work, which, however, happened closely to imitate the Hebrew form. The rival reading arose from adaptation to Aramaic/Syriac idiom, which brought it into agreement with a Targum – especially a Palestinian Targum – that had not attempted to hew so close to the Hebrew in the first place. An example relates to the Hebrew expression השיב נקם at Deut. 32:41,43. In MT, this is construed with the preposition *l-*, duly reflected in many mss of P. Other Syriac mss, however, instead have *'al*, obtaining the more vigorous expression "repay vengeance *upon* (enemies)". That T^N too prefers this preposition betokens no more than shared idiomatic sense; the Syriac reading need not have been inherited from Targum tradition.[117]

Parallels with the Targum in daughter-versions of P

A similar process accounts for cases where one or more Targums agree with a daughter-version made from the Syriac. It has sometimes instead been argued that in these agreements the daughter-version preserves the original text of P, which stood close to the Targums.

We may consider, for example, two passages in Deut. 32 where Vööbus found evidence of P's alleged "Targumisches Profil":[118]

(a) Deut. 32:4   MT ואין עול   P ܘܠܐ ܗܘܐ ܥܘܠܐ

but T°ᴶ ולית קדמוי עוולא לא נפיק, Tᶠ דמן קדמוי שקר; Arab. وليس عنده ظلم[119]
While P reproduced the laconic Hebrew ("there is no wickedness"), both the Targum and the Arabic felt free to add a suffixed preposition: "before him" or "with him".

(b) Deut. 32:12 MT ינחנו (בדד) י'; so P ܘܐܬܟ [ܠܚܘܕܝܗܘܢ,] ܘܕܒܪ ܐܢܘܢ
T° עתיד לאשריותהון בעלמא די הוא עתיד לאתחדתא...

. . .will make them dwell in the world that will be renewed

Ar. وهداهم فى البرية "and he led them in the wilderness"[120]

---

[116] *Pace* Vööbus, *Peschitta und Targumim des Pentateuchs*, p. 82.
[117] *Pace* Vööbus, *Peschitta und Targumim des Pentateuchs*.   [118] Pp. 91, 93.
[119] P. de Lagarde, *Materialien zur Kritik und Geschichte des Pentateuchs*, Leipzig 1867, p. 226.
[120] De Lagarde, ibid.

The two latter versions agree only in providing a destination – lacking in P as in MT – for the verb ינחנו. These destinations, however, are utterly different: T^O takes the verb as future to make a theological point, while the Arabic retains P's past tense and thinks of the desert scene of v.10.

Most of the cases adduced where a non-standard form of the Syriac biblical text agrees with one or more Targums come from patristic citations. These will receive detailed discussion in appendix I to this chapter. We shall find, however, that they offer no support for the view that P is based on a Targum, rather than directly translated from a Hebrew text.

The relationship between P and the Targums in the Prophets

In the Prophets, occasional parallels between P and the Targum have been observed. Here again literary dependence has been posited,[121] but most of the parallels are easily ascribed to polygenesis, plus some instances of common tradition.

As before, lexical traditions may yield parallels like ܓܢܦܐ / גדנפין 'rims' for Heb. מסגרות (1 Kgs. 7:28 etc.). Again, differences between Hebrew and Aramaic may independently require the same adjustment in both P and the Targum, as at Josh. 7:24 –

MT   ...ואת בניו ...ואת הכסף... ויקח יהושע את עכן

Tg.   ...ודבר ית בנוהי...ונסיב ית כספא... ודבר יהושע ית עכן

P   ...ܘܕܒܪ ܠܒܢܘܗܝ ...ܘܢܣܒ ܠܣܐܡܐ... ܘܕܒܪ ܝܫܘܥ ܠܥܟܢ

The reason for the two inserted verbs *w-nsb . . .w-dbr* is simply that Aramaic idiom demands different verbs in the sense "take", depending on the object, as already noted in connection with the Pentateuch.

Again, both P and the Targum may make the same expansion for clarity, as at Isa. 5:21–

MT   בעיניהם (הוי חכמים)

P=Tg.   ܒܥܝܢܝ ܢܦܫܗܘܢ ..., '(woe to those who are wise) in their *own* eyes'

Here P and Tg. agree – without implying interdependence – in making explicit what was implicit in the Hebrew.

Both versions may improve on the logic of the Hebrew, as at 1 Sam. 12:15 –

MT   (the Lord's hand will be against you) and your fathers

P=Tg.   ܐܝܟ ܕܗܘܐ ܥܠ ܐܒܗܝܟܘܢ ... as it was against your fathers

Both translators perceived that the fathers could no longer be threatened.

Finally, both may arrive independently at the same guess at an obscure phrase from the context, as at Mal. 2:12 –

MT   יכרת י' לאיש אשר יעשנה ער וענה מאהלי יעקב

Let the Lord cut off [for] the man who does so . . . from the tents of Jacob

The words represented by dots are taken in both P and Tg. as: "his son and his son's son", which each could have guessed independently.

It is true that some other agreements betoken common origin. For those, however, common tradition is a sufficient explanation. The following are examples of exegetical tradition:

---

[121] C. Peters, "Zur Herkunft der Pešiṭta des ersten Samuel-buches", *Biblica* 22 (1941), pp. 25–34.

1 Sam. 2:22   Here, as at Exod. 38:8, Tg. and P agree in taking הצבאות as women who came to pray.

1 Sam. 21:3   MT מקום פלני אלמני, P ܐܬܪ ܟܣܐ ܘܛܡܝܪ, Tg. אתר כסי וטמיר. While in the Hebrew David is utterly vague, in P and Tg. he speaks of a hidden place. This translation apparently depends on פלא 'hide' (see Deut. 17:8 above) and אלם 'dumb'.[122]

1 Kgs. 1:38, 44 MT והכרתי והפלתי, P ܘܓܪܢܝ ܘܦܣܩܐ = Tg. וקשתיא וקלעיא. This interpretation recurs in P at 1 Chr. 18:17, but not in Samuel.

Isa. 7:2   MT נחה (ארם על אפרים). Both versions see in נחה the formation of an alliance: P ܐܬܚܝܕ, Tg. אתחבר (so also LXX συνεφώνησεν).[123]

Jer. 2:24   MT תאנתה, P=Tg. ܝܪܘܪܐ [אין], as if from תן 'jackal'

In addition, at Judg. 9:37, where MT has טבור (הארץ), P has an obscure form ܬܠܬܗ (ܐܪܥܐ). This is most easily explained as a corruption of ܬܘܩܦܐ, which would agree with תוקפא in the Targum.[124] As noted in chapter 2, the use of 'strength' as a guess for a difficult word is an old device among translators of the Bible into Aramaic, and here both P and Tg. seem to depend on a tradition which treated טבור in this way.

At Mal. 2:16, P and Tg. agree strikingly in inserting a negative, but common tradition is not the ideal explanation, since the sense quite differs:

MT   ובאשת נעוריך אל יבגד :כי שנא שלח... וכסה חמס על לבושו

Tg.   ובאיתת ינקותך לא תשקר: ארי אם סנית לה פטרה...ולא תכסי חטאה בלבושך[125]

> And do not betray the wife of your youth. But if you hate her, divorce her[126] . . .; and do not cover sin with your garment

P   ܘܠܐ ܢܟܕܒ ܒܐܢܬܬ ܛܠܝܘܬܗ ܠܐ ܘܢܟܣܐ

> (And let no man be false to the wife of his youth . . .) and let him not conceal the wicked (man) with his cloak

Tg.'s interpretation is that to retain a hated wife is to spread over her a garment of sin.[127] P, however, offers an altogether different sense: indeed the phrase כי שנא שלח, crucial to Tg.'s interpretation, is not represented in P at all. This difference counts against the hypothesis of common tradition. Instead, it may be that both translators inferred that 'covering violence with a garment' was something that the prophet intended to forbid; hence they independently inserted a negative – even though they interpreted the figure quite differently.

As before we find shared identifications of place names which betoken common tradition, e.g.

Josh. 13:11, 13a   MT מעבת, Tg. אפיקירוס, P ܣܘܦܣ
cf. Josh. 13:13b   MT מעבתי, Tg. אפיקירוס, P ܣܘܦܣܝܐ

---

[122] At 2 Kgs. 6:8, the same Hebrew phrase is rendered identically by Tg. but P is closer to MT: ܐܬܪܐ ܦܠܢ.

[123] This may in fact be a survival of the original sense; see O. Eissfeldt, *Kleine Schriften*, Tübingen 1962–8, vol. 3, pp. 124–8. On Isaiah, see further E.R. Rowlands, "The Targum and the Peshitta version of the Book of Isaiah", *VT* 9 (1959), pp. 178–91.

[124] J.M. Wilkie, "The Peshiṭta Translation of ṭabbûr ha-'areṣ in Judges ix 37", *VT* 1 (1951), p. 144, prefers to emend to ܬܘܢܐ 'chamber'.   [125] See further Gelston, *Twelve Prophets*, p. 189.

[126] R. Judah in TB Giṭ.90b interpreted the phrase likewise: אם שנאתה שלח.

[127] Inevitably the husband would constantly vex her, as Rashi comments on the Hebrew.

Here Tg. refers to Ἐπίκαιρος, one of the five cities "to the east of the river Jordan" mentioned by Ptolemy 5.16.9; P presents a corrupt form. This corruption need not imply mis-copying of a written text of the Targum; it could as easily have occurred in the transmission of a rendering through oral tradition.

1 Kgs. 1:33   MT גיחון (in Jerusalem), P=Tg. ܫܝܠܘܚܐ

Jer. 13:23   MT כושי 'Ethiopian', P ܗܢܕܘܝܐ 'Indian', agreeing with the rabbi Samuel that Heb. כוש bordered on India (TB Meg. 11a).

Obad. 20   MT ספרד, P ܐܣܦܡܝܐ 'Spain'

Some of the traditions encountered in the Torah continue here. Thus the מורא associated with the Exodus remains ܘܠܐ in P – like חזונא in Tg. – at Jer. 32:21. Traditions of place names also continue, such as ܬܠܓܐ for בשן (e.g. Josh. 13:11) or [ܘܐܟܪ] ܐܡܪ for קדש [ברנע] (e.g. Josh. 10:41). Likewise the translational tradition to call God 'mighty' rather than 'rock' reappears in P=Tg. at 1 Sam. 2:2. The combined tradition ܠܗ ܒܚ ܝ for ימים recurs in both versions at 1 Sam. 27:7 (not all Tg. witnesses) and 2 Sam. 14:26.[128]

Overall, however, parallels between P and the Targum are less frequent in these books than in the Torah. In the Latter Prophets, a principal reason is that figurative language is more frequent, and tends to be resolved in the Targum but retained in P. There is thus less evidence here than in the Pentateuch that might be adduced for the view that P is a mere transposition into Syriac of a Palestinian Aramaic prototype. On the basis of his study of Isaiah, Rowlands dismisses the case for a direct relationship between P and the Targum to the Prophets as "completely untenable".[129]

Recently, de Moor and Sepmeijer have suggested, in explanation of the parallels between the Targum and P in Joshua, that P had access to a written copy of the Targum. At the same time, they note many more passages in Joshua where P is independent of the Targum. They conclude that the translator must have been a convert from Judaism to Christianity, who would "make use of the Targum but feel the urge to conceal this fact".[130] So imaginative a hypothesis, however, becomes needless if one instead posits traditions of Aramaic renderings of particular phrases, which were available to P's translator here and there.

The relationship between P and the Targums in Proverbs

In most books of the Writings, parallels between P and the Targums are even less common than in the Prophets. Proverbs is exceptional in that the number and character of the parallels demonstrates literary dependence. It is the Targum, however, that is dependent upon P.[131] As Nöldeke argued, the mixture of Jewish Aramaic with Syriac found in the Targum betokens re-working of an older text, and the pure Syriac of P

---

[128] And also in P alone at Judg. 21:19; 1 Sam. 29:3, 2 Sam. 13:23. The equivalence in P also occurs at Judg. 11:40, where Tg. is similar: מזמן לזמן.

[129] Rowlands, "The Targum and the Peshitta version of the Book of Isaiah", p. 81.

[130] J.C. de Moor and F. Sepmeijer, "The Peshitta and the Targum of Joshua", MPI 8 (1995), pp. 129–76: see p. 174.

[131] Th. Nöldeke, "Das Targum zu den Sprüchen von der Peschita abhängig", *Archiv für Wissenschaftliche Erforschung des Alten Testamentes* II/2 (1872) 246–9. The same conclusion is reached in the detailed study by E.Z. Melammed, "The Targum on Proverbs" (in Hebrew), *Bar-Ilan Annual* 9 (1972), part 1, pp. 18–91.

must take precedence. Moreover, the Targum sometimes agrees with P in following LXX against MT, and that pattern can only derive from P, as at Prov. 7:22b –

MT   וכעכס אל מוסר אויל:

LXX   καὶ ὥσπερ κύων ἐπὶ δέσμους ἢ ὡς ἔλαφος...

    and like a dog in bonds, or like a hart (איל) . . .

P   ...ܐܝܟ ܐܝܟܐ ܕܠܒܐ ܠܐܣܘܪܐ. ܘܐܝܟ ܐܝܠܐ...

Tg.   והיך כלבא לאסורא: והיך אילא...

We must now explain how P could have been borrowed as the basis of a Jewish Targum. Here we must remember that the Targums on the Hagiographa, unlike the Targums on the Torah and Prophets, were of interest to private scholars only: they had no liturgical function nor any public status in the synagogue.

Two incidents relating to Hai Gaon (939–1038) help explain how some Jewish scholar may have come to adopt P as a basis for a Targum on Proverbs. First, we have a responsum from Hai to an enquiry whether the Targums to the Writings shared the origin (and status) of Targum Jonathan to the Prophets. Hai replies that the Targums "found with you" had no public status but were merely the work of private individuals (תרגום של הדיוטות). This is the earliest reference to the extant Targums of the Writings, though it is not clear to which books of the Writings (beyond Esther) Hai's enquirers possessed a Targum, and whether Hai knew them at first hand.[132]

In the second incident, Hai despatched an (albeit reluctant) colleague to consult the Nestorian Catholicos on an obscure phrase in the Writings (Ps.141:5b). The incident is recorded by Judah ben Jacob ibn Aknin, who preserves the citation from P quoted in answer by the Catholicos and reported back to Hai.[133] These incidents show Jewish demand in Hai's day for Aramaic versions of the Writings, and Jewish readiness to view biblical translation as common ground with the Church. It is in that atmosphere that the borrowing of P on Proverbs as a Jewish Targum can be envisaged.

Not surprisingly, the compiler of the Targum on Proverbs also consulted the Hebrew, which enabled him to fill gaps, to remove material not corresponding to the Hebrew, and to translate some verses independently. This stage accounts for the presence of some west-Aramaic elements, side by side with the east-Aramaic derived from P.

There is nothing in the text of the Targum to indicate that the borrowing took place before the Middle Ages.[134] Cases where the reading of the Targum could be viewed as earlier than that of the P mss are rare, and all can be explained on the supposition that the author of the Targum consulted the Hebrew directly,[135] e.g.

    25:20   MT נתר   P ܐܬܪ   Tg. נתרא

---

[132] In a responsum of Hai, edited by L. Ginzberg, *Genizah Studies*, vol. 2 (= *Texts and Studies of the Jewish Theological Seminary of America* 8), New York 1929, pp. 85–7.

[133] Joseph b. Judah b. Jacob ibn ʾAknin, התגלות הסודות והופעת המאורות, Arabic text edited and Hebrew translation by A.S. Halkin, Jerusalem 1964, p. 494.

[134] J.F. Healey, *The Targum of Proverbs* in *The Aramaic Bible*.Vol.15, Edinburgh 1991, surveys the history of this debate (pp. 1–11).

[135] *Pace* Melammed, who would occasionally emend P on the basis of Tg. (p. 89).

Is the Peshitta of Chronicles a Targum?

Agreements with rabbinic exegesis

In P-Chronicles, according to Nöldeke, the Syrians unknowingly preserved "a pure Jewish Targum".[136] His reasons were the many additions, paraphrases and (in his view) rabbinic interpretations found in P-Chronicles, as well as its avoidance of anthropomorphisms. This verdict was wholeheartedly endorsed in the detailed study by his disciple S. Fraenkel, who further adduced many instances where P-Chronicles agrees verbally with the Targum to parallel passages from Samuel and Kings.[137]

Closely echoing his teacher, Fraenkel characterises P-Chronicles as "ein reines und unverfälschtes jüdisches Targum". Some basic characteristics which he imputes to P-Chronicles are, however, wholly atypical of the Targums preserved by the Jews. According to Fraenkel, the translator had no more than a mediocre knowledge of Hebrew; he often supposed a vocalisation of the consonantal text which differed utterly from that of MT; and the *Vorlage* from which he worked was in many places defective, so that he often mistook the consonants and was sometimes forced to omit whole phrases or even lengthy sections.[138] All this suggests that P-Chronicles is not simply a Jewish Targum after all.

Certainly P-Chronicles shows a few striking parallels with rabbinic exegesis, notably:

(a)   2 Chr. 28:24

MT דלתות בית י' becomes "the inner and outer doors that were in the house of the Lord", agreeing with the report in Mishnah Mid. 4:1 that the Temple had two inner and two outer doors.

(b)   2 Chr. 33:6

The verb עונן becomes ܐܘܡ ܚܬܢܐ "close the eyes", agreeing with Sifre on Deut. 18:10 (see appendix II below).

(c) 2 Chr. 33:7

Here MT has פסל הסמל, while P has ܐܠܗܐ ܕܐܪܒܥ ܐܦܩ "four-faced image". As Perles already noticed (pp. 15–16), this reflects an item of Jewish exegesis recorded in TB Sanh. 103b:

R. Johanan said: At first he made it with one face, but subsequently he made it with four faces, so that the Shekhina might see it and be wroth.

This exegesis ingeniously reconciles the singular פסל in this verse with the plural פסילים in v.19. It is introduced: אמר ר' יוחנן, which seems to imply that it originated with R. Johanan, the third-century Palestinian Amora. However, much the same tradition turns up in 2 Baruch 64:3, a work for which a date *c.* 96 CE has recently been suggested:[139]

[136] Th. Nöldeke, *Die alttestamentliche Literatur*, Leipzig 1868, p. 264.
[137] S. Fraenkel, "Die syrische Uebersetzung zu den Büchern der Chronik", *Jahrbücher für protestantische Theologie* 5 (1879), pp. 508–36, 720–59.   [138] Fraenkel, pp. 508, 754–7.
[139] P-M Bogaert, *Apocalypse de Baruch* [=Sources Chrétiennes 144], Paris 1969, pp. 270–95.

And [Manasseh] made an image with five faces, four of them looking to the four winds, and the fifth upon the head of the image, as if against the zeal of the Almighty.

ܘܒܕ ܓܠܦ ܘܥܒܕ ܨܠܡܐ...

As this case well shows, the rabbi to whom a given interpretation is ascribed in the Talmud no doubt transmitted it but need not have invented it.

(d) An item of rabbinic knowledge which the translator overworked can be traced in Mishnah R.H. 3:3–4, which prescribes the blowing of a straight horn at the New Year and a curved horn on fastdays. One of the terms for horn is (whether straight or curved) is חצוצרה. Consequently, the translator of Chronicles parades the phrase 'straight and curved horns' to render not only חצוצרה (1 Chr. 15:28, 2 Chr. 15:14, 20:28, 23:13, 29:26, 28) but also the derivative verb (2 Chr. 7:6) and even חצר 'court-yard' at 1 Chr. 23:28.

Loose or expansive translation

Most of the so-called midrashic elements, however, find no parallel in rabbinic litera-ture, and are simply cases of loose (if sometimes ingenious) translation. Thus midrashic influence is often detected at 2 Chr. 35:23, where MT has וירו הירים למלך יאשיהו and P renders: "and Pharaoh the lame smote Josiah with two arrows". As Nöldeke observes, the two arrows were deduced from the twofold use of the root ירה. That deduction, however, is not *ipso facto* midrashic. The only interpreta-tion found in rabbinic literature (and ascribed in PT Qid. 1:7 to the second-century Rabbi Ishmael) of the repetition of ירה is that Josiah was struck by as many as 300 arrows. A variant, ascribed to later rabbis, speaks instead of 300 lances (לולינות) and adds that Josiah's body became "like a sieve" (TB Taan. 22b). The two arrows in P rather seem due to the translator's own speculation, which started out from the state-ment in 2 Kgs. 23:29 that Pharaoh Necho himself killed Josiah (וַיְמִיתֵהוּ). Hence the phrase וירו הירים could not mean that Josiah was killed by many archers, but instead had to signify the means used by Pharaoh; and from the twofold repetition, two arrows were inferred.

What is often considered a midrashic expansion[140] occurs at 1 Chr. 12:1 –

MT   ואלה הבאים אל דויד לציקלג עוד עצור מפני שאול בן קיש והמה בגבורים עזרי המלחמה

P   And these entered with David into ṢNQLG the city, when he was fleeing from before Saul son of Qish; and they were all standing in strength before David. And if he had wished, they could have killed Saul son of Qish, for they were mighty, and they were men who waged war; but David refused to let them kill Saul.

P writes first that David was fleeing from Saul and then that he restrained his men from slaying Saul. The whole episode indeed looks midrashic. In fact, however, P simply has an extended doublet, arising from two attempts to understand עצור. P first sets aside his lexical knowledge of the root עצר and instead guesses from the

---

[140] Most recently by P.B. Dirksen, in "Some Aspects of the Translation Technique in P-Chronicles" in MPI 8, pp. 17–23: see p. 18.

context, and especially from the following preposition מִפְּנֵי, the sense: "(he was) fleeing". He then goes back, trying to obtain suitable sense from the word itself, a part of עצר "restrain". This, with a glance at 1 Sam. 24:8, suggested that David restrained his followers from killing Saul. Confirming that we are dealing here with two attempts to translate the biblical text, rather than one attempt plus extraneous matter, Saul is twice called "son of Qish", and we likewise have two renderings of the phrase והמה בגבורים: first as ܩܘܡ̣ܘ ܟܠܕܝܐܬܐ ܡܫܪܝ ܗܘܐ and then as ܕܡܫܠܠ ܒܓܠܕ̈ܝ ܗܘܐ.

Although loose translations are undoubtedly frequent in P-Chronicles, the great majority of these show no affinity with rabbinic sources. In many cases, more seriously, they do not bear any semantic relation to MT, nor to any putative Hebrew text remotely resembling MT. In that sense they should not be described as translations at all, but rather as free composition. They suggest that in Chronicles the Hebrew *Vorlage* had suffered damage so extensive that the translator was often reduced to weaving sense round the few words or letters that he could read.

The hypothesis of a damaged *Vorlage* is not unlikely in itself, given the many omissions in P-Chronicles, some quite extensive. The omitted portions include 1 Chr. 2:23, 45, 47–9; 4:7–8, 34–7; 5:12b–13; 7:34–39a; 8:7–8, 15b-22, 26b-27; 16:6; 24:27–30a; 25:4b (from הנני); 2 Chr. 4:11–17,19–22; 27 5:12–13; 24:13–14; 25:22; 26:6c-8a; as well as many parts of verses.[141] These passages pose no particular intrinsic difficulty, and the reason for their omission may be damage to the *Vorlage*. The same hypothesis well explains the many places where P-Chronicles follows the Hebrew text of parallel passages in earlier books rather than the Hebrew of Chronicles itself; of these the most extensive is 2 Chr. 11:5–12:12, which has instead been supplied from 1 Kings 12–14. We have already encountered possible instances of a damaged *Vorlage* in other books, but the most extensive instances are in Chronicles and to a lesser extent in Wisdom.[142] The theory of a damaged *Vorlage* goes back to Fraenkel, who did not, however, exploit its potential to account for the many discrepancies in sense between MT and P in Chronicles.

The so-called loose translations in P-Chronicles thus differ in character from those in the Targums, where a semantic link with the original can normally be traced. The following examples of breakdown of semantic correspondence between P and the Hebrew illustrate this:

(a) 1 Chr. 4:33b

MT זאת מושבתם והתיחשם להם

P   These are the cities of their habitation, and they had a great name, and their habitation was goodly, and quiet and peace were about them

At first sight, P has rendered the line of Hebrew expansively. In fact, however, P's rendering represents the little that the translator could make out not only in this line but

---

[141] In addition, 1Chr. 26:13–27:34 is found in 7a1, 8a1 and 17e1 but omitted in the rest (including 6h13, 9a1, 12a1) and may originally have been omitted; see Appendix II to chapter 6 below.

[142] M.P. Weitzman, "Two Curious Passages in the Peshitta of Wisdom", in B.A. Taylor (ed.), *IX Congress of the International Organisation for LXX and Cognate Studies*, Atlanta 1997, pp. 137–51.

also in the succeeding verses (34–7), which are not otherwise rendered at all. The 'great name' derives from וְהתיח[שם לחם (v.33) and the 'habitation' from the name וּמשובב (v.34, understood as וּמושב). The "quiet and peace" (ܫܠܝܐ ܘܫܠܐ) derive from a glance forward to שקטת ושלוה in v.40; later, when v.40 itself is translated, that Hebrew phrase is rendered similarly (though not identically) as ܫܠܐ ܘܫܠܝܐ.

(b)   1 Chr. 5:1–2

Both the Hebrew and the Syriac state that Reuben's blessing was transferred to Joseph, but they continue differently:

MT   ולא להתיחש לבכרה: כי יהודה גבר באחיו ולנגיד ממנו והבכרה ליוסף

P   and upon these two come blessings, out of all the tribes of Israel: from Judah the king Messiah will come forth,[143] and the birthright will be given to Joseph.

In the final phrase of v.1, the translator seems to have recognised only the first five letters (read as one word ולאלה) at the beginning and בכרה – which he proceeded to 'misread' as ברכה – at the end.[144] The messianic interpretation of נגיד (v.2) may have been influenced by משיח נגיד at Dan. 9:25; how much could be read of the preceding phrase is not clear. Evidently, the translator aimed to reconcile Judah's leadership with Joseph's birthright.

(c)   1 Chr. 7:24–6

MT   ואת אזן שארה: ורפח בנו ורשף בנו ותלח בנו ותחן בנו: לעדן

P   and all those who remained, his daughter healed, for she was a healer and cured their sicknesses. And she healed La'dan . . .

Apparently the translator could only make out שארה: ורפח at the first verse boundary, and nothing more until he reached the name La'dan at the beginning of v.26. He derived שארה from שאר "remainder", and from its ending he inferred the feminine gender. He misread ורפח as ורפא "and healed". The sense of P is derived straightforwardly from these elements.

(d)   1 Chr. 12:23

Here we may reconstruct:

MT   לעזרו עד למחנה   גדול כמחנה אלהים
Legible letters: .. ....   למח.. גדול ..חנ. לה.ם
Construed as: לֶחֶם גדול   חֵן   לחֶם

P   to eat bread before them because David loved them greatly

David is the main subject of the chapter, and the sense was woven about the legible letters, with למחה rearranged as לחם, and חן understood as 'grace'.

---

[143] Although ms 9a1 has ܢܦܘܩ, the future form ܢܦܘܩ read by the remaining mss is supported by the context. As Nöldeke observed, this tense indicates Jewish origin.

[144] Other instances of deliberate misreading, and in particular transposition, were noted in chapter 2.

(e) 1 Chr. 29:7

Here one item among the resources given by the people for the Temple is indicated thus:

MT　ואדרכנים רבו

P　ܘܐܒܪܐ ܛܒܐ ܠܓܘ ܠܦܣܩܬܐ

　　　and good lead for the pipes

It seems that no more than the letters א..כ..נ. in the first word were legible; and these, in the context of building the Temple, suggested the metal ܐܒܪܐ, for use in pipes. The metal required for plumbing was of course lead, as ܐܒܪܐ must here be translated. It is true that usually ܐܒܪܐ means 'tin' while lead is indicated by ܐܒܪܐ; but tin is too brittle to be moulded into pipes shaped as required, and its main use was as a component of alloys with other metals.[145] The use of ܐܒܪܐ for lead is not surprising, since the two metals were associated in antiquity, perhaps on account of their low melting-points; thus the Latin for tin was *plumbum album*. Incidentally, this evidence of the meaning 'lead' for ܐܒܪܐ supports the understanding by Rashi of אנך at Amos 7:7–8 as a plumbline.[146]

(f)　1 Chr. 29:14

MT　וכי מי אני ומי עמי כי נעצר כח להתנדב כזאת כי ממך הכל ומידך נתנו לך

P　　　For what am I, and what is my people? For from all my teachers I have learnt. For it is thy
　　　way of life that helped me, and thou art our hope, O Lord our God.

Though the first five words of the verse were legible, the only words that could be recognised thereafter – and that none too clearly – were כי ממך הכל. In fact, the translator could only make out כ. ממד הכל, which he filled out using Ps. 119:99 [מ]כ]ל] מ]ל]מדין] ה]ש]כל]תי]. Perhaps he thought it fitting that this lacuna in David's last speech should be filled from one of David's psalms. The rest is free composition, based on two theological terms 'way of life' and 'hope'.[147] This treatment of Ps. 119:99 is independent of P-Psalms, which instead renders השכלתי by ܐܣܬܟܠܬ.[148] The citation by Aphrahat[149] of Ps. 119:99 in this form demonstrates Aphrahat's familiarity with P-Chronicles.

(g)　2 Chr. 16:12b

MT and P agree in the preceding half-verse that Asa fell sick in his feet,[150] and in the following verse that he died, but in 12b itself they totally diverge:

MT　עד למעלה חליו וגם בחליו לא דרש את י׳ כי ברפאים

P　ܘܐܬܪܬܚ ܒܝܫ ܠܣܓܘ ܠܥܠ ܡܢ ܚܝܠܗ

---

[145] R.J. Forbes, in C.Singer et al. (eds.), *A History of Technology*, Oxford 1954–84, vol. 2 (1956), pp. 46–7.

[146] On this question, see H.G.M. Williamson, "The Prophet and the Plumbline", *OTS* 26 (1990), pp. 101–21.

[147] On 'hope' see pp. 224–5 below. It is not clear whether the phrase 'way of life' means 'manner of (earthly) life' or 'way to (eternal) life'. Biblical prototypes are דרך החיים (Jer. 21:8) and ארח חיים (Ps. 16:11 etc.).

[148] Since in the previous verse מן is comparative (מאיבי תחכמני), the obvious sense is: "I have become wiser than all my teachers". However, in either book the translator avoids such disrespect. P-Psalms instead has a petition ("make me wiser . . . !") while P-Chronicles does not make מן comparative at all (so also Ben Zoma at Mishnah Aboth 4:1).　　[149] Ed. Parisot, col. 1048.　　[150] So 8a1 9a1; the other mss omit "feet".

Thus P, instead of adding details of Asa's sickness and unbelieving response, writes that he grew weak and fell down inside the house. This seems sheer guesswork, from the reference to infirmity of feet.

(h)   2 Chr. 20:22–3

These verses describe the consequences when Levites sang on the battlefield. MT tells that when they offered praise (תהלה), God set ambushers against the invaders from Ammon, Moab and mount (הר) Seir, who proceeded to attack one another. For all this, P instead writes: "The hills began praising and the mountains began dancing." Apparently P could read only the Hebrew words just specified, and guessed the rest using Ps. 114:4.

(i)   2 Chr. 21:11

ML   ויזן את יושבי ירושלם

> and he caused the inhabitants of Jerusalem to commit whoredom

P   ܘܐܫܩܝ ܐܢܘܢ ܠܢܙܝܪ̈ܝ ܐܘܪܫܠܡ

> and he made the Nazirites of Jerusalem drink wine

This has been viewed as a euphemistic Midrash.[151] More probably, however, the translator misread ויזן as ויין "and wine", and drew on Amos 2:12.

(j) 2 Chr. 25:13 in MT mentions the cities of Judah, then Samaria, then Beth Horon. The translator naturally recognised the first, and also the second (rendered: "the Samaritans"), but could not apparently read the third. He therefore substituted the third ethnic presence of which he knew in the Holy Land, rendering: "the cities of the gentiles" (ܩܘܪ̈ܝܐ ܕܥܡ̈ܡܐ).

Many more instances of breakdown of semantic correspondence can be found in David's prayer in 1 Chr. 29. Of particular interest is the expansion at the end of 1 Chr. 29:19, which as noted above echoes the first paragraph of the Jewish prayer called the Qaddish:

> that Thy great name be sanctified and praised in the world that Thou didst create before those that fear Thee

The Qaddish served as a prayer at the conclusion of a discourse.[152] The motive for this expansion was apparently to compensate for the many earlier lacunae in the rendering of this speech.

Clarifying expansions and Targum tradition

Although the translators in other books of P provide additions from time to time in order to clarify the sense or to solve problems in the text, the translator of Chronicles felt particularly free in this respect, e.g.

---

[151] W.E. Barnes, *An Apparatus Criticus to Chronicles in the Peshitta Version*, Cambridge 1897, p.xii.
[152] See the reference to **יהי שמיה רבא דאגדתא** at TB Sota 49a.

1 Chr. 21:26

MT   וַיַּעֲנֵהוּ בָאֵשׁ מִן הַשָּׁמַיִם

P   and he answered him, and fire came down from heaven and consumed the burnt-offerings that were upon the altar

P here explains what an "answer by fire from heaven" might mean.

1 Chr. 26:10

MT   שֹׁמְרִי הָרֹאשׁ כִּי לֹא הָיָה הַבְּכוֹר וַיְשִׂימֵהוּ אָבִיהוּ

P   and his first-born son died, and his father set up the next one as head, and did not call him by the name of primogeniture

The translator adds an explanation of why there was no first-born (while also making various omissions).

1 Chr. 29:1

Here David's announcement that the Lord had chosen Solomon, the youngest of his sons, demanded a reason, which P supplies: "because he is a wise and understanding youth".

2 Chr. 6:30

MT   וְאַתָּה תִּשְׁמַע מִן הַשָּׁמַיִם מְכוֹן שִׁבְתֶּךָ וְסָלַחְתָּ

P   and you will hearken to the sound *of their prayer* from heaven and you will forgive *their sins*

The extent of this tendency in Chronicles is clear from comparison of parallel passages in other books, e.g.

Ezra 1:1 = 2 Chr. 36:22

MT	P-Ezra	P-Chr.
לכלות דבר י'	ܐܠܗܐ ܦܬܓܡܐ ܕܡܪܝܐ	ܕܢܫܠܡ ܡܠܬܐ ܕܡܪܝܐ
וגם במכתב לאמר	ܟܬܒܐ ܐܡܪ	ܘܐܦ ܟܬܒܐ ܐܡܪ ܗܘܐ ܠܡܐܡܪ

Ezra 1:2 = 2 Chr. 36:23

MT	P-Ezra	P-Chr.
והוא פקד עלי לבנות	ܘܗܘ ܦܩܕ ܥܠܝ ܠܡܒܢܐ	ܘܗܘ ܦܩܕ ܥܠܝ ܕܐܒܢܐ
אלהיו עמו	ܐܠܗܗ ܥܡܗ	ܐܠܗܗ ܠܟ ܡܗ

The renderings in Ezra are noticeably closer to the Hebrew. Thus P-Ezra represents the Hebrew infinitive in the first verse by a verbal noun, while P-Chronicles prefers a clause as is usual in Syriac: "in order that the Lord's word should be fulfilled". P-Chronicles likewise replaces the Hebrew infinitive in the second verse by a clause, while P-Ezra preserves it. Again, the two Hebrew words meaning: "he said in writing" which P-Ezra was content to reproduce, evidently seemed mutually contradictory to P-Chronicles, for he expands to admit both saying and writing: "in writing his name was mentioned (lit. said)". Finally, while P-Ezra accepts the expression "his God is with him", P-Chronicles places greater distance between God and man, rendering: "his God delights in him".[153]

Significantly, however, this expansive tendency is not present in Chronicles at the outset. Quantitative literalism is preserved in the first chapter as closely as in most other biblical books,[154] and begins to break down only in the second chapter. Thus at 1 Chr. 2:14, where the Hebrew has: "David the seventh (son of Jesse)", P writes: "Elihu the seventh, David the eighth", in order to take account of 1 Sam. 16:10, which stated that David had seven older brothers.[155] Again, the nouns "son", "daughter" at 2:23 are expanded to "male son", "female daughter". Significantly, it is at this same point that the translator first betrays difficulty in reading the Hebrew: some verses in this chapter are omitted (1 Chr. 2:23, 45, 47–9), while 1 Chr. 2:52b–55 is drastically abridged. The translator had apparently become aware of deficiencies in his *Vorlage*, and appreciated that he would have to allow himself an unusual degree of freedom in order to remedy them; and since quantitative literalism in such passages was unattainable, the translator felt free to make clarifying additions even where the *Vorlage* was clearly legible. Whether the first chapter of Chronicles was actually intact in his *Vorlage*, or whether he successfully restored it by consulting parallels in Genesis, we cannot tell; but it is in the second chapter that signs of a defective *Vorlage* and additions by the translator appear together.

These expansions sometimes bring P-Chronicles into agreement with the Targum on Chronicles, or on the parallel passage in an earlier book. Usually, however, the agreement betokens nothing more than common concern for clarity and Aramaic idiom, which the translators of the other books in P had to forgo for the sake of quantitative literalism, as at 2 Chr. 8:18 –

MT	יודעי ים
P	ܘܢܚܬܝܢ ܠܚܕܒܘ ܐܠܦܐ ܕܝܡܐ
Tg. to 1 Kgs. 9:27	דאומנין לדברא בימא
[but P to 1 Kgs. 9:27	ܝܕܥܝ ܝܡܐ]

At least two parallels with the Targum on an earlier book, however, cannot be ascribed to coincidence:

(a) 1 Chr. 17:27 (where P follows 2 Sam. 7:29):

MT	ומברכתך יברך בית עבדך לעולם
P-Chron.	ܒܡܟ ܨܕܝܩܐ ܒܗܘܢܐ ܕܥܒܕܝܟ ܘܢܬܒܪܟ ܒܝܬ
Tg-Sam.	ומברכתך יתברכון בתי עבדך צדיקיא לעלמין]

Both these translations explain, following the fall of David's dynasty, that the blessing on his house had been conditional on righteous behaviour (cf. Ps. 136:12).

---

[153] After the final word ויעל, P-Chronicles has an addition not found in P-Ezra: "let him come to me". However, there was no need for such an addition in Ezra, where – unlike Chronicles – the Hebrew goes on to name the destination: "to Jerusalem which is in Judah".

[154] The only departure is the omission of the phrases: "And Jobab died" (v.45), "And Baal Hanan died" (v.50), which in this repetitive passage could be inadvertent.

[155] The name Elihu derives from 1 Chr. 27:18, which mentions Elihu, brother of David.

(b)   2 Chr. 6:14

MT   אין כמוך אלהים בשמים ובארץ

P   there is none like Thee, O Lord, that dwellest in the heaven above and Thy wishes are performed upon the earth below.

Tg. to 1 Kgs. 8:23   את הוא אלהא דשכינתך בשמיא מלעילא ושליט על ארעא מלרע

Both translators share the same explanation of how God can be both in heaven and on earth.

These cases suggest that P-Chronicles may have known some traditional renderings, which would also crop up in Targum Jonathan, of particular phrases in the prophets.

As to the parallels with the Targum on Chronicles itself, which is thought to have been redacted no earlier than *c.* 800 CE,[156] there are very few strong enough to suggest common origin. Notable, however, is the replacement of Jabneh in both versions by Gaza, 30 miles to the south-west, in the list of Philistine cities at 2 Chr. 26:6. Unless this reflects a different *Vorlage*, it seems that both translators drew upon a tradition which balked at including the site of the great Jewish academy among Philistine cities.

Avoidance of anthropomorphisms

P also shows a greater tendency in Chronicles than in other books to use expressions that distance God from man. Thus P makes not God but his angel smite Israel's foes at 1 Chr. 14:11). Again, the expression ܕܚܠܬܐ is sometimes introduced in P-Chronicles as a buffer between God and man; see 1 Chr. 28:2 and 2 Chr. 5:14; 6:2, 18, 20; 7:1–3, 16, 12:13, 33:7.[157]

In this respect again we may contrast P-Chronicles with P-Kings within the section where the former has followed the Hebrew of Kings rather than of Chronicles, e.g.

1 Kgs. 14:5
MT   וי' אמר (אל אחיהו)
P-Kings   ܘܐܡܪ ܠܐܚܝܐ
P-Chronicles   ܘܐܡܪ ܠܐܚܝܐ ܡܪܝܐ ܡܢ ܩܕܡ

and from before the Lord it was said (to Ahijah)

1 Kgs. 14:9
MT   ואתי השלכת אחרי גוך
P-Kings   ܘܠܝ ܫܕܝܬ ܠܒܣܬܪ ܓܘܫܡܟ

and Me you have cast behind your body

P-Chronicles   ܘܕܚܠܬܝ ܫܕܝܬ ܠܒܣܬܪ ܩܕܠܟ

and the fear of Me you have cast behind your neck[158]

---

[156] R. Le Déaut and J. Robert, *Targum des Chroniques*, Rome 1971, p. 27.
[157] N. Séd, "La Shekhinta et ses amis «Araméens»", *Mélanges Antoine Guillaumont*, Geneva 1988, pp. 233–42.
[158] The translator again introduces "fear" (of God) at 1 Chr. 29:18, 2 Chr. 16:9, 2 Chr. 19:4.

All these elements in P-Chronicles are certainly reminiscent of the Targums. One cannot, however, explain them simply by describing P-Chronicles as a Targum, for it differs in too many fundamental respects from the Targums preserved by the Jews. It seems rather that discrete traditions relating to the sense and/or to the proper expression of individual phrases formed part of a Jewish tradition of scholarship in the Aramaic language. Common dependence on that tradition caused P to agree on occasion with rabbinic sources, or with Targum Jonathan on parallel passages, or with the Targum on Chronicles, or with combinations of these. That store of tradition was in some measure available to all the translators of P, but rejected by most for the sake of quantitative literalism. In the case of Chronicles, exceptionally, that ideal was beyond reach, and so the translator was more receptive to elements from that tradition, on which the Midrash and Targums also drew.[159]

Conclusion

The relationship between P and MT in Chronicles is certainly loose at many points. Loose translation, however, cannot be characterised without further ado as 'targumic'. In Chronicles it is almost entirely due to two factors that have nothing to do with influence from the Targums. First, the translator was often unable to read the Hebrew *Vorlage* properly, and this is confirmed by the many omissions, which are decidedly not typical of the Jewish Targums. Second, the considerable freedom which the translator had to assume in order to produce continuous sense, given the poor state of the *Vorlage*, became characteristic even in passages where the *Vorlage* was legible. Thus the P translator of Chronicles goes further than his fellow translators in expanding or tacitly changing the text for the sake of clarity or perceived improvement of sense.

Undeniably, P shows in Chronicles a greater incidence of agreements with Jewish traditional exegesis and with the Targums or rabbinic traditions than in any other book, at least apart from the Pentateuch. However, truly significant agreements are very rare, in relation to the full text of Chronicles. Most of the agreements are instead ascribed easily to polygenesis, through common concern for Aramaic idiom and for general intelligibility. Moreover, P in Chronicles differs from the Jewish Targums in a fundamental respect: it often bears no semantic relationship with MT, or with any hypothetical Hebrew *Vorlage* at all like MT.

All in all, one cannot describe P-Chronicles as "a pure Jewish Targum" without having to revise drastically the definition of Targum. The translators who produced the Jewish Targums had full access to the Hebrew text, and to a rich exegetical tradition. P in Chronicles, by contrast, gives the impression of a valiant effort by an individual working with limited resources: an often unsatisfactory Hebrew text, a sound but far from comprehensive knowledge of the Hebrew language, and a few reminiscences of the Jewish tradition of biblical scholarship in Aramaic. It is a measure of his (albeit

---

[159] The position of Chronicles within P is examined in greater detail by M.P. Weitzman, "Is the Peshitta of Chronicles a Targum?" in P. Flesher (ed.), *Targum Studies*, vol. 2, Atlanta 1998, pp. 159–93.

often misguided) ingenuity that he was usually able to extract good sense and to express it in clear and idiomatic Syriac.

The relationship between P and the Targums elsewhere in the Writings

In the remaining books of the Writings, parallels between P and the Targums are unusual, and easily ascribed either to polygenesis or to common tradition. An example of the latter is the rendering of סלה in Psalms as "for ever" both in P (ܠܥܠܡ, at 3:9, 24:10, 66:7) and in Tg. (לעלמין regularly). It seems that the combination "[praise] + [God] + *selah* " (Ps. 66:4, 68:33, 84:4, 88:11) was equated with the common formula "blessed be the Lord for ever" (Ps. 41:14, 89:53 etc.).

P-Ruth deserves special mention, since it is often dubbed paraphrastic. It is true that P-Ruth has some expansions, but most aim simply to shield the reader from difficulties. Thus the translator may spell out an allusion, e.g.

1:8   עם המתים   ܥܡ ܗܢܘܢ ܕܡܝܬܘ ܠܟ

or give point to an otherwise redundant phrase, e.g.

1:22   השבה משדה מואב   ܕܐܬܗܦܟܬ ܠܡܐܬܐ ܥܡܗ ܒܠܒܐ ܫܠܡܐ

who desired to return with her with a full heart[160]

At 1:13, the expansion results from hesitation between the Hebrew and Greek texts, as noted above. Theological scruples make Orpah return to her people (ܐܢܫܗ̇) rather than her gods at 1:15, and transform Boaz's greeting to: "Peace be with you" (ܫܠܡܐ ܥܡܟܘܢ: contrast MT 'ר עמכם) at 2:4. The only clear element of traditional Jewish exegesis is in fact the rendering, ܡܪܝܐ ܕܡܣܬܝܟ̈ܝܢ ܟܠ for שׁדי at 1:21; the direct source, however, could easily be LXX ὁ ἱκανός. All this is not enough to demonstrate any link with the Targums.

At one stage, the situation in Proverbs – where P provided the basis for a Jewish Targum – seemed set to be repeated in Job. Rabbi Samuel ben Nissim Masnut of Aleppo wrote a biblical commentary in the early thirteenth century, of which the sections on Genesis, Job, Daniel and Ezra-Nehemiah have been published.[161] The commentaries to Genesis, Job and Daniel often cite Aramaic renderings introduced by the formula ת"א (apparently תרגום ארמי = Aramaic translation).[162] H. Yalon remarked briefly that all but five or six of the 80-odd such citations in Genesis come from P.[163] Yalon's observation is correct; many elements in these citations – such as the translated divine name ܡܪܝܐ and the expectation that Esau will repent (ܬܬܘܒ, for MT תריד, at Gen. 27:40) – are so characteristic of P as to exclude the explanation of polygenesis. The editors of Masnut's commentary on Daniel identified there some 120 further citations of P, similarly introduced. Most naturally came from P on Daniel, but three came from Psalms (1:4, 103:5 and 122:5 cited on Dan. 2:35, 4:9 and 7:9 respectively). Four of Masnut's Targum citations in Job likewise come (albeit in corrupt form) from P:

---

[160] It had already been stated in v.6 – where P renders literally – that Ruth returned from Moab.

[161] S. Buber (ed.), *Ma'yan Gannim . . . 'al Sefer Iyyob*, Berlin 1889; Mordechai Ha-Kohen (ed.), *Midrash Bereshit Zuta*, Jerusalem 1962; I.S. Lange and S. Schwartz (eds.), *Midraš Daniel et Midraš Ezra, auctore R. Samuel b. R. Nissim Masnut (saec. xiii)*, Jerusalem 1968.

[162] The abbreviation cannot stand for אחר תרגום; in Daniel there is no other Targum.

[163] Ch. Yalon, "מה הוא ת"א ת' בבראשית זוטא?", *Sinai* 53 (5723), p. 278. The name *Bereshit Zuta* was given by S. Buber to the commentary on Genesis.

Job 13:25a	MT	העלה נדף תערוץ
	P	ܠܘܦܐ ܝܪܒ ܘܢܘܪ ܪܒܬܐ ܘܪܐ ܫܪܒ ܐܘܠ
	Masnut	לטרפא יבישא דנתר דאיש אותי
	contrast Tg.	הטרפא דשקיף תתבר
Job 38:12b	MT	יִדַעְתָּ שַׁחַר מְקֹמוֹ
	P	ܒ.ܝ ܐܘܬ ܐܪܝܐ ܐܘܠ ܡ, ܘܗܒܬܐ ܘܙܦܪܐ
	Masnut	ידע אנת איהא דעתא דשפרא
	contrast Tg.	ידעת לקריצתא אתריה
Job 38:20a	MT	כי תקחנו אל גבולו
	P	ܐ_ ܒ.ܝ ܐܘܠ ܠܬܘܚܘܡܗ
	Masnut	אין ידע תחומיה
	contrast Tg.	ארום תדברניה לתחומיה
Job 39:25c	MT	רעם שרים ותרועה
	P	ܘܗܒܐ ܠܪܘܪܒܐ ܒܨܗܠܐ
	Masnut	ומבזע לרברבנא בצהלה
	contrast Tg.	אכליותא דרברבי ויבבא

Perhaps copies of P in Hebrew transliteration were then in circulation. Masnut never hints that the text is written in a script other than Hebrew or is of Christian provenance.

Evidently, however, rival Jewish Aramaic translations had grown up for most books of the Writings. In Masnut's commentary on Job, the four citations above from P are outnumbered by citations from the Targum to Job familiar today, as well as another Targum which also differed from P. The Targums eventually adopted on the various books of the Writings differ from P in two respects. First, they show less guesswork, as they rest on a better knowledge of Hebrew; and second, they contain sometimes lengthy expansions. The latter tendency may have been no less an advantage over P than the former in the eyes of Jewish scholars: an Aramaic version based on P would add little to the broadly literal translation of the whole Bible into Arabic already provided by Hai's predecessor Sa'adiah (882–942). Proverbs was exceptional in that the result of an expansive approach to its hundreds of isolated couplets would have been unwieldy; in this book, therefore, P had no rival as the basis for a Targum. Elsewhere in the Writings, however, the need for a Targum of the books of the Writings was fulfilled through the more periphrastic Jewish Aramaic versions, or not fulfilled at all.

Is P of western origin?

In favour of the view that P comes from a specifically Palestinian Aramaic prototype, it has been claimed that P contains western features. These comprise west-Aramaic linguistic elements, and exclusive agreements with the Palestinian Targums. These arguments must now be evaluated.

West-Aramaic linguistic elements

In principle, it is difficult to demonstrate that a given linguistic element in P was borrowed from the west, rather than inherited from an older stage in the Aramaic language before the division into eastern and western dialects.[164] This point applies in particular to the accusative particle *yat*, which is the parade example of a supposedly west-Aramaic feature. This particle, which occurs 19 times in P, is not western but archaic, being well attested (as *'yt*) in Aramaic as early as *c.* 800 BCE, in the Zakir inscription. It is used with some frequency by P in S. of S. (5x) and Qohelet (11x), in which books P shows particular preference for Syriac etymological equivalents of other Hebrew elements also, e.g. ܠܘܬ for שׁוּב. Even in these books, however, not every object is marked by ܝܬ, though the original translation may have contained more examples than the extant text: thus at S. of S. 8:11, ܝܗܒܬ may be corrupt for ܝܗܒ ܝܬ (MT: נָתַן אֶת). Outside these books, the remaining usages of ܝܬ are at Gen. 1:1 (2x) and 1 Chr. 4:41 (1x). In both Genesis and Chronicles the translator's original policy was to mark the direct object (apart from named persons) by ܝܬ; but both translators abandoned ܝܬ as archaic almost immediately, and switched to contemporary usage, viz no particle for non-personal accusatives and *l-* for personal ones.[165] In Chronicles, the early chapters consist largely of genealogies, and the first non-personal accusative ("their tents") occurs at 1 Chr. 4:41 – where the translator uses ܝܬ for the only time. In abandoning ܝܬ the translators of Genesis and Chronicles differ from the translator(s) of S. of S. and Qohelet; and the fact that they did not go back to remove its initial occurrences shows a certain informality – or initial instability – in their translation technique.[166]

Another element in P which has been claimed as west-Aramaic is the usage at Prov. 11:31 of ܚܝܐ 'live' (in simple stem) in the sense "be saved" (cf. LXX σῴζεται). This feature is also claimed to indicate that the translator of Proverbs consulted the Peshitta version of the New Testament – specifically, of 1 Peter 4:18 – where western elements are thought to occur.[167] Since it thus impinges on the dating of P, this passage will be discussed in detail in chapter 5, where it is concluded that this usage of ܚܝܐ can be explained as a Graecism rather than as specifically western.

In the Apocrypha too it has been suggested that "the Syriac version seems based on a West Aramaic original", but again the main evidence is the same usage of ܚܝܐ and derivatives. The only other evidence adduced is ܒܚܝܪ, apparently meaning "chosen", in the last verse of the third apocryphal psalm.[168] This usage of Aramaic *bḥr* is indeed common in the west, while the Old Testament Peshitta instead uses ܓܒܐ. In that particular passage, however, two words for 'chosen' were evidently required in the two stichs, and so ܒܚܝܪ had to be used alongside the usual ܓܒܐ.[169]

[164] Thus A. Tal, *The Language of the Targum of the Former Prophets and its Position within the Aramaic Dialects* (Hebrew with English summary: Tel Aviv 1975), pp. 133–7, identified many words common to the Syriac of P and the Aramaic of Targum Jonathan to the Former Prophets. His explanation is that both reflect an (archaic) standard literary Aramaic (pp. x–xi, 141). On the problems of identifying west Aramaic elements, see further L. van Rompay, "Some Preliminary Remarks on the Origins of Classical Syriac as a Standard Language", in G. Goldenberg and S. Raz (eds.), *Semitic and Kushitic Studies*, Wiesbaden 1994, pp. 70–89: 81–2.

[165] T. Nöldeke, *Compendious Syriac Grammar* (tr. J.A. Crichton), London 1904, p. 227. See further I. Avineri, *Syntaxe de la Peshitta sur le Pentateuque* (Hebrew with French summary), Diss. Jerusalem 1973.

[166] This is a more comprehensive explanation of *yāt* at the opening of Genesis than the suggestion in F. Rosenthal, *Die Aramäistische Forschung seit Th. Nöldeke's Veröffentlichungen*, Leiden 1939, pp. 202–3, that the translator desired here "einen besonderen feierlichen Klang". Rosenthal has convincingly disposed of Baumstark's remaining arguments.

[167] J. Joosten, "West Aramaic Elements in the Old Syriac and Peshitta Gospels", *JBL* 110 (1991), pp. 271–89:275.   [168] Joosten, "West Aramaic Elements", p. 273n.

[169] Noth reconstructed the underlying Hebrew words as חסד... בחיר; see M. Noth, "Die fünf syrisch überlieferten apokryphen Psalmen", *ZAW* 48 (NF 7) (1930), pp. 1–23: 15.

Exclusive agreement with Targums of Palestinian provenance

Another argument for P's dependence on a Palestinian Targum is that P shows exclusive agreement with the extant Palestinian Targums. For this purpose agreements are needed which are *not* shared with T⁰; since T⁰ was available in the east, renderings in P which also occur in T⁰ would not prove a specifically western origin for P.[170]

The evidence, presented by Wohl, is meagre indeed.[171] In some passages cited, the syntax of the Hebrew is retained by T⁰ but adjusted in line with Aramaic idiom by both P and the Palestinian Targum(s). Such agreements, however, could easily have arisen through polygenesis. Thus at Exod. 22:22 MT – followed by T⁰ – switches to singular תענה, after a plural address in v.21, while both P and a Palestinian Targum from the Geniza (fragment A) continue the plural. However, the use of different vocabulary by these two translations (P ܬܘܡܐ, A תצערון) counts against the suggestion of dependence.

In other passages both P and one or more Geniza fragments of Palestinian Targum bring out an element implicit in the Hebrew, while T⁰ agrees closely with MT, as at Gen. 38:21 –

MT	איה הקדשה היא בעינים על הדרך
T⁰	אן מקדשתא דהיא בעינים על ארחא
P	ܐܝܟܐ ܗܝ ܙܢܝܬܐ ܗܝ ܕܝܬܒܐ ܥܠ ܐܘܪܚܬܐ
Fragments DE	די [דהות] יתבא...

The choice of the verb 'sit' could have occurred to any number of readers; it was obvious from v.14.

In other passages, T⁰ retains his usual Aramaic equivalent for a Hebrew word, while P and the Palestinian Targums vary it for the sake of nuance. Thus Exod. 7:10 mentions Pharaoh's servants (עבדיו), whom T⁰ duly calls עבדוהי. By contrast, both P and Geniza fragment D reserve that word for the Israelite slaves and so here render otherwise: P ܥܒܕܘܗܝ, D שלטנוי. Likewise at Gen. 37:26, where MT has בצע מה, T⁰ʲ include in their renderings the word ממון, apparently their standard equivalent for בצע (again at Exod. 18:21): the brothers ask how they would gain financially by selling Joseph. P and DE agree in seeing instead a reference to general advantage: P ܡܢܐ ܝܘܬܪܢ, D[E] מה הניא לן. This agreement need not, however, imply common origin; in both cases the verbal differences confirm P's independence.

Elsewhere, P and the Palestinian Targums agree in a straightforward Aramaic/Syriac rendering, but the agreement is nevertheless cited by Wohl as evidence of P's dependence on the Palestinian Targums, simply because both disagree with T⁰. In some cases the reason for T⁰'s disagreement is that it prefers a rarer Aramaic word, albeit of similar meaning, e.g.

Exod. 21:19   MT משענתו, P ܚܘܛܪܗ = A :: T⁰ בוריה

In other cases, T⁰ chooses to bring out an implicit meaning, e.g.

Gen. 43:25   MT צהרים, P ܒܛܗܪܐ = E :: T⁰ בשירותא 'at the meal(time)'

---

[170] We recall that according to Kahle, the main proponent of this argument, T⁰ actually originated in the east.   [171] Wohl presents the evidence on pp. 9–13.

Wohl's arguments are sometimes very subtle, as at Gen. 37:30 –

MT   **הילד איננו ואני אנה אני בא**

P   ܓܠܠܐ ܐܝܟܐ ܗܘ. ܐܝܟܐ ܠܐܝܟܐ ܐܝܢ ܐܝܟܐ.

Where is the boy? And I – whither shall I go?

D   **...ואנה לית אנה ידע להן איזל בתר טליא**

and I do not know where I should go after the boy

According to Wohl, the opening question in P implies dependence on the Palestinian Targum. In fact, however, P could have derived his question from the analogy of the succeeding phrase, especially as a literal translation ("the boy is not") would have made poor Syriac.[172]

All these agreements between P and the Palestinian Targums can of course be ascribed to polygenesis. There are a few other agreements which indicate common origin, but these are sufficiently explained by common tradition, as at Exod. 22:14 –

MT **עאל פסידיה באנגריה** T^J :: ܠܐ ܟܐܢ ܟ = P ܐ ܟ^P, T^O **על באנגריה** = **בא בשכרו**, T^O
While T^O renders literally, P and T^J reflect – albeit in different ways – the exegetical tradition, that a hirer is not liable for losses which he could not reasonably have prevented. At Gen. 4:5 the agreement again betokens shared tradition, though here of the translational sort:

MT **ויחר** (לקין), P ܐܬܟܪܗܬ = A **ובאש** = T^N:: T^{OJ}**ותקף**.

Agreements of this sort fall very far short of demonstrating that P derives from a Palestinian Targum. They are better explained by positing a fund of traditional renderings upon which translators drew at will. Although P's translators had tastes that generally stood closer to those of T^O, there were just a few traditional renderings which they happened to adopt in exclusive agreement with one or more Palestinian Targums.

The theory of origin in Adiabene

We must now consider whether the theory that P was made to answer the needs of the converts in Adiabene is so attractive in itself as to support – as opposed to requiring the support of – the view that P is derived from a Palestinian Targum, rather than a Hebrew source.

The conversion to Judaism of the royal house of Adiabene is reported both by Josephus and by the Midrash; and both refer to a king of Adiabene reading the Torah. According to Josephus (Antiq. 20.44–5 [ii.4]), a Jewish teacher found Izates reading the law of Moses (τὸν Μωυσέος νόμον ἀναγινώσκοντα) and told him that the law was to be not only read but also practised:

if you have not yet read the law about circumcision, and do not know how guilty you are by neglecting it, read it now.

According to Genesis Rabba (46:10), it was instead Izates' own conscience that drove him to undergo circumcision after reading the relevant verse (Gen. 17:11):

---

[172] Wohl is further criticised by Wernberg-Møller, "Prolegomena", pp. 256–9.

King Monobazus and Izates, the sons of Ptolemy (תלמי) were sitting and reading the book of Genesis. When they reached this verse: "And ye shall be circumcised in the flesh of your fore-skin", each turned his face to the wall and began to weep. They both went and were circum-cised.

Despite this discrepancy, both reports agree in implying that Izates possessed a text of the Pentateuch. Arguably, Izates could only have read the Pentateuch in his local Aramaic dialect. Hence the suggestion – first advanced by Perles[173] – that P originated to serve the converts at Adiabene – even though the dialect of Adiabene must have dif-fered noticeably from Syriac, the dialect of Edessa used in P.

Perles suggested that the translation was made in Palestine by a delegation of schol-ars from Adiabene. He found two supposed reminiscences in extant sources. First, Josephus reports that Izates sent his five sons to be educated in the language and learn-ing of the Jews (γλῶτταν τὴν παρὰ ἡμῖν πάτριον καὶ παιδείαν ἀκριβῶς μαθησομένους).[174] Second, Syriac tradition relates that P was translated by a delegation sent (albeit by Abgar of Edessa) to Palestine.[175] The same suggestion was made by Marquart and by Kahle. Kahle, however, thought not of a new translation made directly from Hebrew into the dialect of Adiabene but of a pre-existing translation in western Aramaic brought to the east and there transposed into Syriac.[176]

The suggestion that P was made for the converts at Adiabene is, however, far from proven. First, the accounts of the kings of Adiabene reading the Torah do not mention translation at all. Rather, the wording (ἀναγίνωσκοντα, וקורין) suggests that they were reading the Hebrew text itself. Second, even if the kings of Adiabene could not under-stand Hebrew, we need not posit a continuous written version. The reports of their 'reading' the text may in fact mean that they had the text read to them by a courtier who – like the princes – had learnt Hebrew and could translate *ex tempore*. Third, it is possi-ble that the reports go back to a legend which overlooked the practical question of how Izates could read the Torah.

Moreover, even if we grant that P was made for the converts at Adiabene, P need not be derived from a Palestinian Targum. The expertise to translate direct from the Hebrew may have been available in Adiabene (given Josephus' report of the princes' education in Judea) and it would certainly have been available to a delegation sent to Judea.

Furthermore, there is no internal evidence in P pointing to Adiabene. In particular, the references introduced by P to Nisibis, Harran and Mabbog, though mainly con-fined to Chronicles, instead suggest an origin in Osrhoene.

Of course, if it were clear that P contains west-Aramaic linguistic elements and depends on west-Aramaic Jewish Targums, we would indeed have to locate P in an east-Aramaic centre that had direct connections with Palestine, and Adiabene would be a most suitable location. However, such Palestinian elements in P cannot in fact be demonstrated. Hence there is no stronger case for Adiabene than for any other Syriac-speaking centre which had a Jewish community.

---

[173] J. Perles, *Meletemata*, pp. 7–8.   [174] Jos. *Antiq*.20.3.4 (71).
[175] This tradition is discussed in chapter 5.
[176] P.E. Kahle, *The Cairo Geniza*, 2nd edn, Oxford 1959, pp. 265–83.

P's independence of all known Targums

The many parallels that have been observed between the P and other Syriac literature on the one hand, and the Targums on the other, must be balanced against the many passages where P offers a treatment of the Hebrew without parallel in the extant Jewish Targum tradition. The cases cited here will be restricted to the Torah, on which the arguments for dependence on an Aramaic prototype have concentrated. Here P sometimes differs from the Massoretic pointing and may even 'misread' the consonantal text. Examples:

Gen. 22:2   MT ארץ המוריה, P ܐܪܥܐ ܕܐܡܘܪ̈ܝܐ "land of the Amorites"[177]

Exod. 23:17   MT זכורך "your males", P ܕܘܟܪܢܟ "your memorial (gift)" – unless inner-Syriac corruption from ܕܟܪܝܟ

Exod. 25:18   MT מקשה "turned work" (?), P ܢܣܟܬܐ "molten work", as if from the similar sounding מסכה

Num. 6:25   MT ויחנך, P ܘܢܚܝܟ "may he save your life", reading ויחיך.

Num. 23:18   MT עדי "to me", P ܣܗܕܘܗܝ, vocalising the Hebrew עֵדִי, cf. LXX μάρτυς

Deut. 32:18   MT מחללך, P ܕܫܒܚܟ "who praised thee", reading מהללך

Deut. 33:3   MT בידך, P ܒܪܟ "he blessed", reading ברך

Deut. 33:19   MT שפוני, P ܐܠܦ̈ܐ "ships", as from Heb. שפיני

More examples where P diverges from the Hebrew text presupposed by the Targums, or P interprets the Hebrew through an unrelated Syriac word of similar sound, were discussed in chapter 2; and these underscore P's direct dependence on a Hebrew source, and its independence of the Targums.

The evidence for P's independent treatment of the Hebrew is even more plentiful outside the Pentateuch, and has well been marshalled, for example, by Driver in 1 Samuel[178] and by Gelston in the Twelve Prophets.[179] An example from Isaiah is P's rendering at Isa. 10:26 of צור ערב "rock of Oreb" by the similar-sounding ܛܘܪ ܚܘܪܒ "Mount Horeb", again inexplicable except through direct contact with the Hebrew.

There are also more general contrasts between P and the Targums. Where the plain sense of the Hebrew is evident, P shows greater fidelity than the Targums to the Hebrew text, as emerges particularly from its treatment of poetic passages. In particular, P is committed to quantitative literalism to a greater extent than any targum, even T[O].

Where the Hebrew is obscure, differences again appear between P and the Targums. P strives always for intelligibility, while the Targums may be content to reproduce the form, e.g.

Exod. 8:17   MT כפרת   T[O] כפרתא

P ܚܘܣܝܐ '(place of) atonement'

1 Sam. 7:2   MT וינהו   Tg. ואתנהיאו

P ܘܐܬܟܢܫܘ 'and they cast themselves (after the Lord)'

In obscure passages P is ready to guess, to misread deliberately or even to omit, in order to attain intelligibility within the whole verse. In such passages the Targums instead draw upon the interpretations of the rabbis, whose ingenuity was proof against every difficulty in the Hebrew.

---

[177] So also P at 2 Chr. 3:1. LXX there has ἐν ὄρει τοῦ Αμορια, which may be a transliteration of המוריה rather than imply the same interpretation.

[178] See e.g. S.R. Driver, *Notes on the Hebrew Text and the Topography of the Books of Samuel*, 2nd edn, Oxford 1913, pp. lxxiii–lxxiv.   [179] A. Gelston, *Twelve Prophets*, p. 189.

The contrasting functions of P and the Targums

The parallels between P and the Targums have led to the judgment that "the Syriac translation of certain books of the Old Testament, especially that of the Pentateuch, is not much else than a Jewish Targum".[180] However, as we have noted, there are important differences not only in individual passages but also in general approach. As regards understanding, P is more committed to the exact plain sense, so far as it can be discerned; as regards expression, P is more committed to intelligibility.

These differences in approach stem from a fundamental difference of function between P and the Jewish Targums, despite their being written in closely related dialects and drawing upon common traditions. The Targums were designed to be read and studied *alongside* the Hebrew original, to which access would continue.[181] The Peshitta, by contrast, was designed to *replace* the Hebrew altogether, and so had to be as plain and intelligible as possible.[182] It was thus P, rather than the Targums, which partook of the usual function of a translation, namely to bring the text to those without independent access to the original; and this task demanded high standards both of fidelity and of intelligibility.

This difference in function in turn flows largely from a difference of location: the Targums are ultimately products of Palestine, while P originated in the eastern diaspora. It was only in Palestine that a translator could assume that, alongside his translation, there would always be someone available to identify and expound the plain sense of the Hebrew. Such translators could relax their standards of fidelity, as in the additions found in the Palestinian Targums; or they could sacrifice intelligibility, as in some Targum passages considered above, and in the revisions to the Greek Bible which culminated in Aquila's version.[183] As the Aramaic version of Job from Qumran shows, however, not every Palestinian translation assumed such latitude.

Because of this fundamental difference, it is not helpful to describe P as a Jewish Targum.[184] The term is valid in the elementary sense that it is a translation of the Bible into an Aramaic dialect, probably undertaken by Jews (as argued in chapter 5 below). However, many of the connotations of the term Targum – virtually constant agreement with the Massoretic text (including vocalisation), continual recourse to rabbinic exegesis, frequent loose renderings, Palestinian origin – are misleading in relation to P. For the same reason, the Aramaic version of Job from Qumran should not be termed a Targum. Both P and the latter are *interpretes*, while the Targumists are *expositores*.[185]

---

[180] Kahle, *The Cairo Geniza*, p. 272.

[181] Rabin has likewise argued for "a conception of the Targum more as a guide to the correct understanding of the Hebrew text for those who already understood the words than as a means of giving the meaning of an otherwise unintelligible text". See C. Rabin, "Hebrew and Aramaic in the First Century" in S. Safrai and M. Stern (eds.), *The Jewish People in the First Century*, Assen/Amsterdam 1976, pp. 1007–39, esp. p. 1032.

[182] So already P.A.H. de Boer, *Research into the Text of 1 Samuel I–XVI*, Amsterdam 1938, pp. 42–3.

[183] D. Barthélemy, *Les devanciers d'Aquila* (=SVT 10), Leiden 1963, pp. 266–9.

[184] So e.g. M.H. Goshen-Gottstein in *JSS* 6 (1961), p. 266.

[185] Cf S.P. Brock "Translating the Old Testament", in D.A. Carson and H.G.M. Williamson (eds.), *It is Written: Scripture Citing Scripture: Essays in Honour of Barnabas Lindars*, Cambridge 1988, pp. 87–98; see p. 95.

Summary of conclusions

The conclusions of this long chapter may be summarised as follows. So far as LXX is concerned, polygenesis and common tradition do not suffice to explain the parallels with P. Some literary dependence of P on LXX must be posited, though not in all books and never systematically.

Rather more complicated is the relationship between P and the Targums. Undeniably, there are many parallels, especially in the Torah. Although many of these result from polygenesis, others betoken common origin – which, however, is explained satisfactorily through common traditions, exegetical and translational, attached to individual passages. Primarily, P is a direct translation from Hebrew into Syriac, designed to be straightforward and readable; and normally such traditions were utilised only when they furthered those aims. There is no good evidence that the P translator had any complete Targum at his elbow; nor that there once existed a form of the P text which preceded the text preserved by the biblical mss and stood closer to the Targums. Moreover, there is a basic difference in function: the Targums accompanied the Hebrew original, while P replaced it. It is true that P stands close to the Targums in language, and sometimes in content; but so far as function is concerned, P invites comparison rather with LXX.

Appendix I: Biblical citations in Syriac and the Targums

Introduction

The biblical text of citations in Syriac literature sometimes agrees with one or more of the Targums, and sometimes is expansive or loose by comparison with the text of the mss of P; and these two features may overlap. According to a number of scholars – notably, Baumstark[186] and Vööbus[187] on the Pentateuch, Peters on Psalms[188] and Running on Isaiah[189] – both types of citation preserve traces, lost in the biblical mss, of an earlier stage when the text of P stood closer to the Targum(s). The term *Vetus Syra* is sometimes applied to this supposed earlier stage, by analogy with the Latin Bible – though the *Vetus Syra* is thought of as a single version rather than as a welter of different translations like the *Vetus Latina*.

Where an expansive or loose citation finds no parallel among the Jewish Targums, its expansive or loose character could in fact be due to any of a number of factors, which need to be disentangled. For clarity's sake the conclusions will be anticipated here. First, the citing author may intentionally adapt the biblical text to its new function. Second, he may intersperse the biblical text with comment. Third, his recall of the text may be imperfect, or alternatively he may have intended only to allude rather than quote; in either case the effect is much the same. In particular the author may conflate more than one biblical passage, so that, compared to P, the citation will seem expansive

---

[186] A. Baumstark, "Das Problem der Bibelzitate in der syrischen Übersetzungsliteratur", *Oriens Christianus* 30 (1933), pp. 208–25.   [187] A. Vööbus, *Peschitta und Targumim des Pentateuchs*, Stockholm 1958.
[188] C. Peters, "Pešiṭta-Psalter und Psalmentargum", *Muséon* 5 (1939), pp. 275–96.
[189] L.G. Running, "An Investigation of the Syriac Version of Isaiah", *Andrews University Seminar Studies* 3 (1965), pp. 138–57; 4 (1966), pp. 37–64, 135–48.

or loose. Most of the expansive or loose renderings in patristic sources which have been adduced by Baumstark and his followers can be ascribed to these factors. Less often, the divergence between the citation and the text of P arises because the citation has been mis-copied, or because the author cited scripture after LXX rather than P.

As to those passages where the citation agrees with one or more Targums, the agreement in most cases arises simply from a common desire for clarifying expansion, by contrast with P's concern for quantitative literalism. Yet a few passages remain where the text of a citation indeed shows substantive agreement with a Targum against the biblical mss of P. These have been claimed to represent a stage in the development of P earlier than the text of the biblical mss. However, the text of the biblical mss of P shows no sign of being derived from the text-forms preserved in these citations. Instead, the latter testify to the continuing circulation of phrases from the Targums within the Syriac church, quite independently of P.

Adaptation of the biblical text in patristic citations

A common form of expansive adaptation on the part of citing authors is to use information implicit in the context – rather than external data – in order to fill out terse expressions in P that imitate the Hebrew. This may bring the citation into agreement with the Palestinian Targums against P, but for different reasons: the citing author wanted his argument expressed in fluent rather than compressed language, while in the Palestinian Targums expansions had always been acceptable.

Thus Aphrahat agrees with the Targums in expansive phrases like "with [his] rod *alone*" (Gen. 32:11), or in the addition of ܕܟܪܐ to ܒܪܐ (even though the context already made it clear that a male was meant) at Exod. 1:22. The same factor is at least partly responsible for the agreement (cited by Vööbus[190]) at Deut. 32:21 also:

MT בלא עם "with a no-people" = P ܒܠܐ ܥܡ (5b1: later mss ܒܠܐ ܥܡܐ)

Aphr.[191] ܒܥܡ ܕܠܐ ܥܡ "with a *people that is* not a people"

cf. T^JN‎ ‎באנ[ו]מא דלא אנ[ו]מא

Here, though, an added factor may have been Aphrahat's description of the church as a new people, contrasted with the existing peoples, especially the Jews.

In other cases, the citing author's adjustment of a difficult Syriac expression leads to substitution rather than addition, so that the citation appears loose rather than expansive. We may consider Moses' plea at Exod. 32:32, after the making of the Golden Calf:

MT   ‎ועתה אם תשא חטאתם ואם אין (מחני נא ...)

P   ܗܫܐ ܐܢ ܬܫܒܘܩ ܐܢܬ ܠܗܘܢ ܚܛܗܝܗܘܢ. ܘܐܢ ܠܐ...

now if you will forgive their sins; and if not, (blot me out . . .)

Aphr. I 448   ܐܢ ܫܒܘܩ ܠܥܡܐ ܚܛܗܝܗܘܢ ܘܐܢ ܠܐ...

either forgive the people their sins; and if not, . . .

Aphr. I 772   ܐܢ ܫܒܘܩ ܣܟܠܘܬܐ ܠܥܡܐ ܗܢܐ ܐܘ...

either forgive folly for this people, or . . .

---

[190] *Peschitta und Targumim des Pentateuchs*, pp. 69–104, esp. p. 100.   [191] Vol. 1, 852.24–853.1

MT has two alternative conditional clauses, but with the apodosis of the former suppressed. The construction is reproduced in P. Aphrahat, however, fearing that it would distract readers from his argument, replaces the opening conditional verb by the imperative that is its implied apodosis, albeit slightly differently in the two passages. Now T^FJ likewise introduce the imperative, albeit while also retaining the conditional clause:

וכדון אין תשבוק לחוביהון שבוק ואין לא מחיני כדון...

and now if you will forgive their sins, forgive; and if not, (blot me out now . . .)

The parallel does not prove, however, that Aphrahat knew a biblical text standing closer than P to the Palestinian Targums. Rather, both were more concerned than P with readability, and less with quantitative literalism.

Sometimes the difference between the biblical text and a patristic citation arises from the imposition of grammatical consistency within the latter. For example, when Aphrahat summarises the instructions for the first Passover in Exod. 12:3–5, he begins (like P and MT) in the third person; and he maintains the third person, despite the subsequent transition in P and MT to the second. He thus quotes 5b in the form:

ܢܣܒܘܢ ܐܝܟ ܓܒܪܐ ܡܐ ܐܡܪܐ ܡܢ (col. 505)

while in P the verb is instead ܐܘܒܠ. On other occasions, he imposes grammatical consistency over a whole series of citations of different passages. Thus, citations of Deut. 32:24b and 32:32b appear in the second person in Aphrahat (cols. 468–9), while P and MT have the third. Baumstark suggested that Aphrahat knew a version of Deut. 32 with the second person throughout.[192] However, these citations follow on from a citation (of Deut. 9:24) which upbraids the Israelites in the second person, and it may simply be that Aphrahat continued the second person here so that the transition would not distract attention from his argument.

Similar levelling of grammatical elements has occurred in citations of Deut. 6:4 in a number of Syriac authorities, which have: "Hear O Israel, the Lord *your* God is one Lord", as against the first person plural pronoun found in P and MT.[193] Vööbus here saw a relic of the supposed *Vetus Syra*, though he admits that "this reading is not attested by any of the targumic traditions that have come down to us".[194] In fact, such a change in this fundamental text is most unlikely to go back to any Jewish source. Rather, the citing authors within the Syriac church have assimilated the pronoun "our" to the preceding second person imperative: "Hear!".

The interspersing of comment with the biblical text

A different cause of expansive citations is that the citing author interspersed his own comments with the biblical text. An example is the blame laid by Ephrem upon Eve, in his citation of God's words to Adam at Gen. 3:17:

P mss ܘܐܟܠܬ ܡܢ ܐܝܠܢܐ

Ephrem[195] ܘܐܬܛܦܝܣܬ ܠܩܠܗ ܘܐܟܠܬ ܡܢ ܐܝܠܢܐ

and you *were enticed* to eat from the tree

---

[192] "Ps.-Jonathan zu Dtn 34:6 und die Pentateuchzitate Afrahaṭs", *ZAW* N.F. 18 (1942–3), pp. 99–111: see p. 111.   [193] Evidence in Armenian as well as Syriac is quoted by Vööbus, pp. 20–1.
[194] *Peschitta und Targumim*, pp. 20–1.   [195] Ed. Tonneau, p. 43.

In such cases the expansion is readily ascribed to the citing author rather than any early loose form of the P text.[196]

Such comment may transform the sense of the passage cited, as in Aphrahat's treatment of Job 36:7. The biblical text declares that God is ever mindful of the righteous:

MT לא יגרע מצדיק עיניו (ואת מלכים לכסא)

P ܠܐ ܢܒܨܪ ܚܕ ܙܕܝܩܐ ܡܢ ܩܕܡ ܥܝܢܘܗܝ. (ܡܘܬܒ ܡ̈ܠܟܐ ܥܠ ܟܘܪܣܝܐ)

Aphrahat, however, apparently thought of those passages where P uses ܚܕ ܠܐ (rendering לא יכרת) to indicate that a line or class will never die out, of kings (1 Kgs. 2:4, 8:25, 9:5), priests (Jer. 33:17–18), the Rechabites (Jer. 35:19) and others (e.g. Josh. 9:23, 2 Sam. 3:29). Hence he takes this as a prooftext that every generation has its own righteous people, as his following comment makes clear:

Aphr. ܠܐ[197] ܚܕ ܙܕܝܩܐ ܡܢ ܩܕܡ ܥܝܢ̈ܘܗܝ ܕܡܪܝܐ: ܘܠܐ ܫܠܐ ܥܠܡܐ ܡܢ ܟܐܢܐ

> for the righteous man does not pass away from before the eyes of the Lord, nor does the world lack (lit. cease from) just men

The interpretation is atomistic – as often in rabbinic exegesis – without regard for context.

The tendency to add comment can again bring the cited text into agreement with the Targums, especially the Palestinian Targums. In particular, the parallel pointed out by Baumstark between Aphrahat and the Palestinian Targums at Deut. 34:6 is readily explained in this way. The biblical mss have:

(v.5) ܘܡܝܬ ܬܡܢ ܡܘܫܐ ܥܒܕܗ ܕܡܪܝܐ ܒܐܪܥܐ ܕܡܘܐܒ ܒܡܠܬ ܦܘܡܗ ܕܡܪܝܐ

(v.6a) ܘܩܒܪܗ ܒܚܝܠܐ ܒܐܪܥܐ ܕܡܘܐܒ ܠܘܩܒܠ ܒܝܬ ܦܥܘܪ

However, Aphrahat (col. 380) cites as follows:

(v.5) ܘܡܝܬ ܡܘܫܐ ܒܡܠܬ ܦܘܡܗ ܕܡܪܝܐ

(v.6a) ܘܩܒܪܗ ܒܚܝܠܐ ܒܐܪܥܐ ܕܡܘܐܒ ܠܘܩܒܠ ܒܝܬ ܦܥܘܪ ܐܬܪ ܕܣܟܠ ܐܝܣܪܝܠ

> (5) And Moses died by the word of the mouth of the Lord, (6a) and he buried him in the valley in the land of Moab, opposite Beth-Peor, *where Israel sinned*

Baumstark pointed out that the final phrase, not found in MT, resembles T^J:

> . . . opposite Beth-Peor; so that whenever Peor arises to remind Israel of their sins, he looks upon the burial-place of Moses and is vanquished

He concluded that Aphrahat's biblical text stood closer than that of the biblical ms of P to the Targums.[198]

The additional phrase "where Israel sinned" indeed seems to reflect a more expansive text, akin to the Palestinian Targums. Examination of the whole section in Aphrahat,

[196] On Ephrem in Genesis, see further S. Hidal, *Interpretatio Syriaca. Die Kommentare des Heiligen Ephräm des Syrers zu Genesis und Exodus mit besonderer Berucksichtigung ihrer auslegungsgeschichtlichen Stellung*, Lund 1964.

[197] Ed. Parisot, vol. 2, col. 23. Parisot's note instead suggests Prov. 2:21 ("for the upright dwell upon the earth, and those without blemish remain on it") as the source.

[198] Baumstark detected the same idea, albeit more succinctly, in Geniza Fragment F_2 : "opposite the error of Peor" (so also T^N). However, apart from the standard use of טעוותה 'error' for 'idol' this rendering is straightforward.

however, reveals other expansions, introduc)ed by exactly the same formula ܐܬܪ ܕ– "where". Thus Aphrahat writes that Moses saw the mount of the Jebusites, *where* the divine presence would rest, and that he wept to see Hebron, *where* he would not join his ancestors in burial. The clause "*where* Israel sinned" adds information familiar to any reader of the Bible, in exactly the same way. It need not be indebted to the Palestinian Targums, nor imply that Aphrahat's text differed at all here from the biblical mss of P. In any case, Aphrahat does not claim here to quote P exactly, as his omission of some words in v.5 confirms.

Other adaptations of the biblical text in citations

The citing author may conflate two or more biblical passages, whether through imperfect recall or because he had not intended to quote exactly in the first place. This may give the misleading impression that one of those passages is cited expansively.[199] Thus Aphrahat cites Gen. 7:1 in varying forms, which have been influenced by 6:9, 14 in varying degrees, as Owens has shown:

ܠܟ ܚܙܝܬ [ܕ]ܙܕܝܩ ܘܬܡܝܡ ܒܕܪܐ ܗܢܐ - I 408
ܠܟ ܚܙܝܬ ܕܙܕܝܩ ܐܢܬ ܘܬܡܝܡ ܩܕܡܝ ܒܕܪܐ ܗܢܐ - I 549 [lines 12–15]
ܠܟ ܚܙܝܬ ܕܬܡܝܡ ܐܢܬ ܩܕܡܝ ܒܕܪܐ ܗܢܐ - I 552

Such conflation may also occur on a wider scale, as in another passage studied by Owens, where a citation of Deut. 24:19 is filled out with words – indicated below in round brackets – from Lev. 19:9 or 23:22 –

ܡܐ ܕܚܨܕ ܐܢܬ ܚܨܕܟ. (ܠܐ ܬܠܩܛܘܢ ܫܩܠܬܗܘܢ.) [ܘ]ܥܡܪܐ ܟܕ ܬܛܥܐ ܒܚܩܠܐ ܬܗܦܘܟ ܬܣܒܝܗ̇.[200]

Less often, the text is adapted for theological reasons. Thus at Ps. 99:8c, in relation to Moses, Aaron and Samuel, P has an imperative, apparently addressed to God:

ܦܪܘܥ ܐܢܘܢ ܒܥܒܕܝܗܘܢ[201]

Ephrem, however, has a first person singular future form ܐܦܪܘܥ, as a divine promise: "I shall reward them for their deeds".[202] The citation opens a hymn on the resurrection, which – Ephrem goes on to explain – can be deduced from the text of the Old Testament, through the future tense of this verb. The reason for Ephrem's interchange of the future and imperative verbs may be identity in sound: the opening consonant cluster *pr-* may develop a prosthetic Aleph, as in the medical term ܐܦܪܢܝܛܝܣ (φρενῖτις), so that both verbal forms may have been realised as *epro'*.There is a striking parallel to this inference from an apparently future tense in TB Sanh. 91b, which likewise infers from the tense of the verb ישיר (אז) in Exod. 15:1 that Moses will live again to sing in time to come. Ephrem agrees not only in content, but also in basing his exegesis on an isolated phrase in defiance of context.

A particular theological motive for adaptation was to assimilate to the New Testament text, e.g.

[199] R.J. Owens, *The Genesis and Exodus Citations of Aphrahat the Persian Sage*, Leiden 1983, p. 241.
[200] R.J. Owens, "Aphrahat as a Witness to the Early Syriac Text of Leviticus", MPI 4 (1988), pp. 1–48:20.
[201] MT has a participle from the root נקם; the whole phrase is difficult.
[202] E. Beck (ed.), *Des heiligen Ephraem des Syrers Carmina Nisibena*, part 2, Louvain 1963 (CSCO 240 / Syr 102), p. 115.

Ps. 19:5 –
MT ‎בכל הארץ יצא קום
P ‎ܒܟܠܗ ܐܪܥܐ ܢܦܩ ܫܒܪܬܗܘܢ
Aphr. ‎ܢܦܩ ܒܪܬ ܩܠܐ ܕܣܒܪܬܗ ܕܡܫܝܚܐ... (I 20)
Rom. 10:18 εἰς πᾶσαν τὴν γὴν ἐξῆλθεν ὁ φθόγγος αὐτῶν

The phrase ܒܪܬ ܩܠܐ in Aphrahat reflects φθόγγος in Romans. The latter was derived from LXX (which apparently read – or misread – קולם rather than קום) and taken as the tidings of Christ.

Again, in metrical works the citing author may adapt the biblical text to the metre. For example, in a hymn ascribed to Ephrem,[203] Ps. 50:16a is cited in two lines, each of which needed fourteen syllables, as follows:

ܕܠܚܛܝܐ ܠܗ ܐܡܪ ܠܗ ܐܠܗܐ ܕܡܢܐ ܠܟ
ܡܛܠ ܠܡܬܢܐ ܩܝܡܝ ܘܦܘܩܕܢܝ ܠܡܫܬܥܝܘ

This has been claimed to represent an earlier 'targumic' stage, on the ground that it is fuller than the text of the biblical manuscripts:[204]

ܠܚܛܝܐ ܐܡܪ ܠܗ ܐܠܗܐ ܡܢܐ ܠܟ ܘܠܬܫܥܝܬܐ ܕܦܘܩܕܢܝ

However, the expansions may have been needed simply to reach the required number of syllables.[205]

The intended accuracy of citations from P

As a rule, the citing author may be expected to have striven for greater exactitude where his interest centres on the biblical text, than where the citation illustrates an external theme. Thus, Ephrem's norm in his commentaries is to cite exactly the biblical text on which he is commenting. He is freer, however, in his metrical works, and even in his commentaries a passage other than that on which he is commenting directly may be cited freely. For example, Deut. 20:10 runs thus in the biblical mss:

ܘܡܐ ܕܩܪܒܬ ܐܢܬ ܠܩܪܝܬܐ ܠܡܬܟܬܫܘ ܥܠܝܗ ܐܩܪܐ ܥܠܝܗ ܫܠܡܐ

but Ephrem in his commentary on Exodus cites it in the form

ܗܒ ܫܝܢܐ ܠܥܡܗ ܠܡܕܝܢܬܐ ܕܩܪܒܬ ܐܢܬ ܒܩܕܡܝܢ[206]

and, despite the introduction ܐܡܪ ܠܢ ܕ– (the subject being Moses), this is a mere paraphrase rather than an exact quotation of an older P text. This is confirmed by the use of ܡܕܝܢܬܐ, the regular term for "city" in Ephrem's day, rather than ܩܪܝܬܐ, the original Aramaic usage retained by P-Deuteronomy.

In Aphrahat's Demonstrations, the biblical text tends to be quoted less faithfully than in Ephrem's commentaries, simply because the author's main interest lies elsewhere. Thus he shows different forms of a single verse, such as Isa. 1:11a –

203 Ed. Rom. vi 413.
204 C. Peters, "Pešitta-Psalter und Psalmentargum", *Muséon* 5 (1939), pp. 275–96.
205 For further discussion, see M.P. Weitzman, "The Origin of the Peshitta Psalter", in: J.A. Emerton and S.C. Reif (eds.), *Interpreting the Hebrew Bible.* Fs. E.I.J. Rosenthal, Cambridge 1982, pp. 277–98: 279–80.
206 R.-M. Tonneau (ed.), *S. Ephraemi Syri in Genesim et in Exodum Commentarii*, vol. 1 (Louvain 1955), p. 148.

MT   למה לי רב זבחיכם

P   ܠܡܢܐ ܠܝ ܣܘܓܐܐ ܕܕܒܚܝܟܘܢ

Aphrahat:

I 61   ܠܡ ܚܫܚܝܢ ܠܝ ܣܘܓܐܐ ܕܕܒܚܝܟܘܢ

I 180   = P

I 747   ܠܐ ܨܒܐ ܐܢܐ ܠܝ ܣܘܓܐܐ ܕܕܒܚܝܟܘܢ

It is true that Aphrahat cites Daniel 9 in almost exactly the same form as the biblical mss;[207] but here, exceptionally, his attention was fixed upon the biblical text precisely because of the unusual length of the citation. Most of his citations, by contrast, comprise just one verse or less, as he moves from text to text to build up an argument, and the same accuracy cannot be expected.

A more general problem raised by Owens is that the distinction between a quotation and a general reference is not always straightforward. In Aphrahat, for example, the introductory formula (if any) is not conclusive: in particular, the formula ܐܡܪ ܕ– may be taken either as "he said", followed by direct speech, or as "he said that", with indirect speech. Conversely, even where there is no formula, Aphrahat may fall into the language of scripture.[208]

Text-critical causes of discrepancy between patristic citations and P

Another possible – but rarer – reason why a citation should differ from P is that the one text has suffered in transmission while the other is intact. An example where it is the citation that appears corrupt occurs in Ephrem's commentary on Exodus, where the existing text states of the Hebrew midwives of Exod. 1 that

ܘܒܬܠܗ ܥܡܡܐܘܗܝ ܕܝܢ ܗܘܐ، ܗܘܐ، ܗܘܐ ܕܝܢ ܠܦܘܬ ܓܒܪܐ ܪܒܐ ܗܘܘ،

The opening phrase seems a quotation, but differs from anything in the relevant verses (1:20–1), and the emphatic state of ܥܡܡܐ is odd. The likelihood is that the first word is corrupt from ܘܒܢܬܐ, so that Ephrem's comment means:

and they became houses – that is, a great family

This would relate well to 1:21a –

MT ויעש להם בתים, P ܥܒܕ ܠܗܘܢ ܒܬܐ

as interpreted by two early third-century rabbis:

רב ושמואל חד אמר בתי כהונה ולויה וחד אמר בתי מלכות

Rav and Samuel (disagreed). One said: (He made for them) houses of priestly and levitical office. The other said: houses of royalty.[209]

It seems that the translator intended ܠܗܘܢ as dative: "he made houses for them". Ephrem, however, apparently took it as accusative: "he made them [into] houses".

Conversely, there are a few passages where the biblical mss have a corruption while a citation preserves the original work of the translator, which has not survived in the biblical mss. Instances can be found in Ephrem, and there is even a well-known instance in Išo'dad, as late as the ninth century. The main discussion of these cases appears in chapter 6 below, on the establishment of the text.

---

[207] Ed. Parisot, vol. 1, cols. 872–9.   [208] Owens, *The Genesis and Exodus Citations*, p. 20.
[209] TB Sota 11b.

Citations from sources other than P

Yet another – albeit unusual – reason for discrepancy between a citation and the text of P is that the citing author had a different biblical version in mind. Scripture is sometimes cited after LXX, even once by Aphrahat, at Ps. 37:35 –

MT	ראיתי רשע עריץ ומתערה כאזרח רענן
P	ܡܛܠ ܕܚܙܝܬ ܪܫܝܥܐ ܕܡܫܬܒܗܪ ܘܡܬܬܪܝܡ ܐܝܟ ܐܪܙܐ ܕܠܒܢܐ
Aphr. col. 186	ܚܙܝܬ ܠܪܫܝܥܐ ܕܡܬܬܪܝܡ ܘܡܬܥܠܐ ܐܝܟ ܐܪܙܐ ܕܠܒܢܢ
cf. LXX	εἶδον ἀσεβῆ ὑπερυψούμενον καὶ ἐπαιρόμενον ὡς τὰς κέδρους τοῦ Λίβανου.

Burkitt ingeniously suggested that Aphrahat had been reading a Greek patristic work which quoted the verse according to LXX.[210]

A different version is cited alongside P in the commentary ascribed to Ephrem on Josh. 15:28b –

MT	ובאר שבע ובזיותיה
P	ܘܒܪܫܒܥ ܘܒܪܘܬܐ
"Ephrem"	ܘܒܝܪ ܫܒܥ ܘܩܘܪ̈ܝܗ̇ ܘܕܝܪ̈ܝܗ̇
	and Beersheba and its villages and its enclosures
cf. LXX	καὶ Βηρσαβεε καὶ αἱ κῶμαι αὐτῶν καὶ αἱ ἐπαύλεις αὐτῶν

The commentary continues:

ܗܘ ܩܘܪ̈ܝܗ̇ ܒܕ ܠܐ ܝܕܥܘ ܗܢܘܢ ܕܦܫܩܘ ܠܣܘܪܝܝܐ ܡܢܐ ܐܝܬܘܗ̇، ܗ̇ܝ ܒܪܬ ܩܠܐ ܥܒܪܝܬܐ
ܒܙܝܘܬܝܗ̇ ܦܫܩܘ ܘܐܣܒܪܘ ܕܫܡܐ ܕܡܕܝܢܬܐ ܐܝܬܘܗ̇،

As to this (word) "its villages" – since those who translated into Syriac did not know what that Hebrew word was, they rendered it BZYWTYH, and thought that it was the name of a city.

The text first cited in the commentary is not related to P-Joshua, where villages are instead called ܩܘܪ̈ܝܐ (as in 15:44) and ܩܪܝܬܐ signifies a city. Instead, it goes back to LXX, whose *Vorlage* evidently read בנותיה "its villages" rather than the (probably corrupt) בזיותיה of MT. P differs not, of course, out of ignorance of Hebrew but because it is based on a *Vorlage* like MT. The reading ܒܙܝܘܬܝܗ̇ cited in the commentary agrees with MT exactly, and conceivably preserves the original text of P, of which ܒܪܘܬܐ in the mss is then a corruption. Alternatively, however, it may be due to later consultation of the Hebrew, to which this commentary had some access (as at 1 Sam. 21:8).

Citations after LXX are more frequent in later authors. Thus Jacob of Edessa cites Job 41:25 in a form which is close to LXX and distant from MT:[211]

ܠܐ ܐܝܬ ܘܐܦܠܐ ܡܕܡ ܥܠ ܐܪܥܐ ܕܕܡܐ ܠܗ. ܗܘ ܕܥܒܝܕ ܠܡܬܓܚܟܘ ܡܢ ܡܠܐܟ̈ܝ

compare LXX	οὐκ ἔστιν οὐδὲν ἐπὶ τῆς γῆς ὅμοιον αὐτῷ πεποιημένον ἐγκαταπαίζεσθαι ὑπὸ τῶν ἀγγέλων μου
contrast P	ܘܫܠܝܛ ܥܠ ܥܦܪܐ ܡܗܠܟ
MT	אין על עפר משלו העשוי לבלי חת

It follows that general biblical knowledge need not imply acquaintance with P, rather than another text form. For example, Bar-Daisan knows of Jewish circumcision,[212] and

[210] F.C. Burkitt, in *JTS* 6 (1905), p. 289.
[211] J.-B. Chabot (ed.), *Jacobi Edesseni Hexaemeron*, Paris 1928 (= CSCO 56), p. 23.
[212] Ed. Parisot, Part I, vol. 2, col. 604.

the Hymn of the Soul knows of Egypt as a place of bondage, but such references do not imply even that P yet existed in their day.

The above analysis builds on detailed studies of individual chapters or books, on Exod. 15,[213] Isaiah[214] and Psalms,[215] as well as Owens' work on Aphrahat in Genesis to Leviticus.

Substantive agreements between patristic citations and the Targums

Renderings which agree significantly with one or more Targums against the biblical mss of P occasionally turn up in citations, notably by Ephrem. In his commentary on Genesis, of undisputed authenticity, Ephrem quotes some short phrases which agree with one or other of the Targums. Thus at Gen. 49:23, where MT has בעלי חצים, the P mss are unanimous in ܡܪ̈ܝ ܓܘܕ̈ܐ, "lords of troops". Ephrem knows this text, which he takes to mean the heads of the tribes, i.e. Joseph's own brothers. He then adds, however, that if it is [instead] written "lords of division" (ܡܪ̈ܝ ܦܠܓܘܬܐ), the brothers are still meant. This alternative reading, as Perles (p. 12) already noted, agrees with T^O. However, the P rendering cannot be derived from it, and each reflects a different treatment of the Hebrew: T^O goes back to חצה "divide", while P may be an ancient corruption of ܓܐܪ̈ܐ, a literal translation based on חֵץ "arrow".[216]

At Gen. 15:13, noted by Brock,[217] the agreement is in content though not in wording. Here God tells Abraham that his descendants will be strangers in a foreign land, and T^J comments: חלף דלא הימנת "because you did not believe (sc. the promise of possession of the land)." Ephrem is aware (though opposed) to this view:

ܠܗ ܐܬܐܡܪ ܗܕܐ ܕܥܠ ܦܘܠܗܕܢܘܬܗ ܕܥܠܘܗܝ ܐܢܫܝ̈ܢ ܕܝܢ ܐܡܪܝܢ[218]

Now *some* say that it was on account of his doubt about this that it was said to him

At Gen. 49:10, for MT שילה, the P mss have ܕܝ ܕܓܠܘܬܗ ܗܘ; but the text in Ephrem's commentary adds ܡܠܟܘܬܐ, as does Aphrahat also.[219] Both fathers agree with T^O:

עד דייתי משיחא דדיליה היא מלכותא

In this case it indeed seems as if the text of the P mss derives from the text preserved in the citations. One must recall, however, that quantitative literalism was an important constraint upon P. It is therefore possible that P's translator knew and indeed intended the interpretation familiar from the Targums but felt unable to add ܡܠܟܘܬܐ, which had no counterpart in the Hebrew. See full discussion by T. Jansma, "Ephraem on Genesis XLIX, 10. An Enquiry into the Syriac Text Forms as Presented in his Commentary on Genesis", *Parole de l'Orient* 4 (1973), pp. 247–56.

Other fathers too knew of renderings that had bypassed P and originated in Jewish Aramaic versions. Important evidence on Gen. 3:22 was recently pointed out by

[213] M.D. Koster, *The Peshitta of Exodus*, Assen 1977, pp. 198–212.

[214] A. van der Kooij, *Die alten Textzeugen des Jesajabuches. Ein Beitrag zur Textgeschichte des Alten Testaments*, Göttingen 1981, pp. 260–70.

[215] M.P. Weitzman, "The Origin of the Peshitta Psalter", pp. 277–98; see pp. 278–84.

[216] Although ܓܐܪܐ is cognate with גדוד, it is unlikely that P had in mind the גדוד of v.19, which is instead rendered ܓܝܣܐ. Maori (p. 135) defends the existing text: he takes ܓܐܪܐ to mean "partition" by analogy with גודא in the Babylonian Talmud, and supposes that the translator understood the Hebrew חצים as מחיצה.   [217] Brock, "Jewish Traditions", p. 220.   [218] Ed. Tonneau, p. 70.

[219] Ed. Parisot, p. 60; see Owens, pp. 172–5; Vööbus, pp. 25–7.

Romeny. Here in MT God declares that man had become כְּאַחַד מִמֶּנּוּ, the last word being ambiguous. In P (as in LXX) the suffix was taken as first person plural ("like one of us"). T^O, however, instead took it as third person singular, meaning "like one of his own": knowledge had rendered man unique (יְחִידִי בְעַלְמָא מִנֵּיה). Romeny observes that Eusebius of Emesa knew both renderings. Eusebius writes that, among the Syrians, some agree with LXX while others have the sense: "See, Adam has become one, to have by himself knowledge of good and evil." He thus confirms that the Syrians knew not only P but also a rendering like that of T^O.[220] Brock has noted other Syriac expressions that likewise seem to reflect Jewish Aramaic renderings not found in P, such as "second death".[221]

Jansma has pointed out that such an extra-Peshitta tradition may have been known to Bar-Daisan, who writes that the created world has been placed at the disposal of mankind,

ܒܝܕ ܐܠܗܐ ܘܒܕܡܘܬܐ ܕܐܠܗܐ (ed.Parisot, col. 547)[222]

This is evidently an allusion to Gen. 1:26 or 9:6. The passage which bears greater resemblance is 9:6, where the P mss likewise have a passive, unlike the active construction of MT:

P   ܡܛܠ ܕܒܨܠܡ ܐܠܗܐ ܥܒܝܕ ܒܕܡܘܬܐ ܕܐܠܗܐ .

MT   כִּי בְּצֶלֶם אֱלֹהִים עָשָׂה אֶת־הָאָדָם

In its transliteration ܐܠܗܝܡ, Bar-Daisan's citation differs from the P mss in either passage, which instead read ܐܠܗܐ. However, it agrees in this respect with T^O, which – as Jansma notes – also has a transliteration, according to most manuscripts: בְּצֶלֶם אֱלֹהִים (in both passages). Jansma therefore describes Bar-Daisan's text as "a Syriac quotation which in one respect is related to the Targum of Onkelos rather than to the Peshitta known to us".[223]

At the same time, Bar-Daisan agrees with P in the passive ܥܒܝܕ, which suggested to Jansma that he was also partly dependent on P; but this inference is less secure. The original active construction, preserved in MT and T^O, does not specify the subject, and so could have been changed to passive by P's translator and by Bar-Daisan independently.[224] In any case, it is not certain that P originally had the passive at all: the text cited in Ephrem's commentary has an active verb (ܥܒܕ), as in MT.[225]

These survivals of the Targums do not represent an earlier stage from which the existing text of P was derived. In most cases, they have been cited precisely because P offers an utterly different treatment of the Hebrew. Rather, they reached the church fathers independently of P. Evidently there was a tradition of biblical scholarship in Aramaic which not only fed the Jewish targums themselves but in some passages survived in the church alongside P.[226] As Goshen-Gottstein put it: "we have to reckon with

---

[220] B. ter Haar Romeny, "Eusebius of Emesa and the Early History of the Peshiṭta", paper at Leiden University 19 December 1995. The text of Eusebius here survives in Armenian translation only. See now his *A Syrian in Greek Dress*, Leuven 1997, p. 210.   [221] Brock, "Jewish Traditions".

[222] Although the work was edited by a disciple, these words seem Bar-Daisan's own.

[223] T. Jansma, "The Book of the Laws of Countries and the Peshitta Text of Genesis IX,6", *Parole de l'Orient* 1 (1970), pp. 409–14.

[224] Compare the paraphrase in the passive in Mishnah Aboth 3:14 – שֶׁנֶּאֱמַר: ...חָבִיב אָדָם שֶׁנִּבְרָא בְצֶלֶם... בְּצֶלֶם "...עָשָׂה אֶת־הָאָדָם "beloved is man *who was created* in the image ..."

[225] Note that Bar-Daisan offers no explicit quotation formula, nor any allusion to the particular context – namely murder – of Gen. 9:6.   [226] Brock, "Jewish Traditions", pp. 218–23.

extra-Peshitta traditions which were possibly connected with individual passages and never amounted to a [continuous] 'version' or manuscript".[227]

The 'Ebraya

A number of Syriac biblical commentaries occasionally cite an authority called the 'Ebraya (ܥܒܪܝܐ "the Hebrew"), whose text they contrast with P. The commonest introductory formulae are ܐܡܪ ܥܒܪܝܐ and ܐܫܠܡ ܥܒܪܝܐ.

The 'Ebraya is not cited (at least by that term) in Ephrem's undoubtedly authentic commentaries on Genesis and Exodus. However, it is cited in the commentaries ascribed to him on later books, which are known from the catena compiled by Severus of Edessa and there combined with later material. The 'Ebraya is also cited in further commentary material ascribed (again disputedly) to Ephrem on Genesis, both in Syriac – again in a compilation by Severus[228] – and in Armenian translation.[229] The accepted criterion for authenticity, formulated by Burkitt, is survival in mss that predate the invasions of the seventh century; but, as Murray has urged, the other works – particularly the biblical commentaries – may also contain authentic material.[230]

The functions of the 'Ebraya vary. First, this authority sometimes offers an alternative treatment of the Hebrew, which comes closer than P to MT:

MT	P	'Ebraya	
Gen. 25:25	אדרת	ܟܘܪ̈ܬܐ "ringlets"	ܐܣܛܠܐ
Judg. 5:29	שרותיה	ܚܟܝ̈ܡܬܐ	ܪ̈ܘܪܒܬܐ
1 Sam. 24:4	להסך את רגליו	ܘܕܢܦܢ	ܕܢܟܣܐ ܪ̈ܓܠܘܗܝ
2 Sam. 19:36	שָׁרִים וְשָׁרוֹת	ܫܝܪ̈ܐ ܘܫܝܪ̈ܬܐ[231]	ܙܡܪ̈ܐ ܘܙܡܪ̈ܬܐ

At Amos 6:1, where MT has נְקֻבֵי ראשית הגוים, P instead has an active verb: ܦܪ̈ܫܝ ܠܪܫܐ ܕܥܡ̈ܡܐ, but the 'Ebraya comes somewhat closer with a reflexive: ܦܪ̈ܫܝ ܢܦܫܗܘܢ ܠܪܫܐ ܕܥܡ̈ܡܐ "who appoint *themselves* as heads of nations".

Second, the 'Ebraya and P are sometimes comparably close to MT but mutually different. At 2 Kgs. 8:10, P renders on the basis of the Qere לו: "(say) to him: you will surely live". The 'Ebraya instead rests on the Kethib: "you will surely not live". At Isa. 17:9, חרש is transliterated in P, but translated by the 'Ebraya as "wood". At Job 26:13 we have:

MT	חללה ידו נחש בריח
P	ܘܩܛܠܬ ܐܝܕܗ ܠܚܘܝܐ ܕܥܪܩ
'Ebraya	ܘܒܪܬ ܐܝܕܗ ܠܚܘܝܐ ܡܕܘܕܝܐ

and his hand created the mottled (?) serpent

[227] Review of Vööbus in *JSS* (1961), pp. 266–70: 269.
[228] Ed. Rom., vol. 1, pp. 116–93.
[229] "Ueber den Hebräer Ephraims von Edessa", in P.A. de Lagarde, *Orientalia*, part 2, Göttingen 1880, pp. 43–64 (on Gen. 1–38). The function of these citations ranges over all three main types considered below, though it has occasionally been obscured by the translation process.
[230] F.C. Burkitt, *S. Ephraim's Quotations from the Gospel*. Texts and Studies VII.2, Cambridge 1901, pp. 23–5; R.Murray, *Symbols of Church and Kingdom*, Cambridge 1975, p. 32.
[231] P as cited in the Ephremic work agrees with the consonants of MT, albeit differently pointed as שָׁרִים וְשָׁרוֹת. This text is supported by 9a1 alone among the biblical mss, but seems the original text of P; see discussion in chapter 6 below.

The first Hebrew word is connected with חלל 'slain' by P but with חולל 'travail, bear, create' by the 'Ebraya. The last word of 'Ebraya is rare in Syriac, and its relation to the Hebrew obscure.

A third function of the 'Ebraya is to provide an interpretation known through T⁰ but not P:

MT	P	'Ebraya	Ed. Rom.
Gen. 24:63 לשוח	ܠܡܬܠܐ	ܠܡܨܠܝܘ "to pray"	I.173B
Gen. 36:24 הַיֵּמִם	ܡܝܐ	ܓܢܒܪܐ "the mighty ones"	I.184D

Other citations of the 'Ebraya suggest confusion of various sorts:

(a) In place of the cherubs at Gen. 3:24, the 'Ebraya has ܘܡܙܥܙܥܘܬܐ ܕܘܪܐ "dizziness and hallucination". This seems a recollection of להט in the same verse, taken not as 'flame' but as 'wizardry, illusion', by analogy with the להטים of the Egyptian magicians at Exod. 7:11; TB Ber. 67a likewise explains להט here as כשפים "witchcraft, illusion".[232]

(b) At Deut. 9:26, where MT has "and I prayed" and P duly renders ܘܨܠܝܬ, the 'Ebraya is said to have written ܘܨܡܬ "and I fasted", which is in fact an easy corruption of P's text, induced by the statement in v.18: "I ate no bread".

(c) At 2 Kgs. 3:15, for MT מנגן, P has ܩܝܬܪܐ, which may mean either an instrument or its player; the 'Ebraya wrongly chooses the former and specifies: ܟܢܪܐ.

(d) At Jonah 3:4a, the 'Ebraya is said to have written that Jonah "began to enter Nineveh the city, [a journey of] 40 days";[233] MT has only one day, and confusion has occurred with the prophecy of Nineveh's destruction within 40 days (v.4b).

(e) Finally, at Ezek. 7:17, the reading ascribed to the 'Ebraya coincides with LXX and is thus falsely ascribed, as Assemani already observed in the Roman Edition.

All these cases must be distinguished from cases where the Syriac term ܥܒܪܝܐ refers to the Hebrew language or a Hebrew word.[234] Such references include 1 Sam. 8:11, where the commentary cites the Hebrew form נעצר in Syriac transliteration, rightly noting its relationship with the Syriac verb ܥܨܪ.

Altogether, the material in the Ephremic works supplied by the 'Ebraya varies not only in reliability but also in character, part based directly on the Hebrew text and part on traditional Jewish interpretation. This variety suggests that it was drawn piecemeal – rather than through an unknown written source – from contacts with (perhaps converted) Jews or even inherited from Jewish antecedents of the Syriac church.[235]

The references to the 'Ebraya may well go back in part to Ephrem himself. The commentaries in which they occur, although disputed, occasionally preserve the original reading of P against the biblical mss, as do the undoubted commentaries on Genesis

---

[232] D. Gerson, "Die Commentarien des Ephraem Syrus im Verhältniss zur jüdischen Exegese. Ein Beitrag zur Geschichte der Exegese", *MGWJ* 17 (1868), pp. 15–33, 64–72, 98–109, 141–9: see p. 147n.

[233] Lamy, vol. 2, col. 237.

[234] These relate to the following passages, with references added to the first volume of the Roman edition: Gen. 26:33 (174C), Josh. 13:6 (303C), 15:28 (305B), 1Sam. 8:11 (340D), 21:8 (376E), 23:28(379E), 1 Kgs. 18:44 (498F), 2 Kgs. 3:4 (523E). On 1 Kgs. 7:21 (460a), the commentary explains the Hebrew names Jachin and Boaz, but without using the term "Hebrew".

[235] A. Baumstark, "Griechische und hebräische Bibelzitate in der Pentateucherklärung Išo'dads von Merw", *OrChr* (1911), pp. 1–19. L.van Rompay, "The Christian Syriac Tradition of Interpretation", in M.Sæbø (ed.), *Hebrew Bible/Old Testament: The History of its Interpretation*, Göttingen 1996, p. 616.

and Exodus. Moreover, Ephrem's undisputed commentary on Genesis cites the text of the Targums, as does the 'Ebraya on occasion.

There is in fact one passage in Ephrem's undisputed commentary on Genesis where a corrupt reference to the 'Ebraya has been suspected. Ephrem refers to the Behemoth and remarks:[236]

ܐܦ ܕܘܝܕ ܕܢ̈ܒܪܐ ܐܡܪ ܕܥܠ ܐܠܦ ܛܘܪ̈ܝܢ ܐܬܬܪܣܝܬ ܒܗܡܘܬ

Evidently he refers to Ps. 50:10b, which runs in MT as follows:

בהמות בהררי אלף

Ephrem thus interprets בהמות here as the Behemoth (cf. Job 40:15), and infers that it feeds upon a thousand mountains. Here he differs utterly from P- Psalms, which takes בהמות as a common noun and the last word as "ox": ܘܒܥܝܪܐ ܕܒܛܘܪܐ ܘܬܘܪܐ.[237] Ephrem's understanding is, however, paralleled in TB Baba Batra 74b.

The word ܕܢ̈ܒܪܐ in Ephrem's commentary cannot stand. Payne Smith emends to ܕܒܥܝܪܐ,[238] and the noun ܒܥܝܪܐ indeed occurs in P to the Psalms passage. However, the syntax of the *dalath* is strange, and in any case Ephrem's treatment wholly differs from that of P-Psalms. Jansma instead amended to ܒܥܒܪܝܐ "in the Hebrew", which would be in keeping with a common function of the 'Ebraya elsewhere, namely an interpretation of the Hebrew which differs from P.[239] The same effect may be achieved by a gentler emendation, to ܕܥܒܪ̈ܝܐ (ܕܘܝܕ) "David according to the Hebrews". The construction would be paralleled in the phrase ܕܘܝܕ ܕܡܦܪ̈ܫܐ in the title of the Psalter in various mss, meaning "David according to the separated ones", i.e. on the basis of those who translated the Bible into Greek and worked in separate cells.[240]

The 'Ebraya is also mentioned by later writers, with the same range of functions. Thus it may stand closer than P to MT:

	MT	P	'Ebraya
Judg. 13:17	וכבדנוך	ܘܢܝܩܪܟ	ܘܢܝܩܪܘܢܟ[241]
Ps. 16:2	טובתי בל עליך	ܘܛܒܬܝ ܡܢ ܠܘܬܟ ܗܝ	ܘܛܝܒܘܬܝ ܚܠܦܝܟ ܠܐ ܐܝܬ[242]

It may provide an alternative 'plain sense' for the Hebrew consonantal text:

Exod. 1:19 MT חָיוֹת P ܚ̈ܝܬܐ Ebr apud 9m1 ܚܝ̈ܘܬܐ[243]

Here the 'Ebraya starts out from the alternative vocalisation חַיּוֹת "animals". Sometimes, again, the 'Ebraya offers a rabbinic interpretation, e.g.

Gen. 39:11 MT לעשות מלאכתו P ܠܡܥܒܕ ܥܒܕܐ

Ebr. *apud* Isho'dad explains that Joseph's motive for going to Potiphar's house on a day when no other man would be there was ܠܡܚܫܒܘ ܚܘܫ̈ܒܢܐ ܕܡܪܘܗܝ "to examine his account

[236] Ed. Tonneau, pp. 22–3.

[237] S. Hidal, *Interpretatio Syriaca. Die Kommentare des heiligen Ephräm des Syrers zu Genesis und Exodus mit besonderer Berücksichtigung ihrer auslegungsgeschichtlichen Stellung*, Lund 1974, p. 71.

[238] R. Payne Smith (ed.) *Thesaurus Syriacus*, vol. 2, col. 2773. The emendation is accepted by Tonneau.

[239] T. Jansma, "Beiträge zur Berichtigung einzelner Stellen in Ephraems Genesis-kommentar", *OrChr* 56 (1972), pp. 60–78: 60.

[240] So Barnes in *JTS* 2 (1901), p. 191.

[241] C. van den Eynde (ed.), *Commentaire d' Išo'dad de Merv sur l'ancien Testament. Vol.3: Livre des Sessions*, Louvain 1962 (CSCO 229, Syr. 96), p. 33. The text of the mss seems an old corruption of a text coinciding with the 'Ebraya. The 'Ebraya is cited similarly in the (slightly later) Gannat Busame, a Nestorian compilation perhaps of the 10th century. See G.J. Reinink (ed.), CSCO 502 (Syr. 212), p.xx.

[242] Išo'dad explains: "You need nothing of mine, for you are my benefactor always". See C. van den Eynde (ed.), *Commentaire d' Išo'dad de Merv sur l'Ancien Testament* (CSCO 433, Syr 185), Louvain 1981, p. 34.

[243] W. Wright, *Catalogue of Syriac Manuscripts in the British Museum*, London 1870–2, vol. 1, p. 104.

books".[244] Here the 'Ebraya agrees verbally with T^O.[245] Once more the varied function confirms that the 'Ebraya was never a continuous version in Syriac, but a generic term for information derived by whatever route from Jewish tradition.

Translations from Greek into Syriac

Traces of the putative *Vetus Syra* have sometimes been detected in Syriac translations made from Greek biblical texts. We may begin with an example from the Syrohexapla:
Exod. 15:1 MT ויאמרו לאמר; P ܘܐܡܪܘ; Syrohex. ܘܐܡܪܘ ܠܡܐܡܪ[246]
Vööbus (p. 65) viewed Syrohex. as a trace of "targumisches Profil", apparently because it is fuller than P. However, it could easily have instead been derived from LXX: καὶ εἶπαν λέγοντες.

The putative *Vetus Syra* is also thought to have influenced the Syrolucianic version of Isa. 44:13:

MT   יתארהו בשרד יעשהו במקצעות
LXX[Lucian] καὶ ἐμόρφωσεν αὐτὸ ἐν παραγραφίδι, ἐποίησεν αὐτὸ ἐν παραγωνίσκοις
Syroluc.   ܘܡܬܩܢ ܠܗ ܒܡܫܘܚܬܐ ܘܒܕܝܘܐ ܥܒܕܗ

The Syrolucianic text cannot be derived from P (which all but omits these words), nor does it correspond exactly to the Greek. Hence Delekat detects here a trace of the *Vetus Syra*.[247] In fact, however, Syroluc. could simply be an attempt to render the difficult Greek: the ܡܫܘܚܬܐ ('carpenter's square') apparently corresponds to the last word of Lucian, while ܕܝܘܐ is a vague guess.[248]

Traces of the *Vetus Syra* have also been sought in Syriac translations of Greek patristic works. In translations made before the end of the sixth century, we often find that the text of P is substituted for any Old Testament quotations in the Greek work.[249] Cureton already observed, in his first publication of the Old Syriac Gospels, that "there is a great similarity in many cases between the Peshito of the Old Testament and this text [i.e. Curetonianus] in the places quoted by St. Matthew".[250] The same practice was noted more fully by Baumstark.[251] At the same time, of course, the translator may also be influenced by the Greek text. Elements in the Syriac translation not immediately attributable either to the Old Testament Peshitta or to the Greek text have been ascribed to the putative *Vetus Syra*.

However, one must first verify that the Greek text is not the cause. Thus a trace of the *Vetus Syra* on Ps. 101:1 has been detected in the P version of Hebrews 1:13 –

---

[244] J.-M.Vosté and C. van den Eynde (eds.), *Commentaire d'Išo'dad de Merv sur l'ancien Testament. I: Genèse*, Louvain 1950 (CSCO 126, Syr.67), p. 205. See further C. van den Eynde (tr.), *Commentaire d' Išo'dad de Merv sur l'ancien Testament. I: Genèse*, Louvain 1955 (CSCO 156, Syr.75), p. xxiv.

[245] Others viewed Joseph's intentions less charitably; see discussion in TB Sotah 36b.

[246] P. de Lagarde, *Veteris testamenti ab Origene recensiti fragmenta apud Syros servata quinque*, Göttingen 1880, p. 106.

[247] L. Delekat, "Die syrolukianische Übersetzung des Buches Jesaja und das Postulat eines alttestamentlichen Vetus Syra", *ZAW* 69 (1957), pp. 21–54:31,35.

[248] For further discussion, see R.G. Jenkins, *The Old Testament Quotations of Philoxenus of Mabbug*, Louvain 1989, p. 29.

[249] S.P. Brock, "Towards a History of Syriac Translation Technique", *OCA* 221 (1983), pp. 1–14: 11–12.

[250] W. Cureton, *Remains of a very Antient Recension of the Four Gospels in Syriac*, London 1858, p.lxxxvi.

[251] A. Baumstark, "Das Problem der Bibelzitate in der syrischen Übersetzungsliteratur", *Oriens Christianus* 30 (1933), pp. 208–25.

Gk   ὑποπόδιον τῶν ποδῶν σου

Peshitta   ܩܕܡ ܕܘܟܬܐ ܠ̈ܪܓܠܝܟ

P on Ps. 110:1   ܩܕܡ ܠ̈ܪܓܠܝܟ

The Peshitta of Hebrews indeed adds the word ܕܘܟܬܐ, which is not found in P-Psalms, and is instead ascribed by Peters to the *Vetus Syra*.[252] Instead, however, it may be inspired by the element ὑπο-, or by the variant ὑποκάτω τῶν ποδῶν σου at Matt. 22:24 and Mark 12:36.

Moreover, we have to take account of the general approach of the Syriac translators, who – at least until the end of the sixth century – aimed primarily to convey the sense of the original, rather than imitate the form.[253] Hence, before concluding that a loose citation of a biblical verse goes back to some form of the biblical text older than P, one must allow for the freedom inherent in the translation of the patristic work. The point is illustrated by the biblical citations in the Syriac version of the Ecclesiastical History, made shortly after – if not before – the death of its author Eusebius in about 340 CE.[254] The freedom of this translation was noted above. At I.iii.14, Eusebius quotes Ps. 45:8 after LXX: "God . . . has anointed you with the oil of gladness more than your companions (παρὰ τοὺς μετόχους σου)". P renders the last phrase similarly: ܝܬܝܪ ܡܢ ܚ̈ܒܪܝܟ ("more than your fellows"). However, the Syriac translator of Eusebius has: "God . . . has anointed you more than those who had been anointed":

ܝܬܝܪ ܡܢ ܗܢܘܢ ܕܐܬܡܫܚܘ. . . .

This is taken by Peters as a relic of an early loose or expansive stage of P. However, Eusebius goes on to explain that the 'oil of gladness' indicates the superiority of Christ's anointing over those anointed of old as mere types of him; and it may be that the translator simply adapted the quotation to that exegesis.

"The Syrian" in Greek works

A form of the biblical text is quoted by various Greek fathers under the name ὁ Σύρος: the Syrian. The first to use this term was long thought to be Melito of Sardis (died *c.* 190 CE), in a fragment on Gen. 22:13, which, however, is now known to belong to Eusebius of Emesa (died *c.* 359).[255]

The history of scholarship regarding the Syrian has been ably traced by Romeny.[256] The citations agree sometimes but by no means always with P. Perles was sufficiently impressed by the agreements to identify the two versions, albeit tentatively. He ascribed the disagreements partly to errors of transmission – either of the patristic text or of the text of P – and partly to errors in the process of translating into Greek the (perhaps orally reported) readings of P.[257] Field, however, attached greater importance to the disagreements, and therefore viewed the Syrian as a Greek version made by an anonymous

---

[252] As suggested by C. Peters, "Pešitta-Psalter und Psalmentargum", *Muséon* 52 (1939), pp. 275–96.

[253] S.[P.]Brock, "Aspects of Translation Technique in Antiquity", *Greek Roman and Byzantine Studies* 20 (1979) pp. 69–87, esp. p. 75.

[254] W. Wright and N. McLean, *The Ecclesiastical History of Eusebius in Syriac*, Cambridge 1898, p. ix.

[255] G. Mercati, "A quale tempo risale 'il Siro' dei commentatori greci della Bibbia?", *Biblica* 26 (1945), pp. 1–11: 1–6.

[256] R.B. ter Haar Romeny, "'Quis Sit ὁ Σύρος' Revisited", in A. Salvesen (ed.), *Origen's Hexapla and Fragments*, Tübingen 1998, pp. 390–8.   [257] Perles, *Meletemata*, pp. 49–51.

Syrian scholar, distinct from P though perhaps based on P in part.[258] Rahlfs too distinguished the Syrian from P, advancing the following new argument. At Judg. 12:6, the Hebrew dialectal difference שבלת-סבלת is reproduced in P as ܣܒܠܐ . ܫܒܠܐ, but the Syrian, as cited by Theodoret of Cyrrhus (c. 393–c. 466), uses the quite different opposition σεμβελώ – σεμβλά. Since the latter opposition involves vowels only, Rahlfs inferred that the text of the Syrian was in Greek rather than the Syriac text of P.[259] Sprenger, however, has warned against inferring too much from this passage: it may be the particular opposition expressed in P – between ܫ and ܣ – could not be reproduced in Greek, which has only Sigma, so that Theodoret exceptionally substituted an analogy which Greek could represent, drawn from the variation of vowels of the Syriac dialects.[260] Lehmann has argued that – at least in the usage of Eusebius of Emesa, who yields the earliest extant references – the term "Syrian" most naturally means a version in Syriac, just as Eusebius' references to "the Hebrew" imply access to a Hebrew text. Born in Edessa, Eusebius would have known Syriac; and the parallels with P convinced Lehmann that this was his source.[261]

The Greek text for Eusebius' commentary on the Octateuch survives in fragments alone, but we have a continuous translation into Armenian. The evidence for Genesis – comprising about half of the complete work – has been studied by Romeny, who there found some sixty citations (double the number previously known in Genesis) of the Syrian.[262] Romeny's work confirms the identity of the Syrian with P. In one striking instance, at Gen. 8:7, Romeny finds that the Syrian preserves the original text of P better than any extant ms. Here MT has ויצא יצוא ושוב, and most P mss have a negative before the last verb: ܘܢܦܩ ܘܠܐ ܗܦܟ ܗܘܐ (similarly LXX). In 5b1, however, there is an erasure after the first word, and the next legible word is ܘܗܦܟ. Romeny rightly deduces that 5b1 originally had no negative, and that we should probably reconstruct: ܘܢܦܩ [ܗܦܟ] ܘܗܦܟ, which closely resembles MT and may be considered the original reading of P. What lends probability to this reconstruction is that Eusebius reports that the Syrian, unlike LXX, has no negative here.[263] Remarkably, as Romeny notes, Wellhausen already suspected – on the basis of the Syrian alone and without knowledge of 5b1 – that P originally had no negative here.[264]

Eusebius' citation at Gen. 22:13 is exceptional. He states that the Syrian (and "the Hebrew") have κρεμάμενος φῆσιν, ὡς σαφέστερον τυποῦν(τα) τὸν σταυρόν.[265] This reading is also widely cited in Syriac by Ephrem and later fathers, who write that Abraham found the ram at Gen. 22:13 suspended (ܬܠܐ). In this case, the Syrian clearly

---

[258] F. Field, *Origenis Hexaplorum quae supersunt*, vol. 1 (Oxford 1875), pp. lxxvii–lxxxii.

[259] A. Rahlfs, "Quis Sit ὁ Σύρος", *Nachrichten von der Gesellschaft der Wissenschaften zu Göttingen, Phil.-hist. Klasse* (1915), pp. 420–8.

[260] H.N. Sprenger, *Theodori Mopsuesteni Commentarius in XII Prophetas. Einleitung und Ausgabe*, Wiesbaden 1977, p. 82.

[261] H.J. Lehmann, "The Syriac Translation of the Old Testament as Evidenced around the Middle of the Fourth Century", *SJOT* 1 (1987), pp. 66–86.

[262] R.B. ter Haar Romeny, *A Syrian in Greek Dress. The Use of Greek, Hebrew and Syriac Biblical Texts in Eusebius of Emesa's Commentary on Genesis*, Leuven 1997; see pp. 71–86.

[263] Romeny in MPI 8 (1995), pp. 177–85: 181–2.

[264] J. Wellhausen, in F. Bleek (ed.), *Einleitung in das Alte Testament*, 4th edn, Berlin 1878, p. 604.

[265] Vööbus (*Peschitta und Targumim des Pentateuchs*, pp. 100–1) quotes the Syriac evidence fully. For the Greek, see F. Petit (ed.), *Catenae Graecae in Genesim et in Exodum. I. Catena Sinaitica* [=*Corpus Christianorum. Series Graeca* 2]. Turnhout 1977, p. 189.

differs from P, where the ram is caught (ܐܝܠܐ), as in MT (נֶאֱחַז). Eusebius' explanation (in the form ὡς plus infinitive) suggests that the Syrian here denotes an interpretation – rather than a text – current in Syria, predominantly in Christian circles.[266]

The identity of P with the Syrian seems likely for other fathers, notably Diodore of Tarsus, a disciple of Eusebius,[267] and Theodoret of Cyrrhus. Some of the readings which Theodoret ascribes to the Syrian could in fact only be derived from P, e.g. at Jer. 48:33 –

The Syrian: οὐκέτι οἱ ληνοβατοῦντες κελεύσουσι λέγοντες ἰὰ ἰὰ

P: ܘܠܐ ܢܬܝܢ ܦܩܘܕܝܢ ܘܠܐ ܢܒܣܘܢ ܟܐ ܘܠܐ ܐܡܪܝܢ ܗܝ ܗܝ،

The identity of the Syrian in Theodoret with P has been further argued by Guinot,[268] who is however troubled by some contrary evidence. First, in three instances the Syrian appears to disagree with P; and second, in a passage in book 5 of his *Therapeutica*, Theodoret lists the languages into which the Hebrew Bible has been translated, but does not mention Syriac, which seems odd if he used P as a source.[269]

In fact, however, even in the three refractory passages the Syrian may represent P:

(a)   Ezek. 27:8: The Syrian (and the "Hebrew") are cited as οἱ γείτονές σου "your neighbours", while P has ܥܡܘܪܐ "dwellers" (agreeing with MT יֹשְׁבֵי). These meanings are linked, however, in that the Hebrew word יֹשֵׁב "dweller" may extend to "neighbour". The same range may have been imputed to Syriac ܥܡܘܪܐ. That impression may have been fostered by Jer. 50 [LXX 27]:40, where LXX has ὁμορούσας "neighbours" while P has ܥܡܘܪܐ, both for the plural of יֹשֵׁב.

(b)   Ezek. 27:24: Here Theodoret's starting-point is not P, but Aquila's ἐν μαγώζοις, which he explains as ἐν ἀποκρύφοις σκεύεσιν "in hidden vessels"; and Theodoret adds that the Syrian understood the text likewise.[270] P has ܣܝܡܬܐ ܛܒܬܐ "goodly treasures", which Guinot thought significantly different. Given, however, that an exact citation was never intended, the Greek phrase corresponds to P reasonably well.

(c)   Lam. 3:29: The verse begins: "Let him place his mouth . . ." P continues: ܒܥܦܪܐ. The Syrian is cited by Theodoret as ἐν γῇ, which at first sight differs. Here, however, γῇ must have meant "lump(s) of earth", since Theodoret interprets the phrase thus: "let him bear suffering , as if he had his mouth filled with earth".[271] Thus P and the Syrian in fact correspond well in sense.

As to Theodoret's reticence about P, an oriental who has chosen to write in Greek as a cultural language could well have felt ambivalent about his native dialect and its literature.

Similar ambivalence may be observed in Theodore of Mopsuestia (*c.* 350–428). In his commentary on Psalms he quotes the Syrian as a serious authority.[272] In his later

---

[266] The ram was also so depicted on the floor of the Bet Alpha synagogue (but perhaps under Christian influence) in sixth-century Palestine; see M. Bregman, "The Depiction of the Ram in the Aqedah Mosaic at Beit Alpha" (in Hebrew), *Tarbiz* 51 (1981/2), pp. 306–9.

[267] See L. van Rompay, "L'informateur syrien de Basile de Césarée: à propos de Genèse 1,2", *OCP* 58 (1992), pp. 245–51.

[268] J.-N. Guinot, "Qui est 'le Syrien' dans les commentaires de Théodoret de Cyr?" in E.A. Livingstone, ed. *Papers Presented at the Eleventh International Conference on Patristic Studies Held in Oxford 1991.* Studia Patristica 25 (Louvain 1993), pp. 60–71: 63–4.   [269] Migne, PG 83, col. 948.

[270] οὕτω γὰρ καὶ ὁ Σύρος νοήσας ἡρμήνευσεν...

[271] ὥσπερ γῆς ἔχων πεπληρωμένον τὸ στόμα (PG 81, col. 897).

[272] R. Devreesse, *Le Commentaire de Théodore de Mopsueste sur les Psaumes. (I–LXXX)*, Rome 1939, pp. 91,92,134,134. It is unlikely that *caddis* at Ps. 29:8 (p. 134) is a further 'Syrian' reading.

commentary on the Twelve Prophets, however, he describes the author of P as ἕνα τινὰ ἀφανῆ, whom he constrasts unfavourably with the learned Seventy, whose work was used by the Apostles.[273] It is here that Theodore makes his famous comment on the obscure origin of P: ἡρμήνευται δὲ ταῦτα εἰς μὲν τὴν Σύρων παρ᾽ ὅτου δήποτε, οὐδὲ γὰρ ἔγνωσται μέχρι τῆς τήμερον, ὅστις ποτὲ οὗτός ἐστιν.[274]

Both in the Twelve Prophets and in Psalms, Theodore's citations of the Syrian normally reflect P, though the relation is not always straightforward. In Psalms (where much of Theodore's work survives in Latin only), the Syrian and P may be compared as follows:

(a) At Ps. 16:2 the citation *quoniam bona mea a te sunt* clearly agrees with P, whereas MT and LXX have a negative.

(b) At 16:3b, P agrees closely with MT: "and the glorious ones (ܘܡܝܩܪ̈ܐ), all my desire is in them; their pains shall increase . . . I shall not remember their name". LXX, however, in place of the opening phrase has ἐθαυμάστωσεν παντὰ τὰ θελήματα αὐτοῦ "he made all his desires wondrous (in them)". Theodore presents, as a paraphrase of the "Hebrew" and the Syrian:

> Superbis et magnis . . . id est gentibus . . . admirabilis ostensus es ita, ut omnes voluntates meae fierent in illis, dum te persequente pereunt . . .

This combines the opening verb of LXX with the elements "glorious" and "*my desire(s)*" in MT and P. The latter are Theodore's justification for ascribing this translation to the "Hebrew" and the Syrian.

(c) At 29:6a, the reading *inimicos sicut germina cedrorum* is ascribed to the Syrian. Most of this can readily be derived from P: ܐܝܟ ܥܓ̈ܠܐ in 6a and ܐܪ̈ܙܐ in 5a suggested "calves of cedars", which could have become *sicut germina cedrorum*, while the context identified God's enemies (*inimicos*) as the object of comparison.

(d) At 29:6b, MT has שִׂרְיֹן and P ܣܪܝܢ (cf. Deut. 3:9), yet the Syrian is cited as *Israhel*. This implies that the Hebrew was instead read as יְשֻׁרוּן. Such a reading (or deliberate misreading) must have been known, since LXX has ἠγαπημένος, which is an interpretation of יְשֻׁרוּן, as at Deut. 33:26. In having no connection with P, this reading of the Syrian is exceptional; perhaps again it represents an interpretation current in Syria.

(e) At 60:10a, the Syrian's λεκάνη τῆς καταπατήσεώς μου, which Theodore relates to the trampling of garments by a fuller, agrees with P in the parallel passage 108:10a ܘܡܣܐܢܝ ܕܕܝܫܬܝ, though not here.[275]

(f) At 65:11, the Syrian's δρόσους "dew-drops" – in place of LXX σταγόσιν – seems an interpretation of P ܪܣܝܣܘ̈. Although the latter can mean "drops" in general, it clearly refers at Cant. 5:2 to dew, which there occurs in parallel.

In Theodore's commentary on the Twelve Prophets, two readings show distinctive readings of P:

Hab. 2:11   πάσσαλος "peg" = P ܣܟܬܐ (contrast LXX: beetle)   Sprenger, p. 270

Zeph. 3:1   Ιωνᾶ "Jonah" = P ܝܘܢ (contrast LXX: dove)   Sprenger, p. 295

---

[273] Sprenger, *Theodori Mopsuesteni Commentarius*, p. 284 (on Zeph. 1:5).   [274] Sprenger, p. 283.
[275] Except in the late ms 12a1.

Those responsible for the latter rendering are disparaged as οἱ θαυμαστοὶ μυθολόγοι τῶν Σύρων.

At Zeph. 1:5, P has ܡܠܟܘܡ, and some LXX manuscripts likewise have Μελχομ, while MT is vocalised as בְּמַלְכָּם "in their king". Theodore criticises those who claim ὅτι Μελχὸμ ἐνταῦθα τὸν βασιλέα βούλεται εἰπεῖν. He dismisses this interpretation as a μυθολογία, and ascribes it to "those who gape (κεχηνότων) at the Syrians". It seems that these Syrians had a reference to the god Milcom in their text – just as in P – but interpreted the unfamiliar name as if it were ܒܡܠܟܗܘܢ "in their king".[276]

Translations from Syriac into Arabic

In Arabic translation, the P version of the Old Testament – as well as the New – is cited by 'Ali ibn Rabban al-Tabari, a convert from Christianity, who wrote a defence of Islam *c.* 855.[277] 'Ali Ibn Rabban quotes more than 200 verses from the Old Testament, of which about half come from Isaiah. He refers to his biblical source as "the books of the Syrians which Marcus (i.e. Mark the evangelist) has translated",[278] and some renderings confirm that his source could only have been the Peshitta version, e.g.
Deut. 33:2 –

MT	אשדת למו: אף חבב עמים כל קדשיו בידך
P	ܣܬ ܠܗܘܢ ܘܐܝܟ ܐܣܚ ܘܐܘܪ ܠܬܚܬܟ ܚܠܗ ܘܩܕܝܫܗ, ܟܢ ܡܒܪܟ
Ibn Rabban (p. 74)	فمنحهم العز وحبّبهم الي الشعوب ودعا بجميع قديسيه بالبركة

> He gave them power, and made them to be loved by nations, and called blessings on all his saints (ET, p. 87)

The elements "gave" and "bless" can only have come from P, which offered a vague guess for אשדת and misread בידך as ברך.

A principal motive of Ibn Rabban in citing the biblical text was to show that Muhammad was there mentioned by name. Since the Syriac equivalent of الحمد لله is ܬܫܒܘܚܬܐ ܠܐܠܗܐ, he inferred equivalence between the Syriac root ܫܒܚ and Arabic حمد, and deduced that derivatives of the former indicated Muhammad. The frequency in P of such derivatives (which sometimes serve as drudge words[279]) left Ibn Rabban with a large collection of prooftexts.[280]

In the following further examples, Ibn Rabban cites the Old Testament in a longer form than the P mss, elements not present in P being italicised below:

Isa. 21:8 and the watchman told me *secretly*

Ps. 45:5 for thy law *and thy prescriptions are joined* with the majesty of thy right hand

Ps. 72:11 and all nations shall serve him *with obedience and submissiveness*

According to Peters, who cites the Psalms passages, Ibn Rabban's citations exhibit

---

[276] Sprenger, p. 283.

[277] A. Mingana, *The Book of Religion and Empire by 'Ali Ṭabari.* English translation: Manchester 1922. Arabic text: Manchester 1923.

[278] This tradition of the authorship of P is also known elsewhere in the east; see p. 248 below.

[279] Thus in Psalms the root ܫܒܚ corresponds to some 25 different Hebrew roots, and the form ܫܒܚ alone to Hebrew אדיר, הוד, מהלל, יפה, כבוד, נדיב, פז, רעם, רענן.

[280] For a general treatment of the claim by Muslim authors that Muhammad had been predicted in the Bible, see H. Lazarus-Yafeh, *Intertwined Worlds*, Princeton 1982, pp. 75–110.

"targumartige Breite und Freiheit", and so preserve an early form of the P text. Instead, however, these loose and expansive forms of the Old Testament text may result from Ibn Rabban's own technique of translation into Arabic. There is a simple control: Ibn Rabban's translations from the New Testament. Here we find expansions of the same sort:

Matt. 4:19 (p. 148)	And I will make you *after this day* fishers of men
Matt. 4:21 (p. 148)	He called them *to his faith*
Matt. 12:25 (p. 59)	Every kingdom which is divided against itself shall perish*, and shall not stand*, and every city in which there is disunion *and disagreement shall not last* and shall not be firm
Matt. 21:23 (p. 150)	By what authority doest thou *what we see*?
Matt. 27:40 (p. 151)	Come down from the cross *that we may believe in thee*
Luke 22:35 (p. 143)	*Were ye harmed* and lacked ye in anything?
John 16:13 (p. 140)	and [the Paraclete] will not say anything of his own accord, but will *direct you in all truth*, and tell you of events *and hidden things*

Thus Ibn Rabban's loose and expansive citations from the Old Testament likewise reflect his own technique of translation into Arabic, rather than the early history of P. This is also clear in the second half of Matt. 12:25, where P (following the Greek) repeats a phrase from the first half, while the Arabic translation strives to introduce variety:

Peshitta: ܕܡܬܦܠܓܐ ܥܠ ܢܦܫܗ "(every city) which is divided against itself"

Ibn Rabban (p. 53):   يقع فيها التشتّت والخلاف

in which there is disunion and disagreement (ET, p. 59)

Ibn Rabban's biblical citations were used by later Arabic writers, though not always accurately.[281] How loosely later writers can cite the Old Testament is illustrated by what Abu Nu'aim (died 1038 CE) claims to be a verse from Psalms:[282]

لانتقم من المنافق بالمنافق ثم انتقم من المنافقين جميعا

that I may wreak vengeance on the hypocrite through the hypocrite, and then I shall wreak vengeance on all the hypocrites together

Altogether, therefore, biblical citations in Arabic seem unlikely to illuminate the early history of the Peshitta text.

Conclusion

Despite expectations, citations shed no light on the relationship between P and the Targums. Their interest lies elsewhere. Very occasionally, they preserve an original reading of P which the biblical mss of P have lost. On other rare occasions, they preserve isolated Targum renderings which were never shared by P but were known alongside P in the Syriac church. In by far the majority of cases, however, there is no reason to believe that the biblical text known to the citing authors or translators differed from

[281] D.S. Margoliouth, "On 'The Book of Religion and Empire' by Ali b.Rabban al-Tabari", *Proceedings of the British Academy* 16 (1930), pp. 1–20.
[282] C. Peters, "Arabische Psalmenzitate bei Abū Nu'aim", *Biblica* 20 (1939), pp. 1–9. Peters, who insisted that the citations were exact, could only call this citation a "riddle" (p. 4).

that of the P mss. Almost all the divergences between citations and the text of the biblical mss, can be viewed as adjustments, conscious and unconscious, of a text identical with the latter. Where citations agree with the Targums – particularly the Palestinian Targums – against P, this is because the citing authors and the Palestinian Targums both expand the text to gain explicitness, while P accepts the constraint of quantitative literalism. The citations fall well short of proving the claim that P stands at one remove from the Hebrew, its direct source being an Aramaic translation. P must instead be viewed as a direct translation from the Hebrew.

Appendix II: Parallels with rabbinic sources

Methodology

As noted above, many renderings in P which agree with one or more Targums agree also with rabbinic sources. However, a number of further agreements between P and rabbinic sources have been detected which are not paralleled in the extant Targums. Although far less numerous than the parallels either with LXX or with the Targums, these cases must now be discussed.

As before, the first question is whether the agreement indicates common origin or whether it could be due to polygenesis. Here we must recall that P's translator desired, like the rabbis, to make explicit what was implied (however clearly) in the Hebrew text. Both also desired to harmonise contradictory passages, and both tended to interpret one passage through another, out of a desire for consistency and a belief in the unity of scripture. Moreover, the translator would have applied his own ingenuity to passages presenting rare words or logical difficulties, and this may have led him independently to the same solution as the rabbis, who were after all confronted with the same text.

The likelihood of polygenesis is also affected by the nature of the rabbinic source. In the halachic Midrashim, and later in the Talmuds, the rabbis sometimes present an array of alternative interpretations of the biblical text, which they scrutinise and eliminate in turn, until the one correct interpretation is identified. Since the arrays of interpretations are intended to be exhaustive, the agreement of one of these with P is no proof of common origin.

Another methodological issue affecting the likelihood of influence upon P is the date of the rabbinic material scoured for parallels. In particular, much of the material embedded in medieval rabbinic compilations is later than P (even though much may also be earlier), so that one must be take particular care before inferring influence upon P from parallels found in these compilations only. On the contrary, P was occasionally a source for medieval Jewish scholars, as we have seen in the case of Rabbi Samuel ben Nissim Masnut of Aleppo in the early thirteenth century.

Text-critical issues must also be borne in mind. On the Syriac side, corruption or deliberate change in transmission may have brought the text into agreement with a rabbinic source. This is especially relevant when a reading claimed to exhibit a rabbinic parallel appears in only part of the ms tradition of P, while the remaining mss (or even a single ms) of P present a rival reading that follows MT closely. In such cases, we must pause before assuming that the reading of P which exhibits the rabbinic parallel is original, even if it is attested by the majority of mss. As discussed in chapter 6 below, certain manuscripts – notably, 5b1 in Genesis and Exodus, 6b1 in Leviticus to Deuteronomy, 7pj2 in Numbers, and 9a1 in Leviticus and several later books – often depart from the majority to agree closely with MT in readings which preserve the original text of P.[283]

The first to survey the parallels between P and rabbinic exegesis in detail was again Perles, who inferred that P knew isolated rabbinic traditions attached to individual passages. Heller posited a far more pervasive rabbinic influence, which in his view was the source of many of the translators' techniques. Thus he claimed that P's technique of 'misreading' was derived specifically from the rabbinic device of Al-Tiqre. He also regarded the practice of interpreting one passage through another as intrinsically rabbinic. He even considered that P's treatment of grammatical particles on occasion as interchangeable or redundant was also due to rabbinic influence, even though he acknowledged that no such principle was formulated explicitly in the extant literature of rabbinic Judaism before Ibn Janāḥ (*c.* 1000 CE).[284] What Heller's approach overlooked is that all these adjustments are obvious expedients for any interpreter of a difficult text, and need not betoken common origin, even when the results in individual passages are identical.[285] The first to give proper attention to the problems of methodology was Maori.[286]

Instances in the Pentateuch suggesting common origin

Cases where P agrees not only with rabbinic sources but also with one or more Targums have already been considered. Here we shall be concerned with parallels with rabbinic sources that lack attestation in the Targums.[287] Some of these agreements in understanding are so striking as to imply common origin:

(a)   Exod. 1:10

MT ועלה מן הארץ, P ܢܣܩܘܢ ܠܗ ܡܢ ܐܪܥܐ "they (the Israelites) will make us (Egyptians) go up from the land". Compare the explanation in TB Sotah 11a: "like a man who applies to another a curse really directed against himself". This sense is not found in T[OJFN], though the margin to T[N] has ויתרך יתן וניסוק מן ארעה.[288]

(b)   Exod. 40:17

P adds that the tabernacle was set up ܒܚܕ ܒܫܒܐ "on a Sunday", as in the tradition recorded in TB Shab. 87b and Sifra Shemini *init.* that that day was: ראשון למעשה בראשית.[289]

---

[283] See M.D. Koster, *The Peshitta of Exodus. The Development of its Text in the Course of Fifteen Centuries*, Assen/Amsterdam 1977, pp. 177–97 (on 5b1); A.P. Hayman's review thereof in *JJS* 25 (1980), pp. 263–70 (on 7pj2 and 9a1 in Numbers); and the discussion in chapter 6 below.

[284] Ch. Heller, *Untersuchungen über die Peschîttâ zur gesamten hebräischen Bibel*, Berlin 1911.

[285] As at Ps. 49:10, where both lead to קברם in place of MT (בתימו לעולם) קרבם.

[286] Y. Maori, *The Peshitta Version of the Pentateuch and Early Jewish Exegesis* (in Hebrew), Jerusalem 1995. The view here taken of individual passages does not always agree.

[287] Cases supported by no more than a marginal note in a Targum are included here.

[288] Maori, pp. 137–8.   [289] Maori p. 159.

(c)   Lev. 10:1

MT אֵשׁ זרה "strange fire"; P adds ܕܠܐ ܒܙܒܢܗ "not in its [right] time", agreeing with R.Ishmael's comment in Sifra ad loc. הכניסוה בלא עתה.[290]

(d)   Lev. 19:26

MT לֹא תנחשו : P adds ܟܣܘܡܐ ܐܦܗ, and Sifra ad loc. (unlike any Jewish Targum) also mentions the use of birds in this type of divination:

מנחשים בחולדה ובעופות ובכוכבים.[291]

(e)   Deut. 18:10

MT מעונן: P ܓܕܐܪܐ ܚܙܝ, agreeing with the majority opinion in Sifre ad loc: אלו אוחזים עינים (cf. our "hoodwink"). The same intepretation recurs at 2 Chr. 33:6, though at Lev. 19:26 P's rendering of the same verb is vaguer: ܠܐ ܬܩܨܡܘܢ.

In most of these cases, the apparent motive for drawing on exegetical traditions was to solve an obvious problem within the text. Readers would otherwise have been puzzled at the references to Egyptian fear that the Israelites might leave their land, or to strange fire. The only exegetical tradition whose adoption is not thus explained is the reference at Exod. 40:17 to the erection of the tabernacle on a Sunday.

There are also cases where the rabbinic material is transmitted in Aramaic, and P's resemblance lies in the language rather than the content. Here it is the agreement in expression that implies common origin:

(f)   Gen. 15:11b

MT   וַיַּשֵּׁב אתם אברם

P   ܐܒܪܡ ܠܗܘܢ ܗܘܐ ܡܗܦܟ

Compare the comment in Aramaic ascribed to R. Assi (*c.* 300 CE) in Bereshit Rabba 44:16 –

נסב אברהם מכושה והוה מכש להון ולא הוו מתכשין
ואף על פי כן "וישב אתם אברם" בתשובה

Abraham took a flail and he was (trying to) strike them, but they were not struck; yet even so, 'Abram made them retreat (lit. return)' through repentance

In the first half of the verse, birds of prey came down upon the bodies of the clean birds and animals. To R. Assi this pre-figured the assault of hostile nations upon Israel, and his comment means that repentance is Israel's ultimate weapon. There is a striking agreement in the rendering of the Hebrew verb by the rare root *kšš*. On the other hand, R. Assi's overall understanding differs considerably from P, first in that the patriarch at first failed to repel the birds and second in that the scene is interpreted symbolically. The two appear to share no more than a tradition of an Aramaic equivalent of וַיַּשֵּׁב.

---

[290] Maori, pp. 162–3.   [291] Maori, p. 171.

(g)   Lev. 11:19 // Deut. 14:18

MT דוכיפת, P ܢܘܓܐ ܒܪ. P's term does not occur in the extant Jewish Targums. In TB Git. 68b, however, we find the remark that the bird traditionally translated טורא נגר (as T^OJF indeed render it) is also called תרנגול ברא.[292]

(h)   Lev. 25:36, 37

MT נשך, P ܩܨܨ

P's wording is related to the term ריבית קצוצה found at TB B.M. 61b, and indicates interest deducted in advance from the capital lent (rather than claimed in arrear). We need not infer, however, that P borrowed from the rabbis. The sense of money deducted in advance may have been inferred independently, since a contrast was needed with the term תרבית (or מרבית) which follows in the Hebrew; and the shared root *qṣṣ* may have been the established legal term, older than either P or the Talmud.[293]

Rabbinic parallels in the Pentateuch not implying common origin

Parallels between P and rabbinic sources which demand to be ascribed to common origin are outnumbered by parallels more readily attributable to other causes. Some sample passages will illustrate the methodological issues.

(a)   The first three occurrences of תוך in the Pentateuch are rendered by ܡܨܥܬܐ (Gen. 1:6, 2:9, 3:3), while thereafter the regular equivalent is ܓܘ. It has been suggested that in P's unusual word choice in these three earliest passages reflects rabbinic traditions that the firmament was exactly midway between the upper and lower waters, and that the tree of life was in the very middle of the garden. As illustrated above, however, a translator might change his rendering of a Hebrew word in mid-course, without going back to correct his earlier work; such words are דוד in S. of S., and את in Genesis itself. Thus the change from ܡܨܥܬܐ may therefore be simply another case of initial instability. Perhaps it was initially chosen for its resemblance to Greek (ἐν) μέσῳ but then rejected in favour of the briefer ܓܘ.

(b)   Gen. 3:24

MT וישכן מקדם לגן עדן את הכרבים

For וישכן "and he made dwell", P has ܘܐܗܦܟ "and he made to go about", meaning apparently that God set the cherubs on active patrol of Eden. P's choice of this word has been ascribed to a reminiscence of a rabbinic comment – in its rabbinic Hebrew wording – in Sifre Deut. 40. This states that "the book and the sword came down wrapped (כרוכים) together", meaning that the Torah carries reward for observance but punishment for infringement; and as a prooftext Sifre cites this verse in Genesis, where a whirling sword guards the way to the tree of life, representing the Torah.[294] In

---

[292] I. Prager, *De Veteris Testamenti Versione Syriaca quam Peschittho vocant Quaestiones Criticae*, Göttingen 1875, p. 18 (n.2).   [293] L.A. Rosenthal, "Vermischtes", *ZAW* 16 (1896), p. 316.
[294] Maori, *The Peshitta Version*, pp. 234–5.

no way, however, does P convey the specific lesson of the rabbinic comment. However, the reason for the verb ܐܒܪ̈ in P may instead be simply that the translator thought it dull to write that God "caused the cherubs to dwell" east of Eden, and instead dramatised the text – a tendency noted in chapter 2. In that case, the use of the same root *krk* in both P and Sifre is coincidental; its sense certainly differs completely ('go about' in P but 'wrap' in Sifre).

(c)   At Gen. 45:23, MT states that Joseph sent his father gifts from the "good of Egypt", together with בר ולחם ומזון "corn, bread and food". For this last phrase, P has: ܥܒܘܪ̈ܐ ܘܚܡܪܐ ܘܙܘܕܐ "corn, wine and provisions". It has been suggested that the wine in P reflects a rabbinic tradition attributed to R. Eliezer (*c.* 100 CE) which so identified the "good of Egypt" earlier in the verse (TB Meg. 16b):

שלח לו יין [וישן] שדעת זקנים נוחה הימנו

he sent him (old) wine, which elderly people enjoy[295]

However, the translation technique admits a different explanation: the nouns ܥܒܘܪ̈ܐ ܘܚܡܪܐ often occur together, to render the standard pair דגן ותירוש (e.g. Gen. 27:28, Deut. 7:13). The translators – or possibly early copyists – of P were capable of extending a list by adding associated items. Thus at Gen. 24:35, the servant lists Abraham's possessions, which include camels and asses; but P adds she-asses (ܐܬܢ̈ܐ), which accompanied the other items at Gen. 12:16. Hence ܘܚܡܪܐ could have been inserted in this passage without need for rabbinic influence. It is worth adding that an alternative rabbinic tradition interprets the "good of Egypt" as beans (so Gen. R. 94:2), which do not form part of any standard combination; had these instead appeared in P, rabbinic influence would not have been in doubt.

(d)   Exod. 19:13

MT   במשך היבל המה יעלו בהר

P   ܘܡܐ ܕܢܫܬܠܝ ܩܪܢܐ ܫܪܝ ܠܟܘܢ ܠܡܣܩ ܠܛܘܪܐ

  and when the horn falls silent, it is permitted to you to go up to the mountain

P's understanding of במשך has been thought to reflect the same tradition as in Mekhilta of R. Simeon b. Yohai on this verse: כשיפסוק השופר.[296] This understanding could easily, however, have been reached independently. The giving of the commandments was accompanied by the sound of the horn (19:16), and at that point the Israelites were of course forbidden to ascend the mountain. It would be natural to infer that ascent of the mountain would be permitted once more when the horn fell silent, and to interpret the obscure במשך accordingly. The similar understanding in LXX, Symmachus and Theodotion, who speak of the sound moving away,[297] may likewise be independent.

---

[295] Maori, pp. 130–1.   [296] Maori, pp. 145–7.
[297] LXX: ὅταν αἱ φωναί... ἀπέλθῃ. In Syriac guise, Sym. has the verb ܥܒܪ and Theod. the noun ܡܥܒܪܬܐ.

(e)   Deut. 24:1,3

MT   ושלחה מביתו

P (v.1 [9a1] and v.3)   ܘܢܫܪܝܗ ܡܢ ܒܝܬܗ

P (v.1 [most mss])   ܘܢܫܪܝܗ

This passage is concerned with the laws of divorce, and it has been suggested that the rendering ܘܢܫܪܝܗ "and he will release her" is a deliberate reference to the rabbinic divorce formula:

הרי את מותרת לכל אדם (Mishnah Git. 9:3)

behold thou art released/permitted to any man[298]

However, the combination "release her *from his house*", attested at least once in all mss, ill fits this divorce formula. One may instead suppose that P originally had ܘܢܫܕܪܝܗ "and he will send her" – i.e. a literal translation of ושלחה – of which the existing text ܘܢܫܪܝܗ is an easy corruption. In that case, the translator retained the words "from his house" (as 9a1 still does) in both verses, but a later copyist omitted it in v.3. He may have been rightly suspicious of the expression "release her from his house", and loath to repeat it.

(f)   Deut. 32:10

MT   יסבבנהו יבוננהו יצרנהו כאישון עינו

P   ܐܩܦܗ ܘܪܚܡܗ ܘܢܛܪܗ ܐܝܟ ܒܒܬܐ ܕܥܝܢܐ

      he drew him near[299] and loved him and preserved him like the pupil of [his] eye

It has been claimed that P here echoes a Midrash preserved in Tanhuma Bemidbar 13. According to the first half of the verse, God found Israel in a desert land. The Midrash infers that the world was as a desert until Israel received the Torah, and the words in the second half of the verse are thus explained:

"He surrounded him": he enveloped them in clouds of glory (שהקיפן בע ‏ נני כבוד). "He gave him understanding": he made them understand words of Torah. "He cherished him": happy the ears that heard how much he loved them (חבבן), how much he guarded them, how much he cherished them, as it were even "like the pupil of his eye".

The Syriac equivalences ܐܩܦܗ-סבב and ܪܚܡ-בין are both unique, and both have been ascribed to the influence of the Midrash upon the translator. In particular, it is argued, the phonetic resemblance between ܐܩܦܗ and הקיפן is so striking that P must here be echoing the words of the Midrash, even though the two verbs differ wholly in sense.[300]

However, P shows once more no awareness of the central point of the Midrash – namely that יבוננהו on the basis of בין "understand" refers to Israel's acceptance of the Torah. This suggests that P was not influenced by the Midrash at all. P's renderings of the two verbs יסבבנהו and יבוננהו, which are both difficult in context, can instead be ascribed to guesswork, which provided obvious links between the preceding verb

---

[298] Maori, pp. 231–3.
[299] Compare Prov. 6:22 ܘܟܕ ܐܢܬ ܐܙܠ ܐܢܘܢ ܠܟ "and when you walk, attach them (= my words) to you".   [300] Maori, *The Peshitta Version*, pp. 227–9.

ימצאהו and the succeeding verb יצרנהו thus: "he found him, *drew him near, loved him*, preserved him"). That P does not render יסבבנהו by a Syriac term for "surround" is not surprising, since P does not aim for one-to-one correspondence and instead varies his rendering of a given Hebrew word according to context. Admittedly, the phonetic resemblance between ܐܩܦܗ and הקיפן is not easily put down to coincidence; but it is still harder to suppose that the translator knew the Midrash but echoed it so obliquely.

(g) Deut. 32:26
MT אמרתי אפאיהם
P ܘܐܡܪܬ ܐܝܟܐ ܐܢܘܢ

and I said: Where are they?

Sifre ad loc: אמרתי באפי איה הם
Here again rabbinic influence upon P has been detected.[301] In fact, however, P seems to have reduced the unique אפאיהם to the two easy words: איפה הם. This could easily have occurred to the translator independently. In fact the analysis in Sifre is different, and identifies the noun 'anger': אף+איה+הם.

(h) We must likewise be aware of explanations other than common origin when P agrees with non-rabbinic sources against the rabbinic view, as at Exod. 13:13 –
MT וכל פטר חמר תפדה בשה
P ܘܟܠ ܒܘܟܪܐ [ܕܚܡܪܐ om. 5b1] ܦܬܚ ܪܚܡܐ ܕܒܥܝܪܐ ܒܐܡܪܐ ܬܦܪܘܩܝܘܗܝ
cf. Exod. 34:20 –
MT ופטר חמור תפדה בשה
P ܘܒܘܟܪܐ/ܘܟܠ ܒܘܟܪܐ ܕܒܥܝܪܐ ܬܦܪܘܩ ܒܐܡܪܐ
While the Hebrew allows the first-born ass to be redeemed by offering a lamb, P substitutes the general term ܒܥܝܪܐ "a beast". The rabbis restricted this law to the ass, but Philo, Josephus and Karaite authorities took the ass here to represent all unclean animals, and it has been claimed that P partakes of the same tradition.[302] Against this supposition, however, P makes no mention of uncleanness; we find only ܒܥܝܪܐ "beast". It may be that פטר חמור was originally rendered ܦܬܚ ܪܚܡܐ ܕܚܡܪܐ, but that a copyist was distracted by the phrase ܦܬܚ ܪܚܡܐ ܕܒܥܝܪܐ (for פטר שגר בהמה) in the previous verse. The Syriac text of Exod. 34:20 would later have been conformed thereto.

Rabbinic parallels not attested in all mss of P

The manuscript variants must also be examined before a parallel with rabbinic sources can be said to go back to the translator, as the following examples will illustrate.

301 Maori, p. 205.
302 Philo (*De spec. leg.* I 135f); Josephus (*AJ* IV 4.4), against Mishnah Bek.1:2. See further Maori, p. 142.

(a)   Gen. 8:20

MT   (ויקח) מכל הבהמה הטהורה

P (5b1, Ephrem[303])   ܡܢ ܟܠܗ ܚܝܘܬܐ ܕܟܝܬܐ

P (most witnesses)   ܡܢ ܟܠܗ ܒܥܝܪܐ ܘܚܝܘܬܐ

Victims in Noah's sacrifice after the Flood are here indicated. The usual rendering of בהמה is ܒܥܝܪܐ. On the basis of the majority text, it has been suggested that P here deliberately uses ܚܝܘܬܐ instead, in order to reflect a Jewish tradition that Noah offered up wild as well as domestic animals.[304] The verse was indeed thus interpreted by R. Huna (cent. iii), who commented thereon: חיה בכלל בהמה, and concluded that wild as well as domestic animals were sacrificed before the Tabernacle existed (TB Zeb. 115b). It is simpler to suppose, however, that the translator rendered בהמה by ܒܥܝܪܐ as usual, and that the variant reading ܚܝܘܬܐ [חלה] arises from assimilation to the phrase ܚܝܘܬܐ ܚܝܘܬܐ at the beginning of the preceding verse.

(b)   The majority text of P at Gen. 28:17 exhibits expansions in relation to the Hebrew: "and *Jacob* feared *a great fear* and said: How fearsome is this place *today*". It has been suggested that the expansion "a great fear" reflects the rabbinic interpretation which took Jacob, not the ladder, as the object of the biblical phrase עולים ויורדים בו, and so explained that the angels on the ladder leapt out to threaten him (Gen. R. 68:18 – אפזים בו קפצים בו סוטנים בו).[305] However, the expansions are absent in 5b1, which seems to preserve the original text. The expansions may instead be due to a reviser, who inserted the words 'a great fear' in order to lead up to Jacob's exclamation ("How awesome . . ."), and the word 'today' because Bethel later became an illicit cult-place.

(c)   At Exod. 32:26, Moses stands בשער המחנה "at the gate of the camp". An exact rendering appears in 5b1: ܒܬܪܥܐ ܕܡܫܪܝܬܐ. Most mss, however, instead have ܒܬܪܥܐ ܕܡܫܟܢܐ "at the entrance of the tent (or tabernacle)" – the usual rendering of פתח האהל. It has been suggested that P here reflects a lost Midrash, perhaps echoed faintly in the extant Midrashim.[306] However, it is simpler to suppose that the translator rendered literally (as in 5b1) and that a later copyist who knew of no gate of the Israelite camp substituted the common phrase "entrance of the tent", found shortly afterwards at 33:9.

(d)   At Lev. 20:15 the P mss are again divided:

MT (ואת הבהמה) תהרגו); 6b1 8b1 9a1 ܬܬܩܛܠ; rell. ܬܩܛܠܘ.

Sifra ad loc. and Mishnah Sanh. 4: 4 have been cited as evidence that "P translates according to rabbinic halacha, that the animal should be punished by stoning".[307] However, this rendering need not owe anything to rabbinic influence. It is equally possible that the original translation was literal, as in 6b1 etc., and that a copyist drew the

---

[303] Tonneau, *S. Ephraemi Syri*, p. 61.   [304] Maori, pp. 216–18.

[305] A. Levene, "Quelques exemples intéressants d'exégèse syriaque sur Genèse chapîtres 28,30 et 31", *L'Orient Syrien* 12 (1967), pp. 549–58. No explanation is offered for the expansion "today".

[306] Maori, pp. 280–1.   [307] Maori in MPI 8, p. 111; *The Peshitta Version*, pp. 173–4.

same obvious analogy as the rabbis from the only other case of an animal condemned to death, namely the goring ox which according to Exod. 21:28 must be stoned.

(e)   There are three passages in Leviticus where God commands in the Hebrew the observance of "my sabbaths" (שבתתי). At Lev. 19:3, all P mss instead have "my commandments" (ܦܘܩܕܢܝ). The latter is also the reading of the majority of mss at Lev. 19:30 and 26:2. In each of these last two passages, however, there is one ms which instead reads ܫܒܝ "my sabbaths" as in MT: 9a1 before correction at 19:30, and 6b1 at 26:2.[308]

Maori,[309] following Perles,[310] takes the majority reading (and in Lev. 19:3 the unanimous reading) to represent the original translation. According to these scholars, P here reflects a rabbinic dictum that the Sabbath in these passages represents all the commandments. Such comments can indeed be found in Sifra on two of these passages – Lev. 19:3 and 26:2. In either passage, however, the rabbinic comment forms part of a specific lesson, of which P seems wholly unaware.

Thus, Lev. 19:3 is taken by the rabbis to mean that *although* a man must fear his parents (3a), he must not obey any request of theirs to break the sabbath (3b) or by implication to break any other divine command. That lesson could not have been guessed from P:

ܠܓܒܪ ܡܢ ܕܝ ܐܡܗ ܘܐܒܘܗܝ، ܗܘܐ ܬܕܚܠܘܢ ܘܫܒܝ ܘܩܘܕܫܝ ܬܛܪܘܢ

At Lev. 26:2 the rabbis again refer to a situation of duress:

"You shall keep my sabbaths and fear my temple." Scripture here refers to one who is sold to a heathen (cf. Lev. 25:47), that he should not say: Because my master serves idols, so shall I; because my master commits immorality , so shall I; because my master profanes sabbaths, so shall I. Therefore the Torah says: "You shall not make for yourselves idols, you shall keep my sabbaths and fear my temple." Thus scripture warns concerning all the commandments.

However, the majority text of P offers blandly:

ܘܫܒܝ ܘܩܘܕܫܝ ܬܛܪܘܢ ܐܢܐ ܡܪܝܐ

observe my commandments and fear my sanctuary

In both Lev. 19:3 and 26:2, had the translator really been thinking of the rabbinic interpretation, he would have recognised duress as the essential point. To substitute "commandments" for "sabbaths" without conveying the basic rabbinic lesson would have been a pointless gesture.

In fact, the majority reading in these passages is easily explained without supposing rabbinic influence at all. The injunction ܦܘܩܕܢܝ ܛܪܘ occurs in many neighbouring passages in Leviticus (18:4, 5; 19:19, [37]; 20:8, [22]; 22:21; 25:18; [26:3]). The majority text could therefore be due to a revision to impose uniformity. The revision may have been encouraged by the loss of the importance of the Sabbath for the church. In that case, ܫܒܝ was the original text in all three passages, agreeing straightforwardly with the Hebrew, but traces survive in Lev. 19:30 and 26:2 alone. Such a hypothesis would explain why P has "commandments" at Lev. 19:30 even though no such rabbinic comment on that verse is known.

---

[308] See p. xix of the introduction to the edition.
[309] Maori in MPI 8, pp. 110–11; *The Peshitta Version*, pp. 170–1.   [310] Perles, *Meletemata*, pp. 41–2.

(f)   A more complex case occurs at Gen. 24:55 –

MT   ימים או עשור

P (5b1)   ܢܫܘܬ ܐܘܪ̈ܚܐ ܗܘ ܒܕܓ ܚܕ   "an exact period[311] or 10 months"

cf. T°   עידן בעידן או עסרא ירחין

P (rell)   ܝܪ̈ܚܐ ܥܣܪܐ

Three different arguments have been advanced in order to show rabbinic influence on the majority reading of P, presumed to be original.[312] First, there is a view in Midrash Hagadol – compiled around the thirteenth century but often preserving earlier traditions – that Rebecca's family requested a delay of one year, as was usual for virgins, or at least of one month, as for other brides. That view interprets ימים as "year" and עשור as "month", being approximately one-tenth of the year. The latter indeed agrees with the majority text of P; but what invalidates this parallel is that the word "year" is an integral part of the Midrash but wholly absent from the majority reading of P.

The second argument rests on a targumic citation in Masnut's commentary on Genesis: ת"ש ירח יומין או עשר יומין ("a month of days or ten days"). Here it is ימים rather than עשור that is taken as "month", the sense of the majority text of P. Now most of Masnut's citations introduced ת"ש agree with renderings preserved in the text and annotations of Neofiti, and thus derive from the Palestinian Targum tradition.[313] The present citation belongs to the minority that disagree with all extant Targums; but the suggestion has been made that it too is a fragment of an (otherwise unknown) Targum rendering, which served as the source for P.[314] The essential difference, however, remains: this Targum also presents an alternative alongside "month", while P does not. Nor is the citation in Masnut's commentary textually certain: Masnut has a citation of P (after the majority text) immediately afterwards (ת"א ירח יומין), to which the text of the first citation may have been conformed in transmission.

The third argument for rabbinic influence is also the subtlest. Mishnah Ketubot 5:2 allows a bride time to make preparations before the marriage: one year for a virgin and one month for a widow. In itself, this contradicts the majority reading of P ("one month"), since Rebecca's status would rather have demanded a year. However, a discrepant tradition is recorded in the Talmud (TB Ket. 57b), that a virgin beyond the age of majority is allowed one month only. Now the view is found in Midrash Hagadol that Rebecca was at that point fourteen years old and had thus attained majority – even though the older compilations (e.g. Seder Olam Rabba 1, Bereshit Rabba 57.1) state instead that she was but three years old. Hence, it is argued, the translator held that Rebecca had attained majority (as in Midrash Hagadol), and that a virgin of that age was allowed one month only (with the tradition in the Talmud), and so he specified "one month" as the only proper period of delay! Unfortunately, there is no evidence that the views selected for this syllogism even existed in P's time.

Once it is recognised that 5b1 is capable of preserving the original text, the majority reading can instead be explained very simply as an assimilation to Gen. 29:14 ("and he

---

[311] This expression in the Targums and P indicates an exact year, as discussed above.
[312] Maori in MPI 8, p. 116; *The Peshitta Version*, pp. 118–20.
[313] A. Zimels, "Palestinian Targumim in Secondary Sources" (Hebrew with English summary), *Beer Sheva* 1 (1973), pp. 199–203: 234–5. He does not, however, specify this passage as an example.
[314] Maori in MPI 8, p. 118; *The Peshitta Version*, p. 120.

dwelt with him a month of days"). There we have the same phrase ܢܘܗ ܝܘܡܬܐ, likewise collocated with the verb "dwell" (ܥܡܪ). The reading of 5b1 in fact shows far clearer affinity than the majority text with Jewish exegesis, given its verbal agreement with T^O.

(g)   The variant reading that agrees with the rabbinic source may on occasion be original, as at Exod. 16:29. Here the Hebrew forbids a man to go out "from his place" on the Sabbath, while 5b1 has ܡܢ ܬܚܘܡܗ "from his border". This shows verbal acquaintance with (though not necessarily acceptance of) the rabbinic interpretation, which confined movement on the sabbath to an area called the תחום ("limit"), comprising in the simplest case a circle of 2,000 cubits' radius. The majority mss instead have "(from) the door of his house", which is sometimes thought to indicate Karaite influence. The simplest explanation, however, is that 5b1 has the older reading, and that its rival results from assimilation to Exod. 12:22, which commands in relation to the first Passover: "let none of you go out from the entrance of his tent, until morning".[315]

(h)   An examination of the ms variants is no less necessary when a non-rabbinic interpretation is detected in P. Thus at Deut. 21:22, in relation to a capital offender, we have

MT	והומת ותלית אתו על עץ
P (majority)	ܘܬܩܛܠܝܘܗܝ ܘܬܙܩܦܝܘܗܝ ܥܠ ܩܝܣܐ
P (9a1)	ܘܬܙܩܦܝܘܗܝ ܥܠ ܩܝܣܐ ܘܬܩܛܠܝܘܗܝ

According to the majority text the criminal is put to death by hanging, but 9a1 agrees with MT that only after death is the body to be hanged. The majority text, as Maori observed,[316] gives the same sense as the Temple Scroll:[317]

ותליתמה גם אותו על העץ וימות

It is, however, instead possible that the original translation was literal, as in 9a1, and that a later reviser mistook the hanging for the death penalty itself.

Rabbinic parallels outside the Pentateuch

Agreements with rabbinic sources not reflected in the Targums are rare outside the Pentateuch. However, Perles found at 2 Sam. 24:15 an example which clearly betokens common origin:

MT	מן הבקר ועד עת מועד
Tg.	[מן עידן דמתנכיס תמידא] ועד דמתסק
P	ܡܢ ܨܦܪܐ ܘܥܕܡܐ ܠܥܕܢ ܫܬܐ

The divergence between Tg. and P is almost exactly the same as a disagreement between two third-century rabbis as recorded in TB Ber. 62b:

אמר שמואל סבא... משמיה דר׳ חנינא:
משעת שחיטת התמיד עד שעת זריקתו.
ר׳ יוחנן אמר: עד חצות ממש

---

[315] See Maori, *The Peshitta Version*, pp. 334–5, for further details and a somewhat different view.
[316] Maori, pp. 194–201.
[317] Y. Yadin, *The Temple Scroll* (in Hebrew), Jerusalem 1977; vol. 2, p. 204 (= col 64, ll.10–11)

The Targum understood the Hebrew phrase as the interval between the slaughter and presentation of the daily offering (no doubt of the morning).[318] R.Hanina's understanding is similar if not identical. According to R. Johanan, however, the pestilence continued right up to midday, and with this P agrees exactly ("the sixth hour").

Perles goes on to detect rabbinic definitions of time in P at Ezra 9:4–5, where Ezra is said to pray at the "ninth hour". Here, however, P rather reflects a system of fixed hours of prayer, attested also in Chronicles, and continued in the church as terce, sext and none, as further discussed in chapter 5 below.

Perles also cites Ezek. 44:26. In the preceding verse, a priest is permitted to defile himself for the dead in the case of near relatives only. The texts continue:

MT   ואחרי טהרתו שבעת ימים יספרו לו: וביום באו אל הקדש... יקריב חטאתו

P   ܘܡܢ ܒܬܪ ܘܡܬܕܟܐܢܘܬܗ.....

According to MT, after purification from this defilement the priest must wait seven days, before presenting a sin-offering. However, P instead requires counting from the time of defilement. At first sight this seems to agree with the Baraita quoted in TB Moed Qatan 15b:

ואחרי טהרתו-אחר פרישתו מן המת.שבעת ימים יספרו לו-אלו ז' ימי ספירו

However, the agreement is no more than superficial. Numbers 19 makes it clear that defilement by contact with the dead requires seven days' waiting before purification. All that P and the Baraita have in common is that both were puzzled to find here that seven days' waiting are instead stipulated *after* purification. Their solutions are utterly different. P radically improves on the text: the seven days are to be counted from the defilement. No such option was open to the Baraita, which instead concluded that the verse dealt with a priest who had been defiled not only by contact with the dead but also by leprosy: after his purification from the former, he had to wait a further seven days to be cleansed of the latter. Thus P in fact shows no significant rabbinic parallel.

To the extent that true parallels exist, however, they can be readily ascribed to common tradition, usually exegetical but occasionally translational. Even the former traditions were presumably transmitted in Aramaic: despite the claims regarding Gen. 3:24 and Deut. 32:10, there is no sound evidence that the translators knew exegetical interpretations in rabbinic Hebrew.

Appendix III: P among the Jews in the Middle Ages

There is no evidence that P was known in rabbinic Judaism until the Middle Ages. True, the translations introduced in the Babylonian Talmud by מתרגמינן of phrases from the Torah and Prophets have been claimed to represent P.[319] In fact, however, these translations always agree with the official Targum recognised in the Talmud, namely Onkelos on the Torah and Jonathan on the Prophets; and they agree with P only when the latter coincides with those Jewish Targums. Thus at Num. 29:1, where MT reads יום תרועה and P has ܝܘܡܐ ܕܝܘܒܒܐ, P agrees with the מתרגמינן rendering cited in the Talmud (RH 33b), namely יום יבבא, but only because that is also the rendering of T⁰. Where P

---

[318] This would have taken one hour: see Mishnah Pesachim 5:1.
[319] M. Seligsohn, article Peshiṭta, in *Jewish Encyclopedia* 9 , New York and London 1905, cols. 653–5.

differs from the official Targum, it differs also from the מתרגמין rendering. For example, at Num. 31:50 MT has כומז and P renders ܗܡܢܝܟܐ "neckchains", which differs utterly from the rendering preserved at TB Shab. 64a, namely מחוך, explained as: "something which leads to mockery (גיחוך)" (=T⁰). Similarly at 2 Sam. 5:21, for MT וישאם, P has ܘܫܩܠ ܐܢܘܢ "and he took them" while the מתרגמין rendering is ואוקדינון (TB RH 22b= Tg.). There are many such cases where P disagrees with the rendering cited in the Talmud.[320]

We have already noted how Hai Gaon in the tenth or eleventh century, and Rabbi Samuel Masnut in the thirteenth, consulted P on the canonical books. In later centuries P interested the Jews as an authority for the Apocrypha only. The commentary of Nachmanides (1194–*c.* 1270), rabbi of Gerona, on Gen.1:1 cites P on Wisdom, under the name:

הספר המתורגם הנקרא חוכמתא רבתא דשלמה[321]

The purpose of the quotation is to show that Solomon's wisdom had no source but the Torah. Nachmanides considers this text of Wisdom to be an ancient Jewish translation of a work by Solomon into "very difficult Aramaic" (לשון תרגום חמור מאד).[322] The Jews, he supposed, first handed down the work orally (in Hebrew) but committed it to writing during the Babylonian exile, in their then current Aramaic. The Hebrew was not preserved, since the work was merely Solomon's wisdom and not divinely inspired. Unlike Masnut, Nachmanides is aware of the Christian provenance of the P text, for he adds that it was later copied by Christians (והגוים העתיקוהו).

The text accessible to Nachmanides for his citations of Wisdom (7:5–8a, 7:17–21) was rather corrupt, by comparison with the Syriac biblical manuscripts. Thus in v.18 ܫܘܚܠܦܐ ܕܙܢ̈ܝܐ "changes of things" (a weak translation of τροπῶν ἀλλαγάς) is cited as שולחפי דזנבותא; and Nachmanides explains the second word through Heb. זנב 'tail', so that in his translation into Hebrew the phrase is taken as "slanting of tails" (אלכסונות הזנבות). Similarly in v.20 ܟܝܢܐ 'nature' (of beasts) has been corrupted to מתנא and explained in Hebrew as לחות 'moisture'. Some of these errors may have arisen in the process of transposition into Hebrew script; for, like Masnut, Nachmanides knew P in Hebrew characters only. By contrast, Syriac scholarship among Christian scholars in Europe, which began in the sixteenth century in direct contact with the eastern churches, knew the texts in Syriac script.[323]

Later, on Deut. 21:14, Nachmanides' commentary cites P to Judith 1:7–11 (abridged) under the name מגלת שושן, i.e. the scroll of Susanna, with which his manuscript evidently combined Judith (together with Esther and Ruth) in the biblical section called "Book of Women" in Syriac tradition. The biblical phrase in question is לא תתעמר בה, in relation to a female captive, which, according to Nachmanides,

---

[320] See also MQ 2a (on Isa. 62:5), BQ 116b (on Deut. 28:42), BB 12b (on Exod. 27:8), AZ 17b (on Isa. 41:6) and Bek 50a (on Exod. 30:13).

[321] A. Marx, "An Aramaic Fragment of the Wisdom of Solomon", *JBL* 40 (1921), pp. 57–69. See D. Chavel (ed.), פירוש התורה לרבינו משה בן נחמן (רמב״ן), Jerusalem 1959. The same quotation from P-Wisdom appears in a sermon by Nachmanides; see p. 163 of the edition cited below.

[322] D. Chavel (ed.), כתבי רבנו משה בן נחמן, Jerusalem 1963, vol. 1, p. 182. This occurs in the course of another sermon, on the subject of Qohelet, which Nachmanides delivered in Gerona shortly before he emigrated to the Holy Land in 1267.

[323] On this, see R. Contini, "Gli inizi della linguistica siriaca nell' Europa rinascimentale", *RSO* 68 (1994), pp. 15–30.

means that she must not be treated as a slave. As one item of evidence he cites P-Judith, noting that the phrase עמורי ארעא (i.e. ܥܡܘܪܝ ܕܐܪܥܐ) there means "inhabitants of the land", and suggesting – albeit wrongly – that its primary sense is הנעבדים לארץ "those subjected to the land".

Further evidence of medieval use of P as a source for the apocrypha was discovered by Neubauer in ms Bodl. 2339. This ms contains a Midrash incorporating a Hebrew transcription of the P version of Bel and the Dragon in a fifteenth-century hand (p.vii).[324]

One may doubt, however, whether Samuel b. Hofni (died 1013), Gaon of Sura, knew P.[325] He condemns the interpretation of מטה (MT מִטָּה) at Gen. 47:31 as "staff" (מַטֶּה), claiming that "the translators (or copyists) of the Christians have mis-represented" the text (صحف ناقلي النصاري).[326] P indeed has "staff" here (ܚܘܛܪܗ); and Bloch infers that Samuel b. Hofni knew P and thought it of Christian origin. Neither inference is warranted. The sense "staff" also occurs in LXX (τῆς ῥάβδου αὐτοῦ), to which Samuel b. Hofni could have been referring rather than P; he could reasonably have applied the term "translators of the Christians" to LXX by virtue of its usage in the church, despite its Jewish origin. The LXX rendering underlies Hebrews 11:21: "By faith Jacob . . . bowed in worship over the top of his [Joseph's] staff". The staff was later taken to pre-figure the Cross;[327] and if Christians further took Jacob to pre-figure the Jews, and so argued that Jewish conversion to Christianity was pre-ordained, this could explain how the interpretation in LXX came to Gaon's attention.

Appendix IV: The theory of common dependence on an Imperial Aramaic version

A translation of the whole Hebrew Bible into Imperial Aramaic, with a suggested date in the fourth century BCE, was posited by Beyer in order to explain the parallels between P and the Targums. That putative translation was said to survive in Job alone, as 11QTgJob.

This theory regards P's direct source as an Aramaic version, while avoiding the objection that P altogether lacks the looseness characteristic – in various degrees – of the Targums preserved by Jewish tradition. However, P's treatments of the Hebrew that are without parallel in any Targum are no more easily explained by a prototype in Imperial Aramaic than by a Palestinian Targum. We noted above, for example, P's mis-reading of ויחנך as ויחיך in the priestly blessing; no ancient authoritative translation in Imperial Aramaic could have thus misread this fundamental text. Moreover, the evidence that P's translators sometimes took account of the Greek text as well as the Hebrew counts against derivation from an Imperial Aramaic version.

Nor does detailed textual comparison suggest a common origin for P and the Aramaic version of Job from Qumran,[328] which according to Beyer represents the

---

[324] Included in A. Neubauer, *The Book of Tobit*, Oxford 1878, pp. 39–43.

[325] As claimed by J. Bloch, "The Authorship of the Peshitta", *AJSL* 35 (1981/9), pp. 215–22: 219.

[326] A. Harkavy (ed.), זכרון לראשונים וגם לאחרונים, St Petersburg 1880, part 1, sect. 3, p. 49.

[327] So e.g. Primasius in the sixth century (PL 68, col. 766).

[328] *Le Targum de Job de la Grotte XI de Qumrân*, édité et traduit par J.P.M. van der Ploeg, O.P. et A.S. Van der Woude, Leiden 1971.

putative Imperial Aramaic version. The two translations often differ in their approach to the Hebrew, as at Job 37:11 –

MT   אף ברי יטריח עב יפיץ ענן אורו

11QTgJob   אף בהון ימרק עננין] וינפק מן ענן נורה

> with them also he makes clouds gleam and brings forth his fire from a cloud

P   ܘܐܚܪܝ ܫܬܝܩܐܝܬ ܐܢܘܢ ܦܪ‍ܣ ܐܢܐ ܘܢܓܗܝܢ

> and silently the clouds are stretched out and he extends the clouds of his light

P derives ܦܪܣ "extend" from "scatter", the literal meaning of יפיץ, while the version from Qumran ("bring forth") is much less specific. Again, P's rendering of יטריח ("stretch out") seems a guess based on his treatment of יפיץ, while 11QTgJob appears to combine it with the preceding word ברי ('purity') and renders: "cleanse". P's rendering of ברי (as "silently"[329]), by contrast, is no more than a guess, based on the references in neighbouring verses to God transforming nature by his breath (v.10) or thoughts (v.12) alone. Though there is scope for argument about the details, it is clear that P here owes nothing to any prototype of the version from Qumran. In many other verses from Job the two versions differ no less. They stand closer in the easiest passages, but no closer than would be expected when two independent translators into dialects of the same language confront the same text.

---

[329] Cf Judg. 20:37 ܓܒܠ ܘܫܬܩܘ ܚܝܠܗܘܢ for MT והארב החישו (in which P apparently found חשה "be silent").

4
Unity and diversity in the Peshitta

Introduction

Native traditions

Already in antiquity the Peshitta version of the Old Testament was believed to be the work of more than one translator. Thus a passage already quoted from the commentary attributed to Ephrem (on Joshua 15:28) speaks in the plural of those who translated the Bible into Syriac – though this particular passage hardly goes back to Ephrem himself. Jacob of Edessa (c. 700 CE) too uses plural verbs (ܐܘܟܡ̈ܘ ܐܪܟ̈ܘ). The division of the books according to Isho'dad of Merv (ninth century) into two groups, translated in two different periods, likewise presupposes more than one translator.[1]

It is true that the commentary attributed to Ephrem (on 1 Kgs. 18:44) instead uses the singular: ܐܡܪ ܡܬܪܓܡ. This refers, however, to the translator responsible for that particular passage, and so does not contradict the earlier reference to many translators. Likewise, the references by Theodore of Mopsuestia noted above to the "obscure individual" responsible for P do not necessarily affirm that the translation is a unity. Theodore's point is, rather, that in any given passage the P translation is the work of one individual, rather than the agreed rendering of seventy translators of legendary learning.[2]

Differences in general technique

Modern scholars have found confirmation in the text of P that many translators took part. Here again the starting-point must be Perles' discussion, which is brief and yet fundamental.[3]

Perles pointed out, in the first place, that some books (e.g. Job) are more literally rendered, and others (e.g. Ruth, Chronicles) less so. These impressions certainly bear on our question, but must be treated with caution, for two reasons. First, the possibility that differences in technique are conditioned by the Hebrew text rather than a change of translator must be controlled. For example, there is a strong tendency to abbreviate

---

[1] J.-M. Vosté and C. van den Eynde (eds.), *Commentaire d' Išo'dad de Merv sur l'Ancien Testament: I. Genèse,* CSCO 126 (text) and 156 (French translation), Louvain 1950 and 1955, text, p. 3. On these traditions, see further chapter 5 below.

[2] In the same way Epiphanius deprecates the minor Greek versions as the work of individuals ("De LXX Interpr" in PG 43, cols 374–9), in contrast with the inspired Seventy.

[3] Perles, *Meletemata*, pp. 14–15.

in Ezekiel, especially towards the end, but not in the Twelve Prophets. This need not mean that different translators were involved: perhaps the abbreviating tendency in P-Ezekiel results from the repetitions and technical terms in the Hebrew of that book.

The other reason for caution in the comparison of the conclusions of different investigators is that most books strike a balance between fidelity and intelligibility. Inevitably, some investigators will have been more impressed by the former tendency and others by the latter. Comparison of their perceptions would give an exaggerated impression of diversity within P, unless the primary sources are checked independently.

Perles also pointed out that the books vary in their dependence on LXX and also in their affinities with the Targums. This too is an important consideration, but again other causes for the variation must be controlled. For example, the reason that the Prophets depend more heavily than the Pentateuch upon LXX might be that they were more difficult to translate from the Hebrew alone. Again, the particularly high incidence of parallels with Targums and/or rabbinic traditions in the Pentateuch, Proverbs and Chronicles provides no ground for regarding them as a distinct group, since separate causes operated (as argued above) in each of these three biblical sections.

Different approaches to specific phrases

In addition to the general arguments described above, one may point to varying renderings of the same phrase in different books, as in the following examples mentioned by Perles:

	בין קדש (ל)חול... ובין (ה)טמא (ל)טהור	
Lev. 10:10	ܒܝܬ ܩܘܕܫܐ ܠܚܘܠܛܢܐ ܘܒܝܬ ܠܛܡܐܐ ܠܕܟܝܐ	
Ezek. 22:26	ܒܝܬ ܩܘܕܫܐ ܠܚܘܠܐ ܘܒܝܬ ܛܢܦܐ ܠܕܟܝܐ	
	ויצמד... לבעל פעור	
Num. 25:3	ܘܐܫܬܡܠܝ ܐܝܣܪܐܝܠ ܒܒܥܠ ܦܥܘܪ	
Ps. 106:28	ܥܠ ܕܐܬܢܩܦܘ ܠܦܬܟܪ̈ܐ ܕܦܥܘܪ	
	לא קדמו את... בלחם ובמים	
Deut. 23:5	ܥܠ ܕܠܐ ܩܪܒܘ [ܠܟܘܢ] ܠܚܡܐ ܘܡܝ̈ܐ	
Neh. 13:2	ܠܐ ܐܪܥܘ [ܠܒܢ̈ܝ ܐܝܣܪܐܝܠ] ܒܠܚܡܐ ܘܒܡܝ̈ܐ	
	עזי וזמרת יה (Isa.+ 'י) ויהי לי לישועה	
Exod. 15:2	ܬܘܩܦܐ ܘܬܫܒܘܚܬܐ ܗܘ ܡܪܝܐ ܘܗܘܐ ܠܝ ܦܪܘܩܐ	
Isa. 12:2	ܬܘܩܦܝ ܘܬܫܒܘܚܝ ܡܪܝܐ ܗܘ ܘܗܘܐ ܠܝ ܠܦܘܪܩܢܐ	
Ps. 118:14	ܚܝܠܝ ܘܬܫܒܘܚܝ ܡܪܝܐ ܗܘ. ܗܘ ܗܘܐ ܠܝ ܦܪܘܩܐ	
	כרתי ופלתי	
2 Sam. 8:18	ܚܐܪ̈ܐ ܘܦܠܚ̈ܐ	free men and labourers
1 Kgs. 1:38	ܩܫ̈ܬܐ[4] ܘܫܕܝ ܒܩܠܥܐ	archers and shooters with slings

[4] Compare Tg. קשתיא וקלעיא. As to the former passage, the rendering ܘܦܠܚ̈ܐ for ופלתי of the second word perhaps arises from a misreading of the Hebrew as ופלחי, whence the guess that כרתי was a contrasting term.

Other examples could be added, e.g.

	כתנת פסים	
Gen. 37:3	ܟܘܬܝܢܐ ܕܦ̈ܣܬܐ	coat of long sleeves
2 Sam. 13:18f	ܟܘܬܝܢܐ ܡܚܠܦܬܐ	many-coloured coat

These cases are again suggestive, but we have to control the possibility that they lie within the margins of inconsistency of a single translator. Well-known examples of short textual doublets within books occur in Jeremiah,[5] Ezekiel[6] and Psalms.[7] These are usually rendered consistently, even if on occasion distinctively, e.g.

(קשת וכידון) יחזיקו	ܡܚܝܢ	Jer. 6:23 //50:42
יחול	ܢܬܬܢܝܚ	Jer. 23:19//30:24
שחקים	ܥܕ̈ ܥܢܢܐ	Ps. 57:11//108:5
מחקקי	ܡܠܟܝ	Ps. 60:9//108:9

Yet inconsistency within a single book is not unknown:

(י)רפו (ידיו/ידינו)	ܘܐܬܪܦܝ (Jer. 6:24)	ܘܐܬܪܦܘ (Jer. 50:43)
סער(ת)	ܣܘܥܪܢܐ (Jer. 23:19)	ܥܠܥܠܐ (Jer. 30:24)
כלה	ܓܡܘܪܐ (Jer. 30:11)	ܣܘܦܐ (Jer. 46:28)
יעידני	ܢܩܘܡܘܢܢܝ (Jer. 49:19)	ܢܬܚܪܐ ܒܝ (Jer. 50:44)
רשע (ter)	ܚܛܝܐ (Ezek 3:18)	ܥܘܠܐ (Ezek. 33:8)
ואתה כי הזהרת	ܐܢ ܬܙܗܪ ܕܝܢ (Ezek 3:19)	ܐܢܬ ܕܝܢ ܐܢ ܙܗܪܬܝܗܝ (Ezek. 33:9)
בעונו	ܒܚܛܗ̈ܘܗܝ (Ezek 3:19)	ܒܥܘܠܗ (Ezek. 33:9)
נאלחו	ܘܐܣܬܠܝܘ (Ps. 14:3),	ܘܐܬܛܠܦܘ (Ps. 53:4)
נכון	ܡܛܝܒ (Ps. 57:8)	ܡܬܩܢ (Ps. 108:2)
אעלזה	ܐܬܚܣܢ ܐܢܐ (Ps. 60:8)	ܐܥܫܢ (Ps. 108:8)
סיר רחצי	ܥܛܠܬܐ ܕܪ̈ܓܠܝ (Ps. 60:10)	ܡܘܣܐ ܕܥܛܠܬܐ (Ps. 108:10)
עזרת (מצר)	ܡܥܕܪܢܐ ܥܠ... (Ps. 60:13)	ܣܥܕܐ ܥܠ... (Ps. 108:13)
ושוא	ܕܓܠ (Ps. 60:13)	ܣܪܝܩ (Ps. 108:13)

A lessening of literalism between Ps. 14 and Ps. 53 likewise falls under the heading of inconsistency:

MT	אכלי עמי אכלו לחם
Ps. 14:4 (P)	ܐܟܠ [ܠ]ܥܡܝ ܡܐܟܠ ܠܚܡܐ
Ps. 53:5 (P)	ܐܟܠܝܢ ܕܐܟܠܝܢ ܗܘܘ ܠܥܡܝ ܡܐܟܘܠܬܐ ܕܠܚܡܐ

Thus discrepancies in the rendering of isolated phrases are suggestive of different translators, but not in themselves conclusive.

Unity in diversity

Another important point noted – albeit very briefly – by Perles is that the P version of the Pentateuch was consulted by the translators of later books. We shall in fact see that it was not only the Pentateuch that was so used. Thus, there may be literary links in P between books which go back to different translators.

Altogether, then, Perles thought of a number of different translators, who nevertheless considered themselves engaged on a single project – as native tradition again

[5] 6:12–15//8:10–12; 6:22–4//50:41–3; 10:12–16//51:15–19; 11:20//20:12; 21:9//38:2; 23:5–6//33:15–16; 23:19–20//30:24–5; 30:10–11//46:27–8; 49:19–21//50:44–6; 49:18//50:40. [6] Ezek. 3:17–19//33:7–9.
[7] Ps. 14//53; 40:14–18//70; 57:8–12//108:2–6; 60:7–14//108:7–14.

suggests. His evidence was, however, too scanty to demonstrate the relationships between books in any detail, or to delimit the sections which the different translators undertook (these sections may be technically termed the translation units).

Here, a wider range of evidence will be examined. First, there are Hebrew words which are systematically rendered in different ways in the different books, reflecting the diversity within P. Second, there are renderings common to different books in P and so distinctive that the translators must have used one another's work, or at least depended on interpretative traditions peculiar to the translators' own communities. These links co-exist with the diversity just noted. Finally, the comparison of extended passages that are duplicated in different biblical books may offer clues both to diversity and to linkage between the books, the former through the differences between the two Syriac texts, and the latter through the agreements.

Arranging the biblical books in a graded series

The significance of different renderings of a given Hebrew word

The Hebrew words whose renderings are to be tested – which may be termed 'discriminators' – must be chosen with care. A discriminator must be frequent, since otherwise books cannot be shown to differ in their translation of it systematically. Ideally, the meaning of the Hebrew word should be uniform throughout the Bible. Failing that, the possibility that the Hebrew word is variously rendered because of variations (real or perceived) of meaning, rather than because of differences of policy among the translators, will have to be controlled.

An example of a Hebrew word which can*not* serve as a discriminator is דבר. This has two Syriac renderings, ܡܠܬܐ and ܦܬܓܡܐ; but the choice between these renderings depends on meaning. The basic distinction is that ܦܬܓܡܐ means 'thing' or 'matter', while ܡܠܬܐ means "word";[8] and the rendering is apparently chosen according as a primary reference was perceived to the content or to the words themselves. In particular, either term may be used of the word of God, where both the message and the wording are significant, and even duplicate passages are divided on this point.[9] Thus the choice is based on sometimes subtle perceptions varying from passage to passage, and does not allow us to distinguish translators. The usage of these two Syriac words differs, incidentally, in the Peshitta version of the New Testament, where ܡܠܬܐ is usual and ܦܬܓܡܐ is almost wholly restricted to set expressions for "answer". In the Syrohexapla too, ܡܠܬܐ is much preferred.

Differences in the frequency of alternative grammatical constructions may likewise reflect differences in the underlying Hebrew rather than in translation policy. For example, an argument for Exodus having had its own translator is based on its preference for ordinal numbers, rather than the cardinal plus *dalath*. The statistics are as follows:

[8] Note, however, the set expressions for "answer", where ܦܬܓܡܐ serves, together with verbs ܥܢܐ or ܐܡܪ. Biblical Aramaic already used the causative of חות together with פתגם in the sense "answer" at Dan. 3:16.
[9] Thus the word of the Lord becomes ܦܬܓܡܐ at Isa. 2:3 but ܡܠܬܐ at Mic. 4:2; likewise God's דבר becomes ܦܬܓܡܐ at Ezek. 3:17 but ܡܠܬܐ at 33:7.

	Adjective	Cardinal+ *dalath*	Other[10]
Genesis	15	13	4
Exodus	32	2	21
Leviticus	9	28	4
Numbers	2	35	8
Deuteronomy	2	4	1

Genesis shows a slight preference for the ordinal, but in Exodus that preference is over-whelming. The other books prefer the cardinal plus *dalath*. This pattern has been used as an argument for a separate translator for Exodus.[11] However, the pattern may instead be due to differences in the nature of the underlying Hebrew. It may be, for example, that the cardinal plus *dalath* was the more formal construction. Hence it tended to be preferred in legal contexts, which predominate from Leviticus onwards, and also in calendrical dates and in lists. In Genesis, in particular, the cardinal plus *dalath* is used in the lists of days of creation (1:8–31) and of rivers in Eden (2:14), in the dates of the Flood (7:11, 8:14), and in the account of the birth of Jacob's sons (Gen. 30:12, 17, 19), apparently likewise perceived as a list.[12] The Syriac ordinal, by contrast, was perceived as less formal, and thus better suited to render Hebrew ordinals inciden-tal to a narrative – which happen to be most frequent in Exodus.[13] More important than this particular suggestion is the general problem that the varying incidence of a particular grammatical feature in P may merely reflect the wide variation of content and style in the original.

Nevertheless, one can identify a number of Hebrew words which can validly serve as discriminators; and these are studied below. By definition, a discriminator has at least two alternative Syriac renderings. It will always be found that one of these can be char-acterised as 'conservative' – either because it is the oldest Aramaic term, or because it is the Syriac cognate of the Hebrew word. Any alternative rendering may be contrasted as 'modern' or as an 'innovation'. The reason that such an innovation gained currency will lie in some drawback (e.g. ambiguity) in the conservative rendering. The biblical books vary systematically in the receptivity of their translators to such innovations.

Text-critical aspects

Modern usages may be introduced either by the translators or by later copyists, and for the present study the distinction is crucial. Where the mss divide between the 'conserv-ative' and the 'modern' rendering, we should ascribe the former to the translator and the latter to scribal revision, since copyists were likelier to substitute a 'modern' for a 'conservative' expression than vice versa. In such passages, the 'conservative' rendering

[10] Most cases comprise use of ܐܚܪܝܢ for 'second'; see also Lev. 13:6, 27:32; Num. 2:16, 24; 33:38; Deut. 23:3.
[11] I. Avineri, ?מי תרגם את הפשיטתא לחומש, *Beth Mikra* 65 (1975/6), pp. 303–4.
[12] The translator might not detect a list immediately. Thus, in Gen. 2:14, the less formal ܬܢܝܢ appears for "2nd", but cardinal plus *dalath* for "3rd" and "4th". Again in Gen. 30, the phrase "and she bore Jacob a second son" actually occurs twice, of Bilhah (v. 7) and Zilpah (v. 12); the former is rendered with the less formal ܬܢܝܢ, and it was apparently the latter which triggered the treatment of this account as a list. The only other case of cardinal + *dalath* in Genesis is at 31:22, perhaps by 'hangover' (see p. 182) from Gen. 30.
[13] P's use of Syriac ordinals in the instructions for the first Passover suggests that the passage is viewed as the Israelites' detailed escape plan, and thus as narrative.

is sometimes confined to just one manuscript, or a minority of manuscripts, but still deserves preference. At an early stage in transmission, it seems, a body of new readings which modernised the translators' original work became overwhelmingly popular, so that at many points the original reading is confined to a minority of mss, perhaps a minority of one. This question is discussed in detail in chapter 6.

Words having a conservative and a modern rendering

Conservative and modern words for 'city'

Our first discriminator is עִיר 'city'. P consistently uses ܩܪܝܬܐ in some books, and ܡܕܝܢܬܐ in others. For example, P in Jeremiah has ܩܪܝܬܐ 127 times and ܡܕܝܢܬܐ only twice, while P in Ezekiel has ܡܕܝܢܬܐ 59 times and only once ܩܪܝܬܐ. This difference cannot be due to different meanings in the underlying Hebrew. In both books the Hebrew usually denotes the same city at the same period – Jerusalem around the time of the Babylonian invasion. In fact P in nearly every biblical book comes down firmly on one side or the other, as follows:

	Gen.	Ex.	Lev.	Num.	Deut.	Jos.	Judg.	Sam.	Kgs.	Isa.	Jer.	Ezek.	Dodk.
ܩܪܝܬܐ	45	3	14	49	57	83	53	75	112	34	127	1	2
ܡܕܝܢܬܐ	0	0	0	0	0	55	0	1	2	9	2	59	40

	Ps.	Prov.	Job	Cant.	Ruth	Lam.	Qoh.	Esther	Dan.	Ezra	Neh.	Chr.
ܩܪܝܬܐ	15	0	2	0	0	4	0	3	2	6	15	99
ܡܕܝܢܬܐ	5	3	0	3	4	1	5	7	3	1	4	4

These statistics include components of names (e.g. עִיר דוד). They exclude the few cases where P renders differently (e.g. by ܕܝܪܐ at Prov. 1:21 or even ܩܠ at 2 Sam. 20:19)[14] or not at all (e.g. Gen. 19:14), and also the cases in Chronicles where the whole verse is treated freely or omitted. On the other hand, they include cases like the city Ar (Isa. 15:1), the form מֵעִיר at Hos. 7:4, and even בַּעֲדִי עֶדְיִים at Ezek. 16:7, where the noun עִיר is not normally thought present but was perceived by P. Thus the total of occurrences differs from statistics for the Massoretic text as analysed today.[15]

Some books have a minority of renderings that go against their main policy. The main causes will be discussed below. One of the few books not to opt overwhelmingly for just one of the two alternatives is Joshua, which nevertheless has a clear policy: a Canaanite city was a ܡܕܝܢܬܐ while a city founded by the Israelites was a ܩܪܝܬܐ. By contrast, two books vacillate with no obvious policy between the two alternatives: Isaiah and Psalms.

Hebrew also possesses the synonym קִרְיָה, which is etymologically cognate with ܩܪܝܬܐ. One might have expected that even a translator who avoided ܩܪܝܬܐ for עִיר would feel obliged to translate קִרְיָה by its Syriac cognate. In fact, however, the translators adhere to the same policies as for עִיר:

[14] On this passage see R.P. Gordon, "The Variable Wisdom of Abel: The MT and Versions at 2 Samuel XX 18–19", *VT* 43 (1993), pp. 215–26:222.
[15] Conveniently presented in F.I. Andersen and A.D. Forbes, *The Vocabulary of the Old Testament*, Rome 1989.

	Deut.	Kgs.	Isa.	Jer.	Dodk.	Ps.	Prov.	Job	Lam.	Ezra
ܩܪܝܬܐ	2	2	8	1	1	1	0	1	1	3
ܡܕܝܢܬܐ	0	0	2	0	4	0	4	0	0	4

Thus ܡܕܝܢܬܐ predominates for קריה in P to the Twelve Prophets and to Proverbs, just as for עיר. Evidently these translators felt strongly that ܩܪܝܬܐ did not adequately convey the meaning 'city'.[16]

The original Aramaic for 'city' was of course *qryh*, whence Syriac ܩܪܝܬܐ. Its rival ܡܕܝܢܬܐ originally meant an imperial province, literally a district with its own law-courts, from דין. Such is its usage at Elephantine and in biblical Aramaic. The hellenistic period, however, saw the emergence of cities of unprecedented size, which had to be distinguished from the older settlements that had always been indicated by the term ܩܪܝܬܐ. For the new great cities, ܡܕܝܢܬܐ seemed an appropriate term, for such a city could dominate a whole province.[17] Thus, in the almost contemporary account of the flood of 201 CE, the city of Edessa is called a ܡܕܝܢܬܐ while ܩܘܪܝܐ, plural of ܩܪܝܬܐ, denotes the surrounding villages.[18] Although ܡܕܝܢܬܐ never lost the meaning 'province', it was in some measure demoted in those contexts where it instead means 'city', and ܩܪܝܬܐ shrank in turn, becoming a mere village.[19] Hence ܩܪܝܬܐ is the traditional rendering, but ܡܕܝܢܬܐ the more accurate, and the translators varied in their preference between these rival claims.

This development of the senses of ܡܕܝܢܬܐ and ܩܪܝܬܐ was paralleled at Palmyra, where we have the advantage of dated texts. In the bilingual tariff of 18 April 137 CE, the term for the city of Palmyra is מדיתא – not surprisingly, given that the city lay at an oasis in the Syrian desert, dominating the surrounding territory. By contrast, the tariff indicates surrounding villages by the plural קריא; no duty was paid on goods transported between these and the city (ii 112). The tariff uses מדיתא of other cities also (ii 116). In fact, as early as 24 CE a Palmyrene inscription from Babylon uses מדתא of that city; the inscription marks a statue set up by תנ[ג]רי כלהון די במדינת בבל, which surely means all the merchants in the city, rather than the whole province, of Babylon.[20] This may be the earliest extant occurrence of *mdi(n)ta* as 'city'.

With the exception of the Targum on Proverbs, which depends on P, the Targums normally use קרתא, cognate with ܩܪܝܬܐ, to mean 'city', and not *mdi(n)ta*. Indeed at Gen. 47:21 the Palestinian Targums use the latter for 'countryside': Joseph in Egypt is said to have exchanged the populations of the cities (קוריתא) and the countryside (מדינתא) lest his brothers be stigmatised as wandering strangers.[21]

---

[16] Excluded are the few cases of the rendering ܩܪܬܐ, as well as cases where קריה forms part of a name (here transliteration to ܩܘܪܝܬ is usual).

[17] E.Y. Kutscher, *Words and their History* (Hebrew with English summary), Jerusalem 1961, p. 20.

[18] C. Brockelmann, *Syrische Grammatik*, Leipzig 1912, pp. 21*–23*.

[19] The renderings ܐܝܟ ܩܪܝܬܐ ܕܒܒܠ (Dan. 2:48 3:1) or ܐܝܟܐ ܕܒܒܠ (3:30) for מדינת בבל indicates awareness that ܡܕܝܢܬܐ no longer conveyed adequately the meaning "province", though it is retained in some other passages.

[20] J. Cantineau, "Textes Palmyréniens provenants de la Fouille du Temple de Bêl", *Syria* 12 (1939), pp. 116–41: 122.

[21] In rabbinic Hebrew, both senses – 'city' and 'countryside' – are attested in different passages. The former occurs at Mishnah Ter. 2:5, which allows town onions (בצלים מבני המדינה) to be substituted as heave-offering for village onions, but not vice versa, since the former are the food of the wealthier citizens (פוליטיקין). Rabbi Samuel b. Nahman (*c.* 300 CE) likewise explained מדינה in Est. 9:28 as כרך (TJ Meg. 1:1 fin). Elsewhere, however, מדינה could indicate the provinces as opposed to Jerusalem, e.g. at Mishnah Maaser Sheni 3:4. Some passages (e.g. Mishnah Shekalim 1:3) remain ambiguous.

To return to P, it is likely that all the translators were aware that ܟܪܟܬܐ denoted a larger settlement than ܩܪܝܬܐ. They differed, however, as to which should be the normal equivalent of עיר and קריה. P in some books (e.g. Jeremiah) prefers the more conservative usage, and in other books (e.g. Ezekiel) the more modern. The reason will be considered after some further variations have been examined.

To sum up: a strong preference for ܟܪܟܬܐ is characteristic of Ezekiel, the Twelve Prophets and the Solomonic books, while most of the other books equally strongly prefer ܩܪܝܬܐ. Joshua is split, with ܟܪܟܬܐ for Canaanite and ܩܪܝܬܐ for Israelite settlements. The books of Isaiah and Psalms are also split, but on no clear basis; details appear below. In itself this one word would be of limited significance, were it not part of a coherent pattern in the renderings of a whole series of other Hebrew words.

Conservative and modern renderings of עוֹלָה

Another word differently rendered among the biblical books is עוֹלָה. Here the conservative rendering is ܥܠܬܐ. However, the rival rendering ܝܩܕܐ ܫܠܡܐ, evidently a calque on Greek ὁλοκαύτωμα, was sometimes preferred, perhaps because ܥܠܬܐ also possesses the meaning: 'hill shrine'. Less common renderings are ܝܩܕܐ alone, or ܕܒܚܐ or ܩܘܪܒܢܐ. The two commonest renderings are distributed as follows:

	Gen.	Ex.	Lev.	Num.	Deut.	Jos.	Judg.	Sam.	Kgs.	Isa.	Jer.	Ezek.	Dodk.
ܥܠܬܐ	6	13	27	22	0	1	6	14	17	3	4	1	0
ܝܩܕܐ ܫܠܡܐ	0	2	26	30	6	3	0	0	0	0	0	18	3

	Ps.	Ezra	Neh.	Chr.
ܥܠܬܐ	0	9	1	31
ܝܩܕܐ ܫܠܡܐ	3	0	0	0

It will be seen that the innovation ܝܩܕܐ ܫܠܡܐ for 'burnt-offering' gained wider acceptance than the innovation ܟܪܟܬܐ for 'city'. Ezekiel and the Dodekapropheton, which showed the modern usage for 'city', have the modern rendering for עוֹלָה also. However, that modern rendering for עוֹלָה also appears in a number of books that had the more conservative usage for 'city', notably Leviticus to Deuteronomy. Finally, some historical books (Judges, Samuel, Kings and Chronicles) as well as Jeremiah retain conservative usages for both words. The books thus begin to fall into a graded series, some conservative in rendering both words, some conservative in rendering עיר but modern in rendering עוֹלָה, and some modern in rendering both words.

Leaving aside the Psalter, where linguistic usage tends to vacillate, we may identify the second most modern group as Leviticus, Numbers and Deuteronomy. By contrast, Genesis is wholly conservative. Exodus agrees mainly with Genesis, but occasionally foreshadows the more modern usages of the last three books.

Conservative and modern renderings of גֵּר

Only rarely is גֵּר rendered by its Syriac cognate ܓܝܘܪܐ. Its disadvantage, as Geiger observed, was that this form also carried negative senses of 'alien' and even 'adulterer'.[22]

---

[22] Geiger, *Urschrift und Uebersetzungen der Bibel*, pp. 354–5.

More often we find ܥܡܘܪܐ 'dweller', which goes back to the underlying Hebrew verb גור. Some passages instead have the rendering ܬܘܬܒܐ, which corresponds to the Hebrew synonym תושב.

The most intriguing rendering, however, is the phrase ܐܝܢܐ ܕܡܬܦܢܐ ܠܘܬܝ "he that turns to Me". Although the word גֵּר meant 'resident alien' in the Bible, it developed in rabbinic Hebrew the sense of 'proselyte', which LXX and the Jewish Targums often import into the text. It seems that P likewise finds here the meaning 'proslyte', and is in fact rendering the Greek term προσήλυτος. The latter literally means "one who goes (cf. the archaic aorist ἤλυθον) to (πρός)", without stating the object of the preposition. P's translators take this object as God himself.[23] In its dependence on Greek rather than Hebrew sources, this is the most modern rendering.

The distribution of the renderings is as follows:

	Gen.	Ex.	Lev.	Num.	Deut.	Jos.	Sam.	Isa.	Jer.	Ezek.	Dodk.	Ps.	Job	Chr.
ܪܝܐܠ	0	0	0	0	0	0	1	0	0	0	0	0	1[24]	3[25]
ܪܝܐܣܒ	2	9	6	0	18	2	0	1	2	0	1	3[26]	0	1
...ܪܝܐܦܬܢ	0	0	15	11	3	0	0	0	0	5	2	0	0	0
ܪܒܗܐ	0	3	0	0	1	1	0	0	1	0	0	0	0	0

The basic pattern resembles that for עולה. A rendering which may be characterised as modern is confined to the two most modern groups: Ezekiel with the Twelve Prophets,[27] and Leviticus to Deuteronomy.

There is the complication, due to the changing sense of גר, that the differences of rendering result in part from differences in perceived meaning, rather than differences of translation policy between books. In different passages גר was in fact understood in three different senses:

(a)   strangers who sojourn in Israel without adopting their faith,
(b)   Israelites (or patriarchs or even God) compared to strangers,
(c)   strangers who become proselytes.

These perceived differences of meaning are certainly responsible for some of the variation. Thus in Lev. 19:34 the Israelite is commanded to "love the stranger, for ye were strangers in the land of Egypt". P renders the first by ܐܝܢܐ ܕܡܬܦܢܐ ܠܘܬܝ and the second by ܥܡܘܪܐ, sacrificing the correspondence found in the Hebrew. The situation at Deut. 10:19 is similar.

There is also the possibility that stylistic factors contributed to the variation in rendering. Thus in Deuteronomy, where the גר is mentioned together with other weaker

---

[23] This term is further discussed in chapter 5.
[24] So Job 28:4 (MT גָּר); but at Job 31:32, P has ܐܘܪܚܐ.
[25] At 1 Chr. 9:2 ܪܝܐܠ appears again, to render נתינים. P thus names four groups: Israel(ites), priests, Levites and proselytes. This is reminiscent of the seating order at Qumran according to 1QS 14:3–5:

הכהנים לראשונה והלוים שנים ובני ישראל שלשתם והגר רביעי

Also comparable are the four groups called upon to bless the Lord in Ps. 135:19–20, namely the house of Israel, the house of Aaron, the house of Levi and the fearers of the Lord.

[26] So Ps. 39:13, 94:6, 119:19. At Ps. 146:9, P has ܡܟܝܟܐ, apparently to suit the neighbouring references to the weakest members of society (e.g. the oppressed, the hungry, orphans, widows).

[27] The Solomonic books have no example of this discriminator.

members of society, the one-word rendering ܥܡܘܪܐ is preferred, and the reason may be to avoid undue emphasis on any one item in the list (so Deut. 16:11 etc., and even 5:14).

Nevertheless, differences in translation policy between different books also play a part. In Leviticus to Deuteronomy, Ezekiel and the Minor Prophets – which we already found to form the two most radical groups – the rendering ܐܝܢܐ ܕܡܬܦܢܐ ܠܘܬܝ is predominant.[28] The only other occurrence (or perhaps reminiscence) of that rendering is for the first two occurrences of the verb גור at Isa. 54:15 (discussed on p. 72 above):

MT הן גור יגור אפס מאותי

P ܘܟܠ ܕܡܬܦܢܐ ܡܢ ܐܚܪ̈ܝ ܢܦܠܘܢ ܠܟ

This distribution of the rendering ܐܝܢܐ ܕܡܬܦܢܐ ܠܘܬܝ is not wholly explained by differences in the preceived meaning of גר, nor by stylistic factors, nor even by the need to confine the phrase 'he that turns to Me' to legislation and prophecy. Only differences of translation policy between books can explain why, in the phrase "if a stranger sojourns with thee", P in Lev. 19:33 writes ܐܝܢܐ ܕܡܬܦܢܐ ܠܘܬܝ, but P in Exod. 12:48 has ܬܘܬܒܐ. Again, when Zechariah (7:10) appeals to the people not to oppress the גר, P writes ܐܝܢܐ ܕܡܬܦܢܐ ܠܘܬܝ, but for the same phrase in Jeremiah (7:6), P has ܥܡܘܪܐ. Thus the modern rendering ܐܝܢܐ ܕܡܬܦܢܐ ܠܘܬܝ is characteristic of the translation policy of the books Leviticus to Deuteronomy, Ezekiel and the Minor Prophets, as was ܦܘܪܐ ܥܠܡܐ.

Similarly, the confinement of the conservative rendering ܓܝܘܪܐ to Samuel and Chronicles is also due largely to the general conservatism of these books in P. It is true that גר here in the Hebrew usually had to be taken in sense (a), viz strangers who dwell among the Israelites without joining them;[29] and so one might argue that it was the perceived sense which disposed the translators here to use a term with negative associations. However, there are also clear cases in the less 'conservative' books where the גר remains distinct from Israel, as when he eats forbidden meat (Deut. 14:21) or waxes more prosperous than the Israelites themselves (Lev. 25:47, 49 and Deut. 28:43); and in those books P uses not ܓܝܘܪܐ but ܥܡܘܪܐ or ܬܘܬܒܐ. Conversely, P-Chronicles twice uses ܓܝܘܪܐ where the interpretation 'proselyte' could easily have been admitted, of the sojourners summoned to Asa's sacrifice (2 Chr. 15:9 – Heb. גָּרִים) or to Hezekiah's Passover (2 Chr. 30:25). Thus the usage of ܓܝܘܪܐ in Chronicles – and in Samuel – seems due to the 'conservatism' of these books, rather than any wish to reserve this word for the perceived sense (a).

A text-critical problem must also be addressed. Aphrahat, in an amalgam of Lev. 19:10, 23:22 and Deut. 24:19–21, never uses ܐܝܢܐ ܕܡܬܦܢܐ ܠܘܬܝ but instead has (twice) ܓܝܘܪܐ. It has been suggested that the biblical text familiar to Aphrahat actually read ܓܝܘܪܐ,[30] and moreover that this is a relic of the earlier Jewish Aramaic versions from which P was supposedly derived.[31] However, as we have seen, Aphrahat's citations usually presuppose the same Syriac text as the biblical mss, when allowance is made for

[28] With the exceptions in Deuteronomy noted above. In Mal. 3:5 P has a doublet, with ܥܡܘܪܐ side by side with ܐܝܢܐ ܕܡܬܦܢܐ ܠܘܬܝ.

[29] Note the Amalekite at 2 Sam. 1:13, and the foreigners employed in building the temple (1 Chr. 22:2, 2 Chr. 2:16).

[30] See most recently R.J. Owens, "Aphrahat as Witness to P-Leviticus", MPI 4 (1988), pp. 1–48: 22–5.

[31] A. Baumstark, "Neue orientalistische Probleme biblischer Textgeschichte", *ZDMG* 89 (1935), pp. 89–118:94. The question whether P is a transposition of an earlier version in Jewish Aramaic was discussed on pp. 86ff., 122ff. above.

faulty memory or exegetical need. Aphrahat's wording here may therefore reflect theological rather than textual factors. If (as is argued below) the translators of P were Jews, we can well understand their sensitivity to the negative overtones of ܓܝܘܪܐ, and their preference for terms such as ܫܘܬܦܐ and ܐܢܫ ܕܡܬܬܠܘܐ ܠܗܘܢ wherever reference was perceived to the Jews or the proselytes who had joined them.[32] A Christian writer, however, would have no qualms about applying ܓܝܘܪܐ to a convert to Judaism. Hence the reappearance of ܓܝܘܪܐ in the Syriac versions of the New Testament (Matt. 23:15, Acts 2:11, 6:5, 13:43) to denote Jewish proselytes. Aphrahat too would have found ܓܝܘܪܐ acceptable, and indeed clearer than its substitutes. It may therefore be that Aphrahat read the same text as the biblical manuscripts, but substituted ܓܝܘܪܐ as a neater term.

Conservative and modern renderings of כֶּסֶף

Here we are concerned with כֶּסֶף in the sense of silver metal as opposed to money. This distinction is largely anachronistic in terms of the biblical text itself until after the exile,[33] but was nevertheless perceived by the translators of P. Some retain the native ܟܣܦܐ even where silver metal is meant. Others reserve ܟܣܦܐ to mean 'money' and use ܣܐܡܐ – again a loan word from Greek (ἄσημος) – where silver functions as a material. The statistics follow:

	Gen.	Ex.	Num.	Deut.	Jos.	Sam.	Kgs.	Isa.	Jer.	Ezek.	Dodk.
ܟܣܦܐ	6	28	0	0	0	2	8	2	2	0	0
ܣܐܡܐ	0	2	31	1	7	0	0	8	2	9	14

	Ps.	Prov.	Job	Cant.	Qoh.	Esther	Dan.	Ezra	Chr.
ܟܣܦܐ	1	0	1	1	1	2	2	10	8
ܣܐܡܐ	7	11	0	2	0	0	2	0	10

Where the mss differ, the conservative rendering is viewed as original, since scribes would have tended to substitute the modern rendering rather than vice versa. In Exodus, in particular, where in many places 5b1 alone has ܟܣܦܐ and the majority have ܣܐܡܐ, the former has been adopted.

The innovation ܣܐܡܐ has made even greater progress than ܒܪ ܓܠܝܐ. It is preferred in all the books which have the latter; note that Exodus once more, despite its usual conservatism, occasionally anticipates the modern usage of the later books of the Pentateuch. In addition, however, ܣܐܡܐ also occurs sporadically in Jeremiah and Daniel, and in Chronicles, which had all resisted the innovations discussed so far.

Conservative and modern renderings of גלה

A yet more widely accepted innovation is found among the renderings of the root גלה (including the nouns גּוֹלָה and גָּלוּת) in the sense 'go into exile'. While the most

---

[32] Except perhaps in the conservative translation of Chronicles.
[33] R. Loewe, "The Earliest Biblical Allusion to Coined Money", *Palestine Exploration Quarterly* 87 (1955), pp. 141–50.

conservatively translated books have the cognate Syriac verb ܓܠܐ (with noun ܓܠܘܬܐ), the majority instead use the passive of the verb ܫܒܐ 'capture', with noun ܫܒܝܬܐ. The aversion to ܓܠܐ may be gauged from the Aramaic portions of Daniel, where the Syriac of P normally hews close to the original Aramaic, but pointedly replaces גלותא by ܫܒܝܬܐ (2:25, 5:13, 6:14). The reason for the avoidance of ܓܠܐ may have its ambiguity, given its alternative sense 'reveal'. Its rival could be due to the influence of LXX, which has the passive αἰχμαλωτεύομαι (or αἰχμαλωτίζομαι) for גלה and αἰχμαλωσία for its nouns. The statistics follow:

	Judg.	Sam.	Kgs.	Isa.	Jer.	Ezek.	Dodk.	Lam.	Esther	Dan.	Ezra	Neh.	Chr.
ܓܠܐ	0	1	17	1	0	0	0	2	4	0	1	2	6
ܫܒܐ	1	0	0	3	32	17	18	0	0	3	12	0	1

It will be seen that this innovation has proceeded still further than those mentioned above, with P even in Jeremiah and Daniel coming down firmly on the modern side. These two books form the third most modern group. Meanwhile, the block Ezra-Chronicles is split. As to the earlier historical books, only Kings has more than one occurrence of גלה; it strongly prefers ܓܠܐ.

Conservative and modern renderings of חג, ארצות, ארזן

The word חג possesses the cognate ܚܓܐ, which, however, appears in Judges and Kings alone (the Hebrew word does not occur in Samuel). Other books avoid the cognate, apparently because it could also apply to heathen feasts; instead they have ܥܐܕܐ or the related ܥܕܥܐܕܐ. Mishnaic Hebrew likewise avoids the biblical term חג, substituting יום טוב.

	Ex.	Lev.	Num.	Deut.	Judg.	Kgs.	Isa.	Ezek.	Dodk.	Ps.	Ezra	Neh.	Chr.
ܚܓܐ	2	0	0	0	1	5	1	0	0	0	0	0	0
ܥܐܕܐ	0	0	0	0	0	0	0	0	2	0	1	2	9
ܥܕܥܐܕܐ	10	4	2	7	0	0	1	4	8	2	1	0	0

Here Judges and Kings have the most conservative record.

We may consider at the same time the renderings of the plural of ארץ. Some books simply show the Syriac cognate ܐܪܥܬܐ. In others, however, the translator recognised that the 'lands' of the Bible had become mere provinces in a succession of empires. Such translators therefore render ܡܕܝܢܬܐ 'provinces', or less commonly ܐܬܪܘܬܐ 'places'. For all these translators, ܐܪܥܐ may have meant primarily 'world', and thus lacked a meaningful plural. The distribution is as follows:

	Gen.	Kgs.	Isa.	Jer.	Ezek.	Ps.	Dan.	Ezra	Neh.	Chr.
ܐܪܥܬܐ	6[34]	2	3	3	2	3	1	0	0	0
ܡܕܝܢܬܐ	0	0	0	0	15	0	0	5	2	8
ܐܬܪܘܬܐ	0	0	0	3	0	0	1	0	0	0

---

[34] This includes Gen. 26:3, where 5b1 alone reads ܐܪܥܬܐ, while the others modernise to ܡܕܝܢܬܐ.

Here the 'conservative' rendering dominates not only in Genesis and Kings – two of the most conservative books but also in Isaiah and Psalms, which behaved erratically with respect to the other discriminators. Elsewhere, ܐܪܥܬܐ is avoided, usually in favour of ܡܕܝܢܬܐ. An indication of the aversion to ܐܪܥܬܐ is the rendering of Ezek. 29:12, where God promises to make Egypt "the most desolate of desolate lands, and her cities shall be the most desolate of ruined cities for forty years, and I shall scatter Egypt among the nations and disperse them among all lands". In this single verse P uses ܡܕܝܢܬܐ four times – twice for the plural of עִיר and twice for the plural of אֶרֶץ. Even the singular אֶרֶץ is sometimes rendered by ܡܕܝܢܬܐ (e.g. Qoh. 10:16, 1 Chr. 19:3) or by ܐܬܪܐ (Josh. 9:6, 10:42, 12:1). The alternative substitute ܐܬܪܘܬܐ seems due to the translator of Jeremiah, who apparently assimilated 23:8 ("all the lands where I exiled them") to 8:3 ("all the places where I exiled them").

A similar pattern emerges from the renderings of אָרוֹן (excluding Gen. 50:26, where 'coffin' is meant). In Kings, parts of Samuel, and once in Chronicles, we find the calque ܐܪܘܢܐ, but elsewhere the loan-word ܩܒܘܬܐ (from κιβωτός) has prevailed. The statistics follow:

	Ex.	Lev.	Num.	Deut.	Jos.	Judg.	Sam.	Kgs.	Jer.	Ps.	Chr.
ܐܪܘܢܐ	0	0	0	0	0	0	25	13	0	0	1
ܩܒܘܬܐ	26	1	6	8	30	1	33	1	1	1	50

Again the 'conservative' rendering is best represented in the early historical books Samuel and Kings. It is true that in many other places P-Samuel has the 'modern' rendering, but this is because the book falls into two parts, apparently due to two different translators, as will be discussed below.

In relation to all these three discriminators, the books Ezra to Chronicles show preference for the modern renderings, and here stand apart from Genesis and from the block Judges to Kings. It will also be recalled that Ezra to Chronicles did not eschew the term ܡܕܝܢܬܐ for "city" so strictly. Thus the books Ezra to Chronicles form the fourth most radical group.

Renderings of חֶסֶד and תּוֹרָה

The fifth group, which is least radical, comprises Genesis, Judges, Samuel and Kings. These books resist all the innovations so far considered.

It must be noted, however, that these books do not behave identically. To represent עַשְׁתֹּרֶת, for example, P-Judges uses ܥܣܬܪܐ (2:13, 10:6), a Syriac form which resembles the Hebrew phonetically and occurs in no other book.[35] P-Samuel is less conservative, rendering ܣܬܪܐ 'lurking-places', apparently inferred from a root סתר thought equivalent to סתר.[36] P in Kings is different again, transliterating as ܥܣܬܪܘܬ.[37]

---

[35] This Syriac form also renders אֲשֵׁרָה in Judges (6:25–30). On the renderings of these words in other books, see M.P. Weitzman, "Lexical Clues to the Composition of the Peshitta", M.J. Geller, J.C. Greenfield and M.P. Weitzman (eds.), *Studia Aramaica: New Sources and New Approaches*, Oxford 1995, pp. 217–46: see p. 229.

[36] Note at 1 Sam. 25:20 the rendering ܣܬܪ for סתר. A root סתר (Niph.) occurs at 1 Sam. 5:9, where, however, the context led to the rendering ܐܬܦܣܩ ("broke out").

[37] Here עַשְׁתֹּרֶת is accompanied by the phrase "god (or: abomination) of the Sidonians", which indeed suggests a proper name.

P-Kings is especially conservative in preferring to render חסד by its cognate *ḥesdā*. As this Syriac word has a homonym meaning 'disgrace', the less conservative rendering *ṭaybūtā* is more common overall, as shown below:

	Gen.	Ex.	Num.	Deut.	Jos.	Judg.	Sam.	Kgs.	Isa.	Jer.	Dodk.
ḥesdā	1	0	0	0	0	0	1	4	0	0	0
ṭaybūtā	9	4	2	2	2	1	11	1	5	6	12
raḥmūtā	0	0	0	0	0	0	2	0	0	0	0

	Ps.	Prov.	Job	Ruth	Lam.	Esther	Dan.	Ezra	Neh.	Chr.
ḥesdā	1	0	1	2	1	2	0	1	0	4
ṭaybūtā	68	5	2	0	0	0	2	1	1	10
raḥmūtā	51	3	0	1	1	0	0	0	0	0

Even in Kings the majority of mss have *ṭaybūtā* in every passage, and the four occurrences of *ḥesdā* are attested by 9a1 alone. Other books too show occasional usage of *ḥesdā*.

The renderings of תורה confirm the impression that Kings is the book most conservatively rendered overall. P almost always uses the Greek loanword *nāmōsā*. By contrast, the Jewish Targums use אורייתא, reserving נמוס for human decrees, such as those enacted by Joseph in Egypt (Palestinian Targums on Exod. 1:8) or by the Israelite king (Tg. on 1 Sam. 8:9) or by corrupt priests (Tg. on 1 Sam. 1:13) or by foreigners for themselves (T⁰ on Lev. 18:3) or for subject Israelites (Tg. on Ezek. 20:25). P-Kings is unusual in occasionally using instead the Jewish Aramaic term *ʾōrāytā* (2 Kgs. 22:11; 23:24, 25). One must add, however, that P-Chronicles too shows three occurrences of *ʾōrāytā* (2 Chr. 23:18, 34:14, 15).[38]

Books that resist location in the series

Isaiah and Psalms stand apart as books that treat several of these discriminators with wide inconsistency. For example, they have no clear policy regarding the use of *qritā* and *mdittā*. Thus the same phrase וגנותי על העיר הזאת occurs at Isa. 37:35 and 38:6; in the first passage P has *qritā* and in the second *mdittā*. Again, Jerusalem is called 'city of God' in Psalms both at 46:5 and at 48:2; in the first P renders *mdittā*, in the second *qritā*. To posit more than one translator would not account for the pattern, since, within either book, the occurrences of *mdittā* are widely scattered over the text (amidst more numerous occurrences of *qritā*, not listed here):

    Isaiah: 1:8, 26; 19:2; 32:19; 36:1; 37:26, 35; 38:6
    Psalms: 46:5; 59:7,15; 72:16; 101:8; 122:3

These books are moreover peculiar in combining *mdittā*, the most recent innovation in the list, with such conservative usages as *qaryā* (Isa. 30:29) or *ḥesdā* (Ps. 107:43). Altogether the lack of a coherent policy towards innovations is itself a characteristic of these two books.

---

[38] In all these places a reference was detected to a written book of the Torah; but less conservative translators were content to use *nāmōsā* even then (e.g. Deut. 31:21, Jos. 1:8).

In the case of Job and Lamentations, the problem is rather that the discriminators occur but rarely. What evidence there is, however, tends to place these books too in the broadly conservative category; note especially the occurrence of ܟܣܦܐ for silver metal in Job[39] and the verb ܐܠ in Lamentations.

P-Exodus is intriguing, in that it varies between the conservative choices of Genesis and the more radical choices of Leviticus to Deuteronomy. This mixed behaviour is observed in its renderings of three Hebrew words: חג, כסף, עולה, as follows:

	No. of conservative renderings	No. of modern renderings
חג	2	10
כסף	28	2
עולה	13	4

The four 'modern' renderings of עולה are ܥܠܬܐ ܩܘܪ and ܩܘܪ alone, in two passages each. Both these renderings are also found in Leviticus, where the translator seems to have experimented with all three possible renderings (including ܥܠܐ) before settling down to regular use of ܩܘܪ ܥܠܬܐ.

In Exodus, the modern elements in our texts may be due in part to later scribes. At Exod. 11:2 in particular, the silver (as material of vessels) 'borrowed' by the Israelites is called ܣܐܡܐ in the P mss, but ܟܣܦܐ in Ephrem's commentary,[40] which appears original. However, the mixed behaviour of P-Exodus in relation to three different Hebrew words suggests that scribal change is not the whole explanation. Rather, we could suppose that a single translator of the whole Pentateuch began here to experiment with modern usages tentatively, before returning to take them up fully in the later books of the Pentateuch.

Finally, Ruth twice shows the conservative rendering ܚܘܣܪܐ for חסר, yet decidedly prefers the modern rendering ܩܪܝܬܐ for עיר. This book thus shares characteristics of both the most conservative and the most radical group, and so cannot be fitted into the scheme at all.

Results of the comparisons

The evidence may be summarised in fig. 3. Each biblical book accepts the innovations shown above it and rejects the innovations shown below it. In relation to any innovations shown at its own level, the book is inconsistent. Any book that is inconsistent in respect of innovations at more than one level is represented by a line (ending in an arrow) that spans those levels.

Lamentations and Job belong somewhere in the upper part of the diagram. Isaiah and Psalms, because of their inconsistency, have no fixed position. Only Ruth shows a pattern that cannot be accommodated in the table at all.

---

[39] Not only for כסף but also for בצר 'iron ore' (22:24).
[40] R-M. Tonneau (ed.), *Sancti Ephraemi Syri in Genesim et in Exodum Commentarii* (=CSCO 152, Syr 71), Louvain 1955, p. 140.

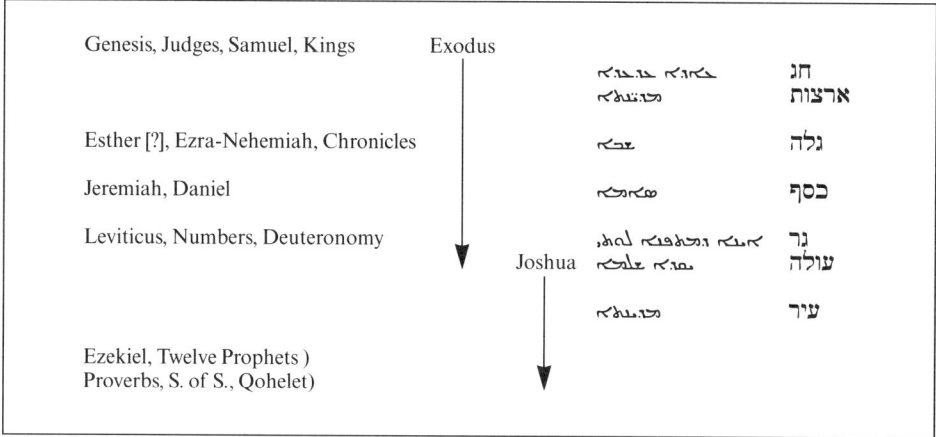

Fig. 3. A scale of biblical books and discriminators.

Interpretation of the series: an implicational scale

The above scale has a twofold aspect. On one side, it is a scale of innovations, running down from the most widely accepted to the least. On the other, it is a scale of books, with those most resistant to innovation at the top and the most modern at the bottom.

The most obvious interpretation of the scale would be chronological. One could suppose, for example, that the reason that עיר is differently rendered in Jeremiah and Ezekiel is that the translator of Jeremiah worked before the usual term for 'city' changed from ܩܪܝܬܐ to ܡܕܝܢܬܐ, while the translator of Ezekiel worked afterwards.

A purely chronological interpretation would lead, however, to the odd conclusion that some historical books, notably Kings, were translated before Leviticus and other books of the Pentateuch. One cannot lightly abandon the expectation that the books were translated in approximately the same order as in the Jewish canon. This is suggested, first of all, by the analogy of the Septuagint and Jewish Targums. Moreover, there is evidence that the P version of books which stand earlier in the canon influenced the P version of books that stand later, even where the latter are more 'conservative' in their language. Furthermore, the absence of Ezra-Chronicles from the Nestorian canon and from the Syriac 'massoretic' tradition seems to confirm that these books, being last in the Jewish canon, were translated last in P, after the canon in Syriac was thought by some to have already closed.[41]

It is not satisfactory, then, to interpret the scale of translators chronologically. Instead, it may be viewed as a scale of conservatism (or conversely of modernism). At any one time, not all writers are equally open to innovation. For example, both the 'conservative' Thucydides and the 'modern' Lysias were contemporaries in Greece in the late fifth-century. Indeed, it is possible for one writer to be more conservative in his language than another who wrote some decades earlier.

Where innovations are entering a language, modern linguistic science tells us that a

[41] R. Beckwith, *The Old Testament Canon of the New Testament Church*, London 1985, p. 309.

scale such as fig. 3 is likely to be observed, if we examine the usage of a number of speakers at one point in time.[42] Such a scale is technically termed 'implicational', since a speaker's acceptance of one innovation implies his acceptance of all the innovations shown above in the scale.

The reason is that linguistic changes – for example, changes in vocabulary – do not sweep through a whole speech community overnight. At any one time, some speakers are more modern – i.e. more receptive to innovation – than others. In principle, the different speakers could be ranked along a scale from the most conservative to the most modern. When an innovation enters the language, it is first adopted by the most modern speakers, through whom it spreads to those who are somewhat more conservative, and onwards to those who are more conservative still. It spreads, in broad terms, along the scale of speakers, starting at the most modern end. (This is of course a model – a simplification from which an analysis can be developed that yields insight into a more complex reality.) Ultimately, the innovation may be adopted even by the most conservative speakers, but this will take time.

At any one moment, a number of different innovations will be spreading from less to more conservative speakers in this way. Since these innovations did not all enter the language (in the sense of being adopted by the most modern speakers) simultaneously, they will not all have progressed along the scale to the same extent. If we take a snapshot of usage at that moment, we shall be able to rank the innovations according to their progress along the scale, and we shall also be able to rank the speakers according to their 'modernism' (i.e. the number of innovations adopted). In short, we shall observe an implicational scale just like fig. 1.

In the case of P we are dealing not with the free utterance of speakers but with translators, each bound by a source text. However, translators must have had their individual views on the proper balance between tradition (which favoured conservative lexical choice) and intelligibility (which would tend to favour modern usage). Hence different translators will place themselves along an implicational scale, no less than speakers.

In relation to P, the implicational scale is found to be subject to two qualifications. First, absolute consistency cannot be expected in any biblical book. Even a translator with a high degree of consistency in the rendering of a particular Hebrew word may occasionally depart from his normal policy. For example, P in Jeremiah twice translates עִיר by ܡܕܝܢܬܐ, despite his usual massive preference for ܩܪܝܬܐ. The reasons for this 'interference' will be investigated below.

Second, the scale is not quite comprehensive. It does not accommodate all translators, or all innovations. In Ruth we found a translator who could not be fitted into the scale: he renders חֶסֶד by ܛܝܒܘ, which according to the scale should imply that he renders עִיר by ܩܪܝܬܐ, and yet he in fact uses ܡܕܝܢܬܐ. As to innovations, an example not consistent with the scale is the use of the Greek loanword ܕܝܬܩܐ to the exclusion of the native (though not cognate) word ܩܝܡܐ to render בְּרִית. This feature is mainly confined to Joshua and Chronicles – a combination that could not have been suspected from fig. 1, where the two books are well separated. Clearly it is an over-simplification to assert that *all* innovations spread into the language by exactly the same route.

---

[42] J.K. Chambers and P. Trudgill, *Dialectology*, Cambridge 1980, pp. 149–54.

In short, it would be wrong to assert that the renderings in P obey immutable laws. To say that they are random, however, would be even further from the truth.

The 'modern' usages (e.g. ܡܕܝܢܬܐ for 'city', ܝܩܕܐ ܫܠܡܐ for 'burnt offering') naturally became normative for later biblical translations into Syriac, of the Apocrypha and New Testament. There are some exceptions, however. The Old Syriac Gospels – and later Syriac versions – retain ܓܠܘܬܐ 'exile' (Matt. 1:11,17) and ܣܐܡܐ 'silver' (Matt. 10:9).[43] Even the Peshitta version of the New Testament has ܐܘܪܝܬܐ, though as a technical term for the written Torah.

'Modern' usage and the influence of the Septuagint

The influence of LXX on P was shown above to vary between books, and the pattern which emerges from Haefeli's survey is still instructive:

Frequent parallels	Ezekiel; the Twelve Prophets; the Solomonic books
Sporadic parallels	Genesis; Joshua; Isaiah; Jeremiah; Psalms; Esther
Few or no parallels	Samuel; Kings; Job; Lamentations; Chronicles
[No assessment offered	Exodus-Deuteronomy; Judges; Ruth; Daniel; Ezra-Nehemiah]

Of course these results were based on studies each restricted to one book, but a correlation between these results and the scale of lexical usage in fig.1 is clear. Conservative lexical choice went with fidelity to the *Hebraica veritas* and hence with reluctance to consult LXX, even when the Hebrew exemplar was obscure (as in Job) or illegible (as in Chronicles). It seems that the LXX version and up-to-date Syriac idiom were viewed as two things which the modern world had to offer, which tended to be adopted or rejected together. Indeed the two could coincide, for some of the 'modern' renderings – namely ܩܝܒܘܬܐ, ܐܠܦ ܕܡܬܩܪܐ ܠܗ, ܝܩܕܐ ܫܠܡܐ . are loanwords or calques from the Greek renderings actually found in LXX.

Sources of interference

The tables above showed that a book which usually favours one rendering may occasionally choose its rival. The main reasons for this may be classified as follows:

Variations of nuance

Normally, גלה 'go into exile' has people as subject. At Judges 18:30, however, the subject is the land. P-Judges is normally conservative and therefore expected to use ܓܠܐ; but the land could not be said to depart into exile. Hence the modern rendering ܐܫܬܒܝ 'be captured' (which could apply to the land as well as people) could not be avoided.

The renderings of עיר may likewise be distorted by variations of nuance. Even though most translators had a definite preference between ܩܪܝܬܐ and ܡܕܝܢܬܐ, they were aware that the latter denoted a greater or mightier settlement than the former. Thus in Lamentations, the mighty Jerusalem of the past is called ܡܕܝܢܬܐ (Lam. 1:1),

---

[43] Here the Peshitta and Harklean versions have the modern ܟܣܦܐ.

but in its ruined state it is called ܩܪܝܬܐ (Lam. 2:12, 15; 5:11). Likewise in Joshua, ܡܕܝܢ̱ܬܐ is used of Canaanite cities and ܩܪܝܬܐ of cities founded by Israelites.[44]

In particular, a contrast in the original may force the translator to use side by side the words employed for the conservative and for the modern rendering. For example, the Hebrew at 1 Sam. 6:18 contrasts עיר מבצר 'fortified city' with כפר הפרזי 'open village'. To bring out the contrast, P had to use ܡܕܝܢ̱ܬܐ of the fortified city, despite his normal practice, and so had ܩܪܝܬܐ available for the village. Again, Jer. 19:15 threatens evil אל העיר הזאת ועל כל עריה, where העיר denotes Jerusalem and עריה its daughter-cities. To point the contrast, P translates the first word by ܡܕܝܢ̱ܬܐ (against normal usage) and reserves ܩܪܝܬܐ for the second. The case is similar at Neh. 11:1, and also at Zech. 7:7 (where 'her cities' contrasts with Jerusalem).

The use of both the conservative and the modern renderings together can also be forced by the occurrence of synonyms in the Hebrew, notably within parallelism. Thus Hab. 2:12 uses עיר in the first line and קריה in the second, which become in P ܡܕܝܢ̱ܬܐ and ܩܪܝܬܐ respectively, though no difference in sense is intended.

Hangover

Although the usual word for 'city' in P on Kings is overwhelmingly ܩܪܝܬܐ, we find ܡܕܝܢ̱ܬܐ at 1 Kings 20:19, 30. This is due to the appearance in the Hebrew of מדינה, which was naturally rendered ܡܕܝܢ̱ܬܐ (in the sense 'province') at 1 Kings 20:14–19; and the word ܡܕܝܢ̱ܬܐ lingered in the memory. Likewise in Ezra the occurrence of מדן in the Aramaic of 4:15 has brought in ܡܕܝܢ̱ܬܐ for עיר at 4:15, 19; by 4:20, however, the normal rendering ܩܪܝܬܐ is back in use. Conversely, in Ezekiel the usual rendering is ܡܕܝܢ̱ܬܐ, but ܩܪܝܬܐ appears at Ezek. 39:3. This is a hangover from 38:13, where MT has כְּפִירֶיהָ but the translator understood כְּפָרֶיהָ 'her villages' and so translated ܩܘܪܝܐ.

Initial instability

A translator may revise his initial policy. The example of ܝܠ, which the translators of Genesis and Chronicles each used in just one verse before abandoning it permanently, was noted on p. 123 above.

Initial instability may be detected in the renderings of עולה in Leviticus and Numbers. In each book the 'conservative' rendering ܥܠܬܐ is frequent towards the beginning, but ܩܘܪܒܢܐ ܕܝܩܕܐ is dominant by the end.[45] The renewed willingness to try ܥܠܬܐ once more at the beginning of Numbers suggests awareness of a new start, if not a new translator.

Differences within P-Samuel

The renderings of ארון in P-Samuel are as follows:
(1)   Up to 1 Sam. 6:11 inclusive, P renders ܩܒܘܬܐ (29 times);
(2)   From 1 Sam. 6:13, the rendering is ܐܪܘܢܐ, which remains up to 2 Sam. 6:16 inclusive (23 times);

---

[44] For detail, see M.P. Weitzman, "Lexical Clues", p. 246.
[45] Occasionally we also find the compromise ܩܘܪܒܢܐ, with or without ܕܝܩܕܐ (or ܠܥܠܬܐ). The detailed pattern is set out in M.P. Weitzman, "Lexical Clues", p. 237.

(3)   The remainder of the book displays rapid alternation: ܣܗܘܒܐ in the next verse (2 Sam. 6:17), ܐܪܘܢܐ at 2 Sam. 7:2, ܣܗܘܒܐ between 2 Sam. 11:11 and 15:25 (3 times) and finally ܐܪܘܢܐ at 2 Sam. 15:29.

So far as the shift in 2 Sam. 6 is concerned, אֲרוֹן is not the only Hebrew word whose rendering suddenly changes at just this point. Up to 2 Sam. 6:13, ויהי is usually rendered (27x) and relatively seldom omitted (10x). From 2 Sam. 7:1 onwards, however, it is usually omitted (20x), and only once rendered (2 Sam. 8:1). (The situation in other books is compared below.) To these we may add a third Hebrew word which has two different renderings in Samuel, with a change of policy just here. The divine title צבאות is transliterated in all seven places where it occurs in Samuel up to and including 2 Sam. 6:2, but from 2 Sam. 6:18 it is rendered ܣܠܝܛܢܐ 'mighty'.

The convergence of these three shifts suggests that a fresh translator may have taken over at this point.[46] This would also explain a certain instability in the renderings of חסד after this breakpoint, as if a new translator were finding his feet: although the usual rendering is ܛܝܒܘܬܐ, we find ܚܣܡ at 2 Sam. 7:15 and ܐܘܫܝ at 2 Sam. 9:1,3, before the regular ܛܝܒܘܬܐ is resumed at 2 Sam. 9:7. Whether yet another change of translator must be posited to explain the change from ܐܪܘܢܐ to ܣܗܘܒܐ somewhere between v. 2 and v. 13 of 1 Sam. 6 is doubtful; this single switch could credibly have been made by one translator.

Further evidence for classification

Agreement patterns that cut across the implicational scale

So far we have discussed innovations whose distribution tends to follow the implicational scale of fig.1, and also the factors that occasionally break that underlying pattern. We now turn to some innovations whose distribution tends to cut systematically across the implicational scale.

We may begin with Hebrew בְּרִית, for which, as already mentioned, the native (though not cognate) rendering ܩܝܡܐ had to compete with the Greek loan-word ܕܝܬܩܐ (διαθήκη), which was first used in LXX for a religious covenant and elsewhere usually denoted a will or other legal settlement. The distribution follows:

	Gen.	Ex.	Lev.	Num.	Deut.	Jos.	Judg.	Sam.	Kgs.	Isa.	Jer.	Ezek.	Dodk.
ܩܝܡܐ	26	12	10	5	26	0	3	13	25	12	14	15	11
ܕܝܬܩܐ	0	0	0	0	0	15	0	0	0	0	7	1	4

	Ps.	Prov.	Job	Dan.	Chr.
ܩܝܡܐ	16	1	1	5	2
ܕܝܬܩܐ	0	0	0	2	13[47]

---

[46] It is worth noting, however, that in the Septuagint a similar shift occurs in the rendering of צבאות. Lucian's recension usually transliterates up to 2 Sam. 6:18 but always has παντοκράτωρ thereafter; see the collations of boc₂e₂ in A.E. Brooke, N. McLean and H.St-J. Thackeray, *The Old Testament in Greek*, vol. 2, Cambridge 1935.

[47] P in Chronicles even adds ܕܝܬܩܐ in some passages where MT does not have בְּרִית (2 Chr. 5:10, 7:22, 29:9). Of the rarer renderings of בְּרִית, one may note ܩܝܡܣ (twice in Nehemiah and 5 times in Chronicles).

In this case Joshua and Chronicles, one relatively modern and one relatively conservative book, unite against the rest in a strong preference for the innovation.[48] It is worth noting that Joshua and Chronicles are further linked by their common policy of translating Heb. זקן as ܩܫܝܫܐ rather than ܣܒܐ.

Another discriminator whose renderings cut across the implicational scale is ויהי, before a phrase or clause of time which introduces another verb. This word is sometimes rendered literally (ܘܗܘܐ), sometimes omitted, and occasionally represented by the adverb ܗܝܕܝܢ 'then', on the following pattern:

	Gen.	Ex.	Lev.	Num.	Deut.	Jos.	Judg.	Sam.	Kgs.	Isa.	Jer.	Ezek.	Dodk.
[rendered]	38	16	1	3	1	0	4	28	15	3	5	2	1
[omitted]	21	5	0	5	4	26	20	30	65	0	15	11	2
ܗܝܕܝܢ	0	0	0	0	0	0	0	0	0	0	0	0	0

	Job	Ruth	Esther	Dan.	Neh.	Chr.
[rendered]	2	3	1	0	1	22
[omitted]	0	0	4	2	0	0
ܗܝܕܝܢ	0	0	0	0	10	2

Here the less conservative rendering – namely omission – is commoner in Kings than in books like Jeremiah, shown as relatively modern in fig.1. The figures for Samuel mask a change occurring somewhere in 2 Sam. 6, discussed above.

Finally we may consider צבאות, where the conservative rendering is most frequent (in absolute terms) in Jeremiah, which in other respects is not among the most conservative books:

	Sam.	Kgs.	Isa.	Jer.	Dodk.	Ps.	Chr.
[transliterated]	7	0	1	12	0	0	0
ܚܝܠܬܐ	4	4	58	64	103	15	3

The distributions for ויהי and צבאות both cut across the scale. In the former case, we observe a difference between Chronicles and the first part of Samuel on the one hand, and the remaining historical books (including Joshua) on the other.

Such cases show that not all innovations entered the language by precisely the same route. Although one group – to which the translators of Ezekiel etc. stood closest – were particularly active in introducing the innovations listed in fig.1, we can detect a minority of innovations – such as ܕܐܬܪܗܡ – which were first adopted by some other group(s).

Small groups of books

There are a number of renderings of which each is characteristic of just one or two books. They do not conflict with the implicational scale, and may allow us to subdivide some of the groups shown in fig.1.

Ironically, the P versions of S. of S. and Qohelet, which express 'city' and 'silver'

---

[48] This rendering has recently been discussed by J.C. de Moor and F. Sepmeijer, "The Peshiṭta and the Targum of Joshua" in MPI 8 (1995), pp. 174–5; see further pp. 243–4 in chapter 5 below.

through modern vocabulary, stand unusually close to the Hebrew in certain other respects.[49] These books are alone in P in regularly using ܬܢ. They also use Syriac words which resemble the Hebrew and seldom appear in other books, such as ܬܘܒ rather than ܗܦܟ for שוב (Cant. 7:1 *quater*, Qoh. 1:6, 7), ܡܩܢܐܬܐ rather than ܛܢܢܐ for קנאה (Qoh. 9:6), and ܙܥܩܬܐ rather than ܝܠܠܬܐ for זעקה (Qoh. 9:17). Again, the construct (rather than emphatic plus *dalath*) is used more frequently in these books than elsewhere. Both books may well go back to the same translator. As no such tendency appears in Proverbs, the Solomonic books cannot form a single translation unit, even though all stand towards the more modern extreme.

The books Ezra, Nehemiah and Chronicles are linked in rendering משוררים by ܡܫܡܫܢܐ "servants", equating with משרתים.[50] We may also note the use of ܗܘܝ for ויהי exclusive to Nehemiah and Chronicles, and the seemingly total freedom of all these books from LXX influence. There is also external evidence for viewing them as a distinct group: they are excluded from the Nestorian canon and from the Syriac 'massoretic' tradition (as noted above) and also from the scholia of Bar Hebraeus. Moreover, Theodore of Mopsuestia rejected (ἐξέβαλεν) them from the biblical canon.[51]

Within this group, Chronicles is distinctive in that the Syriac bears a far looser relationship to MT. As argued in detail above, however, that approach was only acquired in the course of the work of translation, because of the illegible *Vorlage*. It is therefore possible that all books in this group come from the hand of the same translator.

Esther may belong to the same group, not only because this book too relates to the Persian period but also because it was likewise omitted from the Nestorian massoretic ms 9m1. Again like those books it uses both ܩܪܝܬܐ and ܡܕܝܢܬܐ for "city". Unlike them, however, it receives comment in western massoretic mss.

Peculiarities of single books

The singular הבל is rendered by its Syriac cognate ܗܒܠܐ regularly in Qohelet (33x). In Jeremiah the rendering is instead ܠܐ ܡܕܡ (Jer. 2:5, 10:3, 15, 16:19, 51:18). Yet another rendering, namely ܠܗܓܐ 'vapour', going back to the primary meaning of the Hebrew, is usual in Psalms (6 times).[52] This evidence confirms that the three books of Psalms, Jeremiah and Qohelet all stand apart from each other, as was already apparent from fig. 1.

The P version of Job has a number of innovations peculiar to itself: ܛܝܒܐ for חסד (10:12, 36:14, but ܣܘܥܪܐ at 37:13), ܐܟܣܢܝܐ for גר (31:32), and the vague terms ܕܒܚܐ (1:5) or ܩܘܪܒܢܐ (42:8) for עולה. Thus, although P-Job is basically conservative in policy, it seems to differ in origin from the other conservative books.

For completeness, we may note that the biblical books vary also in the incidence of Jewish traditional exegesis, which is highest in the Pentateuch and in Chronicles.

[49] Though even these books have 'free' touches, such as the change from "companions" (חבריך) to (ܥܢ̈ܟܝ)"sheep" at Song 1:7 or from פתגם to ܬܒܥܬܐ 'retribution' at Qoh. 8:11.

[50] Ezra. 2:41,65 etc; Neh. 7:1,44 etc; 1 Chr. 9:33, 2 Chr. 35:15.

[51] According to Leontius of Byzantium, PG 86, col. 1368.

[52] The adjective ܣܪܝܩ (or a derivative) appears in Isa. (2x), Dodk. (1x), Ps. (2x), Pr. (1x), Job (2x) and Lam. (1x). Note also the renderings ܐܒܕܢܐ (Pr. 21:6), ܥܘܠܐ (Pr. 13:11) and ܚܠܠܐ (Isa. 57:13). The plural of הבל, when it has the different nuance of 'idols' (and in P becomes ܕܚ̈ܠܬܐ), may be left aside.

In itself, however, this variation does not indicate different translators. The Pentateuch was always the primary object of Jewish exegesis, and its relatively high incidence in P here may reflect the abundance of material. In Chronicles, it seems rather that the translator's difficulties in recovering the plain sense of his damaged Hebrew *Vorlage* left him receptive to any traditional material available. Finally, the books vary in their attitude towards the Jewish people, as we shall investigate in chapter 5.

The translation units and the relationships between them

The work above has indicated differences in usage in the different books of P. These differences do not of course suffice to indicate the boundaries of the translation units definitively, since one cannot know how much inconsistency to admit in the work of an individual translator. Still, the translation units may be tentatively delimited on the following lines.

Within the Pentateuch, the case is strong for the unity of Leviticus to Deuteronomy. Genesis is so much more conservative as to suggest a different translator. However, given the combination of both types of profile in Exodus, we cannot exclude the alternative hypothesis that the Pentateuch is a unity: the translator began with conservative usages, but in Exodus he began tentatively to abandon some of these, and then adopted the modern usages wholeheartedly in the later books.

Among the Former Prophets, Joshua stands well apart. Judges, Samuel and Kings form a block by virtue of their conservatism, but each has its own peculiarities, and within Samuel two hands can be detected. Of the Latter Prophets, Ezekiel and the Twelve Prophets have identical profiles, and, given also their proximity in the canon, seem due to the same translator. Another possible pair are Jeremiah and Daniel; the profiles are similar, and ܐܝܬܘܬܐ serves for אִצְרוֹת both in Jeremiah and at Dan. 11:42. Isaiah, however, with its varying policy stands apart.

In the Writings, the profiles again vary sufficiently to suggest that almost every book has its own translator. In particular, the profiles in Psalms (mixed), Proverbs (modern) and Job (conservative) are quite different. S. of S. and Qohelet, however, share a distinctively literalist style and probably form a single translation unit. Moreover, as noted above, there is also a case for viewing Ezra, Nehemiah and Chronicles as a single unit, which may also have included Esther. Of course the translation technique of Chronicles is unique, but this may reflect the unusual state of the *Vorlage*, rather than yet another translator.

The search for links among the translation units

The criteria as to whether different translators nevertheless belonged to a single school must be chosen with care. To begin with, we are not concerned with cases where the Hebrew is straightforward and the agreement of the two Syriac texts could be coincidental. For example, the words common to Deut. 24:16 and 2 Kgs. 14:6 are rendered in the former as follows:

ܠܐ ܢܡܘܬܘܢ ܐܒܗܐ ܥܠ ܒܢܝܐ ܘܒܢܝܐ ܠܐ ܢܡܘܬܘܢ ܥܠ ܐܒܗܝܗܘܢ

Kings agrees exactly, except in writing ܒ̈ܢܝܐ for ܒ̈ܢܝܗܘܢ. Yet this almost total agreement is no proof of literary dependence, because two translators could have reached this plain rendering of the Hebrew independently.

Nor are we concerned with cases where the translator in one book could have consulted the Hebrew text, and not necessarily the Peshitta version, of a passage in another book, e.g.

Judg. 5:10 ישבי על מִדִּין והלכי על דרך שיחו
ܘܝܬܒ̈ܝ ܒܒ̈ܬܐ ܘܡܗܠܟ̈ܝ ܒܐܘܪܚܬܐ ܪܢܘ

and ye who sit in houses and walk on the ways: meditate!

Puzzled by מִדִּין, the translator noted the references to "sit" and "go on the way" (and possibly "meditate"), and inferred a connection with Deut. 6:7: "when you sit in your *house*, and go on the way". This understanding is continued in the next verse, where משאבים is rendered ܡܠܦ̈ܢܐ 'teachers'. All this does not, however, demonstrate dependence on the P version of Deuteronomy, as opposed to the Hebrew text.

Again, for the last three words of Jonah 4:8, P substitutes a rendering of a longer passage from the similar context of 1 Kgs. 19:4 –

MT-Jonah טוב מותי מחיי
MT-Kings רב עתה י׳ קח נפשי כי לא טוב אנכי מאבתי
P-Jonah ܫܐܠܐ ܒܐܢܬܘܢ ܡܪܝܐ ܠܡܣܒ ܢܦܫܝ ܡܢܝ. ܡܛܠ ܕܠܐ ܗܘܝܬ ܛܒ ܡܢ ܐܒܗ̈ܝ
P-Kings ܣܓܝ ܠܝ. ܗܫܐ ܡܪܝܐ ܣܒ ܢܦܫܝ ܡܢܝ. ܡܛܠ ܕܠܐ ܗܘܝܬ ܛܒ ܡܢ ܐܒܗ̈ܝ

P-Jonah evidently depends on Kings, but not necessarily in Syriac form; the differing treatment of the opening words instead suggests direct consultation of the Hebrew.[53]

Nor can weight be attached to renderings that are common to many biblical books but could have been derived independently from traditions well attested elsewhere. Such renderings are ܓܢܒܪ̈ܐ for רפאים,[54] or ܫܢܝܢ ܒܫܢܝܢ (or the like) for ימים 'year', which also occur in the Targums.

Three types of evidence are instead relevant. First, different books sometimes agree in ascribing to a particular Hebrew word a meaning unparalleled outside P. Second, even where there is nothing extraordinary in the perceived sense, the manner in which different books of P agree in expressing that sense is sometimes idiosyncratic, and without parallel in Jewish Aramaic versions. Third, there are passages where the translator of one book found in the Hebrew text of a given passage an association which led him to a passage in a different book, which he can be shown to have consulted in the P version and not simply in the Hebrew.

Common understanding of Hebrew words

A number of Hebrew words are understood in a manner common but exclusive to the translators of P. In some cases we can identify the passage where this understanding arose:

(a) Heb. סוללה 'siegeworks' is oddly rendered 'ambush' or 'marauders' in all the books where it occurs (Samuel, Kings, Isaiah, Jeremiah, Ezekiel, Daniel). The only

[53] See further Gelston, *Twelve Prophets*, p. 150.
[54] E.g. Gen. 14:5, Deut. 2:11, Josh. 12:4, Isa. 14:9, Ps. 88:11, Pr. 9:18, Job 26:5.

exception is Jer. 33:4, but even here סוללה is rendered by the near-synonym ܓܝܣܐ 'troop'. The understanding of סוללה as 'ambush' or the like apparently arose from the opening of Jer. 32:34 –

MT   הנה הסללות באו העיר ללכדה

> Behold the siegeworks. They have come to the city to capture it.

Understandably, P did not detect the break, and instead read the Hebrew as a continuous sentence. This suggested that the סוללה was the subject of 'come' and hence animate.

(b) Forms derived from the root חקק 'incise' are rendered by forms from ܒܩܐ 'examine', and in particular by the form ܡܒܩܝܐ, which means "scrutineer" (in the sense of 'prophet', according to Ephrem[55]). This equation appears at Gen. 49:10*, Num. 21:18, Deut. 33:21*, Judg. 5:9*, 14*, Isa. 10:1, 33:22*, Prov. 8:15, 31:5*. The asterisk indicates the form ܡܒܩܝܐ, for which the corresponding Hebrew form is usually מחקק (often taken as 'sceptre'). The origin of the equivalence חקק – ܒܩܐ may be sought in Judges 5, where the phrases חקקי לב (5:15) and חקרי לב (5:16) appear in successive verses. These phrases are almost identical graphically, and also in their context, namely the taunting of the Reubenites for reflecting too long rather than coming to Deborah's aid. Hence a reader of Judges could well have equated the roots חקק and חקר. Now חקר is aptly rendered by ܒܩܐ "examine", and so ܒܩܐ came to represent חקק also.

(c) Subtler is the understanding of the noun עני 'affliction' as the specific ܥܒܕܘܬܐ 'enslavement'. The verb ענה (Piel) 'afflict' first occurs at Gen. 15:13, in a prediction of the Egyptian bondage, and is there duly rendered ܫܥܒܕ. Thence, however, ܥܒܕܘܬܐ 'enslavement' became a common rendering even where the affliction is quite different – e.g. an indifferent husband (Gen. 29:32), infertility (1 Sam. 1:11) or persecution by enemies (Ps. 9:14) – or is altogether more general (Ps. 25:18, Job 30:16, 27; Lam. 3:1,19).[56]

(d) Heb. נדבה – properly a free-will gift – is rendered regularly by ܦܘܪܫܐ '(gift) separated off'. The same Syriac word serves also to render תרומה "(gift) lifted off"; the free-will gift is thus fused with the obligatory portion for the priests. This further use of ܦܘܪܫܐ to render נדבה originated at Exod. 35:29, where that Hebrew word occurs for the first time. The equation תרומה = ܦܘܪܫܐ had occurred just before (at 35:24), and the translator took up the same Syriac word for the term נדבה. This equivalence is repeated later in the Pentateuch, Ezekiel (46:12), Psalms (54:8), Ezra (1:4) and 2 Chr. 35:8.[57] At Judg. 5:9, this unusual understanding led to the rendering of המתנדבים 'who offer themselves' as ܕܦܪܝܫܝܢ 'who are separated, distinguished'.

(e) The word משפתים, is understood as ܫܒܝܠܐ "paths". This understanding originates at Gen. 49:14, where the Hebrew compares Issachar to a bony ass crouching between the משפתים. Apparently the translator looked ahead to the description of Dan three verses later as a serpent upon the path, which last word P rendered likewise by the plural ܫܒܝܠܐ. The same rendering occurs for משפתים at Judg. 5:16.[58]

---

[55] R.-M. Tonneau (ed.), *Sancti Ephraem Syri in Genesim et in Exodum Commentarii*, Louvain 1955 (CSCO 152, Syr 71), p. 113, l.17.
[56] Although other renderings of עני are also found, e.g. ܡܣܟܢܘܬܐ at Ps. 31:8.
[57] Here לנדבה is rendered ܦܘܪܫ.
[58] It may be, however, that the translators instead thought of שפיים, which P often understands as 'paths'.

(f) Not quite exclusive to P, but still noteworthy, is the understanding of חליפה 'change (of garments)' as (ܕܢܚܬܐ) ܙܘܓܐ "pair (of garments)". This first occurs in Gen. 45:22, and seems due to LXX δισσὰς στολάς. It is repeated in Judges (14:12–13), 2 Kings (5:5) and in the latter part of Gen. 45:22 itself, even though LXX does not speak of "twofold" garments in any of these passages.

(g) In 2 Sam. 23 and 1 Chr. 11, we have two parallel lists of David's heroes. In Samuel, P unexpectedly understands adjectives of place to indicate provenance from specific mountains:

	Adjective	**P**	**Hero**
v.11	הררי	"from the king's mountain (country)"[59]	שמה
v.25	החרדי (1°)	"from the king's mountain (country)"	שמה
v.28	האחחי	"from the temple mount"	צלמון
v.33	הררי	"from the mount of olives"	שמה

This curious understanding recurs in Chronicles, despite differences in the forms of the adjectives as well as the identity of the heroes:

v.27	ההרורי	"from the king's mountain (country)"	שמות
v.35	הררי	"from the temple mount"	אחיאם

Most of the adjectives graphically resemble הר – apart from האחחי which, however, is followed by the name מהרי. No doubt Samuel was translated before Chronicles, but it could not be said that P-Chronicles has simply copied P-Samuel. Rather, both seem to share a special tradition which distinguished the nearly homographic adjectives, naming the mountains in a set order.

The origin of two further instances of a special meaning shared by more than one book cannot be traced to any specific passage:

(h) The rendering ܣܦܪܐ "scribe" for שֹׁטֵר is usual in Exodus, Deuteronomy and Joshua, and also occurs twice in Chronicles (1 Chr. 23:4, 2 Chr. 19:11). It derives from association with Syriac ܫܛܪܐ 'document' (or conceivably with the rabbinic Hebrew cognate). This rendering does not derive from rabbinic tradition, which instead views the שֹׁטֵר as an enforcer rather than scholar of the law.

(i) Again, the unclear graphic sequence ארם/אדם was almost everywhere understood by P as Edom(ite), as discussed in detail above.

Common modes of expression in Syriac

Here we are concerned with agreement between different books of P, against the Jewish Aramaic versions, on the choice of expression in Syriac.

We may be able to identify the biblical passage at which such a solution was invented. Thus at Gen. 49:9, MT applies to Judah three different terms for lion:

גור אריה-ארי-לביא

P duly renders the first by ܓܘܪܝܐ ܕܐܪܝܐ and the second by ܐܪܝܐ alone. For the third term he has no new Syriac word, and so repeats ܓܘܪܝܐ ܕܐܪܝܐ. Now the use of ܓܘܪܝܐ ܕܐܪܝܐ for the rarer Hebrew terms for 'lion' is well attested in other books of P,

---

[59] The term הר המלך in rabbinic Hebrew indicates an extensive area north of Jerusalem; see S. Applebaum, *Judea in Hellenistic and Roman Times*, Leiden 1989, pp. 24–8.

and seems to have spread from this passage. It represents לביא (Num. 24:9*, Joel 1:6*), ליש (Isa. 30:6*, Prov. 30:20), שחל (Job 4:10*), and even the mother lioness לָבִיא at Ezek. 19:2. (The asterisk indicates passages where the Hebrew has in a parallel line another word for 'lion', rendered ܐܪܝܐ in P.)[60]

In other cases in which a common policy can be identified as to the choice of Syriac expression, its origin cannot be linked decisively to any particular biblical passage, though often we may reasonably ascribe it to the canonically earliest occurrence:

(a) The most striking example is the Tetragrammaton, which is not transliterated but translated as ܡܪܝܐ "lord", similarly to LXX and against the Targums preserved by rabbinic Judaism.[61]

(b) Again, תורה is almost everywhere rendered by the Greek loanword ܢܡܘܣܐ, while the Jewish Targums use אורייתא and reserve נימוסא for human decrees, as discussed above.

(c) The sacrificial term אשם "trespass offering" is rendered by the colourless ܩܘܪܒܢܐ in all the books where it occurs (Leviticus, Samuel, Ezekiel). This Syriac word is also used for the near-homograph אִשֶּׁה, a generic term for which ܩܘܪܒܢܐ is indeed appropriate; the translators were indifferent to the distinction. Common choices of expression may thus raise the broader question of shared theological attitudes: in this case, an indifference to ritual (of which the obverse was regard for prayer), as will be discussed in chapter 5.

(d) The Hebrew sometimes describes God as מגן 'shield'. The first instance is at Gen. 15:1, where P instead states that God helps (ܡܥܕܪ). P goes on to substitute the same verb at Deut. 33:29 and Prov. 2:7, 30:5. The corresponding *nomen agentis* ܡܥܕܪܢܐ is substituted ten times in the Psalms (plus 2 Sam. 22:3).[62]

(e) Another case where the general (though not the exact) sense was known and different books share a distinctive rendering concerns lists of sacrificial pots. In various books we find the same sequence of three terms – ܡܣܪ̈ܩܬܐ ܐܪܝܐ ܩܣ̈ܘܬܐ – namely at Exod. 27:3 = 38:3, 1 Sam. 2:14, 1 Kgs. 7:40, 45, 2 Kgs. 25:14 = Jer. 52:18, 2 Chr. 35:13, even though the Hebrew terms vary considerably.[63]

(f) A single nuance of (לב) שרירות 'stubbornness' is brought out in the common rendering ܨܒܝܢܐ 'will' – usually in the construct – at Deut. 29:19, six times in Jeremiah (3:17, 7:24, 9:13, 11:8, 16:12, 18:12) and at Ps. 81:13. Again, a common mode of expressing the sense was agreed.

(g) Hebrew סנורים, confined to Gen. 19:11 and 2 Kgs. 6:18, is rendered ܫܪܓܪ̈ܓܝܬܐ ('bedazzlement') in both passages (twice in the verse from Kings). This is an unusual term, formed from ܫܪܓܐ 'lamp', reflecting a derivation of סנורים from נר.

Ultimately, the common policies regarding choice of Syriac expression can be broadened out to include shared attitudes to the task of translation altogether. These were considered in detail in chapter 2, and here we need only recall the major characteristics which set the P translators aside from the Targums transmitted by rabbinic Judaism: quantitative literalism, fidelity to the plain sense even in poetic or figurative passages,

---

[60] The renderings of כפיר can be left aside, since here the rendering ܐܪܝܐ ܘܓܘܪܝܐ is unexceptional. See also Gelston, *Twelve Prophets*, p. 141.   [61] In 11QTgJob, the name is represented by אלהא (e.g. 42:1).
[62] See Joosten in MPI 8 (1995), p. 65n.
[63] M.A. Zipor, "A Striking Translation Technique of the Peshitta", *JSS* 26 (1981), pp. 11–20.

and the deliberate misreading or even omission of difficult passages. In addition, the P translators agree in their general tolerance towards anthropomorphisms, with the same exceptions – notably, of God as shield (as noted above) and of God changing his purpose.

The consultation of passages in different books

In some passages, notably in Job, the translator borrowed the equivalences invented by a colleague in a different book. The direction of influence can be established in the following cases:

Exod. 33:5–6 $\Rightarrow$ Job 10:17a

In Exodus, Heb. עדי is rendered ܙܝܢܐ, as in the Targums. The equivalence was taken up in Job:

MT   תְּחַדֵּשׁ עֵדֶיךָ נֶגְדִּי

P   ܡܚܕܬ ܐܢܬ ܘܡܢ ܠܩܘܒܠܝ

     and you rouse your weaponry against me

It seems that P-Job understood the second Hebrew word as עֶדְיָךְ, which led him to Exodus. The verb ܡܚܕܬ is probably, as Bernstein supposed, a corruption of ܡܚܕܬ "(you) renew".[64]

Deut. 21:17 $\Rightarrow$ Job 20:10b

In Deuteronomy, ראשית אנו "the firstfruits of his strength" is rendered ܪܝ ܝܠܕܗ "the first (lit. head) of his progeny", in line with the context (inheritance rights of sons). This rendering for אונ is later adopted by P in Job:

MT   וְיָדָיו תְּשֵׁבְנָה אוֹנוֹ

P   ܘܐܝܕܘܗܝ, ܢܫܘܛ ܒܠܝܠܕܗ

     and his hands will stretch out against his offspring

The first line of v.10 had stated (in P) that the sons of the wicked would be broken by poverty. Even so, mere guesswork would not have led P-Job to continue that they would be attacked by their own father. Rather, the form אונו put P-Job in mind of the passage in Deuteronomy.

Ps. 4:5, 17:3–4 $\Rightarrow$ Job 31:34c

The Hebrew and Syriac texts in Job may be thus compared:

MT   וְאָדֹם לֹא אֵצֵא פֶתַח

P   ܘܒܡܡܠܠܐ ܕܣܦܘܬܐ ܠܐ ܪܢܝܬ

     and on the speech of lips I did not meditate

---

[64] G.H. Bernstein, "Syrische Studien I. Beiträge zur Berechtigung einzelner Stellen und Wörter in den bisher gedruckten syrischen Werken", *ZDMG* 3 (1849), pp. 385–428: 392.

The concluding verb in P represents the opening verb in the Hebrew; apparently P-Job consulted Ps. 4:5, where ודמו is rendered ܘܪܢܘ "and meditate". This equivalence seems to have originated with the translator of Psalms, who apparently felt that a literal translation ("be silent") would contradict the preceding phrase: "speak in your hearts". Having adopted this equivalence, P-Job then apparently took פתח as the organs of speech (cf. Micah 7:5 פתחי פיך), and selected an expression from another passage in Psalms, namely Ps. 17:3–4, where the context is similar to that of Job, namely protestation of innocence:

MT ...בל יעבר פי: לפעלות אדם בדבר שפתיך...

P ܘܠܐ ܥܒܪܘ ܥܠ ܦܘܡܝ ܥܒ̈ܕܐ ܕܒܢܝ̈ܢܫܐ ܒܡܡܠܠܐ ܕܣܦ̈ܘܬܐ

and the works of man have not passed over my mouth by the speech of lips

Ps. 78:41 ⇒ Job 31:35b

In Psalms, MT has התוו and P ܡܪ̈ܡܪܘ, again on the basis of LXX (παρώξυναν).[65] The same equivalence is adopted for תוי at Job 31:35b, which was evidently thought related:

MT הן תוי שדי יַעֲנֵנִי

P ܠܡܪ̈ܡܪܘܬܗ ܕܐܠܗܐ ܡܟܒܢܝ [= יְעַנְּנִי]

The equation תוי – ܠܡܪ̈ܡܪܬܐ would be otherwise inexplicable.

Psalm 139:23 (and 55:9?) ⇒ Job 20:2

The texts in Job are as follows:

MT לכן שעפי ישיבוני ובעבור חושי בי

P ܡܛܠ ܗܠܟ̈ܬܝ ܐܬܦܢܘܢܝ ܘܡܛܠܬܝ ܟܬܪܘ ܠܝ

for the sake of my steps, answer me; and for my sake, wait for me

To render שעפי, P found the related word שרעפי at Ps. 139:23, which is likewise rendered ܗܠܟ̈ܬܝ, on the basis of LXX τὰς τρίβους μου. The rendering of Heb. חוש "hasten" by its near-opposite ܟܬܪ is likewise characteristic of P in Psalms.[66] This equivalence apparently arose in Psalms, perhaps at Ps. 55:9, where MT has חוש and P follows the guess in LXX: προσεδεχόμην. Alternatively, the reason for this rendering in P-Psalms may be that all forms of this verb occurring in Psalms end with cohortative ה. This may have suggested a connection with the verb חשה, which originally meant "be silent" but could mean 'hesitate' (Judg. 18:9, 2 Kgs. 7:9).

Lam. 3:63 ⇒ Job 30:9a

In Lamentations, Heb. מנגינתם is rendered ܪܢܝܗܘܢ, apparently borrowed from the previous verse, where והגיונם was rendered ܘܪܢܝܢ "and (my enemies' lips) meditate". This equivalence was adopted by P for a similar form in Job:

[65] At Job 31:34c and 31:35b, the translator's uncertainly led him to add an alternative reading. See M.P. Weitzman, "Hebrew and Syriac Texts of the Book of Job", SVT 66 (1997), pp. 381–99.

[66] See Ps. 22:20, 38:23, 40:14=70:2, 55:9, 70:6, 71:12 and (in 9a1 alone) 141:1.

MT ועתה נגינתם הייתי
P ܘܗܫܐ ܪܢܝܢܗܘܢ ܗܘܝܬ

and now I have become their meditation

In the following case the agreement suggests borrowing but evidence of priority is lacking. At both Isa. 16:6 and Jer. 48:30 the Hebrew phrase לא כן בדיו has been taken as: "not so (foresaw) his priests" and expanded in similar terms:

ܠܐ ܗܘܐ ܗܟܢܐ ܒܕܘ ܟܠܘܗܝ ܘܟܘܡܪ̈ܘܗܝ Isa. 16:6

ܘܟܘܡܪ̈ܘܗܝ ܠܐ ܗܘܐ ܗܟܢܐ ܒܕܘ ܟܠܘܗܝ Jer. 48:30

We may distinguish a further group of passages, where the translator faced with a given Hebrew word found a verse in another book where that same word occurred, but adopted the Syriac rendering of a *different* word in that verse:

Exod. 28 ⇒ Job 28:19

In Job, wisdom is compared to two precious stones (שהם and ספיר) which recur in the description of the priestly garments in Exodus 28. Only this association can account for P's treatment of v.19b:

MT בכתם טהור לא תסלה
P ܘܟܐܦ̈ܐ ܕܦܕܬܐ ܠܐ ܫܘ̈ܝܢ ܠܗ̇

The stones of the ephod are not equal to her

The word ܦܕܬܐ identifies the source of P-Job here as P-Exodus. The association again follows the Hebrew from one passage to another, but here creates a new Hebrew-Syriac equivalence.

Deut. 21:18,20 ⇒ Prov. 7:11

The intending adulteress described in MT-Proverbs as המיה וסררת "flighty and rebellious" becomes in P ܡܪܘܕܐ ܘܐܣܘܛܐ "rebellious and gluttonous". These adjectives both occur in the law of the rebellious son in Deuteronomy: ܡܪܘܕܐ represents סורר (v.18), while ܐܣܘܛܐ answers to זולל, in the parents' declaration in v.20 that their son is a glutton. Here, unlike Proverbs, the adjectives "rebellious" and "gluttonous" fit the Hebrew. The translator of Proverbs was evidently guided by the common Hebrew word סורר to the passage in Deuteronomy. However, the Hebrew word זולל, to which corresponds one of the Syriac words carried over from P-Deuteronomy, does not occur in the Proverbs passage at all.

Isa. 38:12 ⇒ Job 7:6a

MT ימי קלו מני ארג
P ܝܘܡ̈ܝ ܩܠܘ ܡܢ ܓܕܕ ܩܘ̈ܡܝ

This seems to depend on the verse in Isaiah, where ארג likewise occurs in the Hebrew, and the root ܓܕ in the Syriac, but for a later word in the verse:

MT   קפדתי כארג חיי מדלה יבצעני

P   ܐܬܦܣܩܬ̈ ܐܝܟ ܢܚ̈ܬ ܚܝ̈ܝ ܘܐܝܟ ܢܝܪܐ ܕܠܐ ܢܬܡܬܚ ܘܢܬܩܛܥ[67]

my life was snapped off like threads, and like a web ready to be cut off

In all these cases, it may seem surprising that anyone who knew his Bible well enough to be able to locate an analogous form in a different book did not know the meaning of the relevant word in the first place. However, to recognise the meaning of a word requires knowledge, while to track down a parallel form requires industry alone. In principle, industry is always in supply, but knowledge of meaning, once lost in a given community, cannot be recovered – except through the unusual possibilities of successful guesswork or recourse to a different community. Here we must beware of judging the ancient translators by the standards of our own knowledge, which has been drawn from many different circles of tradition, including the versions as well as rabbinic and patristic exegesis. The knowledge available in any one circle in antiquity would have been far more restricted.

Transfer of the choice of Syriac expression from passage to passage on an altogether larger scale occurs in texts that are duplicated in the Hebrew Bible, such as 2 Sam. 22 = Ps. 18. These are discussed below.

Syriac text quoted from book to book without reference to the Hebrew

Finally, there are cases where the translator's association runs from the Hebrew text in one book directly to the Syriac text in another. This procedure is of course hardly justifiable, and the association may have been unconscious.

(a)   Num. 5:27 ⇒ Jer. 15:9

In Jeremiah we have

MT   נפחה נפשה   "she breathed out her soul"

P   ܨܒܬ ܟܪܣܗ̇   "her belly swelled"

P's unexpected rendering recalls the fate of the adulteress at Num. 5:27 (cf. 21), where P has an identical phrase, even though MT is wholly different: וצבתה בטנה. Instead of searching for the same Hebrew word in a different book, the translator has followed an association which runs from the Hebrew in Jeremiah to the Syriac in Numbers.

(b)   Exod. 2:12 ⇒ Neh. 13:25

MT-Nehemiah describes the treatment of those who had contracted foreign marriages: ואך מהם אנשים ואמרטם "I smote some of the men and tore out their hair". In P, however, Nehemiah's behaviour is more violent still:

ܘܩܛܠܬ ܡܢܗܘܢ ܓܒܪ̈ܐ ܘܛܫܝܬ ܐܢܘܢ

and I killed some of the men and hid them

---

[67]   See further M.P. Weitzman, "Hebrew and Syriac Texts of Job".

Apparently the translator of Nehemiah was thinking of Exod. 2:12, where Moses smote an Egyptian and hid him in the sand. There P renders:

ܘܩܛܠܗ ܠܡܨܪܝܐ ܘܛܡܪܗ ܒܚܠܐ

and he killed the Egyptian and hid him in the sand

The reason that the translator of Nehemiah thought of this passage is that he associated by sound the Hebrew verb *mrt* in his *Vorlage* with the Syriac verb *ṭmr* in Exodus.

Duplicate texts

Further evidence relating to links among the biblical books comes from those texts that are duplicated in two different books of the Bible. Here we may hope that the differences between the Syriac texts in the two books will highlight differences of translation technique, since the underlying Hebrew texts are almost identical.

Samuel and Psalms

Any hope that the duplicate texts of 2 Sam. 22 and Ps. 18 in P might bring into relief the differences of technique between the translators of Samuel and Psalms is soon dashed. The translations are for the most part identical. Not only do they presuppose the same Hebrew text, despite the differences in the Hebrew of MT. They also choose the same Syriac equivalent at almost every point, and coincidence cannot always be responsible, e.g.

9   מפיו   ܡܢ ܦܘܡܗܘܢ   (as if מפניו)
13   נגדו   ܠܩܘܒܠܗ[68]
36   ונחתה   ܘܐܬܪ

Almost wherever the two books differ in MT, both Syriac texts follow the Hebrew of Psalms, e.g.

	Sam. (MT)	Ps. (MT)	Sam. & Ps. (P)
5	משברי	חבלי	ܚܒܠܐ
8	שמים	הרים	ܛܘܪܐ
13	-	ברד וגחלי אש	ܒܪܕܐ ܘܓܘܡܖܐ ܕܢܘܪܐ

Only in v.3 do differences in the Hebrew give rise to corresponding differences between the two Syriac texts. At this point, a phrase appears in Samuel but not in Psalms, according both to MT and to P, namely:

ܘܡܦܪܘܩܝ ܡܢ ܥܘܠܐ ܦܪܩܬܢܝ[69]   משעי מחמס תשעני

However, P-Samuel's practice of following the Hebrew text of Psalms had already begun in v.2, where it includes a rendering of the words ארחמך י׳ חזקי, which MT has in Psalms but not in Samuel. After v.3, differences in the Hebrew are no longer reflected in the respective texts of P, which instead agree closely.

Occasionally P-Samuel and P-Psalms treat the Hebrew independently, e.g.

v.19 משען   P-Samuel ܣܡܟܬܢܝ   P-Psalms ܣܘܥܪܢܐ

---

[68] The translator was apparently distracted by כתבו (v.12). See M.P. Weitzman, "The Peshiṭta Psalter and its Hebrew *Vorlage*", *VT* 35 (1985), pp. 341–54: p. 342.
[69] MT (again in Samuel only) also has ומנוסי, but this is not represented in P, perhaps because the preceding ܒܝܬ ܓܘܣܝ (for משגבי) covered it.

Here P-Samuel is perhaps guided by similarity of sound, while P-Psalms assumes a derivation from ישׁע "save". Such discrepancies are, however, exceptional.

How can this close correspondence be explained? The virtual unanimity of the manuscript tradition makes it unlikely that the two passages were translated independently and only later harmonised by copyists. Rather, both P-Samuel and P-Psalms are essentially the same translation.

As that translation is based on the Hebrew text of Psalms, the obvious inference is that it originated in P-Psalms, and that P-Samuel (at least in this chapter) was translated later. As Englert concluded: "It is very likely that Psalms was one of the first Old Testament books to be translated into Syriac and that, when II Samuel was translated, the Syriac of II Samuel was made to conform with that of Psalms".[70]

However, this hypothesis fails to explain the occurrence in both Syriac texts of an equivalence which is characteristic of P-Samuel and unknown in P-Psalms, in v.12:

Samuel   וישׁת חשׁך   ܣܬܪܗ ܠܡܛܫܝܐ ܚܕܪܘܗܝ
Psalms   ישׁת חשׁך סתרו   ܣܬܪܗ ܠܡܛܫܝܐ ܡܢ

Now the noun ܛܘܫܝܐ "hiding place" – and indeed the root ܛܫܐ – never recurs in P-Psalms. In P-Samuel, however, the root is not uncommon. At 1 Sam. 25:20 בסתר ההר is rendered ܒܛܠܠܗ ܕܛܘܪܐ. Moreover, as noted above, in Samuel alone the עשׁתרות are called ܛܘܫܝܬܐ "lurking-places", apparently on the supposition that they derive from a root שׁתר which is equivalent to סתר.

We thus have an equivalence characteristic of P-Samuel and alien to P-Psalms, applied to the Hebrew text of Psalms.[71] This supports the reconstruction suggested by Greenberg: the translator of Samuel used the Hebrew of Psalms instead of the Hebrew of Samuel, and his translation was taken over almost unchanged by the translator of Psalms.[72]

No doubt the Syriac translator of Samuel was well aware of the duplicate Hebrew text in Psalms. In verses 2–3 he strove for completeness by combining the Hebrew of both books. However, he soon decided instead simply to follow the Hebrew of Psalms – either because it is generally fuller, or because it was more familiar through regular recitation of the Psalter. Later, when the book of Psalms came to be translated, the text already in P-Samuel was for the most part simply adopted. The translator of Psalms undertook no more than light revision. In v.3, he removed the last few words, which have no counterpart in the Hebrew of Psalms. Thereafter, on rare occasions, he offered an independent treatment of the Hebrew. Other differences between the two texts can be explained as stylistic adjustments of the text of P-Samuel. Altogether, one can maintain the priority of P-Samuel, in keeping with the traditional Jewish order.

We may note also that P-Samuel often stands closer to the Hebrew, and that P-Psalms could be viewed as a revision to improve inner logic or Syriac idiom, e.g.

17   יקחני ימשׁני   P-Samuel ܘܕܠܢܝ ܢܣܒܢܝ, P-Psalms ܘܕܠܢܝ ܫܕܪ

The equivalence משׁה = ܫܕܐ in P-Samuel, known also from Exod. 2:10, seems original, in which case P-Psalms removed a perceived tautology ("he took me and drew me").

---

[70] D.M.C. Englert, *The Peshitto of Second Samuel*, Philadelphia 1949, p. 95. Englert provides a table comparing the Hebrew and Syriac texts on pp. 92–3.

[71] The word סתרו is absent in almost all Hebrew mss of Samuel. The main point, however, concerns not the Hebrew text but the Syriac equivalent.

[72] G. Greenberg, "The Peshitta to 2 Samuel and Psalm 18 – One Translation or Two?", forthcoming.

36   ‫וענ(ו)תך‬ P-Samuel ܣܥܒܕܝ, P-Psalms ܬܘܪܬܢܝ

P-Samuel corresponds closely to the Hebrew, but P-Psalms found it paradoxical in context ("Your humiliation exalts me") and adjusted to "your discipline".

41   ‫ואיבי תתה לי ערף‬

P-Samuel ܠ ܐܢܫ ܠܟܠܕܒܒܝ ... ܘܡܠܕܬܟ P-Psalms ܡܕܡ ܘܗܒ ܠܟܠܕܒܒܝ ... ܘܡܠܕܬܟ

Here P-Psalms resolves an idiom extant in P-Sam.

A seeming indication against the priority of P-Samuel appears in v.46. In both Samuel and Psalms, MT has ‫ממסגרות(יה)‬ while P renders ܡܢ ܪܓܠܬܗܘܢ. This evidently reflects ἀπὸ τῶν τρίβων αὐτῶν, the reading of LXX in Psalms but not in Samuel. We would expect the influence of the LXX version of Psalms to have been exerted through P-Psalms, rather than through P-Samuel. Yet this argument is not conclusive. If P-Samuel followed here the Hebrew of Psalms rather than of Samuel, he may likewise have consulted the Greek of Psalms. Moreover, there is no evidence that LXX-Samuel was available to the translators of P at all; it has left no trace in P-Samuel.[73]

Kings and Isaiah

We must now consider the passages duplicated between 2 Kings 18–20 and Isaiah 36–39, which have been studied by Walter.[74] In MT, the divergence between these passages is more extensive than that between Samuel and Psalms. This divergence is usually reflected in the two Syriac texts. In particular, sections unique to one of the books in MT (e.g. 2 Kgs. 18:14–16, Isa. 38:9–20) remain unique to that book in P. At some points there is greater divergence between the two passages in P than in MT, in that the same Hebrew word is rendered differently, as Walter illustrates (p. 192).

Nevertheless, as Walter has observed, the number and nature of the agreements between the two books in the choice of Syriac rendering cannot be ascribed to coincidence. Walter's comparisons are rightly based on the oldest extant form of the text, which in most cases (especially in Kings) is that of the Florence manuscript 9a1, e.g.

2 Kgs.	Isa.	MT	P (both books)
18:22	36:7	‫המזבח הזה‬	ܥܠ ܡܕܒܚܐ
19:24	37:25	‫בכף פעמי‬	ܦܣܬܐ ܕܪܓܠܝ
19:28	37:29	‫ושאננך‬	ܘܫܠܝܘܬܟ

Evidently, the Syriac version in one book has been utilised in the other.

According to Walter, the translation of Isaiah came first, and influenced P-Kings. In favour of this view, Walter points to passages where the Hebrew presupposed by both texts is that of Isaiah rather than Kings:[75]

2 Kgs.	Isa.	MT (Kgs.)	MT (Isa.)	P (both books)
18:25	36:10	‫המקום הזה‬	‫הארץ הזאת‬	ܐܪܥܐ ܗܕܐ
19:23	37:24	‫מלון‬	‫מרום‬	ܪܘܡܐ
20:13	39:2	‫וישמע‬	‫וישמח‬	ܘܚܕܝ

---

[73] The same Syriac equivalence has been borrowed by P at Mic. 7:17, the one remaining occurrence of this word. P's source in Micah cannot be LXX-Micah (ἐν συγκλεισμῷ αὐτῶν).

[74] D.M. Walter, "The Use of Sources in the Peshiṭta of Kings", MPI 8 (1995), pp. 187–204.

[75] Though, as Walter notes, in 19:23 and 20:13 one or more mss of MT-Kings agree with Isaiah.

There is another very clear case where P-Kings presupposes the Hebrew of Isaiah, though it lies outside the main duplicate section:

2 Kgs. 16:5 (MT)   ‏...למלחמה ויצרו על אחז ולא יכלו להלחם

Isa. 7:1 (MT)   ‏...למלחמה עליה ולא יכל להלחם עליה

P (both passages)   ‏...ܠܩܪܒܐ ܥܠܝܗ ܘܠܐ ܐܬܡܨܝܘ ܕܢܬܟܬܫܘܢ ܥܠܝܗ

Walter also argues that the Hebrew-Syriac equivalences characteristic of Isaiah have sometimes influenced the translator of Kings, notably:

(a) P-Kings almost always renders ‏עיר‎ by ‏ܩܪܝܬܐ‎, while P-Isaiah varies between this and ‏ܡܕܝܢܬܐ‎. However, P-Kings has ‏ܡܕܝܢܬܐ‎ at 2 Kgs. 19:25, within the duplicate section, agreeing with P-Isaiah at the parallel point (Isa. 37:26). This according to Walter betokens the influence of P-Isaiah.

(b) It will be recalled that in rendering the noun ‏דבר‎ the translators tend to use ‏ܦܬܓܡܐ‎ for 'matter' and ‏ܡܠܬܐ‎ for mere words. P-Isaiah duly uses ‏ܡܠܬܐ‎ of the Assyrians' words from the first (Isa. 36:13 onward), so indicating their emptiness. P-Kings, however, first calls these words ‏ܦܬܓܡܐ‎ (2 Kgs. 18:27–28), and only later ‏ܡܠܬܐ‎ (2 Kgs. 18:37 and thereafter). Walter infers that the translator of P-Kings was influenced by P-Isaiah, from which he learnt belatedly to use ‏ܡܠܬܐ‎ for empty words.

Walter's evidence for the priority of P-Isaiah is impressive, but not conclusive. That P-Kings sometimes rests on the Hebrew text of Isaiah is certain; but, as the discussion on 2 Samuel 22 showed, the fact that P in one book presupposes the Hebrew text of another need not imply dependence on the P version of that other book. Nor do the claimed traces in P-Kings of the translation technique of P-Isaiah demonstrate dependence. At 2 Kgs. 19:25, it remains possible that the translator himself used ‏ܩܪܝܬܐ‎, and that ‏ܡܕܝܢܬܐ‎ is due to a copyist who assimilated to Isaiah. The change would have been tempting, since ‏ܡܕܝܢܬܐ‎ better suited P's adjective ‏ܥܫܝܢܬܐ‎ (MT: ‏בצרות‎ ‏ערים‎). As to the distinction between ‏ܦܬܓܡܐ‎ and ‏ܡܠܬܐ‎, the usage of the latter for empty words was already known to P-Kings, since he so terms the words of the false prophets at 1 Kgs. 22:23 (*ter*). A possible reason for his not using it at 2 Kgs. 18:27–28 is that the Assyrian envoy is himself speaking and here referring to the words of his own king. Here, we may suppose, P chooses the more respectful term ‏ܦܬܓܡܐ‎, and not until the Assyrians' words are mentioned by the biblical narrator or by the Israelites does he term them mere ‏ܡܠܬܐ‎.

Moreover, arguments similar to Walter's could be mounted in the opposite direction. In one passage, the two Syriac texts on balance stand closer to the Hebrew of Kings than of Isaiah:

2 Kgs. 20:7   ‏קחו דבלת תאנים ויקחו וישימו על השחין

Isa. 38:21   ‏ישאו דבלת תאנים וימרחו על השחין

P (both passages)   ‏ܢܣܒܘ ܕܒܠܬܐ ܕܬܐܢܐ ܘܣܡܘ ܥܠ ܫܘܚܢܐ

As to characteristic equivalences, we may consider the renderings of Hebrew ‏לאמר‎ immediately before direct speech. P-Kings uses the Syriac infinitive ‏ܠܡܐܡܪ‎ in 13 passages according to all mss, while in another two this usage survives in 9a1 alone.[76] In Isaiah, by contrast, the Hebrew infinitive ‏לאמר‎ – which appears 28 times – is almost

---

[76] 1 Kgs. 2:4; 6:11; 12:22–23; 15:18; 16:1; 17:8; 18:1; 21:17,28; 2 Kgs. 10:1; 20:4; 22:3; plus occurrences in 9a1 only at 1 Kgs. 17:2 and 2 Kgs. 3:7.

always either replaced by a finite verb or omitted altogether. There are just two exceptions, both of which fall within the duplicated sections. One is Isa. 38:4, where the parallel in Kings likewise has ܠܡܐܡܪ, which could have been the source for P-Isaiah. The other occurrence of ܠܡܐܡܪ for לאמר in P-Isaiah is at the end of 37:9, as attested by two mss (7a1 9l6), though the rest displace it to the middle of v.10. Admittedly, in the parallel at the end of 2 Kgs. 19:9, the extant mss do not render לאמר by ܠܡܐܡܪ: instead, 9a1 (and part of its family) has a finite verb (ܘܐܡܪ) while the rest omit. Still, it remains possible that P-Kings too once had ܠܡܐܡܪ here and that the ms variants represent two ways of removing this Hebraism.[77] At all events, the fact that this usage in P-Isaiah is confined to the passages duplicated in Kings demands explanation.

A further argument for the priority of P-Kings is that (at least on the evidence of 9a1) it stands closer than P-Isaiah to the Hebrew, e.g.

2 Kgs. 18:24 = Isa. 36:9

MT   לרכב ולפרשים

P-Kgs.   ܘܥܠ ܡܪܟܒܬܐ ܘܥܠ ܦܪܫܐ

P-Isa.   ܦܪܫܐ ܘܡܪܟܒܬܐ ܥܠ ܘܐܢܬ

2 Kgs. 18:26=Isa. 36:11

MT   אשר על החומה

P-Kgs.   ܕܥܠ ܫܘܪܐ

P-Isa.   ܕܩܝܡܝܢ ܥܠ ܫܘܪܐ

2 Kgs. 19:3 = Isa. 37:3

MT   (כי באו) בנים עד משבר

P-Kgs.   ܠܬܒܪܐ ܒܢܝܐ

P-Isa.   ܒܢܝܐ ܠܬܒܪܐ

The text of P-Isaiah could be viewed in such cases as an idiomatic revision of that of P-Kings.

It deserves to be said that Walter's case for the influence of P-Isaiah upon the *majority* text of P-Kings remains strong. However, it is not at all certain that P-Isaiah already influenced the *original* text of P-Kings, as represented by 9a1. The evidence admits at least as well the priority of P-Kings over P-Isaiah, in accordance with the Jewish canonical order.

Kings and Jeremiah

The final chapters of Kings and Jeremiah (2 Kgs. 25, Jer. 52) are very similar in the Hebrew, though again not so similar as the texts of 2 Samuel 22 and Psalm 18. For the first few verses there is further parallel material in Jer. 39:1–10.

---

[77] A similar case occurs at 1 Kgs. 1:13, where MT has לאמר while 9a1 has a finite verb and the majority omit.

Here again the Syriac texts tend to reflect the divergence of the Hebrew texts. Moreover, even the same Hebrew text may be treated independently in the two books, e.g.

	MT	P-Kgs	P-Jer.
2 Kgs. 25:2=Jer. 52:5	וַתָּבֹא (הָעִיר בַּמָּצוֹר)	ܘܐܬܚܒܫܬ	ܘܥܠܬ
2 Kgs. 25:17=Jer. 52:22	שְׂבָכָה	ܣܪܝܓܐ	ܚܘܝܪܐ

In particular, each translator has imposed his own preferred usage for ordinals:

2 Kgs. 25   ܫܬܝܬܝܐ, ܫܒܝܥܝܬܐ (v.1); ܥܣܝܪܝܐ (vv.3,8)

Jer. 52   ܕܬܪܝܢ, ܕܬܫܥ (v.4); ܕܚܡܫܐ (vv.6,12)

These follow the normal usages of either book: adjectives in P-Kings, as at 1 Kgs. 6:38, 12:12; and *dalath* with the cardinal in P-Jeremiah, as at Jer. 28:1, 41:1.

Once again, however, there are some similarities too close to be accidental, e.g.

2 Kgs. 25:12   לְכֹרְמִים וּלְיֹגְבִים   (6ph1 ܠܦܠܚܐ) ܠܦܠܚܐ ܠܟܪܡܐ

Jer. 39:10   כְּרָמִים וְיֹגֵבִים   ܟܪܡܐ ܘܦܠܚܘܬܐ

Jer. 52:16   לְכֹרְמִים וּלְיֹגְבִים   ܠܟܪܡܐ ܘܠܦܠܚܘܬܐ

Here too Walter is inclined to regard P-Kings as the borrower, albeit "at most to a very minor degree".[78] In support, he points out one passage where P-Kings presupposes the Hebrew text of Jeremiah:

2 Kgs. 25:4 (most Heb. mss)   הַלַּיְלָה

Jer. 39:4=52:7   [וַ]יִּבְרְחוּ וַיֵּצְאוּ לַיְלָה

P (all passages)   ܥܪܩܘ ܘܢܦܩܘ ܡܢ ܡܕܝܢܬܐ ܒܠܠܝܐ

In fact, however, we can find evidence for the priority of P-Kings, in the renderings of two items in the temple, as will be explained below:

(a)   Heb. מְכוֹנָה properly denotes a wheeled stand, of which the temple had ten, for the ten lavers. However, the word was instead understood in the Syriac texts of both books as "basin", though the terms differ: ܠܩܢܐ at 2 Kgs. 25:13,16, and ܐܓܢܐ at Jer. 52:17.[79]

(b)   Heb. כֹּתֶרֶת properly indicates each of the capitals above the temple pillars. In P, however, we find ܐܓܢܐ "basin" again, both in P-Kings and in P-Jeremiah (2 Kgs. 25:17 *ter*; Jer. 52:22 *ter*), which here agree verbally.

Both equivalences can in fact be traced to P-Kings, in the detailed account of the temple in 1 Kgs. 7. The translator did not understand the description in 1 Kgs. 7:27–37 of the מְכוֹנָה as a wheeled stand, and instead thought it a basin (ܐܓܢܐ), with much the same function as the bronze sea that immediately preceded. As to כֹּתֶרֶת, P-Kings had until that point used ܓܘܝܬܐ, derived from ܓܙܪ "cut", apparently to denote a crowning slab.[80] At 7:31, however, כֹּתֶרֶת occurs in the description of the wheeled stands, which the translator instead thought were basins. The architectural sense was clearly unsuitable, and so the כֹּתֶרֶת too had to become an ܐܓܢܐ 'basin'. The translator was not to know of the archaeological discoveries from Cyprus which suggest that

---

[78]   Walter, "The Peshiṭta of Kings", p. 203.

[79]   At Jer. 52:20, however, where the twelve brazen cattle are beneath the מְכֹנוֹת in MT, P places them beneath ܣܦܘܬܗ ܕܝܡܐ "the rims of the (brazen) sea". This long rendering perhaps seeks to combine MT with LXX ὑποκάτω τῆς θαλάσσης.

[80]   This Syriac word first appears at 1 Kgs. 6:36, where MT has כְּרֻתֹת, which the translator evidently derived from כרת "cut". It again represents כֹּתֶרֶת at 7:2,12. Evidently כֹּתֶרֶת was considered an equivalent form.

this כתרת was a circular frame which surmounted the stand and into which the laver fitted.[81]

The sense 'basin' continues to be attached both to מכונה and to כתרת in P-Kings. In 2 Kgs. 25:13,16 מכונה is again understood in this way, although the different term ܠܡܕ is used. Likewise כתרת continues to be understood as 'basin' (ܐܓܢܐ), so that the temple pillars are surmounted according to P by basins (1 Kgs. 7:41–42).[82] Thus ܐܓܢܐ for כתרת at 2 Kgs. 25:17 *ter* simply maintains an equivalence already characteristic of P-Kings (from 1 Kgs. 7:31 onward). The use of the same equivalence כתרת – ܐܓܢܐ at Jer. 52:22 *ter* can hardly be explained except on the basis of borrowing from P-Kings. P-Jeremiah is unlikely to have alighted on ܐܓܢܐ 'bowl' as an independent guess for כתרת, because the context is instead architectural, being a description of the temple pillars. The translator of Jeremiah must therefore be the borrower.[83]

As to the agreement between P-Kings and P-Jeremiah in understanding מכונה as a basin (Jer. 52:17 = 2 Kgs. 25:13), it is true that coincidence could in theory be responsible. First, the immediately preceding item is the bronze sea; moreover, P already at Jer. 27:19 renders המכנות as ܡܟܘܢܐ, which again are receptacle for liquids, mentioned immediately after the bronze sea. Given, however, the proven dependence of P-Jeremiah upon P-Kings regarding כתרת, such dependence is a likely explanation for the agreement regarding מכונה also.

Finally, a lexicographic problem deserves mention. Some modern dictionaries record "capital (of pillar)" and even "wheeled stand" among the meanings of ܐܓܢܐ; but this presupposes that the translator knew the true meaning of these two Hebrew terms. It is likelier that he was simply guessing the meaning 'basin' for both words. Thus ܐܓܢܐ renders כתרת and מכונה in successive verses, at 1 Kgs. 7:42,43; and readers could not have been intended to understand it instead as "capital" in the first verse and "wheeled stand" in the second.

In general, P-Jeremiah tends, like P-Isaiah, to depart farther than P-Kings from the Hebrew, and to that extent gives the impression of a stylistic revision of P-Kings, e.g.

2 Kgs. 25:11=Jer. 39:9=Jer. 52:15

MT   ואת הנפלים אשר נפלו

P-Kgs. ܘܢܦܠ ܕܢܦܠܐ; P-Jer. 39 ܘܕܐܪܟܐ ܕܢܦܠܘ; P-Jer. 52 ܘܡܢ ܕܢܦܠܘ

2 Kgs. 25:19=Jer. 52:25

MT   אשר היה פקיד

P-Kgs. ܕܗܘܐ ܦܩܝܕ   P-Jer ܕܗܘܐ ܡܫܠܛ ܘܗܐ

---

[81] Plates are reproduced in C.F. Burney, *Notes on the Hebrew Text of the Book of Kings*, Oxford 1903, figs. 1–2.

[82] The translator may have been encouraged by the combination גלת הכתרת, where the range of the first noun indeed covers "bowl, basin".

[83] The alternative supposition that P-Jeremiah offered an independent translation, which a copyist later replaced by ܐܓܢܐ in conformity with P-Kings, is unlikely; there was little incentive for a copyist to impose the term "basin" in an architectural context.

2 Kgs. 25:30=Jer. 52:34

MT   ואַרֻחָתוֹ אֲרֻחַת תָּמִיד נִתְּנָה לּוֹ מֵאֵת מֶלֶךְ בְּבָל דְּבַר יוֹם בְּיוֹמוֹ

P-Kgs.   ܘܣܝܒܪܬܗ ܣܝܒܪܬܐ ܐܡܝܢܬܐ ܐܬܝܗܒܬ ܠܗ ܡܢ ܩܕܡ ܡܠܟܐ ܕܒܒܠ ܟܠ ܝܘܡ ܒܝܘܡܗ

and as his food, food was always given to him from before the king of Babylon every
day

P-Jer.   ܘܣܝܒܪܬܗ ܘܗܝ ܗܘܐ ܡܢ ܩܕܡ ܡܠܟܐ ܕܒܒܠ ܟܠ ܝܘܡ ܒܝܘܡܗ ܐܡܝܢܐܝܬ

and his allowance was issued from before the king of Babylon every day continually

Chronicles and the earlier books

The duplicates between Chronicles and the earlier books, though more extensive, are
less enlightening, because frequent discrepancies in the Hebrew wording disturb the
comparison. Of particular interest, however, are those parts of 1 Kgs. 12–14 which
P-Chronicles substituted for an apparently illegible passage in his *Vorlage*. This passage
thus survives in two Syriac translations, in P-Kings and in P-Chronicles. The two translations appear independent. Comparison shows, as already remarked, that the translator of Chronicles did not share the concern of P-Kings for quantitative literalism. On
the other hand, he was sometimes readier to imitate the Hebrew form. Thus P-
Chronicles, unlike his colleague, renders the particle נָא (1 Kgs. 14:2), as well as וַיְהִי
before a temporal clause (1 Kgs. 14:6); and at (1 Kgs. 14:7) he translates נָתַן (which
means "render") by Syr. ܢܣܒ "give" rather than by the more idiomatic ܝܗܒ as in P-
Kings. These contrasts well illustrate Barr's thesis that literalism has many dimensions:
one translation may be more literal than another in one respect, and less so in another.

In addition, there are of course many parallels in the Hebrew between Chronicles
and earlier books; and there are many brief passages where P-Chronicles follows the
Hebrew text of an earlier book rather than the Hebrew of Chronicles. The duplicates
involving Chronicles are not comparable, however, with other cases of duplicate passages. In those other cases, the Syriac text of the first book to be translated provided a
base for the translation in the second. In Chronicles, by contrast, where the translator
looks to an earlier book he always consults the *Hebrew* text; and although he shares
with his predecessors an idiosyncratic understanding of certain Hebrew words and
certain characteristic choices of expression, there is no evidence that he consulted their
translations at all.[84]

More than one reason may be suggested for the independent approach of P-
Chronicles. First, the translator had not struck the same balance as his predecessors
between the rival virtues of fidelity and intelligibility, and he may have felt – rightly –
that extracts from their work would sit badly with his own. Second, to use the text of P
in earlier books would have forced him to work with three source-books: the Hebrew of
Chronicles, the Hebrew of the earlier book (without which he could not have traced
any parallels) and the P version of that earlier book. Although P-Jeremiah seems to
have followed such a procedure in his final chapter, the translator of Chronicles may
have decided at the outset this would be too cumbersome an undertaking for his own

---

[84] On 2 Chr. 23:5 see p. 296 in chapter 6 below.

much lengthier task. Third, as discussed in chapter 3, the partial illegibility of the *Vorlage* sometimes left the translator scope to express his own religious sentiments; and a supplementary source text may have been an unwelcome constraint.

Summary

P has been shown to be the work of different translators; the number perhaps lies in the region of fifteen. This diversity, however, is only part of the picture. There is also a network of linking features which unite all these translators, and show them to have been working on the same greater project.

First, the translators of different books share an understanding not attested elsewhere of certain recurring Hebrew words. Second, they choose the same Syriac renderings for certain Hebrew words which raise problems of expression rather than understanding. Third, in certain passages the translator has followed an association to another passage in a different book for which the P version already existed, and has utilised that version. Finally, almost all share a simultaneous concern both for fidelity (notably including quantitative literalism) and plain intelligibility.

In the first category, the sense distinctive to the P translators moved sometimes from a book earlier in the canon to a later book, and sometimes in the opposite direction. Thus, the understanding of מחקק as ܡܒܕܩܢܐ in Gen. 49 derives from information in Judges 5, while the translator of Judges 5 obtained his understanding of משפתים as ܫܒܝܠܐ from Gen. 49. In view of this reciprocal relationship, it cannot be that all these unusual meanings were invented during the translation process; for we cannot maintain at the same time that P-Genesis depends on P-Judges and that P-Judges depends on P-Genesis. Rather, we need to posit a stage preliminary to the translation itself, in which the community that was eventually to produce the translation built up its own understanding of the Hebrew text, and in particular worked out the meaning of certain Hebrew words through wide reading of the Hebrew Bible – sometimes with curious results.[85] The fruits of that effort were later passed on to the translators.

In the second and third categories, however, as in duplicate passages, we always find that the book which stands earlier in the canon has influenced the later. This is consistent with Beckwith's suggestion – which is in any case intrinsically probable – that the books were translated in substantially the order traditional among the Jews. Beckwith himself adds the qualification that "books which contained important testimony to Jesus and to Christianity, and were needed for the lectionary, would naturally tend to jump the queue";[86] but the evidence seems consistent with the hypothesis even without that qualification.

Of course the Jewish canonical order varies somewhat between the witnesses; but much is common to them all, such as the placing of Ezra-Nehemiah and Chronicles at the end.[87] In so far as the order varies among the witnesses to the Jewish tradition, we can sometimes reconstruct the position of P's translators. The many borrowings in

---

[85] By the same token, the translation of סוללה in Samuel and Kings by 'ambush', which is apparently based on Jer. 32:34, need not imply that Jeremiah was translated first.

[86] Beckwith, *The Old Testament Canon of the New Testament Church*, London 1985, p. 309.

[87] See the masterly survey by R. Beckwith, *The Old Testament Canon*, pp. 198–211.

P-Job from P-Psalms show that Job was translated later, in accordance with one line of Jewish tradition. This is despite the fact that some Syriac biblical mss (notably 7a1 and 8a1) place Job far earlier, immediately after the Pentateuch, in accordance with a different Jewish tradition which named the author of Job as Moses himself.[88] Again, the fact that P-Job once seems influenced by P-Lamentations suggests that Lamentations was translated earlier, as an appendix to Jeremiah; and although most Jewish witnesses contradict this, Jerome in his "Helmed Prologue" to the Vulgate on Samuel and Kings attests just such a Jewish ordering, where Kinoth (i.e. Lamentations) was combined with Jeremiah.[89]

Where P in one book has influenced P in another, how did the link operate? This question interlocks with that of the time taken to complete the translation of the whole Bible. At one extreme, we could think of the links as purely literary: any given translator had access to his predecessors' work in writing only, too long an interval having elapsed for him to consult them personally. In that case, it would be dangerous to combine evidence from different books in order to reconstruct the community's beliefs, since that evidence might be spread over a long period. At the other extreme, we could think of the translation of the different books being accomplished quickly enough to allow the translators to consult among themselves. In that case, we could speak of a school of contemporary translators, and safely combine evidence from different books.[90]

The latter view is favoured by such passages as Job 20:2, where a translator renders a difficult Hebrew word on the basis of another occurrence in a different book. In the days before concordances, it might have been difficult for the translator to discover the parallel alone. However, if the translators proceeded with fair speed, then each could have consulted his predecessors in person; and this would have made the discovery of such parallels possible, though even then not easy. Even if they did not equal the feat claimed by Jerome, of translating the Solomonic books within three days,[91] the translators could have completed the whole Hebrew Bible within a single generation. The time taken to complete the translation will be considered further in chapter 5, together with the wider questions of dating.

Finally, the common view that the books of P differ too widely in translation technique to permit any uniform evaluation of the version,[92] and that variety is even more marked in P than in either LXX or the Targums,[93] must be rejected. One reason that such an impression could arise was the concentration upon those features of translation technique which divide the biblical books in P (such as use of LXX) rather

[88] Some rabbis, quoted in TB Baba Batra 15a-b, make Job a contemporary of Moses. Exodus Rabba 1:9 likewise places him in Pharaoh's court and explains that he suffered for his failure to protest at the killing of Israelite children. However, the listing in TB Baba Batra 14b places Job after Psalms, and this is supported by alternative views (set out on fol. 15b) that make him a contemporary of Solomon or even of Ahasuerus.

[89] The Latin text is conveniently found in R. Weber (ed.), *Biblia Sacra iuxta Vulgatam Versionem*, 2 vols., Stuttgart 1969, p. 364. For English translation and discussion, see Beckwith, pp. 119–21.

[90] This model does not exclude the possibility of some overlap in time between the work of different translators.

[91] "Itaque longa aegrotatione fractus, ne penitus hoc anno reticerem . . ., *tridui opus* vestro nomini consacravi, interpretationem videlicet trium Salomonis voluminum . . ." (from the prologue, included in Weber's edition, p. 957). In his prologue to Tobit, Jerome similarly states that to translate that book "unius diei laborem arripui".   [92] O. Eissfeldt, *The Old Testament: An Introduction*, Oxford 1974, p. 700.

[93] Roberts, *The Old Testament Text and Versions*, Cardiff 1951, pp. 214, 221.

than those which unite them. Another reason was that different investigators were differently impressed by the balance between fidelity and intelligibility which characterises P in nearly every book: some stressed P's freedom, and others its fidelity, whence an exaggerated perception of diversity. It would be better to view P as the work of a number of different translators, who nevertheless considered themselves colleagues in a single school.

5
The background of the Peshitta

Introduction

The community background of P has long been debated. On the one hand, the fact that the translation was made from the Hebrew, as well as its contacts with the Targums and Jewish traditional exegesis, suggest a Jewish context. On the other hand, the translation has been preserved by the church alone, and there is no evidence of its use in the synagogue. As discussed in chapter 3, a few medieval Jewish scholars showed academic interest in P, but this has no bearing on the origin of the version.

General considerations of this sort do not suffice to indicate the community background of P, and opinion remains divided between the hypotheses of Jewish and Christian origin. We must instead examine P's rendering of individual passages throughout the Hebrew Bible, searching for changes of substance, or at least of emphasis, which might reflect the theology of the translator(s). Such clues are rare, because P translates literally (though without sacrificing intelligibility) for the most part. Nevertheless, theologically significant passages are more numerous than previous discussions have allowed. Here we shall attempt to describe the faith of the translators from the internal evidence of the translation. We shall then review the available evidence of its time and place. Correlating all these findings, we shall attempt a reconstruction of the historical setting of the translation. Finally, we shall – with all due reserve – trace the roots of the translators' faith back to the period of the Hebrew Bible, and also follow that faith forwards into the Syriac-speaking church to which we owe the transmission of the version.

Arguments for Jewish origin

A primary argument for Jewish origin is that the translation was made from a Hebrew text, while the church invested authority in the Greek Bible. This is clear from mistakes in P only explicable on the basis of a Hebrew *Vorlage*; for example, at Num. 6:25 ויחנך "may He be gracious to thee" was read ויחיך "may He preserve thee"). Of course the use of a Hebrew *Vorlage* by a Christian scholar is not impossible, as shown by the examples of Origen or Jerome, who appreciated the importance of the Hebrew.[1] Still, the use of a Hebrew *Vorlage* decidedly favours Jewish origin.

---

[1] So H.J.W. Drijvers, "Syrian Christianity and Judaism", in J. Lieu, J. North and T. Rajak (eds.), *The Jews among Pagans and Christians in the Roman Empire*, London & New York 1992, pp. 124–46.

Jewish origin is further suggested by the examples of Jewish exegesis in P, as discussed in chapter 3. The evidence was first marshalled by Perles, and although it has sometimes been overstated,[2] P exhibits many striking parallels with rabbinic sources and with Jewish Targums, as Maori's rightly "minimalist" study shows.[3] The parallels do not prove, however, that P originated within rabbinic Judaism, which preserved the texts exhibiting the parallels. First, not everything preserved by rabbinic Judaism originated there; biblical exegesis and translation were part of an older and broader movement. Second, material of rabbinic origin could circulate elsewhere: a satisfying solution to a textual problem, an appealing lesson or a happy Aramaic rendering of a difficult Hebrew phrase could easily have been transplanted from rabbinic Judaism to other movements.

In particular, the presence of some Jewish exegesis in P is still compatible with an origin in a Christian community that had Jewish roots or Jewish contacts. For example the earlier Syriac versions of Matt. 23:5 translate φυλακτήρια by the authentic Jewish term, viz "(the straps of) their Tephillin" (ܐܫܩܠܬܗܘܢ – so Old Syriac and Peshitta). Again, Jerome in his commentary on Hos. 3:2 has a homiletic explanation – the 15 shekels symbolise the date of Passover on the 15th of Nisan – which reappears in TB Hullin 92a.[4]

Arguments for Christian origin

No more conclusive, however, are the arguments often proposed in favour of Christian origin, and familiar from Roberts's influential book,[5] which here depends on Bloch.[6] Some renderings, as we shall see, could be read as references to Christ, or appear to echo the New Testament. Values which (at least at first sight) fit the church rather than the Synagogue have also been detected, notably an "air of negligence apparent in the translation of the Levitical law, particularly in the sections concerning clean and unclean animals".[7] We shall return to such passages, which are certainly of theological interest. For the moment, however, we should note that they do not prove Christian origin outright. First, some of the arguments are factually wrong. In particular, as regards dietary laws, Emerton has shown that P in fact identifies all the creatures in accordance with Jewish tradition, apart from a few forbidden birds. These gaps in the translator's ornithology do not in themselves prove that he was not a practising Jew.[8] Second, phrases that could lend themselves to Christian interpretation are not necessarily Christian in origin. Thirdly, ideas that some have assumed to be exclusive to Christianity may have existed also in certain currents of Judaism.

Previous generations, then, could not agree on the question of Jewish versus Christian origin. For them, Judaism was represented by the rabbinic texts –

---

[2] In particular, Perles's category of "Jewish" euphemisms is pressed too far, e.g. to explain P's omission of 2 Chr. 20:22–5. Again, on *Meletemata* p. 17, Perles writes that P moved Ezra's gathering from the twentieth day of the seventh month to the tenth day, the Day of Atonement; but in fact both P and MT have the ninth month.   [3] See discussion in chapter 3 above.   [4] PL 25, col. 843.

[5] B.J. Roberts, *The Old Testament Text and Versions*, p. 222.

[6] J. Bloch, "The Authorship of the Peshitta", *AJSL* 35 (1918/19), pp. 215–22:219.

[7] S. Davidson, *Lectures on Biblical Criticism*, Edinburgh 1839, p. 60

[8] J.A. Emerton, "Unclean Birds and the Origin of the Peshitta", *JSS* 7 (1962), pp. 204–11.

Mishnah, Midrash, Talmud – and so the alternatives were either this rabbinic Judaism or Christianity. The problem was that much of the evidence, as we shall see, fits neither alternative well. The explanation lies in the diversity which the last few decades have revealed within both religions. In particular, not all Judaism was rabbinic. It follows that, rather than devise a litmus test between two possibilities called "Judaism" and "Christianity", we have to build up a theological profile of the translation, and only then compare it with the different movements, Jewish and Christian, known to us.

Identification with the Jewish people in the Peshitta of Chronicles

Chronicles may seem an odd point to begin, especially as its canonicity was questioned in the Syriac church. It was excluded from the Nestorian canon, so that the Nestorian Isho'dad (cent. ix) remarks that the Old Testament has twenty-two books only "if one includes Chronicles, as the Jews and Greeks do".[9] Chronicles was also excluded from the Syriac scholarly tradition stretching from the "massoretic" manuscripts of the Bible to the scholia of Bar Hebraeus.[10] It demands our attention, however, because in Chronicles P diverges far more from MT than in any other book. Elsewhere, P translates in a more or less straightforward fashion, with very little explicit theological (or other) comment. In Chronicles, however, the translator was not able to hide behind the text, because, as argued in chapter 3 above, his Hebrew *Vorlage* had suffered damage. This forced him to guess and so reveal his attitudes; or it might even be said that this loosened the constraint of the text, and allowed the translator to express his own feelings.

First, the translator links himself with past generations of Jews, and shares the grief and shame of Israel in exile, as at 1 Chr. 29:15–16:

MT   for we are before thee strangers and sojourners like all our forefathers; our days on earth are like a shadow and there is no hope. Lord our God, all this wealth that we have prepared to build thee a house for thy holy name is from thy hand, and all is thine.

P   and we are sojourners before thee, insignificant (ܚܣܝܪܝܢ) in the world; and thou didst rule over our fathers formerly and command them by which way they should go, that they might live; and thee do we praise, O Lord our God, that thou mayest save us from all the nations that harm and revile us, saying: "Where is your God that ye worship?"[11]

This falls within David's prayer (1 Chr. 29:10–19), much of which in P has been freely composed by the translator, presumably faced with a largely illegible Hebrew text. For P's gloom there is no warrant in the Hebrew, where David has joyously appointed Solomon as his successor and collected treasure for the temple. The

---

[9] J.-M. Vosté and C. van den Eynde, *Commentaire d'Isho'dad de Merv sur l'ancien Testament. I: Genèse*, Louvain 1950 (=CSCO 126 / Syr. 67), p. 3. See further the masterly review of the evidence by R. Beckwith, *The Old Testament Canon of the New Testament Church*, London 1985, pp. 307–9.

[10] C. Brovender, *The Syriac Shemahe Manuscripts: A Typological and Comparative Study*, Diss. Jerusalem 1976, pp. 38–72. Brovender shows that these manuscripts (for which "massoretic" is not a happy designation) embodied a "collected Syriac exegesis" (p. xiii), which Bar Hebraeus later incorporated in his scholia.

[11] Cf. Ps. 42:11, 79:10, 115:2, Joel 2:17, Mic. 7:10, as well as (closer in time) 3 Baruch 1:2.

translator's tolerance of the anachronism of making David cry out from exile demonstrates the depth of his own grief.

Another reference to the exile appears in P at 2 Chr. 15:5–7:

and in those former times, when we feared not our God, there was no peace . . . for great evil came upon all the inhabitants of the earth, and we were scattered in every nation and among different cities and lands, for we had forsaken the Lord our God and refused to hearken to his servants the prophets; and he too has requited us for our deeds.

These references to the sin and exile of the Jews find no counterpart in the Hebrew, which is instead written in the third person, refers to the discomfiture of all nations, and ends on a note of hope:

Now in those times, there was no peace for him that went out, or him that came in; for there were great disturbances upon all the inhabitants of the lands. And they were dashed, nation against nation and city against city; for God had confused them with every trouble. Now, be you strong, and let not your hands be weak; for there is a reward for your work.

P here is thus no longer translation at all, but (at least in part) free composition.

A further reference to the exile is introduced at 1 Chr. 16:20 –

MT   ויתהלכו מגוי אל גוי

P   ܘܐܬܬܒܪܬܘܢ ܡܢ ܥܡܐ ܠܥܡܐ

and you were led captive from nation to nation.

We must remember that exile meant not only political helplessness but also disgrace and guilt. Ezekiel had declared that the nations would know that Israel had been exiled for their sins (39:23). Dan. 9:7–8 is a confession before God: "Ours is the shame . . . upon the men of Judah . . . in all the lands to which you expelled them, for their rebellion against you". A Jewish prayer recited at every festival acknowledges: "because of our sins we were exiled from our land".[12] Once more, the illegible *Vorlage* functioned much like the psychologist's ink-blot: it led the translator to reveal his own mind.

It might be argued that P-Chronicles is instead the work of a Christian who gloated over the exile of the Jews as proof of their rejection (so e.g. Tertullian, Adv. Marcion 3.23.4; Aphrahat, Dem. 19). However, a hostile propagandist could hardly have simulated the heartfelt ring of the prayers above,[13] or placed in God's mouth the promise that "the sons of wickedness shall not exile him again" (1 Chr. 17:9).[14] Even a Jewish Christian is unlikely to have felt such sorrow at the plight of the Jews as is expressed in P on 2 Chr. 15:5–7 above. Jewish Christianity is characterised by retention of Jewish laws – something hardly typical of P in Chronicles, as we shall see – rather than by Jewish national identification.[15]

The participation in Jewish suffering identifies the translator of Chronicles as a Jew, and a positive reference to the historical Israel at 2 Chr. 6:18 confirms this:

---

[12] Baer, *Seder Avodat Yisra'el*, Rödelheim 1868, p. 352.
[13] Note also P's rendering of verse 14 in David's prayer: "for thy way of life helped me, and thou art our hope, Lord God".   [14] This was achieved by 'misreading' לבבלתו as לנלתו.
[15] Thus Origen observes that "the Jewish converts have not deserted the law of their fathers, inasmuch as they live according to its prescriptions" – Contra Celsum 2.1.

MT   כי האמנם ישב אלהים את האדם על הארץ

> can indeed God dwell with man on earth?

P   ܡܛܠ ܕܒܗܝܡܢܘܬܐ ܐܝܟ, ܡܪܝܐ ܐܫܪܝ ܫܟܝܢܬܗ ܥܠ ܐܝܣܪܐܝܠ ܥܡܗ ܥܠ ܐܪܥܐ

> for in faith the Lord caused his presence to dwell upon his people Israel on earth

Hebrew אמנם "indeed" was interpreted as אמונה "faith". Compare the statement (discussed below) introduced by P at 2 Chr. 31:18, that "all Israel were sanctified in faith".

The attitude to Jewish law in the Peshitta of Chronicles

Though the translator identified with the Jewish people, he nevertheless departs on occasion from rabbinic and even Pentateuchal norms.

The calendar

The Hebrew text of Chronicles tells of Solomon's seven-day feast which marked the dedication of the Temple. It was immediately followed by the seven-day feast of Tabernacles, with a closing festival (Heb. עצרת) on the eighth day. Solomon then dismissed the people "on the twenty-third day of the seventh month" (2 Chr. 7:10). P agrees that Solomon feasted for two weeks, though in v.9 he seems to invert their order ("seven days of the festival and seven days of the dedication of the house") and makes no reference to a closing festival. The surprise in P comes in v.10:

MT   וביום עשרים ושלשה לחדש השביעי שלח את העם

> and on the 23rd day of the seventh month he dismissed the people

P   ܘܒܝܘܡܐ ܕܣܗܪܐ ܡܠܝܐ ܗܘ ܕܬܫܪܝ ܩܕܡܝܐ, ܫܪܐ ܡܠܟܐ ܠܥܡܐ

> and on the day of the full moon of Tishri the king dismissed the people

MT accords with the fact that Tabernacles begins of the 15th day of Tishri and lasts eight days. In P, however, the people are instead dismissed on the full moon of Tishri, i.e. the fifteenth day.[16] This is the first day of Tabernacles, and yet the translator was under the impression that Tabernacles had already ended a day (or eight days) before that date.

Again, the Hebrew at 2 Chr. 8:13 tells us that Solomon offered sacrifice on the feasts of Unleavened Bread, Pentecost and Tabernacles. For Pentecost (Heb. חג השבעות), however, P writes: "the feast of the fast" (ܥܐܕܐ ܕܨܘܡܐ). Fasting on Pentecost is forbidden in rabbinic Judaism; according to TB Pes. 68a, it was one of the three days in the year when even the ascetic Mar son of Rabina did not fast. Fraenkel's seems the likeliest explanation of P's rendering, namely that the translator confused this feast with the Day of Atonement. Fraenkel did not try, however, to account for this elementary mistake.[17]

---

[16]   Compare 1 Kgs. 12:32, where בחמשה עשר יום בחדש is rendered ܒܚܡܫܬ ܥܣܪ ܒܣܗܪܐ.
[17]   S. Fraenkel, "Die syrische Uebersetzung zu den Büchern der Chronik", *Jahrbücher für protestantische Theologie* 5 (1879), pp. 508–36, 720–59; see pp. 727–8.

Finally, the vague translation of "Passover" as "festival" (ܥܐܕܐ) in 2 Chr. 30 and 35 confirms the impression of indifference to halachah.

Priests and Temple

In relation to the Temple cult we again find striking departures from rabbinic and even biblical norms, e.g.

2 Chr. 13:11

MT   ומנורת הזהב ונרתיה לבער בערב בערב

P   ܘܡܢܪܬܐ ܕܕܗܒܐ ܘܫܪܓܝܗܘܢ. ܘܛܠܝܐ ܡܢܗܪ ܗܘܐ ܠܗܘܢ ܟܠ ܪܡܫ ܘܪܡܫ

> and the candelabra of gold and their lamps, and a boy lamplighter would light them every evening.

P's statement that the candelabrum was lit up by a "boy lamplighter" is contradicted by the Mishnah *Tamid* 3:9, which imposed this task on the priests themselves. It seems that the *Vorlage* was unclear and the translator hesitated between reading לבער or לנער.

2 Chr. 31:3

MT   לעלות הבקר והערב

P   ܠܥܠܬܐ ܕܬܘܪܐ ܕܨܦܪܐ ܘܪܡܫܐ

P here identifies the animals for the 'continual' sacrifice (the Tamid) as bulls, instead of the lambs prescribed at Num. 28:3. Again P was unsure which vocabulary item stood in the consonantal text: בֹּקֶר 'morning' (correctly, as in MT) or בָּקָר 'cattle, bulls'.

2 Chr. 31:18–19

MT   ... (כי באמונתם יתקדשו) קדש: ולבני אהרן הכהנים בשדי מגרש עריהם
       בכל עיר ועיר

P   ܡܛܠ ܕܩܕܝܫܝܢ ܗܘܘ ܒܢܘܗܝ ܕܐܗܪܘܢ ܟܗܢܐ. ܩܕܝܫ ܗܘܐ ܒܣܪܗܘܢ.
     ܘܠܢܫܐ ܠܐ ܩܪܒܝܢ ܗܘܘ. ܘܡܬܟܪܟܝܢ ܗܘܘ ܒܟܠ ܡܕܝܢܐ ܘܡܕܝܢܐ...

> for holy were the sons of Aaron the priest; holy was their flesh; and they drew not nigh unto women; and they would go about in every city . . .

The statements in P about the priests seem to result from difficulty in reading the Hebrew *Vorlage*. The translator mistook the consonants בשדי "in the fields" for בשר "flesh", whence the holy flesh of the priests. The reference to not drawing nigh to women is indebted to Exod. 19:15, as Brock remarks.[18] However, the reason that it was introduced here is that the translator apparently connected מגרש ("common-land" for grazing animals) with "divorce" (expressed in Hebrew through the same root גרש "drive out"), whence "celibacy".

---

[18] S.P. Brock, "Jewish Traditions", p. 217.

One cannot suppose that the translator was here thinking of the priests' hours of service in the Temple alone, for there entry was forbidden not only to women but to all non-priests (Num. 18:4, Neh. 6:11). P is asserting rather that the priests led a celibate life. This is alien to rabbinic Judaism, but is reminiscent of the Essenes, who considered themselves priests, and, according to Josephus (War 2.8.2.[120]), were celibate.

Prayer and its hours

Yet with regard to certain other commandments, the translator is well informed, even assiduous. He often introduces the idea of prayer. For example, at 1 Chr. 16:29 the sense of the Hebrew ("and come before Him") is expanded in the Syriac: "with the prayer of your mouths". References to musical instruments (apart from animal horns) in divine service are almost always removed – having perhaps been abolished in mourning for the Temple[19] – and replaced by terms for 'praise', 'voice' and 'mouth', i.e. by spoken prayer (1 Chr. 15:28, 16:5; 2 Chr. 20:28, 29:25–6, 30:21).[20] At 1 Chr. 16:42, P departs from the Hebrew to stress that "righteous men offered praise not with instruments [five are listed] but with goodly mouth and pure and perfect prayer and righteousness and integrity". Those who according to the Hebrew "sought" (דרש or בקש) or "returned to" (שוב) the Lord are said instead to have "prayed before Him" (1 Chr. 22:19, 2 Chr. 15:4, 15 etc.).[21]

P's treatment of 2 Chr. 14:3 is instructive. Here king Asa, having suppressed heathen worship, calls upon the Jews as follows:

MT   לדרוש את י׳ אלהי אבותיהם ולעשות התורה והמצוה

> to seek the Lord the God of their fathers and to perform the Torah and the commandments.

P   ܥܠ ܢܨܠܐ ܩܕܡ ܡܪܝܐ ܐܠܗܐ ܕܐܒܗܝܢ

> Come let us pray before the Lord God of our fathers.

The second half of Asa's plea, for performance of the Torah, is simply omitted.[22]

Finding his text of David's prayer in 1 Chr. 29 largely illegible, the translator composed large sections of it for himself. As the basis for its conclusion he used the first paragraph of the Jewish prayer called the Qaddish, as noted above:

P   ܕܢܬܩܕܫ ܫܡܟ ܪܒܐ ܘܢܫܬܒܚ ܒܥܠܡܐ ܕܒܪܝܬ ܩܕܡ ܕܚܠܝܟ

> that Thy great name be sanctified and praised in the world that Thou didst create before those that fear Thee.

This is by far the earliest extant evidence for the opening of the first paragraph of the Qaddish, the next being in Seder Amram Gaon (died 875 CE). Only the second paragraph is quoted in the Talmud.[23]

---

[19] According to the Mishnah, "when the Sanhedrin ceased, singing ceased at the wedding feasts" (Sota 9:11), and "during the war of Vespasian they forbade . . . the wedding-drum (אירוס)" (Sota 9:14).

[20] The instruments are retained only at 1 Chr. 15:19, 21. At 2 Chr. 20:28 נבלים become praises but the כנרות remain.

[21] Compare LXX at Isa. 66:20, where the Israelites bring offerings not "in a pure vessel" (so MT) but μετὰ ψαλμῶν.   [22] Conceivably, however, the Hebrew was illegible at this point.

[23] On P's treatment of 1 Chr. 29 in detail, see M.P. Weitzman, "Is the Peshitta of Chronicles a Targum?", *Targum Studies*, ed. P. Flesher, 2(1998), pp. 159–93. On the Qaddish, see id., "The Qaddish Prayer and the Peshitta of Chronicles" (Hebrew) in H. Ben-Shammai (ed.), *Hebrew and Arabic Studies in honour of Joshua Blau*, Tel Aviv & Jerusalem 1993, pp. 261–90.

That prayer was not a mere substitute for the Temple service but had actually superseded it emerges from the words which P puts into Hezekiah's mouth at 2 Chr. 30:18–19 –

MT י׳ הטוב יכפר בעד:
כל לבבו הכין לדרוש האלהים י׳ אלהי אבתיו ולא כטהרת הקדש:

> May the good Lord atone for all who set his heart to seek God, the Lord, God of his fathers, even if not according to the purity of (i.e. required for) the sanctuary

P ܐܠܗܐ ܛܒܐ ܢܚܣܐ ܥܠ ܟܠܗ ܥܡܐ ܕܐܝܣܪܝܠ.
ܡܛܠ ܕܐܬܩܢܢ ܠܒܢ ܠܡܨܠܝܘ ܠܡܪܝܐ ܐܠܗܐ ܕܐܒܗܬܢ. ܩܘܕܫܐ ܠܐ ܗܘܐ ܕܟܐ ܡܢܢ

> May the good God .atone for all the people of Israel. Because we have set our hearts to pray to the Lord, God of our fathers, the sanctuary is no purer than we are.

Thus P continues the prayer, while the Hebrew, however obscure, reverts to narrative. P stresses the power of prayer again in v.21, where the priests and Levites praised God בכלי עז, while P writes ܒܬܫܒܚܬܐ ܕܦܘܡܗܘܢ "with the praises of their mouth".

The hours specified for prayer are set out in P's rendering of the final phrase of 1 Chr. 15:21, which lists the Levites whose duties were specified thus:

MT בכנרות על השמינית לנצח

> to play with harps upon the *šemīnīt*[24]

P ܗܠܝܢ ܡܫܒܚܝܢ ܒܟܢܪܐ ܟܠ ܝܘܡ ܒܝܘܡ ܒܫܥܝܢ ܬܠܬ ܘܒܫܬ ܘܒܬܫܥ

> these would utter praise on the harps every day at the third, sixth and ninth hours.

Thus, in place of the obscure ordinal in the Hebrew, P refers to the third, sixth and ninth hours of the day as hours of prayer. These hours are alien to rabbinic Judaism, which specifies not points but intervals of time; for example, the morning prayer may be said at any time between dawn and noon (Mishnah Ber. 4:1). In the church, however, these canonical hours of prayer – terce, sext and none – are well established. Clement of Alexandria noted that "some fix hours for prayer, such as the third, sixth and ninth" (Stromata 7:7). Tertullian commends these hours, because of their importance (see below) in the New Testament and because their number recalls the Trinity (De Oratione 25). These hours indeed appear as designated for prayer from the earliest days of the church.[25] Peter prayed at the sixth hour, i.e. at noon (Acts 10:9). The ninth hour is called the "hour of prayer" (Acts 3:1). This was the hour when Cornelius prayed even as a "God-fearer" attached to the Jewish community, i.e. before his conversion to Christianity. It was also the hour of Jesus' final prayer (Matt. 27:46, Mark 15:34, Luke 23:44–46). The observance of these hours of prayer by Cornelius, and their occurrence in P, suggest that they originated within certain currents of Judaism – distinct from rabbinic Judaism – before being adopted by the church.

The same system also shaped P's translation of Ezra 9:4–5. According to MT, Ezra sat appalled until the time of the evening sacrifice (מנחת הערב) and then prayed. In P, however, the time of his prayer is instead the "ninth hour" (ܬܫܥ ܫܥܝܢ). This does

[24] This word, literally "eighth", is a musical term of which the meaning is now lost; the usual explanation is "eight-stringed instrument".

[25] Diadache 8 commends prayer thrice daily but without specifying hours.

not reflect the rabbinic definition of the normal time for presenting the evening meal-offering as half an hour after the ninth hour;[26] for the half-hour difference cannot be overlooked. Rather, it picks up one of the canonical hours mentioned in P-Chronicles.

Other religious values

Another commandment evidently important to the translator was charity, for at 1 Chr. 23:5 he writes, apparently on the basis of free composition in the face of an illegible Hebrew text:

ܘܐܩܝܡ ܕܘܝܕ ܥܠ ܡܣܟܢܐ ܘܥܠ ܚܫܝܟܐ: ܡܦܪܢܣܢܐ. ܘܣܥܘܪܐ.
ܕܢܗܘܘܢ ܙܢܝܢ ܘܡܦܪܢܣܝܢ ܡܣܟܢܐ: ܚܕ ܥܠ ܥܣܪܐ.
ܘܡܕܡ ܠܐ ܡܚܣܪܝܢ ܠܗܘܢ.

and David set, over the poor and needy, providers and overseers who might feed and provide for the poor – one [provider] over ten [needy people] – and they let them lack nothing.

This stands in the place of the report in MT that David had appointed 4,000 Levites as gatekeepers and another 4,000 to praise God with musical instruments.

At 2 Chr. 31:10 another reference to charity is introduced by P. Heaps of priestly and Levitical dues had been brought, and their prospective recipients are told:

MT מהחל התרומה לביא בית י׳ אכול ושבוע והותר עד לרוב כי י׳ ברך עמו...

> since the dues first entered the house of the Lord, (we) have had enough to eat, even to spare, exceedingly; for the Lord has blessed his people . . .

P ܫܪܝܐ ܗܝ ܠܟܘܢ ܪܡܫܬܐ ܗܕܐ ܠܡܐܟܠ. ܡܛܠ ܕܠܒܝܬܗ ܕܡܪܝܐ ܥܠܬ.
ܘܐܟܘܠܘ ܘܣܒܥܘ. ܘܕܝܬܪ ܡܢܗ ܗܒܘ ܠܡܣܟܢܐ ܘܠܚܫܝܟܐ. ܡܛܠ ܕܡܪܝܐ ܒܪܟ ܠܥܡܗ...

> This offering is permitted for you to eat, because it has come into the house of the Lord; so eat and be satisfied; and what remains of it, give to the poor and needy, for the Lord has blessed his people . . .

P takes הותר as הַיֶּתֶר 'the surplus', and calls for its distribution to the poor.

Study was another value commended by the translator. At 1 Chr. 8:40, where MT speaks of multiplying (מַרְבִּים) children and grandchildren, P instead speaks of educating them:

> ܘܡܠܦܝܢ ܗܘܘ ܒܢܝܗܘܢ ܘܒܢܝ ܒܢܝܗܘܢ
>
> and they were teaching their children and their children's children

instead vocalising the Hebrew as מְרַבִּים in the Aramaic sense "raise (children)". P also understands משנה as 'study' at 1 Chr. 5:12 and 2 Chr. 34:22, agreeing with the Targum on Chronicles in both and also with Tg. to 2 Kgs. 22:14, a passage parallel to the latter. At 2 Chr. 30:3, the words לְמַדַּי וְהָעָם (which in fact belong to two different phrases) were rendered ܘܡܠܦܢܘܗܝ, ܕܥܡܐ "and the teachers of the people", as if the Hebrew had been מְלַמְּדֵי הָעָם.

It seems likely that prayer, charity and study were all seen as replacing sacrifice. Such

[26] I.e. after the elapse of 9½ 'hours' in a day divided into 12 'hours', between dawn and nightfall (Mishnah Pes. 5:1).

views are also attested within rabbinic Judaism, albeit together with constant hope for the restoration of sacrifice. According to one rabbinic opinion cited in TB Ber.32b, the morning and afternoon prayers were instituted on the basis of the daily sacrifices.[27] Yet at the same time a rival opinion saw the daily prayers as a far older and hence more honoured institution, introduced by the patriarchs themselves. Thus R. Eliezer considered prayer actually greater than sacrifice. At Qumran too, the Manual of Discipline calls prayer **תרומת שפתים** ("offering of the lips"), valued above sacrifice (9:5).

The same R. Eliezer also declared charity superior to all sacrifice, on the basis of Prov. 21:3 (TB Suk. 49b). He accounted on similar lines for the reference at Ezek 41:22 to the altar as a table:

> So long as the Temple stood, the altar atoned for Israel; but now, a man's table atones for him.

In this way he explained R.Judah's dictum that a man can hope to extend his lifespan by lingering at his table, because a poor man may come and be fed.[28]

Study too was a substitute for sacrifice. According to R.Assi, God promised Abraham that the sacrifices would atone for Israel's sins; and when Abraham objected that the Temple would not stand for ever, God replied (TB Taan. 27b):

> I have already ordained for them the order of sacrifices. When they read them before me, I count it for them as if they had offered them before me, and I forgive them for all their sins.

Indeed, study was considered superior to sacrifice. David was assured that one day's study of the Torah on his part was more pleasing to God than a thousand burnt-offerings that Solomon would sacrifice (TB Shab. 30a). Accordingly, "we may not suspend the education of children even for the re-building of the Temple" (TB Shab. 119b; cf. TB Meg. 16b).

Finally, we may note the theme of faith which is introduced into P-Chronicles. At 1 Chr. 29:17, P twice substitutes inward faith for the "rectitude" (i.e. upright action) of the Hebrew –

MT וידעתי אלהי כי אתה בחן לבב ומישרים תרצה אני בישר לבבי התנדבתי כל אלה

P ܘܝܕܥ ܐܢܐ ܐܠܗܝ، ܕܐܢܬ ܒܿܨܐ ܐܢܬ ܠܒܐ. ܘܒܗܝܡܢܘܬܐ ܐܢܬ ܪܥܐ.
ܘܐܢܐ ܒܗܝܡܢܘܬܐ ܕܠܒܝ ܫܒܚܬ ܗܠܝܢ ܟܠܗܝܢ

And I know, O God, that Thou searchest the heart, and delightest in faith; and I by the faith of my heart have uttered all this praise[29]

Also relevant here is the last part of 2 Chr. 31:18 –

MT לכל קהל כי באמונתם יתקדשו קדש

P ܘܠܟܠܗ ܥܡܐ ܕܐܝܣܪܝܠ ܕܒܗܝܡܢܘܬܐ ܡܬܩܕܫܝܢ ܗܘܘ

... and to all the people of Israel, who were sanctified in faith

MT is speaking of priests, and here declares that their whole company hallowed themselves in their **אמונה** – i.e. either conscientiously, or because of their permanent standing. P instead introduces faith, ascribed to all Israel.

[27] Likewise, on the basis of Hos. 14:3, prayer is deemed as efficacious as the sacrifice of cattle (TB Yoma 86b). [28] TB Ber. 55a. This saying was also transmitted by R. Johanan.
[29] For the equivalence **נדב** ܫܒܚ, compare Jgs. 5:2.

We may also recall the reference at 2 Chr. 6:18 to Israel's faith. The rabbinic sources, although they of course value faith, generally prefer to stress observance.[30]

Those renderings in P which suggest conflict with rabbinic observance belong to two distinct categories. Some embody a halachah which we know (or can presume) to have actually been practised in non-rabbinic circles. For example, in view of the external parallels, the rendering at 1 Chr. 15:21 must reflect a real practice of praying at the third, sixth and ninth hours. There are of course many other sources that attest divergence from rabbinic halachah. Thus Josephus (e.g. *AJ* 4.280) and Philo (e.g. *De Spec. Leg.* 3,182,195) do not interpret "eye for an eye" invariably, like the rabbis (TB B.Q.84a), to mean monetary compensation. The apocryphal book of Susannah in a capital case demands death for witnesses whose testimony is broken down under examination, in contrast to Mishnah Mak. 1:4. Above all, the Dead Sea Scrolls differed from rabbinic halachah in the calendar and much else. That P-Chronicles too should have diverged from rabbinic halachah need occasion no surprise.

By contrast, it would be rash to suppose that the translator was actually familiar with a practice of fasting on Pentecost or deputing a boy to light the Temple lamp. It seems rather that the many guesses which the partially illegible text forced upon the translator happened to include some which bore on halachic matters. What we have in such a case could be called a pseudo-halachah. Here the content of the guess is noteworthy, but more important is the translator's ignorance of rabbinic norms. The references to a daily sacrifice of bulls and (probably) to a celibate priesthood fall under this heading of pseudo-halachah.

Religious values outside Peshitta Chronicles

We must now examine the other biblical books in P, to see whether similar attitudes apply. Outside Chronicles, such indications are far less frequent, since the translator is better able to hide behind the text. However, what evidence that we shall find is consistent with the attitudes in Chronicles, except in one area, namely the attitude towards the Jewish people.

Prayer

As in Chronicles, prayer is elsewhere too introduced occasionally in the translation, as at Ps. 37:7 –

MT   דּוֹם לי' והתחולל לו

be silent for the Lord and wait (?) for him

P   ,ܡܘܗܝ ܡܢ ܘܨܠܐ ܘܗܘ ܕܡܪܝܐ ܒܥܝ

Entreat the Lord and pray before Him

(cf. LXX ἱκέτευσον for the second verb).

Again at Ps. 71:14, P makes the Psalmist declare that he will always pray, rather than wait in hope as in MT אֲיַחֵל. To "seek (Heb. דרש) the Lord" becomes to "pray before

---

[30] It agrees with this that the Targums sometimes insert פולחנא 'service', e.g. at Deut. 7:4 ("lest they remove your son *from my service*, MT מאחרי); in such cases P is instead literal.

the Lord" at Ezra 6:21, as often in Chronicles. The "fixed times" (עתים מזמנים) of Ezra 10:14 become in P "the time for prayer" (ܥܕܢܐ ܕܨܠܘܬܐ). At Neh. 9:17, MT describes God as "slow to anger and abundant in lovingkindness"; P instead calls him "far from anger and near to supplication" (ܘܪܚܝܩ ܐܦܘܗܝ ܡܢ ܪܘܓܙܐ ܘܩܪܝܒ ܠܒܥܘܬܐ).

In some further passages where P introduces prayer, the Targum agrees. An example occurs at Gen. 30:8, where MT has the root פתל "twist, wrestle" but both versions think instead of the noun תפלה:

MT   נפתולי אלהים נפתלתי עם אחתי

P   ܒܥܝܬ ܡܢ ܡܪܝܐ. ܘܐܬܟܫܦܬ ܥܡ ܚܬܝ

I sought from the Lord and I supplicated with my sister

cf. Tᴼ   קביל י' בעותי באתחננותי בצלותי חמידת דיהי לי ולד כאחתי

God has accepted my request, when I entreated in my prayer; I desired that I should have a child like my sister.

Again, at Exod. 38:8 and 1 Sam. 2:22 the Hebrew speaks of the women who served –הצבא(ו)ת – at the entrance of the Tent of Meeting. P instead calls them the women who came to pray (ܢܫܐ ܕܐܬܝܢ ܠܡܨܠܝܘ); the relevant Targums agree in both places.

That sacrifice is supplanted by prayer is clearly stated in the Peshitta version of the Apocrypha, at Ecclus. 32:8 [35:6].[31] While LXX reads: "the offering of a just man anoints the altar", P renders: "the sacrifices of just men are the prayer of their mouths". On the next two verses in Ecclus. (32:9–10), P represents charity as a further substitute for sacrifice:

LXX   The sacrifice (θυσία) of a just man is accepted . . . with a good eye glorify the Lord.

P   ܡܘܗܒܬܐ ܕܓܒܪܐ ܛܒܐ ܡܬܩܒܠܐ . . . ܒܥܝܢܐ ܛܒܐ ܗܒ ܠܡܣܟܢܐ

The gift of a good man is accepted . . . with a good eye give to the poor[32]

All this is reminiscent of P-Chronicles, where P likewise commends charity, and where the translator makes elementary errors regarding the sacrificial cult and the priests.

Sacrifice and Temple

According to Davidson, P is negligent in rendering the "Levitical law" in general, and the dietary laws in particular.[33] Carelessness in relation to the dietary laws had earlier been claimed by Hirzel;[34] and although Emerton has well disposed of this particular charge,[35] a certain negligence can indeed be detected in P's rendering of the sacrificial laws. In fact, an indifferent or even hostile attitude to sacrifice – and to the priesthood

---

[31] M.M. Winter, "The Origins of Ben Sira in Syriac", *VT* 27 (1977), pp. 237–53, 494–507: 239.
[32] Winter, loc.cit. The Syriac is cited from P.A. de Lagarde (ed.), *Libri Veteris Testamenti Apocryphi Syriace*, Leipzig 1861.   [33] S. Davidson, *Lectures in Biblical Criticism*, Edinburgh 1839, p. 60.
[34] L. Hirzel, *De Pentateuchi Versionis Syriacae Quam Peschito Vocant Indole Commentatio Critico-Exegetica*, Leipzig 1825, pp. 127f.
[35] J.A. Emerton, "Unclean Birds and the Origin of the Peshitta", *JSS* 7 (1962), pp. 204–11.

and Temple – can be traced right through the Peshitta of the Old Testament and into the Apocrypha.

Throughout the Peshitta (e.g. Lev. 5, 1 Sam. 6:3, Ezek. 46:20), the "guilt-offering" (אשם) is termed merely "offering" (ܩܘܪܒܢܐ), as if it were no different from אִשֶּׁה. In Leviticus, the "peace-offerings" (שלמים) are repeatedly mistaken for a burnt-offering and so rendered ܥܠܬܐ.[36] Apparently the common root *šlm* which this Hebrew word shared with ܡܣܩܐ ܥܠܬܐ, P's frequent term for a burnt-offering, suggested that the two were interchangeable; and the translator had no prior halachic knowledge to prevent this confusion. Elsewhere שלמים may become the vague ܩܘܪܒܢܐ 'offering'[37] or "sacrifices" ܕܒ̈ܚܬܐ (Josh. 8:31). The indifference of the translator at Josh. 22:23 is especially clear. The tribes who build an altar east of the Jordan undertake, according to the Hebrew, never "to offer on it burnt-offering (עולה) or meal-offering (מנחה) nor to make on it peace-offerings (זבחי שלמים)". P sweeps away these details in a brief rendering: "nor shall we offer on it sacrifices or other worship (ܕܒ̈ܚܬܐ ܐܘ ܦܘܠܚܢ ܐܚܪܝܢ)".

Similarly, the ניחוחין of Ezra 6:10 become vague ܩܘܪ̈ܒܢܐ. Another reference to offerings in Ezra (at 3:5) is eliminated:

MT וכל מתנדב נדבה לי׳

and all those who made voluntary offerings to the Lord

P ܘܠܟܠ ܡ̇ܢ ܕܨܒܐ ܨܒܝܢܐ ܕܡܪܝܐ

and to all who desired the will of the Lord

Indifference to the cult verges on disrespect in two passages:

(a) Jer. 7:4–5

MT היכל י׳ המה: כי אם היטיב תיטיבו את דרכיכם ואת מעלליכם אם עשו תעשו משפט...

P ... ܗܝܟܠܗ ܐܢܬܘܢ ܕܡܪܝܐ: ܐܢ ܬܫܦܪܘܢ ܐܘܪ̈ܚܬܟܘܢ ܘܥܒ̈ܕܝܟܘܢ. ܘܐܢ ܬܥܒܕܘܢ ܕܝܢܐ

You are the temple of the Lord, if you improve your ways and deeds and practise justice . . .

The first phrase in MT is in the third person: "they" denotes the false words in which the Jews trust, which are: "the Temple of the Lord". P however addresses his readers in the second person, telling them that they themselves are the temple, if they will only pursue social justice. This implies that the physical Temple is obsolete. We may recall the מקדש אדם ("temple of men") at Qumran (4QFlor 6). A yet closer parallel appears in Paul, at 1 Cor. 3:16: "Do you not know that you are the temple of the Lord and the spirit of God dwells in you?"[38] A more distant parallel is Deut. Rabba 5:3, where David is assured that his performance of righteousness and justice are more pleasing to God than the Temple would ever be:

א״ל הקב״ה הצדקה והדינין שאתה עושה חביבין עלי מבית המקדש

36 Lev. 3:6, 9; 4:10, 26, 31, 35; 7:11–37 (10 times in this passage).

37 Exod. 20:24; Num. 29:39; Josh. 22:27; Ezek 43:27; 45:15, 17; 46:2, 12.

38 Compare Eph. 2:21.

(b)   Ezek. 45:20

MT   וכן תעשה בשבעה בחדש מאיש שנה ומפתי

P   ܘܗܟܢܐ ܢܥܒܕ ܒܫܒܥܐ ܒܝܪܚܐ ܡܛܠ ܓܒܪܐ ܣܟܠܐ ܘܛܥܝܐ

and so shall a foolish and erring man do on the seventh of the month

Here the sacrificial ritual for the new moon of the first month has to be repeated on the seventh day. The last three words are difficult, and mean literally: "from a man in error and a simpleton." Most translations understand "from" as "on behalf of", or in some other way avoid disrespect to the ritual; but P's translation characterises the performer of the ritual as foolish.

At Psalm 48:14, that disrespect, or rather hostility, is directed to Jerusalem:

MT   פסגו ארמנותיה

P   ܘܥܩܘܪܘ ܣܚܪ̈ܬܗ

In the Hebrew, the readers (evidently worshippers) are urged to go about (literally "separate") the palaces of Jerusalem. P, however, is a summons to uproot them. The calls to surround Zion and mark its ramparts (vv.13–14) now read like commands to prepare for a military assault, and to recount the outcome to future generations (v.15). Etymologically, "uproot" is a credible rendering of פסג, which can mean "dismember" in Jewish Aramaic.[39]

Aversion not only to sacrifice but to the law in general emerges clearly in two books of the Apocrypha. In Sir. (Ecclus.) 32, the commendation of sacrifice in the Hebrew original is systematically suppressed, in favour of prayer and obedience to God's will. Many further favourable references to sacrifice are omitted, surely deliberately, in P, at 7:31, 14:11, 38:11, 45:21, 50:19–22. The promised "covenant of Phineas" (50:24), and the account of Simon's glorious priestly attire and sacrificial duty (45:9–15), are likewise dropped. Furthermore, favourable references to the law are replaced by "way" (35:24) or "word" (44:20), or altered otherwise (41:8) or eliminated altogether (35:16, 36:2–3).[40] Likewise, as Drijvers points out, the original of Wisdom 2:10 charges the wicked with sins against the law, but works of law become themselves the charge against the wicked in P.[41]

Negligence of the Law

In Chronicles, a number of renderings were found that suggested indifference to rabbinic halachah in a number of areas. More such renderings can be found in other books, despite the parallels revealed elsewhere by Perles and Maori with rabbinic halachah. For the most part these renderings in P are pseudo-halachot – i.e. guesses ventured by the translator where the context happened to be legal – rather than hard evidence of non-rabbinic practice. Examples:

---

[39] e.g. Lam. Rabba 5:6 ומפסיג ליה אברים אברים.
[40] Winter, "The origins of Ben Sira in Syriac", pp. 494–8.
[41] H.J.W. Drijvers, "The Peshitta of *Sapientia Salomonis*", in H.L.Vanstiphout et al (eds.), *Scripta Signa Vocis: Festschr. J.H.Hospers*, Groningen 1986, pp. 15–30.

Exod. 23:11

MT　וְהַשְּׁבִיעִת תִּשְׁמְטֶנָּה וּנְטַשְׁתָּהּ

P　ܘܒܫܒܬܐ ܬܗܦܟܝܗ ܘܬܫܒܩܝܗ

and (in) the seventh year, you will plough it and leave it

P thus permits ploughing the land in the sabbatical year, which the rabbis forbade (Mishnah Shebi'it 1:4). It is not satisfactory to emend the text to ܬܘܒܕܝܗ,[42] since the resulting sense ("destroy") is unsuitable and bears no relation to the Hebrew.

Lev. 19:27

MT　לֹא תַקִּפוּ פְּאַת רֹאשְׁכֶם

P　ܠܐ ܬܪܒܘܢ ܣܥܪܐ ܕܪܝܫܟܘܢ

While the Hebrew forbids rounding (i.e. cutting) the hair of the temples, P forbids growing the hair long. This could be sheer guesswork, based on the norm in P's society.[43]

Deut. 23:2

Two categories of men here forbidden ever to be accepted as converts to Israel are פְּצוּעַ דַּכָּא and כְּרוּת שָׁפְכָה, both phrases indicating mutilation of the privy parts. P falsely uses the single term ܓܝܪܐ "adulterer" to cover both. This seems a guess based on the exclusion in the next verse of the מַמְזֵר, which P rightly renders ܒܪ ܓܘܪܐ "child of adultery".

Deut. 25:6

MT　יָקוּם עַל שֵׁם אָחִיו הַמֵּת

P　ܢܩܘܡ ܥܠ ܫܡܐ ܕܐܚܘܗܝ, ܕܡܝܬ

The subject is the first-born child of a widow in levirate marriage. P understands that the child shall take the name of his dead uncle. This interpretation appears also in Josephus[44] but is rejected by Sifre, which instead takes the text to mean that the child becomes the dead brother's heir. It is possible that P derived this interpretation from non-rabbinic circles, but alternatively it may have been inferred directly from the word שֵׁם in the biblical text.

Hag. 2:13

MT　טְמֵא נֶפֶשׁ "one defiled by a person (i.e. corpse)"

P　ܐܝܢܐ ܕܛܡܐܐ ܢܦܫܗ "one whose soul is impure"

There is of course no concept of an impure soul in rabbinic law.

---

[42] So tentatively Maori (*The Peshitta Version of the Pentateuch*, p. 31n.), following Heller.
[43] The idea that long hair makes one look unkempt (מנוול) appears also in TB Taanit 17a. According to Deut. Rabba 2.18, however, long plaits indicate idolatry: העושה בלורית אינו מגדלה אלא לשמה של עבודה זרה.　[44] τὸν παῖδα ... τῷ τοῦ τεθνεῶτος καλέσας ὀνόματι ... – *AJ* 4.8.23 (254).

Neh. 10:32

MT ועמי הארץ המביאים את המקחות
וכל שבר ביום השבת למכור לא נקח מהם בשבת...

P ܘܡܢ ܥܡ̈ܡܐ ܕܐܪܥܐ ܕܡܝܬܝܢ ܠܐ ܢܣܒܘܢ.
ܘܟܠ ܕܡܘܓܪ ܒܥܝܪܐ ܒܝܘܡܐ ܕܫܒܬܐ: ܐܓܪܐ ܠܐ ܢܣܒ.

> and from the nations who bring, they shall not take (i.e. buy); and whoever hires out a beast on the sabbath day shall take no reward.

In the Hebrew, the Jews agree that "we shall not take" from any foreigners who bring goods or grain for sale on the sabbath. The translator, however, evidently mistook Heb. שבר "grain" for the verb שכר "hire"; it did not trouble him that neither the hiring nor the work performed by the beast that was hired was permitted on the sabbath.

Also relevant here is the regular rendering of the measure "ephah" (frequent in sacrificial laws) by "seah", at Exod. 16:36, Lev. 5:11, 6:13, Num. 5:15 etc. This is only one third of the quantity prescribed by the rabbis (Mishnah Men.6:6) and stipulated by rabbinic Targums such as T^{O} in these biblical passages.

Significant too are some difficult Hebrew passages in halachic contexts where P offers a mere guess while a translator concerned with halachah would be expected to utilise the established halachic sense. For that reason, the fact that P always guesses at טוטפת, rather than translating as "phylacteries", tends to suggest indifference to ritual. At Exod. 13:16, P writes ܕܘܟܪܢܐ "memorial", in line with v.9 of the same chapter (where MT has זכרון). In Deut. 6:8, 11:18 we find another vague translation ܪܘܫܡܐ "mark", which may be a guess based on Heb. אות "sign" in the same verse.

Probably not significant, however, are P's literal translations that contradict the rabbinic interpretation, such as "Thou shalt not seethe a kid in its mother's milk" (Exod. 23:19 etc.), while the Jewish Targums instead have: "Do not eat meat with milk." In themselves these need not indicate indifference to ritual, since no translator could take full account of the halachic tradition attached to every passage by rabbinic (or indeed other) halachah.

Faith and eternal life

Finally, the value of religious faith introduced in Chronicles also appears occasionally in other books. At Ps. 17:15, the Psalmist hopes to awaken to the image of God, but P instead writes of his faith:

MT אשבעה בהקיץ תמונתך

P ܘܐܣܒܥ ܡܐ ܕܐܬܬܥܝܪܬ ܗܝܡܢܘܬܟ

> and I shall be satisfied when the faith of thee is awakened

At Prov. 19:8, faith replaces understanding:

MT שמר תבונה למצא טוב

P ܕܢܛܪ ܗܝܡܢܘܬܐ ܡܫܟܚ ܠܛܒܬܐ

> he who observes faith finds what is good.

Faith on man's part also replaces the loyalty (אמת) shown by God to man:

(a)   Jer. 33:6

MT   וגליתי להם עתרת שלום ואמת

P   ܘܐܓܠܐ ܠܗܘܢ ܫܒܝܠܐ ܕܫܠܡܐ ܘܡܗܝܡܢܘܬܐ

   and I shall reveal to them the paths of peace and faith

(b)   Ps. 26:3

MT   והתהלכתי באמתך

P   ܘܗܠܟܬ ܒܡܗܝܡܢܘܬܟ

   and I have walked in faith

Relevant here too is Ruth 4:6, noted above in chapter 3, where Boaz's rival cannot redeem "because of my lack of faith". This corresponds to nothing in the Hebrew, and although it seems due instead to a misreading of LXX, it nevertheless betokens a preoccupation with faith.

   This faith includes belief in eternal life. Thus, verses are sometimes reinterpreted to affirm belief in resurrection:

(a)   Ps. 48:15

MT   הוא ינהגנו על מות

P   ܗܘ ܢܕܒܪܢ ܠܥܠ ܡܢ ܡܘܬܐ

   he will lead us beyond death

(b)   Ps. 49:9f

MT   וחדל לעולם: ויחי עוד לנצח לא יראה השחת:

   and he is ever unable to live for ever without seeing destruction

P   ܠܐܐ ܠܥܠܡ ܕܬܐܚܐ ܠܥܠܡ ܘܠܐ ܬܚܙܐ ܚܒܠܐ

   Labour continually that thou mayest live for ever and not see destruction

(c)   Ps. 88:11

MT   הלמתים תעשה פלא

   For the dead shalt thou perform wonders?

P   ܗܐ ܠܡܝܬܐ ܬܥܒܕ ܐܢܬ ܓܢܒܪܘܬܐ

   Behold for the dead thou wilt perform wonders

The Hebrew adds further despairing questions, transformed by P into triumphant affirmations.

(d) Job 30:23

MT כי ידעתי מות תשיבני ובית מועד לכל חי

For I know that Thou wilt bring me back to death, to the place appointed for all the living

P ܡܟܝܠ ܝܕܥ ܐܢܐ ܕܡܢ ܡܘܬܐ ܬܗܦܟܢܝ܆ ܠܒܝܬ ܘܥܕܐ ܕܟܠܗܘܢ ܚܝ̈ܐ

Now I know that Thou wilt bring me back from death, to the meeting place of all the living

Compare Job 28:13, where the Hebrew denies that wisdom can be found in the land of the living (ארץ החיים), while P declares that wisdom is found in the "land of life" alone.

(e) Job 42:6

MT על כן אמאס ונחמתי על עפר ואפר

Therefore I reject (my complaint) and repent upon dust and ashes

P ܡܛܠ ܗܢܐ ܐܫܬܘܩ܆ ܘܐܬܢܚܡ ܥܠ ܥܦܪܐ ܘܥܠ ܩܛܡܐ.

Therefore I shall be silent, and I shall be resurrected upon dust and ashes

P uses the root *nḥm*, as in MT; and although the Syriac verb ܢܚܡ means 'comfort' in P on Sirach (Ecclus.) 48:24, the usual Syriac meaning 'resurrect' is confirmed for this passage by the reference to Job's future resurrection in the appendix to Job in LXX (discussed below). That reference was arguably derived from an "Aramaic book" which might likewise have influenced P.

There are messianic statements in the Hebrew Bible which P preserves, or even explicates; thus at Num. 24:17 שבט is taken as ܪܝܫܐ (cf. LXX "man", T^O "Messiah"). These, however, tell us little about P's own theology. More important are the eschatological references which seem to have originated with P, e.g.

(a) Prov. 31:25

MT ותשחק ליום אחרון

and she laughs at tomorrow

P ܘܬܚܕܐ ܒܝܘܡܐ ܐܚܪܝܐ

and she will rejoice at the last day

(b) Job 19:25

MT ואני ידעתי גאלי חי ואחרון על עפר יקום

And I know that my redeemer liveth and that he will arise last on the ground[45]

P ܘܐܢܐ ܝܕܥ ܐܢܐ ܕܦܪܘܩܝ ܚܝ ܗܘ܆ ܘܒܣܘܦܐ ܥܠ ܐܪܥܐ ܢܬܓܠܐ

And I know that my redeemer liveth, and in the end he will be revealed on earth

[45] Apparently this means: "I know that my defender will have the last word in court."

The second half in MT apparently means that Job's defender will speak last in court, but in P the expectation is eschatological.

One may also note here the introduction of ܣܒܪܐ "hope". A number of instances occur in Proverbs:

(a)   2:7

MT   וצפן לישרים תושיה

P   ܘܢܛܪ ܣܒܪܐ ܠܟܠܗܘܢ ܬܪܝܨܝܢ

He preserves hope for the righteous

(b)   8:21

MT   להנחיל אהבי יש

P   ܕܐܘܪܬ ܠܪܚܡܝ ܣܒܪܐ

that I may let those that love me inherit hope

Likewise eschatological is R. Joshua b. Levi's deduction, from the same verse, that every righteous person will inherit 310 worlds – 310 being the numerical value of יש (Mishnah Uq. 3:12).

(c)   10:24.

MT   ותאות צדיקים יתן

P   ܘܣܒܪܐ ܕܟܐܢܐ ܡܬܝܗܒ ܠܗܘܢ

and hope is given to the righteous

(d)   11:3

MT   תמת ישרים תנחם

P   ܣܒܪܐ ܕܬܪܝܨܐ ܢܬܩܢ

the hope of the upright shall be established

(e)   13:12

MT   ועץ חיים תאוה באה

P   ܘܐܝܠܢܐ ܕܚܝܐ ܡܝܬܐ ܣܒܪܐ

and the tree of life brings hope

In two of these passages from Proverbs (10:24, 13:12), the sense 'hope' was reached by misreading of תאוה "desire" as תקוה "hope". The same happens at Ps. 10:17 –

MT   תאות ענוים שמעת י'

P   ܣܒܪܐ ܕܡܣܟܢܐ ܫܡܥ ܐܢܬ ܡܪܝܐ

Thou heedest the hope of the poor, O Lord

Elsewhere the noun "hope" (ܣܒܪܐ) is introduced in P-Psalms in place of the epithet "refuge" (מחסה) applied to God (Ps. 62:8, 142:6). The corresponding Syriac verb (ܣܒܪ) is also occasionally introduced by P. At Ps. 34:6 in MT, the righteous look to God and are radiant (ונהרו); P instead is a call to look to God and hope in him (ܣܒܪܘ ܒܗ). Again, Ps. 52:8 in MT contains the phrase ועליו ישחקו: the righteous will laugh at the wicked man condemned in the Psalm. P, however, preferred to write: ܘܢܣܒܪܘܢ ܒܡܪܝܐ "and they will hope in the Lord".

P-Psalms also twice introduces the related ܣܒܪܬܐ "good news" (eventually applied to the gospels[46]):

19:5

MT   בכל הארץ יצא קום

P   ܒܟܠܗ ܐܪܥܐ ܢܦܩܬ ܣܒܪܬܗܘܢ

      in all the earth their good news went forth

This passage is further discussed in chapter 3 above, p. 134.

68:11

MT   אדני יתן אמר המבשרות צבא רב

P   ܡܪܝܐ ܢܬܠ ܡܠܬܐ ܠܡܣܒܪܢܐ ܒܚܝܠܐ ܪܒܐ

      the Lord will give the word of good news with great might

In some passages where the Hebrew noun בֶּטַח properly means physical security, P instead has 'hope' (ܣܒܪܐ), the link being the root בטח. Examples occur at Deut. 12:10, Isa. 30:15, 32:17, Ezek. 28:26, 34:27f*, Hos. 2:20*, Mic. 2:8* – and also in Psalms (78:53*) and Proverbs (1:33, 3:23, 10:9). At Deut. 12:10, for example, righteous Israel is to dwell not in outward security but in hope. This rendering seems to have come in from LXX, which has ἐλπίς in those passages marked by an asterisk. It is conceivable that the prayer within the weekday 'Amida that there should be no hope for the sectarians (ולמינים אל תהי תקוה) was first directed against a non-rabbinic group whose watchword was hope.[47]

Such eschatological hope fostered disdain for earthly wealth. At Prov. 22:7 P inverts the sense of the Hebrew, proclaiming instead that "the poor will rule over the rich". Similar inversion, resulting likewise in condemnation of riches, occurs at Prov. 14:23, within a couplet inserted by the translator on the basis of the Greek:

ܘܐܝܢܐ ܕܡܣܟܢ ܒܝܢ ܒܡܐܟܘܠܬܗ ܢܫܠܐ ܢܗܘܐ ܘܢܒܣܡ. ܟܠ ܟܐܒ ܗܘ ܡܪܝܐ ܡܐܣܐ

and he that is poor with regard to his sustenance will be tranquil and happy (lit. pleasant). All pain the Lord heals.

---

[46] Origen (*Contra Celsum* I.62) quotes both these passages (albeit from LXX) to show that the apostles were divinely inspired.

[47] Rather as the statement that Ephraim "sinned through Baal and died" (Hos. 13:1) may be directed against the myth of Baal's resurrection; see J. Day, "Resurrection imagery from Baal to the Book of Daniel", *SVT* 66 (1997), pp. 125–33. This rabbinic prayer is called ברכת המינים in TB Ber. 28b; it was first directed against sectarians, though later against informers (מלשינים).

This derives from LXX (for v.23b):

ὁ δὲ ἡδὺς καὶ ἀνάλγητος ἐν ἐνδείᾳ ἔσται

but the pleasure-taking (lit. sweet) and the one without (regard for) pain will be in need

However, the words "sweet" and "need(y)" have been inverted, and a theological explanation provided for being without pain.[48] A positive reference to wealth is also suppressed by P in another line adopted from the Greek, after 11:16 –

LXX   οἱ δὲ ἀνδρεῖοι ἐρείδονται πλούτῳ "and the brave are supported by *wealth*"

P   ܪ̈ܚܡܝ ܚܘܟܡܬܐ ܘ "and the mighty support *knowledge*"

Similarly Qohelet's remark (10:19) that "money is an answer to (יַעֲנֶה) everything" becomes in P: "money humbles (יְעַנֶּה) and misleads [the living] in all".

P-Chronicles likewise qualifies David's wealth as being merely "of (this) world" (1 Chr. 29:28). Disapproval of wealth recurs at 2 Chr. 26:16. The Hebrew indicates the cause of Uzziah's pride, which led him to usurp the priestly office, in the one word וּכְחֶזְקָתוֹ "and when he became mighty"; P instead writes ܡܕ ܥܬܪ ܗܘܐ ܒܩܢܝܢܐ "and when he had become rich in possessions".

The same tendency occurs in the Apocrypha. The commendation of poverty is amply documented by Winter in P on Ecclesiasticus,[49] and that of humility (ܡܟܝܟܘܬܐ) is noted by Drijvers in P at Wisdom 2:19.[50] Ecclus. 37:4 in P refers to the evanescent "wealth of the world", as in Chronicles (noted above).[51] Poverty is of course commended in other movements also: notably, at Qumran (1QH 10:22–30), at Enoch 94:8 and at Matt. 5:3.

Israel outside Chronicles

In P of Chronicles, the translator identified himself as a Jew, sharing the sufferings of Israel. In the other books we shall find both parallels and contrasts to this attitude.

Identification with the Jewish people

An attitude much like that found in Chronicles appears in P's expansion of Ezra 9:14–15. In the Hebrew, Ezra is contrite at Jewish intermarriage. In P, however, Ezra bewails his people's sinfulness in general and pleads for their very survival:

MT   Shall we again disobey thy commandments and intermarry with peoples [that practise] such abominations? Wouldst thou not be so angry with us as to destroy us without remnant or survivor? Lord God of Israel, thou art just, for we have been left as a remnant today; behold we are before thee in our guilt; one cannot stand before thee on its account.

P   We have turned aside and transgressed thy commandments and gone and cleaved to these unclean nations and done according to their deeds. But thou art merciful. Be not wroth

---

[48] This was pointed out by Joosten in MPI 8 (Leiden 1995), pp. 67–8.
[49] Winter, "The Origins of Ben Sira in Syriac", pp. 245–9.
[50] Drijvers "The Peshitta of *Sapientia Salomonis*", p. 18.
[51] Winter considers that the translation of Ecclesiasticus was made by Ebionites and later (towards the end of the fourth century) worked over by an orthodox Christian hostile to Arianism. R.J. Owens, "The Early Syriac Text of Ben Sira in the Demonstrations of Aphrahat", *JSS* 34 (1989), pp. 39–76, argues that this is too specific, but accepts Winter's evidence for a Christian origin.

with us. Forgive our sins before thee ... Leave for us remnants in the world for there is none like Thee, lest we perish. O Lord, God of Israel, thou art just, for thou hast left of us a remnant as today. Lo we stand and confess our sins before thee, for one cannot speak before thee [even] one word concerning this.

The equivalence of disgrace and exile emerges also at Dan. 9:16 –

MT   כי בחטאינו ובעונות אבותינו ירושלם ועמך לחרפה לכל סביבתינו

> for through our sins and our fathers' iniquities Jerusalem and thy people (have become) a reproach for all about us.

P   ܡܛܠ ܕܒܚܛܗܝܢ ܘܒܥܘܠܐ ܕܐܒܗܬܢ ܐܬܒܕܪ ܥܡܟ ܠܟܠ ܐܬܪ

> for through our sins and our fathers' wickedness thy people has been scattered to every place.

A similar change occurs in a passage of P-Daniel translated from the Greek, at Dan. 3:37(Greek)–

LXX/Theod.   καὶ ἐσμὲν ταπεινοὶ ἐν πάσῃ τῇ γῇ σήμερον διὰ τὰς ἁμαρτίας ἡμῶν

> and we are lowly in all the earth today because of our sins

P   ܘܗܐ ܡܒܕܪܝܢ ܚܢܢ ܝܘܡܢܐ ܒܟܠܗ ܐܪܥܐ ܡܛܠ ܚܛܗܝܢ ܘܥܘܠܢ

> and we are scattered today in all the earth because of our transgressions and sins

It is noteworthy that the books which show this awareness of exile – Daniel and Ezra – stand like Chronicles late in the Jewish canonical order.

Another indication of Jewish identity, but without awareness of exile, is P's rendering of Lev. 18:21 and 20:2–5 noted above, forbidding union with a "foreign woman". A Christian translator would have had no need of a prohibition against union with foreign races. For Jews, however, these were the only passages (though the rabbis denied even this) interpretable as a general prohibition of intermarriage.

Identification with the Jews appears also in P's nationalistic stance at Isa. 19:25, where the universalism of the original is overturned:

MT   Blessed be my people Egypt and the work of my hands Assyria and my heritage Israel

P: ܒܪܝܟ ܥܡܝ ܕܒܡܨܪܝܢ, ܘܥܒܕ ܐܝܕܝ ܕܒܐܬܘܪ, ܘܝܪܬܘܬܝ ܐܝܣܪܝܠ

> Blessed be my people which is in Egypt and the work of my hands (which is in) Assyria and my heritage Israel

Thus Egypt and Assyria are no longer peoples, but centres of the contemporary diaspora. The same sense appears in LXX, which may have influenced P here.[52]

Alienation from the Jewish people

Despite these cases of identification with the Jews as a people, we also find passages which instead suggest alienation:

---

[52] Whereas LXX and P thought of the contemporary diaspora, the Targum looks back into history: "Blessed be my people that I brought out of Egypt. Because they sinned before me, I exiled them to Assyria; but as they have repented, they are called my people and my inheritance, Israel."

(a) Isa. 28:13

MT ...והיה להם דבר י׳ צו לצו... קו לקו

P ܘܗܘܬ ܠܗܘܢ ܡܠܬܗ ܕܡܪܝܐ܆ ܬܟܡܬܐ ܥܠ ܬܟܡܬܐ... ܘܬܘܩܒܐ ܥܠ ܬܘܩܒܐ...

the word of the Lord was for them dung upon dung . . . and vomit upon vomit . . .

The preceding verses seem to identify the Hebrew words צו and קו with incomprehensible speech (לעגי שפה), though their exact meaning remains uncertain. P, however, identifies them with צאה and קיא, which occur in v.8. Compare Theodotion: δεισαλία... ἐμετός ("filth . . . vomit").

(b) Isa. 40:.2

MT כי מלאה צבאה כי נרצה עונה

that she has served her term, her penalty is paid

P ܡܛܠ ܕܐܬܡܠܝܬ ܚܝܠܐ ܘܨܒܬ ܒܚܛܝܬܐ

for she was filled with force and delighted in sin

Here the Heb. passive נרצה is replaced by an active, meaning "delight".

(c) Isa. 40:7

MT יבש חציר... אכן חציר העם

P ܝܒܫ ܥܣܒܐ... ܗܟܢܐ ܗܘ ܥܣܒܗ ܕܥܡܐ ܗܢܐ

The grass withers . . .; so is the grass of this people

The Hebrew referred to the mortality of people in general, but P singles out the prophet's own people.

(d) Ezek. 37:12

God's promise to revive the dead is addressed in the Hebrew to "my people" – which phrase P omits.

(e) Ps. 105:43

MT ויוצא עמו בששון ברנה את בחיריו

P ܐܦܩ ܠܥܡܗ ܒܚܕܘܬܐ. ܘܒܬܫܒܘܚܬܐ ܠܓܒ̈ܪܘܗܝ

he brought out his people with joy, and with song his young men

The Hebrew uses the term "elect" of the Jewish people, but the translator avoids this equation, by rendering בחיריו "his elect" by בחוריו "his young men". This contrasts with his eagerness to introduce the term "elect" to indicate his own group, as shown below.

(f) Ps. 106:5

MT   לראות בטובת בחיריך לשמח בשמחת גויך

to see the prosperity of your chosen ones, to rejoice in the joy of your people

P   ܢܫܘܐ ܕܢܚܙܐ܀ ܒܛܒܬܐ ܕܓܒܝܟ: ܘܢܚܕܐ ܒܚܕܘܬܟ

that we may look upon the prosperity of your chosen ones, and rejoice in your joy

Here again the term "elect" is used of the Jews in MT and not in P. In this case, P avoided calling the Jews the elect by simply not mentioning them.

Identification as a sub-community

A number of passages suggest that the translators, rather than identifying with the Jewish people as such, saw themselves as an elect sub-community. In a number of passages in the Psalms, the translator introduces the term 'elect', which seems a self-reference:

(a) 30:5   ܘܗܒܘ ܠܡܪܝܐ ܓܒܘܗܝ,

Sing unto the Lord, O his elect

(b) 31:22   ܒܪܝܟ ܗܘ ܡܪܝܐ ܕܓܒܐ ܠܗ ܓܒܝܐ ܒܡܕܝܢܬܐ ܥܫܝܢܬܐ

Blessed be the Lord, who chose for himself the elect in a mighty city

(c) 32:6   ܡܛܠ ܗܢܐ ܢܨܠܐ ܠܟ ܟܠ ܕܓܒܐ ܐܢܬ ܠܗ ܐܟܙܢܐ ܕܒܙܒܢܐ ܡܩܒܠܐ

Therefore every one who is chosen by thee shall pray to thee at an acceptable time

(d) 50:5   ܐܬܟܢܫܘ ܠܘܬܗ ܓܒܘܗܝ,

Gather unto him, O his elect

In all these passages "elect" corresponds to MT חסיד "pious" – except at 31:22, where MT has הִפְלִיא חַסְדּוֹ but the translator again perceived the element חסיד and so understood the phrase as הִפְלָה חֲסִידָיו "he separated out his pious ones".

(e–f) The preoccupation with election appears in two further passages from Psalms:

Ps. 47:5 (MT)	יבחר לנו את נחלתנו	'he chose our unheritance for us'
Ps. 68:20 (MT)	יעמס לנו	'he carries us'
Both passages (P)	ܐܓܒܝܢ ܝܪܬܘܬܗ	'he chose us as his inheritance'

In both passages, the translator P claims – with no warrant in the Hebrew – to belong to the elect.

The terminology of election of Israel, though found in the Bible, was systematically dropped by the rabbis of the tannaitic period, who feared that sects could utilise it in order each to claim to be the elect *among* Israel. Such claims were indeed made, among others, by the Dead Sea Sect and the early Church. In reaction, T⁰ even recasts the biblical statements that God "chose" Israel, declaring instead that God "was pleased" with them. Only during the third century was election terminology resumed in the synagogue, when the claims of the church had to be answered and not just studiously ignored.[53] If the translator of Psalms was Jewish, his use of the term "elect" – presumably before the third century[54] – would suggest allegiance to a non-rabbinic group.

This new election seems expressed as the formation of a new congregation at Mal. 3:17 –

MT   והיו לי אמר י׳ צבאות ליום אשר אני עשה סגלה

P   ܘܢܗܘܘܢ ܠܝ ... ܠܝܘܡܐ ܕܥܒܕ ܐܢܐ ܥܡܐ ܚܕܬܐ

They [the fearers of God] shall be Mine on the day that I make a congregation

P's interpretation, that God will one day choose a new community, is not adopted by LXX, Tg. or by rabbinic tradition, which instead identify the סגלה as the יום – the day set for judgment. Three verses later it is stated that the sun of righteousness will shine upon those who fear the Lord. According to MT, this sun will have healing in its wings. In P, however, the sun of righteousness will have healing "on its tongue", and so may indicate the group's teacher.

The formation of a new congregation is also implied by P at Isa. 5:7 –

MT   ואיש יהודה נטע שעשועיו

and the men of Judah are the plant of his delight

P   ܘܓܒܪܐ ܕܝܗܘܕܐ ܢܨܒܬܐ ܚܕܬܐ ܘܚܒܝܒܬܐ

and the men from Judah are a new and beloved plant

P's source for the element "new" is evidently LXX (νεόφυτον); but, by introducing the preposition "from", P applies it to a new community.[55]

Two more self-references in Isaiah to a group standing outside the mainstream of Israel belong here:

(a)   10:22

MT   שאר ישוב בו כליון חרוץ שוטף צדקה

a remnant will return of them; destruction is decreed, overflowing with justice

P   ܫܪܟܐ ܢܦܢܘܢ ܡܢܗܘܢ . ܓܝܙ ܡܦܣܩ ܘܓܝܙ ܒܙܕܝܩܘܬܐ

a remnant of them shall return,[56] cutting and lopping off and sweeping away in righteousness

This militant remnant in P is of course alien to the Hebrew.

[53] M.P. Weitzman, "Usage and Avoidance of the Term 'Chosen People'" (Hebrew with English summary), מחקרים בלשון = Language Studies (Jerusalem) 4 (1991), pp. xv–xvi, 101–28.
[54] The question of the date of P is further discussed below.
[55] This rendering was noted by A. van der Kooij, *Die alten Textzeugen des Jesajabuches*, Freiburg 1981, p. 279.   [56] This may alternatively mean: "repent, turn to God".

(b)   59:20

MT   ובא לציון גואל ולשבי פשע ביעקב

    and a redeemer shall come to Zion and to those who turn from iniquity in Jacob

P   ܘܢܐܬܐ ܠܨܗܝܘܢ ܦܪܘܩܐ: ܘܢܦܢܐ ܥܘܠܐ ܡܢ ܝܥܩܘܒ

    and to Zion shall come a redeemer, and those who turn iniquity away from Jacob

This too may be a self-reference, in which the community sees itself working with the redeemer to remove iniquity from Jacob.[57]

    Finally, P again insists on a sub-community at Dan. 12:1. There in the Hebrew, Daniel is promised:

ימלט עמך כל הנמצא כתוב בספר

The Hebrew suggests, or at least admits the possibility, that the two subjects – 'your people' and 'all found written in the book' – stand in apposition, or in other words that all Israel are written in the book. However, P takes care to state explicitly that *only* those who are inscribed in the book will be saved:

ܢܫܬܘܙܒ ܡܢ ܒܢܝ ܥܡܟ ܟܠ ܕܢܫܬܟܚ ܕܟܬܝܒ ܒܣܦܪܐ

there will be saved, of the children of your people, any who is found to be inscribed in the book

One may contrast the rabbis' insistence that "all Israel have a portion in the world to come" (Mishnah Sanhedrin 10:1). By contrast, the translators in the passages considered above seem an introspective sub-community, who did not expect salvation for their people at large.

High regard for the nations

The obverse of the negative attitude towards the Jews as a people is a high regard for the nations. This is attested in various passages, e.g.

Isa. 52:15

MT   כן יזה גוים רבים

P   ܗܘ ܡܕܟܐ ܠܥܡܡܐ ܣܓܝܐܐ

    This one [i.e. the Servant] cleanses many nations

Hebrew יזה was taken as "sprinkle" and understood in a ritual sense, in disagreement with both LXX and Tg.

---

[57] The same verse is quoted in Romans 11:26, but differently interpreted: the deliverer himself would remove wickedness from Jacob.

Ps. 35:18

MT   בעם עצום אהללך

in a great nation I shall praise you

P   ܘܒܥܡܐ ܣܓܝܐܐ ܐܘܪܒ ܠܝ

among many nations I shall sing to Thee

Ps. 65:6

MT   אלהי ישענו מבטח כל קצוי ארץ וים רחקים

P   ܐܠܗܐ ܦܪܘܩܢ. ܣܒܪܐ ܕܟܠܗܘܢ ܣܘܦܝܗ ܕܐܪܥܐ ܘܕܥܡܡܐ ܪܚܝܩܐ

God our saviour, hope of all the ends of the earth and of distant nations

Thus י‍ם "sea" was understood as עם "people", again changed to plural.

Ps. 107:32

MT   וירממוהו בקהל עם

P   ܫܒܚܘܗܝ ܒܟܢܫܐ ܕܥܡܡܐ،

Praise Him in the assembly of the nations

This positive attitude would also explain P's treatment of Isaac's promise to Esau at Gen. 27:40 –

MT   והיה כאשר תריד ופרקת עלו מעל צוארך

The rare word for what Esau would do in order to free himself from Jacob's yoke is usually understood as "grow restive", but evidently puzzled ancient interpreters. T[J] renders: "if you beguile them and bring them low so that they do not observe the commandments . . .". T[O[F]] express the same idea more concisely by changing the subject: "when they (the Jews) transgress the Torah".[58] P, by contrast, renders ܬܬܘܒ "you will repent", and is alone in ascribing this spiritual potential to Esau.

A subtle shift by P in relation to Abraham confirms this regard for the nations, as pointed out by van der Kooij, at Gen. 17:4–5:

MT   אב המון גוים

P   ܐܒܐ ܠܣܘܓܐܐ ܕܥܡܡܐ

MT calls Abraham the father *of* a multitude of nations, i.e. a physical ancestor of the Jews and various other nations. P, however, makes him a father *unto* a multitude of nations, i.e. a spiritual inspiration whom all nations can claim.[59]

A further connection between Abraham and the nations might be found at Gen. 17:27, though the sense is not certain. According to MT, the only men circumcised together with Abraham were members of his own household, and these included some

---

[58] For further variety compare תאדר "gain glory" in the Samaritan text, and καθέλῃς "bring down" in LXX (= תֹרִיד)...

[59] A. van der Kooij, *Abraham, vader van/voor een menigte volkeren*, Inaugural Lecture, Leiden 1990, pp. 18–22.

slaves bought from foreigners. However, P seems to state[60] that foreigners even outside Abraham's household underwent this first circumcision:

MT   וכל אנשי ביתו יליד בית ומקנת כסף מאת בן נכר נמלו אתו

P   ܘܟܠܗܘܢ ܐܢܫ̈ܝ ܒܝܬܗ ܘܕܙܒܝܢ̈ܝ ܟܣܦܐ ܡܢ ܒܪ ܢܘܟܖ̈ܝܐ ܓܙܪ ܥܡܗ

and all the men of his house, and those bought by his money, *and also* some children of foreigners, he circumcised with him[61]

When we reach P on Wisdom of Solomon, the preference for the nations is very clear. The promise of the original Greek (3:8) that the righteous "shall judge nations and have dominion over peoples" becomes in P: "the nations will exult and the peoples will rejoice." As Drijvers observes, the nations are now the true righteous, and this implies that the godless whom the book proceeds to contrast are the Jews.[62]

Another aspect of P's universalism is a high regard for the proselyte, denoted in many books as ܐܢܫ ܕܡܬܦܢܐ ܠܘܬܝ "he that turns to Me". As noted in chapter 4, the Greek προσήλυτος means "one who has come unto", but does not state the object of the preposition. LXX (at Lev. 19:33 and Num. 9:14) takes the object of πρός as Israel (προσελεύσονται σοι). Josephus, in describing a female convert as νομίμοις προσεληλυθυῖαν τοῖς Ἰουδαϊκοῖς (*AJ* 18.82), thinks rather of the laws. Philo's statement that the proselyte enters καινῇ καὶ φιλοθέῳ πολιτείᾳ combines both. According to P, however, the proselyte turns to God himself.

One biblical antecedent for the proselyte's title is Isa. 45:22: "turn unto Me (פנו אלי) and be saved, all ye [unto] the ends of the earth." The Targum there renders אתפנו למימרי, which P's phrase for 'proselyte' seems to echo, even though P in that passage renders quite differently as ܐܬܦܢܘ.[63] The same passage is also echoed in the plea in the 'Alenu prayer להפנות אליך כל רשעי ארץ.[64] Another biblical anctecedent is Ruth 2:12, where Ruth is said to have come to take refuge under God's wings. This direct link of the proselyte with God himself is affirmed centuries later in Maimonides' message to the proselyte Obadiah:

for since you have entered beneath the wings of the divine presence and attached yourself to him, there is no difference between us and you . . . Further, do not belittle your lineage: if we trace our descent to Abraham, Isaac and Jacob, your connection is with Him by Whose word the universe came into being.[65]

Other theological concerns

A few other changes in P that seem theologically motivated may be noted here. First, special regard for angels appears in P-Daniel. The 'man' who speaks to Daniel is said to be clothed not in linen (MT בדים) but in "glory" (10:5; 12:6,7); these are early

---

[60] Unlike any of the rabbinic sources claimed by Maori (*The Peshitta Version of the Pentateuch*, p. 113) to show that P is here influenced by Jewish traditional exegesis.

[61] P could instead mean that Abraham circumcised those bought with his money *even* from children of foreigners; but then the added particle ܘܐܦ would serve little purpose.

[62] H.J.W. Drijvers, "The Peshitta of *Sapientia Salomonis*", pp. 15–30: see p. 18.

[63] This seems yet another case where the Targum on a particular phrase was known independently of P to the Syriac-speaking community.   [64] S. Baer, *Seder Avodat Yisra'el*, Rödelheim 1868, p. 132.

[65] A. Freimann (ed.), *Moses ben Maimon – Responsa*, Jerusalem 1934, no.42 (p. 41).

examples of the common figure of the robe of glory in Syriac literature.[66] This man is girt also in "glory of praise" (MT אופז כתם – 10:5), and "his appearance was different with none like him" (MT וגויתו כתרשיש).

Second, the משכילים ("those who understand") in Daniel 11–12, who will be radiant at the eschaton (Dan. 12:3), undergo changes in the translation. They are wholly replaced by "the righteous" at Dan. 11:33 and by the "doers of good deeds" (ܚܕ̈ܐ, ܠܬ̈ܐ) at 12:10. At Dan. 12:3, P combines the "doers of good deeds" with a faithful rendering: ܚܕ̈ܐ, ܠܬ̈ܐ ܘܡܣܟܠ̈ܐ. These adjustments to the term משכילים may be anti-gnostic. A protest against gnosticism may also be intended in the phrase cited by P on 1 Chr. 29:19 from the Qaddish prayer: "that your great name may be sanctified and praised in the world that you created . . ."

Finally, the elevation of David in the Hebrew of Chronicles is carried even further in P, which denies that David killed any Ammonites (1 Chr. 20:3) and comments that "David did right before the Lord, departing not from all that he commanded him, all the days of his life" (1 Chr. 29:30).[67] The reference introduced at 1 Chr. 23:5 to David's works of charity likewise commends him.

Combination of evidence from different books

The evidence in the sections above has been drawn from various biblical books. In particular, much is derived from P-Chronicles. To what extent can we combine this evidence and apply it to P as a whole?

In chapter 4 a network of links was pointed out between different books, and this network was found to include Chronicles. A number of unusual features link Chronicles with the other books: the understanding of שטרים as ܣܦܪ̈ܐ 'scribes' and of נדב as ܦܪܫ 'separate', the mountain provenances attributed to David's heroes, the replacement of Aram by Edom, the use of three particular words for sacred pots, and of course the use of ܢܡܘܣܐ for divine law and the translation of the Tetragrammaton. All these were peculiar to the community which produced the translation, and in particular are alien to the Targums transmitted by rabbinic Judaism. Similarly alien to those Targums are certain religious values common to P in Chronicles and in the other books, such as the importance of prayer at the expense of sacrifice, or disdain for wealth (cf. 2 Chr. 26:16). The references to Corinthian bronze, which fall both within and outside Chronicles, suggest a further link.[68] Altogether, therefore, there is ample justification for drawing an overall picture of the religious outlook of the translators, on the basis of the evidence from the various books.

Peshitta and Targum

Before reaching any conclusion about the community background of P, we have to consider its place in relation to the Targums preserved by rabbinic Judaism. As noted

---

[66] S.P. Brock, "Clothing metaphors as a means of theological expression in Syriac tradition", in M. Schmidt (ed.), *Typus, Symbol, Allegorie bei den östlichen Vätern und ihren Parallelen im Mittelalter*, Regensburg 1982, pp. 11–38: 15.

[67] P.B. Dirksen, "Some Aspects of the Translation Technique in Peshitta Chronicles", in MPI 8 (Leiden 1995), pp. 17–23.   [68] 1 Kgs. 7:45; Ezra. 8:27; 1 Chr. 29:7.

above, there are verbal parallels between P and the Targums which imply common traditions relating both to the meaning of the Hebrew and to the proper choice of words in Aramaic to render particular words or phrases. On the other hand, P often translates independently of any known Targum, and even covers books for which no Targum exists. Moreover, whereas P seems designed to replace the Hebrew, the Targums assume continuing access thereto.

Biblical translation into Aramaic not an exclusively rabbinic institution

The Targums owe their survival today to rabbinic Judaism. This need not mean, however, that they were exclusively – or even primarily – a rabbinic institution. Indeed, of all Jewish groups, the rabbis least needed a translation. The attentive exegesis of the rabbis had to be applied to the original text. Rarely do they refer to any Targum. According to R.Judah (cited in TB Qid. 49a), translation was innately unsatisfactory:

המתרגם פסוק כצורתו הרי זה בדאי והמוסיף עליו הרי זה מחרף ומגדף

Whoever translates literally deceives; whoever expands is a blasphemer.

For the rabbis, the specific purpose of the Targum was to make the public lections accessible to those who could not understand Hebrew. As Rashi later put it, "the purpose of the Targum is only to inform women and the ignorant, who do not understand Hebrew" (on TB Meg. 21b). One rabbi, it is true, enjoins study of the weekly lection in advance, twice in Hebrew and once in an Aramaic Targum (TB Ber.8a). The primary consideration was not, however, the intrinsic value of the Targum, but the need for proper respect and attention throughout the public reading, as shown by the companion saying, against leaving the synagogue during the reading.

Beyond this liturgical necessity, the Targums were of little interest to the rabbis. In rabbinic tradition, the first Targum was supplied by an outsider, the proselyte Onkelos. The Targum on the Prophets was not altogether welcomed by the rabbis, possibly because it went beyond purely liturgical needs, by covering the whole text rather than the extracts chosen for public reading.[69] When Jonathan ben Uzziel made it, the earth trembled, and God cried: "Who reveals My secrets to the sons of man?" (TB Meg. 3a).

It would not be surprising, therefore, if the first impetus to translate the Bible into Aramaic came from non-rabbinic groups. Occasional translations of which the rabbis disapproved were indeed preserved among the Targums. Well-known instances are found in T^J – and shared by P – at Lev. 18:21 and Lev. 20 (discussed above). Again at Lev. 22:28, the commandment not to sacrifice a new-born animal until the eighth day is given an introduction condemned by the rabbis: "Just as our father is merciful in heaven, be ye merciful on earth" (cf. TJ Ber. 5:3). Likewise, the Targum at Isa. 12:3 promises "new doctrine from the elect of righteousness", despite rabbinic distaste for the term 'elect'.[70] An oft-quoted Targum on Ruth 1:17 refers, against rabbinic law (Mishnah Sanh. 7:1), to capital punishment by hanging (צליבת קיסא).

---

[69] R. Beckwith, *The Old Testament Canon of the New Testament Church*, London 1985, p. 140.
[70] A close parallel to the term "elect of righteousness" is instead found in Mandaic, in a passage from the Right Ginza cited by E.S. Drower and R. Macuch, *A Mandaic Dictionary*, Oxford 1963, p. 54: *nibihrun bhiria zidqa* "let the proven (or elect) of the Righteousness prove themselves".

Thus the institution of Targum was not confined to rabbinic Judaism. This accounts for the survival, in the Syriac church, of renderings from the Targums not paralleled in P, and of elements derived from such renderings, as noted in chapter 3.

The inclusion of the Writings (Hagiographa) in P

In fact the inclusion of the Writings in P suggests an origin outside rather than within rabbinic Judaism. The rabbis' attitude to translation of the Writings into Aramaic was predominantly negative. Although Mishnah Shab. 16:1 rules that such translations may be saved from fire on the sabbath, the parallel Tosefta and the Talmudic discussion record that some rabbis forbade it. Gamliel I forbade written translation of the Writings into any language other than Greek (Mishnah Meg. 1:8).[71] Thus, when a written translation on Job was brought before him, Gamliel I had it buried. It was at the table of "Johanan (the son of) the excommunicate (נזוף)" that his grandson Gamliel II found another Aramaic version of Job, which he likewise destroyed (TB Shab. 115a). These incidents, together with the discovery of an Aramaic version of Job at Qumran, show that Targums on the Writings existed but were confined to non-rabbinic Jewish circles.

Rabbinic Judaism in fact for centuries lacked Aramaic versions to nearly every book of the Writings. Of course such versions can now be found in printed editions of rabbinic Bibles and so are familiar to scholarship today; but, as will be argued below, they were not supplied until the Middle Ages. The only exceptional book is Esther, for which a Targum is quoted at Soferim 13:6. This absence of Aramaic versions of the Writings has left its mark in Jewish liturgy. Thus, the Jewish Kedushah prayer includes Isa. 6:3, Ezek. 3:12 and Ps. 146:10. Its substitute the Kedushah de-Sedra, however, in which each verse is given together with Aramaic translation, replaces the verse from Psalms by Exod. 15:18, and so strangely cites the Prophets before the Torah. We may deduce that there was no Targum of the Writings, or at least none accepted by the rabbis or their Pharisaic forebears, when the Kedushah de-Sedra was composed.[72] Abudarham actually commented, as late as the fourteenth century: "There is no Targum of the Writings".[73]

Such Targums had, however, been gaining currency. The first known reference appears in the responsum by Hai Gaon (939–1038 CE) in Babylonia. As discussed in chapter 3 above there is no indication that Hai himself knew directly a Targum on any book of the Writings except Esther.[74] In France, a century later, Rashi still knew of no Targum to the Writings, for he states explicitly (on TB Meg. 21b) that none exists. His biblical commentaries cite no such Targum (except on Esther), though he sometimes coincides with these Targums in his interpretation.[75] However, these Targums must have reached France soon afterwards, for the Tosaphists (again on TB Meg. 21b)

---

[71] The rabbinic sources use the term תרגום, which however there connotes translation alone, rather than the specific features – looseness, expansive tendency – now associated with the term Targum.

[72] Part of this prayer is cited in 2 Macc. 1:3–5 and is therefore goes back at least to 143 BCE. See D. Flusser, "Sanktus und Gloria", in *Festschr. Otto Michel*, Leiden 1963, p. 151.

[73] S.A. Wertheimer (ed.), *Abudarham's Commentary on the Liturgy* (in Hebrew), Jerusalem 1953, p. 122.

[74] Targum Sheni (apparently) on Esther 1:3,10 is cited in his comment on Deut. 3:4.

[75] E.g. in taking דמו (Ps. 35:15) as "draw blood" or יקחך (Job 15:12) as "teach thee". For a different view, see P. Churgin, *The Targum to Hagiographa* (in Hebrew), New York 1945.

contradict Rashi's statement. Rashi's own grandson Rashbam also cites Targums to the Writings several times; for example, on Exod. 15:2 he cites the Targum to Job 4:15.

The rabbis of the era of the Mishnah and Talmud, by contrast, disapproved of translations of the Writings on principle. As TB Meg. 3a puts it, Jonathan promised not to proceed from the Prophets to translate the Writings because these include prophecies of the end-time (קץ). These misgivings apparently arose from fear that a resourceful translator could purvey sectarian ideas under the very guise of Scripture. The freedom which translators allowed themselves may be gauged from that even earlier "Aramaic book" quoted in the appendix to Job in LXX. This identifies Job with Jobab (Gen. 36:33), but – more importantly – begins by declaring that he will be resurrected.[76]

In the case of the Pentateuch and Prophets, which were read publicly, fears of sectarian infiltration had to be balanced against the congregation's need to understand the text. The rabbis exercised control by marking out Onkelos on the Torah and Jonathan on the Prophets as authorised translations. These were regarded as made "from the mouth of" prophets or eminent rabbis (TB Meg. 3a), and were cited by the formula מתרגמינן ("we translate").

The Writings, by contrast, were not read publicly (apart from Esther), and here the rabbis had no need for Targums of these books. The fact that for some books (Daniel and Ezra-Nehemiah) no Targum was ever produced may be ascribed to their disapproval of translation. The usual explanation – viz that these books contain Aramaic portions – is not compelling, since the Hebrew portions bristle with obscurities that demand explanation. Only in the geonic period did individual scholars within rabbinic Judaism attempt to complete the Aramaic Bible.

To summarise, the parallels between P and the Targums may favour the view that P is of Jewish origin, but not necessarily of rabbinic origin. Moreover, the inclusion in P of the Writings, as well as P's many divergences from all known Targums, tip the balance in favour of non-rabbinic origin.

The case for origin within rabbinic Judaism

If only for the sake of completeness, we must now consider the remaining evidence for the two rival theories of P's origin: either in rabbinic Judaism, or in Christianity.

The evidence for a specifically rabbinic origin consists of the parallels with the Targums and (often overlapping with these) with rabbinic literature. Before inferring that P originated within rabbinic Judaism, however, we must ask three questions:

(a)   Are parallels with rabbinic sources characteristic of P?
(b)   Although the parallels survive today in rabbinic sources, are they of specifically rabbinic origin?
(c)   What was the provenance of the rabbinic parallels so far as P's translators were concerned?

---

[76] The reference to the resurrection in LXX runs: γέγραπται δὲ αὐτὸν πάλιν ἀναστήσεσθαι μεθ᾽ ὧν ὁ κύριος ἀνίστησιν. Οὗτος ἑρμηνεύεται ἐκ τῆς Συριακῆς βίβλου. This indebtedness to a "Syrian book" is no less likely to apply to Job's resurrection than to the following section, which identifies him with Jobab. The syntax is improved by emending οὗτος to οὕτως.

Are parallels with rabbinic sources characteristic of P?

Even in the Torah, parallels with rabbinic sources are not numerous in relation to the length of the text.[77] In the other biblical books, such parallels are rare. Moreover, we have already noted many passages which puzzled the translator but could have been elucidated through rabbinic exegesis, and many cases where P understands the text in a manner that contradicts rabbinic halachah. The rabbis would also have protested at the frequent recourse to LXX, which led to the addition of lines and even lengthy passages not found in MT.

P also differs fundamentally from the rabbis in its treatment of seeming anomalies or inconsistencies in the biblical text. Thus Gen. 2:4 refers first to "heaven and earth" but then to "earth and heaven"; and at Exod. 24:7 the Israelites promise to "do and hear" all the commandments, against the logical order. The rabbis accounted for these anomalies thoughtfully. Thus Gen. 2:4 was interpreted to mean that heaven and earth were created simultaneously (TB Hag. 12a), and Exod. 24:7 to mean that the Israelites accepted the Torah so eagerly that they promised to perform it before they even knew its content (TB Shab. 88a). Targums familiar with rabbinic exegesis but lacking space to set out such interpretations at least preserve the anomalies. P, however, simply corrects them away: thus he imposes "heaven and earth", "hear and do", as if the biblical text were simply mistaken. This radical attitude, of which many more examples were shown in chapter 2, separates P cleanly from rabbinic exegesis.

In its general tolerance of anthropomorphisms, P differs from the Targums and hence presumably from rabbinic norms. On one occasion, however, P would have been condemned by the rabbis for over-sensitivity, namely in relation to Boaz's greeting at Ruth 2:4 –

MT   עמכם י׳

P   ܫܠܡܐ ܥܡܟܘܢ

    may peace be with you

At Mishnah Ber.9:5 the rabbis commend the use of this greeting, even though it included the Tetragrammaton. By contrast, the sectaries at Qumran sometimes substituted אל for the Tetragrammaton in biblical citations (e.g. 1QS 2:16, CD 20:19); and just such a substitution appears in P.[78]

If there were any example of a passage known to be controversial in which P followed an interpretation which distinguished the rabbis from any other Jewish movement, that would be evidence of a specifically rabbinic character. There seems, however, to be no convincing example. In particular, P seems aware that controversy surrounds the phrase ממחרת השבת in Lev. 23, which prescribes the date of the Omer offering and the commencement of the seven weeks' counting until Pentecost.[79] He thus does not render it literally. On the other hand, he does not clarify his own position:

(v.11)   ܡܢ ܒܬܪ ܝܘܡܐ ܐܚܪܢܐ – probably conflated from two expressions for "on the morrow", namely ܝܘܡܐ ܐܚܪܢܐ and ܒܬܪ ܝܘܡܐ.[80]

(v.15)   ܡܢ ܒܬܪ ܝܘܡܐ – "on the morrow"

(v.16)   ܒܬܪ ܫܒܘܥܐ [ܫܒܝܥܝܐ] – "after the (seventh) week"

---

[77] Maori claimed fewer than 200, some of which were queried above.

[78] Though the reapers' reply is translated faithfully ("may the Lord bless thee").

[79] The rabbis took it as the morrow of the first day of Passover, which was a day of rest, while the Sadducees and others took it as the morrow of the Sabbath during Passover week.

[80] So Maori, *The Peshitta Version of the Pentateuch*, p. 178.

In none of these verses does P specify the date of which the morrow is meant. The preceding context indeed mentions the first day of Passover (vv.6,7), but also the whole Passover week (vv.6,8a) and (most recently) its seventh day (v.8b); and P shows no clear choice. LXX leaves his own interpretation in v.11 far clearer: τῇ ἐπαύριον τῆς πρώτης "on the morrow of the first day".[81] It may be added that even if P had clearly sided with the rabbis, as does LXX in v.11, this would show only that he knew the dominant interpretation, and not necessarily that he – or for that matter the translator of LXX – was a committed follower of rabbinic Judaism.

The origin of the parallels with rabbinic sources

Some of the exegetical traditions which P shares with rabbinic sources can be shown to pre-date the emergence of rabbinic Judaism. Two are known from Jubilees, a non-rabbinic source going back at least to the second century BCE. Of these, one is at Gen. 22:12 –

MT   ידעתי (with God as subject)

P   ܐܘܕܥܬ "I have made known"[82]

It is true that this understanding is found in Gen.Rabba 56. : "I have made it known to all that you love me". However, it is as old as Jubilees 18:16: "and I have shown to all that you are faithful to me in all that I have said to you". The motive was, of course, to preserve divine omniscience.

    The other case relates to Lev. 18:21 and 20:2–4. Here the Hebrew forbids the passing of one's seed to Moloch, while P finds a condemnation of procreation with foreign women. The same intepretation was upheld by R.Ishmael early in the second century CE (TJ Meg. 4:4). It had lost favour, however, by the end of that century and is condemned in the Mishnah (Meg. 4:4). It nevertheless survived in T^J (and the margin of T^N). The biblical texts at Lev. 18:21 follow, with the rabbinic texts:

MT   ומזרעך לא תתן להעביר למלך

T^J ומן זרעך לא תתן בתשמישתא לציד בת עממין למעברא לפולחנא אוחרא

Meg 4:4   ומזרעך לא תתן לאעברא בארמיותא

TJ Meg 4:10   זה שהוא נושא ארמית ומעמיד ממנה בנים מעמיד אויבים למקום

P   ܗܡ ܘܙܪܥ ܠܐ ܐܝܬ ܘܐܘܟ ܐܝܟ ܠܗܒܠܐ ܘܣܘ ܐܘܣܒ

A kindred interpretation already appears in Jubilees 30:10, namely that a man who gives his daughter in marriage to a gentile has "given of his seed to Moloch". The application of this verse to foreign marriage thus predates the rise of rabbinic Judaism. Its survival in T^J tends to confirm that Targum was not a specifically rabbinic institution, so that non-rabbinic elements may crop up even in the targums preserved by the Jews.[83]

    Where an exegetical tradition common to P and rabbinic sources appears also in LXX, we may again posit pre-rabbinic origin. Thus P's understanding of קשיטה (Gen.

---

[81] Though LXX in v.15 is instead literal: ἀπὸ τῆς ἐπαύριον τῶν σαββάτων.

[82] The form was originally intended in the first person, even though a vocalisation according to the second person (*awda't*) has become traditional; cf. S.P. Brock, "Genesis 22 in Syriac Tradition", in P. Casetti et al., *Mélanges Dominique Barthélemy*, Göttingen 1981, pp. 1–30:3.

[83] G. Vermes, "Leviticus 18:21 in Ancient Bible Exegesis" in E. Fleischer and J.J. Petuchowski (eds.), *Studies in Aggadah, Targum and Jewish Liturgy in Memory of Joseph Heinemann*, Jerusalem 1981, pp. 108–24.

33:19) as "sheep" is paralleled not only in Gen.R. 79.7 but also in LXX (ἀμνῶν).[84] The suggestion that exegetical traditions shared with rabbinic sources were in fact pre-rabbinic would not have offended the rabbis themselves, who claimed that their interpretations were not invented but had long been the common property of all Israel.

Whether any of the translational traditions which P shares with the Targums were likewise pre-rabbinic cannot be proved, for lack of evidence. In itself, however, this is a reasonable possibility, since biblical translation into Aramaic was certainly not an exclusively rabbinic activity, as the Qumran evidence shows. All in all, the parallels with rabbinic sources do not prove that the translators were indebted to rabbinic Judaism specifically.

Separate from the question of the origin of the material common to P and rabbinic sources is the question of whence P obtained that material. As argued below, the likeliest date for the making of P is the latter part of the second century CE. By that time, rabbinic Judaism had become dominant. However, not all other varieties of Judaism had yet died out. It was argued in chapter 3 that a fund of biblical scholarship, including exegetical and translational traditions of individual passages, had long been in wide circulation. That fund would have remained accessible to almost all Jewish movements still surviving. Indeed, as pointed out above, it was not beyond reach even in the Syriac-speaking church of Ephrem's day. Thus the provenance of the traditions adopted by P – like their origin – is not necessarily rabbinic. Even if it were, that would only prove contact with rabbinic Judaism, rather than rabbinic origin.

The case for origin within Christianity

It has long been pointed out – notably by Bloch[85] – that some passages in P could be read as specific references to Christ. None, however, is beyond dispute:

(a) Isa. 7:14

P   ܗܐ ܒܬܘܠܬܐ ܒܛܢܐ ܘܝܠܕܐ ܒܪܐ

     Behold a virgin shall conceive and bear a son

The rendering 'virgin' is of course too specific in relation to MT עלמה, but it coincides with LXX παρθένος, and may merely reflect the influence of that version.

(b) Isa. 15:9–16:1

MT ולשארית אדמה: שלחו כר משל ארץ

P   ܠܒ ܫܐܪܐ ܕܐܪܥܐ: ܫܕܪ[ܘ] ܠܒܪ ܫܠܝܛܐ ܕܐܪܥܐ

     and to the rest of the earth, send the son of the ruler of the earth

Messianic interpretation of this passage in one way or another was widespread, as attested both by Targ. ("they shall bring tribute to the King Messiah") and by Vulg.

---

[84] See Maori, *The Peshitta Version of the Pentateuch*, p. 123, for further references.
[85] J. Bloch, "The Authorship of the Peshitta", *AJSL* 35 (1918/19), pp. 215–22.

(emitte [domine] agnum dominatorem terrae). P has replaced בר by בר 'son', which here looks like a Christian touch. Instead, however, it may be a deliberate misreading in order to make some sense of a very difficult text.

(c)   Isa. 25:6

MT   משתה שמנים משתה שמרים שמנים ממחים שמרים מזקקים

P   ܪܐܬܐ ܘܪܬܐ ܢܒܝܠ ܐܝܟ ܘܐܬܐ ܘܐܬܐ ܢܬܘܣ ܘܐܬܐ ܘܚܬܐ

    a rich feast, a feast set aside and rich (or: heavenly) of our heavenly and mighty redeemer

P has rendered שמנים ממחים by two Syriac words of similar sound: ܚܣܝܢ ܫܡܝܢ "our heavenly redeemer". The redeemer is taken by van der Kooij to be Christ.[86] Note, however, that elsewhere this title may indicate God (Isa. 60:16 [9a1], Wis. 16:7). In any case, the use of similar-sounding Syriac words is a known technique in difficult Hebrew texts of this sort.

(d)   Isa. 25:7

MT   ובלע... והמסכה הנסוכה על כל הגוים

P   ܘܢܒܠܥ...ܘܢܟܣܬܐ ܘܕܒܝܚܬܐ ܕܥܠ ܐܦܝ ܟܠܗܘܢ ܥܡ̈ܡܐ

    and the sacrifice slaughtered for all the peoples . . . shall be swallowed

The Hebrew forms המסכה הנסוכה "web woven" are interpreted through derivatives of the similar-sounding Syriac root ܢܟܣ "slaughter, sacrifice". This passage too is considered Christian by van der Kooij (p. 276). Following that line one might take the "swallowing" of this sacrifice to refer to the Eucharist. Once again, however, the translator may simply have been applying his usual techniques to these rare words, one by one.

(e)   Isa. 53:8

MT   מפשע עמי נגע למו

    through the sin of my people, a stroke to them

P   ܘܡܢ ܥܘܠܐ ܕܥܡܝ ܩܪܒ ܠܗ

    and some of the wicked ones of my people touched him

P's differences from MT in several grammatical points might have been intended to fit the passion narrative. On the other hand, however, the translator might simply have been striving once more to obtain good sense.[87]

---

[86]   Van der Kooij *Die alten Textzeugen des Jesajabuches*, p. 274.
[87]   On the background of Peshitta Isaiah see now A. Gelston "Was the Peshitta of Isaiah of Christian Origin?" in C.C. Broyles and C.A. Evans (eds.) *Writing and Reading the Scroll of Isaiah* [= SVT 70], vol. 2, Leiden 1997, pp. 563–82.

(f)   Zech. 12:10

MT   והביטו אלי את אשר דקרו

and they shall look to me, the one that they pierced

P   ܘܢܚܘܪܘܢ ܠܘܬܝ܂ ܒܗ̇ܘ ܕܕܩܪܘ

and they shall look to me through him that they pierced

The verse is applied at John 19:37 to Jesus' death: "they shall look upon the one that they pierced". P too seems Christian, though the nuance differs, namely that mankind will look to God ("me") *through* a pierced one. Yet a Christian reference is by no means certain. The translator may have changed the preposition, as often elsewhere, simply to make sense of the puzzling Hebrew text.[88]

(g)   Ps. 2:12

MT   נשקו בר

P   ܢܫܩܘ ܒܪܐ "kiss the son"

(h)   Ps. 110:3

MT   לך טל ילדתיך

P   ܠܟ ܛܠܝܐ ܝܠܕܬܟ "thee O child I have begotten".

In both passages, a Hebrew word difficult in itself or in context is replaced by a Syriac word of similar sound (ܒܪܐ and ܛܠܝܐ respectively). Both passages in P could be read as references to Christ. The possibility remains, however, that they are word-by-word renderings forced on the translator in difficult passages and not necessarily reflecting his conscious beliefs.

(i)   Dan. 9:24

MT   ולמשח קדש קדשים

P   ܘܠܡܫܝܚܐ ܩܕܘܫ ܩܘܕ̈ܫܝܢ

and for the Messiah, holy of holies

Thus P vocalises וְלַמָשֵׁחַ rather than וְלִמְשֹׁחַ "to anoint" (so MT). Wyngarden observes that the holiness of the Messiah seems a Christian idea.[89] However, the reason that P thought of the Messiah may have simply have been the mention of משיח in v.26.

(j)   Dan. 9:26

MT   יכרת משיח "the anointed one will be cut off"

P   ܢܬܩܛܠ ܡܫܝܚܐ "the Messiah will be slain"

P goes on, like the Hebrew, to say that that the holy city would be destroyed with (=by?) "the king that cometh . . . its end will be in destruction . . . he will annul the sacrifices . . .

---

[88] A not dissimilar intepretation occurs in TB Sukk. 52a, where this verse is taken as referring to the Messiah "son of Joseph" who would be slain.

[89] M.J. Wyngarden, *The Syriac Version of the Book of Daniel*, Leipzig 1923, p. 30.

it will remain in desolation". According to Aphrahat, this verse refers to the slaying of Christ and the subsequent destruction of the second Temple.[90] Wyngarden too identifies P's slain Messiah with Christ. However, P is simply a literal translation, or nearly so, of the Hebrew, and need be no more Christian than Aquila's ἐξολοθρευθήσεται ἠλειμμένος.[91]

As well as references to Christ, an echo of the New Testament text has been detected in P at Hos. 13:14 –

MT   אהי דבריך מות

P   ܐܝܟܐ ܗܝ ܕܝܢܟܝ ܘܢܨܚܢܟܝ ܡܘܬܐ

         Where then is your justification/victory, O death?

cf. LXX   ποῦ ἡ δίκη σου, θάνατε; "Where is your justification, O death?"

cf. 1 Cor. 15:55   ποῦ σου, θάνατε, ὁ νῖκος; "Where, O death, is thy victory?"

That P was following 1 Corinthians rather than LXX is not, however, a safe inference. Given the range of meaning of ܢܨܚܢܐ, P could be understood to agree with either. Indeed, that range of meaning may explain how an Aramaic speaker like Paul transmuted δίκη into νῖκος.

All the above passages are compatible with a Christian context, but none is unequivocally Christian. There is no explicitly Christian reference in P to compare with, say, Jerome's introduction of "Jesus" to render ישעה "salvation" in his *Psalterium iuxta Hebraeos*,[92] or to the addition of ἀπὸ ξύλου in Justin Martyr's text of Ps. 96:10.

In all the above passages, the original was difficult, and P adheres closely to the Hebrew or, at Isa. 7:14 and Hos. 13:14, to the Greek. Even at Dan. 9:26 "slay" is an obvious explanation of "cut off". In any of these passages, therefore, one could suppose that a Jewish translator, unable to fathom the sense of the original, conveyed what he could of the form, word by word. The resulting overall sense might not have been his primary concern, in these unusually difficult passages. Hence these cases, even cumulatively, fall short of demonstrating Christian origin.

We may leave aside the Christian reference claimed at Isa. 53:2, where P makes the Jews confess: "we deceived him" [ܐܛܥܝܢܗ]. This is in fact an easy corruption of ܪܓܝܢܗ, "(that) we desire him", which would have been a literal translation of the Hebrew.

The use of the loan-word ܕܝܬܩܐ (rather than the native ܩܝܡܐ) for "covenant", which appears regularly in Joshua and Chronicles, has also been ascribed to New Testament influence.[93] It is sufficiently explained, however, by the general influence upon P of the vocabulary of LXX. Even the usage of ܕܝܬܩܐ in the reference to a new covenant at Jer. 31:30 [31] is no proof of Christian origin; P is a straightforward translation of the Hebrew. It is likewise wrong to detect Christian influence in P's faithful rendering of Isa. 9:5, no matter how significant that verse became for Christianity;

---

[90] Aphrahat's demonstrations, in I. Parisot et al. (eds.), *Patrologia Syriaca* I. 1–2 (Paris 1894–1907), vol. 1, col. 885.

[91] On the two passages from Daniel, see R.A. Taylor, *The Peshiṭta of Daniel*, Leiden 1994 [= MPI 7], pp. 9–11, 244. Taylor too regards neither passage as convincing evidence of Christian origin.

[92] There the name Jesus is introduced where the Hebrew has nouns ישע or ישועה, at Ps. 51:14, 79:9, 85:5, 95:1, 149:4. On Hos. 13:14 see also Gelston, *Twelve Prophets*, pp. 154–5.

[93] J.C. De Moor and F. Sepmeijer, "The Peshiṭta and the Targum of Joshua", MPI 8 (Leiden 1995), pp. 129–76:174–5.

such literal translations need no more be Christian than the underlying Hebrew texts themselves.[94] Elements well attested in second-century Judaism as well as Christianity – such as invocation of God as "our father" – are likewise irrelevant.[95]

Finally, it is worth noting a rendering which actually proved awkward to Christian interpreters, at Isa. 53:9 –

MT   ויתן את רשעים קברו ואת עשיר במתיו

P   ܡܗܘܬܗ ܒܟܠܗ ܘܥܬܝܪܐ ܩܒܪܗ ܪܫܝܥܐ ܝܗܒ

    a wicked man gave his grave, even a rich man at his death

Here P ignored את and so made the wicked man and the rich man the subjects. He did not, however, further adjust the Hebrew by inverting those subjects, so as to make the rich man responsible for the Servant's grave and the wicked man for his death, and thus to apply the verse to Jesus.[96]

In the P version of the Apocryphal books of Sirach and Wisdom, by contrast, some convincing Christian references seem present. Winter points to the hope in Ecclus 48:10 that Elijah would "evangelise" (ܠܡܣܒܪܘ, rather than Heb. להכין "establish") the tribes of Jacob. Drijvers (pp. 24–5) shows how P transforms the sense of Wis. 14:5–7, ending thus:

LXX   εὐλόγηται γὰρ ξύλον, δι᾽ οὗ γίνεται δικαιοσύνη

    For blessed is the wood through which righteousness comes

P   ܟܐܢܘܬܐ ܡܢܗ ܕܡܢ ܗܘ ܩܝܣܐ ܗܘ ܡܒܪܟ ܡܟܝܠ

    For blessed is the wood from which the righteous man appears

The glorification of the gentiles over Israel also appears even more clearly here than in the canonical books.[97]

The faith of the translators

Let us now review, in the light of the evidence assembled above, the two alternative hypotheses with which we began.

The hypothesis of Christian origin could hardly apply to Ezra and Chronicles, in which books the translator identifies himself with the Jews. Now these books were in all probability among the last to be translated, as discussed in chapter 4; and as communities tended to convert from Judaism to Christianity rather than the reverse, a Jewish origin for Ezra and Chronicles would imply a Jewish origin for the earlier books also.

Only by setting up a complex hypothesis could one instead argue for the Christian

---

[94] *Pace* Bloch, "The Authorship of the Peshitta", p. 219.

[95] *Pace* De Moor and Sepmeijer, "The Peshitta and the Targum of Joshua", p. 175. On the rabbinic side, note R. Akiba's prayer addressed to אבינו מלכנו (TB Taan. 25b).

[96] For explanations, see D.B. Bundy, "The Peshitta of Isaiah 53:9 and the Syrian Commentators", *Oriens Christianus* 67 (1983), pp. 32–45.

[97] M. Winter, "The Origins of Ben Sira in Syriac", *VT* 27 (1977), pp. 237–53, 494–507, on which see R.J. Owens, "The Early Syriac Text of Ben Sira in the Demonstrations of Aphrahat", *JSS* 34 (1989), pp. 39–75; H.J.W. Drijvers, "The Peshitta of *Sapientia Salomonis*", pp. 15–30.

origin of the earlier books, given the marks of Jewish origin in Ezra and Chronicles. For example, it could be urged that Ezra (and Nehemiah) and Chronicles should be treated separately, since they share some peculiarities (e.g. the rendering of "singers" as "servants") as shown in detail in chapter 4 above. On this view, perhaps a Christian community translated the biblical books in roughly the traditional Jewish sequence and stopped short of Ezra-Chronicles. Later, having forgotten Hebrew, they commissioned Jews – or recent converts from Judaism – to complete the translation. An alternative hypothesis is that P on Ezra-Chronicles is all that survives of an old Jewish translation of the whole Bible into Syriac. The Christians made a new translation of every book except Ezra-Chronicles, which were of lesser interest or authority.

There are difficulties, however, in viewing P on Ezra-Chronicles either as an afterthought or as the sole relic of a Jewish translation of the whole Hebrew Bible. On the former hypothesis, the earlier books were translated by Christians but the last few were given over either to Jews or to converts who still remembered Hebrew. However, if these last few books were translated by Jews, then these must have worked together with the Christians in surprising harmony, given the censorious attitude which the *ex hypothesi* Christian translators had already shown in the earlier books; and if the last few books were translated by recent converts, then we have to be surprised at their continued heartfelt identification with the plight of the Jewish people. This leaves the hypothesis that P on Ezra-Chronicles is all that survives of an old Jewish translation of the whole Bible. However, the remarkable homogeneity of the manuscript tradition of P is then hard to explain. Had an earlier Jewish version existed, one would have expected many passages where two substantially different alternative renderings survive, each independently derived from the Hebrew, representing the old version and the new. In fact, however, such passages are few indeed; they are discussed in appendix I to chapter 6.

The subordinate role of LXX in the making of P also favours Jewish rather than Christian origin. The church did not yet fully appreciate the *Hebraica veritas*, and cherished LXX as its Old Testament. It is hard to see why Christian translators should instead have given primacy to the Hebrew, and thereby produced a version often at odds with LXX.

A Jewish origin is thus likelier. Indeed, the translators of P identify with the Jewish people, at least in some books. And yet they do not represent rabbinic Judaism. We need only recall their three fixed hours of daily prayer, their depreciation of sacrifice, and their emphasis on faith and hope rather than observance.

A non-rabbinic form of Judaism would account for all these features. A similar combination of Jewish identification with neglect of ritual was also known to Philo (De Peregr. Abr. 89–93), who complains that some Jews believed that they had penetrated to the inner meaning of the commandments and therefore "casually neglected" (ῥαθύμως ὠλιγώρησαν) their observance. No doubt other Jews were lax in observance even without the benefit of such a philosophical system. One could indeed cite the book of Esther, whose heroine's acts betray no hint of Jewish observance.

Again, the combination of high regard for the nations with disdain for those Jews of differing beliefs was not unknown among Jewish groups. Indeed, it is only to be expected in a non-rabbinic group that lacked any rapport with rabbinic Judaism, which now commanded majority allegiance. In particular, such an attitude is parallelled in the Enoch literature. In Enoch 89–90, the Jews and their ancestors are represented by clean animals, mainly sheep. However, those Jews outside the writer's group are called "blinded sheep", ultimately to be burnt. Although many unclean beasts and birds – representing aggressive gentiles – will likewise be destroyed, there will also be "beasts of the earth and birds of the heaven" who are pleasing to God (90:33) and are eventually transformed to white bulls, i.e. to the pristine righteousness of Adam in Eden (90:38).

We also have to account for the striking inconsistency within P in its attitude to the Jewish people as a whole – now antipathy, now contrite self-identification. Perhaps the explanation is that the translation covers two stages in the history of the community. In the first, represented by all but the latest books, the community – whatever its physical location – was estranged spiritually from the main Jewish centres in the Holy Land and Babylon. They were a defiant minority, whose religion revolved about their own elect community and personal salvation. They felt alienated from the majority of Jews, whose hopes centred on the restoration of the Jews as a nation, and who respected the rabbinic academies and the observance of Jewish ritual practice in detail. Indeed, the community represented by P held out greater hope for the gentiles, whom they believed could come directly to God. However, by the second stage, represented by P in Daniel as well as in Ezra-Chronicles, some catastrophe (perhaps the massacre under Trajan) had reminded the community that they were part of the Jewish people. They now identified with the Jews in general, and keenly felt their shame and vulnerability in exile.

A different hypothesis to explain the inconsistent attitude towards the Jewish people might be that the translation is the work of Jews but has undergone Christian interpolation. However, a Christian interpolator might have been expected to introduce clear references to Christian belief, and yet – as shown above – there are none in the P version of the canonical books. Furthermore, most of the P passages interpretable as Christian (or as hostile to Israel) seem to have been derived from the Hebrew text, whereas a Christian interpolator would presumably have instead viewed the Greek Bible as authoritative.

All in all, then, the likeliest explanation is that P on the whole Hebrew Bible is of non-rabbinic Jewish origin. The translators seem to represent a closed community, estranged from the Jewish people as a whole. Their practice of working out their own – sometimes extravagant – solutions to difficulties in the Hebrew (such as the word מחקקק), with no external check, reinforces the impression of isolation. So too does their inability to replace their damaged Hebrew text of Chronicles, following the argument in chapter 3 above. As we shall see in chapter 6, the revision of the text of P in the earliest centuries of its existence likewise suggests a closed group of scholars with little access to the outside world. If so, then the introspective nature of Syriac-speaking Christianity has deep roots, reaching back to the Jewish community represented by P.

This survey of the translators' ideas must now be set in a historical framework. Only then will it be possible to venture to explain how the Old Testament Peshitta, despite its Jewish origin, came to be transmitted by the eastern churches exclusively.

The place of the translation

The next stage must be to survey the evidence on the place and time of the translation. A number of indications favour Edessa, or at least its province Osrhoene, as the place of origin. One of the native traditions (cited below) locates the translation there, under "Abgar the believing king". Moreover, the language in which P has been transmitted agrees with that of inscriptions found at Edessa – though the same dialect may have been current over a wider area at the time of the translation. Again, as van der Kooij has well argued, the fact that the translators knew Greek as well as Hebrew accords well with an origin at Edessa, whose educated citizens – including Jews – had known Greek ever since the city was re-founded by Seleucus I.[98]

Moreover, the translation introduces references to places in the neighbourhood of Edessa – namely to Harran, Mabbog and Nisibis – as discussed in chapter 2.[99] In addition, the rendering of Heb. אשרה by ܢܡܪܐ "leopard" (2 Chr. 31:1 etc.) suggests familiarity with a leopard-cult, such as is reported in the sixth century by Jacob of Serug in Harran.[100] It is true that P contains other topographic matter – e.g. the frequent rendering Matnin for Bashan, or the identification of Antioch as the northern extreme of the promised land – which instead points to Palestine; but these may be derived from earlier tradition. It is also true that the Palestinian Targums Pseudo-Jonathan and Neofiti likewise introduce the name Nisibis – as well as Ctesiphon, Adiabene and even Edessa – at Gen. 10:10–11;[101] but these Targums have an altogether broader perspective, ranging from Germany to India.

An origin at Edessa would not conflict with the suggestion made earlier, that the different books represent a Jewish community's changing attitudes to the Jewish people at large: first alienation, then self-identification. It is true that Edessa stood on the celebrated silk road that connected Antioch and the Mediterranean seaboard with India and the Far East, and enjoyed close relations with Nisibis and other Jewish centres to the east.[102] All this, however, is still compatible with an alienation from the larger community, if its values – such as the observance of rabbinic Judaism and the hope for national restoration – differed from their own. The second stage, in which the community identifies with the Jewish people in exile, is also perfectly credible in Edessa.

Against this stands the theory that P originated further east in Adiabene. Had there been cogent evidence that P depends fundamentally on the Palestinian Targums, then Adiabene would indeed have been a likely place of origin, since Adiabene lay in the east and yet had close ties to Palestine. In fact, however, the parallels with the Targums are no more striking than might be expected in any Jewish community that spoke an Aramaic dialect and had some access to the tradition of biblical scholarship in Aramaic. Nor would an origin in Adiabene well explain the translators' knowledge of Greek. All in all, therefore, the likeliest place of origin is Edessa.

---

[98] Van der Kooij, *Die alten Textzeugen*, p. 292. For details of the inscriptions see J.B. Segal, *Edessa. The Blessed City*, Oxford 1970, pp. 27, 30, 42.

[99] Admittedly, these are confined to P-Chronicles, apart from the mention of Mabbog at 2 Kgs. 23:29.

[100] J.P.P. Martin, "Discours de Jacques de Saroug sur la chute des idoles", *ZDMG* 29 (1875), pp. 107–47: p. 110 (line 54).

[101] These somehow served as sources to Ephrem, whose commentary to Genesis shows the same identifications of Edessa, Nisibis, Ctesiphon and Adiabene (ed. Tonneau, p. 65). See Brock, "Jewish Traditions", p. 219.   [102] J.B. Segal, *Edessa*, p. 4.

The date of the translation

We must now examine the evidence for the period of P. There is some that indicates a specific date or period; such items of evidence are external traditions about the origin of P, and references to contemporary events within P. Other evidence may provide a latest possible date; examples are citations of P in outside works, and the nature of the Hebrew *Vorlage* behind P. Yet other evidence may provide an earliest possible date; such are Latin loanwords, and citations of outside sources within P. Grammatical elements may suggest either a latest or an earliest possible date for P, depending on whether it is their obsolescence or their introduction that can be dated.

Tradition

As already remarked, neither Aphrahat nor Ephrem in the fourth century provides any information on the origin of P, and Theodore of Mopsuestia (*c.* 350–428 CE) stated explicitly that nothing was known. However, Jacob of Edessa (*c.* 700 CE) reports that the translation originated in the time of Abgar, king of Edessa who was remembered as a contemporary of Christ:

ܗ̄ ܐܡܪ ܡܪܝ، ܝܥܩܘܒ: ܕܐܕܝ، ܫܠܝܚܐ ܘܐܒܓܪ ܡܠܟܐ ܡܗܝܡܢܐ ܫܕܪܘ ܓܒܪ̈ܐ ܠܐܘܪܫܠܡ
ܘܠܐܬܪܐ ܕܦܠܣܛܝܢܐ. ܘܐܦܩܘ ܘܐܥܒܪܘ ܠܕܝܐܬܝܩܝ، ܥܬܝܩܬܐ ܡܢ ܠܫܢܐ ܥܒܪܝܐ ܠܠܫܢܐ ܣܘܪܝܝܐ

Addai the apostle and Abgar the believing king sent a man (men?) to Jerusalem and to the region of Palestine, and they translated[103] the Old Testament from the Hebrew language to the Syriac language.

This saying does not appear in any extant work of Jacob, but is quoted with approval in Jacob's name by Moses bar Kepa (died 903). [104] The same tradition is recalled by Barhebraeus commenting on Ps. 10:5, where Jacob is said to have mentioned "those translators who were sent by Addai the apostle and Abgar, king of Edessa, to Palestine and translated scripture".[105] This may be called the dominant view in the west.

In the east, however, the dominant tradition is that P was produced by Mark the Evangelist. This view appears in Syriac in the Gannat Bussame:

ܡܫܠܡܝܢ ܕܝܢ ܬܘܒ ܐܢܫ̈ܝܢ: ܕܟܬ̈ܒܐ ܕܥܬܝܩܬܐ ܡܢ ܥܒܪܝܐ ܠܣܘܪܝܝܐ ܗܘ
ܗܘܝܘ ܡܪܩܘܣ ܬܪܓܡ ܐܦܩ ܘܥܒܪ ܐܢܘܢ ܠܘܬ ܝܥܩܘܒ ܐܚܘܗܝ ܕܡܪܢ
ܘܠܘܬ ܫܠܝ̈ܚܐ. ܘܫܒܚܘ ܐܢܘܢ ܘܫܕܪܘ. ܘܐܫܠܡܘ ܐܢܘܢ ܠܗܘܢ ܠܒܢ̈ܝ ܣܘܪܝܐ.
ܦܠܚ ܕܝܢ ܒܡܣܒܪܬܐ ܘܐܦ ܥܡ ܦܛܪܘܣ ܟܕ ܐܝܬܘܗܝ، ܥܡܗ ܒܪܗܘܡܐ.

Again, people have a tradition that the writings of the Old Testament were translated from Hebrew into Syriac by Mark himself, who presented them before Jacob, brother of our Lord and before the apostles; and they approved them and sent them and handed them over to the people of Syria. He then worked on the Gospel, together with Peter, when he was with him in Rome.[106]

[103] Lit. "brought out and across"; cf. ܡܦܩܢܘܬܐ 'translation', and the combination ܐܦܩ ܬܪܓܡ below.

[104] G. Diettrich, *Eine jakobitische Einleitung in den Psalter* (=BZAW 5), Giessen 1901, p. 115. See also L. Schlimme, *Der Hexaemeronkommentar des Moses ber Kepha: Einleitung, Übersetzung und Untersuchungen*, Wiesbaden 1977, vol. 1, p. 172.

[105] P. de Lagarde, *Praetermissorum Libri Duo*, Göttingen 1879, p. 110. Presuming the psalm division in LXX correct, Jacob explained that when these translators found a διάψαλμα after Ps. 9:20 they mistakenly thought that a new psalm began there.

[106] Ms Rylands Syr. 41, p. 260.

The same tradition appears in the defence of Islam written in *c.* 855 by ʻAli ibn Rabban al-Tabari, already mentioned in chapter 3. Ibn Rabban's biblical citations are based on P, and he refers to his biblical source as "the books of the Syrians which Marcus (i.e. Mark the evangelist) has translated".[107]

For the book of Genesis alone, a pseudepigraph attributed to Zacharias Rhetor but completed in 569 CE indicates a far earlier date, namely the fall of Samaria:

ܟܢܫܐ ܕܝܢ ܣܘܪܝܝܐ. ܐܝܟ ܕܐܡܪ ܠܐܦܝܦܢܝܘܣ ܐܦܣܩܘܦܐ ܕܩܘܦܪܘܣ ܕܒܪܝܬܐ. ܡܢ
ܚܕ ܡܢ ܟܗܢܐ ܕܓܠܝ ܫܠܡܢܐܣܪ ܡܠܟܐ: ܐܝܢܐ ܕܐܫܬܕܪ ܠܥܡܐ ܕܫܡܪܝܐ. ܕܐܝܬ ܗܘܘ ܡܢ ܒܒܠ...
ܘܐܬܬܘܬܒܘ ܒܐܪܥܐ ܕܐܝܣܪܐܝܠ ܚܠܦܝܗܘܢ. ܘܕܚܠܘ ܡܢ ܚܒܠܐ ܕܐܪ̈ܝܘܬܐ... ܘܫܐܠܘ ܢܡܘܣܐ.
ܐܬܟܬܒ ܒܠܫܢܐ ܣܘܪܝܝܐ.

Now the Syriac volume of Genesis, as was said by Epiphanius bishop of Cyprus, was written in the Syriac language by one of the priests whom king Shalmaneser exiled, and who was sent to the people of the Samaritans, who were from Babylon . . . and settled in the land of Israel in its stead, and were afraid at the lions' destruction . . . and requested the Law.[108]

Whereas the above writers each offer a single date, we find no fewer than three in Ishoʻdad (*c.* 850), and also in the opening of Barhebraeus' scholia – even though the latter in his commentary on Psalms accepts Jacob's straightforward dating to Abgar's age. A related account is offered by Theodore bar Koni, at the end of the eighth century.[109]

Barhebraeus (1226–86) reports:

ܥܠܘܗܝ ܕܝܢ ܕܗܢܐ ܣܘܪܝܝܐ. ܬܠ̈ܬ ܡܣܒܪܢܘܬܐ ܗ̈ܘܝ.
ܚܕܐ ܕܒ̈ܝܘܡܝ ܕܫܠܝܡܘܢ ܘܚܝܪܡ ܡ̈ܠܟܐ ܐܬܬܦܩܬ.
ܕܬܪܬܝܢ ܕܐܣܐ ܟܗܢܐ ܗܘ ܦܫܩܗ ܐܡܬܝ ܕܫܕܪܗ ܐܬܘܪܝܐ ܠܫܡܪܝܢ:
ܕܬܠ̈ܬ ܕܒܝܘ̈ܡܝ ܐܕܝ ܫܠܝܚܐ ܘܐܒܓܪ ܡܠܟܐ ܕܐܘܪܗܝ ܐܬܦܫܩܬ.

Concerning this Syriac (version), there are three opinions; one, that it was brought out in the time of kings Solomon and Hiram; second, that Asa the priest translated it when the Assyrian sent him to Samaria; third, that it was rendered in the days of Addai the apostle and Abgar the king of Edessa.[110]

The second and third theories had each already circulated separately, as already noted, while the first – which implies that Solomon had the version prepared at Hiram's request – carried P back earlier still.

Thanks to a tradition that Hiram survived into and indeed beyond the age of Assyrian domination, Theodore bar Koni was able to combine the first two theories into one. He also supplies motives for the translation:

Some say that the Scriptures were translated in the time of Hiram, who remained alive until the Return; and because of his love for David he desired to acquire the scriptures of the Hebrews.

107 A. Mingana, *The Book of Religion and Empire by ʻAli Ṭabari*. English translation: Manchester 1922, p. 95. Arabic text: Manchester 1923, p. 81.

108 E.W. Brooks (ed.), *Historia Ecclesiastica Zachariae Rhetori Vulgo Adscripta*, Paris 1919 (reprinted Louvain 1953), vol. 1 (=CSCO 83/Syr. 38), pp. 12–13.

109 R. Hespel and R. Draguet, *Théodore bar Koni. Livre des Scolies. I. Mimrê I–V*, Louvain 1981 (CSCO 431, Syr. 187), pp. 1–2.

110 M. Sprengling and W.C. Graham (eds.), *Barhebraeus' Scholia on the Old Testament. Part I: Genesis – II Samuel*, Chicago 1931, pp. 4–5.

And some say that the apostles translated them, desiring to improve mankind through their preaching among every people and in every language.[111]

According to Theodore and Barhebraeus, all the biblical books were translated in a single period, whichever of the three. Isho'dad, however, offers an account which divides them between two different periods:

> The Torah – it is said – and Joshua, Judges, Ruth, Samuel, David (i.e. Psalms), Proverbs, Qoheleth, S. of S. and Job were translated in the time of Solomon, at the request of his friend Hiram king of Tyre; and the books of the rest of the Old Testament, together with the New, (were translated) in the time of Abgar, king of Edessa, under the care of Addai and the rest of the apostles. Others, however, say that they were translated by one of the priests, called Asya, whom the Assyrian king sent to Samaria.[112]

As Vosté remarks, the scheme of three alternatives preserved by Barhebraeus was known already to Isho'dad, who, however, appreciated that some books of the Hebrew Bible were composed after Solomon's day, and some even after the fall of Samaria. Isho'dad therefore ascribed whatever books he could to Solomon's time, and all the rest to Abgar's; and he also noted the rival dating.[113]

What is the historical worth of these traditions? That the datings to the time of Solomon or even to the fall of Samaria were impossibly early was already appreciated by Isho'dad. However, the fact that the dominant theories in both the east and the west, though different, agree on a date in the first century CE might seem impressive. Unfortunately, the literary sources of both theories are too obvious. The motif of co-operation with scholars from Jerusalem, in the western tradition, echoes Aristeas's account of the origin of LXX (though in the former account these scholars are consulted in Jerusalem while in the latter they are despatched abroad); while the casting of Mark the Evangelist as the translator reflects the statement by Papias (*c.* 140 CE), elaborated by later fathers, that Mark served Peter as an interpreter.[114]

It is worth noting that Barhebraeus adds:

.ܠܘܬ ܕܝܠܗܘܢ ܗܝܕܐ ܦܫܝܛܬܐ ܕܐܝܬ܊ܝ ܐܘܟ.

܊ܘܥܘܬܐ ܐܝܟ ܕܐܡܪ ܐܘܣܒܝܘܣ ܕܩܣܪܝܐ ܐܘܪܝܓܢܝܣ ܐܫܟܚ:

ܗ. ܗ̇ܘ ܕܠܘܬ ܚܕܐ ܣܒܬܐ ܒܟܠ ܐܬܪ

For this Peshitta ('simple') translation, which corresponds to [the text] of the Jews, and as Eusebius of Caesarea said, Origen found it with a certain widow, is in the hands of the Syrians everywhere.[115]

Eusebius does not in fact mention P at all, but he tells us something similar about Symmachus' version: Origen obtained it from a lady called Juliana, who had received it from Symmachus himself.[116] The same story is later told in greater detail by Palladius

[111] A. Scher, *Theodorus bar Koni, Liber Scholiorum 1*, Paris–Leipzig 1910 (=CSCO 55, Syr. 19), p. 280.
[112] J.-M. Vosté and C. van den Eynde (eds.), *Commentaire d' Isho'dad de Merv sur l'Ancien Testament: I. Genèse*, CSCO 126 (text), Louvain 1950, p. 3.
[113] C. van den Eynde (ed.), *Commentaire d' Isho'dad de Merv sur l'Ancien Testament: I. Genèse*, CSCO 156 (French translation), Louvain 1955, p. 4 (with n.1).
[114] See B.H. Streeter, *The Primitive Church*, London 1929, pp. 17ff. The same tradition is cited by Eusebius, *Hist. Eccl.* 3.39.15, who uses the term ἑρμηνευτής; this appears in the Syriac translation as ܡܦܫܩܢܐ.
[115] Sprengling and Graham (eds.), *Barhebraeus' Scholia on the Old Testament*, pp. 1–3.
[116] *Hist. Eccl.* 6.17.

(in 419–20 CE), who describes Juliana as a virgin in Caesarea (in Cappadocia).[117] The lady's celibacy provides a further link between this story and Barhebraeus' account. Given, however, that as there is a variant reading ܐܪܡܠܬܐ, it is conceivable that the original text in fact had not "widow" but ܐܪܡܝܬܐ "an Aramaean woman", i.e. one whose mother tongue was Aramaic; both extant readings would be easy corruptions of this.[118]

If only for completeness, we must also review here the few references to P which allegedly appear in rabbinic literature. The supposed references to P under מתרגמין, and in the report at Genesis Rabba 46:10 that the king of Adiabene read the Torah, were discussed in chapter 3. A reference to P has also been detected in the report (Palestinian Talmud to Megilla 1:9) that an inn-keeper offered an Aramaic rendering of a Greek translation of the Bible:

בורגני אחד בידא להם ארמית מתוך יוונית

Of course, P is based primarily on the Hebrew text, not the Greek, but the mistaken belief that the direct source of P was Greek appears also in Syriac tradition, in the colophons of some mss of P. Might this rabbinic passage therefore refer to P, as Perles suggested tentatively?[119] Against that view, the verb בידא "invented" would suggest an *ex tempore* rendering of a sample, rather than citation from a pre-existing continuous version. In any case, the text is uncertain, and the parallel account in Esther Rabba on Est. 1:22 mentions Latin (לשון רומי) rather than Aramaic.

References to contemporary events

Occasionally we glimpse the world powers of the translators' day. Thus ששך at Jer. 25:26 becomes ܐܪܫܟܝ 'Arsaces' and at 51:41 ܐܪܫܟܝܬܐ 'the Arsacid city'. The Arsacids ruled Persia from 250 BCE to 230 CE. This interval is too long to narrow the date of P appreciably. It is noteworthy, however, that the translators took pains to introduce the Parthians in this particular context, and thus to present them as successors to the Babylonians – for ששך is evidently a by-name for בבל – rather than to the benign Persians.[120]

There may also be references to Rome, under the code-name Edom. As noted in chapter 2, Duval detected a reference to Roman domination in P at Ps. 12:9, where "children of man" (אָדָם) become "children of Edom".[121]

According to van der Kooij, as noted above, the frequent substitution of Edom for Aram alludes to the status of Syria in the translator's day as a province of Rome. Moreover, the fact that references to Aram beyond the Euphrates are translated unchanged indicates a date between 117 CE, when Roman rule was bounded by the Euphrates, and 165 CE, when it was extended into Mesopotamia.[122] Indeed, van der Kooij thinks even greater precision possible. In P on Isaiah, he finds that P has added references, beyond those in MT, to the expected fall of a world power:

---

[117] C. Butler (ed.), *The Lausiac History of Palladius*, Cambridge 1898–1904, vol. 2, p. 160. Palladius claims to have read the account in Origen's own hand, in a note inscribed ἐν βιβλίῳ στιχηρῷ, apparently a copy of the Bible arranged in lines.

[118] A corruption from ܐܪܡܝܬܐ (albeit in the sense 'heathen') to ܐܪܡܠܬܐ occurs in the Old Syriac Gospels at Mark 7:26.   [119] Perles, *Meletemata*, p. 4.

[120] The Parthians are introduced by name (ܦܪܬܘܝܐ) to render פרתמים at Dan. 1:3, again in Babylon. However, the same equivalence occurs in the context of Ahasuerus' court, at Est. 1:3, 6:9.

[121] R. Duval, "Notes sur la Peschitto. I, Edom et Rome", *REJ* 14 (1887), pp. 49–51.

[122] Debevoise, *A Political History of Parthia*, Chicago 1938, p. 246.

Isa. 25:7

MT   ובלע בהר הזה פני הלוט הלוט על כל העמים

P   ܘܢܒܠܥ ܒܛܘܪܐ ܗܢܐ ܐܦ ܥܠܝܐ ܕܐܬܚܝܠ ܗܘܐ ܥܠ ܟܠܗܘܢ ܥܡܡܐ

and on this mountain even *the ruler who was empowered* over all the nations will be swallowed

Isa. 33:21

MT   וצי אדיר לא יעברנו

P   ܘܣܦܝܢܬܐ ܕܓܢܒܪܐ ܠܐ ܬܥܒܪܝܘܗܝ ܒܗ

and the mighty one who is found will not pass through it[123]

Hence van der Kooij would date the translation to a point when the fall of Rome seemed a real possibility. This might have appeared so around 162 CE, when the Parthian king Vologases III briefly conquered Armenia, Cappadocia and Syria following the death of Antoninus Pius. Van der Kooij thus inclines to date P, at least in Isaiah, to about 162 CE.[124]

The argument is attractive but not conclusive. The underlying suggestion that Edom was substituted for Aram in order to indicate Rome, and hence Syria as a Roman province, was examined in the excursus to chapter 2. As to the references to the imminent fall of the world power, this is a theme of the Hebrew text of Isaiah itself in chapter 25, and immediately after chapter 33. P's use of that theme as the basis of guessed renderings in these two difficult passages need not therefore reflect his own expectations of the eschaton.

A further reference to contemporary events is the theme of exile as disgrace in P, primarily in Chronicles but also elsewhere. These suggest a date after 70 CE, and probably at least some decades later, since the tone of the references in P suggests that all hope of a speedy restoration – as occurred after the fall of the first Temple – had died away.

Citations of P

Citations of P in outside writers may be hoped to establish a latest possible date. Interest thus centres on the earliest works to cite P.

Where the Old Testament is quoted in the New, the Old Syriac Gospels – as noted in chapter 3 – tend not to follow the Greek text of the New Testament but instead to import the text of the Peshitta of the Old Testament. If the Old Syriac Gospels are dated to around 200 CE,[125] then P of the Old Testament – or at least of the books there quoted – must be at least as early.

That limit can be carried back a few decades earlier, because this practice of following the Peshitta of the Old Testament rather than the Greek text of the New Testament

---

[123] Van der Kooij sees here another reference to the world tyrant. In fact, however, ܫܟܚ is an unremarkable rendering of אדיר (as e.g. at Ps. 136:18), while צי was 'misread' as a derivative of מצא.

[124] Van der Kooij, *Die alten Textzeugen*, p. 295.

[125] F.C. Burkitt, *Evangelion da-Mepharreshe*, Cambridge 1904, vol. 1, p. 209.

probably goes back to Tatian's Diatessaron, which was complete by about 170 CE. In the one passage (Matt.21:5=Zech. 9:9) where a reliable Syriac text of the Diatessaron survives in a passage containing an Old Testament quotation, Brock found that the Diatessaron stood even closer to the Old Testament Peshitta than do the Old Syriac Gospels.[126] Brock suggested that the practice of using P as the textual basis for Old Testament passages cited in the New originated with Tatian himself, because "in the primitive Judaeo-Christian church the authority of the Old Testament was greater than that of the (still emerging) New Testament". The reason that, in passages containing an Old Testament quotation, the Old Syriac Gospels likewise follow the Old Testament Peshitta (albeit less faithfully) is that they depend in some measure on the Diatessaron.[127]

Joosten has rightly drawn out the implication that the Peshitta version of those books of the Old Testament that are quoted in the Diatessaron already existed, and indeed had already attained authoritative status, by around 170 CE. Joosten has shown, with full listings, how the Old Testament Peshitta – by preference to the Greek text of the New Testament – has influenced both the Old Syriac and Peshitta versions of the Gospels. Following Brock, he considers that this influence was mediated through the Diatessaron.[128] His argument implies a date no later than *c.* 170 CE for the books cited: the Pentateuch, the Latter Prophets and the Psalms.

Another early writer who provides a biblical citation in Syriac is Bar-Daisan, born in 154 CE. His citation of Gen. 9:6 does not agree well with P but rather with T^O, as already discussed in chapter 3; the implications for the dating of P are considered below.

In the early fourth century, P is cited by Aphrahat in all canonical books of the Old Testament, except for a few short enough to have been excluded by chance. A little later, Ephrem's commentaries on Genesis and Exodus cite these books extensively. Significantly, however, Ephrem no longer understood the particle ܝܬ in Gen. 1:1, as his comment shows:

ܝܬ ܫܡܝܐ ܘܝܬ ܐܪܥ. ܗܘ ܕܝܢ ܗܘܝܐ ܫܡܝܐ ܕܝܕܥܝܢ ܘܗܘܝܐ ܐܪܥ ܕܝܕܥܝܢ

Ephrem explains that the heaven and earth created on the first day are the very heaven and earth familiar to every generation; and, by the same token, the whole creation account is no allegory but literally meant.[129] The fact that the particle had become obsolete suggests that Genesis was translated no later than *c.* 200 CE.[130]

[126] Ephraem, *Comm. Diatessaron* xviii.1. See L. Leloir (ed. and tr.), *Saint Éphrem: Commentaire de l'Évangile Concordant*, Dublin 1963, p. 204.

[127] S.P. Brock, "Limitations of Syriac in Representing Greek", contributed to B.M. Metzger, *The Early Versions of the New Testament*, Oxford 1977, pp. 96–8.

[128] J. Joosten, "The Old Testament Quotations in the Old Syriac and Peshitta Gospels", *Textus* 15 (1990), pp. 55–76. (esp.76, n.42).

[129] R.-M. Tonneau (ed.), *Sancti Ephraem Syri in Genesim et in Exodum Commentarii* [CSCO 152, Syr.71], Louvain 1955, p. 8.

[130] There are many other phrases in P which Ephrem glosses correctly; for example, he explains ܡܟܣ ܘܡܟܣ (Gen. 1:2) as ܪܟܝܗܘ ...ܟܡܪ, or ܚܒܘܪ (Gen. 30:14) as "a root with fragrant, edible fruits like apples". Ephrem's need to gloss particular words need not in itself indicate a long interval since P was made, but rather that the relevant words in P were unusual from the first, especially if they followed the Hebrew or a standard Jewish Aramaic rendering.

Nature of the Hebrew text

A latest possible date for P has been inferred from the close but not complete agreement of the Hebrew *Vorlage* of P with MT. That pattern suggests a date shortly before the standardisation of MT, which is often associated with R.Akiba. Hence the inference that P "is unlikely to have been made much later than 100 CE."[131]

However, the translation technique is not so literal as to determine the text of the *Vorlage* with sufficient precision for this purpose. One could argue for an earlier date, since – as some 'model' copies from Qumran show – a text very much like MT existed perhaps 200 years before Akiba, though it had not yet been adopted as standard.[132] Conversely, one could argue for a later date, since, as the Vulgate shows, non-massoretic Hebrew readings (so far as can be inferred from the Latin version) were still circulating in the fourth century.

Citations in P

Citations in P establish an earliest possible date for the translation, at least in the biblical book containing the citation. Hence interest centres on the latest works cited in P. Almost all the works arguably quoted, however, are too early to be helpful.

In the many biblical books where LXX is cited, P must be later than that version. However, even the latest relevant books of LXX, such as Proverbs, still pre-date the turn of the era, so that this argument hardly narrows the range of dates for P. The promise of greater precision might seem to be held out by the cases where P is influenced by Theodotion, as occurs frequently in Daniel and also at Isa. 28:7. Epiphanius (c. 315–403) dated Theodotion to the reign of the emperor Commodus (180–92 CE).[133] As is well known, however, Theodotionic readings turn up in earlier sources, where – according to the widely accepted reconstruction by Barthélemy – they are now thought to reflect a revision already made in the last century BC.[134] Hence these too fail to provide a useful earliest possible date for P.

Nor is the range much narrowed by the reference to the "four-faced idol" introduced at 2 Chr. 33:7. As discussed in chapter 3, essentially the same tradition can be traced back to 2 Baruch, probably towards the end of the first century CE. Indeed, the tradition could be older still.

A further problem is that we may suspect that P's translator is quoting but be unsure of the source, as at Job 20:22 –

MT   במלאות שפקו יצר לו

P   ܒܟܝܠܐ ܕܟܝܠ ܢܬܦܪܥ

by the measure that he measured he will be punished

Here P seems to guessing a sense for the obscure Hebrew, by stretching the Hebrew words "fullness" and "sufficiency" to "measure". Now the expression "measure for measure" first occurs in texts later than the Hebrew Bible, such as Mishnah Sota 1:7

[131] Gelston, *The Peshitta of the Twelve Prophets*, pp. 192–3.
[132] Tov describes these texts as proto-Masoretic (p. 115).
[133] Epiphanius, *De Mensuris*; see PG 43, col. 265.
[134] S. Jellicoe, *The Septuagint and Modern Study*, Oxford 1968, pp. 87–94.

and Mark 4:24 (even though the idea itself is biblical). As P's source cannot be identified with any confidence, however, the passage sheds no new light on the date.

At Prov. 11:31, as noted above, it has been suggested that the translator uses a western element not found elsewhere in the Old Testament Peshitta, and that he must therefore have consulted the Peshitta version of the New Testament – specifically, of 1 Peter 4:18 – where western elements are thought to occur.[135] The Syriac text in both passages is identical:

ܐܢ ܙܕܝܩܐ ܠܡܚܣܢ ܚܝܐ ܪܫܝܥܐ ܘܚܛܝܐ ܐܝܟܐ ܡܫܬܟܚ

if the righteous man hardly lives, where is the wicked man and sinner to be found?

The Greek text of 1 Peter follows LXX in Proverbs:
εἰ ὁ μὲν δίκαιος μόλις σῴζεται, ὁ ἀσεβὴς καὶ ἁμαρτωλὸς ποῦ φανεῖται;
The use of ܚܝܐ (and derivatives) in the sense "save" – with the Aph'el as active and the simple stem as passive – is very common in the Old Syriac Gospels and the Peshitta version of the New Testament, but this is the only secure instance in P of the Old Testament.[136] The same usage also occurs in the P version of the Apocrypha, and is frequent in the Christian Palestinian Aramaic Bible, in both the Old and New Testaments. It is not found in Jewish Aramaic.

However, this usage of ܚܝܐ need not be western and therefore alien to classical Syriac. Rather, it seems a Grecism. It is confined to translations from Greek, and it may be a representation of σῴζω, which is the underlying verb in P of the Apocrypha,[137] in the Syriac New Testament versions, in the Greek-based Christian Palestinian Aramaic versions of both the Old and New Testaments, and also in this isolated Old Testament reference.[138] The Greek verb σῴζω was rightly analysed as σῶς with causative suffix –ιζω. The minimal meaning of σῶς is "alive", so that the adjective may be rendered by Syr. ܚܝ. Thus at 2 Macc. 12:24, where Timotheus pleads ἐξαφεῖναι σῶον ("to be released unharmed"), P renders his request ܕܢܫܒܩܘܢܗܝ، ܟܕ ܚܝ. That σῴζω originally meant "allow to live" was known also to the Septuagint translators, who use it to render חיה in the Qal (Ezek. 33:12 – with Greek passive), Pi'el (Ps. 30:3, Prov. 15:27) and Hiph'il (Gen. 47:25).

It would thus have been natural for P to represent the Greek active verb σῴζω by the causative of ܚܝܐ. The Greek passive had no exact counterpart, since no suitable passive causative form yet existed; thus the passive of σῴζω had to be represented by ܚܝܐ in simple stem. It is true that the use of ܚܝܐ in the sense 'be saved' is unique in the Peshitta of the Old Testament; but that is because Prov. 11:31 is exceptional in being translated from the Greek rather than the Hebrew. The rendering of σῴζω by ܚܝܐ can thus be viewed as a tradition which begins here and circulated among translators from Greek

135 J. Joosten, "West Aramaic Elements in the Old Syriac and Peshitta Gospels", *JBL* 110 (1991), pp. 271–89:275.

136 Places where ܚܝܐ represents Hebrew חיה must be left aside and the nuance is in any case different (e.g. "give life", "spare the life of", "revive"). The occurrence of ܡܚܝܢܐ at Isa. 25:6 may also be classified here: MT has the obscure ממחים, and it is not clear that "saviour" rather than "lifegiver" is intended.

137 Cases where ܚܝܐ Aph. instead means "revive" – e.g. Sir. 48:5 – must be considered separately.

138 In the Old Testament there is another possible occurrence of ܚܝܐ as "save" at Isa. 60:16, where for MT מושיעך וגואלך 9a1 has ܦܪܘܩܟܝ ܘܡܚܝܢܟܝ but the other mss ܦܪܘܩܟܝ ܘܡܦܨܝܢܟܝ. If 9a1 preserves the original text, ܡܚܝܢܐ may again represent σῴζω; compare LXX ὁ σῴζων σε καὶ ἐξαιρούμενός σε (despite the different order).

into Syriac, from the Old Testament into the New and from the east to the west. The priority of 1 Peter over Proverbs is in any case unlikely as there is no evidence that 1 Peter was known in the Syriac church even by the fourth century: unlike Proverbs, it is never cited either by Aphrahat or by Ephrem.[139]

Another citation in P which bears on the question of date appears in the final phrase of 1 Chr. 29:19 according to P. This text shows close verbal agreement with the first paragraph of the Aramaic prayer of the Jews called the Qaddish, as noted above. In particular, both texts lay emphasis on this created world: "may your/his great name be sanctified in the world that you/he created". This conflicts with the rabbinic insistence during the Second Temple period that blessings should contain the word עולם not once but twice, to refute those heretics – no doubt the Sadducees – who insisted that this was the only world. This controversy is reported in the Mishnah (Ber. 9:5) –

כל חותמי ברכות שהיו במקדש היו אומרים: "מן העולם".

משקלקלו המינים ואמרו: "אין עולם אלא אחד" התקינו שיהו אומרין "מן העולם ועד העולם"

Yet this world is stressed exclusively in the Qaddish. The reason seems to be that at some time after the Second Temple period a new threat arose, from gnostics who taught that this world was not God's work. This, it may be argued, led the rabbis of that age to stress the created world alone, against their predecessors' policy. In the rabbinic sources, the first exponent of protest against the gnostic view of the world is Bar Kappara at the beginning of the third century (e.g. in Gen.Rabba 1:1). It is unlikely that a protest would have been inserted into the liturgy much earlier. This suggests a date no earlier than *c.* 200 CE for the P version of the particular book of Chronicles.

Vocabulary

Loanwords may yield an earliest possible date for P, namely the earliest attestation of the borrowed word in the source language. Unfortunately, loanwords from Greek are too early to be of use. A little more helpful are the references to Corinthian bronze (ܢܚܫܐ ܩܘܪܢܬܝܐ), introduced three times in P, for different Hebrew expressions:

1 Kgs. 7:45   נחשת ממרט
Ezra 8:27   נחשת מצהב
1 Chr. 29:7   נחשת רבו

Corinthian bronze is first mentioned by Cicero (died 43 BCE), but the bulk of the literary references belong to the first century CE. Pliny (Hist. Nat. 34:1) places the Corinthian first in his list of bronzes, valuing it "before silver and almost before gold". He calls it an alloy of gold, silver and copper (34:3, 37:12), with which the explanation of Bar Bahlul in Arabic broadly agrees ("part silver, part gold and part copper").[140] Josephus records that the most precious gate to the sanctuary in Jerusalem was of Corinthian bronze (War 5, 201). Altogether, P's reference in Chronicles to Corinthian bronze can hardly be earlier than the first century CE.[141]

---

[139] R. Murray, *Symbols of Church and Kingdom*, Cambridge 1975, p. 20.
[140] R. Duval (ed.), *Lexicon Syriacum auctore Hassano bar Bahlule*, 3 vols., Paris 1888–1901, p. 1238
[141] For full discussion, see D.M. Jacobson and M.P. Weitzman, "What was Corinthian Bronze?", *American Journal of Archaeology* 96 (1992), pp. 237–47:241; "Black Bronze and the 'Corinthian Alloy'", *Classical Quarterly* 45 (1995), pp. 580–3.

Of Latin loanwords, we may note the word ܩܪܘܟܐ for 'chariot', occurring in both conservative and modern books of P – in Exodus (14:6), Joshua (11:4–9; 24:6), 1 Kings (10:25, 20:33), Isaiah (66:20) and 2 Chronicles (35:24). This is a loanword from Latin *carruca*, attested no earlier than Pliny (fl. 79 CE), in Hist. Nat 33:140. The Latin itself derives from *carrus*, a borrowing from Celtic already known to Caesar. The *carruca*, however, was a specifically Roman adaptation of the Celtic vehicle, and its absence from extant Latin literature before the first century CE is hardly accidental. Incidentally, whereas the Latin *carruca* was used by civilians, the ܩܪܘܟܐ in P is a war chariot.

Grammar

Grammatical elements could in principle help to date the translation, if we can date when they entered the Syriac language, or alternatively when they became obsolete. Unfortunately, it is difficult to ascertain these dates with sufficient precision.

One feature in P which might imply a latest possible date is the archaic demonstrative ܗܠܝܢ at Esther 1:5 and 1 Chr. 9:1. In either passage this form is attested by one ms only, while the rest have ܗܢܘܢ. The form ܗܠܝܢ appears elsewhere in Syriac only in the Old Syriac Gospels and in the older ms (of 462 CE) of the translation of the Ecclesiastical History of Eusebius; in the later ms (probably of the sixth century), all four occurrences are replaced by ܗܢܘܢ.[142] So far as the scanty data suggest, ܗܠܝܢ was a neutral type of demonstrative, used either alone ("the aforesaid") or with *dalath* ("those who, those of"). It served alongside the nearer form ܗܠܝܢ and the farther form ܗܢܘܢ, but was eventually supplanted by the latter. However, although in classical Syriac it had fallen out of use, the moment of its obsolescence cannot be determined accurately enough to narrow the range of possible dates for P.

Conversely, we may search P for new grammatical features whose entry to the Syriac language could be dated. An example is the passive participle plus *lamadh* with personal suffix, used as a perfect:

Prov. 13:22 ܐܝܠܝܢ ܕܠܐ ܚܙܐ ܠܗܘܢ ܡܥܡܪܐ those who have never seen a dwelling-place

Job 38:22 ܘܐܘܨܪܐ ܕܒܪܕܐ ܚܙܐ ܠܟ and have you ever seen the treasuries of hail?

Ruth 2:8 ܠܐ ܫܡܝܥ ܠܟ ܒܡܬܠܐ have you never heard in a proverb . . .

According to Kutscher, this feature was imported from Persian. An earliest possible date for P would be provided by the date of this borrowing – which is, however, not known accurately enough to help us.[143]

A further problem is that the original grammar may have been changed by later copyists. Thus, the 3sm future in P is throughout *nqbr*, for which the first dateable occurrence is in the Edessene bill of sale from Dura Europos (243 CE); before that, the

[142] See L. van Rompay, "Some Preliminary Remarks on the Origins of Classical Syriac as a Standard Language", in G. Goldenberg and S. Raz (eds.), *Semitic and Cushitic Studies*, Wiesbaden 1994, pp. 70–89: 76.
[143] E.Y. Kutscher, "Two 'Passive' Constructions in Aramaic in the Light of Persian", *Proceedings of the International Conference on Semitic Studies in Jerusalem 1965*, Jerusalem 1969, pp. 132–51:140. This feature was drawn to my attention by Prof. Joosten.

inscriptions (up to the late second century) show *yqbr*.[144] Yet this does not guarantee a date as late as *c.* 200 CE for P; for *nqbr* may have been imposed throughout by later copyists for an original *yqbr*.

Summary

The likeliest place of origin is Edessa. As to the period of the translation, the evidence is compatible with a date *c.* 150 for the earlier books of the Hebrew Bible. This would recognise the use of P in the earlier books by Tatian, but also at the same time the reserve of Bar-Daisan.

As to the date of the last books, the quotation of the Qaddish in P-Chronicles suggests a date no earlier than *c.* 200. On the other hand, Chronicles cannot have been translated more than about fifty years after the earlier books, since it was found in chapter 4 to be among the most conservative in lexical usage. Moreover, it shows a number of links in translation technique with the earlier books.

None of the evidence for a date as early as *c.* 150 CE applies to Ezra-Nehemiah. It is better to view these books as contemporary with Chronicles.[145] This whole group would then have been translated later than the majority of the Bible, in keeping with its place in the Jewish canonical order. That would help to explain why these books were excluded from comment in the massoretic mss and in the scholia of Bar Hebraeus, and rejected from the eastern canon.

Historical reconstruction

Having considered the translators' values, and the evidence for the historical setting of the version, we can venture a historical reconstruction. The Judaism of P is non-rabbinic and indeed anti-ritual. Where might it have originated? From a traditional Jewish viewpoint, P's Judaism represents a mere falling away from a pre-existing rabbinic standard. It is however worth considering an alternative possibility: the origins of the translators' religion may lie in a popular anti-cultic movement that goes back to biblical times.

Practices of worship suggest a possible reconstruction. In the Pentateuch sacrifice is prescribed twice daily, and prayer is not prescribed at all, and pre-exilic practice in the Temple no doubt followed this model. It may be, however, that at the same time the Levites in the provinces developed an independent regular cult consisting of prayer "evening and morning and noon-day" (Ps. 55:18). Such a prayer-cult would presumably have accompanied by sacrifice before Josiah's reform, but afterwards the prayer-cult would have been the sole means of regular worship there in the provinces. We may surmise that it was conducted by Levites who found no livelihood at the temple in Jerusalem (2 Kgs. 23:9). It was the prayer-cult that enabled the religion of Israel to survive the destruction of the Temple in Jerusalem. The gates of prayer remained open; and thus, during the Babylonian exile, Daniel would turn to Jerusalem in prayer three times every day (Dan. 6:11).

---

[144] H.J.W. Drijvers, *Old-Syriac (Edessean) Inscriptions*, Leiden 1972, p. 18.

[145] Esther, which joins them in being excluded from the Nestorian massora 9m1, may have been translated not much earlier.

The importance of regular prayer was recognised in the worship of the Second Temple. Sacrifice was of course restored; but prayer now became equally an integral part of worship, led as ever by the Levites. Chronicles justifies regular prayer by tracing psalmody and the Levitical choirs back to David, at the origin of the Temple.

So far as the relative status of prayer and sacrifice is concerned, two lines of tradition can be discerned. There is one line that regards prayer as dependent on sacrifice. On that view, the hours of prayer were aligned with those of sacrifice, and so reduced to two. Thus at Qumran, prayer was offered twice daily – at daybreak and nightfall (1QS 10:1 ff, 1QH 12:4–7, 1QM 14:13–14), the points when sacrifice had been offered (Jubilees 6:14).[146] Wisdom 16:28 bids us "rise before the sun to give thanks and pray as daylight dawns", and Judith prayed at the moment (ἄρτι) when the evening incense was offered in the Temple (Jud. 9:1). This attitude is found also among the rabbis, who remembered an ancient practice of reciting the morning prayer at sunrise.[147] They themselves, however, extended the times of prayer, so that the morning prayer could be said until midday, and the second prayer all afternoon.[148]

All this time the original prayer-cult – without any connection with sacrifice and so thrice daily as always – had survived, especially in the diaspora. To P it is central. It appealed to God-fearers, and doubtless to full converts, among the gentiles. Despite the victory of the rabbinic system among the Jews, the prayer-cult survived in the church.

The prayer-cult was not merely characterised by thrice daily hours of prayer. Having grown up away from the central sanctuary, it may have tended to depreciate not only sacrifice but ritual in general, and instead to emphasise inward faith. Such an attitude can already be detected in Proverbs. That book, like P, refers favourably to prayer (15:8,29), while sacrifice is presented negatively throughout. The wicked man's sacrifice is an abomination (15:8, 21:27). Sacrifice is inferior to just behaviour (21:3), and may even be a prelude to immorality (7:14). It is true that Prov. 3:9, 10 commends payment of first-fruits, but this seems a social rather than cultic obligation. Again like P, Proverbs prefers to emphasise faith (3:6, 16:20, 28:25, 29:25). It is not suggested here that P was especially influenced by Proverbs. Rather, both independently reflect the values of the prayer-cult. Other well-known biblical passages critical of the sacrificial cult (Isa. 1:11, Jer. 7:22, Hos. 6:6, Amos 5:21–2, Mic. 6:7, Ps. 40:7, 50:9–14, 51:18) may be influenced by the same movement.

Jews whose practice was confined to the prayer-cult could well have come to adopt Christianity. Christianity would have preserved their dearest religious values – prayer, charity and faith – and yet given them a rationale for continuing to neglect ritual. This may be the case for the community represented by P. In that case, the reason why a Jewish translation came to be transmitted by the eastern churches is simple: a Jewish community converted to Christianity, bringing with it a version of the Hebrew Bible.

---

[146] But see J.A. Jungmann, "Altchristliche Gebetsordnung im Lichte des Regelbuches von 'En Fešcha", *Zeitschrift für Katholische Theologie* 75 (1953), pp. 215–19, for a contrary view.

[147] TB Ber. 26a: ותיקין היו גומרין אותה עם הנץ החמה, as reported by R. Johanan; i.e. the 'ancient ones' used to complete the Shema as the sun was rising, and to proceed immediately to the Amidah. The rabbis themselves refer to the service as שחרית, from שחר 'dawn'.

[148] They argued that the whole period in which the sacrifice could legitimately be brought, including the time needed to complete it, was an acceptable time for the relevant prayer. It is worth noting that R. Judah b.Ilai is stricter and so, for example, extends the morning prayer to the fourth hour only.

The alternative is to suppose that Christians took P over from a Jewish community with which they were otherwise unconnected. This seems improbable, given the many places where P diverges from LXX, which would have been familiar and presumably authoritative for these Christians. A Christian community would have tolerated these discrepancies, however, if they saw themselves as the descendants or otherwise as the continuation of a Jewish group for whom P had become authoritative.

This movement from prayer-cult to Christianity can perhaps be paralleled in the Epistle to the Hebrews, written to prevent the relapse of newly converted Christians. The intended recipients of the letter must have been of Jewish origin, in view of the traditional title of the epistle and the assumption throughout that its recipients accept the authority of the Hebrew Bible. Yet the author expresses no concern that they might revert to Jewish ritual observance. The hypothesis that their background had been a non-rabbinic Judaism like that of P would explain this combination. It would also explain other elements – apart of course from the belief in Christ – which the author expects his readers to share: faith (6:12, and chapter 11), hope (6:11, 19; 7:19), the elevation of prayer and charity as true sacrifice (13:15–16), and the view of scriptural laws as mere symbols (9:9) or shadows (10:1). It is altogether fitting that Hebrews (10:5–7) should quote Psalm 40:7 to argue that God does not desire sacrifice. A line can be traced from the Israelite prayer-cult which (on the present reconstruction) inspired those verses, through the non-rabbinic Judaism with which the audience of Hebrews had grown up, to the Christian faith of the author of the letter.

The community addressed in Hebrews is usually located in the west (cf. 13:24), but this process of conversion from non-rabbinic Judaism to Christianity may have repeated itself all over the diaspora. The severing of links with the Jewish people may have been due to despair at at their interminable exile following the destruction of the second temple. After the first temple was destroyed, restoration was predicted by Jeremiah (25:11–12; 29:10) within 70 years and accomplished even sooner. Likewise in the first decades after 70 C.E, hope persisted for speedy restoration, as expressed in 2 Baruch (23–30, 80–82) and 4 Ezra (4–6), works usually dated around the end of the first century CE. Again, 4 Baruch, dateable to the opening decades of the second century, looked forward to restoration 66 years after the destruction, i.e. in 136 CE.[149]

No such hope, however, relieves the references to exile in P. With the expiry of the full 70 years, and the failure of the uprising under Trajan and of the Bar Cochba revolt, many must have lost hope. The Christian arguments – still being purveyed two centuries later by Aphrahat – that the biblical prophecies of ingathering were spent, that the Messiah had already come, and that the historical Israel had been rejected, must have seemed increasingly convincing. It would not have been surprising, then, if the Jewish community responsible for P finally accepted that argument.[150] Conversion to Christianity would have made no great difference to their practice: it preserved their existing values of prayer, charity and faith in God, and it gave them a rationale for

---

[149] These books are translated and introduced by A.F.J. Klijn, B.M. Metzger and S.E. Robinson respectively, in J.H. Charlesworth (ed.), *The Old Testament Pseudepigrapha*, 2 vols., New York 1983.

[150] The P version of the Apocrypha seems to have been made later, when the community was already evangelised.

continuing to neglect the ritual demands of Judaism. Thus the community brought its biblical version into the church of the east.

The special position of Ezra-Nehemiah and Chronicles may illuminate the course of the community's conversion to Christianity. It was suggested above that most of the biblical books in P are to be dated to *c.* 150 CE, but the books Ezra-Chronicles to *c.* 200 CE. It will then follow that, before the last books had even been translated, the earlier books were already being used in the church. The Jewish community responsible for the translation was haemorrhaging.

Those who remained in that Jewish community went on doggedly to translate those outstanding books. The despair voiced in the P version of Ezra and Chronicles may reflect the massive ongoing defections, as well as the failure of the Jewish uprisings of the second century. Perhaps the translator of Chronicles welcomed the opportunity provided by the damaged Hebrew *Vorlage* to express his own reaction to the crisis. This might explain why he did not resort to LXX or search harder for another Hebrew exemplar.[151]

After the translation of Ezra-Chronicles had been completed, more members of that Jewish community went over to the church. They brought with them the translation of these last books. However, some formal act of self-definition by the earlier converts had already taken place – perhaps shortly after Tatian's mission – whereby they had renounced their old community, and (leaving aside the question of their New Testament) had adopted as their Bible the existing books of the Peshitta Old Testament. That collection had not included Ezra to Chronicles; and when the later generation of converts brought in these last books, there were those in the church who considered that the limits of the Old Testament in Syriac had already been defined. Moreover, these books were known to be the work of that very Jewish community from which the new Christian community had parted company. In this way we could explain how the books Ezra-Chronicles never attained the same status in the Syriac Church as the earlier books of the Old Testament.

Those Jews who continued to hope for the fulfilment of the biblical prophecies of restoration became convinced that survival now depended on observance of the Torah and adherence to the rabbinic commandments. These are the Jews of whom Aphrahat speaks in the fourth century. They observe the dietary laws prescribed by the rabbis, who forbade all gentile cooking and gentile wine.[152] It is difficult to accept Neusner's view that the Jews known to Aphrahat practised a Judaism based on the Hebrew Bible alone.[153] Aphrahat's references to dietary laws show rather that the Jews who had not joined the church by the fourth century were precisely those who accepted rabbinic halachah.

Despite its Jewish origin, P was altogether rejected by the Jews. One reason, as in the case of LXX, was that it had become the Bible of a church. The other reason was that it was too 'simple' to reflect the rabbinic interpretations that had become dominant. The similarity in name between the Peshitta and the Peshat movement of interpretation of the Hebrew Bible in France and Spain in the eleventh and twelfth centuries is not quite

---

[151] I owe this suggestion to Dr Gillian Greenberg.
[152] Aphrahat, vol. I, col. 733; cf. Mishnah Abodah Zarah 2:4,6.
[153] J. Neusner, *Aphrahat and Judaism*, Leiden 1971, p. 147.

fortuitous, even though there is of course no direct connection between the two. Both were interested primarily in the plain sense of the Hebrew text; and neither the use of P nor the Peshat movement became established within rabbinic Judaism, because the quest for the plain sense threatened the rabbis' interpretations of scripture and ultimately their authority. Only in the thirteenth century was P re-discovered by Jewish scholars; but again the involvement was brief.

6
The establishment of the text

The primary witnesses to the text of P are the biblical manuscripts in Syriac which have come down to us from the fifth century CE onward. We also have biblical citations in Syriac within patristic writings, and in Arabic within works translated from Syriac. These witnesses do not offer an absolutely uniform text. This fact raises the question of how far – and on what principles – we may hope to work back from the extant witnesses to the translators' original work. It also challenges us to explain in historical terms the phenomenon of divergence among the extant witnesses, and the observed patterns of agreement and disagreement.

The goal of textual criticism

To explain the variation among the mss, it is simplest to assume that they all go back ultimately to a single original text. On that view there was just one translator, and in principle one translation, at every point of the text. This does not exclude the possibility that a translator may occasionally have left doublets, or that different books (or parts of books) are the work of different translators. Given this assumption of an Urtext, i.e. a single original text at every point, the differences among the mss arose in the course of scribal transmission, partly through unconscious mistakes, and partly through conscious attempts to 'improve' the original translator's work. (Here any change from the original text will be dubbed an 'error', even if the scribe intended it as a deliberate improvement.) The aim of textual criticism will then be to recover that unique Urtext.

The alternative is not to assume a unique Urtext, or at least not at every point in the text, and so to view the ms variants as "different and equally valid attempts to reproduce a Syriac version of a single Hebrew *Vorlage*".[1] On this view there were multiple translation attempts from the first, at least at some points in the text. In that case, the aim of textual criticism would be to recover these alternative translations, each of which has its own point of contact with the Hebrew. However, the nature of the variants among the mss of P provides little justification for this hypothesis. There are few if any variant readings which cannot be explained through inner-Syriac development and which instead imply more than one point of contact with the Hebrew; this point is considered in detail in appendix I to this chapter. We may therefore proceed on the hypothesis of a single Urtext.

[1] D.J. Lane in *Journal of Biblical Literature* 103 (1984), p. 108.

The recovery of an Urtext

The basic stages

We may begin by considering the general problem of reconstructing an Urtext from the varying texts of different mss, without specific reference to P.[2] In principle, there are two stages. First, where the extant authorities disagree, a choice must be made. In this way we may hope to construct from the extant manuscripts a text better and earlier than any one of them. Even if we make the right choice in every passage, however, there is no guarantee that the resulting text will be that of the original itself. It is possible – indeed likely – that some errors arose so early as to have tainted all the extant manuscripts. Hence the need for the second stage: emendation, in order to improve the text that can be constructed from the extant readings.

Intrinsic criteria to discriminate between rival readings

The first stage is to choose between the rival readings in every variant passage, i.e. at every point in the text where the manuscripts disagree. Here we must begin with those passages where a confident choice can be made. Such passages may be called determinate, and the remaining variant passages indeterminate. The available criteria for basing such choices are of two types. First, there is authenticity, based on our independent knowledge of what the author might be expected to write. In general, writers may be expected to observe the rules of grammar and (in poetry) metre, and to be consistent with the content and linguistic usage of their other writings. Rather different expectations will apply to translators, who are bound by their source text. The other type of criterion may be called direction, and is based on our independent knowledge of the changes likely to have been made by scribes. Every one of the alternative readings needs to be accounted for, and the criterion of direction favours whichever reading best explains the origin of its rivals.[3]

To be adopted, a reading must reach a minimum standard on both criteria. One cannot adopt a reading of which the author was not capable, however well it would account for the rival reading(s); nor can one be content with a reading that leaves its rivals inexplicable, whatever its own merits. Where more than one of the rival readings reaches this minimum standard on both criteria, we shall have to compare the respective merits of each variant on the two criteria combined, in the hope of thus identifying the better reading. The two types of criterion can both be called intrinsic, since they rest on the intrinsic qualities of the readings rather than any judgment as to the worth of the manuscripts presenting them.

In every passage where the manuscripts diverge, both types of intrinsic criterion – authenticity and direction – have to be considered. The danger is that these two types of argument may cancel each other out: the reading which best appeals to us as authentic

---

[2] See more fully M. Weitzman, "The Analysis of Open Traditions", *Studies in Bibliography* 38 (1985), pp. 82–120.

[3] The adages *lectio difficilior potior* and *lectio brevior potior* are examples of this principle, and are only valid to the extent that they exemplify it: scribes tend to simplify difficult readings, or to expand the text. However, a *lectio difficilior* comprising nonsense due to corruption, or a *lectio brevior* due to scribal omission, fails to explain its rival(s) and so has no claim to originality.

is all too often the likeliest at the same time to have been invented by a copyist. Hence the particular value of criteria of authenticity that were not available to copyists down the centuries. Examples in classical Greek literature are certain metrical laws governing iambic hexameters, which were forgotten in late antiquity and first re-discovered by Porson two centuries ago.[4]

Unfortunately, intrinsic criteria are unlikely to suffice to identify the best reading in every variant passage. We therefore need a means of inferring from the determinate passages which reading is correct in the remaining (indeterminate) passages. The basis for that inference is that, over the passages where intrinsic criteria determine the choice, we may establish a track record of the degree of textual reliability of different manuscripts, and of different combinations of manuscripts. This information will help us to reach a decision in the remaining passages, on a principle of analogy: a combination of manuscripts, or even a single manuscript, which alone preserves the true reading in a passage where we *can* distinguish truth from error on intrinsic grounds deserves a serious hearing in passages where we can*not*.[5] This criterion may be called distributional, being based not on the intrinsic virtues of a reading but on the particular combination of mss that attest it.

Conventional approaches to the choice between rival readings

It is usual to base distributional inferences on a reconstructed genealogy of the manuscripts, called a stemma.[6] On that approach, one must first establish the genealogy, which then provides the basis for discriminating between rival readings in the indeterminate passages. It may happen, for example, that we have four manuscripts ABCD. Suppose that (as almost always) we are able to demonstrate some errors common to all the mss, which can only be removed by conjectural emendation. Suppose further that each manuscript is also found to show some errors peculiar to itself. In addition, let there be just one combination of mss which are found to share errors not found elsewhere, namely CD. On that basis, a stemma would be drawn as in fig. 4, with an overall common ancestor ω to explain the errors of the whole tradition, and an exclusive common ancestor (γ) for C and D to explain the errors exclusive and common to these two mss.

In indeterminate passages where the manuscripts AB agree against CD, one will then reject the joint reading of CD, presuming it to go back no further than γ. Instead one will follow the joint reading of AB, which share no ancestor but ω, the latest common ancestor of all the mss.

Conventional scholarship thus proceeds in successive stages: from the agreements in error detectable among the determinate passages to a history, and from that history to a policy for discriminating between readings in indeterminate passages. It is preferable, however, to streamline this logic. The reason that an exclusive common ancestor was ever posited for C and D was that these two mss had been caught in exclusive and

---

[4] On these laws, see M.L. West, *Greek Metre*, Oxford 1982, p. 42.
[5] To be precise, in order to be established as a unique carrier of true readings, the ms or combination needs to occur in a passage where there are only two rival readings.
[6] See the classic exposition by P. Maas, *Textual Criticism*, tr. B. Flower, Oxford 1958.

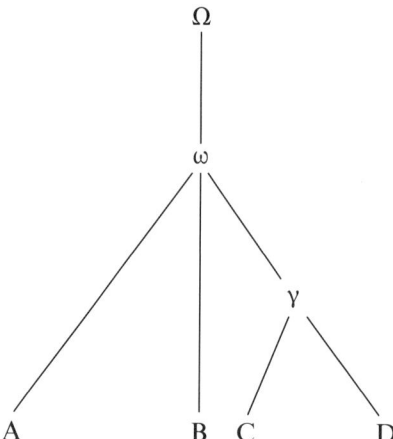

Fig.4. Example of stemma.

common error; and the reason that no such ancestor was posited for AB is that they were never so caught. Thus the underlying reason for preferring AB to CD in an indeterminate passage is that AB have never been caught in exclusive common error elsewhere while CD have. Ultimately, therefore, the reasoning is not historical but analogical. It could be applied straight from the determinate passages to the indeterminate, even without a stemma. In other words, the critical policy is not based on the history; rather, both can be derived independently from the choices to which the intrinsic criteria lead in the determinate passages.

The advantage of unbundling history and critical policy is that, even where the history is too complex for any stemma to be reconstructed, we may still hope to derive a critical policy for the indeterminate passages. This would be based directly on the impression which the determinate passages give of the worth of different mss and ms combinations.

Identifying distributional criteria

On the basis of the analogical reasoning set out above, distributional criteria are developed by tracking the performance of individual mss, and of combinations of mss, over the determinate passages. Of course, the distributional criteria that we may develop are no more secure than our judgment in identifying and pronouncing on the determinate passages from which they derive.

Distributional arguments can be either positive or negative. Positively, we may discover a combination of mss, and perhaps even a single mss, that preserves the true reading exclusively in some passages where intrinsic considerations suffice to distinguish truth from error. We may then infer that that ms or combination – with or without the support of further mss – is capable of likewise preserving the true reading in passages where intrinsic considerations are inconclusive. As to the negative

---

[7] The technical term for the copyist's source ms.

argument, there are some combinations of mss, including single mss, whose exclusive readings are never found correct, so far as can be judged from the determinate passages. We shall therefore be reluctant, in the indeterminate passages, to accept any reading exclusive to such a ms or combination as original.

Intuitively it may seem that numerical support should constitute an important and even an overriding distributional criterion. In particular, we may sometimes find that the reading which appears true by the intrinsic criteria survives in just one ms, against the agreement of the majority, and we may question whether this can really be so.

The answer is that it is perfectly possible. A simple case occurs where the extant mss belong to two independent branches, of which one is represented by a single ms and the other by a fertile tradition. In this case that single ms will repeatedly offer correct readings not extant elsewhere, though no doubt there will also be passages where that single ms has an error of which the majority are free.

One may also encounter a more complex situation, where the true reading survives in a single ms at one point in the text and in another single ms at another point. This situation can arise when it was common for a scribe not to copy a single exemplar[7] mechanically but to compare one or more additional exemplars and to adopt attractive readings from these. In a text transmitted in this fashion, plausible errors (or 'improvements' of the text) might thus gain wide currency, and the true reading, if not lost altogether, might become confined to isolated pockets or even to a single ms, and not necessarily the same ms in every passage.

Even if the scribes who compared additional mss were infallible in their choice between rival readings, the result could still be that the true reading survives uniquely now in one single ms, now in another. The scenario here is that all extant mss come from one family, and bear the errors already found in its latest common ancestor, but that another family, independent of that ancestor and free of its errors, long survived alongside the first, before finally dying out. In that case, the scribes who produced the mss (lost or extant) of the one family with extant representatives had the opportunity to remove piecemeal the errors inherited from that family's common ancestor, by substituting correct readings that were preserved in the now extinct independent family. Since different scribes searched for such readings independently, and perhaps not systematically, the result may be once more the unique preservation of the correct reading now in one ms or combination, now in another.

Whether the cause is the spread of good readings or of bad, the phenomenon of unique preservation of the correct reading in different mss at different points of the text is frequent in classical and patristic literature – for example in Homer[8] and Aeschylus,[9] or in the *Ecclesiastical History* of Eusebius.[10] In textual criticism, it is not always right to follow the majority. We should therefore be prepared for a similar possibility in the textual criticism of P.

Another distributional criterion which seems intuitively important is age. In principle, of course, age and textual worth are likely to be correlated. The relationship is not, however, absolute. A late ms may have been copied from an early exemplar; conversely,

---

[8] G. Pasquali, *Storia della tradizione e critica del testo*, 2nd edn, Florence 1952, p. 211.
[9] R.D. Dawe, *The Collation and Investigation of Manuscripts of Aeschylus*, Cambridge 1964, chapter 5.
[10] E. Schwartz (ed.), *Eusebius' Werke*, vol. 2, part 3, Leipzig 1909, p. cxlvi.

one careless copyist can degrade the text more than a long succession of careful ones. As Pasquali has reminded us: *recentiores, non deteriores*.[11] On the other hand, one must admit that the likelihood that an attractive reading has arisen through conjecture rather than faithful transmission increases as one nears modern times.

How powerful are the distributional criteria?

We cannot expect intrinsic criteria to determine the correct reading in more than a minority of the variant passages. We may therefore ask in what proportion of the remaining passages the choice between the rival readings is likely to be decided by the distributional criteria.

There is no general answer to this question. At the most favourable extreme, we could imagine a tradition where just three mss survive, and where – among the determinate passages – any reading attested by at least two of those mss is correct. In that case, one could identify the original reading in the indeterminate passages mechanically, by following the agreement of any two of the three mss. The genealogy would also be clear: three mss, each derived directly and independently from the original. Dom Quentin tried to establish just such a *règle de fer* to reconstruct the text of the Vulgate, on the basis of the agreement of any two out of three designated principal mss. Unfortunately, a situation so tidy is unlikely in real life, especially in relation to biblical texts, if only because of the tendency of scribes not to copy one exemplar mechanically but to compare others in order to improve the text.[12] Not surprisingly, Quentin's approach was found wanting and abandoned by his successors.[13]

At the other extreme, one could imagine a situation where the scribes compared different exemplars with such enthusiasm (rather than discrimination) that readings good or bad might be transferred anywhere. In that case, the true reading might turn up in one combination of mss in a certain passage, and in a different combination in another, without any regular pattern. There would be no scope whatsoever for distributional arguments, nor historical reconstruction.

In practice, the situation lies between these extremes. Usually, a number of ms combinations (possibly including single mss) can be identified, each of which preserves the true reading exclusively in some determinate passages and *may* therefore do the same in the indeterminate passages. Other combinations of mss are found to have no good readings exclusive to themselves, over the determinate passages, and so are unlikely to present good readings exclusively over the indeterminate passages. Ideally, when faced with variant readings, we should like to see one of them attested by a ms combination of the former type, and its rival attested by a ms combination of the latter type. The

---

[11] Pasquali, *Storia della tradizione*, pp. 43–108.

[12] Another reason is that textual traditions in three (or more) primary branches are rare. Most have just two primary branches, and so fail to decide cases where these two offer different readings. This phenomenon was pointed out by the Romance scholar Joseph Bédier.

[13] H. Quentin, *Mémoire sur l'établissment du texte de la Vulgate*, Rome and Paris 1922. Genesis-Numbers were edited by Quentin in accordance with the principles there set down. The edition of Deuteronomy, which he had supervised for some time until his death in 1935, adheres in the main to the same system. However, two of the three principal mss are not extant beyond Deuteronomy, and the editors did not venture to devise a new "iron rule" for the later books. An explanation and critique of Quentin's method are included in M. Weitzman, "The Analysis of Open Traditions", pp. 88–91.

choice would then be clear. More often, however, it will not be possible to decide between the rival readings on this basis, either because neither rival reading is supported by a combination of the former type or because both are.

Constructing a textual history

In relation to historical reconstruction, our results are again likely to be partial. If every scribe were content to follow one exemplar, then a family of mss of common descent would be easily distinguished by a series of exclusive errors inherited from its latest common ancestor. Where scribes made a practice of comparing more than one exemplar, however, the boundaries between families become blurred, in two ways. First, some of the errors inherited from the ancestor of a given family will spread to certain mss belonging to other families. Second, some of the errors that stood in that ancestor will be removed from certain members of the family through comparison of outside mss. Thus the distinctive errors of the ancestor will not be confined to its descendants, but on the other hand will not appear in all its descendants. The larger the family, the greater scope for both phenomena, and hence the harder the family will be to delimit. Hence we are likely to be able to do no more than identify the smallest groups (in effect, small sub-families) which agree regularly in exclusive error, and so to establish the lowest branchings only of the genealogical tree.[14] The genealogical relationships *between* those small groups are likely to elude us. This is only to be expected: where scribes were wont to compare two or more exemplars, any genealogical tree embracing all the extant mss and purporting to show the ancestry of each ms would inevitably be too simplistic to be of use. As we shall see, however, there may be alternative means of gaining insight into the relationships between the manuscripts.

Identifying determinate passages in P: the intrinsic criteria

Authenticity: the significance of agreement with MT

The criterion of authenticity requires independent judgment of what the translator may have been expected to write. Had we instead been dealing with free composition in a well-documented dialect, criteria such as clear style and idiomatic use of language would have been appropriate. However, P is a translation, on the nature of which – particularly, the balance struck between fidelity and intelligibility – we must not pronounce in advance.

Our starting-point in considering what the authors – i.e. P's translators – might have been expected to write must instead be the fact that P is a translation of some form of the text of the Hebrew Bible. The Hebrew *Vorlage* of P is of course lost, and no doubt differed in places from MT. However, both that *Vorlage* and MT derive ultimately from a common source. Hence, when a particular manuscript of P agrees with MT, the simplest explanation of that agreement will be that it reflects the common source of MT and of P's *Vorlage*. This argument would apply equally to agreement with any other

---

[14] By convention the tree is drawn with the root at the top.

extant form of the Hebrew text, such as a fragment from Qumran.[15] Thus, agreement in form or in content with MT, or with any other extant Hebrew text, should in principle count in favour of a reading. Of course, P is at its most useful to students of the Hebrew text of the Bible where it does *not* agree with any extant form of the Hebrew; but this cannot weigh with us as we set about reconstructing the oldest text of P.

In theory one could mount a countervailing argument of direction: agreement with the Hebrew is due to later scribal revision after the Hebrew. That possibility is remote, however, because there is no direct evidence that those who copied the Syriac text had any access to the Hebrew (as is discussed further below). So far as our evidence goes, scribal revision was based rather on Greek forms of the biblical text. This dichotomy between the Hebrew source used by the translator and the Greek text used by revisers is indeed valuable. The situation is different in the Apocrypha (with the partial exception of Ecclesiasticus) and New Testament, where both the translator and the reviser would have used the Greek text. As Emerton stated the problem:

Agreement between the Peshitta and the Greek may be interpreted in two different ways. It may be suggested either that a Syriac reading which stands closer than another to the Greek is more original, or that it is a later correction. It is sometimes impossible to decide between the two possibilities.[16]

The investigator of P in the canonical books of the Hebrew Bible is indeed fortunate by comparison.

Apart from formal agreement with extant Hebrew texts, an equally important aspect of authenticity is translation technique. Although the translators did not impose upon themselves any rule of one-to-one correspondence between Hebrew and Syriac vocabulary items, we may still expect the translator to be consistent in his Syriac rendering of a given Hebrew word, other things being equal. Of course we must allow here for the various factors that can cause inconsistency, such as differences in the meaning of the Hebrew word in different passages, [17] or even a desire for stylistic variation. Nevertheless, in the absence of any such identifiable factor, the use of the translator's characteristic equivalences will be a mark of authenticity. Conversely, an equivalence not characteristic of the translator (again in the absence of a specific explanation) will be suspicious, even when there is agreement with the Hebrew. Thus at Ps. 74:12b we have:

MT   ואלהים מלכי מקדם פעל ישועות בקרב הארץ

P [majority][18]   ܐܠܗ ܝܠܢ ܡܠܟܢ ܗܘ ܕܦܩܕ ܡܢ ܩܕܝܡ ܥܠ ܦܘܪܩܢܗ ܕܝܥܩܘܒ

       Our God is our king, who commanded of old concerning the salvation of Jacob.

A[=7a1] T[b]   ܐܠܗ ܝܠܢ ܡܠܟܢ ܗܘ ܕ[ܥ]ܒܕ ܦܘܪܩܢܐ ܒܡܨܥܬܗ ܕܐܪܥܐ

       Our God is our king, who wrought salvation in the midst of the earth

The second reading agrees with MT, while the first differs considerably. Nevertheless, the word ܡܨܥܬܗ found in the second reading is never attested elsewhere in Psalms,

---

[15] In theory it would apply to agreement with LXX also, but there would be a countervailing argument based on direction, since copyists of P were capable of accommodation to LXX.

[16] J.A. Emerton, *The Peshitta of the Wisdom of Solomon* (= Studia Postbiblica 2), Leiden 1959, p. xxxvi.

[17] A. van der Kooij, "On the Significance of MS 5b1 for Peshiṭta Genesis", in MPI 4 (1988), pp. 183–99.

[18] On the basis of the collations and sigla of Barnes's edition.

which instead uses ܟܐܠ (for both קרב and תוך). It seems rather that the translator was unable to read the last four words, owing to damage to the Hebrew *Vorlage*, and so guessed on the basis of Ps. 44:5. This implies that the majority are correct after all. The reading that agrees with MT is then a later correction, perhaps from LXX.[19] As this example shows, agreement with MT does not in itself demonstrate authenticity.

Again at Job 30:19 we have:

MT   הרני לחמר ואתמשל כעפר ואפר

P [majority]   ܐܘܕܡܝܢܝ ܠܛܝܢܐ. ܘܐܬܕܡܝܬ ܐܝܟ ܥܦܪܐ ܘܩܛܡܐ.

they compared me to mire, and I was likened to dust and ashes

For the first word, 12a1 and some later mss instead have ܐܪܡܝܘܢܝ "they threw me". Formally, this reading is closer to MT הרני, which likewise comes from a verbal root (ירה) originally meaning 'throw'. However, in context that Syriac reading yields poor sense; and, given that the translator could have guessed a meaning for the obscure הרני on the light of the parallel verb ("and I was likened . . ."), the majority reading is the more authentic.

The need to consider translation technique as well as proximity to MT means that little importance can be attached to agreement with the Hebrew in features that the translator himself was not careful to reproduce. Such are the presence/absence of *waw* and other particles, variation in number or suffixes, and other grammatical points.[20]

All in all, however, the criterion of agreement with MT is indeed valuable. It is applicable in a good proportion of variant passages. Moreover, as will be argued in detail below, it was largely inaccessible to copyists. It must be checked against translation technique and the distributional criteria; but if all else is equal, the reading that agrees with MT deserves preference.

The criterion of direction

Direction is concerned with the changes that a scribe might be expected to make. Copyists have tended to replace Hebraisms by constructions in keeping with Syriac idiom, and also to remove inconsistencies and other difficulties in the text. In that they depart from the original text, these readings must be termed errors; but they would not have appeared so to the scribes.

In particular, copyists have striven to smooth the style. To this end they might adjust grammatical particles, notably by the addition or omission of *d*- or *w*-. This tendency may even cause more extensive changes, as at Ps. 109:27 –

MT כי ידך זאת; Nestorian mss (LNm) ܕܐܝܕܟ ܗܝ, ܗܕܐ; rell. ܕܓܠܝܬ ܗܝ, ܗܕܐ
The former reading is closer to MT, while the other is an attempt to improve the syntax.

Another scribal change is assimilation to parallel passages, as at Lam. 2:20[21] –

MT   (יהרג) במקדש (ה')

DAP*vidFBO   (ܢܬܩܛܠ) ܒܡܩܕܫܗ (ܕܡܪܝܐ)

Pc and later mss: ܒܡܩܕܫܐ

____

[19] See further M.P. Weitzman, "The Peshitta Psalter and its Hebrew *Vorlage*", *VT* 35 (1985), pp. 341–54.

[20] As pointed out by S.P. Brock, "Text History and Text Division in Peshiṭta Isaiah" in MPI 4 (1988), pp. 49–80: 60–1.

[21] After the collations and sigla of B.Albrektson, *Studies in the Text and Theology of the Book of Lamentations with a Critical Edition of the Peshitta Text*, Lund 1963.

The older mss give the same sense as MT, while the younger have assimilated to Lam. 2:4 just above:

ܘܩܛܠ ܟܠ ܪ̈ܓܝܓܬ ܥܝ̈ܢܐ ܒܡܫܟܢܐ ܕܒܪܬ ܨܗܝܘܢ

At least in Psalms, where the text was used for divine service, we sometimes find adaptation for use in the church:

Ps. 51:20 את ציון; majority ܠܨܗܝܘܢ "Zion"; BJβδ ܠܥܕܬܟ "thy church".
Ps. 51:21 פרים, majority ܬܘܪ̈ܐ "bulls"; m ܩܘܪ̈ܒܢܐ "offerings"

Scribes might also assimilate to LXX, as discussed in chapter 3 above. When some mss agree with MT and the others with LXX, authenticity counts in favour of the former and direction against the latter, so that the choice is particularly clear, as at Ps. 39:7 –

MT	ולא ידע מי אספם	
cf. P variant	ܘܠܐ ܝܕܥ ܡܢܘ ܟܢܫ ܠܗܘܢ	[9a1, Nestorian mss]
LXX	καὶ οὐ γινώσκει τίνι συνάξει αὐτά	
cf. P variant	...ܠܡܢܘ ܟܢܫ ܠܗܘܢ	[6t 1 7a1 8a1 and other western mss]

Although the mss supporting the second variant are older by far, the intrinsic criteria clearly favour the first variant.

Scribes have also changed the text by inadvertent miscopying. Where one variant reading can only be explained as a corruption of its rival, the choice is clear, as at Cant. 8:14 –

MT ברח; ܘܗܒ ܐܬܐ 6h17 7a1 8a1 12a1; ܐܬܗܦܟܝ 8a1^{c} 9c1 9h1 and later mss

The reading ܘܗܒ ܐܬܐ bears no semantic relation to the Hebrew, and in context yields poor syntax; it altogether lacks authenticity. By contrast, the word ܐܬܗܦܟܝ "turn" is not alien to P in this book; it recurs in all mss in the similar verse 2:17, where MT has סב. Although the root ברח does not recur in the book, ܐܬܗܦܟܝ would be an acceptable rendering in this context. As for direction, one could argue against ܐܬܗܦܟܝ that it results from assimilation to 2:17.[22] Since, however, ܘܗܒ ܐܬܐ is ruled out of court on authenticity grounds, we must regard ܐܬܗܦܟܝ as original, so long as the rival reading ܘܗܒ ܐܬܐ is then explicable – which it is, on the following lines. The reading ܐܬܗܦܟܝ underwent an error which can easily occur in the later Syriac scripts: ܗ was misread ܐܘ. At the beginning of the resulting ܐܬܐܘܦܟܝ, the scribe thought that he could distinguish the word ܐܬܐ. The remaining letters ܘܦܟܝ then seemed an error for ܘܗܒ; and in order to produce some sense, the scribe inverted these two words, whence ܘܗܒ ܐܬܐ. Thus the original reading here survives in the later tradition only – a phenomenon further considered below.

Finally, scribes have sometimes been thought capable of conforming the Syriac text to MT. That possibility must now be considered.

The hypothesis of revision of individual mss after MT

The case for unique preservation

In a number of biblical books, a single ms is found to depart from the majority and to agree uniquely with MT. The evaluation of these cases has proved controversial. A

22 So D.J. Lane, "'The Curtains of Solomon': Some Notes on the 'Syriacing' of ŠÎR-HAŠŠÎRÎM", MPI 8 (1995), pp. 73–84: 79.

celebrated ms in this category is 5b1 in Genesis and Exodus, which offers many unique agreements with MT, ascribed by Barnes to scribal revision but by Pinkerton to unique preservation of the original text.[23] Another is 9a1 in all books where the first hand survives (Leviticus-Hosea, Psalms, Lamentations and Chronicles).[24] Here again Barnes supposed revision after the Hebrew, but unique preservation was instead posited by Diettrich.[25] The behaviour of two other mss in different books – 8h5 in Ezra-Nehemiah and 10f1 in Esther – is similar.

In order to account for the unique agreements with MT, we have to choose between two possible scenarios:

(a) The original translation stood relatively close to the Hebrew, and sometimes survives in a single ms, while the variant readings of the majority are due to scribal change, whether conscious or not;

(b) The original translation was a relatively loose rendering of the Hebrew, and readings in single mss that stand closer than the majority to MT are due to later accommodation to the Hebrew.

Thus textual criticism and translation technique are interlocking questions.

If Syriac scribes were indeed wont to revise after the Hebrew, then the arguments set out above for viewing agreement with MT as a mark of authenticity are countered by an argument of direction, that the agreement could have been imposed by revisers. Whether copyists revised after the Hebrew, or whether the original translation was the sole point of contact with the Hebrew, is thus a central question in the textual criticism of P.

That individual scribes should have wished to revise P after the Hebrew is not inconceivable. As we have seen, Syriac tradition was aware that P had been translated ultimately from Hebrew, even if some viewed LXX as an intermediate link. Hence some scholar intent on improving the text of P might have tried to conform it to the Hebrew.

Moreover, there are precedents for such revision in other ancient versions. In LXX, correction after the Hebrew is as old as the fragments recovered from Qumran,[26] and was probably the main purpose of Origen's Hexapla.[27] Revision after the Hebrew has also been detected in some mss of the Vulgate. In the *Psalterium iuxta Hebraeos*, E. Power concluded that "the Codex Hubertianus, the oldest of the Theodulfian Mss.,

---

[23] W.E. Barnes, "A New Edition of the Pentateuch in Syriac", *JTS* 15 (1914), pp. 41–4; J. Pinkerton, "The Origin and the Early History of the Syriac Pentateuch", *JTS* 15 (1914), pp. 14–41. The latter view was advanced even earlier by Ceriani, *Le Edizioni*, p. 9.

[24] The ms is undated. S.E. Assemanus, *Bibliothecae Mediceae Laurentianae et Palatinae codicum mss. orientalium catalogus*, Florence 1742, pp. 49–50, attributed it to the sixth century. Barnes, "Chronicles", p. xxix preferred the ninth by reason of the cursive script which, however, still admits an earlier date. See now K. Jenner, "A Review of the Methods by which Syriac Biblical and Related Manuscripts have been Described and Analysed," *Aram* 5 (1993), pp. 255–66:264. The Leiden siglum 9a1, in accordance with the editors' usual policy, adopts the later date in cases of doubt.

[25] Barnes, "Chronicles", p.xxx; idem (ed.), *The Peshitta Psalter according to the West Syrian Text*, Cambridge 1904, p.xviii. Contrast G. Diettrich, *Ein Apparatus criticus zur Pešitto zum Propheten Jesaia* [= BZAW 8], Giessen 1905, pp. xxxi–xxxii. See further M.P.Weitzman, "The Originality of Unique Readings in Peshitta MS 9a1", in MPI 4 (1988), pp. 225–58.

[26] E.Tov, *The Greek Minor Prophets Scroll from Naḥal Ḥever (8ḤevXIIgr)* [= DJD 8], Oxford 1990; D. Barthélemy, *Les devanciers d'Aquila*, Leiden 1963.

[27] S.P. Brock, "Origen's Aims as a Textual Critic of the Old Testament", *Studia Patristica* 10 (1970), pp. 215–8.

had been extensively corrected from the Hebrew" and moreover that "a number of Theodulfian and allied Mss. of the ninth century had lost some of the Hubertian corrections and at the same time incorporated in the text of the Psalter a number of new corrections from the Hebrew".[28]

If we are to show that unique agreements with the Hebrew result from preservation rather than revision, further arguments apart from the agreement with the Hebrew must be found. Here two types of situations can be identified as critical. In the first, the majority reading can only be explained as a corruption of the unique reading that agrees with MT. As the majority reading is without authenticity, the reading of the single ms must be original, e.g.

(a)   Gen. 48:4

MT   הנני מפרך
5b1   ܐܠ ܐܢܐ ܡܒܪܟ ܗܐ
rell.   ܐܠ ܐܢܐ ܡܗܢܟ ܗܐ

       behold I bless thee

The majority reading bears no semantic relation with the Hebrew. It can only be explained as a corruption of 5b1's reading, which agrees with the Hebrew. That corruption is in part an assimilation to the last word of the previous verse (ܡܗܒܕܟ).[29]

(b)   2 Sam. 19:36

MT   שָׁרִים וְשָׁרוֹת
9a1   ܫܝܪܐ ܘܫܝܪܬܐ
rell.   ܫܝ ܘܫܝܪܬܐ

       one and another (fem.)

No semantic path can be traced from the Hebrew text to the majority reading, which thus lacks any authenticity. The reading of 9a1, by contrast, is readily derivable from the Hebrew, on the assumption that the translator read it as שָׁרִים וְשָׁרוֹת. The equation of שָׁר with ܫܝܪܐ recurs in v.7 of the same chapter, even though the usual Syriac equivalent is ܙܡܪ. The reading of 9a1 must be original, because the majority reading cannot be explained except as a corruption of it.

(c)   2 Kgs. 22:14

MT specifies the quarter of Jerusalem where the prophetess Huldah dwelt: במשנה. The majority have ܒܬܟܫܦܬܐ, meaning that she dwelt (or sat) "in supplication"; but this bears no semantic relation with the Hebrew. Now 9a1 instead makes her sit ܒܬܢܝܬܐ "in repetition", or in effect: "in study". This Syriac rendering and the Hebrew come from

---

[28] E. Power, "Corrections from the Hebrew in the Theodulfian Mss of the Vulgate", *Biblica* 5 (1924), pp. 233–58; see p. 234. Hubertianus is dateable to the eighth or ninth century.
[29] See further van der Kooij in MPI 4 (1988), p. 195.

cognate roots. The reading ܕܝܢܘܬܐ of 9a1 is also supported by the commentary ascribed to Ephrem, by the Targum (בבית אלפנא) and by P at the parallel passage 2 Chr. 34:22 (ܕܝܠܘܬܐ).[30] Once more the majority reading can only be explained through the reading that agrees with MT.

(d)   Esther 8:3

MT ותבך; 10f1 ܘܒܟܬ; rell. ܘܒܟܐ.

Here 10f1 clearly agrees with MT, unlike the majority reading. The latter can in fact be easily explained as a corruption of the text preserved in 10f1. What induced the corruption was that the next word is ܘܐܬܚܢܢܬ in all mss, to represent the next Hebrew word ותתחנן "and she supplicated".

In the second critical situation, the unique reading is so characteristic of the translator's own system of Hebrew-Syriac equivalences that it could not have been supplied by a reviser, e.g.

(a)   Gen. 24:55

MT   (תשב הנער אתנו) ימים או עשור

5b1   ܥܣܪܐ ܐܘ ܬܪܝܢ ܝܘܡܝܢ

rell.   ܝܘܡܬܐ ܥܣܪ

Reference is here made to the length of the delay requested by Rebecca's family before she departed with Abraham's servant. The rendering of ימים by ܬܪܝܢ ܝܘܡܝܢ is characteristic of P; it appears in all P mss at Num. 9:22, and the rendering at Exod. 13:10 and Lev. 25:29 is similar: ܡܢ ܝܘܡ ܠܝܘܡ. The authenticity of this reading is further supported by the verbal agreement of T⁰. A Syriac reviser bent on conforming the text to the Hebrew would not have known or desired this rendering; instead, he might have written ܝܘܡܬܐ, or perhaps ܥܕܢܐ. The majority reading is easily explained by assimilation to Gen. 29:14: "and he dwelt with him a month of days". The attempt to view it instead as a reflection of rabbinic exegesis and hence as authentic was discussed in chapter 3.

(b)   Ps. 141:1

MT חושה לי

9a1 ܟܬܪ ܠܝ, rell. ܐܣܬܪܗܒ.

The rendering of חוש (which of course really means "hasten") by ܟܬܪ ("wait") is a peculiarity of P-Psalms (22:20 etc.), though it was also borrowed by the translator of Job at Job 20:2, as noted above. A reviser after the Hebrew would have been unlikely to know of, or to wish to imitate, this peculiarity of the translator; instead he would have supplied an accurate translation meaning "hasten to me". Hence the reading of 9a1 is original, while the majority substitute a more straightforward expression.

In this connection we may consider the controversy surrounding the rival readings

---

[30] For details, see M. Weitzman, "Originality", p. 237.

[Syriac] and [Syriac] where reference is made to silver metal. Six times in Genesis and 28 times in Exodus, 5b1 has [Syriac] while the majority have [Syriac]. Likewise at 2 Kgs. 25:15 9a1 has [Syriac] and the majority [Syriac]; and in Ezra 1:11 5:14 8h5 alone has [Syriac] and the rest [Syriac].[31] In all these places MT has כסף, meaning silver metal.

So far as authenticity is concerned, van der Kooij has shown that the translator sometimes used different Syriac words to distinguish different nuances of the same Hebrew word. On authenticity grounds, we could well argue that the translator of Genesis deliberately varied his usage according to sense: [Syriac] for silver metal and [Syriac] for 'money'. On the other hand, one could instead argue that the consistent use of [Syriac] is authentic, and that the translation may have been made before [Syriac] – a loanword from Greek ἄσημος – came into Syriac in order to specify silver metal.

On authenticity grounds, then, either reading is acceptable. However, we must also consider direction. We can easily understand why scribes would change an original [Syriac] to [Syriac], where silver metal was meant. But why should anyone wish to change [Syriac] to [Syriac]? It has been suggested that such a change might result from the influence of Hebrew, or of another Aramaic dialect where [Syriac] indicated silver material as well as currency;[32] but there is no independent evidence for either process. Hence priority must go to [Syriac]. This agrees with the findings in chapter 4: where the mss are unanimous, we find [Syriac] in the more conservative books (e.g. Samuel, Kings) and [Syriac] in the more modern (e.g. Proverbs).

The impression that ancient material survives in the mss that agree uniquely with MT is confirmed by ancient linguistic forms. Thus 9a1 has the deficient spelling [Syriac] for an *Ayin Waw* verb form (Isa. 19:1), a feature otherwise confined to the oldest mss of Syriac literature. Again, the archaic demonstrative [Syriac] (cf. Biblical Aramaic אִלֵּךְ) is attested uniquely by 9a1 at 1 Chr. 9:1 and by 10f1 at Esther 1:5, while the remaining mss have [Syriac] (as observed in chapter 5 above). As scribes were far likelier to modernise than archaise, the form [Syriac] must be original, despite being attested in a single ms.

A further text-critical question raised by this last replacement is whether the original translation had many more cases of [Syriac], which were later displaced by [Syriac] in all extant mss. It was argued above that [Syriac] was a neutral demonstrative which fell out of use. Now each occurrence of [Syriac] in a ms of P stands near the beginning of the relevant book; and this suggests that the relevant translators used it at the outset but soon discontinued its use as obsolescent, just as the translators of Genesis and Chronicles renounced the particle [Syriac]. If so, few if any cases of [Syriac] in the original translation have been altogether lost.

As Koster has pointed out, there are some further linguistic usages in which those mss which elsewhere agree uniquely with MT depart from the rest. In some places where the majority have [Syriac] for "finish", these mss have [Syriac], at Gen. 24:45, 27:30 Exod. 31:18, 34:33 (5b1), and 1 Kgs. 8:54 (9a1).[33] Again, for the noun זִיז we find [Syriac] in 5b1 alone at Exod. 17:5, and in 9a1 alone in Judg. 2:7, whilst the other manuscripts

[31] C. Moss, "The Peshitta Version of Ezra", *Le Muséon* 46 (1933), pp. 55–110: 78.
[32] Van der Kooij, MPI 4 (1988), pp. 191,198.
[33] M.D. Koster, "Peshitta Revisited: a Reassessment of its Value as a Version", *JSS* 38 (1993), pp. 235–68: 263.

have ܘܢܚܐ. Given the recurrence of this pattern in different books, it seems that in these usages the minority reading is again the older.

The origin of the majority readings

If we are to show that the unique agreements with MT give the original reading, we must also explain how the majority readings arose. In many cases, the cause is a desire to improve clarity. Here the revisers follow in the footsteps of the translators. For example, in the conversation between Isaac and Esau at Gen. 27:35–6, there is one instance of an addition (underlined below) to indicate the speaker in all mss including 5b1, but there are many more instances (italicised below) where such an addition appears in all mss except 5b1. It would seem that the translator made just the one (underlined) addition, while the revisers went further in the same direction:

And *his father* said *to him*: "Your brother entered in guile and took your blessings." And <u>Esau</u> said: "Truly was his name called Jacob, for he cheated me twice. He took my birthright and now he has received my blessings." And *Esau* said to *his father*: For me have you not left a blessing?

In many other cases the majority reading can readily be attributed to mechanical mis-copying, assimilation to other biblical passages, or a desire to improve the text, linguistically or logically. Some cases were given above, but some additional examples deserve note:

(a) Lev. 11:19

MT עֲטַלֵּף   6b1 ܦܘܪܫܘܢܐ rell. ܠܛܘܣܐ

Here 6b1 alone has "bat" as in MT, while the rest show the substitution "peacock". The motive was logical improvement: a bat has no place in a list of birds, and moreover a law against eating it might have seemed superfluous. The peacock may have been chosen as substitute because of its affinity with the "wild rooster" ܬܪܢܓܠܐ ܒܪܐ which immediately precedes.[34]

(b) Lev. 15:17

MT עוֹר   9a1* ܘܡܫܟܐ; rell. ܘܡܬܟܐ, preceded by *waw*, *dalath* or ܐܘ.

The reading of 9a1* relates directly to the Hebrew, while the majority reading is an easy corruption, influenced by a similar-looking word in a nearby verse: ܡܬܟܐ in the similar context of v.23 (MT מִשְׁכָּב). The scribe of 9a1 has in fact gone back to correct his text to ܘܡܬܟܐ, so that we catch the majority reading in the act of supplanting the older text.

(c) 1 Kgs. 6:37

MT יֻסַּד   9a1 ܐܬܫܬܠ rell. ܐܬܫܬܐܣ

Here the translator used ܫܬܠ in the sense "found", as occasionally elsewhere in P (Isa. 44:28, Job 4:19) and sometimes in the Targums (e.g. at Exod. 9:18). This old sense was

---

[34] The link between these two birds was noted by Maori, *The Peshitta Version*, p. 333. According to Maori, however, the reading "peacock" is original, and the link was utilised by the translator himself.

later forgotten, since the usual sense is of course "complete". The motive of the majority text is then linguistic improvement: to substitute an unambiguous word.

(d)   Ps. 110:4

MT עַל דִּבְרָתִי מַלְכִּי צֶדֶק

9a1 ܐܠ ܡܠܟܐܘ ܘܡܠܟܝܨܕܩ

rell. ܟܕܡܘܬܗ ܘܡܠܟܝܨܕܩ

The majority reading arises from assimilation to a New Testament passage, namely Hebrews 7:15 κατὰ τὴν ὁμοιότητα Μελχισεδεκ. The Peshitta version of Hebrews likewise has ܟܕܡܘܬܗ ܕܡܠܟܝܨܕܩ in all citations and echoes of this verse.

The alternative hypothesis: revision after the Hebrew

If the regular agreements with MT in single mss are not due to unique preservation, they must indeed result from revision after the Hebrew. That supposition, however, is open to many difficulties.

First, if mss like 5b1 really bear the marks of revision after the Hebrew, we would expect to find some features demonstrably alien to the translator's usage as known from elsewhere – rather as the reviser who supplied 7a1's reading at Ps. 74:12b betrayed himself by using ܡܨܥܬܐ rather than ܓܘܐ. However, there are no convincing instances. Instead, as noted above, these unique readings agree not only with MT but also with the Syriac equivalences used by the translator elsewhere.

Second, we would also expect revision to be consistently done. Instead, we tend to find an agreement with MT next to an obvious *dis*agreement. For example, in the instructions for building the Tabernacle in Exod. 25–6, 5b1 agrees from time to time uniquely with MT, but at the same time tends alone to replace the second person future verbs by imperatives, herein departing from MT.

A third point against the hypothesis of revision after MT is that the phenomenon of regular agreement in a single Syriac ms with the Hebrew text repeats itself in different biblical books and in different mss – namely 5b1, 8h5, 9a1 and 10f1. To explain all these cases through a series of independent revisions after the Hebrew text is not easy.

Fourth, even though in theory the Syriac-speaking church may have received Jewish converts who knew enough Hebrew to perform such a revision, we have no hard evidence that that church ever called upon such expertise. The commentaries ascribed to Ephrem show knowledge of a few Hebrew words, but do not indicate the capacity to produce the regular agreements with MT found in 5b1 or 9a1. Even Jacob of Edessa would not have been equal to the task, to judge by his statement that Hosanna in Hebrew means "save me".[35]

The only evidence of possible revision after the Hebrew occurs in certain passages where a whole verse or an even longer section is omitted in some mss, while the other mss supply wording based on a Hebrew text. Here it can be argued that the original translator omitted the passage, but, shortly after he had completed his task, a colleague

---

[35] See W. Wright in *Journal of Sacred Literature* (Jan 1867), pp. 430ff.; *Catalogue of the Syriac Mss in the British Museum*, p. 430. Wright's description of Jacob as "equally conversant with Syriac, Greek and Hebrew" seems charitable.

detected the omission and tried to make it good on the basis of the Hebrew. Two such instances – in 1 Chr. 26:13–27, 34 and Judg. 20:20–1 – are discussed in appendix II to this chapter; there may be a third in 2 Sam. 19:12.

We may also consider the revision hypothesis in relation to the apocryphal book of Maccabees. In 1 Macc. 1:1–14: 25, the text of 7a1 often departs from the majority. In many such passages, 7a1 stands closer to the Greek, to which it is therefore thought to have been conformed.[36] This greater affinity with the Greek, however, could equally be ascribed to unique preservation, which would also explain other features of this text. First, the translator strove – as is clear from passages where all mss agree – to restore names to their Semitic form rather than transcribe them from the Greek; and in its unique readings 7a1 sometimes outdoes the other mss in this authentic tendency.[37] Second, the names found in the other mss are sometimes best explained as corruptions of those found in 7a1, e.g.

1 Macc. 3:13   Σήρων   7a1 ܣܝܪܘܢ   rell. ܣܝܪܘܡ [38]

Finally, as Nöldeke observed, only 7a1 shows the ancient form ܚܣܝܕܝܐ rather than ܚܕܝܡ at 1 Mac. 8:15.[39] All this suggests that 7a1 preserves on occasion the original text, which was later smoothed out or corrupted by the other mss – although elsewhere it no doubt also contains some corruptions of its own. The estimation of 7a1's unique readings as the more ancient goes back to Ceriani.[40]

History of modern scholarship

It remains to trace the course of modern scholarship on this point. The idea that a P ms which agreed with the Hebrew had instead been conformed to the Hebrew originated in Cornill's commentary on Ezekiel; in that book 7a1 alone agreed with the Hebrew against the printed editions, which were the only other authorities that he knew. By examining other mss, Barnes proved that 7a1 was not isolated after all, so proving – even to Cornill – that 7a1 had not been conformed to the Hebrew.[41] Yet Barnes himself accepted the underlying assumption that agreements with MT in one isolated ms were probably due to revision. Accordingly, when he encountered unique agreements with MT – first in 9a1 in Chronicles, Psalms[42] and 2 Kings,[43] and later in 5b1 in Genesis and Exodus – he inferred revision. Other revision theories – that 9a1 had been conformed to LXX[44] or to the minor Greek versions[45] – were prompted by the same respect for numerical strength.

---

[36] G. Schmidt, "Die beiden Syrischen Übersetzungen des I. Maccabäerbuches", *ZAW* 17 (1897–8), pp. 1–47, 233–62: 234. A. Penna, "I nomi propri dei primi due libri dei Maccabei nella Peshiṭṭa", *RSO* 40 (1965), pp. 13–41: 23.   [37] The evidence is amply documented by Penna.

[38] More speculatively, the remarkable variety of Syriac readings in the three passages where the Greek has Ἀσιδαῖοι (1 Macc. 2:42; 7:13; 2 Macc. 14:6) could be explained as scribal developments from the straight-forward transliteration ܚܣܝܕܝܐ found in 7a1 (except at 2 Macc. 14:6, where 7a1 is no longer distinctive). Two of the rival readings are ܚܣܝܕܐ and thence ܚܠܝܡܐ (under the influence of the following ܕܝܣܢܐ); another is ܚܘܣܝܐ (perhaps a misguided correction rather than a straight corruption of ܚܣܝܕܐ), and thence ܚܘܣܝܐ.   [39] *Literarisches Centralblatt für Deutschland* 17 (1883), pp. 569–71.

[40] Ceriani, *Le Edizioni*, p. 16.

[41] W.E. Barnes, *An Apparatus Criticus to Chronicles in the Peshitta Version*, Cambridge 1897, pp. xx–xxvi.

[42] W.E. Barnes (ed.), *The Peshitta Psalter according to the West Syrian Text*, Cambridge 1904.

[43] W.E. Barnes, "The Peshitta Version of 2 Kings", *JTS* 6 (1904/5), pp. 220–32; 11(1910), pp. 533–42.

[44] So (very tentatively) Albrektson, *Studies in the Text and Theology of Lamentations*, p. 28.

[45] F.C. Burkitt in *JTS* 6 (1905), pp. 286–90: 287–8.

Supporters of the majority text have also invoked the influential view (discussed in chapter 3) that P was derived from an older Targum. Their argument is that the majority text, being fuller, is more like a Targum and hence closer to the supposedly earliest state of P:

It is more reasonable to assume that a Targum-like version would be gradually refined and brought into line with the Hebrew text than vice versa. What, after all, would be the purpose of introducing a 'Targum' for the use of the Christian Church?[46]

The fallacy in that argument lies in the epithet "Targum-like" applied to the text of the majority. That text does not stand any closer than the text of the single ms to any Targum, in respect of content. The only feature which it shares with the Targums is an occasional tendency to expand – which, however, is by no means confined to the Targums, as shown in chapter 3 above. Any such adjective as "Targum-like" applied to the majority text can only confuse.

The manuscript inter-relations in different biblical books – an overview

Introduction

Application of the intrinsic criteria allows us to form an overview of the situation which we face in the attempt to recover the original text of P in the different biblical books. Here we shall not concern ourselves with the long history of textual transmission, nor examine any individual book in depth. Instead we shall search for patterns, in relation to the survival of the original text, that repeat themselves in the different books.

The textual variation among the earlier mss – before *c.* 800 CE – can be explained if we posit a body of new readings which were generated during the first few centuries of P's existence, in order to improve the text in respect of inner logic or Syriac idiom. These new readings appealed to copyists and became widely adopted. At many points in the text, the original text must be sought in whatever mss escaped the effects of this scribal zeal.

In considering the impact of the new readings upon the ms tradition, we may identify three separate factors that would cause variation between biblical books. The first concerns the production of new readings: more were generated in certain books (and indeed in certain passages) than in others. Evidently the revisers responsible for the new readings found some books or passages of particular interest, or in particular need of revision.

The second factor concerns the absorption of the new readings into the mss. Although the new readings have been widely adopted, a minority of mss are relatively free of them, prime examples being 5b1 and 9a1. It may be that the scribes to whom we owe the existence of that minority worked too early, or were geographically too isolated, to be fully exposed to the new readings. At all events, none of these mss is altogether immune to the new readings, and their propensity to absorb them may have varied between books.

---

[46] B.J. Roberts, *The Old Testament Text and Versions*, Cardiff 1951, p. 219.

The third factor is survival. It was largely chance that determined how many mss – if any – would survive which were relatively free of the new readings, and which mss would survive alongside them.

The last factor led to the most obvious discrepancies between biblical books. In some, we have no ms at all that regularly preserves the old readings. In most books, however, we have just one such ms. Sometimes further evidence of the old readings survives alongside, e.g. in Ephrem's citations (as we shall see) or in a palimpsest. From Leviticus 15:14 until the end of Deuteronomy we are unusually fortunate, in that two mss – 6b1 and 9a1 – survive, each of which regularly preserves old readings.

Books without a regular unique carrier: the example of Job

We may begin with books like Job, for which no ms has survived which regularly preserves old readings against the majority. In the search for determinate passages, we can often use the criterion of agreement with MT, e.g.

35:2 חשבת

P variants: ܐܬܚܫܒܬ "you were considered" [6h8* 7a1 8a1^{c}]

ܐܬܚܒܫܬ "you were bound" [6h8^{c}.20 8a1*][47]

The former reading, agreeing with MT, is original. The latter is due to miscopying, partly influenced by the sequel: " . . .in judgment, for you said: 'I am more righteous than God'".

In Job, readings unique to a single ms usually prove to be scribal errors, but a small minority are correct, e.g.

1:15 ואת הילדים הכו = 6h20 ܘܠܛܠܝ̈ܐ ܩܛܠܘ , rell. ܘܛܠܝ̈ܐ ܐܬܩܛܠܘ

6:14 שדי =1111 ܕܐܠܗܐ, rell. ܕܡܠܟܐ[48]

22:18 רשעים =6h20 ܕܪ̈ܫܝܥܐ, rell. ܕܥܘ̈ܠܐ

33:3 לבי =913 ܕܠܒܝ, rell. ܕܦܘܡܝ

34:10 ושדי =6h20 ܠܐܠܗܐ, rell. ܠܗ

39:21 בכח =7a1 ܒܚܝܠܐ, rell ܒܚܩܠܐ (a corruption induced by בעמק in the parallel line).

Thus the true reading is usually that of the majority, as expected, but occasionally survives in a single mss – 6h20, 7a1, or one of the lectionaries 913 and 1111 – or in the later mss alone. In a few other passages the true reading survives in some combination of the above.

The variation at 7:7 poses a dilemma. Here 1111 closely follows MT, while in the other mss the sense is reversed by omission of the negative:

MT זכר כי רוח חיי לא תשוב עיני לראות טוב

Remember that my life is wind; my eye shall not again see good

P[1111] ܐܬܕܟܪ ܕܪܘܚܐ ܚܝܐ ܗܝ. ܘܠܐ ܬܗܦܘܟ ܥܝܢܝ ܠܡܚܙܐ ܛܒܬܐ.

P[rell.] . . . . ܘܬܗܦܘܟ . . . .

Remember that the spirit lives, and my eye shall return to behold good

47 Each reading has further support among manuscripts of the ninth or later centuries.

48 Syr. ܐܠܗܐ is the normal rendering of שדי in P-Job, though where אל or אלוה – which had to be rendered ܐܠܗܐ – occurs in the preceding or following line, the rendering ܫܡܝܐ often serves instead as a B-word. Never is שדי rendered by ܡܠܟܐ.

The text of the majority thus introduced belief in life after death. This may be due to change by copyists, in which case the original text again survives in 1111 alone. On the other hand it may be due to the translator, who (as we saw above) introduces belief in life after death at 30:23 and 42:6. In that case, 1111's reading may reflect influence from LXX (καὶ οὐκέτι ἐπανελεύσεται...).

Most readings in which the younger mss agree against the older are errors, as expected, e.g.

2:9   MT אלהים = older mss ܐܠܗܐ, younger ܐܠܗܝܢ

38:12   MT בקר = older mss ܒܨܦܪܐ, younger ܠܨܦܪܐ "at dawn"

Occasionally, however, the younger mss alone preserve the original reading. This is not altogether surprising, since their shared text derives from a lost earlier ms, which – like any other early ms – could occasionally have preserved the original text alone. For example, at 9:18b all P mss have ܕܐܫܒܥܢܝ ܡܪܪܐ "for he filled me with bitter things", following MT. The older mss all continue: ܘܐܪܘܝܢܝ ܓܕܕܐ "and he sated me with wormwood", an obvious addition from Lam. 3:15. Only the younger mss (8a1ᶜ 10c1.4 11c1) are free of this addition. Again, at 41:18 MT has חרב and only the younger mss likewise have ܚܪܒܐ (apparently meaning "desolation"); the rest have the corruption ܚܫܟܐ "pit, darkness".

The list of mss which preserve the true reading thus varies from passage to passage. The true reading is preserved now by the majority but now by a single particular ms, now by another, now by the younger mss alone, and now by some combination of these. In yet other passages it has been ousted altogether and can only be recovered by emendation. This lack of pattern reflects the unpredictable fashion in which the new readings spread. Besides Job, we find a similar situation in most of the Twelve Prophets (Joel-Malachi), Daniel, Ruth and the Solomonic books

Books with a single regular carrier: overview

We now turn to books that have one regular unique carrier of old readings. The identity of these carriers varies between biblical books:

5b1   Genesis, Exodus
8h5   Ezra, Nehemiah
9a1   Joshua-Kings, Isaiah-Ezekiel, Hosea, Psalms, Lamentations, Chronicles
10f1   Esther

The opening folios (plus a few others) of 5b1 in Genesis are in a later hand, but have the same textual character, and were apparently copied from the original hand. By contrast, the fifth-century text of Numbers-Deuteronomy in a different hand, bound together with Genesis-Exodus and thus also called 5b1, is not a carrier of unique true readings. As to 9a1, the readings exclusive to the portions added by later hands do not appear original.

In these biblical books, the original reading at a series of points in the text survives in no ms other than the unique carrier. Nevertheless the latter occasionally has other support, e.g. from Ephrem's citations, the Malkite lectionary ms 10l1 (in Exodus)[49] or the palimpsest 5ph1 (in Isaiah).[50]

---

[49] M.D. Koster, *The Peshitta of Exodus: The Development of its Text in the Course of Fifteen Centuries*, Assen/Amsterdam 1977, pp. 99–101, 186.
[50] S.P. Brock, "Text History and Text Division in Peshitta Isaiah", MPI 4 (1988), pp. 49–80: see p. 55.

Among books that have a single regular carrier, the incidence of good readings uniquely preserved varies greatly between books. That incidence is, for example, higher in Kings than in Judges, higher in Jeremiah than in Ezekiel, and indeed higher in Genesis than in Exodus. This variation seems due to the first factor identified above: the revisors responsible for the new readings seem to have been particularly drawn to certain books, and indeed to certain passages within books. Hence the many variants in Gen. 24, or the major expansion of one particular verse – namely Gen. 28:17 – in the majority text.

The particularly high incidence of unique readings in 9a1 in Kings and Jeremiah suggests that these books attracted special attention. Perhaps the reason lies in their content. It may be that Syriac biblical scholars treated these two books – which end almost identically – as a pair, and studied them together, learning from Kings about the sins and downfall of the Jews, and seeing in Jeremiah the life of a type of Christ.[51] Here it may be significant that Aphrahat cites Kings more frequently – in relation to its length – than any other of the historical books. Alternatively, the reason that these books caught the revisers' attention may have been that they seemed particularly in need of revision. Jeremiah is the most conservatively translated of the Latter Prophets, and Kings the most conservatively translated of the whole Hebrew Bible, as argued in chapter 4 above. In particular, each book exhibited Hebraic constructions in its opening verses. Already at 1 Kgs. 1:2 we have:

MT   יבקשו לאדני המלך נערה בתולה

P (9a1)   ܢܒܥܘܢ ܠܡܪܝ ܡܠܟܐ ܥܠܝܡܬܐ ܒܬܘܠܬܐ

Unlike Hebrew and earlier Aramaic dialects, classical Syriac does not use an indefinite third person plural subject instead of the passive; hence in the majority text ܗܘܐ ܥܒܕܘܗܝ ܡܪܝܐ is prefaced (cf. 1 Sam. 16:16), providing a subject for the third person plural verb. In Jeremiah likewise, the Hebraic syntax already jarred at Jer. 1:4 –

MT   ויהי דבר י׳ אלי לאמר

P (9a1)   ܘܗܘܐ ܦܬܓܡܗ ܕܡܪܝܐ ܥܠܝ ܠܡܐܡܪ

All mss but 9a1 move ܥܠܝ to follow the verb directly.[52] It is possible that some supervisor who reviewed the Syriac style of each book decided on such grounds to give priority to the revision of Kings and Jeremiah.

The example of Genesis

In Genesis the regular carrier – 5b1 – often preserves the true reading uniquely, as Pinkerton showed.[53] In some further passages, it is joined casually by other mss in the true reading, e.g.

19:25   הערים (2°); so 5b1 911 ܩܘܪܝܐ; rell. ܩܪܝܐ

41:57   בכל הארץ; rendered without addition in 5b1 916; rell. add ܕܡܨܪܝܢ

43:17   האיש; 5b1 8b1 ܓܒܪܐ; rell. ܠܒܝܬܐ

This is precisely the outcome to be expected if we take a situation like that of Job – where the truth may survive now in one ms and now in another – and add one ms which preserves the original reading on a regular basis.

---

[51] I owe this suggestion to Dr Gillian Greenberg.
[52] The same occurs soon afterwards, at Jer. 1:11, and often thereafter in the book.
[53] Koster's careful treatment of 5b1's unique readings in Exodus (pp. 55–114) is also directly relevant.

Of course the regular carrier is not infallible. Where it errs, the majority will usually preserve the true reading. Cases where the truth instead survives uniquely in a different ms are rare, e.g.

(a) 30:13

MT   כי אשרוני בנות   "for daughters counted me happy"
P (maj)   ܪܚܒܣܝ ܟܢܐ   "for the house(hold) praised me"
10g 1   ܪܚܒܣܝ ܒܢܬܐ   "for daughters praised me"

The corruption from ܒܢܬܐ to ܟܢܐ arose partly from the difficulty of identifying the "daughters" and partly from the identity of the masculine singular and feminine plural verb forms.

(b) 39:11

MT   ויבא הביתה; only 8b1 is free of the added subject ܝܘܣܦ.
Unlike Job, Genesis offers no convincing instance where the later P-mss have the better reading.[54]

Overall, thanks to the survival of a regular carrier, the situation in Genesis shows greater regularity than in Job. The true reading usually survives in that carrier, either alone or with others. Almost everywhere else, it is preserved by the majority of the mss (if the text common to the younger mss is counted as a single witness).

The example of Isaiah

In general, the regular carriers have by definition absorbed fewer new readings than the remaining mss. However, the absorption rate must have varied between books. In the widely read book of Isaiah, 9a1 still has the status of regular unique carrier, but here it has absorbed more new readings (as well as some even later readings that had become popular in the west) than in the other books.[55] We cannot tell how many of these new readings were adopted by the scribe of 9a1 himself, and how many already stood in his exemplar. If 9a1 (as well as its ancestors) was unusually hospitable in Isaiah to the new readings, this would explain 9a1's relatively low incidence of unique preservation in this book, coupled with high incidence of good readings in other single mss, e.g.

9:16   ירחם   =6h5 ܢܪܚܡ   rell. ܢܚܣܐ
17:12   ישאון   =5ph1 ܢܗܡܝܢ   rell. om.
20:2   ישעיהו =9l6 ܐܫܥܝܐ   rell. add. ܢܒܝܐ
21:17   גבורי   =6h3 ܓܢܒܪܝ   rell. ܓܢܒܪܐ
23:15   ונשכחת =6h3.5 7a1 8a1 ܘܬܬܛܥܝܢ   rell. ܘܬܛܥܐ
62:5   יבעלוך =9l5 1l14 ܢܒܥܠܟܝ   rell. pr. ܘܐܝܟ

Again, the true reading may be lost in 9a1 and yet survive in the later mss, either alone or together with an older ms:

---

[54] Though there is a possible example at 31:29, where the later mss (starting with 10b1 and 10g 1) have ܐܝܬܝܗܘܢ ܠ while the earlier have ܐܝܬܝܗܘܢ alone, for MT השמר לך.   [55] Cf Brock in MPI 4 (1988), p. 52.

49:1 שמעו =9d 1 etc. ܫܡܥܝܢ rell. ܫܬܘܡܥܝܢ
13:2 פתחי =8a1 9d 1 etc. ܒܬܪ̈ܥܐ rell. ܒܬܪ̈ܥܝܟܝ[56]

Thus the position in Isaiah is less regular than in Genesis but more so than in Job. In Isaiah, the regular carrier is itself so affected by the new readings that its status is diminished.

Books with two regular carriers

From Lev. 15:14 till the end of Deuteronomy, we have two mss – 6b1 and 9a1 – that regularly preserve old readings. At Lev. 23:26, for example, only 6b1 and 9a1 are free of the addition : "Speak with the children of Israel and say to them". Singly too these mss may preserve the original reading, e.g.

Num. 11:18

MT ואל העם תאמר "and to the people thou shalt say"
9a1* ܘܐܡܪ ܠܥܡܐ "and say to the people"
rell. ܘܐܡܪ ܡܘܫܐ ܠܥܡܐ "and Moses said to the people"

Deut. 19:20
MT כדבר הזה, 6b1 ܐܝܟ ܦܬܓܡܐ ܗܢܐ, rell. om. ܐܝܟ

In Numbers the old readings of 6b1 and 9a1 receive support from the palimpsest 7pj2, where extant. This palimpsest even preserves uniquely some old readings which all other mss had lost, as discovered by Hayman,[57] e.g.
1:20 לגלגלתם כל זכר = 7pj2 ܠܓܓܘܠܬܗܘܢ ܟܠ ܕܟܪܐ; rell. ܟܠ ܕܟܪܐ ܠܓܓܘܠܬܗܘܢ (as 1:2)
3:7 לפני אהל מועד; all mss but 7pj2 preface with ܩܕܡ ܡܕܒܚܐ
Yet despite these regular representatives of the older text, we must still allow for the occasional unique survival of the true reading in a different ms, as at Num. 9:20 –
MT ימים מספר, 9l4 ܡܢܝܢܬܐ ܕܝܘܡܢܐ, rell. ܡܢܝܢܬܐ ܕܝܘܡܬܐ
Again at Deut. 16:3, before the section on the Feast of Weeks, nearly all mss – including 6b1 9a1 – have the title ܦܢܛܩܘܣܛܐ (ܥܠ) or the like. Only 9l6 is free of these words, which cannot be due to the translator, who instead calls the festival ܕܫܒܘ̈ܥܐ ܥܐܕܐ.

The derivation and application of distributional arguments

Where intrinsic criteria are insufficient to distinguish truth from error, one may hope to choose between rival readings on the basis of some prior assessment of the value of the mss or combination of mss which support each reading. These are the distributional criteria, which depend on the extent to which the relevant mss or combinations were found to show the correct reading over the determinate passages.

[56] Thus 8a1 9d 1 etc. have "let them enter the gates of nobles", as MT, while the others have: "let nobles enter thy gates". [57] A.P. Hayman in *JSS* 25 (1980), pp. 263–70.

The positive distributional argument

The distributional criteria can be applied either positively or negatively, as already noted. The positive argument is that a ms or combination found to preserve the true reading in the determinate passages may do the same elsewhere. In many passages, each of the rival readings can claim the support of such a ms or combination. The distributional evidence is then inconclusive, but at least bids us keep an open mind, as at Ps. 141:5 –

MT   יהלמני צדיק חסד ויוכיחני) שמן ראש אל יני ראשי (כי עוד ותפלתי ברעותיהם)

LXX   ἔλαιον δὲ ἁμαρτωλοῦ μὴ λιπανάτω τὴν κεφαλήν μου

P (9a1)   (ܘܠܥܒܕ ܘܢܪܝܫܐ ܘܢܗܘܡܢܝ.) ܡܫܚܐ ܠܪܝܫܝ ܢܗܘܗ. (ܘܟܠ ܕܢܒܠܗ, ܟܠ ܚܛܐܗ ܘܟܠܗܘܢ)

        . . .let oil anoint my head . . .

P (rell.)   ...ܡܫܚܐ ܕܪܫܝܥܐ ܠܪܝܫܝ ܠܐ ܢܗܘ.....

        . . .let the oil of the wicked not anoint my head . . .

Apparently LXX found רשע in his *Vorlage* rather than ראש. The majority text largely agrees; and it is usually taken as the work of the translator, who is supposed either to have found רשע likewise in his Hebrew text or to have followed LXX. However, given 9a1's capacity for unique preservation, its reading here deserves further consideration. In this difficult verse, the translator also omitted the two words חסד and עוד. He also shows a tendency to render just once a word that is repeated in the Hebrew, as at 27:8 –

MT   בקשו פני את פניך י' אבקש

P   ܗܘܝ ܠܩܦܝܟ ܐܦ̈ܝ ܒܥܘ

If he treated the repetition ראש ... ראשי at 141:5 in the same way, and in addition offered a converse translation to improve the perceived sense,[58] he would have produced the text of 9a1. In that case, the majority text arose through assimilation to LXX. This hypothesis would explain the odd word-order (subject, object, verb); this is the order of the words actually translated: שמן ראש יני ... .

The negative distributional argument

The negative type of distributional argument relates to ms combinations whose shared exclusive readings are always found incorrect among the determinate passages: by analogy, we should be reluctant to follow their shared exclusive readings in indeterminate passages. In addition, these combinations are of historical interest, in that they imply a shared exclusive ancestor in which those shared incorrect readings already stood.

One such combination comprises the western mss (other than 9a1) in Psalms. Despite their number and age, their shared exclusive readings are inferior in those passages where we can judge, namely Ps. 39:7 (discussed above) and 104:1 (where the rival reading is supported by Ephrem, as discussed below). This warns us against bowing immediately to their age at Ps. 68:19 –

---

[58] The addition or removal of a negative is well attested in P elsewhere in Psalms and other books (see pp. 26, 34, 38 in chapter 2 above).

MT	לקחת מתנות באדם
P (most western mss)	ܘܝܗܒܬ ܡܘܗܒܬܐ ܠܒ̈ܢܝ ܐܢܫܐ [6t1 7a1 8a1 etc.]
cf. Targum	יהבתא להון מתנן לבני נשא
P (9a1 + eastern mss)	ܘܢܣܒܬ ܡܘܗܒܬܐ ܠܒ̈ܢܝ ܐܢܫܐ [8a1[c] 9a1 12t1.4 etc.]
LXX	ἔλαβες δόματα ἐν ἀνθρώπῳ
but Eph. 4:8	ἔδωκεν δόματα τοῖς ἀνθρώποις

In the western Syriac readings, God no longer receives, but gives: the verb has been changed to ܝܗܒ. However, the eastern reading means much the same: the preposition has likewise become 'to', so that giving is still signified, even though the verb is unchanged.[59] On authenticity grounds, either reading is credible: to reach the desired sense, the translator might have varied the preposition alone, or might also have changed the verb for added clarity. Directionality favours the eastern reading, which can hardly be due to assimilation to MT or LXX, as the preposition would then have also been revised to 'in'; the western reading, by contrast, could have arisen from assimilation to Ephesians. Still, directionality is not conclusive, since assimilation need not be invoked at all: either reading is an easy corruption of the other. What counts more for the reading of 9a1 and the eastern mss is the superior performance of that combination over the determinate passages.[60]

Another combination whose exclusive shared readings are never clearly correct, and are sometimes plainly incorrect, is the pair 6h7 8a1 in Judges, studied by Dirksen.[61] Examples of shared errors are:[62]

	MT	= rell.	6h7+8a1
3:25	נפל	ܪܡܐ	add. ܥܠ ܐܦ̈ܘܗܝ
4:5	ובין בית אל	ܘܒܝܬ ܒܝܬ ܐܝܠ	ܘܒܝܬ ܐܝܠ
11:3	ריקים	ܣܪ̈ܝܩܐ	ܣܪ̈ܝܩܐ ܘܦ̈ܚܝܙܐ
16:23	בידנו	ܒܐܝܕܢ	ܒܐܝ̈ܕܝܢ

Extended discussion of a passage in Judges to which this distributional criterion is applied appears in appendix II.

These shared errors bear not only on the establishment of the text but also on its history. Thus the errors common and exclusive to the western mss in Psalms testify to textual standardisation in the west, which established a number of erroneous readings there. The errors common and exclusive to 6h7 and 8a1 imply a common ancestor which originated or inherited them. Other regular cases of agreement in error allow the identification of particular families among the later mss, notably in Exodus,[63] Judges[64]

[59] As e.g. at Exod. 27:19 ܘܢܣܒܘܢ ܠܟ ܡܫܚܐ "and let them bring you oil".

[60] Barnes (*Apparatus Criticus*, pp. xlii f.) reaches the opposite conclusion. He finds no convincing case elsewhere of assimilation to the New Testament text; but it is hard to explain otherwise the variant ܒܕܡܘܬܗ ܕܡܠܟܝܙܕܩ at Ps. 110:4.

[61] P.B. Dirksen, "The Ancient Peshiṭta MSS of Judges and their Variant Readings", MPI 4 (1988), pp. 127–46; see p. 144. [62] Witnesses only occasionally available, such as 6ph11, are ignored here.

[63] Koster, *The Peshiṭta of Exodus.* In a review entitled "The Peshitta and its Manuscripts", *BO* 37 (1980), pp. 13–16, M.H. Goshen-Gottstein criticised Koster's conclusion not for its substance but because it ran counter to an unpublished thesis unmentioned by Koster. Koster's crushing reply, entitled "Which came first – the chicken or the egg? The Development of the Text of the Peshiṭta", appeared in MPI 4 (1988), pp. 183–99.

[64] P.B. Dirksen, *The Transmission of the Text in the Peshiṭta Manuscripts of the Book of Judges*, Leiden 1972 (=MPI 1).

and the Twelve Prophets.[65] In Leviticus and Qohelet, Lane has correlated these data with the geographical provenance of the mss.[66]

The intrinsic criteria discussed above – authenticity and direction – together with distributional arguments should determine in most variant passages the choice of reading to be placed in the main text. However, any critical edition would need some formal convention to choose between rival readings in passages where all the criteria taken together are inconclusive. Such conventions have been used in the Leiden edition as the primary means of selection. In the volumes published up to 1977, the text of 7a1 was printed in the text except that evident scribal errors were corrected; in the volumes published later, the reading adopted was whichever commanded a majority among mss prior to 1000 CE. This more recent convention can be retained as a last resort. If, however, the criteria discussed above are properly applied, it should not often be needed, and its main disadvantage – namely inconsistency between different passages following the vagaries of ms survival in each[67] – should be avoidable.

Emendation on the basis of external Syriac evidence

The biblical text in external citations was examined in chapter 3 above in relation to the theory that these preserve a text which stood close to the Targum tradition. Here the question is rather different: do citations ever preserve an earlier text than the biblical mss of P?
Aphrahat
There are a few cases where Aphrahat may preserve the original text against the biblical mss:

			MT	Aphrahat	Mss
Lev.	25	20	תאמרו	ܐܡܪܝܢ	ܐܡܪܝܢ ܐܢܬܘܢ
Nah.	2	14	והבערתי	ܘܐܘܩܕ	ܘܐܘܩܕ
Dan.	9	19	סלחה	ܚܣܐ[68]	ܚܣܐ

Again, Gideon's foes in Judges 6 included the בני קדם. The biblical mss call them ܒܢܝ ܩܕܡ (i.e. people of Qadesh) at Judg. 6:3,33;7:12. Aphrahat, however, calls them ܒܢܝ ܩܕܡ,[69] which may have been P's original reading; the text of the biblical mss can be ascribed to corruption.

Ephrem: authentic commentaries on Genesis and Exodus

Ephrem too may retain an original reading lost in the biblical mss, e.g.

	MT	Ephrem	mss
Gen. 9:22	בחוץ	ܒܫܘܩܐ	om.
Gen. 49:6	וברצונם	ܘܒܨܒܝܢܗܘܢ	ܘܒܨܒܝܢܗܘܢ
Gen. 49:13	חוף	ܣܦܪܐ	ܫܦܪܐ

[65] A. Gelston, *The Peshiṭta of the Twelve Prophets*, Oxford 1987, pp. 26–64.
[66] D.J. Lane, The *Peshiṭta of Leviticus,* Leiden 1994 [= MPI 6].
[67] An example is the fluctuation between ܢܚܝ ܪܝܫ and ܢܚܝ ܡܝܐܬܐ for רֵיח נִיחֹחַ in the main text of P-Leviticus in the Leiden edition.
[68] Cf. ܚܣܐ "purify me" at Ps. 25:11 (MT תחסל). At Amos 7:2, however, ܚܣܐ may be the unsuffixed imperative plus precative ܢ (MT סלח נא). The usual rendering for סלח, however, is ܫܒܩ.
[69] Ed. Parisot, col. 489, l.23.

At Gen. 49:6, the reading of the biblical mss arose under the influence of ܢܘܦܫܝ in the preceding phrase; in the other cases, scribal error is responsible.

Ephrem also seems to have the older reading at Gen. 4:7b:

MT   ואליך תשוקתו ואתה תמשל בו

> and to you is his desire, and you will rule over him

P [mss]   ܐܢܬ ܬܬܦܢܐ ܠܘܬܗ ܘܗܘ ܢܫܬܠܛ ܒܟ

> you will turn to him, and he will rule over you

Ephrem   ܘܗܘ ܗܒܝܠ ܢܬܦܢܐ ܠܘܬܟ ܒܝܕ ܨܒܝܢܗ ܡܐ ܕܢܐܙܠ ܥܡܟ ܠܥܘܡܩܐ. ܘܐܢܬ ܬܫܬܠܛ ܒܗ ܗܘ ܒܚܛܝܬܐ. ܗܢܘ ܕܝܢ ܬܬܦܨܚ ܒܗ܀

> And he, Abel, will turn to you – through his willingness when he goes with you to the valley. And you will have power over it – over the sin; that is, you will gratify yourself thereby.

Although the last phrase is difficult,[70] it is clear that Ephrem presupposes a biblical text closer to MT than that of the biblical mss:

ܘܗܘ ... ܢܬܦܢܐ ܠܘܬܟ ... ܘܐܢܬ ܬܫܬܠܛ ܒܗ...

This seems original, while the text of the biblical mss has been influenced by Gen. 3:16 (P): "and to your husband you will turn, and he will have power over you."

Again at Exod. 11:2, where MT speaks of כלי כסף וכלי זהב "vessels of silver and of gold" which the Israelites were to borrow, Ephrem cites the Syriac as ܡܐܢܝ ܟܣܦܐ ܘܡܐܢܝ ܕܗܒܐ,[71] against the agreed reading ܡܐܢܐ ܕܣܐܡܐ ܘܡܐܢܐ ܕܕܗܒܐ in the biblical mss. Ephrem thus shows the older usage ܟܣܦܐ for silver metal, which according to 5b1 is usual in Exodus, even though 5b1 itself here exceptionally has ܣܐܡܐ with all other mss. Ephrem's use of ܟܣܦܐ thus seems original (unlike his word order).

We may also compare Exod. 17:16 –

MT   כי יד על כס יה

P   ܗܐ ܐܝܕܐ ܥܠ ܟܘܪܣܝܐ

Ephrem   ܗܐ ܐܝܕܐ ܕܝܗ ܥܠ ܟܘܪܣܝܐ

Ephrem explains his biblical text to mean that God's hand is on the seat of judgment, to wage eternal battle against Amalek. Ephrem seems to preserve the original text of P. The translator retained the name Jah at Exod. 15:2, and although in Ephrem's citation it is attached to the hand rather than (as in MT) to the throne, P was well capable of such transpositions for the sake of desired sense. In that case, the biblical mss go back to a faulty copy in which the word ܕܝܗ had fallen out.[72]

Also relevant is Exod. 18:12, where MT states vaguely that Jethro "took" (ויקח) sacrifices for God, while the P mss have ܘܩܪܒ, specifying that he offered them up there and then. Now Ephrem's commentary (p. 148) runs as follows:

---

[70] The sense 'gratify yourself' may be justified for Syr. ܬܬܦܨܚ on the basis of P at Num. 25:3 (see p. 71 above). The catena claimed to include Ephrem's comment on Gen. 4:7b quotes the biblical text twice: first in the same form as the P mss and then as in Ephrem's undoubtedly authentic commentary. The latter quotation is introduced ܐܝܟ ܕܟܬܒ; its second clause is interpreted to mean that Cain would had nothing to gain by killing Abel, since in any event "'you will rule over him', as you are first-born". (Ed.Rom., vol. 1, p. 143 CD).   [71] Ed. Tonneau, p. 140.

[72] This passage was pointed out by Hidal (*Interpretatio Syriaca*, pp. 15–16), who does not question the text of the P mss and suggests that Ephrem was here influenced by the Hebrew.

ܘܢܣܒ ܝܬܪܘܢ ܕܒ̈ܚܐ ܠܡܪܝܐ.
ܐܘ ܒܝܕ ܡܘܫܐ ܩܪܒ ܐܢܘܢ. ܐܘ ܡܦܪܫ ܦܪܫ ܕܒܐܬܪܐ ܕܢܓܒܐ ܒܗ ܡܪܝܐ ܢܕܒܚܘܢ ܐܢܘܢ ܒܗ

"And Jethro took sacrifices for the Lord". Either he offered them through Moses, or he set them apart, so that they might sacrifice them in the place that the Lord would choose.

The biblical text cited by Ephrem had ܘܢܣܒ "and he took". This agrees with MT and seems original, while the mss of P show an obvious enough interpretation of it, which also occurred to Ephrem.

The incidence of readings older than those of the biblical mss seems far higher in Ephrem than in Aphrahat. Thus Aphrahat refers to the silver which the Israelites took from Egypt as ܣܐܡܐ,[73] while Ephrem as noted above retains the old term ܟܣܦܐ.

Other patristic sources

The citations in the commentary on Isaiah attributed to Ephrem were studied by Diettrich.[74] Even though its authenticity is disputed, this commentary presents a number of readings that seem superior to the text of the biblical mss. A notable example occurs at Isa. 10:27 –

MT וחבל על מפני שמן

P ܘܢܬܚܒܠ ܢܝܪܐ ܡܢ ܩܕܡ ܡܘ̈ܫܚܐ (or ܡܘܫܚܐ)

and the yoke shall be destroyed from before the heifer(s)

However, the commentary ascribed to Ephrem explains:

ܐܬܘܪܝܐ ܢܬܚܒܠ ܡܢ ܩܕܡ ܚܙܩܝܐ ܕܡܫܝܚ ܗܘܐ

The Assyrian shall be destroyed from before Hezekiah, who was anointed

This implies the reading ܡܫܚܐ 'oil', which would agree in sense with the Hebrew, and of which ܡܘܫܚܐ 'heifer' in the biblical mss is an easy corruption. The reading ܡܫܚܐ actually appears in the lemma in the Roman edition,[75] but the main textual evidence comes from the comment itself. Thus ܡܫܚܐ seems the original reading, of which the text of the biblical mss is a corruption.

Other cases pointed out by Diettrich include forms of names:

	MT	"Eph."	bibl. mss.
7:19	הבתות	ܕܒܬܘܬ	ܕܢܬܘܬ
10:28	במגרון	ܡܓܪܐ	ܡܓܕܘ

In theory, of course, the forms of the biblical text ascribed to Ephrem in this commentary might have arisen centuries later and so may have benefited from consultation of LXX or even from Hebrew contacts. Overall, however, there is a good chance that this commentary preserves further original readings, and it deserves examination in other biblical books.

An old reading is preserved even in the ninth-century commentary by Isho'dad at Zech. 11:4 –

73 Ed. Parisot, vol. 1, col. 372, l.25.
74 *Ein Apparatus criticus zur Pešitto zum Propheten Jesaia*, pp. xxviii-xxix.
75 Though in B.L. Add.12144, fol.72b, the lemma is reported – despite the comment – as ܡܘܫܚܐ, as in the biblical mss.

MT צאן ההרגה
P mss ܠܥܢܐ ܡܬܢܟܣܬܐ
Isho'dad knows the text of the mss, but notes that the 'Ebraya has ܡܛܠܠܬܐ, and he continues:

ܘܗܟܢ ܙܕܩ ܠܡܩܪܐ ܘܐܦ ܒܟܬܒܐ ܥܬܝܩܐ ܕܣܘܪܝܝܐ ܗܟܢ ܟܬܝܒ

and thus it is right to read; and it is also written thus in old manuscripts of the Syriac

The reading recommended by Isho'dad is evidently original.[76]

That citations occasionally preserve a reading lost in the main ms tradition is a phenomenon also known from classical literature. A well-known example is line 1167 of Antigone, which fell out of all manuscripts of Sophocles but survived in citations by Athenaeus (*c.* 200 CE) and Eustathius (cent. xii)[77]

Cases where a citation agrees with part of the manuscript tradition

In some of the passages where one of the biblical mss departs from the rest to agree with MT, we have a citation by an early Syriac author. We can then see which of these rival readings the citation supports.

Aphrahat

For the most part, Aphrahat tends to attest the majority readings, e.g.

			MT	single ms=MT	ms	majority =Aphr.	ref.
Gen.	7	1	י'	ܡܪܝܐ	8/5b1	ܐܠܗܐ	I 408
Exod.	20	2	הוצאתיך	ܕܐܦܩܬܟ	5b1	ܕܐܦܩܬܟ	I [25], 61
Exod.	20	11	יום השבת	ܘܝܘܡܐ ܕܫܒܬܐ	5b1	ܘܝܘܡܐ ܫܒܝܥܝܐ	I 541
1 Kgs.	6	1	הבית לי'	ܒܝܬܐ ܠܡܪܝܐ	9a1	ܒܝܬܗ ܕܡܪܝܐ	I 88 (mss. AC)
2 Kgs.	3	17	תראו	ܬܚܙܘܢ	9a1	om.	I 300
2 Kgs.	19	35	במחנה אשור	ܡܢ ܡܫܪܝܬܐ ܕܐܬܘܪ	9a1	ܒܡܫܪܝܬܗ ܕܐܬܘܪܝܐ	I 132
Isa.	10	6	חנף	ܚܢܦܐ	9a1	ܚܠܦܐ	I 189
Jer.	6	16	#	#	9a1	(2) ܘܚܙܘ	I 512
Jer.	9	25	יהודה	ܐܝܗܘܕܐ	9a1	ܐܝܗܘܕܝܐ	I 480
Jer.	18	7	#	#	9a1	ܘܠܡܣܚܦܘ (Aph: ܘܠܡܣܚܦܗ)	I 69 [329]

Again at Isa. 5:2, where MT has ויעזקהו שרק, the older reading ܘܣܝܓܗ ܥܒܘܪܐ is found in 6h3, 7a1, 8a1 only, while Aphrahat (I 861) has the later reading of the majority: ܘܣܝܓ ܒܗ ܥܒܘܪܐ.

Cases where Aphrahat supports the agreement of a single ms with MT are less frequent, e.g.

			MT	ms=MT=Aphr.	ms	majority	ref. (Parisot)
Gen.	11	26	שבעים	ܫܒܥܝܢ	10/5b1	add. ܘܚܡܫ[78]	II 81
Exod.	4	23	שלח	ܫܕܪ(ܕ)	5b1	ܕܫܕܪܬ	I 773,789,845
Exod.	4	23	לשלחו	ܠܡܫܕܪܘ	5b1	add. ܠܒܪܝ	I 789
2 Kgs.	20	19	שלום.. יהיה	ܫܠܡܐ.. ܢܗܘܐ	9a1	ܢܗܘܐ ܫܠܡܐ	I 969

76 C. van den Eynde (ed.), *Commentaire d' Išo'dad de Merv sur l'ancien Testament*, vol. 4, CSCO 303 (Syr 128), Louvain 1969, p. 129. See also Gelston, *Twelve Prophets*, p. 96, and Brock in MPI 4, p. 60.

77 On this and further examples, see L.D. Reynolds and N.G.Wilson, *Scribes and Scholars*, Oxford 1974, 2nd edn., pp. 197–8.

78 Cf. Gen. 12:4.

Ephrem: authentic commentaries on Genesis and Exodus

Ephrem's commentaries of undoubted authenticity, on Genesis and Exodus, tend to support 5b1's unique agreements with MT. Some of the following instances are quoted from Pinkerton,[79] while others have been pointed out by Janson.[80] Notes indicate passages to which the majority readings show assimilation:

	MT	5b1=MT=Ephr.	ref. (Tonneau)		majority
Gen. 8:20	הבהמה	ܒܥܝܪܐ	p. 61	ܚܝܘܬܐ	
Gen. 17:6	ממך	ܡܢܟ	p. 73	ܡܢ ܚܨܝܟ	cf. Gen. 35:11
Gen. 18:20	רבה	ܣܓܝܬ	p. 76	ܥܠܬ ܩܕܡܝ	cf. Gen. 18:21
Gen. 19:16	האנשים	ܓܒܪܐ	p. 78	ܡܠܐܟܐ	cf. Gen. 19:1
Gen. 35:1	אלהים	ܐܠܗܐ	p. 95	ܡܪܝܐ	
Gen. 41:57	בכל הארץ	ܒܟܠܗ ܐܪܥܐ	p. 101[81]	add. ܕܡܨܪܝܢ	
Exod. 32:26	(בשער) המחנה	ܕܡܫܪܝܬܐ	p. 155	ܕܡܫܟܢܐ[82]	

Also of interest is Ephrem's citation of Ps. 104:1 in his Prose Refutations:

MT	י׳ אלהי גדלת מאד
9a1 and Nestorian witnesses	ܡܪܝܐ ܐܠܗܐ ܪܒܬ ܠܟ
Most western mss from 6th century onward	...ܪܒ ܠܟ

The reading cited by Ephrem is not that of the oldest mss. Rather it agrees with MT, and also with 9a1, a unique carrier in Psalms, here joined by the Nestorian authorities.[83]

Other commentaries ascribed to Ephrem

A few readings attested in just one of the biblical mss are likewise supported by the commentaries attributed to Ephrem on later biblical books:

	MT	unique reading	in ms	majority reading	ref in Ed.Rom.
2 Sam. 19:36	שרים ושרות	ܫܐܪ̈ܐ ܘܫܐܪ̈ܬܐ	9a1	ܫܪ̈ܐ ܘܫܪ̈ܝܬܐ	I 423A
2 Kgs. 22:14	במשנה	ܒܬܢܝܢܬܐ	9a1	ܒܬܢܝܢܘܬܐ	I 565B

Such readings tend to confirm that the commentaries contain material genuinely due to Ephrem.

Emendation with aid of MT

Methodology

The text of P as recovered from the extant sources – even including patristic citations – is in frequent need of emendation. Already in 1869, Nöldeke feared that only a

[79] J. Pinkerton, "The Origin and the Early History of the Syriac Pentateuch", *JTS* 15 (1914), pp. 14–51.

[80] A.G.P. Janson, "Ephrem the Syrian and the Early History of the Peshitta", lecture at Leiden University, 19 December 1995.

[81] According to MT, the famine was severe in all the earth (בכל הארץ). This was translated exactly as ܒܟܠܗ ܐܪܥܐ. Some scribe, however, misunderstood ܐܪܥܐ as land and so expanded: "land of Egypt". Ephrem by contrast emphasises that the famine was *not* confined to Egypt.

[82] See discussion in chapter 3 above.

[83] C.W. Mitchell (ed.), *St Ephraim's Prose Refutations*, 2 vols., London and Oxford 1912–21, i, p. 41, lines 9–11.

minority of the corruptions in the old printed editions of P could be remedied through recourse to mss, since the greater part had originated during the centuries immediately after the translation was made, for which we have no manuscript. The corruptions already present in the biblical citations in Aphrahat and Ephrem testified to the "careless and arbitrary" handling of the text of P during the earliest centuries of its existence.[84]

Haefeli in turn closed his monograph on P with a call to give up the attempt to reconstruct the original text, unless more ancient material was discovered, either in biblical mss more ancient than those then known or in patristic citations.[85] A similar note of caution is sounded by de Boer[86] and by Lane.[87]

It is true that there are a number of errors which appear in every extant ms. This is the almost inevitable consequence of the hazards, natural and man-made, which threatened the survival of mss. It may well be that more than one direct copy was made from the original translation; but only one such copy has left progeny extant today, and so all extant mss are tainted by its errors. In fact the latest common ancestor of the extant mss may be two or more generations removed from the original, all collateral lines having now died out; and in that case all extant mss will bear the errors accumulated over two or more transcriptions.[88]

Thus a comparison of the surviving Syriac biblical mss cannot take us all the way back to the Urtext. Patristic citations, which are occasional and in any case often bear the same errors, offer only limited help. Yet we can open up a second front, because the translation was made from a Hebrew *Vorlage* which, although not identical with MT, shared a common origin. This may give us a basis to improve on the evidence of the extant mss through emendation. The point was well appreciated by Bernstein, who proposed some convincing emendations of the Syriac text with the aid of MT.[89] A number of scholars have followed the same route.[90]

Emendation is not to be undertaken lightly, and once again we must consider authenticity and direction. Under the first heading, we ask whether the text of the mss really is unacceptable as a credible rendering of the Hebrew, and the proposed emendation clearly superior. Here textual criticism once again interlocks with translation technique. Under the second heading, we ask whether the existing text is a credible scribal development from the proposed emendation.

Both questions allow room for subjectivity, illustrated by the following passages:

---

[84] *Literarisches Centralblatt* 41, 2 October 1869, as quoted and translated by P.A.H. de Boer, "Towards an Edition of the Syriac Version of the Old Testament", *VT* 31 (1981), pp. 346–57: 347. This was Nöldeke's response to Ceriani's survey of the manuscript evidence.

[85] L. Haefeli, *Die Peschitta des alten Testamentes*, Münster 1927, pp. 115–16.

[86] De Boer, "Towards an edition", p. 355: "An attempt to reconstruct 'the' Peshitta version enters the danger zone in which easy wishful thinking, or unrealistic ideas about the purity and perfection of the first, original copy call the tune".

[87] D.J. Lane, "Text, Scholar and Church: The Place of the Leiden Peshitta within the Context of Scholastically and Ecclesiastically Definitive Versions", *JSS* 38 (1993), pp. 33–47:46: "The search for *the* Peshitta is a search for a chimaera … an attempt to discover the sun by study of a dial".

[88] A similar phenomenon affects the male line in human families: the stock of surnames is constantly being eroded, as male lines become extinct, even though the population itself may be rising. On the early study of this phenomenon, see D.G. Kendall, "The Genealogy of Genealogy: Branching Processes before (and after) 1873", *Bulletin of the London Mathematical Society* 7 (1975), pp. 225–53.

[89] G.H. Bernstein, "Syrische Studien 1", *ZDMG* 3 (1849), pp. 385–428.

[90] So e.g. Gelston, *Twelve Prophets*, pp. 98–100.

1 Sam. 2:29

Here a man of God rebukes Eli and his family, in God's name, for their contempt towards "my sacrifices and meal-offerings which I commanded". In MT, the phrase continues with the Hebrew word מעון "dwelling-place", which, however, does not fit well syntactically. In the P mss, we instead find ܒܡܕܒܪܐ "in the wilderness". One could argue that this is original: if God "came forth from Sinai"(Deut. 33:2), then the translator may have identified his dwelling-place as the wilderness. On the other hand, P seldom wanders so far in his interpretations, and the usual rendering of מעון – occurring even three verses later at 1 Sam. 2:32 – is ܡܥܡܪܐ. Thus we could instead argue that the original text of P had ܒܡܥܡܪܐ "in the dwelling-place" – a faithful if not immediately meaningful rendering of the Hebrew. In that case, an early copyist corrupted the text to ܒܡܕܒܪܐ with a glance at Lev. 7:38, which records how the commandment for the Israelites to offer their sacrifices was given in the wilderness of Sinai. If the emendation is right, P will have been unusually literal at this point; but the text was obscure, and palaeographically the change is credible.

Job 3:22

MT השמחים אלי גיל ישישו כי ימצאו קבר

P ܘܚܕܝܢ ܘܡܬܦܨܚܝܢ ܘܪܘܙܝܢ ܟܕ ܡܫܟܚܝܢ ܩܒܪܐ

who rejoice and gather together and exult when they find a grave

Whence the gathering together? Rignell suggested that the translator read גל "heap" rather than גיל "joy", and interpreted "unto a heap" as "gather together".[91] Such an interpretation, however, seems uncharacteristically subtle. It may instead be that the translator reduced the three terms for rejoicing to two, namely ܘܚܕܝܢ ܘܪܘܙܝܢ, and that ܘܡܬܦܨܚܝܢ is a corrupt dittography of ܡܫܟܚܝܢ later in the verse.

Judges 5:14

MT אחריך בנימין בעממיך

P mss ܒܬܪܟ ܒܢܝܡܝܢ ܒܚܘܒܟ

after thee Benjamin in thy love

What are we to make of the last word? In meaning, the extant text bears no relation to the Hebrew. Moreover, the term ܚܘܒܐ for "love" is almost wholly alien to P in the Old Testament, which instead uses ܪܚܡܬܐ, as Joosten has reminded us.[92] Hence a strong case for emendation. On the other hand, an emendation which achieves the same sense as MT will not easily explain the existing text. Specifically, if we emend to ܒܥܡܡܝܟ – a literal translation – we shall have to suppose quite serious scribal corruption, whereby the ܒ together with the right-hand part of the first ܡ became the two strokes of ܚ, and so on. Overall, though, emendation is probably the least difficult solution.

---

[91] So G. Rignell, *The Peshitta to the Book of Job*, Kristianstad 1994, p. 27.
[92] J. Joosten, "Doublet Translations in Peshitta Proverbs" in MPI 8 (1995), pp. 63–72; see p. 65. The only biblical occurrence of ܚܘܒܐ noted by Joosten is at Prov. 15:17.

Examples

There are many passages where emendation by conjecture can be more confidently proposed, for example:

Lev. 1:16

MT וְהֵסִיר אֶת־מֻרְאָתוֹ; P mss ܡܘܡܬܗ ܡܘܡܬܗ; cj ...ܢܘܚܬܐ "and he shall take away . . ."
There are further passages in Leviticus (e.g. 3:4) where MT has the Hiphil of סור and the P mss have a form of ܢܚܒ which may in fact represent an original Aph'el of ܢܚܒ.

Lev. 24:8

MT בְּיוֹם הַשַּׁבָּת; mss ܫܬܐ ܕܫܬܐ "on the sixth (day)" cj ܫܒܬܐ ܕ̈ܫܒܬܐ
Here the day is specified on which the shewbread has to be presented each week. Perles defends the existing text by referring to Sifra ad loc. and TB Men. 97a, which state that the staves that held the loaves were set out on Friday. However, it is the actual presentation of the loaves that is meant here, and the rabbinic sources fully endorse the biblical commandment that this was done on the Sabbath itself.

Deut. 22:9

MT (לֹא תִזְרַע) כַּרְמְךָ (כִּלְאָיִם) "do not sow your vineyard with mixed seeds"
P mss ܬܘܡܟ "your furrow"; cj ܟܪܡܟ "your vineyard"
The emendation restores correspondence with MT. The existing text seems a corruption due partly to the influence of Lev. 19:19, which forbids mixed seeds in the field, though a different Syriac word is used there: ܚܩܠܬܟ "your fields" for Heb. שָׂדְךָ.

Josh. 15:12

MT הַיָּמָּה הַגָּדוֹל; mss ܠܝܡܐ; cj ܝܡܐ ܪܒܐ
The reading of the mss is then an assimilation to the Meribah of Num. 20:13 etc.

Judg. 13:17

MT וְכִבַּדְנוּךָ; mss ܘܢܘܡܝܟ; cj ܘܢܫܡܥ
This conjecture agrees with the reading ascribed to the 'Ebraya as noted above.

2 Kgs. 11:6

MT סוּר; mss ܣܘܪܐ; cj ܣܝܪܐ
This is the name of a temple gate. The Syriac form is unique, and was interpreted by Barhebraeus as ܟܣܝܐ "hidden".[93] Instead, however, we could suppose that P-Kings read his *Vorlage* as סִיר "pot". For this he offered ܩܕܣܐ, the usual translation, to which

---

[93] A. Morgenstern, *Die Scholien des Gregorius Abulfarag . . . zum Buch der Könige*, 1895.

the existing text in Kings should be emended. This hypothesis is supported by P in the parallel at 2 Chr. 23:5, where MT has שער היסוד but P has: "gate of the cooks (ܛܒ̈ܚܐ)", which seems an interpretation, with this translator's greater freedom, of "gate of the pot". The starting-point "pot" for the translator of P-Chronicles may have come independently from the Hebrew of Kings (often consulted by P-Chronicles), perhaps in the same copy; or it could in theory derive from consultation of P-Kings.

Isa. 24:23

MT זקניו; mss ܩܕܝܫܘܗܝ, cj ܣܒܘܗܝ
The existing text of P offers a sense significantly different from MT: God's glory will appear not to his elders but to his saints. However, the change could have arisen so easily through textual corruption that it cannot safely be ascribed to the translator.[94]

Amos 8:6

MT נעלים; mss ܡܣܐܢܐ; cj ܣܐܢܐ
The poor are sold for "sweepings" according to the mss, but the emendation would give "shoes", as at the parallel at 2:6.

Hab. 1:12

MT לא נמות "we shall not die"; P ܕܠܐ ܢܡܘܣ "without law"
Here God is addressed. Mekilta Shir. 6 presents MT's reading as a Tiqqun Sopherim for לא תמות: that God will not die was too obvious to state. The P manuscripts declare: "Thou art without law, O God." It may be that P's *Vorlage* agreed with MT; the translator wrote ܠܐ ܢܡܘܣ, intended as "we shall not die"; later scribes, however, understood it in the third person, applied to God, yielding a sense again found repugnant; and the existing text results from deliberate distortion, partly inspired by Christian opposition to the Jewish law.[95]

2 Chr. 21:19

MT שרפה; mss ܐܘܩܕܐ; cj ܝܩܕܐ (which renders שרפה in the similar context of 2 Chr. 16:14).
At 1 Sam. 22:19 we find the first of a cluster of serious semantic differences between MT and P which cannot be ascribed either to a different *Vorlage* or to translation technique, and rather seem due to inner-Syriac corruption:

MT   ואת נב עיר הכהנים הכה לפי חרב

P   ܘܝܗܒ ܠܗ ܠܢܘܒ ܩܪܝܬܐ ܕܟܗ̈ܢܐ. ܘܡܚܐ ܒܦܘܡܐ ܕܚܪܒܐ

and he gave him (i.e. Doeg) the city of the priests, and he slew with the edge of the sword

. . .

---

[94] See van der Kooij, *Die alten Textzeugen des Jesajabuches*, Göttingen 1981, p. 280, for a different view.
[95] See further Gelston, *Twelve Prophets*, p. 119.

That P does not represent the name of the city, and instead states that it was given to Doeg, is suspicious. It seems that ܘܝܗܒ is a corruption from ܘܠܢܘܒ (or simply ܘܢܘܒ) and that the original translation was close to MT:

ܘܠܢܘܒ ܩܪܝܬܐ ܕܟܗܢܐ ܩܛܠ ܒܦܘܡܐ ܕܚܪܒܐ

and Nob, city of the priests, he slew with the edge of the sword.

This case is of interest because everywhere else in the extant text of P the city is called not ܢܘܒ but ܢܚܒ. This latter change assimilates the name to that (wrongly) introduced by P at Ezek. 47:20 –

MT עד נכח לבוא חמת

P ܥܕܡܐ ܠܢܚܒ ܕܐܬܐ ܡܥܠܢܐ ܕܚܡܬ

This forms part of the process of levelling names, discussed in chapter 2 above. Evidently the corruption at 1 Sam. 22:19 of ܘܠܢܘܒ to ܘܝܗܒ antedates that process, and shows it to be due to later scribes rather than the original translators.

The cluster of putative corruptions continues into 1 Sam. 23:

	MT	P (mss)	conjecture
17	למשנה	ܘܬܢܝܐ	ܬܢܝܢܐ
19	בגבעת החכילה	ܒܓܒܥܬ ܒܚܝܠܐ	ܒܓܒܥܬ ܚܟܝܠܐ
22	(וראו את מקומו...) הכינו	ܛܒܘ ܒܬܗ	ܛܝܒܘ
28	סלע המחלקות	ܫܘܪܐ ܦܠܓܘܬܐ	ܫܠܥܐ ܕܦܠܓܘܬܐ

The evident corruptions in vv.17, 19, 22 and 28 suggest that a page in an early copy was damaged, so that the next copyist sometimes had to guess at the text. Such a hypothesis would justify even bolder emendations to explain further discrepancies in v.3 and v.18:

	MT	P (mss)	conjecture
3	ביהודה	ܒܝ ܝܗܘܕ	ܒܝܗܘܕ[96]
18	וישב דוד בחרשה	ܝܬܒ ܒܥܘܪܐ ܒܥܘܡܩܐ	ܘܝܬܒ ܕܘܝܕ ܒܚܪܫܐ[97]

Scholarly activity too led to changes in the text. These include the insertion of titles and colophons, to mark the boundaries of books and their constituent sections. Some books include a note of their midpoint, based apparently on the space taken up rather than (as in Jewish tradition) on the number of verses. Thus the midpoints of Isaiah and Chronicles are noted (albeit not by all mss) immediately before Isa. 35:3 and 2 Chr. 6:1 respectively, unlike Isa. 33:21 and 1 Chr. 27:25 in MT.[98] In Ezekiel the results coincide at Ezek. 26:1.

These scholarly notes may have mistakenly become incorporated into the text. Thus the note at Isa. 35:3 runs:

ܘܡܪܬܝܢܐ ܘܠܘܒܒܐ ܕܡܚܝܠܐ ܕܐܬܐ ܦܪܘܩܐ ܘܦܪܩ ܠܗܘܢ

admonition and encouragement of the weak, that the saviour will come and deliver them

This was originally a title of the latter part of Isaiah, but has since merged with the text. Something similar may have happened to God's words to Aaron at Num. 18:20 –

96 Used as at Neh. 2:7 to specify the territory rather than the tribe of Judah.

97 The extant reading ܥܘܡܩܐ 'valley' may reflect the offer of the Qeilites in v.18 to hand David over if Saul would come down to them.

98 This is the midpoint if we do not include the section 1 Chr. 26:13–27:34, which may be among the many passages omitted by the original translator; see Appendix II following this chapter.

MT   אני חלקך ונחלתך בתוך בני ישראל

P   אלא פלגא ויהתכון ונחלתכון דבני ישראל, הי דרומא ואקדשא דמריא,

but your portion and possession among the children of Israel is the heave-offerings and holy things of the Lord.

T⁰   מתנן די יהבית לך אינון חלקך ואחסנתך בנו בני ישראל

At first sight, P has taken refuge in periphrasis, much like T⁰, to avoid anthropomorphism. Expansion on this scale, however, is not typical of P, which moreover (unlike T⁰) has no difficulty with the very similar statement at Deut. 18:2 that "the Lord is his (i.e. the priest's) possession". Here we note that neighbouring sections have been supplied – albeit probably secondarily – with titles: "the passage of the division of Korah" (16:1), "on the whole offerings of purification" (19:1). Now chapter 18 has no title, but the final words of P's reading above would make a very fitting one: "the heave-offerings and holy things of the Lord". Hence it seems that P originally rendered literally here too:

אנא פלגתכון ונחלתכון בגו בני ישראל

I am your portion and possession among the children of Israel

Later, we may suppose that the title of Num. 18 was accidentally displaced to this point, and then absorbed into the text. As it became the subject, אנא then became corrupted to אלא.[99]

Daniel 7–11 has been provided with historical notes maintaining the original identification of the four kingdoms as Babylon, Media, Persia and Greece, the final enemy being named Antiochus. In the west, by contrast, Rome was the fourth kingdom, in both Jewish and Christian tradition (Josephus Antiq. 10.11.7 [276]; Mekilta Bahodesh 9; Matt. 24:15).[100]

It must be emphasised that emendation should only be proposed after every possible attempt to accept the text as it stands. Here the text of Job 4:19 is apposite –

MT   אף שכני בתי חמר אשר בעפר יסודם

P   אף עמרי בתי חצפא דבעפרא דבחצפא משתכללין

even those who dwell in houses of clay which . . .

The Syriac relative clause (left for the moment untranslated) would normally mean: "which are completed in dust". Finding this sense unsatisfactory, Bernstein emended the verb משתכללין to משתחרין "are whitewashed", on the basis of مكلسة in the Syriac-based Arabic version.[101] However, this emendation lacks any semantic connection with the Hebrew, and it is in fact unnecessary. The Syriac verb can also mean "lay foundations", as at 1 Kgs. 6:37 discussed above, so that the relative clause can be translated as it stands: "which are founded on dust". The interest of Bernstein's suggestion is rather that it explains how the translator into Arabic might have 'misread' a Syriac text that baffled him.

---

[99] Cf. Gen. 24:27, where the P mss again have אלא for MT אנכי, and the original text was perhaps אנא.

[100] Aphrahat too identifies the fourth kingdom with Rome, treated as a continuation of Greece, and so places the climax in 70 CE. See J. Parisot (ed.), *Aphraatis Sapientis Persae Demonstrationes*, in *Patrologia Syriaca*, Paris 1894–1907, part 1, vol. 1, cols. 872–82.   [101] Bernstein, "Syrische Studien 1", p. 391.

Emendation must also be kept within bounds. Thus at Deut. 16:20 MT has צדק צדק תרדף but the P mss all have: "in righteousness judge thy neighbour", which instead follows Lev. 19:15. We may well suspect that the substitution is due to a copyist; but an editor would be over-stepping the mark if he replaced this text with his own translation of the line from Deuteronomy. Similarly, the extant text of P contains a number of additional phrases (by comparison with MT) which recall parallel passages, and these likewise may have been inserted by copyists, e.g. "Aaron and his sons shall eat it" (Lev. 10:18, cf. 8:31) and "who killed his neighbour without wishing" (Num. 35:6, cf. Deut. 19:4). Once more, however, these phrases could not be omitted from an edition. Again, as noted in chapter 2, there seems to have been a systematic attempt to impose uniformity on names, by assimilating them to other names known within the closed field of P, as when Saul's daughter מרב is everywhere called ܢܕܒ. That all this goes back to the original translator is unlikely; yet it would be beyond the editor's brief to prepare a text with these names corrected on the basis of MT.

The text of the fourth-century fathers

It is worth noting that, in some places where emendation seems needed, Aphrahat and Ephrem already had the corrupt text. For example, at Gen. 16:2 Sarah expresses the hope אבנה, that she may be "built up" through her handmaid's child. In P she instead wishes: ܐܬܒܝܐ "I shall be comforted". This bears only a distant semantic relationship to the Hebrew, and is more easily explained as a corruption of ܘܐܬܒܢܐ, which would render the Hebrew exactly. However, already in the fourth century Ephrem had the same text as the mss, as his comment makes clear. Ephrem makes Sarah protest to Abraham that she now has to endure Hagar's insults, in bitter contrast to her original hopes –

ܡܛܠ ܒܘܝܐܐ ܗܘ ܓܝܪ ܕܢܗܘܐ ܠܝ ܡܢܗ̇ ܝܗܒܬܗ̇ ܠܟ

for it was for the sake of the consolation that I would have from her that I gave her to you

Similarly at Gen. 30:3 the barren Rachel offers her handmaid to her husband, so that she may be "built up" (ואבנה) through her handmaid's children. In the mss of P, Rachel's hope once more is ܘܐܬܒܝܐ "and I shall be comforted", again apparently for an original ܐܬܒܢܐ. Yet the reading of the mss is again presupposed by Ephrem. When Leah later offers her own handmaid, Ephrem makes Jacob at first refuse, saying:

ܠܟܝ ܐܝܬ ܗܘ ܠܟܝ ܒܘܝܐܐ ܕܐܝܬ ܗܘ ܠܟܝ ܒܢ̈ܝܐ

you (already) have consolation because you *do* have children

An example of a corruption in the biblical mss which is already shared by Aphrahat occurs at Isaiah 9:12: –

MT ויתאבכו גאות עשן

P ܘܢܬܟܪܟܘܢ ܓܒ̈ܝܐ ܒܬܢܢܐ

and the elect will be enveloped in smoke

Here ܓܒ̈ܝܐ "the elect" would be an uncharacteristically loose rendering for גאות "pride". Instead it seems a corruption of ܓܐ̈ܝܐ, which would correspond accurately with the Hebrew.[102] Yet Aphrahat has the same text as the mss, for in his discussion of the sufferings of the righteous he explains that there are times when there is such wickedness in the world that the punishment spills over even upon the righteous; and, with a clear allusion to this passage:

ܗܒܝ̈ܐ ܒܥ̈ܢܐ ܕܒܘܢܐ

the elect are enveloped in the smoke[103]

Cases of this sort create a problem of presentation for the modern editor of P, because of his dual audience: scholars of the Old Testament and of Syriac-speaking Christianity. The former group need to reach back to the translation itself, as a witness to the lost Hebrew *Vorlage* and its exegesis. If they suspect that the Syriac text has suffered in transmission, they will wish to emend it. For the latter group, however, readings that became corrupted before even the earliest extant patristic writings are of limited relevance: so far as the eastern churches are concerned, ܒܥ̈ܢܐ *is* the reading of P. Perhaps the best compromise for a critical edition is to record conjectures in a special apparatus, and to present in the main text the best reading that can be recovered from the extant witnesses. This would contrast with the Göttingen edition of LXX, whose editors are sufficiently confident of emendations to place them in the main text.

Historical interpretation

The observed patterns of right and wrong readings must now be explained in historical terms, in relation both to the genealogy of the extant mss and to developments in the Syriac-speaking church.

The origin of the new readings

The history begins with the Urtext: the original translation. This was as literal as possible, within the demands of intelligibility. If many of the unique agreements of single mss (such as 5b1) preserve the original text against the majority of mss, it follows that in many passages new readings arose, which all but displaced the old. These new readings are already dominant in Aphrahat, but not in Ephrem. They consisted, in large measure, of stylistic adjustments and clarifying additions, since the original translation had sometimes been constrained by quantitative literalism. The new readings gained wide currency, so that in most books there is only one ms that regularly preserves the corresponding old readings, though even such a ms will not be altogether free of the new.

The origin of these new readings takes us back to the earliest stages of transmission. These include the earliest centuries of P's circulation within the Syriac-speaking church, as well as an even earlier stage of transmission within a Jewish community, and the process of the adoption of the version by the Church. Those responsible for the new readings did not know, or perhaps did not care, that they were moving away from the Hebrew original. They evidently did not regard the Syriac text before them as

---

[102] Compare ܒܚܠܝܐ ܪܐܙܐ for עטרת גאות at Isa. 28:1,3.   [103] Ed. Parisot, vol. 2, col. 12.

letter-perfect, but rather as an imperfect version of Scripture which it was their task to render more accessible.

This is indeed a radical attitude, and one can detect some continuity with the radicalism of the translators themselves, who were prepared to misread or improve on the Hebrew text in the interests of good sense. A parallel to the copyists' radicalism can also be drawn with the 'vernacular' copies of the Hebrew text from Qumran. In both, the copyists speak the same language as that of the sacred text, and they do not hesitate to update its language and to make it more accessible in other ways also. A parallel revision process may have been the standardisation of the Syriac language itself shortly before the fifth century.[104]

It would be interesting to know more about the background of these early revisers. They seem to have been a closed group of scholars, rather like the translators before them. The revision operates within the closed field of the Peshitta text, without reference to any outside authority – as attested for example, by the odd changes of biblical names.

The new readings created in effect a second edition of P. As Walter notes, this term is justified by the fact that most of the new readings represent intentional changes, even though some result from corruption.[105] Significantly, the new readings include added section headings, which suggest an official attempt to promulgate the text in a new form, incorporating the new readings.

The revision process which led to the new readings could have gone farther, in the sense that many passages remain that invite stylistic improvement or harmonisation. It may be that the process was arrested by the adoption at some early stage of a particular ms as standard. More probably, however, the revision was halted by the schisms of the fifth century.

The spread of the new readings

In the eyes of the modern investigator, the new readings are errors, because they depart from the original text. To scribes, however, they would have appeared superior, because they resulted in a fuller and more idomatic text, and ironed out the inner contradictions of the Hebrew original.

The mechanism whereby the new readings spread so widely is that many a scribe was aware that the ms from which he was copying might contain errors, and therefore consulted an alternative source. This alternative source was often a second ms; in other cases, however, it was a text that the scribe had learnt elsewhere by heart – an ability that we in the west tend to underestimate. In either case, it often happened that one of the scribe's sources presented the old reading and the other source the new. Because it appeared superior, the new reading was usually preferred, and would even survive any subsequent scrutiny of the copy by a supervisor.

---

[104] Thus Nöldeke (*Compendious Syriac Grammar*, p. xxxii) posits "scholastic regulation" to explain the settled appearance of the language and orthography already in the fifth century. See also, however, L.van Rompay, "Some preliminary remarks on the origins of classical Syriac as a standard language: the Syriac version of Eusebius of Caesarea's Eccesiastical History", in G. Goldenberg and S. Raz (ed.), *Semitic and Kushitic Studies*, pp. 70–89.

[105] D.M. Walter, "The use of sources in the Peshitta of Kings", MPI 8 (1995), pp. 187–204.

Such processes of textual admixture occasionally left traces in the copy, where an alternative reading is noted in the margin or a new reading imposed after erasure. Indeed we sometimes catch the new reading entering a ms in just this way. An instance was noted above at Lev. 15:17, where the old reading ܡܫܟ (corresponding to MT עוֹר 'skin') survived into 9a1 only, and even there a supralinear Beth was added by the first hand to yield the majority reading ܡܫܟ.

One clue that helps us trace the spread of the new readings is that they are dominant in Aphrahat but not in Ephrem. This seems surprising. Ephrem worked in Nisibis and Edessa, two great centres of Syriac Christianity, while Aphrahat was in the eastern outskirts. If the text was undergoing revision, one would have expected Ephrem to know of and adopt the new readings well before Aphrahat.

Another clue is that those mss which regularly preserve old readings come from west-Syriac centres, in so far as any information survives. Thus 5b1 was written at Amid; 8h5 is from Qartmin, the present monastery of Mar Gabriel in Tur 'Abdin;[106] and 9a1 is in a Serta hand. Two of the other mss, though written primarily in Estrangelo, show some western features: 10f1 forms some letters in the Serta fashion, while 6b1 has occasional Jacobite vowels. What may be the latest of these mss, namely 10l1, is known to be Malkite, and so to represent the west of the Syriac speech area. The provenance of the palimpsest 7pj2 is unfortunately unknown.

Together, these clues suggest that the new readings originated at some prestigious centre in the east, perhaps at Mar Mattai itself, during the third century, and spread westwards only gradually. In the fourth century they were known to Aphrahat in the east but not yet to Ephrem. Also in the west, the biblical citations in the Greek text of Eusebius of Emesa (died 359) – which, as Romeny has discovered, reflect the P text then known – are again predominantly of the older type.[107] Even at the end of the fifth century, Philoxenus of Mabbogh still shows some familiarity with the old readings lost in all biblical mss but 5b1.[108]

By the sixth century, the new readings must have spread over most of the Syriac-speaking area, since most mss of that era or later have them. They took many centuries, however, to gain full acceptance in the west, so that a few mss retain old readings regularly (though not invariably), while others join them sporadically. The adoption of the new readings in the west must have been close to completion by the twelfth century, when even the Malkite text is based on the new readings, as shown, for example, by the Psalter 12t 2.

Even in the west, however, some old readings have been altogether driven out by the new. Examples of such new readings are the systematic changes of names, such as NKH for the city-name NWB, and others discussed in chapter 2.

Textual convergence from the ninth century onward

The ninth century witnessed a standardisation of the text of P. Among mss produced in or after that time, the eastern mss are almost uniform in text, and most western mss are

---

[106] A.N. Palmer, *Monk and Mason on the Tigris Frontier: The Early History of Tur 'Abdin*, Cambridge 1990.
[107] R.B. ter Haar Romeny, "Techniques of Translation and Transmission in the Earliest Text Forms of the Syriac Version of Genesis", in MPI 8 (1995), pp. 177–86; *A Syrian in Greek Dress*, pp. 75–7.
[108] R.G. Jenkins, *The OT Quotations of Philoxenus of Mabbug*, Louvain 1989, p. 75.

of the same type – except in the special case of Psalms, discussed below. A division can thus be made between older and younger mss – though the older mss form a far looser grouping than the younger.

The text found in both the east and the west from the ninth century onwards has been termed the textus receptus,[109] or the standard text.[110] These terms assume too much, as Dirksen observes, because the standardisation was not absolute.[111] Some mss in the west escaped it, at least in some degree, and so lack the readings characteristic of the majority of ninth-century and later mss. Witnesses free (or relatively free) of the standardisation include the western massoretic mss, which therefore cannot be viewed as the norm by which the text was standardised, despite the function of the Hebrew Massora.[112] Other later western mss that depart from the text common to the majority of ninth-century and later mss are 12a1 and various mss covering individual books, e.g. 16g6 in Lamentations. Nor should it be forgotten that western mss from the ninth century or later include two of our regular unique carriers of old readings, namely 9a1 and 10f1. Thus, from the ninth century onward, all mss in the east exhibit a single type of text, but the situation is more varied in the west.

As expected, the text of the majority of ninth-century and later mss incorporates most of the new readings that arose in the opening centuries. In other passages, however, it has further new readings of its own; and conversely, it very occasionally preserves an ancient reading lost by the rest, as at Song 8:14 (cited above). Thus it is not derived exclusively from the text of the extant older mss.

A number of phenomena thus demand explanation in historical terms. The first is the fact that the western texts are less homogeneous than the eastern. The relative uniformity of the eastern witnesses reflects an effort to standardise the text through careful comparison of different copies. Less effort was expended on this in the west, where LXX was accessible and often enjoyed greater prestige. Thus Philoxenus of Mabbog considered the Septuagint to be the most accurate (ܚܬܝܬܐ), true (ܫܪܝܪܐ) and correct (ܬܪܝܨܐ) of all Old Testament versions, as well as being the text used by Jesus and his disciples in the Gospels and Acts;[113] and of course the Greek Bible in various forms was translated into Syriac to rival P. No wonder, then, that in the west the text of P was not preserved with such homogeneity.

What is remarkable, however, is that the schisms which broke the Syriac-speaking church into mutually hostile sects are not reflected in a clear textual division between east and west. In principle, one might have expected local text-types to develop. In the Vulgate, by comparison, we find distinctive local texts – e.g. Spanish, Transalpine,

[109] So Koster, *The Peshitta of Exodus*, p. 2 et passim.
[110] So Gelston, *The Peshitta of the Twelve Prophets*, pp. 64–5.
[111] P.B. Dirksen's review of Gelston in *BO* 46 (1989), pp. 152–4; "Some Remarks in Connection with the Peshitta of Kings", in A.S. van der Woude ed., *New Avenues in the Study of the Old Testament*, OTS 25, Leiden 1989, pp. 2–28 (see p. 28).
[112] *Pace* M.H. Goshen-Gottstein, "Prolegomena to a Critical Edition of the Peshitta", *Scripta Hierosolymitana* 8 (Jerusalem 1961) 26–67. Goshen-Gottstein later accepted that these mss "have nothing to do with textual sub-crystallisations" and rejected the modern term "massoretic mss" altogether, instead adoping the native term: Shemahe mss. See "The Peshitta and its Manuscripts", *BO* 37 (1980), pp. 13–16. This term was used in the thesis by his pupil C. Brovender, *The Syriac Shemahe Manuscripts – a Typological and Comparative Study*, diss. Jerusalem 1976 (Hebrew with English summary).
[113] G. Diettrich, *Eine jakobitische Einleitung in den Psalter* (=BZAW 5), Giessen 1901, p. 115. This work also quotes the contrary view that P is more accurate because Hebrew is akin (ܩܪܝܒ ܗܘ) to Syriac.

Insular – despite the interaction that must have occurred between these different communities within the Catholic Church. In the case of P, the geographical separation between east and west was reinforced by the political division between the Roman Empire and Persia, and by sectarian opposition. The absence of a textual division between east and west thus demands explanation.

An important point is made here by Jenner, who points out that the ninth century was a period of flowering of philological activity in which Moslems, Christians and Jews all participated. In particular, the Syrians of the east and the west consulted together in the realm of biblical scholarship, which could be viewed as common ground. The readiness in the west to accept Nestorian scholarship is attested by the Syriac Masora, which appears (to judge from the extant evidence) first in the east (in 9m1) and then in the west.[114] Scholarship travelled also in the opposite direction. The Syrohexapla, despite its monophysite origin, was copied for the Nestorian patriarch Timothy I (died 823),[115] and is also frequently cited by Isho'dad.[116] Timothy also sought the loan of the monophysites' manuscript – or in his words ܟܬܒܐ ܕܝܘܡܬܐ – of Gregory of Nazianzus, in order to collate his own copy.[117] Continuing co-operation between the two sects in the twelfth and thirteenth centuries contributed to a veritable renaissance of Syrian scholarship.[118]

It may have been during this period that scholars in the west compared their own biblical texts with eastern mss. The greater homogeneity of those mss would have impressed them as a token of faithful transmission. Where the western mss were divided, the western scholars would have chosen whichever reading enjoyed eastern support. In that way, the eastern text became widespread in the west also, though its supremacy never became absolute.

The book of Psalms was exceptional in its textual history. As in the other books, a body of new readings arose in the earliest centuries, and sometimes the only ms free of these is 9a1. Thereafter, however, there were separate movements towards standardisation in the east and in the west, owing to the use of the Psalms in divine service, though the western text never became so uniform as the eastern. Textual comparison from the ninth century onward may have introduced eastern readings into various western mss, but in this book the Syrians of the west did not adopt the eastern text as standard.

According to Jenner, the fact that in most biblical books the eastern text was also adopted in the west is due to political factors. Jenner points out that the Nestorian Catholicos was granted judicial power over all Christians under Islam, and would have been concerned about the integrity of the biblical text, which was fundamental not only for all Christians but also in theological disputation with Islam. Jenner therefore suggests that the Catholicos may have wished to demonstrate his authority by imposing a uniform biblical text for all Syriac-speaking Christians. However, had a show of authority been intended, the Catholicos might have been expected to concentrate on

---

[114] K.D. Jenner, "Some Introductory Remarks concerning the study of 8a1", *MPI* 4 (1988), pp. 200–224: see 209–211.

[115] O. Braun, "Ein Brief des Katholikos Timotheos I über biblische Studien des 9 Jahrhunderts", *OrChr* 1 (1901), pp. 299–313; see p. 300. This letter is also noted for its report of a ninth-century discovery of Dead Sea scrolls.   [116] CSCO 156 (Syr 75), p.xxiii.

[117] O. Braun (ed.), *Timothei Patriarchae I Epistulae 1*, Paris 1914 (=CSCO ii 67), p. 123.

[118] P. Kawerau, *Die jakobitische Kirche im Zeitalter der syrischen Renaissance*, Berlin 1955, pp. 70–2.

the Psalms, the book most often read in the Old Testament. Instead it is here out of all biblical books that diversity between eastern and western texts is most obvious.

An alternative explanation of the standardisation of the text from the ninth century onward is offered by Dirksen, who notes that most of our old mss reached the west not from the heartland of Syriac-speaking Christianity (viz Syria and Iraq) but from the monastery of St Mary Deipara at Der es-Suryan in Egypt. So generously, according to Dirksen, did the Syrians of the west donate biblical mss to this monastery, particularly in the ninth and tenth centuries, that they themselves became short of copies of the biblical text, and were forced to copy texts of the eastern type.[119] It seems preferable, however, with Lane, to view the precious collection of mss at the monastery of St Mary Deipara as the effect, rather than the cause, of the standardisation of the text. Where the text traditional among the Nestorians prevailed, the Syrians of the west were unable to continue using the older mss, and so deposited them at the distant monastery at Der es-Suryan, which enjoyed close relations with the monophysite Syrians of Takrit.[120]

We must be thankful that the goal of standardisation was not pursued in the west so zealously as in the east. Hence the survival of old readings, regularly in some mss and sporadically in others.

A simplified model of the textual history

From the complex development of the text in Exodus, Koster has extracted three successive stages:

Stage 1: (partly preserved by) the unique carriers
Stage 2: the other ancient mss up to the ninth century
Stage 3: the textus receptus[121]

At the beginning of this line we may add (as Stage 0) the Urtext itself. As a first approximation to represent the whole history of P, this model is helpful, and not in Exodus alone – so long as its limitations are borne in mind.

First, the second stage is not sharply defined. It is far less homogeneous than either the first stage (which in any most books is represented by one ms) or the third (whose the mss cohere far more closely).

Second, the three stages are not strictly successive in time: the onset of a new stage did not end the production of mss representing the old. Thus mss representing the second stage, and even the first, continue to be produced in the west after the rise of the third. Again, in some books the first stage is represented by a single ms which is chronologically later than the mss of the second.[122]

Third, although the later stages in principle derive from the earlier, such relations of direct dependence do not apply among their extant representatives. Thus 5b1 cannot be the ancestor of the extant mss of the second stage in Exodus, for it shows many errors

---

[119] P.B. Dirksen, "East and West", pp. 480–4.
[120] D.J. Lane, *The Peshiṭta of Leviticus*, Leiden 1994 [=MPI 6], p. 158.
[121] So the diagram (first inspired by Dirksen's work) shown in M.D. Koster, "Peshitta revisited: a reassessment of its value as a version", *JSS* 38 (1993), pp. 235–68: 266. Dirksen's reservations about the term 'textus receptus' were aired above.
[122] This is often true of 9a1; Esther (where 10f1 represents Koster's first stage) is even more striking.

of which the latter are free. Those second stage mss must instead derive from a different first stage ms, now lost. Likewise, in many books the mss representing the third stage preserve readings lost in the older mss; again they cannot derive from the extant mss of the second stage or even of the first.

In all these respects, the complicated textual history has been deliberately simplified, in order to provide a helpful overview. In addition to this model, Koster has provided a detailed analysis of the mss in P-Exodus, which is fundamental also to the detailed history of the text in other biblical books.

History of modern scholarship

Finally, we may trace the history of scholarship regarding the supposed distinction between eastern and western texts. Such a distinction seemed intuitively obvious in the two mutually hostile sects, the Nestorian and the Monophysite. Thus Rahlfs took it for granted that any mutual influence between the eastern and western texts was "so gut wie ausgeschlossen", and he inferred that any reading attested on both sides would have to pre-date the schism.[123] Rahlfs may have been inspired by Barhebraeus, whose comment on Ps. 10:5 he cites as evidence that eastern and western texts were considered distinct.[124]

The absence of any boundary between eastern and western texts was first demonstrated in 1963, in Albrektson's study of Lamentations.[125] It has since been confirmed in book after book – notably, in Judges, Isaiah and the Minor Prophets. The Psalter is the only exception. As the crowning indignity to Rahlfs, Dirksen has shown it likely that the authority which Rahlfs selected to represent the eastern text, namely the Urmi edition, is in fact essentially a western text.[126]

The main reason that Rahlfs' theory was not challenged earlier was that the evidence from the first books to be investigated happened to be consistent with it, because of various special factors. In Chronicles there was just one Nestorian ms, which like almost any ms had some unique readings. These could be thought to represent an established eastern tradition,[127] whereas in fact they may instead have arisen at a relatively recent stage in transmission. In Wisdom the position was essentially the same: there were four Nestorian mss – 16e1, 17e1, 18e1 and 19e1 – which were closely related and showed some exclusive shared readings. The latter were consistent with the hypothesis of a distinctive Nestorian tradition,[128] even though they might instead have originated no earlier than the sixteenth century itself.

The evidence from Psalms was also consistent with Rahlfs's expectations, since here, exceptionally, there actually exist "two groups of MSS, to which the names respectively of Nestorian and Early Jacobite may be justly applied. The boundary is indeed ill-defined,

---

[123] A. Rahlfs, "Beiträge zur Textkritik der Peschita", *ZAW* 9 (1889), pp. 161–210: 165.

[124] Barhebraeus speaks of ܢܣ̈ܝ̇ܢܐ ܚܕܢܝܬܐ ܘܐܚ̈ܕܬܐ. See P. de Lagarde, *Praetermissorum Libri Duo*, Göttingen 1879, p. 110.

[125] One eastern ms (E) and one western (S) are identical in text, and differ only in externals, notably that E introduces each verse with a letter of the alphabet.

[126] P.[B.] Dirksen, "The Urmiah Edition of the Peshitta: The Story behind the Text", *Textus* 18 (1995), pp. 1–11.   [127] Cf. Barnes, *An Apparatus Criticus to Chronicles*, pp. xxx–xxxi.

[128] J.A. Emerton (ed.), *The Peshitta of the Wisdom of Solomon*, Studia Post-Biblica 2, Leiden 1959, p.xlv.

but the existence of the groups cannot be denied."[129] Psalms was used in the liturgy more than any other book, and it is not surprising that the Syrians of the east and of the west should each have gone some way towards evolving a distinctive text – though as in other books greater uniformity was achieved in the east.[130] It is noteworthy, however, that although the division itself was confirmed in Psalms, the implications that Rahlfs had drawn for the reconstruction of the text were not. Barnes soon discovered that a reading attested on both sides of the east–west divide was not necessarily original, and he had to conclude sorrowfully that "the history of the Peshitta is a history of never ceasing admixture of texts" (p. xli).

There is just one situation – confined to Psalms – which resembles that described by Rahlfs, though not at all in the form that he envisaged. A plausible error gained wide currency in the west, but did not reach either the eastern centres or the relatively insulated western community that produced 9a1. The agreement of 9a1 and the eastern mss then gives the correct reading, often despite the greater antiquity of the rival mss. Such agreement does not betoken admixture. Rather, it represents the closest that the mss of P come in practice to the situation envisaged by Rahlfs, where the agreement of mss from two communities that developed separately guarantees the original text. This is very far, however, from the general canon which Rahlfs had sought to establish.

The other reason for the persistence of Rahlfs's theory of an east–west division was that it seemed too obvious to need testing. Thus Diettrich in his study of Isaiah simply assumed that the eastern and western mss constituted different groups in relation to text, and never tried to prove this by specifying readings that distinguished the two. Instead, he discussed in detail the relationships between the mss *within* either group separately (pp. xvii–xix, xxiv–xxvi). One bit of evidence discovered by Diettrich in fact contradicted his assumed boundary: the western ms 12d1 (T) agrees closely with the eastern mss of the same era. Diettrich's response was to put this ms into the eastern category, despite its serta hand and its predominantly western spelling ܠܪ݂ܝܫܐ.[131]

All in all, the balance of opinion on some central questions – notably the absence of a textual division between east and west, and the originality of unique readings – has changed sharply since the Leiden project was first launched. In this light the decision of the Leiden editors to concentrate in the first place on recording all the rival readings, rather than proceeding immediately to decide priority, appears a wise one. Inevitably, of course, one reading appears in the text of the Leiden edition, the rest in the apparatus; but this carries no judgment as to priority. As de Boer emphasised: "The text printed in this edition – it must be stated *expressis verbis* – ought to be used in exegetical and textual study together with the apparatuses".[132] The reading placed in the text of the edition is instead chosen on strictly objective lines.[133] Had the editors gone further and attempted to decide between right and wrong from the outset, the choice of readings in the edition would almost certainly have rested on theories that have since been

---

[129] Barnes, *The Peshitta Psalter*, p.xxxvi.   [130] Dirksen, "East and West", *VT* 35 (1985), pp. 468–84: 473.

[131] There are, however, occasional eastern vowel signs.

[132] See part 1, fasc. 6 of the Leiden edition (Leiden 1977), p. VIII. De Boer enlarges on this in "Towards an Edition of the Syriac Version of the Old Testament", *VT* 31 (1981), pp. 346–57:356.

[133] At times, individual editors have broken the formal rules, evidently in order to promote what they considered the earliest reading. For example, at Gen. 30:31 the text has ܒܢܬܐ on the sole authority of 10g1, agreeing with MT בּוֹנֶה, while the majority reading ܒܥܬܐ is relegated to the apparatus.

questioned. For example, the unique agreements of 5b1 with MT in Genesis-Exodus might have been relegated to the apparatus, not with a specific reminder to consider them as carefully as the readings in the text, but as a token of their rejection by the editor. By their realism, together with their industry, the collaborators to the Leiden edition have laid an abiding foundation for Peshitta research.

Appendix I: Single Urtext or Multiple Origin?

Almost all the variants in mss of P are readily explained through scribal developments, conscious or unconscious. They are thus fully compatible with the hypothesis of a uniquely defined Urtext. A few variants, however, suggest at first sight more than one point of contact with the Hebrew, and so deserve further scrutiny.

(a) At Exod. 3:16, where God is the subject, the texts offer:

MT נראה אלי, 5b1 ܠ ܐܬܚܙܝ, rell. ܐܬܓܠܝ ܠܝ

While 5b1 renders the Hebrew simply, the majority have a respectful circumlocution which originated in the Palestinian Targum tradition. Both renderings of ראה Niph. in relation to God are known elsewhere in P: ܐܬܓܠܝ ܠ is usual (8x) in Genesis, and serves also for נקרה (of God) at Exod. 3:18; and ܐܬܚܙܝ, ܠ is usual (5x) elsewhere in Exodus.[134] We need not posit two independent translations of the Hebrew in this passage: instead, one may be original and the other an assimilation to a parallel passage. It may thus be that 5b1 is original while the others conform to Exod. 3:18; or the majority may be original while 5b1 conforms to Exod. 4:1 (where all mss show ܐܬܚܙܝ, for נראה).

(b) In rendering the phrase ריח ניחח in Leviticus, the mss are continually divided between ܪܝܚܐ ܕܢܝܚܐ and ܪܝܚܐ ܕܣܘܬܐ. Likewise at Gen. 8:21, 8/5b1 has the first phrase only while the other mss preface it with the second. The two need not be independent treatments of the Hebrew; the second may instead reflect LXX ὀσμὴ εὐωδίας.

(c) At Num. 21:30, for the difficult ונירם in MT, the P mss divide between ܥܘܠ̈ܬܐ and ܣܩܠܬܐ. These look like alternative interpretations of ניר, as "yoke" and as "tilled ground"; the first derives from the sense of ניר in Aramaic and Syriac and may underlie T° מלכו, while the second is the sense of the Hebrew at Hos. 10:12 etc. It could instead be argued, however, that ܥܘܠ̈ܬܐ is alone original, while ܣܩܠܬܐ is a corruption, partly induced by the reference to "fields of Moab" at Gen. 36:25.[135] This view gains support from the fact that the sense "tilled ground" for ניר is never elsewhere recognised by P, which instead usually has ܢܝܪܐ (as for נר), even in the obviously agricultural contexts of Jer. 4:3 and Hos. 10:12.

(d) In both of the parallel passages 2 Kgs. 19:24 and Isa. 37:25, for יארי מצור in MT, 9a1 has ܢܗܪ̈ܘܬܐ ܕܚܣܢܐ while the rest have ܢܗܪ̈ܘܬܐ ܕܨܘܪ. Each is a credible treatment of the Hebrew: 9a1's rendering is paralleled in the Targum, while the equation of מצור with ܨܘܪ recurs at Ps. 31:22 (where MT has עיר מצור). It does not follow, however, that there were two alternative Syriac translations from the first, in either passage. First, either reading is a credible inner-Syriac corruption of the other. Second, even if ܕܚܣܢܐ and ܕܨܘܪ are independent translations of מצור, it may be that one was used in

---

[134] For tabulation and discussion see S.P. Brock, "A Palestinian Targum Feature in Syriac", *JJS* 46 (1995), pp. 271–82.   [135] The previous verse in Numbers begins: "Woe to you, Moab".

Kings and the other in Isaiah, and that copyists later imposed uniformity, in different directions. In that case, ܚܣܝܢܐ is probably the original reading in Isaiah (given that מָצוֹר יְאֹרֵי is rendered ܢܗܪܘܬܐ ܚܣܝܢܐ at Isa. 19:6), and therefore ܡܚܣܢܐ in Kings.

(e) At Hos. 11:8, MT has אֲמַגֶּנְךָ while the P mss divide between ܐܣܬܪܟ (in the majority) and ܐܥܨܪܟ (9a1). Although it has been suggested that these are alternative renderings of the Hebrew,[136] the second reading can instead be explained as a simple corruption of the first. The reason for preferring ܐܣܬܪܟ is that it lies closer semantically both to MT (literally "shield") and to P's rendering of אֶתֶּנְךָ in the preceding phrase, namely ܐܫܠܡܟ.

(f) In the light of these cases, we finally consider Gen. 6:2,4. Here MT has בְּנֵי הָאֱלֹהִים while the P mss are divided, with ܒܢܝ ܐܠܗܐ ܕܝܢܐ in most mss but ܒܢܝ ܓܢܒܪܐ in 8/5b1. These are two independent treatments of the Hebrew: the majority transliterate while 8/5b1 takes אֱלֹהִים as 'judges', as did R. Simeon bar Yohai in the mid-second century CE (Gen. Rabba 26:5). Before concluding, however, that P presented here two alternative renderings from the first, we must compare the citations in Ephrem's commentary,[137] which presents – or at least comes close to presenting – both variant readings: ܒܢܝ ܐܠܗܐ in v.2 and ܓܢܒܪܐ in v.4. This suggests that the original text of P was uniquely defined at both points after all, on the following hypothesis. The translator wrote ܒܢܝ ܐܠܗܐ ܕܝܢܐ in v.2 and ܒܢܝ ܓܢܒܪܐ in v.4; Ephrem preserves this inconsistency, though he replaces ܐܠܗܐ ܕܝܢܐ by its obvious Syriac cognate and abbreviates the second rendering; the biblical manuscripts impose consistency between the two verses, with 8/5b1 showing one reading and the remaining mss the other.

On this view, the case is similar to (d) above, where the same word was rendered differently in two parallel passages. Here, however, the translator is supposed to have offered two very different renderings of the same Hebrew phrase within three verses; and this may strain belief. However, similar examples can be found elsewhere, as noted in chapter 2. We may recall in particular the two different meanings given to תּוֹעֲבַת מִצְרַיִם within a single verse: first the abomination of the Egyptians, then their object of awe. On Gen. 6:1–4 see now A. van der Kooij, "Peshitta Genesis 6: 'Sons of God' – Angels or Judges?', *Journal of Northwest Semitic Languages* 23 (1997), pp. 43–51. According to van der Kooij, ܒܢܝ ܐܠܗܐ is the original reading both in v.2 and in v.4.

All in all, then, there is probably not a single variant which implies unambiguously more than one point of contact with the Hebrew; nor, as we have seen in chapter 3, does the wider textual variation in the indirect tradition support the hypothesis of a multiple origin for P. There is, however, occasional evidence – as the next appendix shows – that the translators may have checked each other's work against the Hebrew.

Appendix II: Two extensive variations

The most extensive variant among the mss of P concerns 1 Chr. 26:13–27:34. This section is present in 7a1, 8a1 and 17e1 only. The oldest ms is unfortunately missing in

---

[136] D.J. Lane in *JBL* 103 (1984), p. 108.
[137] R.-M. Tonneau (ed.), *Sancti Ephraem Syri in Genesim et in Exodum Commentarii*, CSCO 152 (Syr 71), Louvain 1955, sections 6.3, 5 (pp. 55, 57).

this part of Chronicles.[138] However, it contains a note marking the end of 2 Chr. 5:14 as the midpoint of the book, which can only be so if the disputed section is not included. Here we recall that the midpoints of books noted in mss of P (notably Isaiah) seem based on the space occupied by the text.[139]

This section was translated from the Hebrew, but the authenticity of the translation technique is suspect, since the form of the Hebrew is reproduced here far more closely than elsewhere in P-Chronicles (at least from 1 Chr. 2 onward). In particular, clarifying expansions are lacking, e.g.

1 Chr. 26:18

MT לפרבר למערב ארבעה למסלה שנים לפרבר
P ܠܦܪܒܪ ܠܡܥܪܒܐ ܐܪܒܥܐ ܠܡܫܠܬܐ ܬܪܝܢ. ܠܦܪܒܪ.
This hews so close to the Hebrew as to lack meaning, and פרבר is transliterated – a device not used outside this section in P-Chronicles.[140]

1 Chr. 27:6 –

MT הוא בניהו גבור השלשים ועל השלשים ומחלקתו עמיזבד בנו
P ܗܘ ܒܢܝܐ ܓܢܒܪܐ ܕܬܠܬܝܢ. ܘܥܠ ܬܠܬܝܢ. ܘܦܠܓܘܬܗ ܕܥܡܝܙܒܕ ܒܪܗ.
Here again P corresponds to the Hebrew so closely as to be obscure; the "thirty" are left unexplained and the final phrase does not make immediate sense.[141]

Again, some particular usages in this section differ from those elsewhere in P-Chronicles. The form ראובני, indicating the members of the tribe collectively, is rendered ܫܒܛܐ ܕܒܝܬ ܪܘܒܝܠ elsewhere in P-Chronicles (1 Chr. 5:6, 26, 12:37); this section, however, uses the adjective ܪܘܒܝܠܝܐ (1 Chr. 27:16) or ܒܢܝ ܪܘܒܝܠ (1 Chr. 26:32). The phrase כקטן כגדול is rendered literally by ܙܥܘܪܐ ܐܝܟ ܪܒܐ at 1 Chr. 26:13 within the section, but more idiomatically – in an analogous context – by ܙܥܘܪܐ ܐܝܟ ܡܣܟܢܐ at 1 Chr. 25:8 outside. At 1 Chr. 26:27, we find the verbal noun ܚܘܠܡܐ, never found elsewhere in this book:
MT לחזק לבית י״, P ܠܚܘܠܡܐ ܕܒܝܬܗ ܕܡܪܝܐ
The noun שֹׁטֵר (1 Chr. 26:29, 27:1) is here rendered ܫܠܝܛܐ, rather than ܣܦܪܐ as usual elsewhere in P, including 1 Chr. 23:4, 2 Chr. 19:11. The authenticity of this long passage is thus uncertain.

How would the rival reading – which here means the omission of the whole section – perform by the criterion of authenticity? In any other book, omission on such a scale would be decidedly unauthentic. P-Chronicles, however, exhibits a number of omissions, such as 2 Chr. 4:11–17,19–22. Thus omission is not *ipso facto* unauthentic here, though it must be admitted that no other omission in P-Chronicles is so long.

We now turn to the criterion of direction, which at first sight favours the longer text;

[138] This is 6h13, missing from 1 Chr. 22:8 to 2 Chr. 5:14.
[139] A quick check is provided by Lee's printed text, which lacks the disputed section. There Chronicles begins in the upper part of p. 334 and ends in the upper part of p. 392; and the end of 2 Chr. 5:14, noted as the half-way point, is exactly midway, in the upper part of p. 363.
[140] The phrase דברי הימים is also transliterated (as ܕܒܪܝ ܗܝܡܝܢ), at 1 Chr. 27:24.
[141] Note also the disfigurement of the name עמיזבד.

it is easier for a copyist to lose a passage than to supply it. Yet directionality is not clear-cut here, precisely because the variation is so extensive. In favour of the shorter text, we could attribute this uniquely long omission to the original translator, and argue that because of its very length it was detected by a colleague – whose approach happened to be more literalist – and made good on the basis of the Hebrew. If so, then the colleague's ability still to consult the Hebrew suggests that little time had elapsed since the original translation.[142] However, the 'patch' never became fully established in the manuscript tradition. This hypothesis would explain those elements in the disputed passage which contrast with the usual technique of P-Chronicles.

It remains to explain how the original translator could have omitted the passage in the first place. The first verse of this section, namely 1 Chr. 26:13, resembles the earlier verse 1 Chr. 25:8. Both open ויפילו גורלות and include the phrase כקטן כגדול. It may be that on reaching 1 Chr. 26:13 the translator thought that he had come upon a passage that duplicated – or even contradicted – a passage that he had already translated. In that case he would have skipped the rest of the lists and proceeded straight to the next narrative, immediately after 1 Chr. 27:34. Hence the omission of this whole section. Such a step is in keeping with the radicalism forced upon the translator of Chronicles by the generally poor state of his *Vorlage*.

To suggest that the *Vorlage* was hopelessly illegible in this section would be less satisfactory. First, at 1 Chr. 2:13–14, MT names Jesse's seven sons, with David as the seventh; but P supplies an additional brother before David, no doubt because 1 Sam. 16:10 stated that David had seven elder brothers. P calls the additional brother Elihu, which name could only have been inferred from the phrase אליהו מאחי דויד at 1 Chr. 27:18. Thus, whoever translated the rest of Chronicles must have had some access to the Hebrew text of the disputed section. Second, whoever translated the disputed section had access to a Hebrew copy of Chronicles that was legible in this section; and unless that copy had just come to light, it must equally have been available to whoever translated the remainder of the book. The original translator's omission of this section would thus not have been due to the illegibility of the *Vorlage* directly, but rather to the radical attitude which he had to adopt in the face of that illegibility in order to discharge his task.

We must now turn to the distributional criteria. The disputed section is confined to mss 7a1, 8a1 and 17e1. There are no convincing instances where, singly or together, these mss exclusively preserve the correct text.[143] On the other hand, there are cases where the truth is preserved in 9a1 alone, which is one of the witnesses to the shorter text. Thus the distributional argument favours the shorter text – which is also admissible on authenticity grounds. If the shorter text is original, however, the longer is still almost as ancient.

Far less extensive, but no less problematic, is the variation at Judg. 20:20–1. Here we find some material confined to a few mss (6h7 6ph11[1] 8a1*), followed by further

[142] A colleague would presumably have used the same Hebrew text as the translator. That the Hebrew text was legible in this section, unlike many others in Chronicles, need not contradict this; the *Vorlage* need not have been uniformly damaged throughout.

[143] Barnes, *An Apparatus Criticus to Chronicles*, (who did not collate 8a1) thought that 7a1 and 17e1 together sometimes alone preserved the truth, but all the instances that he quotes (on p. xxxi) concern prepositions or other minor matters.

material common to all the mss. The Syriac text, together with what appear to be the corresponding Hebrew words, may be tabulated as follows:

6h7 6ph11[1] 8a 1* only:

ܘܢܦܩܘ ܒܢܝ̈ ܒܢܝܡܝܢ ܡܢ ܓܒܥܬ	ויצא איש ישראל	20a α
ܠܡܬܟܬܫܘ ܥܡ ܒܢܝ̈ ܝܣܪܝܠ	למלחמה עם בנימן	20a β
ܘܣܕܪܘ ܒܢܝ̈ ܝܣܪܐܝܠ	ויערכו (אתם) איש ישראל	20b α
ܩܪܒܐ (ܥܡܗܘܢ) ܥܠ ܓܒܥܬ	מלחמה אל גבעה	20b β

Common to all manuscripts:

ܘܢܦܩܘ ܒܢܝ̈ ܒܢܝܡܝܢ ܡܢ ܓܒܥܬ	ויצאו בני בנימן מן הגבעה	21a
ܘܐܣܬܕܪܘ ܠܘܩܒܠ ܝܣܪܝܠ	ויערכו את[ם] איש ישראל	20b α
ܘܐܪܡܝܘ ܡܢ ܝܣܪܝܠ ܒܝܘܡܐ ܗܘ	וישחיתו בישראל ביום ההוא	21b α
ܕܐܩܪܒܘ ܥܡܗܘܢ	למלחמה	20a β1
ܬܪܝܢ ܘܥܣܪ̈ܝܢ ܐܠܦܝܢ ܓܒܪ̈ܝܢ ܥܠ ܐܪܥܐ	שנים ועשרים אלף איש ארצה	21b β

At first sight, 6h7 etc. preserve v.20 while the other mss do not. This would obviously make the text of the former more authentic. Closer inspection shows that matters are not so simple. In the text common to all the mss, two phrases from v.20 are actually embedded. Moreover, the material confined to 6h7 etc. is not a straightforward rendering of v.20: the opening phrase has been modified so that the Israelites do not go out to fight the Benjamites, as in MT, but vice versa. It is also noteworthy that quantitatively the complete text of 6h7 etc. does not correspond to the Hebrew much closer than does the majority text. The majority text is eight words shorter than MT, but the text of 6h7 etc. is five words longer than MT, because it duplicates those phrases from v.20 already rendered in the material common to all the mss. In summary, the criterion of correspondence with MT – which is one aspect of authenticity – favours the longer text; but the case is not overwhelming.

The other aspect of authenticity concerns the translation technique. In Judges, as usually elsewhere, P strives for clarity. By this criterion, the shorter text is more authentic, for it is easier to follow. In v.19, the Israelites encamp outside Gibeah, and the shorter text provides a vivid sequel: the Benjamites make a sortie and defeat them. Now the Hebrew text in this whole passage is heavy with repetitions, and many modern commentators suspect that two accounts have been combined. In one account, the Israelites encamp outside Gibeah and are suddenly overwhelmed by the Benjamites (vv.19, 21); in the other, the Israelites take the initiative and attack Gibeah itself, where they are beaten back (v.20).[144] It may be that P's translator, like many moderns, considered that the logical sequel to v.19 was v.21, to which he proceeded immediately, salvaging from v.20 those few phrases that did not directly contradict his general account. By comparison, the longer text is confusing – in making the Benjamites sally forth from Gibeah twice – and to that extent less authentic.

The criterion of direction favours the longer text, as Dirksen observes;[145] a scribe's eye could easily have jumped from the first occurrence of ܘܢܦܩܘ ܒܢܝ̈ ܒܢܝܡܝܢ ܡܢ ܓܒܥܬ to

[144] So e.g. F.C. Burney, *The Book of Judges with Introduction and Notes*, London 1918, p. 476.

[145] P.B. Dirksen, "The Ancient Peshiṭta Manuscripts of Judges and their Variant Readings" in *Peshitta Symposium I*, pp. 127–46.

the second. However, the priority of the shorter text cannot be excluded, because the discrepancy with the Hebrew is so extensive that a colleague might have detected it. One could then imagine a colleague adding the whole of v.20 (leaving alone those parts already present) and switching the roles of the Israelites and Benjamites to conform with v.21.

Altogether, the intrinsic criteria – of authenticity and direction – yield no certain conclusion. The distributional criteria, however, suggest a decision. Dirksen's examination of the variants in Judges shows that the shared exclusive readings of 6h7 and 8a1 do not appear preferable in any other passage. By contrast, the mss supporting the shorter text, especially in combination, have a better track record.[146] On balance, therefore, the shorter text seems the older, even though Dirksen himself inclines to support the longer on grounds of direction. One must admit, however, that the decision is finely balanced.

Appendix III: Modelling the relations among the witnesses

The development of the text over the centuries is a complex process, which we might better understand if it could be simplified without loss of its essential features. Whereas Koster's representation of the ms inter-relations was linear, we may obtain a more detailed model by introducing a second dimension.

Given a geographical map, it is easy to measure the distance between every possible pair of cities, and to compile a table of inter-city distances. A computer technique, pioneered by Kruskal,[147] makes possible the reverse process: starting from the table of distances, we may obtain a map showing the location of the cities. The same method can even be applied to entities – like manuscripts – for which the very existence of a map was not clear in advance. All that is needed is a table showing the distances – in our case, the degrees of textual divergence – between each pair. On the resulting map, then, the distance shown between each pair of mss will reflect, as closely as possible, the degree of textual dissimilarity between that pair. Figs. 6 and 7 (see pp. 320 and 321) are the "maps" obtained for the P mss in Lamentations and Psalms respectively.[148]

The obvious definition of textual dissimilarity between two mss is the number of disagreements between them. However, some mss may be defective or fragmentary, so that it will not be possible to compare every pair of ms in every variant passage, i.e. in every passage where textual variation exists among the extant manuscripts. To adjust for this, we may define the degree of textual dissimilarity between two mss as the number of disagreements expressed as a percentage of the number of variant passages where both mss are extant. From a table showing these indices of textual dissimilarity between

---

[146] On p. 141, Dirksen enumerates 11 cases where 6h7 and 8a1 agree against the other ancient mss. The four which he finds determinate are listed in the body of this chapter. Six more were indeterminate, and the other is the present passage.

[147] J.B. Kruskal, "Multidimensional Scaling by Optimising Goodness-of-Fit to a Nonmetric Hypothesis", *Psychometrika* (1962), pp. 125–40.

[148] For an application to the mss of Isaiah, see M.P. Weitzman, "The Analysis of Manuscript Traditions: Isaiah (Peshitta Version) and Matthew", in *Actes du Second Colloque International "Bible et Informatique: méthodes, outils, résultats", Jérusalem, 9–13 juin 1988*, Paris-Geneva 1989, pp. 641–52. The textual history in this book seems to have been so complex as to make the map less informative here than elsewhere.

each pair of witnesses, the diagram can be obtained by a standard statistical procedure, described in the next appendix.

In each diagram a location is given not only to the extant mss but also to the original (Ω). Although the original is lost, its reading can be reconstructed – or so the critic believes – in the determinate passages. As for any other fragmentary witness, therefore, we can calculate its index of textual dissimilarity with every other ms, and so locate it on the map. For statistical analysis it is better for the data to be copious – even if they include a little 'grit' – than sparse. We therefore need to take a maximalist view of what constitutes a determinate passage. Any passage where one of the variant readings stands closer than its rival(s) to MT, whether in form or in content, will be taken as determinate, the reading of Ω being whichever reading agrees with MT. Elsewhere, the text of Ω is treated as missing. The criterion of agreement with MT may occasionally be false: the similarity of a Syriac reading to MT may be due, for example, to revision after LXX or to coincidence. Over the great majority of passages, however, the criterion is likely to give correct results, since in general the translator is likelier to have followed his Hebrew *Vorlage* than to have departed systematically from it.

The relative bearings of the different mss from the location of the original (Ω) can be interpreted in historical terms. A path radiating outwards from Ω can be interpreted as a line of descent, on which the ancestor stands closer than its descendant to Ω. Conversely, mss lying at very different bearings from Ω will have come down to us by routes that are relatively independent. Those ms pairs which differ most in their bearing from Ω are of particular interest, since their texts show the greatest degree of mutual independence.[149] Where they agree in text, their common reading will normally be correct; and where they diverge, the truth may survive in either of them, even perhaps alone. This reasoning is developed further in Appendix IV.

Model of the manuscript relations in Lamentations

The map for Lamentations is based on Albrektson's collations.[150] Massoretic mss are represented by lower-case letters. In addition, the sigla for eastern mss are here italicised.

Koster's three phases can be detected in Lamentations no less than in Exodus. F (9a1) often agrees uniquely with MT and corresponds to Koster's first stage, while the other mss up to the ninth century correspond to Koster's second stage. However, the second stage group is widely distributed over the map, confirming its relative heterogeneity. Near the top of the map we may identify a concentration which includes all the eastern mss but also most of the later western mss (SJNCTEGHKLMQa).[151] This reflects the widespread standardisation that occurred from the ninth century onward. At the same time, it is clear from the map that some western mss escaped the standardisation, and in particular that the western massoretic mss never served as a norm to standardise the text in the west.

---

[149] The special interest attaching to such 'mutually opposed' mss was first pointed out by M. Bévenot, *The Tradition of Manuscripts: A Study in the Transmission of St Cyprian's Treatises*, Oxford 1961 (reprinted Westport CT 1979), pp. 148–50.

[150] B. Albrektson, *Studies in the Text and Theology of the Book of Lamentations*, Lund 1963.

[151] Of the remaining mss, P shows the closest affinity with this group.

Whereas F stands at one extreme bearing from Ω, two other western mss stand at the other: O (16a6) differs most in bearing, with B (12a1) in a similar direction. This suggests that the greatest degree of textual independence can be found between F on the one hand and BO on the other. Hence we may expect readings common to FBO to be original, and we may even expect the original reading to survive on occasion in F alone or BO alone. In this short book the only two variations in which FBO agree against the rest concern Seyame, but in both FBO stand closer to MT:

	MT	FBO	rell.
Lam. 2:6	מועד	ܥܐܕܐ	ܥܐ̈ܕܐ
Lam. 3:12	לַחֵץ	ܠܓܐܪܐ	ܠܓܐܪ̈ܐ

There are also places where the text unique to 9a1 can claim to be original, notably:

	MT	F (9a1)	rell.
Lam. 1:18	שמעו נא	ܫܡܥܘ ܢܐ	ܫܡܥܘ
Lam. 2:7	כיום מועד	ܐܝܟ ܝܘܡܐ ܕܥܐܕܐ	ܐܝܟ ܕܒܝܘܡܐ ܕܥܐܕܐ
Lam. 4:12	צר ואויב	ܐܠܘܨܐ ܘܒܥܠܕܒܒܐ	ܒܥܠܕܒܒܐ ܘܐܠܘܨܐ

Conversely, at Lam. 5:10 the reading unique to BO may be original:

MT עורנו כתנור נכמרו
BO ܡܫ̈ܟܢ ܐܝܟ ܬܢܘܪܐ ܐܬܩܦܕܘ
rell. ܡܫ̈ܟܢ ܐܝܟ ܕܡܢ ܬܢܘܪܐ ܐܬܩܦܕܘ

One must remember, however, that the map is no more than suggestive. In this case, the identification of F on the one hand and BO on the other – all western mss of the ninth century or later – as 'maximally opposed' recognises that the eastern text drove out certain good readings, which became confined to isolated pockets in the west. However, we must not view the agreement of F with BO as automatically correct: both may instead bear a plausible reading that became current in the west but did not infect all other extant mss.

Model of the manuscript relations in Psalms

The map of Psalms (fig.7, page 321) is based mainly on the collations of Barnes, who includes printed editions as well as quotations from various ecclesiastical writers: Aphrahat, Philoxenus of Mabbog, Daniel of Salah, Moses bar Kepha and Barhebraeus.[152] One ms – 8a1* – has been added from Walter's collations.

The horizontal axis of the map can be interpreted geographically, with the western mss on one side and the eastern on the other. This division between the two groups reflects separate standardisation in the east and in the west. Even so, the western group – which includes Jacobite, Malkite and Maronite texts – is far looser than the eastern.

Distance from Ω on the map reflects textual deterioration. As expected, the older mss tend to stand closer to Ω. However, the correlation is not perfect; in particular, the massoretic ms Z (10m1) has an especially pure form of the western type of text.

Standing at the most extreme bearings from Ω are 9a1 on one side and the Nestorian

[152] Apart from Aphrahat, these are cited respectively from: E.A.Wallis Budge (ed.), *The Discourses of Philoxenus, Bishop of Mabbôgh*, London 1894; ms B.L.Add.17125 and Diettrich's collations in the next-mentioned work; G.Diettrich, *Eine jakobitische Einleitung in den Psalter*, Giessen 1901; P.de Lagarde (ed.), *Praetermissorum Libri Duo*, Göttingen 1879.

authorities on the other. The western mss, though these include the oldest, stand within a relatively narrow 'wedge' – bordered by broken lines on the map – between those two extreme bearings. This suggests that the combination of 9a1 and the Nestorian group will usually be correct, and also that either may on occasion preserve the original text alone. Passages where the agreement of 9a1 and the Nestorian witnesses gave the better reading were noted above, at Ps. 39:7 and 104:1. Elsewhere the truth may survive in 9a1 alone, as at Ps. 69:11 –

MT ואבכה בצום נפשי, 9a1 ܟܒܫܬ ܨܥܪ ܢܦܫܝ ܒܨܘܡܐ, rell. ܟܒܫܬ...,

or in the Nestorian authorities alone, as at Ps. 94:8 –

MT בערים בעם, eastern mss ܒܥܝܪܐ ܒܥܡܐ, rell. ܒܥܝܪܐ܂ ܒܥܡܐ.

All this implies that the western mss, though these include the oldest, add little to the combined testimony of 9a1 and the eastern mss.[153] This conclusion seems valid throughout the Psalter, though Ps. 51:13 is exceptional:

MT רוח קדשך, ܘܪܘܚ ܩܘܕܫܟ CHQS (+Aphrahat), rell. ܩܘܕܫܟ ܘܪܘܚ

Although CHQS are western, their reading preserves the native feminine gender of 'spirit' and so appears original.

The locations of the ecclesiastical writers are tentative, being based on sparse references. Aphrahat's text, though close to Ω, stands squarely within the 'wedge' that covers the western mss. In this book Aphrahat preserves no good reading absent from the biblical mss, and at Ps. 41:2 he already has a 'new reading' which later recurs among the western mss.[154] The location of Barhebraeus towards the 'east' of the map reflects the incursion of eastern readings into the western text by his time. For the same reason Lee's edition, nominally western, stands away to the 'east' of the other western authorities.

In the emergence of a distinctive western text, the book of Psalms is exceptional. For the most part, the typical pattern is that of Lamentations.

Conclusion

The map is a heuristic device, rather than a foundation for rigorous argument. It reveals the main groupings and their degree of inner cohesion. It highlights those pairs of mss which are least often caught together in error, and whose agreement is therefore likeliest to give the original reading in passages where intrinsic criteria fail. The lines radiating outwards from Ω further suggest outlines of textual history. Ultimately, however, the map is no more than a simplified representation of the complex relations among the mss; and in the last analysis, every variant reading must be treated on its own merits.

Appendix IV: The rationale of the manuscript map

It often happened – not least in biblical texts – that a scribe copied one main ms source but drew at the same time upon a second, or upon his independent knowledge of the text, in order to remove any errors in his main source. This procedure is often called

---

[153] For more detailed treatment, see M.P. Weitzman, "The Originality of Unique Readings in Peshiṭta ms 9a1", MPI 4 (1988), pp. 225–58.

[154] This is the insertion of *dalath* to link the two verse halves, recurring in ABDHJR.

'contamination', though the term is excessively pejorative, as many good readings might otherwise have perished. It can lead to a bewildering variety of patterns of agreement and disagreement between mss (except in relation to the smallest sub-families), which prevents the construction of any meaningful stemma or genealogical tree of the mss. The map is an alternative representation which may shed light on the relationships between the mss.

A simplified model

Let us first imagine a ms tradition in which the original Ω survives, together with two mss A and B. For simplicity, assume that none of these mss has any lacunae, and that at any point in the text there are never more than two alternative readings. We could take these three authorities by pairs and count the disagreements between each pair – i.e. how many times A differs from Ω or B from Ω or A from B. We could then draw a triangle on which each ms is represented by a point and the distance between any pair of points equals the number of disagreements between the corresponding mss.

The shape of that triangle, and in particular the angle which the points A and B subtend at Ω would reflect the degree of textual independence between A and B, and this would have implications both for critical policy and for history. Basically, the wider the angle subtended at Ω the greater the degree of textual independence between A and B. In one hypothetical extreme, the angle is zero and the triangle collapses into a line, with one copy in the middle, as below:

$$\Omega\text{———}A\text{——}B \text{ or } \Omega\text{———}B\text{——}A$$

The first diagram means that B never agrees with Ω against A. Thus B has some errors of which A is free, but no good readings not also found in A. In the reconstruction of Ω, B may be ignored. In historical terms, B is (or might as well be) derived from A. The situation in the second diagram is similar.

In the other hypothetical extreme, the angle subtended Ω is 180°. Once more the triangle collapses into a line, but now with Ω in the middle, as below:

$$A\text{———}\Omega\text{——— }B$$

This diagram means that the two mss never err together. Where one commits an error, the other is needed to correct it. Both mss are indispensable. In historical terms, the two mss descend from Ω by wholly independent routes.

In practice, the angle which the two points A and B subtend at Ω will lie between the two extremes values of zero and 180°. The greater the angle – i.e. the more different the bearings of the points A and B as viewed from the original – the greater the degree of textual independence between the two. The reasoning is explained more fully in the mathematical note below.

The case where a scribe mingles readings from two sources is illustrated as follows. Suppose a different ms tradition, where the original and three extant mss ABC survive. A and B err together once, and in addition each has four errors of which the other is free. C is a mixed copy, based on both A and B. By consulting B, C eliminates three of the errors peculiar to A, retaining one plausible false reading only. Similarly, he corrects away all but one of the errors peculiar to B. The one error common to A and B is naturally repeated in C.

Using 0 for a correct reading and 1 for an error, we may represent the readings in the nine passages as follows:

Manuscript	Passage no.									No. of Errors
	1	2	3	4	5	6	7	8	9	
Ω	0	0	0	0	0	0	0	0	0	0
A	1	1	1	1	1	0	0	0	0	5
B	1	0	0	0	0	1	1	1	1	5
C	1	0	0	0	1	0	0	0	1	3

Then the numbers of disagreements between the various pairs of mss are as follows:

$$\Omega A = \Omega B = 5; \ \Omega C = 3; \ AB = 8; \ AC = BC = 4$$

These are represented by the following figure:

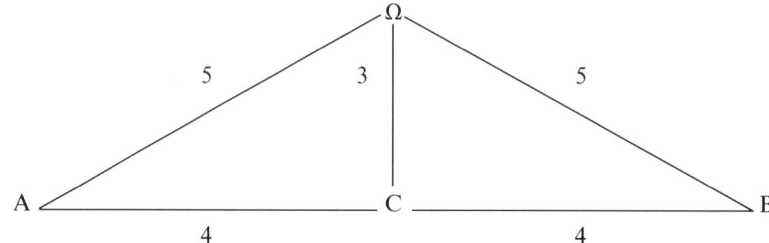

Fig. 5. Example of manuscript map.

C is a relatively successful mixture, in that the scribe made the right decision in six out of the eight passages where he had a choice between the readings of A and B. Had he been less successful, C would have been located at a greater distance from Ω.

It will be noted that the mixed ms C falls within a wedge bounded by the lines that run to each of its two sources (A and B) from Ω. Even though C resembles Ω more closely than does either A or B, it is the pair A and B which shows the greatest degree of mutual independence. These two mss, which lie along the edges of the wedge, together present every good reading that can be found in the ms located within it. Moreover, there are some places where one or other of them preserves the true reading uniquely: in this instance, passage no. 9 in A and passage no. 5 in B. The eclectic text C adds nothing to their joint testimony, even though it contains fewer errors than either.

Let us now consider the sort of extensive ms tradition that occurs in practice. Suppose that the investigator of such a tradition had a diagram on which every ms (including the original) was represented by a point, such that the distances between these points equalled the distances between the corresponding mss. The angles subtended at Ω would then indicate any case where one ms depended on another, or where two mss were of independent ancestry, and so on. The main relationships between the mss would be evident at a glance.

Unfortunately, there are good reasons why such a model is not fully attainable in practice. There are situations, however, where an acceptable approximation may be attained.

Problems and solutions

Two problems were mentioned in the last appendix. First, some mss may be defective. The index of disagreement between two mss should therefore be re-defined as the number of disagreements between the two mss, expressed as a percentage of the number of variant passages where both mss are available. This re-definition would not affect any of the angles in the figures above.

The second problem was that the original, whose position has to be shown on the diagram, is in fact lost. In principle, we may regard the original as a defective witness, available in the determinate passages only. Indices of disagreement can then be obtained – as just explained – and used to locate the original on the map. It must be added, however, that if there are not enough determinate passages, this difficulty will be insurmountable.

There is a third major problem. A map in two dimensions on which the distance between every pair of points equals exactly the index of disagreement between the corresponding mss cannot usually be drawn.[155] However, the computer technique called multidimensional scaling will produce a two-dimensional map in which the distances correspond to the "true" distances in the data as closely as can be attained. The degree to which the distances on the map have to be changed from the true distances is measured by a statistic called the "stress".[156] The stress may prove unacceptably large; that is, it may not prove possible to draw a map at all on which the distances shown bear acceptable resemblance to the data. If the stress is small, however, then the location of the mss on the map, and in particular the angles subtended at Ω will suggest inferences of the sort described above.

This approach comes into its own when the texts of two particular mss can be identified as the 'poles' between which the texts of the remaining mss lie. These two mss will be 'poles' in the sense that they never (or very rarely) agree together in error, except in passages where the true reading has been lost altogether.[157] Each remaining ms can be treated as a mixture of the two 'polar' texts, in the sense that all its good readings are found in one or other of these two. In that case, each of these mixtures will have just two essential characteristics: (a) its degree of overall resemblance to one of the polar texts rather than the other, and (b) the success of the mixture in choosing the better rather than the inferior readings. These two characteristics can be well represented on a two-dimensional map, essentially like figs. 6 and 7 (see pp. 320 and 321).

It may be emphasised that, on this approach, the polar mss need not themselves be the sources of all the other extant mss. They need not even be the most ancient of the extant mss; for example, they may even be late representatives of families otherwise now extinct. What matters is that these two mss together present all (or nearly all) the good readings that have survived.

In other textual situations, where the mss cannot be regarded as varying mixtures of two polar texts, the two-dimensional map will not be useful. At one extreme, it will not

---

[155] In general, the number of dimensions needed is one less than the number of mss, for an exact solution; and even then complex numbers may be involved.

[156] It should be added that the terms 'distance' and 'stress' can be defined in more than one way, and that the approaches – and results – of different computer programs for generating the map may differ somewhat.

[157] This was probably inherited from some remote ancestor common to all extant mss.

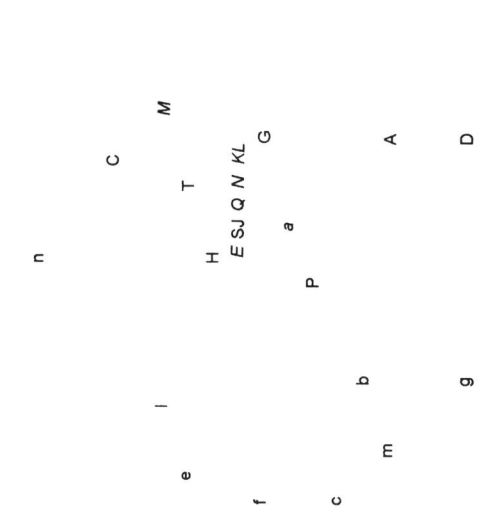

Fig. 6. Manuscript map for Lamentations.

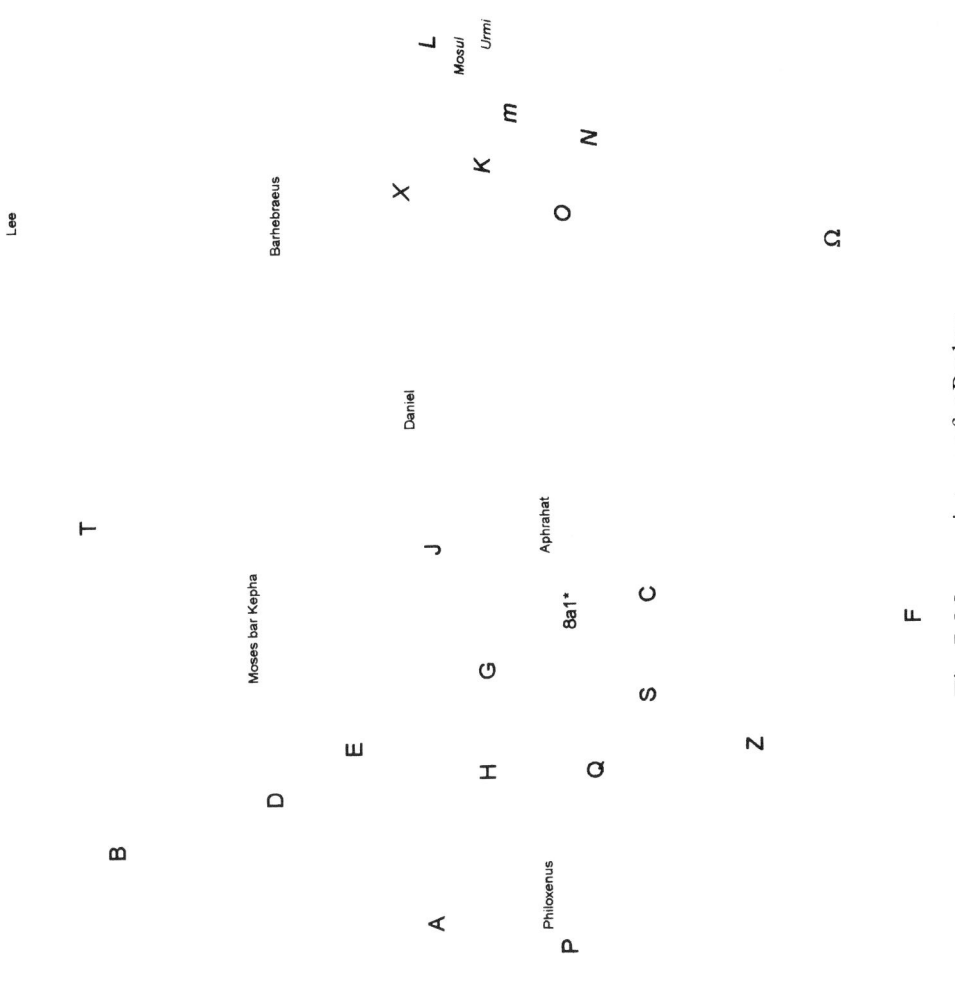

Fig. 7. Manuscript map for Psalms.

work when *no* textual admixture has occurred; for in that case the various branches and sub-branches will remain distinct, each branching will require in principle a dimension of its own, and reduction to just two dimensions will involve unacceptably high distortion. At the other extreme, the method is also inapplicable to texts such as Greek tragedies, where readings travelled in so many different directions that no two witnesses can be identified which together present all (or nearly all) the good readings that have survived. In such cases too, reduction to just two dimensions would be unacceptably simplistic.

In the case of P, however, the two-dimensional map is potentially fruitful, at least in books where there is one regular unique carrier. That ms will then be one pole, and the other will be whichever ms (or close-knit group) has the fewest errors in common with it. In Psalms, for example, the greatest degree of textual independence can be found between one western authority (again 9a1) on the one hand, and the close-knit group of eastern authorities on the other.

In compiling the statistics, we need to eliminate orthographic variants where a scribe was likelier to follow his own habits than his exemplar(s). We should also omit readings unique to a single ms, since these too tell us nothing of the relations *between* the mss. An exception must be made for unique readings which we judge correct. These should be included among the determinate passages, because among the authorities to be shown in the map they are not unique after all: each appears not only in a single extant ms but also in the fragmentary 'original'.

Mathematical note

The reason that the angle subtended at Ω is so informative is as follows. Let us suppose that A and B have common errors in e passages; A errs alone in a passages; B errs alone in b passages. Then the total numbers of disagreements are:

$\Omega A = e + a$ $\Omega B = e + b$ $AB = a + b$

The formula for the angle subtended at Ω is then:

$2 \arcsin \sqrt{\{[a/(a+e)].[b/(b+e)]\}}$

If the angle at Ω is 0, so that the three points stand in a straight line, then either $a=0$ or $b=0$. If $a=0$, then A has no errors that are not shared by B, and A stands in the middle. If $b=0$, the situation is analogous. In either case, the ms farther from Ω has no good readings that cannot be found in the ms nearer to Ω.

At the other extreme, the angle at Ω might be 180°. In that case the three points again stand in a straight line, but now with Ω in the middle. The required condition is $e=0$. This means that mss A and B never err together; they are wholly independent. The situation in practice lies between these two extremes: the greater the angle between the points representing two mss, the greater their degree of mutual independence in text.

INDEX OF REFERENCES

GENERAL INDEX

Note: The following abbreviations are used in the index: LXX = Septuagint; MT = Massoretic text. Headwords in italics indicate discriminator words, while page references in *italics* refer to diagrams.

University of Cambridge
Oriental publications published for the
Faculty of Oriental Studies